LET'S GO

PAGES PACKED WITH ESSENTIAL INFORMATION

"Value-packed, unbeatable, accurate, and comprehensive."

—The Los Angeles Times

"The guides are aimed not only at young budget travelers but at the independent traveler; a sort of streetwise cookbook for traveling alone."

—The New York Times

"Unbeatable; good sight-seeing advice; up-to-date info on restaurants, hotels, and inns; a commitment to money-saving travel; and a wry style that brightens nearly every page."

—The Washington Post

THE BEST TRAVEL BARGAINS IN YOUR BUDGET

"All the dirt, dirt cheap."

—People

"Let's Go follows the creed that you don't have to toss your life's savings to the wind to travel—unless you want to."

—The Salt Lake Tribune

REAL ADVICE FOR REAL EXPERIENCES

"The writers seem to have experienced every rooster-packed bus and lunar-surfaced mattress about which they write."

—The New York Times

"[Let's Go's] devoted updaters really walk the walk (and thumb the ride, and trek the trail). Learn how to fish, haggle, find work—anywhere."

—Food & Wine

"A world-wise traveling companion—always ready with friendly advice and helpful hints, all sprinkled with a bit of wit."

—The Philadelphia Inquirer

A GUIDE WITH A SPIRIT AND A SOCIAL CONSCIENCE

"Lighthearted and sophisticated, informative and fun to read. [Let's Go] helps the novice traveler navigate like a knowledgeable old hand."

—Atlanta Journal-Constitution

"The serious mission at the book's core reveals itself in exhortations to respect the culture and the environment—and, if possible, to visit as a volunteer, a student, or a teacher rather than a tourist."

—San Francisco Chronicle

LET'S GO PUBLICATIONS

TRAVEL GUIDES

Australia
Austria & Switzerland
Brazil
Britain
California
Central America
Chile
China
Costa Rica
Costa Rica, Nicaragua & Panama
Eastern Europe
Ecuador
Egypt
Europe
France
Germany
Greece
Guatemala & Belize
Hawaii
India & Nepal
Ireland
Israel
Italy
Japan
Mexico
New Zealand
Peru
Puerto Rico
Southeast Asia
Spain & Portugal with Morocco
Thailand
USA
Vietnam
Western Europe

Yucatan Peninsula

ROADTRIP GUIDE

Roadtripping USA

ADVENTURE GUIDES

Alaska
Pacific Northwest
Southwest USA

CITY GUIDES

Amsterdam
Barcelona
Berlin, Prague & Budapest
Boston
Buenos Aires
Florence
London
London, Oxford, Cambridge & Edinburgh
New York City
Paris
Rome
San Francisco
Washington, DC

POCKET CITY GUIDES

Amsterdam
Berlin
Boston
Chicago
London
New York City
Paris
San Francisco
Venice
Washington, DC

LET'S GO

LONDON, OXFORD, CAMBRIDGE & EDINBURGH

RESEARCHERS
JACK HOLKEBOER
SARA S. O'ROURKE

MARY POTTER **MANAGING EDITOR**
JESSE BARRON **RESEARCH MANAGER**

EDITORS
COURTNEY A. FISKE
SARA PLANA
RUSSELL FORD RENNIE
CHARLIE E. RIGGS
OLGA I. ZHULINA

RESEARCHERS

Jack Holkeboer   *Oxford, Brighton, Bath, Stratford, Edinburgh,*
                            Cambridge, Gloucestery Ely

Let's Go's in-house wunderkind, Jack is the only researcher whose notes would have to be published with a Parental Advisory sticker. Some researchers content themselves with being tourists; Jack is unusual in that he actually became British this summer. Remember how James Brown called his pompadour "fried, dyed, and laid on the side?" Jack's style is wry, dry, and made for the guide. See what we did there? Jack can tell a real ale from an imitation by putting his ear to the glass.

Sara S. O'Rourke   *London*

To cover London last time, we hired two researchers for eight weeks each. This year, Sara O'Rourke did the whole city in seven. We have no idea how she pulled this off. What's more, Sara still had time to attend auctions at Sotheby's, find us all the best galleries in South London, and charm her way into the East End's most exclusive VIP lines. A taxonomist of London hipsters, the smartest person in the tavern, the girl with the sharpest eye for the avant-garde—okay, so we have some idea how she did 16 weeks in seven. If you ever need to talk to Sara, you can find her at the gelato shop.

STAFF WRITERS

Kyle Bean   Catherine Humphreville
Sanders Bernstein   Meagan Michelson
Molly Donovan   C. Harker Rhodes

CONTENTS

PRICE RANGES
LONDON

1 **2** **3** **4** **5**

Our researchers list establishments in order of value from best to worst, honoring our favorites with the Let's Go thumbs-up (▨). Because the best *value* is not always the cheapest *price*, we use a system of price ranges based on a rough expectation of what you will spend. For **accommodations,** we base our range on the cheapest price for which a single traveler can stay for one night. For **restaurants,** we estimate the average amount one traveler will spend in one sitting. The table below tells you what you'll *typically* find in London at the corresponding price range, but keep in mind that no system can allow for the quirks of individual establishments.

ACCOMMODATIONS	RANGE	WHAT YOU'RE *LIKELY* TO FIND
❶	under £26	Campgrounds and dorm rooms, both in hostels and actual universities. Expect bunk beds and a communal bath. You may have to provide or rent towels and sheets.
❷	£27-42	Upper-end hostels. You may have a private bathroom, or there may be a sink in your room and a communal shower in the hall.
❸	£43-57	A small room with a private bath, probably in a budget hotel. Should have decent amenities, such as phone and TV. Breakfast may be included in the price of the room.
❹	£58-77	Similar to 3, but will have more amenities or be more centrally located. A room in this range should have charm.
❺	over £77	Large hotels or upscale chains. Excellent B&Bs. A splurge for budget travelers, but you deserve to be pampered once in a while.

FOOD	RANGE	WHAT YOU'RE *LIKELY* TO FIND
❶	under £6	Mostly street-corner stands, food trolleys, sandwiches, takeaway, and tea shopds. Rarely a sit-down meal.
❷	£6-12	Pub grub, fish 'n' chips, chips 'n' fish, and cheap ethnic eateries. Could be sit-down or takeaway.
❸	£13-18	Mid-priced entrees, fancier pubs and higher quality ethnic food. Most Indian places are in this range. You'll probably have a waiter or waitress, so the tip will bump you up a few £s.
❹	£19-24	As in 3, higher prices are related to better service. Includes some fancier restaurants and most gastro-pubs (fish 'n' frîtes, anyone?).
❺	over £24	Elegant restaurants. You'll probably need to take off your T-shirt. Don't keep it off! Put on one of those nice shirts, with buttons.

PRICE RANGES

OXFORD, CAMBRIDGE, AND EDINBURGH

Our researchers list establishments in order of value from best to worst, honoring our favorites with the Let's Go thumbs-up (⬛). Because the best *value* is not always the cheapest *price*, we use a system of price ranges based on a rough expectation of what you will spend. For **accommodations**, we base our range on the cheapest price for which a single traveler can stay for one night. For **restaurants**, we estimate the average amount one traveler will spend in one sitting. The table below tells you what you'll *typically* find in Oxford, Cambridge, and Edinburgh at the corresponding price range, but keep in mind that no system can allow for the quirks of individual establishments.

ACCOMMODATIONS	RANGE	WHAT YOU'RE *LIKELY* TO FIND
❶	under £20	Campgrounds and dorm rooms, both in hostels and actual universities. Expect bunk beds and a communal bath. You may have to provide or rent towels and sheets.
❷	£20-27	Upper-end hostels and lower-end B&Bs. You may have an ensuite bath or communal facilities. Breakfast and some amenities, like TVs, may be included.
❸	£28-34	A small room with a private bath. Should have decent amenities, such as phones and TVs. Breakfast may be included.
❹	£35-42	Should have bigger rooms than a ❸, with more amenities or in a more convenient location. Breakfast probably included.
❺	over £42	Large hotels, upscale chains, nice B&Bs, and even castles. If it's a ❺ and it doesn't have the perks you want, you've paid too much.

FOOD	RANGE	WHAT YOU'RE *LIKELY* TO FIND
❶	under £6	Mostly street-corner stands, food trolleys, sandwiches, takeaway, and tea shops. Rarely a sit-down meal.
❷	£6-12	Sandwiches, pizza, appetizers at a bar, or low-priced entrees. Most ethnic eateries are a ❷. Either takeaway or sit-down, but only slightly more fashionable decor than a ❶.
❸	£13-18	Mid-priced entrees, good pub grub, and more upscale ethnic eateries. Since you'll likely have the luxury of a waiter, tip will set you back a little extra.
❹	£19-24	A somewhat fancy restaurant. Entrees tend to be heartier or more elaborate, but you're really paying for decor and ambience. Few restaurants in this range have a dress code, but some may look down on T-shirts and sandals.
❺	over £24	Your meal might cost more than your room, but there's a reason—it's something fabulous, famous, or both. Nicer outfits may be expected. Don't come here expecting a PB&J!

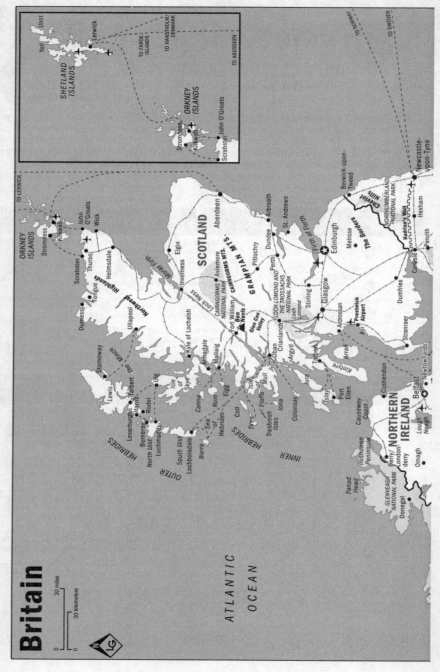

Britain

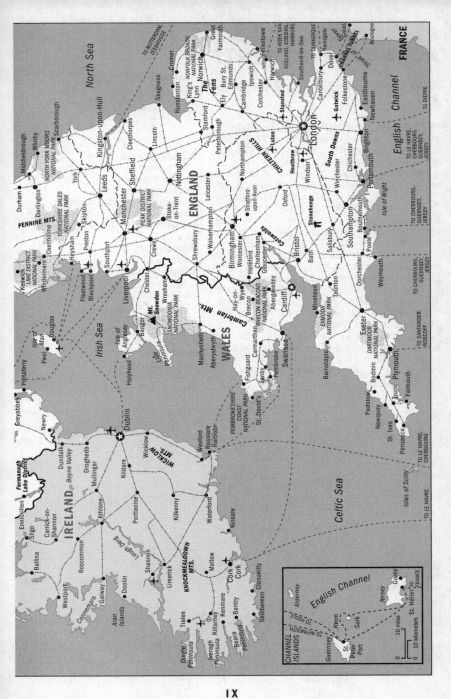

ACKNOWLEDGMENTS

JESSE THANKS: Sara and Jack for all their hard work.

THE EDITORS THANK: The Ed Team would first and foremost like to thank our lord (Jay-C) and savior (Starbucks, Terry's Chocolate Orange). We also owe gratitude to Barack Obama (peace be upon Him), the Oxford comma, the water cooler, bagel/payday Fridays, the HSA "SummerFun" team for being so inclusive, Rotio (wherefore art thou Rotio?), the real Robinson Crusoe, the Cambridge weather and defective umbrellas, BoltBus, Henry Louis Gates, Jr. (sorry 'bout the phone call), the office blog, gratuitous nudity, the 20-20-20 rule and bananas (no more eye twitches), the Portuguese flag, trips to the beach (ha!), sunbathing recently-married Mormon final club alums, non-existent free food in the square, dog-star puns, and last but not least, America. The local time in Tehran is 1:21am.

But seriously, to the MEs and RMs, our researchers (and all their wisdom on tablecloths and hipsters), LGHQ, HSA, our significant others (future, Canadian, and otherwise), and families (thanks Mom).

Publishing Director
Laura M. Gordon
Editorial Director
Dwight Livingstone Curtis
Publicity and Marketing Director
Vanessa J. Dube
Production and Design Director
Rebecca Lieberman
Cartography Director
Anthony Rotio
Website Director
Lukáš Tóth
Managing Editors
Ashley Laporte, Iya Megre,
Mary Potter, Nathaniel Rakich
Technology Project Manager
C. Alexander Tremblay
Director of IT
David Fulton-Howard
Financial Associates
Catherine Humphreville, Jun Li

Managing Editor
Mary Potter
Research Manager
Jesse Barron
Editors
Courtney A. Fiske, Sara Plana, Russell Ford Rennie, Charlie E. Riggs, Olga I. Zhulina
Typesetter
Rebecca Lieberman

President
Daniel Lee
General Manager
Jim McKellar

DISCOVER LONDON, OXFORD, CAMBRIDGE, AND EDINBURGH

For a while, Britain was grim. After nearly a millennium as a unified geographical entity, at the height of an Empire that controlled a quarter of the globe, these poor kids were slammed with two world wars, the rapid dismantling of their colonies, and the postwar Austerity rationing program—not to mention raw memory of the Blitz—that made 1940s London the headquarters of world drabness. What had happened to the source of the English-speaking world's greatest literature, the farthest northern reach of the Roman Empire, the last international stronghold of private life, the greatest naval power in history, the global king of the 19th-century economy?

And what has happened to it since? Like its greatest poet, who spent his last years sitting alone, blind, writing *Paradise Lost*, 20th-century Britain turned inward and whipped up a capital city that is the envy of world while maintaining rural areas of stunning natural beauty and disarmingly polite inn-keepers. Britain doesn't put on its hat when it goes out anymore, but that's partly because it doesn't go out: the nation that conquered the world sits back and lets the world come to it.

 DON'T GET CAUGHT WITH YOUR PANTS DOWN: In Britain, the adjective "naked" describes a person without an umbrella.

WHEN TO GO

Britain's popularity as a tourist destination makes it wise to plan around high season (June-Aug.). Spring or autumn (Apr.-May and Sept.-Oct.) are also appealing times to visit; the weather is still pleasant, and flights are cheaper. If you intend to visit the cities and spend time indoors, the low season (Nov.-Mar.) is cheapest. Keep in mind, however, that sights and accommodations often run reduced hours or close completely, especially in rural areas.

Whenever you go, it will rain. Have warm, waterproof clothing on hand at all times. Relatively speaking, April is the driest month. The mild weather has few extremes: excluding Highland altitudes, temperatures average around 15-20°C (60-70°F) in summer and 5-7°C (40-45°F) in winter. During the winter, snow often causes roads to close in Scotland and in the northern regions of England and Wales. Note that the British Isles are farther north than you may think: Newcastle is on the same latitude as Moscow. In Scotland, the midsummer sun lasts almost all day, and in winter sets as early as 3:45pm.

If you want to see the colleges at Oxford and Cambridge, be aware that graduation often closes the campuses to visitors. On the other hand, Commencement week celebrations are a spectacle in their own right.

WHAT TO DO

🏛 FAMOUS SIDEKICKS FOR $200

One of the advantages of having a big empire is that you collect a lot of weird antiques. Britain's museums are some of the best in the world, and a few days in London will make up for majoring in English instead of Art History. But it may not tell you what's going on with art today; is it just us, or do most museums have only really old paintings? Where are all the new paintings? They are in London's hundreds of galleries, including world-famous spaces like White Cube. Here are our favorite major museums, each paired with a gallery that is the Pimm's to its lemonade.

BATMEN	ROBINS
🎨 **BRITISH MUSEUM.** The funny thing about the British Museum is that there's almost nothing British in it. Founded in 1753 as the personal collection of Sir Hans Sloane, the museum juxtaposes Victorian Anglocentrism with a more modern, take on multi-culturalism.	🎨 **WOOLFF GALLERY.** This gallery features new and established contemporary artists and designers, including Banksy, David Wheeler, Victoria Rose, Ben Young, and Russell Wes, and work in a variety of mediums, including paint, print, photography, ceramic, porcelain, and graffiti.
🎨 **TATE MODERN.** Sir Giles Gilbert Scott's boorish, mammoth building was formerly the Bankside power station. Inside, though, you'll find some of the best modern art in the world.	🎨 **HAYWARD GALLERY.** This stark concrete building is a distinctive maze of blocks, which brilliant curators fill with contemporary art and the occasional foray into the art of the early or mid-20th century.
🎨 **NATIONAL GALLERY.** Founded by an Act of Parliament in 1824, with 38 pictures displayed in a townhouse. Over the years it has become one of the world's grandest museums.	🎨 **WHITECHAPEL ART GALLERY.** Whitechapel has been an outlet for the area's political ferment, artistic innovation, and social change since it first jump-started the Pop Art movement in the 1950s.
🎨 **NATIONAL PORTRAIT GALLERY.** This artistic Who's Who in Britain began in 1856 and is now *the* place to see fresh new artwork alongside centuries-old portraiture. Also be sure to check out the sleek new Ondaatje Wing, which was completed in 2000.	🎨 **BRUNEI GALLERY.** Affiliated with the SOAS, this beautiful three-story space is devoted to carefully and elaborately crafted exhibitions of African and Asian art and culture. As its patron is the Sultan of Brunei, you'd expect nothing less.
🎨 **VICTORIA AND ALBERT MUSEUM.** As the largest museum of decorative (and not so decorative) arts in the world, the V&A rivals the British Museum for the sheer size and diversity of its holdings.	🎨 **WHITE CUBE.** A Hoxton Square (and art scene) institution, this stark white building has showcased some of the biggest names in international contemporary art. Its impressive list of alums includes Chuck Close and Damien Hirst.
🎨 **HUNTERIAN MUSEUM.** John Hunter, considered the founder of modern surgery, had a keen interest in the anatomy of all living things. This museum holds his vast collection of both human and animal fetuses, intestines, and teeth.	🎨 **VICTORIA MIRO.** Though a bit out of the way, Victoria Miro is worth a visit. The gallery features works from young artists that make the most of its sprawling warehouse venue—think large installation pieces, not oil paintings.
🎨 **ROYAL ACADEMY OF ARTS.** The incredibly popular Summer Exhibition (Jun.-Aug.), which has been held every year since 1769, is open to any artist for submission. It showcases an unparalleled range of contemporary art in every medium, most of which is available for purchase.	🎨 **THE PHOTOGRAPHER'S GALLERY.** The largest public gallery in London devoted entirely to photography, the Photographer's Gallery never fails to please and inspire. Displays usually feature a single artist's work, ranging from classic landscape to socially conscious photography.
🎨 **BRITISH LIBRARY GALLERIES.** In the Literature Corner, find Shakespeare's first folio, Lewis Carroll's handwritten manuscript of *Alice in Wonderland* (donated by the real life "Alice" herself), and Virginia Woolf's crazed handwritten notes for *Mrs. Dalloway* (then called *The Hours*).	🎨 **PARISOL UNIT: FOUNDATION FOR CONTEMPORARY ART.** Once a struggling art gallery, this privately funded charity has reestablished itself on the East End scene and now features four innovative exhibits per year, usually of work by international contemporary artists.

BATMEN	ROBINS
▧ **NATIONAL GALLERY OF SCOTLAND.** This gallery has a superb collection of works by Renaissance, Romantic, and Impressionist masters.	▧ **MUSEUM OF CHILDHOOD.** Displays an array of antique and contemporary childhood toys, from 19th-century dollhouses to 1990s Teletubbies.
▧ **SCOTTISH NATIONAL PORTRAIT GALLERY.** The gallery displays the stern faces of the famous men and women who have shaped Scotland's history. Highlights include renegade Bonnie Prince Charlie, royal troublemaker Mary, Queen of Scots, and wordsmith Robert Louis Stevenson.	▧ **PEOPLE'S STORY MUSEUM.** With a beautiful clock face above the Royal Mile, this building once served as a prison and gallows for "elite" criminals. Now it houses the People's Story Museum, which offers an eye-opening look at the life of Edinburgh's working classes.

▨ HEY CHIPS! IT'S ME, FISH

George Orwell pulled a fast one when he wrote about a pub called the "Moon Under Water": "The thing that most appeals to me about the Moon Under Water is what people call its 'atmosphere,'" he wrote in 1946. From Orwell's description, the MUW does come off well: it has Victorian decor and "barmaids" who know the regulars by name, it sells tobacco as well as cigarettes, it serves beer in china glasses, "you can walk around without constantly ducking to avoid flying darts," and so on. Sounds good, right? Well, old George Orwell made up the Moon. MUW, as you suspected, is the Platonic pub, a fantasyland where you can have stout on draught and sausages (so many pubs only have one or the other), where the garden has little green metal tables and little children are exiled in their strollers to the swing set, built specifically for them, so they don't bother the grownups during lunch.

Orwell was right about many things, but he might have been surprised about the gastro-pub craze that has recently filled Britain's pub kitchens with *haute cuisine* chefs, impresarios, and just plain maniacs (a bar made of ice?). Here we present our favorite pubs alongside their less Orwellian counterparts. One of them just may be your Moon Under Water.

FISH AND CHIPS	POISSON ET FRITES
▧ **FRENCH HOUSE** (SOHO). Frequented by everyone from Maurice Chevalier and Charlie Chaplin to Salvador Dalí and Dylan Thomas. During WWII, this SOHO institution became the unofficial gathering place of the French Resistance.	▧ **ABSOLUT ICEBAR** (Mayfair and St. James's). The entire bar and its contents are constructed completely out of Swedish-imported ice and undergo a full renovation every 6 months. It replaced a bar made entirely out of the Wicked Witch of the West, which had melted.
▧ **THE OLD BANK OF ENGLAND** (Holborn). Even Orwell might bend the rules for this pub, opened on the premises of the 19th-century Bank of England. In winter, if the first meat pie on the menu doesn't appeal to you, there are always 10 other choices.	▧ **22 BELOW** (Mayfair and St. James's). This hidden, amber-hued night spot is worth searching for. Entertaining comedy nights and oversized fresh fruit martinis. Orwell would have had a fit; you'll probably have a second round.
▧ **YE OLDE CHESHIRE CHEESE** (Holborn). Once a haunt of greats like Johnson, Dickens, Tennyson, Twain, Conan Doyle, and the minor poet Teddy Roosevelt. Each room serves a different cuisine. Now why is it called the Cheese?	▧ **VATS** (Bloomsbury). Move through the wooden foyer to the classic main bar, flanked by an antique reading desk piled high with wine-related volumes. Delicious and innovative food. The wine list is so long that there is no wine list.
▧ **THE GEORGE INN** (South Bank). Shakespeare's Moon Under Water. Seriously: WILLIAM SHAKESPEARE used to drink BEER at this pub. Wow.	▧ **THE COURT LONDON** (Bloomsbury). A lighthearted pub that's all about students, with pool tables, televised sporting events, and regular DJ nights.

FISH AND CHIPS	POISSON ET FRITES
THE EAGLE (Cambridge). Cambridge's oldest pub. What would Orwell say about the barmaid who insisted that Watson and Crick settle their outstanding 4 shilling tab when the two researchers rushed in to announce the discovery of DNA?	**LA RAZA** (Cambridge). Barcelona in Cambridge: cheap tapas served at a long glittering bar gilded with blue light.
THE TURF TAVERN (Oxford). It was here that Bob Hawke, future prime minister of Australia, downed a yard of ale (over 2 pints) in a record 11 seconds as an Oxford undergrad. Well done, Bob.	**JERICHO TAVERN** (Oxford). An upstairs venue where Radiohead had its debut gig in 1984. Specialty beer served in a heated beer garden.
LAMB AND FLAG (Oxford). Founded in 1617 as the Lamb Inn, this pub also has its share of literary history. Graham Greene was a regular, and Thomas Hardy set part of *Jude the Obscure* here.	**ST. ALDATES TAVERN** (Oxford). The ceiling is plastered with a year's worth of ale labels. Your count isn't off: that's over 1200 labels.
THE EAGLE AND CHILD (Oxford). "The Inklings," a group of 20th-century writers that included C.S. Lewis and J.R.R. Tolkien, referred to this spot as the "Bird and Baby."	**FREVD'S** (Oxford). Pronounced Freud's—an Oxford institution where you eat beneath the vaulted ceiling of a 19th-century church. Gourmet pizzas are a nice break from pub fare.
CHEQUERS INN (Oxford). Built in 1260, the building was originally the home of a money-lender; the name comes from the checkerboard, the ancient Roman symbol of that line of work.	**KAZBAR** (Oxford). Cushions and dim lighting make this tapas bar a good place for beer and *patatas con chorizo*.

⊗ THE WIDE WORLD OF SPORT

Football (soccer, if you must) fanatics are everywhere: the queen is an Arsenal fan and the police run a national hooligan hotline. Incidentally, no one is absolutely sure where the word hooligan comes from. It was used in a popular music-hall song from the 1890s about an Irish family, which may explain its slightly uncomfortable connotations toward the Irish. British football is crazy enough to make a hooligan of almost everyone; you may find yourself wishing that other sports, like cricket, had something more of the hooligan about them. Cricketers play their interminable games at London's Lords grounds, and the world's longest cricket marathon was played at Devon for 17hr. 34min. The Royal Ascot horse races and the Henley regatta draw Britain's blue-bloods, and the revered coastal "links" of Saint Andrews attract golf enthusiasts from all other.

A SPORTING AFFAIR
LONDON FOOTBALL. The big three London teams are Arsenal, Chelsea, and Tottenham Hotspur. Tickets can be a little on the expensive side (€30+), but if you're looking to drink beer and shout and wave flags while men in better shape than you run around in short shorts, you can't spend your money more wisely.
LONDON RUGBY. Three big London teams play from August to May on weekend afternoons. They are the London Wasps, the NEC Harlequins, and the Saracens (Hooligans, Saracens; the world of London sports is not the most politically correct).
LONDON CRICKET. Middlesex and Surrey are the main London teams; their grounds at Lord's and the Oval, respectively, are also used to host international test matches in which England traditionally loses abysmally. Cricket is very slow, takes a long time to play, and must be seen to be believed.
LONDON TENNIS. Demand for tickets at "The Championships" (Wimbledon) so exceeds supply that pre-sold tickets are lotteried in December; only 500 Centre, No. 1, and No. 2 Court tickets are saved for each day (except during the Final Four, when none are saved). Even Rafael Nadal couldn't get a ticket for the 2009 Championships, which is why he pulled out of the tournament (don't believe all that "knee problem" baloney).

A SPORTING AFFAIR

SCOTTISH HIGHLAND GAMES. The Scottish Highland games, which occur annually, are nothing like what you've seen in London. Games include cabertossing, bagpipes playing, and an epic game of tug of war. They take place each year on the first Saturday in September.

◼ CHURCH AND STATE

Restraint was not a popular concept among early Britons. They never held back when a fortress, castle, or cathedral could be defiantly built or defiantly razed. Edward I of England had a rough time containing the Welsh; his "iron ring" of fortresses mark the northwestern Welsh coast. Closer to home, London, Cambridge, Oxford, and Edinburgh have churches, fortresses, parliaments, and towers to impress even the most jaded sightseer. Here's a nice pairing, of the sacred with the profane—each church is matched with an interesting secular structure (or, if you look at it the other way, each annoying secular building is matched with a gorgeous church).

THE SACRED	THE PROFANE
SAINT PAUL'S CATHEDRAL. Architect Christopher Wren's masterpiece is the fifth cathedral to occupy the site; the original was built in AD 604. Today, majestic St. Paul's remains a cornerstone of London's architectural and historical legacy, as well as an obvious tourist magnet.	**TOWER OF LONDON.** Check out the turrets and towers of this multi-functional block—it has served as palace, prison, royal mint, and living museum over the past 900 years. It's still guarded by Beefeaters, who protect it from tourists.
SAINT MARY LE-BOW. Saint Mary's bells rang the City curfew and wake-up call daily from 1334 to 1874. To be a true Cockney, one must have been born within earshot of the bells.	**GUILDHALL.** Excavations in the 1990s revealed the remains of a Roman amphitheater below the Yard of what used to be the administrative center of the London Corporation.
SAINT BARTHOLEMEW THE GREAT. Take this, All Hallows: though you claim to be the oldest church in London, you are but the oldest site on which there has been a church! This, in fact, is the grandfather of them all—the oldest church in London.	**THE CHARTERHOUSE.** Originally a 14th-century Carthusian monastery, the Charterhouse and its walls were built around the communal grave of thousands of victims of the 1349 Black Death.
SOUTHWARK CATHEDRAL. Shakespeare's brother Edmund is buried here, and a rare stained-glass window along the right side of the nave depicts characters from Shakespearean plays.	**SHAKESPEARE'S GLOBE THEATRE.** The original Globe burned down, but this replica is perfect, down to the standing-room only seats for groundlings.
WESTMINSTER CATHEDRAL. With a distinguished history as a burial place for the Who's Who of medieval Britain, Westminster is an important stop on any tour.	**BUCKINGHAM PALACE.** 'Allo!
CHRIST CHRUCH COLLEGE, OXFORD. "The House" has Oxford's grandest quad and its most distinguished students, counting 13 past prime ministers among its alumni. To catch these distinguished gentlemen at their finest, visit during the massive bender that is commencement week.	**CHRIST CHURCH CHAPEL.** The only church in England to serve as both a cathedral and college chapel, it was founded in AD 730 by Oxford's patron saint, St. Frideswide, who built a convent here in honor of two miracles: the blinding of her persistent suitor and his subsequent recovery.
CARFAX TOWER. The tower marks the center of premodern Oxford. A climb up its 99 (very narrow) stairs affords a superb view of the spires and surrounding countryside.	**UNIVERSITY CHURCH OF SAINT MARY THE VIRGIN.** Oxford used to use this church for exams and meetings; now they have to use it to actually go to church.
KING'S COLLEGE CAMBRIDGE. King's College was founded by Henry VI in 1441 as a partner school to Eton; only in 1873 did the college begin admitting students from other prep schools.	**ROUND CHURCH.** The Round Church is one of five surviving circular churches in England and the second-oldest building in Cambridge

ESSENTIALS

PLANNING YOUR TRIP

ENTRANCE REQUIREMENTS
Passport (p. 7). Required for all foreign nationals, although they may not be checked for citizens of the EU.
Visa (p. 8). Not required of citizens of Australia, Canada, New Zealand, the US, and many other Western countries for stays longer than six months. If you are unsure, call your local embassy or complete an inquiry at www.ukvisas.gov.uk.
Inoculations (p. 16). No specific inoculation, vaccination, certificate, or International Certificate of Vaccination (ICV) is required, but check to see if an ICV is required upon re-entry into your own country.
Work Permit (p. 8). Required for all foreigners planning to work in the UK.

EMBASSIES AND CONSULATES

UK CONSULAR SERVICES ABROAD

For addresses of British embassies in countries not listed here, consult the **Foreign and Commonwealth Office** (☎020 7008 1500; www.fco.gov.uk). Some cities have a British consulate that can fulfill most embassy functions.

Australia: Embassy, Commonwealth Ave., Yarralumla, ACT 2600 (☎2 6270 6666; www.ukinaustralia.fco.gov.uk). **Consular Section** (UK passports and visas), Piccadilly House, 39 Brindabella Circuit, Brindabella Business Park, Canberra Airport, Canberra ACT 2609 (☎1902 941 555). **Consulates General** in Brisbane, Melbourne, Perth, and Sydney; **Consulate** in Adelaide.

Canada: Embassy, 80 Elgin St., Ottawa, ON K1P 5K7 (☎613-237-1530; www.ukincanada.fco.gov.uk/). **Consulate General,** 777 Bay St., Ste. 2800, Toronto, ON M5G 2G2 (☎416-593-1290). Other offices in Montreal and Vancouver; **Honorary Consuls** in Quebec City, St. John's, and Winnipeg.

Ireland: Embassy, 29 Merrion Rd., Dublin 4 (☎1 205 3700; www.britishembassyinireland.fco.gov.uk).

New Zealand: Embassy, 44 Hill St., Thorndon, Wellington 6011 (☎+64 4 924 2888; www.ukinnewzealand.fco.gov.uk); mail to P.O. Box 1812, Wellington 6140. **Consulate General:** 151 Queen St., Auckland (☎9 303 2973); mail to Private Bag 92014, Auckland.

US: Embassy, 3100 Massachusetts Ave. NW, Washington, DC 20008 (☎+1-202-588-7800; www.ukinusa.fco.gov.uk). **Consulate General:** 845 3rd Ave., New York City, NY 10022 (☎212-745-0200). Other offices in Atlanta, Boston, Chicago, Houston, Los Angeles, and San Francisco. **Consulates** in Dallas, Denver, Miami, and Seattle.

CONSULAR SERVICES IN THE UK

Australia: Australia House, The Strand, London WC2B 4LA (☎020 7379 4334; www.australia.org.uk). Passport office (☎020 7887 5816; www.uk.embassy.gov.au).

Canada: 38 Grosvenor Sq., London W1K 4AA (☎020 7258 6600; www.canada.org.uk).

Ireland: 17 Grosvenor Pl., London SW1X 7HR (☎020 7235 2171; www.embassyofireland.co.uk).

New Zealand: 80 Haymarket, London SW1Y 4TQ (☎020 7930 8422; www.nzembassy.com).

US: 24 Grosvenor Sq., London W1A 1AE (☎020 7499 9000; www.usembassy.org.uk). **Consulates** in Belfast, Cardiff, and Edinburgh.

TOURIST OFFICES

VISITBRITAIN

Formerly known as the British Tourist Authority (BTA), **VisitBritain** oversees UK tourist boards and solicits tourism. The main office is located at Thames Tower, Blacks Rd., London W6 9EL (☎020 8846 9000; www.visitbritain.com).

Australia: 15 Blue St., Level 2, North Sydney, NSW 2060 (☎+61 1300 858 589; www.visitbritain.com/au).

Canada: 5915 Airport Rd., Ste. 120, Mississauga, ON L4V 1T1 (☎+1-888-847-4885; www.visitbritain.com/ca).

New Zealand: IAG House, 17th fl., 151 Queen St., Auckland 1 (☎+64 9 309 1899; www.visitbritain.com/nz).

US: 551 5th Ave., Ste. 701, New York City, NY 10176 (☎+1-212-986-1188; www.visitbritain.com/us). Other offices in Chicago and Los Angeles.

WITHIN THE UK

Britain Visitor Centre, 1 Lower Regent St., Haymarket, London SW1Y 4XT (☎020 8846 9000).

VisitScotland, Ocean Point One, 94 Ocean Dr., Leith, Edinburgh EH6 6JH (☎0131 472 2222; www.visitscotland.com).

DOCUMENTS AND FORMALITIES

PASSPORTS

REQUIREMENTS

Citizens of Australia, Canada, Ireland, New Zealand, and the US need valid passports to enter the UK and to re-enter their home countries. Britain does not allow entrance if the holder's passport expires in under six months; returning home with an expired passport is illegal and may result in a fine. Your passport will prove your most convenient method of identification and, if the photo was taken long ago, a source of humorous conversation.

NEW PASSPORTS

Citizens of Australia, Canada, Ireland, New Zealand, and the US can apply for a passport at any passport office or at selected post offices and courts of law. Citizens of these countries may also download passport applications from the official website of their country's government or passport office. Any new passport or renewal applications must be filed well in advance of the departure date, though most passport offices offer rush services for a steep fee. Note, however, that "rushed" passports still take up to two weeks to arrive.

 BRITAIN AND EUROPE. The EU's policy of **freedom of movement** means that most border controls have been abolished and visa policies harmonized under a 1985 treaty called the **Schengen Agreement.** Most EU states are already members of Schengen, but Ireland and the UK are not, and travel to these countries may still require you to present a visa or passport, depending on your home country and the length of your stay. Britain and Ireland have formed a common travel area, abolishing passport controls between the two island nations.

PASSPORT MAINTENANCE

Photocopy the page of your passport with your photo as well as your visas, traveler's check serial numbers, and any other important documents. Carry one set of copies in a safe place, apart from the originals, and leave another set at home.

If you lose your passport, immediately notify the local police and your home country's nearest embassy or consulate. To expedite its replacement, you must show ID and proof of citizenship; it also helps to know all information previously recorded in the passport. In some cases, a replacement may take weeks to process, and it may be valid only for a limited time. Any visas stamped in your old passport will be lost forever. In an emergency, ask for immediate temporary traveling papers that will permit you to re-enter your home country.

VISAS AND WORK PERMITS

VISAS

Visa requirements vary by country, and citizens of certain countries will need a visa merely to pass through the UK. Citizens of Australia, Canada, New Zealand, and the US do not need a visa for stays of up to 100 days. Those staying longer than 100 days may purchase a six-month visa for £65 from **visa application centers (VACs)** around the world, generally located in large urban centers and run in collaboration with private companies.

Travelers planning on longer stays will face Britain's complicated and ever-changing patchwork of immigration laws. The Home Office runs a website (www.ukvisas.gov.uk) that is exceedingly helpful in negotiating this process. Applicants are divided into five tiers, with priority given to skilled workers. Entering the UK to study requires a special visa. For more information, see the **Beyond Tourism** chapter (p. 34).

Double-check entrance requirements at the nearest UK embassy or consulate (p. 6) for up-to-date info before departure. US citizens can also consult http://travel.state.gov.

WORK PERMITS

Admittance to a country as a traveler does not include the right to work, which is authorized only by a work permit. For more information, see the **Beyond Tourism** chapter (p. 34).

IDENTIFICATION

When you travel, always carry at least two forms of identification on your person, including a photo ID. A passport and a driver's license will usually suffice.

Never carry all of your IDs together; split them up in case of theft or loss and keep photocopies in your luggage and at home.

STUDENT, TEACHER, AND YOUTH IDENTIFICATION

The **International Student Identity Card (ISIC)**, the most widely accepted form of student ID, provides discounts on some sights, accommodations, food, and transportation, access to a 24hr. emergency help line, and insurance benefits for US cardholders. ISIC cardholders in London, for example, can gain free entry into some museums and discounts at the Shakespeare Globe Theatre or the London Zoo. Applicants must be full-time secondary or post-secondary school students at least 12 years old. Because of the proliferation of fake ISICs, some services (particularly airlines) require additional proof of student identity. For travelers who are under 26 years old but are not students, the **International Youth Travel Card (IYTC)** also offers many of the same benefits as the ISIC.

Each of these identity cards costs US$22. ISICs and IYTCs are valid for one year from the date of issue. To learn more about ISICs and IYTCs, try www.myisic.com. Many student travel agencies (p. 17) issue the cards; for a list of issuing agencies or more information, see the **International Student Travel Confederation (ISTC)** website (www.istc.org).

The **International Student Exchange Card (ISE Card)** is a similar identification card available to students, faculty, and children aged 12 to 26. The card provides discounts, medical benefits, access to a 24hr. emergency help line, and reduced airfares. An ISE Card costs US$25; visit www.isecard.com for more info.

CUSTOMS

Upon entering the UK, you must declare certain items from abroad and pay a duty on the value of those articles if they exceed the allowance established by the UK's customs service. Goods and gifts purchased at duty-free shops abroad are not exempt from duty or sales tax; "duty-free" means that you won't pay tax in the country of purchase. Duty-free allowances were abolished for travel between EU member states on June 30, 1999, but still exist for those arriving from outside the EU. Upon returning home, you must likewise declare all articles acquired abroad and pay a duty on the value of articles in excess of your home country's allowance. Jot down a list of any valuables brought from home and register them with customs before traveling abroad. It's a good idea to keep receipts for all goods acquired abroad.

If you're leaving Britain for a non-EU country, you can claim back any **value added tax** paid (see **Taxes**, p. 12). For information about traveling with pets, consult the **UK Department for Environment, Food, and Rural Affairs** (www.defra.gov.uk/animalh/quarantine/index.htm).

MONEY

CURRENCY AND EXCHANGE

The currency chart below is based on August 2009 exchange rates. Check the currency converter on websites like www.xe.com or www.bloomberg.com for the latest exchange rates.

ESSENTIALS

POUNDS (£)		
AUS$1 = £0.50		£1 = AUS$2.00
CDN$1 = £0.55		£1 = CDN$1.81
EUR€1 = £0.86		£1 = EUR€1.16
NZ$1 = £0.41		£1 = NZ$2.45
US$1 = £0.60		£1 = US$1.65

As a general rule, it's cheaper to convert money in the UK than at home. While currency exchange will probably be available in your arrival airport, it's wise to bring enough foreign currency to last for at least 24-72hr.

When changing money abroad, try to go only to banks or currency exchanges that have at most a 5% margin between their buy and sell prices. Since you lose money with every transaction, it makes sense to convert large sums at once.

If you use traveler's checks or bills, carry some in small denominations (the equivalent of US$50 or less) for times when you are forced to exchange money at poor rates, but bring a range of denominations since charges may be applied per check cashed. Store your money in a variety of forms; ideally, at any given time you will be carrying some cash, some traveler's checks, and an ATM and/ or credit card. All travelers should also consider carrying some US dollars (about US$50 worth), which are often preferred by local tellers.

TRAVELER'S CHECKS

Traveler's checks are one of the safest and most convenient means of carrying funds. **American Express** and **Visa** are the best-recognized brands. Many banks and agencies sell them for a small commission. Check issuers provide refunds if the checks are lost or stolen, and many provide additional services, such as toll-free refund hotlines abroad, emergency message services, and assistance with lost and stolen credit cards or passports. Traveler's checks are readily accepted in the UK, though some hostels and B&Bs accept only cash. Ask about toll-free refund hotlines and the location of refund centers when purchasing checks. Remember: always carry emergency cash.

American Express: Checks available with commission at AmEx offices and select banks (www.americanexpress.com). AmEx cardholders can also purchase checks by phone (☎+1-800-528-4800). Cheques for Two can be signed by either of 2 people traveling together. For purchase locations or more information, contact AmEx's service centers: in Australia ☎2 9271 8666, in Canada and the US 800-528-4800, in New Zealand 9 583 8300, in the UK 1273 571 600.

Visa: Checks available at banks worldwide. For the location of the nearest office, call the Visa Travelers Cheque Global Refund and Assistance Center: in the UK ☎800 895 078, in the US 800-227-6811; elsewhere, call the UK collect at 2079 378 091. Checks available in American, British, Canadian, European, and Japanese currencies, among others. Visa also offers TravelMoney, a prepaid debit card that can be reloaded online or by phone. For more information on Visa travel services, see http://usa.visa.com/personal/using_visa/travel_with_visa.html.

CREDIT, DEBIT, AND ATM CARDS

Where they are accepted, credit cards often offer superior exchange rates—up to 5% better than the retail rate used by banks and other currency-exchange establishments. Credit cards may also offer services such as insurance or emergency help and are sometimes required to reserve hotel rooms or rental cars. **MasterCard** and **Visa** are the most frequently accepted; **American Express** cards work at some ATMs and at AmEx offices and major airports.

The use of ATM cards is widespread in the UK. Depending on the system that your bank at home uses, you can most likely access your personal bank account from abroad. ATMs get the same wholesale exchange rate as credit cards, but there is often a limit on the amount of money you can withdraw per day (usually around US$500). There is also typically a surcharge of US$1-5 per withdrawal, so it (literally) pays to be efficient. A debit card can be used wherever its associated credit card company is accepted.

The two major international money networks are **MasterCard/Maestro/Cirrus** (for ATM locations ☎+1-800-424-7787; www.mastercard.com) and **Visa/PLUS** (for ATM locations visit http://visa.via.infonow.net/locator/global/). Most ATMs charge a transaction fee that is paid to the bank that owns the ATM, although **Barclays** banks around the UK offer free withdrawals for accounts from Bank of America, Scotiabank, and Westpac. It is a good idea to contact your bank or credit card company before going abroad; frequent charges in a foreign country can sometimes prompt a fraud alert, which will freeze your account.

GETTING MONEY FROM HOME

If you run out of money while traveling, the easiest and cheapest solution is to have someone back home make a deposit to your bank account. Otherwise, consider one of the following options.

WIRING MONEY

It is possible to arrange a **bank money transfer,** which means asking a bank back home to wire money to a bank in the UK. This is the cheapest way to transfer cash, but it's also the slowest, usually taking several days or more. Note that some banks may only release your funds in local currency, potentially sticking you with a poor exchange rate; inquire about this in advance. Money transfer services like **Western Union** are faster and more convenient than bank transfers—but also much pricier. Western Union has many locations worldwide. To find one, visit www.westernunion.com or call in Australia ☎1800 173 833, in Canada and the US 800-325-6000, or in the UK 0800 735 1815. To wire money using a credit card, call in Canada and the US ☎800-CALL-CASH, in the UK 0800 833 833. Money transfer services are also available to **American Express** cardholders and at selected **Thomas Cook** offices.

US STATE DEPARTMENT (US CITIZENS ONLY)

In serious emergencies only, the US State Department will forward money within hours to the nearest consular office, which will then disburse it according to instructions for a US$30 fee. If you wish to use this service, you must contact the Overseas Citizens Services division of the US State Department (☎+1-202-501-4444, from US 888-407-4747).

COSTS

The cost of your trip will vary considerably, depending on where you visit, how you travel, and where you stay. The most significant expenses will probably be your round-trip (return) airfare to Britain (see **Getting to the UK: By Plane,** p. 17) and accommodations (see **Accommodations,** p. 27).

STAYING ON A BUDGET

To give you a general idea, a bare-bones day in London, Oxford, Cambridge, or Edinburgh (sleeping in hostels/guesthouses, buying food at supermarkets) would cost about US$65 (£40); a slightly more comfortable day (sleeping in hostels/guesthouses and the occasional budget hotel, eating one meal per day at a restaurant, going out at night) would cost US$110 (£69); and, for a luxurious day, the sky's the limit. Don't forget to factor in emergency reserve funds (at least US$200) when planning how much money you'll need.

TIPS FOR SAVING MONEY

Some simpler ways include looking for free entertainment, splitting accommodation and food costs with trustworthy fellow travelers, and buying food in supermarkets rather than eating out. Bring a **sleep sack** (folding a large sheet in half length-wise and sewing the seam will work) to avoid charges for linens in hostels and do your **laundry** in the sink (unless you're explicitly prohibited from doing so). Museums often have certain days once a month or once a week when admission is free; plan accordingly. If you are eligible, consider getting an ISIC or an IYTC (p. 9); many sights and museums offer reduced admission to students and youths. For getting around quickly, bikes are the most economical option. Renting a bike is cheaper than renting a moped or scooter. Drinking at bars and clubs quickly becomes expensive. It's cheaper to buy alcohol at a supermarket and imbibe before going out. That said, don't go overboard. Though staying within your budget is important, don't do so at the expense of your health or a great travel experience.

 CONCESSIONS. Some sights offer admission at reduced prices for students, seniors, and the unemployed. These discounted prices are known in the UK as concessions and appear throughout *Let's Go.*

TIPPING AND BARGAINING.

Tips in restaurants are often included in the bill (sometimes as a "service charge"). If gratuity is not included, you should tip your server about 12.5%. Taxi drivers should receive a 10% tip, and bellhops and chambermaids usually expect £1-3. To the great relief of many budget travelers, tipping is not expected at pubs and bars in Britain.

TAXES

The UK has a 17.5% **value added tax (VAT),** a sales tax applied to everything but food, books, medicine, and children's clothing. The tax is included in the amount indicated on the price tag. The prices stated in *Let's Go* include VAT. Upon exiting Britain, non-EU citizens can reclaim VAT (minus an administrative fee) through the **Retail Export Scheme,** although the complex procedure is probably only worthwhile for large purchases. You can obtain refunds only for goods you take out of the country (not for accommodations or meals). Participating shops display a "Tax-Free Shopping" sign and may have a minimum purchase of £50-100 before they offer refunds. To claim a refund, fill out the form you are given in the shop and present it with the goods and receipts at customs upon departure (look for the Tax-Free Refund desk at the airport). At peak times, this process can take up to an hour. You must leave the country within three months of your purchase in order to claim a refund, and you must apply before leaving the UK.

PACKING

Pack lightly: lay out only what you think you absolutely need, then take half the clothes and twice the money. The **Travelite FAQ** (www.travelite.org) is a good resource for tips on traveling light. The online **Universal Packing List** (http://upl.codeq.info) will generate a customized list of suggested items based on your trip length, the expected climate, your planned activities, and other factors.

CONVERTERS AND ADAPTERS. Electricity is 230 volts AC in the UK, enough to fry any 120V North American appliance. 220/240V electrical appliances won't work with a 120V current, either. Americans and Canadians should buy an **adapter** (which changes the shape of the plug; US$5) and a **converter** (which changes the voltage; US$10-30). Don't make the mistake of using only an appliance (unless appliance instructions explicitly state otherwise). Europeans, New Zealanders, and Australians (who use 230V at home) won't need a converter but will need a set of adapters to use anything electrical. For more on all things adaptable, check out http://kropla.com/electric.htm.

SAFETY AND HEALTH

GENERAL ADVICE

In any type of crisis, the most important thing to do is **stay calm.** Your country's embassy abroad (p. 7) is usually your best resource in an emergency; registering with that embassy upon arrival in the country is a good idea. The government offices listed in the **Travel Advisories** box (p. 14) can provide information on the services they offer their citizens in case of emergencies abroad.

LOCAL LAWS AND POLICE

The police are a highly visible presence in London, Oxford, Cambridge, and Edinburgh. There are three types of police officers in the UK: regular officers with full police powers, special constables who work only part-time but have full police powers, and police community support officers (PCSO) who have limited police power and focus on community maintenance and safety. The national emergency numbers are ☎999 or ☎112. Numbers for local police stations are listed in each chapter of this guide.

DRUGS AND ALCOHOL

Remember that you will be subject to British laws during your travels. If you carry insulin, syringes, or prescription drugs, it is vital to have a copy of the prescriptions and a note from your doctor.

The Brits love to drink, and the pub scene is unavoidable. In trying to keep up with the locals, keep in mind that the **Imperial pint** is 20 oz., as opposed to the 16 oz. US pint. The drinking age in the UK is 18 (14 to enter, 16 for beer and wine with food). **Smoking** is banned in all enclosed public spaces in Britain, including pubs and restaurants.

SPECIFIC CONCERNS

TERRORISM

The Anti-Terrorism Crime and Security Act 2001, passed in the aftermath of the September 11, 2001 attacks, outlaws certain terrorist groups and gives police extended powers to investigate terrorism. Britain is committed to an extensive program of prevention and prosecution. More information is available from the Foreign and Commonwealth Office (see box below) and the Home Office (☎020 7035 4848; www.homeoffice.gov.uk). Britain raised its terrorist alert level to "elevated" after the London tube bombings of July 7, 2005, and the city stepped up security considerably in order to deter future attacks. In August 2006, the UK raised its threat assessment level again after government authorities thwarted an attack on planes departing from UK airports. In the immediate aftermath, airport security was bolstered, and liquids and many electronics were banned in aircraft cabins.

The US State Department website (www.state.gov) provides information on the current situation and on flight regulations. To have advisories emailed to you, register with your home embassy or consulate when you arrive in the UK. The box below lists offices to contact and websites to visit to get the most updated list of your government's advisories about travel.

TRAVEL ADVISORIES. The following government offices provide travel information and advisories by telephone, by fax, or via the web:
Australian Department of Foreign Affairs and Trade: ☎+61 2 6261 1111; www.dfat.gov.au.
Canadian Department of Foreign Affairs and International Trade (DFAIT): ☎+1-800-267-8376; www.dfait-maeci.gc.ca.
New Zealand Ministry of Foreign Affairs: ☎+64 4 439 8000; www.mfat.govt.nz.
United Kingdom Foreign and Commonwealth Office: ☎+44 20 7008 1500; www.fco.gov.uk.
US Department of State: ☎+1-888-407-4747, 202-501-4444 from abroad; http://travel.state.gov.

PERSONAL SAFETY

EXPLORING AND TRAVELING

To avoid unwanted attention, try to blend in as much as possible. Respecting local customs (in many cases, dressing more conservatively than you would at home) may ward off would-be hecklers. Familiarize yourself with your surroundings before setting out and carry yourself with confidence. Check maps in shops and restaurants rather than on the street. If you are traveling alone, be sure someone at home knows your itinerary and **never tell anyone you meet that you're by yourself.** When walking at night, stick to busy, well-lit streets and avoid dark alleyways. If you ever feel uncomfortable, leave the area as quickly and directly as you can. There is no sure-fire way to avoid all the threatening situations that you might encounter while traveling, but a good **self-defense course** will give you concrete ways to react to unwanted advances. **Impact & Prepare** (www.prepare-inc.com), and **Model Mugging** (www.modelmugging.org) can refer you to local self-defense courses in Australia, Canada, Switzerland, and the US.

If you are using a car, learn local driving signals and wear a seat belt. Children under 40 lb. should ride only in specially designed car seats, available for a small fee from most car-rental agencies. Study route maps before you hit the road and, if you plan on spending a lot of time driving, consider bringing spare parts. Park your vehicle in a garage or well-traveled area and use a steering-wheel locking device.

Common sense is the simplest prescription for good health while you travel. Drink lots of fluids to prevent dehydration and constipation and wear sturdy, broken-in shoes and clean socks.

POSSESSIONS AND VALUABLES

Never leave your belongings unattended; crime can occur in even the most safe-looking hostel or hotel. Bring your own padlock for hostel lockers and don't ever store valuables in a locker. Be particularly careful on buses and trains; horror stories abound about determined thieves who wait for travelers to fall asleep. Carry your bag or purse in front of you where you can see it. When traveling with others, sleep in alternate shifts. When alone, be careful in selecting a train compartment: never stay in an empty one and always use a lock to secure your pack to the luggage rack. Use extra caution if traveling at night or on overnight trains. Try to sleep on top bunks with your luggage stored above you (if not in bed with you) and keep important documents and other valuables on you at all times.

There are a few steps you can take to minimize the financial risk associated with traveling. First, **bring as little with you as possible.** Second, buy a few combination **padlocks** to secure your belongings either in your pack or in a hostel or train-station locker. Third, **carry as little cash as possible.** Keep your traveler's checks and ATM/credit cards in a **money belt**—not a "fanny pack," hipster—along with your passport and ID cards. Fourth, **keep a small cash reserve separate from your primary stash.** This should be about US$50 (US dollars or euro are best) sewn into or stored in the depths of your pack, along with your traveler's check numbers and photocopies of your important documents.

In large cities, **con artists** often work in groups and may involve children in their schemes. Beware of certain classics: sob stories that require money, rolls of bills "found" on the street, mustard spilled (or saliva spit) onto your shoulder to distract you while they snatch your bag. **Never let your passport or your bags out of your sight.** Hostel workers will sometimes stand at bus and train arrival points to recruit tired and disoriented travelers to their hostel; never believe strangers who tell you that theirs is the only hostel open. Beware of **pickpockets** in city crowds, especially on public transportation. Also, be alert in public telephone booths. If you must say your calling-card number, do so very quietly; if you punch it in, make sure no one can look over your shoulder.

If you will be traveling with electronic devices, such as a laptop computer or MP3 player, check whether your homeowner's insurance covers loss, theft, or damage when you travel. If not, you might consider purchasing a separate low-cost insurance policy. **Safeware** (☎ +1-800-800-1492; www.safeware.com) specializes in covering computers and charges US$90 for 90-day comprehensive international travel coverage up to US$4000.

STAYING HEALTHY

In your passport, write the names of any people you wish to be contacted in case of a medical emergency and list any allergies or medical conditions. Matching a prescription to a foreign equivalent is not always easy, safe, or possible, so, if you take **prescription drugs,** carry up-to-date prescriptions or a statement from your doctor stating the medications' trade names, manufacturers, chemical names, and dosages. While traveling, be sure to keep all medication with you in your carry-on luggage.

IMMUNIZATIONS AND PRECAUTIONS

While no injections are required for entry to the UK, travelers should make sure that the following vaccines are up to date: MMR (for measles, mumps, and rubella); DTaP or Td (for diphtheria, tetanus, and pertussis); IPV (for polio); Hib (for *Haemophilus influenzae* B); and HepB (for Hepatitis B). For recommendations on immunizations and prophylaxis, consult the Centers for Disease Control and Prevention (CDC; below) in the US or the equivalent in your home country and check with a doctor for guidance.

USEFUL ORGANIZATIONS AND PUBLICATIONS

The American **Centers for Disease Control and Prevention (CDC;** ☎+1-800-CDC-INFO/232-4636; www.cdc.gov/travel) maintains an international travelers' hotline and an informative website. Consult the appropriate government agency of your home country for consular information sheets on health, entry requirements, and other issues for various countries (see the listings in the box on **Travel Advisories,** p. 14). For quick information on health and other travel warnings, call the **Overseas Citizens Services** (☎+1-202-647-5225) or contact a passport agency, embassy, or consulate abroad. For information on medical evacuation services and travel insurance firms, see the US government's website at http://travel.state.gov/travel/abroad_health.html or the **British Foreign and Commonwealth Office** (www.fco.gov.uk). For general health information, contact the **American Red Cross** (☎+1-202-303-5000; www.redcross.org).

ONCE IN THE UK

MEDICAL CARE ON THE ROAD

Medical aid is readily available and of excellent quality in the UK. For minor ailments, **chemists** (pharmacies) are easy to find. The ubiquitous Boots chain has a blue logo. **Late-night pharmacies** are rare even in big cities. Most major hospitals have a **24hr. emergency room** (called a "casualty department" or "A&E," short for Accident and Emergency).

In Britain, the state-run **National Health Service (NHS)** encompasses the majority of health-care centers (☎020 7210 4850; www.doh.gov.uk/nhs.htm). The cities in this guide have private hospitals, but these cater to the wealthy and are not often equipped with full surgical staff or complete casualty units. Access to free care is based on residence, not on British citizenship or payment of taxes; those working legally or undertaking long-term study in the UK may also be eligible. Health insurance is a must for all other visitors.

If you are concerned about obtaining medical assistance while traveling, you may wish to employ special support services. The **International Association for Medical Assistance to Travelers (IAMAT;** US ☎+1-716-754-4883, Canada +1-416-652-0137; www.iamat.org) has free membership, lists English-speaking doctors worldwide, and offers details on immunization requirements and sanitation.

Those with medical conditions (such as diabetes, allergies to antibiotics, epilepsy, or heart conditions) may want to obtain a **MedicAlert** membership (US$40 per year), which includes, among other things, a stainless-steel ID tag and a 24hr. helpline. Contact the MedicAlert Foundation International (from US ☎888-633-4298, outside US +1-209-668-3333; www.medicalert.org).

WOMEN'S HEALTH

Tampons, pads, and contraceptive devices are widely available, though your favorite brand may not be stocked—bring extras of anything you can't live without. **Abortion** is legal in the United Kingdom only in cases when the mother's health is in danger or if the child is likely to suffer from a severe mental or physical disability. Women who need an abortion or emergency contraception while in the UK should contact the **Family Planning Association (FPA;** ☎0845 122 8690; www.fpa.org.uk; available M-F 9am-6pm).

GETTING TO THE UK

BY PLANE

When it comes to airfare, a little effort can save you a bundle. For those with flexibility and patience, **standby flights** are one way to save; be prepared to spend all day at the airport for a week or more before finally boarding a plane. Call major airline companies for details (see **Commercial Airlines, p. 18**). Tickets sold by consolidators are also good deals, but last-minute specials and airfare wars often beat these fares. The key is to hunt around, be flexible, and ask about discounts. Students, seniors, and those under 26 should never pay full price for a ticket.

AIRFARES

Airfares to the UK peak between June and September; holidays are also expensive. The cheapest times to travel are November to February. Midweek (M-Th morning) round-trip flights run cheaper than weekend flights, but they are generally more crowded and less likely to permit frequent-flier upgrades. Not fixing a return date ("open return") or arriving in and departing from different cities ("open-jaw") can be pricier than round-trip flights. Patching one-way flights together is the most expensive way to travel. International flights to Cambridge and Oxford are hard to come by; London and, to a lesser extent, Edinburgh are more easily accessed from the sky.

Fares for round-trip flights to London from the US or Canadian east coast cost US$500-1200, US$300-700 in the low season (Nov.-Feb.); from the US or Canadian west coast US$700-1500/500-900; from Australia AUS$1800 and up; from New Zealand NZ$1600 and up.

BUDGET AND STUDENT TRAVEL AGENCIES

While knowledgeable agents specializing in flights to the UK can make your life easy, they may not spend the time to find you the lowest possible fare—they get paid on commission. Travelers holding ISICs and IYTCs (p. 9) qualify for big discounts from student travel agencies. Most flights from budget agencies are on major airlines.

The Adventure Travel Company, 124 MacDougal St., New York City, NY 10021, USA (☎+1-212-674-2887; www.theadventuretravelcompany.com). Offices across Canada and the US including New York City, San Diego, San Francisco, and Seattle.

STA Travel, 2871 Broadway, New York City, NY 10025, USA (24hr. reservations and info ☎+1-800-781-4040; www.statravel.com). A student and youth travel organization with offices worldwide, including US offices in Los Angeles, New York City, Seattle, Wash-

ESSENTIALS

ington, DC and a number of other college towns. Ticket booking, travel insurance, rail-passes, and more. Walk-in offices are located throughout Australia (☎134 782), New Zealand (☎800 474 400), and the UK (☎8712 230 0040).

 FLIGHT PLANNING ON THE INTERNET. The internet may be the budget traveler's dream when it comes to finding and booking bargain fares, but the array of options can be overwhelming. Many airline sites offer special last-minute deals on the web. Try **Virgin Atlantic** (www.virgin-atlantic.com), BMI (www.flybmi.com), or **British Airways** (www.ba/com).

STA (www.statravel.com) and **StudentUniverse** (www.studentuniverse.com) provide quotes on student tickets, while **Orbitz** (www.orbitz.com), **Expedia** (www.expedia.com), and **Travelocity** (www.travelocity.com) offer full travel services. **Priceline** (www.priceline.com) lets you specify a price and obligates you to buy any ticket that meets or beats it; **Hotwire** (www.hotwire.com) offers bargain fares but won't reveal the airline or flight times until you buy. Other sites that compile deals include www.bestfares.com, www.flights.com, www.lowestfare.com, www.onetravel.com, and www.travelzoo.com.

Cheapflights (www.cheapflights.co.uk) is a useful search engine for find-ing—you guessed it—cheap flights. **Booking Buddy** (www.bookingbuddy.com), **Kayak** (www.kayak.com), and **SideStep** (www.sidestep.com) are online tools that let you enter your trip information and search multiple sites at once. Let's Go does not endorse any of these websites. As always, be cautious and research companies before you hand over your credit card number.

COMMERCIAL AIRLINES

TRAVELING FROM NORTH AMERICA

Crossing the pond? Standard commercial carriers like **American** (☎800-433-7300; www.aa.com), **United** (☎800-538-2929; www.ual.com), and **Northwest** (☎800-225-2525; www.nwa.com) will probably offer the most convenient flights, but they may not be the cheapest. Check **Air France** (☎800-237-2747; www.airfrance.us), **Alitalia** (☎800-223-5730; www.alitaliausa.com), **British Airways** (☎800-247-9297; www.britishairways.com), and **Lufthansa** (☎800-399-5838; www.lufthansa.com) for cheap tickets from destinations throughout the US to all over Europe. You might find an even better deal on one of the following airlines, if any of their limited departure points is convenient for you.

Aer Lingus: ☎800-474-7424; www.aerlingus.ie. Affordable flights from Boston, Chicago, Orlando, New York City, San Francisco, and Washington D.C. to Birmingham, Bristol, Lon-don, Manchester, Glasgow, Dublin, and Shannon.

Icelandair: ☎800-223-5500; www.icelandair.com. Departs Boston, Minneapolis, New York City, Orlando, and Seattle with stopovers in Iceland.

TRAVELING FROM AUSTRALIA AND NEW ZEALAND

Air New Zealand: New Zealand ☎800 737 000; www.airnz.co.nz. Flights from Auckland to London and Edinburgh.

Qantas Air: Australia ☎13 13 13, New Zealand ☎800 808 767; www.qantas.com.au. Flights from Australia and New Zealand to London for around AUS$1200.

Singapore Air: Australia ☎13 10 11, from New Zealand ☎800 808 909; www.singaporeair.com. Flies from Auckland, Christchurch, Melbourne, Perth, and Sydney to London, all through Singapore.

Thai Airways: Australia ☎1300 65 19 60, New Zealand ☎9 256 8518; www.thaiair.com. Auckland, Melbourne, Perth, and Sydney to London, all through Bangkok.

BUDGET AIRLINES

For travelers who don't place a premium on convenience, we recommend ▨budget airlines as the best way to jet around the UK and throughout Europe. Travelers can often snag these tickets for illogically low prices (i.e., less than the price of a meal in the airport food court), but you get what you pay for: namely, minimalist service and no frills. In addition, many budget airlines fly out of smaller regional airports several kilometers out of town. You'll have to buy shuttle tickets to reach the airports of many of these airlines, so plan on adding an hour or so to your travel time. After round-trip shuttle tickets and fees for services that might come standard on other airlines, that €1 sale fare can suddenly jump to €20-100. Still, it's possible save money even if you live outside the continent by hopping a cheap flight to anywhere in Europe and using budget airlines to reach your final desti-nation. Prices vary dramatically; shop around, book months ahead, pack light, and stay flexible to nab the best fares. For a more detailed list of these airlines by country, check out www.whichbudget.com.

bmibaby: from the UK ☎9111 545 454, elsewhere +44 870 126 6726; www.bmibaby.com. Flights to UK destinations from throughout Europe. Dublin to London £80.

easyJet: ☎+44 871 244 2366; www.easyjet.com. Athens, Barcelona, Madrid, Nice, Palma, and Zurich to London (£72-145).

Ryanair: from Ireland ☎0818 30 30 30, UK 0871 246 0000; www.ryanair.com. From major European cities to destinations all over the UK.

SkyEurope: from the UK ☎0906 680 0065, elsewhere +352 27 00 27 28; www.skyeurope.com. Flights in 19 countries around Europe. Prague to London £33.

Wizz Air: from the UK ☎0904 475 9500, from Ireland ☎1550 475 970; www.wizzair.com. European cities to London and Liverpool.

BY CHUNNEL

Traversing 32 mi. under the sea, the Chunnel is undoubtedly the fastest, most convenient, and least scenic route from Britain to France.

Trains: Eurostar, Times House, Bravingtons Walk, Regent Quarter, London N1 9AW, UK (from the UK ☎08705 186 186, from elsewhere ☎+44 1233 617 575; www.eurostar.com). Frequent trains between the continent and London. Paris to London (3½hr., £60-160).

Buses: Eurolines (www.eurolines.com) provides bus-ferry combinations to London.

Cars: Eurotunnel, Ashford Rd., Folkestone, Kent CT18 8XX (☎08705 35 35 35; www.eurotunnel.co.uk). Shuttles cars and passengers between Kent and Nord-Pas-de-Calais. Return fares range UK£100-250 for a car, depending on length of stay. Book online or via phone. Travelers with cars can also look into sea crossings by ferry (below).

BY FERRY

The fares below are one-way for adult foot passengers unless otherwise noted. Though standard return fares are usually just twice the one-way fare, fixed-period returns (usually within 5 days) are almost invariably cheaper. Ferries run year-round unless otherwise noted. Bikes are usually free, although you may have to pay up to UK£30 in high season. For a camper/trailer supplement, you will have to add UK£20-140 to the "with car" fare. If more than one price is quoted, the quote in pounds is valid for departures from the UK. A directory of ferries in this region can be found at www.seaview.co.uk/ferries.html.

Brittany Ferries: ☎0871 244 0744, France 8 25 82 88 28; www.brittany-ferries.com. Between Plymouth and Roscoff, FRA, and Santander, ESP; Portsmouth and St. Malo, FRA and Caen, FRA; Poole and Cherbourg, FRA; Cork and Roscoff, FRA.

Irish Ferries: ☎08705 171 717, France 1 56 93 43 40, Ireland 818 300 400; www.irishferries.ie. Between Holyhead and Dublin (12hr., £30).

Norfolkline, ☎0870 870 1020; www.norfolkline-ferries.com. Between Dover and Calais, FRA and Dunkirk, FRA (equally convenient but less busy).

P&O Ferries: ☎08716 645 645; www.poferries.com. Daily ferries between Hull and Rotterdam, NTH and Zeebrugge, BEL; Dover and Calais, FRA; Portsmouth and Le Havre, FRA, and Bilbao, ESP; and several Britain-Ireland routes.

SeaFrance: France ☎8 25 08 25 05; www.seafrance.com. Between Dover and Calais, FRA (1½hr., 15 per day, £7-11).

Stena Line: ☎08705 707 070; www.stenaline.co.uk. Between: Harwich and Hook of Holland, NTH; Fishguard and Rosslare; Holyhead and Dublin and Dún Laoghaire.

GETTING AROUND THE UK

TRAVELINE. An essential resource, **Traveline** (☎0871 200 2233; www.traveline.org.uk) offers comprehensive and impartial information for travel planning throughout the UK—whether by train, bus, or ferry.

BY TRAIN

Great Britain's train network crisscrosses the length and breadth of the island. In cities with more than one train station, the city name is given first, followed by the station name (for example, "London Piccadilly" and "London Victoria" are London's two major stations). In general, traveling by train costs more than by bus. Railpasses covering specific regions are sometimes available from local train stations and may include bus and ferry travel. Prices and schedules often change; find up-to-date information from **National Rail Inquiries** (☎08457 484 950) or online at www.nationalrail.co.uk.

TICKET TYPES

The array of tickets available for British trains is bewildering, and prices aren't always set logically—buying an unlimited day pass to the region may cost less than buying a one-way ticket. Prices rise on weekends and may be higher before 9:30am. Purchase tickets before boarding, except at unstaffed train stations, where tickets are bought on the train. There are several types of **discount** tickets. **APEX (Advance Purchase Excursion)** tickets must be bought at least seven days in advance (2 days for ScotRail); **SuperAdvance** tickets must be purchased before 6pm the day before you travel. **Saver** tickets are valid anytime with return trips within a month but may be restricted to certain trains at peak times; SuperSaver tickets are similar but are only valid at off-peak times (usually M-Th, Su, and holidays). It may seem daunting, but the general rule of thumb is simple: planning a week or more in advance can make a £30-60 difference.

BRITRAIL PASSES

If you plan to travel a great deal on trains within Britain, the **BritRail Pass** can be a good buy. Eurail Passes are not valid in Britain, but there is often a discount on Eurostar passes if you have proof of Eurail purchase at the ticket office. BritRail Passes are only available outside Britain; you must buy them before you depart. They allow unlimited train travel in England, Wales, and Scotland, regardless of which company is operating the trains, but they do not work in Northern Ireland or on Eurostar. Travelers under 26 should ask for a **Youth Pass** for a 25% discount on standard and first classes; **seniors** (over 60) should ask for a 15% discount on first class only. **Children** from ages five to 15 can travel free with each adult pass, as long as you ask for the **Family Pass** (free). All children under five travel free. The **Party Discount** gets the third through ninth travelers in a party a 50% discount on their railpasses. Check with BritRail (☎+1-866-BRIT-RAIL; www.britrail.com) or one of the distributors for details on other passes. Prices listed below do not include shipping costs (around US$15 for delivery in 2-3 days, US$25 for priority delivery).

BritRail + Ireland Pass: Includes all trains in Britain, Northern Ireland, and the Republic of Ireland, plus a round-trip Stena or Irish Ferries sea crossing. No discounts apply. Travel within a 1-month period. Any 5 days standard class US$469, 1st class US$699; any 10 days US$839/1245.

BritRail Scottish Freedom Pass: Includes all Scottish trains, the Glasgow Underground, and Caledonian MacBrayne and Strathclyde ferry services. No discounts apply. Standard class only. 4 days within any 8 days US$235; 8 days within any 15 days US$315.

England Consecutive: Travel for consecutive days, only in England. 4 days standard class US$199, 1st class US$299; 8 days US$285/429; 15 days US$429/645; 22 days US$545/815; 1 month US$639/959.

England Flexipass: Travel within a 2-month period, only in England. Any 4 days standard class US$255, 1st class US$379; any 8 days US$369/549.

London Plus Pass: Travel between London and several popular daytrip locations, including Cambridge, Oxford, and Windsor. 2 days within any 8 days standard-class US$139, 1st class US$209; 4 days within any 8 days US$225/289; 7 days within any 15 days US$269/369.

BRITRAIL DISTRIBUTORS

The distributors listed below will either sell you passes directly or tell you where to buy them; you can also ask travel agents for more information.

Australia: Rail Plus, 10-16 Queen St., Level 4, Melbourne, Victoria 3000 (☎3 9642 8644; www.railplus.com.au). Concorde International Travel, 403 George St., Sydney, NSW 2000 (☎1300 656 777; www.concorde.com.au).

Canada and the US: Rail Europe, 44 South Broadway, White Plains, NY 10601 (☎800-361-7245 or 877-257-2887; www.raileurope.com). The North American distributor for BritRail.

Ireland: USIT, 19-21 Aston Quay, O'Connell Bridge, Dublin 2 (☎1 602 1904; www.usit.ie).

RAIL DISCOUNT CARDS

Unlike BritRail passes, these can be purchased in the UK. Passes are valid for one year and generally offer one-third off standard fares. They are available for young people (£26; must be 16-25 or a full-time student), seniors (£26; must be over 60), families (£26), and people with disabilities (£18). Visit the **Railcards** website (www.railcard.co.uk) for details.

ESSENTIALS

BY BUS AND COACH

The British distinguish between **buses** (short local routes) and **coaches** (long distances). *Let's Go London, Oxford, Cambridge & Edinburgh* uses the term "buses" for both. Regional **passes** offer unlimited travel within a given area for a certain number of days; these are often called Rovers, Ramblers, or Explorers, and they usually offer cost-effective travel. Plan ahead and book tickets online to take advantage of discounts.

BUSES

Long-distance bus travel in the UK is extensive and cheap. **National Express** (☎08705 808 080; www.nationalexpress.com) is the principal operator of long-distance bus services in Britain, although **Scottish Citylink** (☎08705 505 050; www.citylink.co.uk) has extensive coverage in Scotland. Discounts are available for seniors (over 50), students, and young people (16-25). For those who plan far ahead, the best option is National Express's **Fun Fares,** only available online, which offer a limited number of seats on buses from London starting at £1. A similar option is **Megabus** (☎0900 160 0900; www.megabus.com), which also offers the £1 price but runs fewer buses. Tourist Information Centres carry timetables for regional buses and will help befuddled travelers decipher them.

BY CAR

Cars offer speed, freedom, access to the countryside, and an escape from the town-to-town mentality of trains. Although a single traveler won't save by renting a car, four usually will. If you can't decide between train and car travel, you may benefit from a combination of the two. Fly-and-drive packages are also often available from travel agents or airline/rental agency partnerships.

Before setting off, know the rules of the road in the UK (e.g., drive on the left). For a primer on British road signs and conventions, check out www.direct.gov.uk/en/TravelAndTransport/Highwaycode. The **Association for Safe International Road Travel** (**ASIRT**; ☎+1-301-983-5252; www.asirt.org) can provide more specific information about road conditions. ASIRT considers road travel to be relatively safe in the UK. Britons use unleaded gas almost exclusively.

DRIVING PERMITS AND CAR INSURANCE

If you plan to drive a car while in the UK, you must be over 17 and have a valid foreign driver's license.

Most credit cards cover standard insurance. If you rent, lease, or borrow a car, you will need a **green card,** or **International Insurance Certificate,** to certify that you have liability insurance and that it applies abroad. Green cards can be obtained at car-rental agencies, car dealers (for those leasing cars), some travel agents, and some border crossings. Rental agencies may require you to purchase theft insurance in countries that they consider to have a high risk of auto theft.

RENTING A CAR

To rent, or "hire," a car in the UK, you need to be at least 21 years old. Some agencies require renters to be 25, and most charge those 21-24 an additional insurance fee (around £10-15 per day). Small local operations occasionally rent to people under 21, but be sure to ask about the insurance coverage and deductible and always check the fine print.

You can rent a car from a US-based firm (Avis, Budget, or Hertz) with British offices, from a European-based company with local representatives or from a tour operator (Auto Europe, Europe By Car, and Kemwel Holiday Autos) that will arrange a rental for you from a European company at its own rates. Multinationals offer greater flexibility, but tour operators often strike better deals. It is always significantly less expensive to reserve a car from the US than from Europe. Ask airlines about special fly-and-drive packages; you may get up to a week of free or discounted rental. Reserve ahead and pay in advance if at all possible. Always check if prices quoted include tax and collision insurance; some credit card companies provide insurance, allowing their customers to decline the collision damage waiver.

Arnold Clark (☎0845 607 4500; www.arnoldclarkrental.co.uk).

Auto Europe (☎+1-888-223-5555 or 207-842-2000; www.autoeurope.com).

Avis (UK ☎08700 100 287; www.avis.com).

Budget (US ☎800-472-3325, UK ☎8701 565 656; www.budgetrentacar.com).

easyCar (☎09063 333 333; www.easycar.co.uk).

Europe by Car (☎+1-800-223-1516 or 212-581-3040; www.europebycar.com).

Hertz (☎+1-800-654-3001; www.hertz.com).

Kemwel (☎+1-877-820-0668 or 800-678-0678; www.kemwel.com).

LEASING A CAR

For longer than 17 days, leasing can be cheaper than renting; it is often the only option for those aged 18 to 21. The cheapest leases are agreements to buy the car and then sell it back to the manufacturer at a prearranged price. As far as you're concerned, though, it's a lease and doesn't entail enormous financial transactions. Leases generally include insurance coverage and are not taxed. Expect to pay around ₤150-300 (depending on size of car) per month. Contact Auto Europe, Europe by Car, or Kemwel (above) before you go.

ON THE ROAD

You must be 17 to drive in the UK. Be sure you can handle **driving on the left side** of the road and driving **manual transmission** ("stick shift" is far more common than automatic). Be particularly cautious at **roundabouts** (rotary interchanges) and remember to give way to traffic from the right.

Petrol (gasoline) prices vary, but they average about ₤1 per liter and increase during the summer and in urban areas like London. The country is covered by a high-speed system of **motorways** ("M-roads," some of them tolled) that connect London with major cities around the country. These are supplemented by a tight web of "A-roads" and "B-roads" that connect towns: A-roads are the main routes, while B-roads are narrower but often more scenic. Distances on road signs are in miles (1 mi. = 1.6km). Speed limits are marked at the beginning of town areas; upon leaving, you'll see a circular sign with a slash through it, signaling the end of the restriction. Drivers and all passengers are required to wear **seat belts** in the UK.

Since a controversial 2003 reform, driving in central **London** is taxed at a stiff ₤8 per day during weekday working hours. Parking in London can be nightmarish. The **Highway Code,** which details Britain's driving regulations, is accessible online (www.highwaycode.gov.uk) or can be purchased at most large bookstores or newsstands.

ESSENTIALS

DANGERS

Driving in rural areas often requires caution on single-lane roads, many of which are scarcely wide enough for two cars to pass. These roads have occasional "passing places," which cars use to make way for passing vehicles. Cars flash their lights to signal that they will pull aside; the other car should take the right of way. The Scottish Highlands, Northumberland, Yorkshire, the Lake District, and parts of Wales all have roads on steep inclines, which drivers should take slowly in a low gear. Beware livestock along remote countryside roads.

CAR ASSISTANCE

In the event of a breakdown, contact the **Automobile Association** (**AA;** ☎0161 495 8945, emergency breakdown 08457 887 766; www.theaa.com). For emergencies, call ☎**999.**

 LET'S NOT GO. Let's Go never recommends hitchhiking; hitchers risk theft, assault, sexual harassment, and unsafe driving.

KEEPING IN TOUCH

BY EMAIL AND INTERNET

Internet access is ubiquitous in big cities, common in towns, and sparse in rural areas. You can find access in the cybercafes, in coffee shops (particularly chains such as Caffe Nero and Starbucks), and in public libraries. Sneaky travelers use computers in media shops like PC World to check email quickly.

Although in some places it's possible to forge a remote link with your home server, in most cases this is a much slower (and thus more expensive) option than taking advantage of free **web-based email accounts** (e.g., www.gmail.com). **Internet cafes** and the occasional free internet terminal at a public library or university are listed in the **Practical Information** sections of major cities. For lists of additional cybercafes in Britain, check out www.cybercaptive.com.

 WARY WI-FI. Wireless hot spots make internet access possible in public and remote places. Unfortunately, they also pose security risks. Hot spots are public, open networks that use unencrypted, unsecured connections. They are susceptible to hacks and "packet sniffing"—the theft of passwords and other private information. To prevent problems, disable "ad hoc" mode, turn off file sharing and network discovery, encrypt your email, turn on your firewall, beware of phony networks, and watch for over-the-shoulder creeps.

BY TELEPHONE

CALLING HOME FROM THE UK

Prepaid phone cards are a common and relatively inexpensive means of calling abroad. Each one comes with a Personal Identification Number (PIN) and a toll-free access number. To purchase prepaid phone cards, check online for the best rates; www.callingcards.com is a good place to start.

Online providers generally send your access number and PIN via email, with no actual "card" involved. You can also call home with prepaid phone cards purchased in the UK.

PLACING INTERNATIONAL CALLS. To call Britain from home or to call home from Britain, dial:

1. The **international dialing prefix.** To call from **Australia,** dial 0011; **Canada** or the **US,** 011; **Ireland, New Zealand,** or the **UK,** 00.
2. The **country code** of the country you want to call. To call **Australia,** dial 61; **Canada** or the **US,** 1; **Ireland,** 353; **New Zealand,** 64; the **UK,** 44.
3. The **city/area code.** *Let's Go* lists the city/area codes for cities and towns in the UK opposite the city or town name, next to a ☎, as well as in every phone number. If the first digit is a zero (e.g., 020 for London), **omit the zero** when calling from abroad (e.g., dial 20 from the US).
4. The **local number.**

Examples: To call the US embassy in London from New York City, dial ☎011 44 20 7499 9000. To call the British embassy in Washington from London, dial ☎00 1 202 588 7800. To call the US embassy in London from London, dial ☎020 7499 9000.

Another option is to purchase a **calling card,** linked to a major national telecommunications service in your home country. Calls are billed collect or to your account. Cards generally come with instructions for dialing both domestically and internationally.

Placing a collect call through an international operator can be expensive but may be necessary in case of an emergency. You can frequently call collect without even possessing a company's calling card just by calling its access number and following the instructions.

CALLING WITHIN THE UK

The simplest way to call within the country is to use a coin-operated phone. Prepaid phone cards (available at newspaper kiosks, train stations, and convenience stores) usually save time and money in the long run. Phone rates typically tend to be highest in the morning, lower in the evening, and lowest on Sundays and late at night. On some public phones, you can swipe the magnetic strip on your phone card, or even your credit card, to pay for calls.

To make a call within a city or town, dial the phone code and the number. For **directory inquiries,** call ☎118 500 (or any of the myriad other 118 services, such as ☎118 118 or 118 888). The services normally charge a 50p connection fee and cost 15p per minute.

PHONE CODES

The first three numbers of a British phone code identify the type of number being called. **Premium rate calls,** costing about 50p per minute, can be identified by the ☎090 phone code. **Freephone** (toll-free) numbers have a ☎080 code. Numbers that begin with an ☎084 code incur the **local call rate,** while the ☎087 code incurs the **national call rate** (these two rates are not significantly different for short calls). Calling a **mobile phone** (cell phone) is more expensive than a regular phone call. Mobile phone numbers carry ☎077, 078, or 079 codes, and pager numbers begin with ☎076.

ESSENTIALS

PUBLIC PHONES

Public pay phones in Britain are mostly run by **BT Group** (formerly British Telecom). Public phones charge a minimum of 30p for calls and don't accept 1p, 2p, or 5p coins. The dial tone is a continuous purring sound; a repeated double-tone means the line is ringing. A series of harsh beeps will warn you to insert more money when your time is up. For the rest of the call, the digital display ticks off your credit. You may use any remaining credit on a second call by pressing the "follow on call" button (often marked "FC"). Otherwise, once you hang up, your remaining phone-card credit is rounded down to the nearest 10p. Pay phones do not give change, so use your smallest coins.

CELLULAR PHONES

The international standard for cell phones is **Global System for Mobile Communication (GSM).** To make and receive calls in the UK, you will need a GSM-compatible phone and a **SIM (Subscriber Identity Module) card,** a country-specific, thumbnail-size chip that gives you a local phone number and plugs you into the local network. Many SIM cards are prepaid, and incoming calls are frequently free. You can buy additional cards or vouchers (usually available at convenience stores) to "top up" your phone. For more information on GSM phones, check out www.telestial.com. Companies like **Cellular Abroad** (www.cellularabroad.com) rent cell phones that work in destinations around the world.

 GSM PHONES. Just having a GSM phone doesn't mean you're necessarily good to go when you travel abroad. The majority of GSM phones sold in the US operate on a different frequency (1900) than international phones (900/1800) and will not work abroad. Tri-band phones work on all three frequencies (900/1800/1900) and will operate through most of the world. Additionally, some GSM phones are SIM-locked and will only accept SIM cards from a single carrier. You'll need a SIM-unlocked phone to use a SIM card from a local carrier when you travel.

TIME DIFFERENCES

The UK is on Greenwich Mean Time (GMT) and observes Daylight Saving Time between the last Sunday of March and the last Sunday of October: in March, the clock moves 1hr. later; in October, the clock moves 1hr. earlier.

BY MAIL

SENDING MAIL HOME FROM THE UK

Airmail is the best way to send mail home from Britain. **Aerogrammes,** printed sheets that fold into envelopes and travel via airmail, are available at post offices. Write *"par avion,"* on the front or swing by any post office for a free "Airmail" label. Most post offices will charge exorbitant fees or simply refuse to send aerogrammes with enclosures. For priority shipping, ask for **Airsure;** it costs £4.20 on top of the actual postage, but your letter will get on the next available flight. Surface mail is by far the cheapest and slowest way to send mail. It takes one to two months to cross the Atlantic and one to three to cross the Pacific—good for heavy items you won't need for a while, like souvenirs that you've acquired along the way.

Royal Mail has taken great care to standardize its international rates. To check how much a shipment will cost, use the Royal Mail Postal Calculator at www. royalmail.com. Allow five days for regular airmail home to Australia, Canada, and the US. Postcards/aerograms cost 56p, as do letters weighing up to 20g.

SENDING MAIL TO THE UK

To ensure timely delivery, mark envelopes "airmail," or *"par avion."* In addition to the standard postage system whose rates are listed below, **Federal Express** (☎+1-800-463-3339; www.fedex.com) handles express mail services between the UK and most other countries. Sending a postcard within the UK costs 25p, while sending letters (up to 100g) domestically requires 30p.

There are several ways to arrange pickup of letters sent to you while you are abroad. Mail can be sent via **Poste Restante** (General Delivery) to almost any city or town in the UK with a post office. Address Poste Restante letters like so:

William SHAKESPEARE
Poste Restante
Stratford-upon-Avon CV37 6PU
United Kingdom

The mail will go to a special desk in the central post office, unless you specify a post office by street address or postal code. It's best to use the largest post office, since mail may be sent there regardless. Bring your passport (or other photo ID) for pickup; if the clerks insist that there is nothing for you, ask them to check under your first name as well. *Let's Go* lists post offices in the **Practical Information** section for each city and most towns.

American Express has travel offices throughout the world that offer a free **Client Letter Service** (mail held up to 30 days and forwarded upon request) for cardholders who contact them in advance. Some offices provide these services to non-cardholders (especially AmEx Travelers Cheque holders), but call ahead to make sure. For a complete list of AmEx locations, call ☎+1-800-528-4800 or visit www.amextravelresources.com.

ACCOMMODATIONS

HOSTELS

Many hostels are laid out dorm-style, often with large single-sex rooms and bunk beds, although private rooms that sleep from two to four are becoming more common. They sometimes have kitchens and utensils for your use, breakfast and other meals, storage areas, laundry facilities, internet, transportation to airports, and bike or moped rentals. However, there can be drawbacks: some hostels impose a maximum stay, close during certain daytime "lockout" hours, have a curfew, don't accept reservations, or, less frequently, require that you do chores. In the UK, a dorm bed in a hostel will average around £15-20 in Oxford, Cambridge, and Edinburgh, and £20-25 in London.

ESSENTIALS

HOSTELLING INTERNATIONAL

Joining the youth hostel association in your own country (listed below) automatically grants you membership privileges in **Hostelling International (HI)**, a federation of national hosteling associations. Non-HI members may be allowed to stay in some hostels, but they will have to pay an extra £3 to do so. HI's umbrella organization's website (www.hihostels.com), which lists the web addresses and phone numbers of all national associations, can be a great place to begin researching hosteling in a specific region. Other hostelling websites include www.hostels.com and www.hostelplanet.com.

Most HI hostels also honor **guest memberships**—you'll get a blank card with space for six validation stamps. Each night you'll pay a nonmember supplement and earn one guest stamp; six stamps make you a member. Most student travel agencies (p. 17) sell HI cards, as do all of the national hosteling organizations listed below.

An Óige (Irish Youth Hostel Association), 61 Mountjoy St., Dublin 7 (☎1 830 4555; www.anoige.ie). €20, under 18 €10.

Australian Youth Hostels Association (AYHA), 422 Kent St., Sydney, NSW 2000 (☎2 9261 1111; www.yha.com.au). AUS$42, under 26 AUS$32.

Hostelling International-Canada (HI-C), 205 Catherine St., Ste. 400, Ottawa, ON K2P 1C3 (☎613-237-7884; www.hihostels.ca). CDN$35, under 18 free.

Hostelling International Northern Ireland (HINI), 22-32 Donegall Rd., Belfast BT12 5JN (☎28 9032 4733; www.hini.org.uk). UK£15, under 25 £10.

Scottish Youth Hostels Association (SYHA), 7 Glebe Cres., Stirling FK8 2JA (☎01786 891 400; www.syha.org.uk). £9, student and under 16 free.

Youth Hostels Association (England and Wales), Trevelyan House, Dimple Rd., Matlock, Derbyshire DE4 3YH (☎1629 592 600; www.yha.org.uk). £16, under 26 £10.

Youth Hostels Association of New Zealand Inc. (YHANZ), Level 1, 166 Moorhouse Ave., P.O. Box 436, Christchurch (☎3 379 9970, in NZ 0800 278 299; www.yha.org.nz). NZ$40, under 18 free.

Hostelling International-USA, 8401 Colesville Rd., Ste. 600, Silver Spring, MD 20910 (☎301-495-1240; www.hiayh.org). US$28, under 18 free.

BED AND BREAKFASTS (B&BS)

For a cozy alternative to impersonal hotel rooms, B&Bs (private homes with rooms available to travelers) range from acceptable to sublime. B&B owners sometimes go out of their way to be accommodating, giving personalized tours, helping with travel plans, or serving home-cooked meals. Some B&Bs, however, do not provide private bathrooms **(ensuite)** and most do not have phones. A **double** room has one large bed for two people; a **twin** has two separate beds. *Let's Go* lists B&B prices by room type.

You can book B&Bs by calling directly or asking the local Tourist Information Centre (TIC) to help you find accommodations; most can also book B&Bs in other towns. TICs usually charge a 10% deposit on the first night's or the entire stay's price, deductible from the amount you pay the proprietor. Occasionally a flat booking fee of £1-5 is added. Rooms in B&Bs generally cost £25-40 for a single and £45-60 for a double. Many websites provide B&B listings; check out **InnFinder** (www.inncrawler.com), **InnSite** (www.innsite.com), or **BedandBreakfast.com** (www.bedandbreakfast.com). The British tourist boards operate a B&B **rating system,** using a scale of one to five diamonds (in England) or stars (in Scotland and Wales). Rated accommodations are part of the tourist board's booking system, but it costs money to be rated and some perfectly good B&Bs choose not to participate.

OTHER TYPES OF ACCOMMODATIONS

HOTELS

Hotel singles in the UK cost about US$140 (£112) per night, doubles US$152 (£95). If you make **reservations** in writing, indicate your night of arrival and the number of nights you plan to stay. The hotel will send you a confirmation and may request payment for the first night.

HOME EXCHANGES AND HOSPITALITY CLUBS

Home exchange offers the traveler various types of homes (houses, apartments, condominiums, even castles in some cases), plus the opportunity to live like a native and to cut down on accommodation fees. For more information, contact **HomeExchange.com Inc.** (☎+1-310-798-3864 or toll-free 800-877-8723; www.homeexchange.com) or **Intervac International Home Exchange** (☎0845 260 5776; www.intervac.com).

Hospitality clubs link their members with individuals or families abroad who are willing to host travelers for free or for a small fee to promote cultural exchange and general good karma. In exchange, members usually must be willing to host travelers in their own homes; a small fee may also be required. **The Hospitality Club** (www.hospitalityclub.org) is a good place to start. **Servas** (www.servas.org) is an established, more formal organization and requires a fee and an interview to join. An internet search will find many similar organizations, some of which cater to special interests (e.g., women, GLBT travelers, or members of certain professions). As always, use common sense when planning to stay with or host someone you do not know.

LONG-TERM ACCOMMODATIONS

Travelers planning to stay in the UK for extended periods of time may find it most cost-effective to rent an apartment. A basic one-bedroom (or studio) apartment in London will range about £400-600 per month, in Cambridge Oxford, and Edinburgh about £300-500. **Housepals UK** (www.housepals.co.uk) and **Gumtree** (www.gumtree.co.uk) both have extensive listings of available apartments and rooms for sublet. Many students opt to stay in hostels instead of flats (see **Hostels,** p. 27).

SPECIFIC CONCERNS

TRAVELING ALONE

Traveling alone can be extremely beneficial, providing a sense of independence and a greater opportunity to connect with locals. On the other hand, solo travelers are more vulnerable targets of harassment and theft. For more information on staying safe when traveling solo, see **Exploring and Traveling,** p. 14. Maintain regular contact with someone at home who knows your itinerary and always research your destination before traveling.

WOMEN TRAVELERS

Women exploring on their own inevitably face some additional safety concerns. Single women can consider staying in hostels that offer single rooms that lock from the inside or in religious organizations with single-sex rooms. It's a good idea to stick to centrally located accommodations and to avoid solitary late-night treks or metro rides. Always carry extra cash for a phone call, bus, or taxi. Hitchhiking is never safe for lone women or even for two women traveling together. Look as if you know where you're going and approach older women or couples for directions if you're lost or feeling uncomfortable in your surroundings. Generally, the less you look like a tourist, the better off you'll be. Dress conservatively, especially in rural areas. Wearing a conspicuous **wedding band** sometimes helps to prevent unwanted advances.

Your best answer to verbal harassment is no answer at all; feigning deafness, sitting motionless, and staring straight ahead at nothing in particular will usually do the trick. The extremely persistent can sometimes be dissuaded by a firm, loud, and very public "Go away!" Don't hesitate to seek out a police officer or a passerby if you are being harassed. Memorize the emergency numbers in places you visit and consider carrying a whistle on your keychain. Mace and pepper sprays are illegal in Britain.

The national emergency number is ☎999. **Rape Crisis UK and Ireland** (a full list of helplines can be found at www.rapecrisis.org.uk, www.rapecrisisscotland. org.uk in Scotland) provides referrals to local rape crisis and sexual abuse counseling services throughout the UK. A self-defense course will both prepare you for a potential attack and raise your level of awareness of your surroundings (see **Personal Safety,** p. 14).

GLBT TRAVELERS

Large cities like the ones covered in this guide are comparatively very open to the GLBT community. The magazine *Time Out* has gay and lesbian listings, and numerous periodicals make it easy to learn about the current concerns of Britain's gay community. The *Pink Paper* (www.pinkpaper.com) is available free from newsstands in larger cities. Listed below are contact organizations, mail-order catalogs, and publishers that offer materials addressing some specific concerns. **Out and About** (www.planetout.com) offers a comprehensive website and a weekly newsletter geared toward GLBT travelers.

Gay's the Word, 66 Marchmont St., London WC1N 1AB, UK (☎+44 20 7278 7654; http://freespace.virgin.net/gays.theword). The largest gay and lesbian bookshop in the UK, with both fiction and nonfiction titles. Mail-order service available.

Giovanni's Room, 345 S. 12th St., Philadelphia, PA 19107, USA (☎+1-215-923-2960; www.giovannisroom.com). An international lesbian and gay bookstore with mail-order service (carries many of the publications listed below).

International Lesbian and Gay Association (ILGA), 17 Rue de la Charité, 1210 Brussels, Belgium (☎+32 2 502 2471; www.ilga.org). Provides political information, such as homosexuality laws of individual countries.

London Lesbian and Gay Switchboard (☎020 7837 7324; www.llgs.org.uk). Confidential advice, information, and referrals. Open 24hr.

> **ADDITIONAL GLBT RESOURCES**
> *Damron Men's Travel Guide, Damron Women's Traveller, Damron Accommodations Guide, Damron City Guide,* and *Damron Women's Traveller.* Published annually by Damron Travel Guides. For info, call ☎+1-415-255-0404 or visit www.damron.com.
> *The Gay Vacation Guide: The Best Trips and How to Plan Them,* by Mark Chesnut. Kensington Books.
> *Gayellow Pages USA/Canada,* by Frances Green. Gayellow Pages. Also publishes regional editions. Visit Gayellow pages online at http://gayellowpages.com.
> *Spartacus International Gay Guide 2009,* by Bruno Gmunder Verlag.

TRAVELERS WITH DISABILITIES

Travelers with disabilities should inform airlines and hotels of their disabilities when making reservations, as some time may be needed to prepare special accommodations. Call ahead to restaurants, museums, and other facilities to find out if they are wheelchair accessible. Guide-dog owners should inquire as to the quarantine policies of each destination country.

Rail is probably the most convenient form of transport for disabled travelers in the UK: many stations have ramps, and some trains have wheelchair lifts, special seating areas, and specially equipped toilets. The National Rail website (www.nationalrail.co.uk) provides general information for travelers with disabilities and assistance phone numbers; it also describes the **Disabled Persons Railcard** (£18 for one year), which cuts one-third off most fares and guarantees other benefits at participating hotels. Most **bus** companies will provide assistance if notified ahead of time. All National Express coaches entering service after 2005 must be equipped with a wheelchair lift or ramp; call the **Additional Needs Help Line** (☎0121 423 8479) for information or consult www.nationalexpress.com. The London **Underground** is slowly improving accessibility, and all of London's public buses became wheelchair-accessible in January 2006; **Transport for London: Access and Mobility** (☎020 7222 1234) can provide more information on public transportation throughout the city. For those who wish to rent cars, some major car-rental agencies (e.g., Hertz) offer hand-controlled vehicles.

The British Tourist Boards rate accommodations and attractions using the **National Accessible Scheme (NAS),** which designates three categories of accessibility. Look for the NAS symbols in Tourist Board guidebooks or ask a sight directly for their ranking. Many theaters and performance venues have space for wheelchairs; some larger theatrical performances include special facilities for the hearing-impaired. Book ahead to guarantee special provisions.

Traveling by public transport in London with a disability is getting easier. While the Underground is almost exclusively accessible via numerous stairs and can be extremely crowded during peak travel times, new stations are beginning to incorporate lifts. Jubilee line trains are wheelchair-accessible at all new stations between Westminster and Stratford. The Docklands Light Railway has lifts, escalators, and/or ramps at every station, and all platforms are level with the train for free-step access; there is also a designated wheelchair area on each train. All city buses, except for routes 9 and 15, have wheelchair-accessible ramps and designated spaces for riding while on board. The wheelchair-accessible Stationlink buses follow a similar route to the Circle Line; routes 205 and 705 travel from Paddington, Euston, St. Pancras, and King's Cross to Liverpool St., London Bridge, Waterloo, and Victoria. All black taxis are wheelchair-accessible. The following companies offer tours, services, and information for travelers with disabilities.

Accessible Journeys, 35 W. Sellers Ave., Ridley Park, PA 19078, USA (☎+1-800-846-4537; www.disabilitytravel.com). Designs tours for wheelchair users and slow walkers. The site has tips and forums for all travelers.

Flying Wheels Travel, 143 W. Bridge St., Owatonna, MN 55060, USA (☎+1-877-451-5006; www.flyingwheelstravel.com). Specializes in escorted trips to Europe for people with physical disabilities; plans custom trips worldwide.

The Guided Tour, Inc., 7900 Old York Rd., Ste. 111B, Elkins Park, PA 19027, USA (☎+1-800-783-5841; www.guidedtour.com). Organizes travel programs for persons with developmental and physical challenges in the UK.

Mobility International USA (MIUSA), 132 E. Broadway, Ste. 343, Eugene, OR 97401, USA (☎+1-541-343-1284; www.miusa.org). Provides a variety of books and other publications containing information for travelers with disabilities.

Society for Accessible Travel and Hospitality (SATH), 347 5th Ave., Ste. 605, New York City, NY 10016, USA (☎+1-212-447-7284; www.sath.org). An advocacy group that publishes free online travel information. Annual membership US$49, students and seniors US$29.

DIETARY CONCERNS

Vegetarian travelers should not have any trouble finding meals in London, Oxford, Cambridge, or Edinburgh. Virtually all restaurants, even pubs, have vegetarian selections, and many cater specifically to vegetarians or to organic-food diets. *Let's Go* notes restaurants with good vegetarian selections.

The travel section of **The Vegetarian Resource Group's** website, at www.vrg.org/travel, has a comprehensive list of organizations and websites that are geared toward helping vegetarians and vegans traveling abroad. For more information, visit your local bookstore and pick up *The Vegetarian Traveler: Where to Stay if You're Vegetarian, Vegan and Environmentally Sensitive*, by Jed and Susan Civic or *Vegetarian London*, by Alex Bourke. Vegetarians will also find numerous resources on the web; try www.vegdining.com, www.happycow.net, and www.vegetariansabroad.com, for starters. The **Vegetarian Society of the UK** (☎0161 925 2000) is another good resource.

The prevalence of South Asian and Middle Eastern communities has made **halal** restaurants, butchers, and groceries common in large cities. Your own mosque or Muslim community organization may have lists of Muslim institutions or halal eateries. Travelers looking for halal food may find the **Halal Food Authority** (www.halalfoodauthority.co.uk) and www.zabihah.com useful.

Travelers who keep **kosher** should contact synagogues in larger cities for information on kosher restaurants. Your own synagogue or college Hillel should have access to lists of Jewish institutions across the UK. Check http://shamash.org for a detailed database of kosher restaurants around the world, including major cities in the UK. If you are strict in your observance, you may have to prepare your own food on the road, although orthodox communities in North London (in neighborhoods such as **Golders Green** or **Stamford Hill**), Leeds, and Manchester provide a market for kosher restaurants and grocers. A good resource is the *Jewish Travel Guide*, edited by Michael Zaidner (Vallentine Mitchell; US$18).

LET'S GO ONLINE. Plan your next trip on our newly redesigned website, **www.letsgo.com.** It features the latest travel info on your favorite destinations as well as tons of interactive features: make your own itinerary, read blogs from our trusty Researchers, browse our photo library, watch exclusive videos, check out our newsletter, find travel deals, and buy new guides. We're always updating and adding new features, so check back often!

BEYOND TOURISM

A PHILOSOPHY FOR TRAVELERS

HIGHLIGHTS OF BEYOND TOURISM IN LONDON, OXFORD, CAMBRIDGE, AND EDINBURGH

CONJURE your inner Harry Potter as a student at **Oxford**...or is it Hogwart's? (p. 41).

GO FOR THE GOLD and lend a hand in **2012 Olympic Games** preparations (p. 39).

COMBAT homelessness and **poverty** in Edinburgh or London (p. 36).

STUDY inside that "wooden O," **Shakespeare's Globe Theatre,** through KCL (p. 41).

FLIP to our "Giving Back" sidebar features for even more regional Beyond Tourism opportunities.

As a tourist, you are always a foreigner. Sure, hostel-hopping and sightseeing can be great fun, but connecting with a foreign country through studying, volunteering, or working can extend your travels beyond tourist traps. We don't like to brag, but this is what's different about a *Let's Go* traveler. Instead of feeling like a stranger in a strange land, you can understand England or Scotland like a local. Instead of being that tourist asking for directions, you can be the one who gives them (and correctly!). All the while, you get the satisfaction of leaving England or Scotland in better shape than you found it. It's not wishful thinking—it's Beyond Tourism.

As a **volunteer** in London, Oxford, Cambridge, or Edinburgh, you can roll up your sleeves, cinch down your Captain Planet belt, and get your hands dirty combating urban poverty, teaching children about plants at a local botanical garden, or supporting the visual and performing arts. This chapter is chock-full of ways to get involved, whether you're looking to pitch in for a day or run away from home for a life of British activism.

Ahh, to **study** abroad! It's a student's dream, and when you find yourself reading Virginia Woolf on the South Bank while enjoying a soft-serve cone from the ice-cream truck, it actually makes you feel sorry for those poor tourists who don't get to do any homework while they're here. From Bloomsbury to Shakespeare's Globe Theatre, London is a city brimming with literary history and, of course, many students travel to Britain to study English literature. Still, universities in England and Scotland offer quality programs in a variety of disciplines. You can study everything from folklore to physics at one of the oldest universities in the English-speaking world: Cambridge, Oxford, or St. Andrews, just a couple of hours from Scotland's capital city. Perhaps you'd like to dabble in biotechnology at the University of Edinburgh, or, if economics is your cup of tea, spend a summer or a year studying accounting, finance, or management at the London School of Economics.

Working abroad is one of the best ways to immerse yourself in a new culture, meet locals, and learn to appreciate a non-US currency. Yes, we know you're on vacation, but these aren't your normal desk jobs. (Plus, it doesn't hurt that it helps pay for more globetrotting.) Visitors can find work teaching or lending a hand in local pubs. British nannies may not actually ride umbrellas over London Mary Poppins-style, but working as a live-in au pair provides an opportunity to become close to a family and a particular place.

 SHARE YOUR EXPERIENCE. Have you had a particularly enjoyable volunteer, study, or work experience that you'd like to share with other travelers? Post it to our website, www.letsgo.com!

VOLUNTEERING

Feel like saving the world this week? Volunteering can be a powerful and fulfilling experience, especially when combined with the ⬛thrill of traveling in a new place. Although the UK is considered wealthy by world standards, there are many aid organizations that need volunteers. In the UK's major cities, you can work to improve large urban communities that suffer from poverty and housing shortages. If "going green" is more your scene, there are ways to lend a hand in landscape and wildlife conservation, even from metropolitan centers. Alternatively, those enamored with British arts and culture might volunteer at a local theater organization or museum.

Most people who volunteer in Britain do so on a short-term basis at organizations that make use of drop-in or once-a-week volunteers. The best way to find opportunities that match your interests and schedule may be to check with local or national volunteer centers. **CharitiesDirect.com** offers extensive listings and profiles on thousands of charities in the UK and can serve as an excellent tool for researching volunteering options. **Volunteering England** (☎0845 305 6979; www.volunteering.org.uk) provides links to local charities and sponsors **Volunteers' Week,** which recognizes and recruits volunteers throughout Britain. The **Cambridge and District Volunteer Centre** (☎012 23 35 65 49; www.cam-volunteer.org.uk) is a registered charity that recruits volunteers across Cambridge and South Cambs. Their website has information on 300+ volunteer roles in hospitals, community groups, and other organizations. **Volunteer Development Scotland** (☎01786 479 593; www.vds.org.uk) lets you connect with other volunteers in the area to share your experiences and learn about new opportunities. As always, read up before heading out.

Those looking for longer, more intensive volunteer opportunities usually choose to go through a parent organization that takes care of logistical details and often provides a group environment and support system—for a fee. There are two main types of organizations (religious and secular) although there are rarely restrictions on participation for either. Websites like **www.volunteerabroad.com, www.servenet.org,** and **www.idealist.org** allow you to search for volunteer openings both in your country and abroad.

I HAVE TO PAY TO VOLUNTEER? Many volunteers are surprised to learn that some organizations require large fees or "donations," but don't go calling them scams just yet. While such fees may seem ridiculous at first, they often keep the organization afloat, covering airfare, room, board, and administrative expenses for the volunteers. (Other organizations must rely on private donations and government subsidies.) If you're concerned about how a program spends its fees, request an annual report or finance account. A reputable organization won't refuse to inform you of how volunteer money is spent. Pay-to-volunteer programs might be a good idea for young travelers who are looking for more support and structure (such as pre-arranged transportation and housing) or anyone who would rather not deal with the uncertainty of creating a volunteer experience from scratch.

URBAN ISSUES AND COMMUNITY OUTREACH

Homelessness and poverty are pertinent issues in any of the world's thriving urban communities. In the UK, as in the US, numerous organizations work to combat and alleviate the affects of these cruel realities. The UK offers countless other social service opportunities, as well, including mentoring underprivileged youth. The list below represents just a few of the resources you can use to discover a community volunteering opportunity that suits you.

ActionAid UK, Head Office, Hamlyn House, Macdonald Road, London N19 5PG (☎020 7561 7561; www.actionaid.org.uk). A member of ActionAid International. Volunteers often work at festivals, spreading the message: "Bollocks to Poverty!"

Christian Aid: Central Office, 35 Lower Marsh, Waterloo, London SE1 7RL (☎020 7620 4444; www.christianaid.org.uk). **Scotland, Edinburgh Office,** 41 George IV Bridge, Edinburgh EH1 1EL (☎0131 220 1254). Work in various fundraising and leadership roles. Responsibilities might include publicity for the organization and running events.

Citizens Advice Bureau, Myddelton House, 115-123 Pentonville Road, London N1 9LZ (☎020 7833 2181, volunteer hotline 0845 126 4264; www.citizensadvice.org.uk). Volunteers help address issues from employment to finance to personal relationships.

Community Service Volunteers, 237 Pentonville Road, London N1 9NJ (☎020 7278 6601; www.csv.org.uk). Part- and full-time volunteer opportunities with the community's homeless, disabled, and underprivileged youth. 16+.

Oxfam, Oxfam House, John Smith Drive, Cowley, Oxford OX4 2JY (☎0186 547 2602; www.oxfam.org.uk). A member of Oxfam International, a group of 13 organizations working to combat poverty and injustice around the world.

Shelter, 88 Old Street, London EC1V 9HU (england.shelter.org.uk). **Shelter Scotland,** 6 South Charlotte Street, Edinburgh, EH2 4AW (scotland.shelter.org.uk). A charity organization dedicated to combating homelessness. Volunteer at one of their many second-hand shops throughout the UK.

DISABILITIES AND SPECIAL NEEDS

In 2002, the Disability Rights Commission launched an Educating for Equality campaign in Britain designed to ensure equal rights of individuals with disabilities in the education system. Despite this progressive measure and increasing attitudes of acceptance and tolerance, those possessing physical and mental handicaps continue to face discrimination. Volunteers can work with one of the multiple organizations concerned with aiding the special needs of these individuals and fostering a culture of mutual respect. More volunteer opportunities related to arts programs for the disabled are also available with the upcoming London 2012 Olympic and Paralympic Games.

Kith and Kids, The Irish Centre, Pretoria Rd., London N17 8DX (☎020 8801 7432; www.kithandkids.org.uk). Tasks include helping disabled youth during community outings, leading sports and art activities, and helping 18+ members find employment.

Leonard Cheshire Disability, Head Office, 66 South Lambeth Road, London SW8 1RL (☎020 3242 0200; www.lcdisability.org) **Scotland Office**, Murrayburgh House, 17 Corstorphine Road, Edinburgh, EH12 6DD (☎0131 346 9040). Volunteer opportunities include mentoring and participating in outdoor activities with disabled people.

Skill, National Bureau for Students with Disabilities, Unit 3, Floor 3, Radisson Court, 219 Long Ln., London SE1 4PR (☎020 7450 0620; www.skill.org.uk). Promotes opportunities for people with any disability in learning and employment.

Vitalise, London Office, 12 City Forum, 250 City Rd., London EC1V 8AF (☎0845 345 1972; www.vitalise.org.uk). Residential volunteers care for disabled people for 1-2 weeks. Nearly all opportunities 16+.

REFUGEE AND IMMIGRANT ISSUES

Asylum Welcome, 276A Cowley Rd., Oxford OX4 1UR (☎0186 572 2082; www.asylum-welcome.org). Connects volunteers to youth and family work, office reception, fundraising, research, media, and advocacy projects. Membership £10.

Jesuit Refugee Service (JRS), 6 Melior St., London SE1 3QP (☎020 7357 0974; www.jrsuk.net). Volunteers visit detainees or help with administrative work in the London office. JRS provides training, supplies simple lunches, and covers local travel expenses.

London Detainee Support Group, Unit 3R, Leroy House, 436 Essex Rd., London N1 3QP (☎020 7226 3114; www.ldsg.org.uk). Gives support and mentorship to detainees in London. 6-month min. commitment. Volunteers work at detention centers in Colnbrrok and Harmondsworth.

Refugee Action, The Old Fire Station, 150 Waterloo Rd., London SE1 8SB (☎020 7654 7700; www.refugee-action.org.uk). Fundraising, administration, research, and interpreting positions available for volunteers.

PLANTS AND ANIMALS

Friends of the Earth, 26-28 Underwood Street, London N1 7JQ (☎020 7490 1555; www.foe.co.uk). Volunteers help with administrative support and various publicity tasks.

IN RECENT NEWS

HOME OF THE RANGE

In May 2009, the British Sportsman's Association went up in arms over the choice of shooting range for the London 2012 Olympics. They protested the organizing committee's decision to switch the locale from Bisley in Surrey to the Royal Artillery Barracks in southeast London. These angry marksmen aren't firing blanks; if Bisley isn't chosen to host the Olympic shooting, the Sporting Association claims that it will urge British shooting fans to boycott the Games, thus leaving the shooting stands short-handed.

Though the choice of shooting range may not seem like much of a reason to get fired up, local shooting enthusiasts have good reason to favor Bisley. Bisley has long been regarded as the home of British shooting: it hosted the event at the 1908 Olympics and Commonwealth Games. Furthermore, funding from the Olympics would enable significant and permanent improvements to the Bisley site. If the competition is held at the Royal Artillery Barracks, on the other hand, the new £30 million ranges will be torn down immediately after the Games end.

London Olympics officials have resisted the sportsman's pleas, pointing out that the Royal Artillery Barracks have their own historical connection with shooting, and are far closer to the rest of the Olympic Village. At least for now, it doesn't look like Bisley has much of a shot.

London Wildlife Trust, Skyline House, 200 Union Street, London SE1 0LX (☎020 7261 0447; www.wildlondon.org.uk). Several opportunities available, from one-time events to more regular volunteering tasks, like leading locals on a weekly nature walk.

Royal Botanic Gardens, Kew Richmond, Surrey TW9 3AB (☎020 8332 5000; www.kew.org). Volunteer opportunities include teaching children and school groups about plants, and assisting with horticultural maintenance.

Thames 21, Walbrook Wharf, City of London Corporation, 78 - 83 Upper Thames Street, London EC4R 3TD (☎020 7248 7171; www.thames21.org.uk). Participate in one of the many clean-ups held yearly. Check out the online events calendar for opportunities.

The British Trust for Conservation Volunteers, London Regional Office, 80 York Way, Kings Cross. London N1 9AG (☎020 7278 4294; www.btcv.org.uk). Many opportunities, ranging from one-day to more regular commitments. Help create or conserve green spaces in England's bustling capital.

Trees for Cities, Prince Consort Lodge, Kennington Park, Kennington Park Place, London SE11 4AS (☎020 7587 1320; www.treesforcities.org). Range of volunteer possibilities, from weekend and evening fundraisers to weekday planting and maintenance projects.

ART AND CULTURE

Many people head to Britain to revel in the rich artistic, literary, and performative traditions of the region. Below are a few of the ways volunteers can become involved in the visual and performing arts in England's capital city. It's a bit of a challenge to find arts volunteer opportunities online, so your best bet is to investigate local theaters and organizations once in Britain.

Arcola Theatre, 27 Arcola St., London E8 2DJ (☎020 7503 1646; www.arcolatheatre.com). Volunteers can work as ushers, or at the theater cafe/bar. Unpaid internships are available in several fields, including management, production, and youth/community events.

London Arts Festival, Studio 10., 77 Beak St., London W1F 9DB (☎0207 900 3226; www.londonartsfestival.org). Begun in 2006, the festival aims to introduce the London public to national and international artists. Email info@londonartsfestival.org to learn about available volunteer opportunities.

Somerset House, Somerset House Trust, South Building, Somerset House, Strand, London WC2R 1LA (☎020 7845 4600; www.somersethouse.org.uk). For those interested in museums, galleries, art, history, and public events. Volunteers can contribute to educational workshops and public talks, and provide administrative support.

The Art Fund, Millais House, 7 Cromwell Place, London SW7 2JN (☎020 7225 4800; www.artfund.org). An organization dedicated to saving art. Several volunteer positions available, including administration, publicity, and event-planning.

LONDON 2012 OLYMPIC GAMES

The Summer Olympic Games don't officially hit London until July 2010, but the Olympic handover ceremony in Beijing in August 2008 marked the beginning of the "olympiad"—four years of planning and celebration preceding the Summer Games. London 2012 will depend on the help of up to 70,000 volunteers, and those eager to help out with the Games are already signing up online or seeking long-term work with the city's planning and preparation.

Olympic Delivery Authority (ODA), 1 Churchill Pl., Canary Wharf, London E14 5LN (☎020 0201 2000; www.london-2012.co.uk/ODA). ODA has already begun work developing the venues and infrastructure for the Games, including the construction of the Olympic Park. Seeking volunteers in multiple areas, from language services to medical care. See website for available positions.

The London Organizing Committee of the Olympic Games (LOCOG), 1 Churchill Pl., Canary Wharf, London E14 5LN (☎020 0201 2000; www.london-2012.co.uk/LOCOG). Responsible for preparing and staging the Games, as well as test events taking place in 2011. Recruiting and training volunteers. Contract procurement begins in 2009.

The Volunteering Programme, 1 Churchill Pl., Canary Wharf, London E14 5LN (☎020 0201 2000; www.london2012.com/get-involved/volunteering). The program will select a wide-range of volunteers from across the UK. Specialist volunteers will be needed for such things as sport and medical training, while generalist volunteers will help with Village operations and uniform distribution. Applications open in 2010. The website also contains information on Olympic volunteering in your local community.

STUDYING

 VISA INFORMATION. As of November 2003, citizens of Australia, Canada, New Zealand, and the US require a visa if they plan to study in the UK for longer than 6 months. Consult www.ukvisas.gov.uk to determine if you require a visa. Immigration officials will request a letter of acceptance from your UK university and proof of funding for your first year of study, as well as a valid passport, from all people wishing to study in the UK. When and where you should apply for a visa varies, depending on whether you are inside or outside the United Kingdom. The visa fee for those outside the United Kingdom is £145. See the above website for further information.

It's completely natural to want to play hooky on the first day of school when it's raining and first period Trigonometry is meeting in the old cafeteria, but when your campus is London and your meal plan revolves around pubs and exotic restaurants (not to mention scrumptious scones with jam and tea) what could be better than the student life? A growing number of students report that studying abroad is the highlight of their learning careers. If you've never studied abroad, you don't know what you're missing—and, if you have studied abroad, you do know what you're missing.

Study-abroad programs range from basic language and culture courses to university-level classes, often for college credit (sweet, right?). In order to choose a program that best fits your needs, research as much as you can before making your decision—determine costs and duration as well as what kinds of students participate in the program and what sorts of accommodations are provided. The **British Council** (☎ 0161 957 7755; www.britishcouncil.org/new) is an invaluable source of information. The **Council on International Educational Exchange** (☎1-207-553-4000; www.ciee.org) offers a searchable online, containing 118 programs in 40 countries. Devoted to international student mobility, the **Council for International Education**, 9-17 St. Albans Pl., London N1 ONX (☎020 7107 9922; www.ukcosa.org.uk), is another important resource.

For accommodations, dorm life provides a better opportunity to mingle with fellow students, but there is less of a chance to experience the local scene. If you live with a family, you could potentially build lifelong friendships with locals and experience day-to-day life in more depth, but you might also get stuck sharing a room with their pet iguana. Conditions can vary greatly from family to family, so, as in most things, make sure to research your options.

UNIVERSITIES

Tens of thousands of international students study abroad in the UK every year, drawn by the prestige of some of the world's oldest, most renowned universities. Apply early, as larger institutions fill up fast. You can search **www.studyabroad.com** for various semester-abroad programs that meet your criteria, including your desired location and focus of study. If you're a college student, your friendly neighborhood study-abroad office is often the best place to start.

AMERICAN PROGRAMS

American Institute for Foreign Study (AIFS), River Plaza, 9 W. Broad St., Stamford, CT 06902, USA (☎+1-866-906-2437; www.aifs.com). Organizes programs for high-school and college study in universities in Britain.

Arcadia University for Education Abroad, 450 S. Easton Rd., Glenside, PA 19038, USA (☎+1-866-927-2234; www.arcadia.edu/cea). Operates programs at many universities throughout Britain. Costs and duration vary widely.

Butler University Institute for Study Abroad, 1100 W. 42nd St., Ste. 305, Indianapolis, IN 46208, USA (☎+1-317-940-9336 or 800-858-0229; www.ifsa-butler.org). Arranges term-time, year-long, and summer study at British universities. Prices vary by location.

Central College Abroad, Office of International Education, 812 University, Pella, IA 50219, USA (☎+1-800-831-3629; central.edu/abroad). Offers internships as well as summer, semester, and year-long programs in Britain. Prices vary by location.

Council on International Educational Exchange (CIEE), 300 Fore St., Portland, ME 04101, USA (☎+1-207-553-4000 or 800-40-STUDY/407-8839; www.ciee.org). One of the most comprehensive resources for work, academic, and internship programs around the world, including in Britain.

The Experiment in International Living (☎+1-800-345-2929; www.experimentinternational.org) 3- to 5-week summer programs run by the School for International Training (SIT), offering high-school students cross-cultural homestays. Immerses students in Britain's rich artistic tradition, in such fields as film and theater (US$6600-6700).

UK PROGRAMS

Many universities accommodate international students for summer, single-term, or full-year study. Those listed below are only a few that open their gates to foreign students; the British Council has information on additional universities. Prices listed are an estimate of fees for non-EU citizens. In some cases, room and board are not included.

King's College London, King's College London, Strand, London WC2R 2LS (☎020 7836 5454; www.kcl.ac.uk). Main campus on the Strand; Guy's and Waterloo Campuses located across Thames. World-renowned War Studies Department. In conjunction with Globe Education Practitioners and Courses Faculty, KCL offers a 2-wk. course at Shakespeare's Globe Theatre to study abroad students in the English department. Semester (£5100-9750) and year-long (£11,300-14,100) programs for international students.

London School of Economics, Undergraduate Admissions, London School of Economics and Political Science, Houghton Street, London WC2A 2AE (☎020 7955 7125; www.lse.ac.uk). Year-long courses for international students (£12,840).

University of Cambridge, Admissions Office (CAO), Fitzwilliam House, 32 Trumpington Street, Cambridge CB2 1QY (☎01223 333 308; www.cam.ac.uk). Open to overseas applicants for summer (£875-1315) or year-long study (£9747-12,768).

University of Edinburgh, The International Office, University of Edinburgh, 57, George Square, EH8 9JU (☎0131 650 4296; www.ed.ac.uk). Offers summer programs (£1900-2100) and year-long courses (£10,550) for international students.

University College London, Gower St., London WC1E 6BT (☎020 7679 2000; www.ucl.ac.uk). Located in the center of London. UCL offers both semester (£5315-8503) and year-long (£11,810-15,460) programs.

University of Oxford, Undergraduate Admissions Office, University Offices, Wellington Square. Oxford OX1 2JD (☎0186 528 8000; www.ox.ac.uk). Summer programs, ranging from 2 to 6 weeks (£2595-7225), as well as year-long courses (£5875-12,325).

University of St. Andrews, Admissions Office, St. Katharine's West, 16 The Scores, KY16 9AX (☎ 0133 446 3324; www.st-andrews.ac.uk). Just under a 2-hr. drive from Edinburgh. Welcomes students for term-time study. Also houses the **Scottish Studies Summer Program** (☎0133 446 2275). Courses in history, art history, literature, and music of the region for high school students (£2800 all-inclusive).

WORKING

We haven't yet found money growing on trees, but we do have a team of dedicated Researchers looking high and low. In the meantime, Britain is filled with great opportunities to earn a living and travel at the same time. As with volunteering, work opportunities tend to fall into two categories. Some travelers want long-term jobs that allow them to integrate into a community, while others seek out short-term jobs to finance the next leg of their travels. In Britain, travelers looking for long-term jobs might be interested in teaching or working as a live-in au pair. Short-term jobs include farming and pub work. **Transitions Abroad** (www.transitionsabroad.com) offers updated online listings for work over any duration. NB: working abroad often requires a special work visa.

MORE VISA INFORMATION. European Economic Area (EEA) nationals (member countries include EU member states and Iceland, Liechtenstein, and Norway) are able to work freely in the UK, without a work permit. In fact, under the new points-based system, the obtainment of a UK work permit applies only to Romanian and Bulgarian nationals. If you are at least 17 years old, live in a Commonwealth country (including Australia, Canada, and New Zealand), and your grandparents were born in the UK, you can apply for UK Ancestry Employment (make sure you have all the relevant birth certificates that can prove your connection to the UK). Britain recently introduced a new points-based system to manage the migration of people heading to the UK to work or study. The new system involves a 5-tier framework, ranging from youth mobility and temporary workers to highly-skilled workers. Various qualifications determine the number of points people at each tier receive, and whether they are able to enter and stay in the UK. Each of the categories varies in their stipulations, entry-clearance checks, and the rights to which they entitle applicants. Furthermore, due to updated immigration laws, the British Universities North America Club (BUNAC) recently eliminated their special Blue Card program for American students wishing to work in the UK. The working holiday visa has also essentially been eliminated. Young people who wish to travel to Britain for a working holiday are likely to fall under Tier 5 of the Points Based system (youth mobility). If you want to apply to work in the UK, determine which tier you belong to using the points based calculator at www.ukba.homeoffice.gov.uk/pointscalculator. Visit www.ukba.homeoffice.gov.uk for further information.

LONG-TERM WORK

If you're planning on spending a substantial amount of time (more than 3 months) working in Britain search for a job well in advance. International placement agencies are often the easiest way to find employment abroad, especially for those interested in teaching. Although they are often only available to college students, **internships** are a good way to ease into working abroad. Many students say the interning experience is well worth it, despite low pay (if you're lucky enough to get paid at all). Be wary of advertisements for companies offering to get you a job abroad for a fee—often times, these same listings are available online or in newspapers. Some reputable organizations include:

Anders Elite, 2nd Floor, New London House, 6 London Street, London EC3R 7LP (☎ 020 7680 3100; www.anderselite.com). Large job placement agency with 13 offices across Britain.

Hansard Scholar Programme, 40-43 Chancery Lane, London WC2A 1JA (☎020 7438 1222; www.hansardsociety.org). Combines classes at the London School of Economics with internships in British government (£6850-7450).

International Association for the Exchange of Students for Technical Experience (IAESTE), 10 Spring Gardens, London SW1A 2BN (☎020 7389 4114; www.iaeste.org). Chances are that your home country has a local office, too; contact it to apply for hands-on technical internships in Britain. You must be a college student studying science, technology, engineering, agriculture, or applied arts (check their website for a list of accepted fields of study). "Cost of living allowance" covers most non-travel expenses. Most programs last 8-12 weeks.

International Cooperative Education, 15 Spiros Way, Menlo Park, CA 94025, USA (☎+1-650-323-4944; www.icemenlo.com). Finds summer jobs for students in Britain. Semester- and year-long commitments also available. Costs include a US$250 application fee and a US$900 placement fee.

TEACHING

While some elite private American schools offer competitive salaries, teaching jobs abroad often pay more in personal satisfaction and emotional fulfillment than in actual cash. Perhaps this is why volunteering as a teacher instead of getting paid is a popular option. Even then, teachers sometimes receive some sort of a daily stipend to help with living expenses.

The British school system comprises **state** (public, government-funded), **public** (independent, privately funded, despite the name), and **international** (both state and public, often for children of expatriates) schools as well as universities. The academic year is divided into **autumn** (September to Christmas), **spring** (early January to Easter), and **summer** (Easter to late July) terms. Applications to teach at state schools must pass through local governments, while public and international schools must be applied to individually.

To obtain a permanent teaching position in state-maintained schools in England, you must have **Qualified Teacher Status (QTS)**, which usually entails a bachelor's degree and some sort of postgraduate teacher training. The government-run **Training and Development Agency for Schools** (☎ 0845 600 0991; www.tda.gov.uk) manages teacher qualifications. Teachers certified in the European Economic Area (EEA) generally qualify for QTS. The **General Teaching Council for Scotland** (☎0131 314 6000; www.gtcs.org.uk) regulates the teaching profession in Scotland and requires different qualifications for primary- and secondary-school certification. For information on teaching opportunities and certification requirements, see **www.teachinginscotland.com,** a website run by the Scottish government. The **British Council** has extensive information for prospective teachers in the UK generally. **Placement agencies** or **university fellowship programs** are the best resources for finding teaching jobs. The alternative is to contact schools directly or to try your luck once you arrive in Britain. In the latter case, the best time to look is several weeks before the start of the school year. The following organizations are helpful in placing teachers in Britain.

Council for International Exchange of Scholars, 3007 Tilden St. NW, Stw. 5L. Washington DC 20008, USA (☎+1-202-686-4000; www.cies.org). Administers the Fulbright program for faculty and professionals.

Eteach UK Limited, Norwich House, South Wing, Knoll Road, Camberley, Surrey GU15 3SY (www.eteach.com). Recruitment service for teachers.

European Council of International Schools, 21B Lavant Street, Petersfield, Hampshire GU32 3EL (☎0173 026 8244; www.ecis.org). Runs recruitment services for international schools in the UK and elsewhere.

International Schools Services (ISS), 15 Roszel Road, P.O. Box 5910, Princeton, NJ 08543, USA (☎+1-609-452-0990; www.iss.edu). Hires teachers for approximately 200 overseas schools, including some in Britain. Candidates should have teaching experience and a bachelor's degree. 2-year commitment is the norm.

Teacher Recruitment Solutions, Pennineway Offices (1), 87-89 Saffron Hill, London, EC1N 8QU (☎0845 833 1934; www.teachers.eu.com). International recruitment agency that lists positions across the country and provides info on jobs in the UK.

AU PAIR WORK

Au pairs are typically women (although sometimes men) aged 18-27 who work as live-in nannies, caring for children and doing light housework in foreign countries in exchange for room, board, and a small spending allowance or stipend. One perk of the job is that it allows you to get to know Britain without large travel expenses. Drawbacks, however, can include mediocre pay and long hours. Most au pairs receive anywhere between £200 and £300 per month in spending money. Much of the au pair experience depends on the family with which you are placed. The agencies below are a good starting point for looking for employment:

Au Pair UK (www.aupair.uk.com). Connects host families with prospective au pairs.

Almondbury Au Pair Agency, 4 Napier Road, London W14 8LQ (☎01803 380 795; www.aupair-agency.com). Lists job openings in the UK.

Childcare International, Trafalgar House, Grenville Pl., London NW7 3SA, UK (☎+44 20 8906 3116; www.childint.co.uk).

InterExchange, 161 6th Ave., New York, NY 10013, USA (☎+1-212-924-0446 or 800-AU-PAIRS/287-2477; www.interexchange.org).

SHORT-TERM WORK

If you're more of a dishwasher than an au pair, or if you'd just like to work an odd job for a few weeks to fund another month of traveling, short-term work might be right up your alley. One popular option is to work several hours a day at a hostel in exchange for free or discounted room and/or board. Most often, these short-term jobs are found by word of mouth or by expressing interest to the owner of a hostel or restaurant. Due to high turnover in the tourism industry, many places are eager for help, even if it is only temporary.

SeasonWorkers.com, Houdini Media Ltd., PO BOX 29132, Dunfermline KY11 4YU (☎0845 643 9338; seasonworkers.com). Lists many short-term jobs, as well as course and volunteer opportunities in several countries around the world, including England.

Transitionsabroad.com, 18 Hulst Road, Amherst, MA 01002, USA (www.transitionsabroad.com). Includes an extensive list of short-term employers in the UK and Ireland.

YHA (Youth Hostel Association) and its Scottish counterpart **SYHA** (www.yha.org.uk, www.syha.org.uk). Both list job openings on their websites and short-term workers from a pool of globetrotters. It's a good idea to ask at individual hostels as well.

BEYOND TOURISM

LONDON

English is London's official language, but you can go hours without hearing it—there are over 300 languages spoken in Europe's most international city. The Administrative capital of Britain and the financial center of Europe, London works hard, but only so it can play hard. No one seems to notice that the Tube closes at 12:30am.

Of course, tradition and hierarchy are central to London's character; you'll hear a lot about Henri VII and his women, Shakespeare's Globe, and William's and Harry's whereabouts. But the city also has keeps its edge and elegance: from the Beatles to the Stones, from Damien Hirst to Gwenyth Paltrow, from Vivienne Westwood to Charles Dickens—if its flashy, trashy, or downright genius, it likely came from London.

A mix of old and new, tradition and rebellion, tourist-trap and working world, London resists definition. But whatever it is, we can't get enough.

NEIGHBORHOODS OF LONDON

While Greater London consists of 32 boroughs, the City of Westminster, and the City of London, *Let's Go* focuses on central London and divides this area into 12 neighborhoods as well as North, South, East, and West London.

THE CITY OF LONDON

For most of its history, the City of London *was* London, and though urban sprawl has caused the border to bulge, the "Square Mile" remains as tight-knit as ever, with its own mayor, separate jurisdiction, and even sway over the queen, who must ask permission of the lord mayor before entering. Today, the decidedly corporate vibe is punctuated by pretty gardens and must-see sights like the Tower of London and St. Paul's. **Upper** and **Lower Thames Street** run along the Thames to the Tower of London, **Aldersgate Street** passes by the Barbican Centre on its way to Clerkenwell, and **Ludgate Hill** connects Fleet St. to St. Paul's Cathedral. ⊖Bank and ⊖St. Paul's are close to most sights; use ⊖Tower Hill for eastern stops.

EAST LONDON

With cutting edge galleries, deliciously affordable markets and restaurants, a raging nightlife scene, and some of the best vintage and boutique shopping in the world, the **East End** is the heart of East London and also its star—up and coming and going nowhere. In the 19th century, the expansion of London and the nearby docks made this area, just east of the City, a natural gathering point for immigrants, including waves of Huguenots, Ashkenzi Jews, Irish weavers, and Bangladeshis. Eventually, the East End became synonymous with overcrowding, poverty, and disease, and it suffered further damage during World War II. The plus side of this, however, is that the area has remained one of the last affordable areas in central London, attracting cutting edge artists and musicians, including the Young British Artists and Gilbert and George. Today the area is undergoing massive refurbishment for the 2012 Olympics, which some fear will ruin its endearing edge; most, however, are confident in the area's staying power. Meanwhile, there's no reason to get off the elevated

Docklands Light Railway (DLR) trains in **Docklands** until they reach **Greenwich,** home to sights that document its maritime past. Greenwich was also once the favorite residence of Queen Elizabeth. ⊖Old St. and ⊖Liverpool St. are best for the East End. Farther east, Tube lines serve ⊖Canary Wharf and ⊖Wapping. The DLR will take you to ⊖Greenwich.

HOLBORN AND CLERKENWELL

London's second-oldest area, Holborn was the first part of the city settled by Saxons—**Aldwych,** on the western edge, is Anglo-Saxon for "old port." Stately **Fleet Street** remains synonymous with the British press even though the newspapers have moved out and banks, law firms, and upscale pubs have moved in. Clerkenwell, a monastic center until Henry VIII closed the Priory of St. John, began as a resort destination, then devolved into Dickensian slums, before storming back onto the scene as a popular spot for fine dining and raging nightlife. Holborn is served by ⊖Holborn, ⊖Farringdon, ⊖Chancery Ln., and ⊖Temple. In Clerkenwell, everything is near ⊖Farringdon; southern and eastern parts can be reached from ⊖Barbican, western parts can be reached by ⊖Chancery Ln., and northern parts can be reached by ⊖Angel.

THE SOUTH BANK

Just across the river from the City, the South Bank has long been the center of London's entertainment industry. In Shakespeare's time it accommodated the lowest of low culture, but today it reigns at the top of the cultural heap. Theater and art giants the Globe and Tate Modern are here, as are the Hayward Gallery, National Theatre, and National Film Theatre. Farther inland, what were once industrial sweatshops are now giving way to posh restaurants and quirky bars and clubs. Cross the Thames on **Waterloo Road, Blackfriars Road, Borough High Street,** or **Tower Bridge Road.** Dominated by wharves and warehouses in the 19th and early 20th centuries, the South Bank was rebuilt after its destruction in WWII. Now, the "Millennium Mile" stretches from the London Eye in the west to Butlers Wharf in the east. Use ⊖Waterloo for inland attractions, ⊖Southwark for Bankside, and ⊖London Bridge for Borough and Butlers Wharf. Also check out the **"Millennium Mile" Walking Tour** of the South Bank.

SOUTH LONDON

Historically maligned for being "dodgy," areas of South London are now hot spots for upscale dining and all-night parties. Once a swanky suburb, **Brixton** has been urbanized, showcasing the charm of its vibrant and maze-like Afro-Caribbean market and a variety of increasingly popular bars and clubs. **Stockwell** and **Vauxhall** offer pubs, while **Dulwich** and **Forest Hill** have quiet streets and offbeat museums. **Clapham** is experiencing a boom in night-life and culture, featuring upscale clubs and pubs for lounging and dancing. Many sites seem to thrive on their remote locations in sketchier areas, so make sure to put safety first and travel in groups. ⊖Stockwell, ⊖Brixton, and the ⊖Claphams serve the area. For access to some areas, overland rail service from ⊖Victoria, ⊖Waterloo, and ⊖London Bridge is necessary. From ⊖Brixton, the P4 bus will take you to all the Dulwich sites.

WESTMINSTER

Westminster, with its spires and parks, feels like the heart of the old British Empire. It is, after all, home to the Houses of Parliament and the queen—convenient for diehard tourists who want to cram all of London's biggest sights into one day. Apart from the grandeur of **Westminster Abbey** and the bureaucracy of **Whitehall,** however, the district is down-to-earth and even a bit grimy—thousands of commuting workers make ⊖Victoria the busiest Tube station in the city. South of Victoria, **Pimlico** is residential, with row after row of B&Bs, cutesy restaurants, and stuffy shops. ⊖Westminster is near most sights; use ⊖St. James's Park for Buckingham Palace and ⊖Pimlico for accommodations and for the Tate Britain.

THE WEST END

If Westminster is the heart of historical London, then the West End is at the center of just about everything else. The biggest, brightest, and boldest (although not always best) of London nightlife, theater, shopping, and eating can all be found within this tough-to-define district, wedged between royal regalia to the south and financial powerhouses to the northeast.

See a world-renowned musical at one of over 30 major theaters in the area (the Broadway of London), head to **Chinatown** for some dim sum, or venture into the side streets of **Soho** for vintage and vinyl. If it's nightlife you're craving, **Old Compton Street** has plenty of bars and nightclubs, while **Covent Garden** is the place to nurse a glass of wine on a terrace along cobble-stone streets. Oxford Street, Leicester Square, and Shaftesbury Avenue contain taxis and tour buses, unnecessary pomp and circumstance, and dirt and grime.

If none of this sounds like your cup of tea, you can always cruise the posh streets of **Mayfair** and **Saint James's,** which offer a more distinct—if more expensive—taste than the more touristed areas of the West End. Wind your way among upscale arcades, world famous galleries, and designer shops, or spend a little time in central **Trafalgar Square** to bask in the glory of Britain's days as an imperial power. The Tube is best for getting in and out of the West End. Use ⊖Charing Cross for Trafalgar Sq.; the stops are often only a few blocks apart. Once you've made it, buses are the best way to get around; stops can be found along any major thoroughfare.

BLOOMSBURY

Bloomsbury is London's intellectual powerhouse, home to the British Museum, near **Russell Square,** the British Library, on **Euston Road,** and University College London, on **Gower Street.** The area was a famous haunt of 20th-century intellectuals—and, as a result, is filled to the brim with specialty bookshops—but its squares are some of the best places to throw books aside in the name of picnics and suntans. Meanwhile, Charlotte Street in the east is a destination for anyone looking for a relaxing drink, a delicious meal, or peaceful people watching. ⊖King's Cross is the biggest interchange but not the most convenient. ⊖Goodge St. and ⊖Russell Sq. are central; ⊖Euston, ⊖Euston Sq., and ⊖Warren St. hit the north border.

MARYLEBONE AND REGENT'S PARK

Marylebone (MAR-leh-bone) is defined by its eclectic borders. Adjacent to academic Bloomsbury in the east, beautiful **Portland Place** stands as an architectural wonder. To the west, **Edgware Road** houses London's largest Lebanese population and boasts many Middle Eastern eateries, shops, and markets. **Marylebone Road** should be avoided except as a gateway to romantic Regent's Park, while **Marylebone High Street** is full of preppy cafes, pubs, restaurants, and boutiques. ⊖Baker St. is convenient for northern sights; ⊖Bond St. covers the south. There are two separate ⊖Edgware Rd. stations, but they aren't far apart.

NORTH LONDON

What *Let's Go* calls North London is actually a group of distinct neighborhoods, all of which lie to the north of Central London. Once the centers of London's counter-culture movement, **Camden Town** and **Islington** are now slightly less ragingly punk. The former has kept some of its edge, with underground venues, a grunge vibe, and endearingly chaotic markets; the latter has gone boho, with posh restaurants, cute boutiques, and upscale pubs and clubs. **Hampstead** and **Highgate** still feel like small villages, but border the beautiful and expansive Hampstead Heath and are great for a day of window-shopping or picnicking. **Saint John's Wood** and **Maida Vale** are wealthy, residential extensions of Marylebone and Bayswater. The Tube stops are ⊖Camden Town for (surprise) Camden Town, ⊖Kentish Town for Camden, ⊖Angel for Islington, and ⊖Kilburn and ⊖Swiss Cottage for St. John's Wood and Maida Vale.

BAYSWATER

Aside from being a cheap place to sleep, Bayswater is nondescript. Rows of Georgian mansions line the quiet streets, which are filled with residences and hotels of all calibers. The main drags of **Westbourne Grove** and **Queensway** are frequented by teenage mall-hoppers, while Bayswater Road borders the beautiful Kensington Gardens and Hyde Park. Use ⊖Bayswater for the west, ⊖Paddington and ⊖Lancaster Gate for the east. There are two separate ⊖Paddington stations: the Hammersmith & City line runs from the Paddington train station and the others run from a station underground.

NOTTING HILL

Once the stopping point for those traveling between London and Uxbridge, Notting Hill is now known for its high-end fashion boutiques and upscale restaurants, most of which are located on or near **Westbourne Grove**. Meanwhile, its mix of mansions and artsy hangouts means that celebrity sightings—notably of Gwyneth and Posh Spice—have become commonplace. The district is dominated by **Portobello Road,** filled with cafes, shops, and bars, but is best known for its extensive market, which brings thousands of eager buyers every weekend. ⊖Notting Hill Gate serves the south, while ⊖Ladbroke Grove deposits you near Portobello Rd.

KENSINGTON AND EARL'S COURT

The former stomping ground of Princess Di, Kensington is divided into two distinct areas. To the west is the **Kensington High Street,** dominated by clothing chains of all types, while to the east lies sprawling Hyde Park, along with the museums and colleges of **South Kensington's** "Albertopolis." South Kensington is filled with white Victorian houses, flashy cars, and stuffy shops and boutiques. In the 1960s and 70s, Earl's Court was mainly the destination of Aussie backpackers and London's gay population, though others have since caught on to its combination of cheap accommodations and transportation links, and Soho has taken up the rainbow flag. Because this is one of central London's larger neighborhoods, public transportation is necessary to get around. Tube stations are helpfully named: ❷High St. Kensington for High St., ❷South Kensington for the South Kensington museums, and ❷Earl's Court for Earl's Court.

KNIGHTSBRIDGE AND BELGRAVIA

Knightsbridge and Belgravia are smug and expensive. The primary draw is window-shopping on **Sloane Street** and **Brompton Road** at stores like Harrods and Harvey Nichols. Belgravia lies east of Sloane St., sporting 19th-century mansions occupied by millionaires and embassies. ❷Knightsbridge is near the shops; most hotels in Belgravia are close to ❷Victoria, but the north end of the neighborhood is closest to ❷Hyde Park Corner.

CHELSEA

Chelsea would like to be considered London's artistic bohemia, a desire rooted in the 60s and 70s, when **King's Road** was the birthplace of the miniskirt and punk rock. Unfortunately, though, the wealthy Chelsea of today has no stomach for radicalism, which it keeps safely contained in the always-cutting-edge Saatchi Gallery. Meanwhile, King's Rd. and **Sloane Square** are chock full of pricey boutiques, fancy chains, and bars and restaurants at which to see and be seen. ❷Sloane Sq. to the east and ❷South Kensington to the north will put you close to most attractions. Taking a bus is critical during bad weather; most run from ❷Sloane Sq. down King's Rd. on their way from ❷Knightsbridge or ❷Victoria.

WEST LONDON

West London is more of a geographical description than a contained and coherent neighborhood, and most people venture here with a destination in mind—this isn't the place for delightful discovery. Stretching for miles before petering out in the nearby hills, the area is intersected by the Thames, which changes course so often and so sharply that communities have developed almost in isolation from their neighbors. **Shepherd's Bush,** one of these relatively autonomous districts, distinguishes itself as home to a number of well-known concert halls and theaters like the 02, as well as the Westfield Shopping Center, the largest urban shopping mall in Europe. **Hammersmith** is also composed largely of shopping malls and entertainment venues, but it has a number of pleasant parks and pubs along the Thames. To the north, **White City** is home to the world-famous BBC, while farther west **Kew** hosts the Royal Botanic Gardens. Historically, the western reaches of the Thames were fashionable spots for country retreats, and the river still winds through the grounds of stately homes and former palaces. The District Line goes to most sights, though you'll be heading into zones 3-4.

LET'S GO PICKS

BEST OVERPRICED SIGHT: The Tower of London (p. 103) may be over £10, but, of the big-name sights, it provides the most bang for your buck.

BEST WAY TO SEE A SIGHT FOR FREE: Attending the Evensong service at St. Paul's Cathedral (p. 102) gets you into the building, although you won't be able to see the crypt.

BEST VIEW/STAIRS RATIO: Monument (p. 105) in the City provides an amazing view as well as a certificate of achievement for getting to the top.

BEST PLACE TO BE SCHOLARLY: Buy a book at Sotheran's of Sackville St. (p. 176) and then head to Bloomsbury to pick up some vibes from past resident Virginia Woolf and current residents at the University College London (p. 128).

BEST LIVE JAZZ: Ronnie Scott's (p. 165) has long hosted the best names in jazz, with a great house band to boot.

BEST WWII THROWBACK: The Cabinet War Rooms (p. 144) are a remarkable preservation of Churchill and Co.'s headquarters and memorabilia.

BEST PLACE TO PIG OUT: The Taste festival has the best of London's cuisine in an all-you-can eat bonanza.

BEST PLACE FOR A PINT: Clerkenwell's Jerusalem Tavern (p. 190) or Holborn's Ye Olde Cheshire Cheese (p. 191).

BEST PLACE TO ESCAPE THE RAIN: Strike back with a quality fightin' brolly from James Smith & Sons (p. 181).

BEST PLACE TO CHILL OUT: The Absolut Icebar (p. 195) keeps their drinks—and everything else in the bar—on ice.

BEST PLACE TO ESCAPE THE HASSLE: Relax in Regent's Park's rose gardens (p. 129) or duck through the secluded passageway into The Temple.

LIFE AND TIMES

HISTORY

OH HEY, BRUTE. Like that of all great cities, London's history begins with an invasion, a legend, and a hero who may or may not have been all that heroic. According to the Anglo-Saxon historian Geoffrey of Monmouth, **Brutus of Troy** founded London. In Geoffrey's version of the city's history, Brutus gained control of early London after defeating Gog and Magog, the giants who called London home.

Scholars acknowledge that the Brutus-Gog-Magog love triangle may not be completely accurate; they do agree, however, that London was founded by Romans during an invasion in AD 43. Prior to this date, no permanent settlement had ever existed in the marshy area surrounding the Thames that became known as "Londinium" and, eventually, London.

Paganism reigned in Londinium for centuries until Saint Eorcenwald became Bishop in 675. Since then, Londoners have largely accepted Christianity, though disagreements over Catholicism versus Protestantism have been bloody. In the early part of the AD seventh century, Londoners built St. Paul's Cathedral.

WHY CAN'T WE BE FRIENDS. London became a bustling center for trade by the AD ninth century, and its prosperity attracted the powerful and dangerous Vikings, who pillaged the city in the winters of 871 and 872. In 1017, the Danish **King Canute** took the throne. Canute allowed Danish merchants to settle and trade in London, and the city thrived. After Canute's death, **Edward the Confessor** took control of the country, moving his court to Westminster Abbey.

London's medieval period began in 1066, when William of Normandy, also known as **William the Conqueror,** was crowned King of England at Westminster Abbey. In the decades that followed, London's population continued to grow, as did its number of now-famous buildings: the Tower of London, Baynard Castle, Montfichet's Castle, the Palace of Westminster, and the London Bridge all sprang up as if over night.

OFF WITH THEIR HEADS. Medieval London was a mostly peaceful place, with a few notable exceptions. In 1381, a group of serfs led by **Wat Tyler** joined together and stormed the Tower of London, executing the Lord Chancellor, the Archbishop, and the Lord Treasurer. Though the revolt in itself is considered unsuccessful, the statement the peasants made was clear: serfdom would no longer be tolerated in London.

Tudor London was dominated by religious controversies and property reallocations. After severing England's ties with the Catholic Church, Henry VIII dissolved the monasteries, expelling countless priests and monks from their homes. The remainder of the Tudor years saw cultural and economic prosperity in London. Monopoly companies, such as the **East India Company,** made the city their headquarters. Writers, actors, and artists thrived under **Queen Elizabeth's** rule.

London continued to expand physically in the 17th century, as **Fleet Street** became a center for performance, **Lincoln's Inn Fields** became a public park, and **Covent Garden** a public marketplace.

RESTORATION, PLAGUE, AND FIRE. Despite economic and cultural growth, London remained an incredibly backward city in terms of sanitation and safety. These shortcomings led to two disasters in the years following the restoration of Charles II to the throne: first, the **Plague** of 1665 and second, the **Great Fire of London** in 1666. Aggravated by London's terrible sewage system and shoddy health policies, the plague spread quickly and voraciously through the city, eventually killing 100,000 people. More death and destruction occurred the following year when a small bakeshop near the London Bridge caught fire. The fire spread to the riverside, where it destroyed the water wheel at the bridge, cutting off the city's water supply. After four days, only one fifth of the city's land remained.

The **Rebuilding of London Act** in 1667 attempted to prevent similar catastrophes in the future.

IN RECENT NEWS

TRAVELING IN STYLE

The Tube is many things—including more than just a bit stuffy on hot summer days. But now the Tube can also be a source of artistic inspiration.

Thanks to a number of cultural initiatives, the Tube is undergoing a transportation transformation, and while it might still be just a way to get from point A to point B, due to its new celebration of the ABCs (see "Notes from the Underground," p. 55) and even pointillism, you might now enjoy the wait for your train. In 2000, the Underground began its Platform for Arts campaign, designed to visually spiff up many of the stations around town. Tottenham Court Rd., for example, is outfitted in colorful (if overwhelming) mosaics while Russell Sq. hosts a number of subtle tile designs. Many of the stations bear markers of the attractions around them: profiles of Sherlock Holmes decorate Baker St. (near to his museum) while Oval, in close proximity to the cricket ground, is peppered with cricketers in various stances. But perhaps most popular is Gloucester Rd., whose large, unused platform features four mural or sculpture exhibits each year. Meanwhile, the Tube has recently gone even further with its Go to the Gallery initiative by sponsoring a number of posters designed by London galleries. Look for adornments at South Ken, Southwark, and Earl's Court.

With all of these stylish improvements, traveling underground has never looked brighter.

According to the Act, houses could only be built of brick or stone and London's streets became wider and safer. London continued to grow, and by 1800, London was home to one million people. By 1900, the population had grown to 6.7 million.

SEWAGE. For all its post-Rebuilding repair, London still needed some work. The city's terrible sewage system, which dumped waste directly into the Thames, led to the nickname "The Great Stink."

At the beginning of the 20th century, London was a polarized city. On the one hand, it was the capital of the world, with incomparable trade, expensive ocean liners, and wonderful music. The wealthiest of the wealthy lived in London, but times hadn't completely changed under Victoria's rule: poor people still lived in London's streets and in the workhouses. A sense of disillusionment, which only increased with the coming of the **World Wars,** pervaded the city.

LONDON PRIDE. London was most severely affected by WWII and **the Blitz,** which razed much of the city. The East End bore the brunt of the destruction. People emerged from bomb shelters and tube stations to behold a city that looked completely different form the one they had left mere hours before.

Londoners remained undaunted by the destruction. Optimism and energy suffused the city. In 1948, London hosted the Summer Olympics. The post-war years also saw the development of London's **immigrant communities:** Caribbean peoples settled in Notting Hill, Chinese in SOHO, Sikhs in Southall, and Cypriots in Finsbury. London continued to modernize and improve, enacting the **Clean Air Act** in 1956 after the **Great Smog of 1952** killed over 4,000 people. London's iconic double-decker trolley buses, run on electricity, first hit the city streets in 1956.

HOTTEST IN THE WORLD RIGHT NOW, JUST TOUCHED DOWN IN LONDON TOWN. Since then, London has continued to construct innovative new buildings and technologies. The **Thames Barrier,** which controls flooding along the river, was completed in 1982. In 2000, the **Millennium Dome** was revealed to the public. The **London Eye,** a Ferris wheel that has become a modern icon, now draws four million visitors per year.

According to census estimates, roughly 40% of Londoners were born outside the UK, and London is the most ethnically diverse region in the UK. It has an extensive public transportation network and its airport, Heathrow International, is the world's third busiest. In 2007, New York Magazine named London the 21st century's "Capital of the World." In the early years of the new millennium, London has once again made a push for global prominence. Modern building initiatives have added skyscrapers to the London skyline; modern art, cinema, and theater movements have softened the city's reputed "stiff upper lip" as it becomes increasingly open to change and modernization.

CULTURE AND THE ARTS

THEATER

During Queen Elizabeth's rule, the city's first permanent theaters, including **The Theatre, The Rose, The Swan,** and **The Globe,** were erected. Since the 16th century, numerous other theaters have cropped up around the city. Several of the city's current theaters were constructed with the help of Royal licenses or charters, such as the **Theatre Royal, Drury Lane,** and the **Theatre Royal Haymarket.**

London currently has a booming theater enterprise, which is divided into three distinct parts: The West End, the National Theater/Globe Theater, and the Fringe. The theaters of **the West End** produce large, commercial favorites, and tickets range from 15 to 60 pounds. The **National Theater** is subsidized, so its productions are often slightly riskier, featuring unknown playwrights and actors. Shakespeare's **Globe Theater,** renovated in 1997, is a thatched-roofed theater that runs throughout the spring and summer months. **The Fringe** produces smaller plays in pub theaters and clubs, and tickets are much less expensive than those of the West End's theaters. London's theater culture is another testament to the city's constant change and expansion.

MUSIC

The London Symphony Orchestra, The Royal Philharmonic Orchestra, and the BBC Concerts perform in established venues throughout the city: the Barbican Arts Centre, Cadogan Hall, and the Royal Albert Hall, respectively. London is also home to two main opera houses: the Royal Opera House and the Coliseum Theatre. Ancient instruments are scattered throughout London's historical sites, many of them in the city's ancient churches. The world's largest pipe organ resides in Westminster's Royal Albert Hall. The city has more music colleges and conservatories than you can shake a baton at.

In the mid-20th century the **British Invasion** gave us the Rolling Stones, The Beatles, the Monkees, and a million other rock and roll bands with long hair. Punk rock sprang up in Chelsea in the late 1970s when the Sex Pistols and the Clash played their first shows.

London still produces chart-topping groups and solo singers every year, including Coldplay, Keane, Amy Winehouse, and Natasha Bedingfield. While mainstream artists such as these continue to dominate the global soundstage, London also hosts plenty of underground music movements.

FILM

London is home to several major film studios, including Pinewood, Ealing, Shepperton, Elstree, and Leavesden. Soho and central London also house a special effects and post-production community. In addition to producing films, London schools train future stars of the silver screen at **RADA** and the **London Academy of Music and Dramatic Art.** The London Film School, founded in 1956, is the oldest international school of film.

Some of the most renowned filmmakers in the world, including **Charlie Chaplin** and **Alfred Hitchcock,** have resided and worked in London. Just as London became a staple character in many literary works, so too has it become a backdrop and a production set. Several contemporary hits have been filmed in London, including *Alfie, Blackmail,* and the Oscar-nominated *Match Point, Closer,* and *Dirty Pretty Things.* London celebrates film each year at the annual **London Film Festival** in October.

SPORTS

London is home to many professional sports teams, the most popular of which are its football teams. Football has only grown in popularity throughout the 20th and 21st centuries.

The League, founded in 1888, is the oldest competition in the history of world football. In 1992, the top 22 clubs branched out to form the **Premier League. Wembley Stadium,** constructed in 1924 and located in London, is the home of the English national football team. Professional football stars such as David Beckham enjoy hero status in London's streets and around the world.

Other popular London sports include Rugby and Cricket. Rugby is known as the "father of American football," and its rules are a sort of mixture of North American soccer and North American football. (Ironic, no?)

Every year, London hosts the **Wimbledon Tennis Championships**, one of the premier sporting competitions for professional tennis players. London is also home to the **Oxford and Cambridge Boat Race**, a rowing regatta that occurs on the Thames, and the annual **London Marathon**.

✈ INTERCITY TRANSPORTATION

THE AIRPORTS

HEATHROW

Heathrow (☎087 0000 0123; www.baa.co.uk/main/airports/heathrow), 15min. from central London, is just what you'd expect from one of the world's busiest international airports. Airlines and destinations are divvied up among its four terminals as listed below, with a few exceptions—if in doubt, check with the airline.

Terminal 1: Domestic flights and British Airways' European destinations, except for flights to Amsterdam and Paris. Also British Airways flights to Tokyo, Hong Kong, Johannesburg, San Francisco, and Los Angeles.

Terminal 2: All non-British Airways flights to Europe with the exception of Air Malta and KLM; British Airways flights to Basel.

Terminal 3: Intercontinental flights, except British Airways, Qantas, and Sri Lankan Airlines; British Airways flights to Miami.

Terminal 4: British Airways intercontinental flights and services to Amsterdam and Paris; Air Malta; KLM; Qantas; Sri Lankan Airlines; and any other flights that won't squeeze into terminals 1, 2, or 3.

TRANSPORTATION TO AND FROM CENTRAL LONDON

UNDERGROUND. The cheapest and best way to get to London, Heathrow's two Tube stations form a loop on the end of the Piccadilly Line. Trains stop first at Heathrow Terminal 4 and then at Heathrow Terminals 1, 2, and 3 (both Zone 6) before swinging back toward central London. For those with heavy luggage, note that stairs are prevalent in most Tube stations. (☎08453 309 880; www.thetube.com. 40-70min. in to central London, every 4-5min. Cost around £4, depending on where you are going.)

 CARTING YOUR LUGGAGE. The walk from Heathrow's international terminals to the Tube can be quite long. Take advantage of the free luggage carts, which can be pushed most of the way.

TRAIN. The Heathrow Express provides a speedy (15min.) but expensive connection from Heathrow to Paddington station. An added bonus is check-in facilities at Paddington. (☎08456 001 515; www.heathrowexpress.co.uk., daily every 15min. 5:10am-11:40pm. Railpasses and Travelcards not valid. £16.50, round-trip £32; £2 extra if bought on the train. Ask about day returns, student discounts, and group specials. AmEx/MC/V.) The new **Heathrow Connect** is bit longer but also cheaper than the Express (at £7.40 and 25min. to Paddington); it offers direct routes from Paddington, Ealing Broadway, West Ealing, Hanwell, Southall, and Hayes to Terminals 1, 2, and 3. For Terminal 4, take

the first Heathrow Express train. (☎08456 786 975;
www.heathrowconnect.com. Daily every 30min.
5:30am-midnight. Railcards accepted.)

BUS. While cheaper than trains, buses take longer and can end up in traffic—making them not
very worth it. The National Express runs between
Heathrow and Victoria Coach Station. (☎08705 808
080; www.nationalexpress.com. 40-85min., approx.
every 20min. 5:35am-9:35pm Heathrow-Victoria,
7:15am-11:30pm Victoria-Heathrow. Railpasses and
Travelcards not valid. From £8; ages 3-15 half price.
AmEx/MC/V.)

TAXI. Metered fares to central London are unlikely to be
under £70, and journey times are never under one hour.

GATWICK

Gatwick (☎08700 002 468; www.baa.co.uk) is
much farther from London (30 minutes south),
but numerous swift and affordable train services
make it easy to get to. Transport facilities are concentrated in the South Terminal; a free monorail
shuttle connects the South Terminal to the newer
North Terminal, which has better shops and restaurants.

TRANSPORTATION TO AND FROM CENTRAL LONDON

TRAIN. The Gatwick Express runs non-stop service to Victoria station. (☎08456 001 515;
www.gatwickexpress.com. 30-35min., daily
every 15 min. 5am-11:45pm. £16.90, round-trip
£28.80; ages 5-15 £8.45/14.40; tickets available for
purchase on the train.) Additionally, Thameslink
commuter trains head regularly to King's Cross,
stopping in London Bridge and Blackfriars. Beware
that Thameslink stations typically have lots of
stairs. (☎08457 484 950; www.thameslink.co.uk.
50min., daily every 30min., £10.)

BUSES, SHUTTLES, AND TAXIS—OH MY. Road service is slow and unpredictable. National Express's
Airbus A5 takes roughly 1hr. to travel to Victoria
bus station but can also be much longer with a
wait at Brighton. (Contact details same as for
Heathrow. Daily every hr. 4:50am to 10:15pm
from Gatwick, 7am-11:30pm from Victoria. From
£6.20.) You should never take a taxi from Gatwick
to London; the trip will take over an hour and cost
at least £90. If you have heavy bags, take the train
to Victoria and catch a taxi from there.

TRAIN AND BUS STATIONS

London has nine mainline train stations, where a number of privatized companies run through. For impartial advice, call National Rail Enquiries (24hr. ☎08457 484 950). International services are dominated by Eurolines, which offers regular links to all major European cities. (☎08705 143 219; www.eurolines.co.uk.) Victoria Coach Station, Buckingham Palace Rd., is the hub of Britain's long-distance bus network. National Express is the largest operator of intercity services. (☎0870 580 8080; www.nationalexpress.com.) Much of the area around London is served by Green Line coaches, which leave from the Eccleston Bridge mall behind Victoria station. Purchase tickets from the driver. (☎08706 087 261; www.greenline.co.uk.)

LOCAL TRANSPORTATION

Despite its daily interruptions, London's public transportation under the **Transport of London** (☎020 7222 1234; www.tfl.gov.uk) is remarkably efficient—and it's getting better. New fares are generally introduced in January. Free maps of the Underground network and of bus routes are available at Tube stations and Transport for London information centers.

ZONES. The public-transport network is divided into a series of concentric zones; ticket prices depend on the zones passed during a journey. To confuse matters, there are two different zoning systems. The Tube, rail, and Docklands Light Railway (DLR) network operates on a system of six zones, with Zone 1 the most central. Buses reduce this to four zones. Bus Zones 1, 2, and 3 are the same as for the Tube, and Bus Zone 4 encompasses Tube Zones 4, 5, and 6.

TRAVEL PASSES

You're almost bound to save money by investing in one of London's travel passes, based on the zone system. You probably won't need a pass beyond Zone 2. Passes can be purchased at Tube, DLR, and commuter rail stations. Avoid ticket touts hawking secondhand One-Day Travelcards, LT Cards, and Bus Passes; there's no guarantee the ticket will work, it's illegal, and it's just not worth it.

All children under 16 travel free on buses and trams in Greater London. On the Tube, all children under the age of five travel for free; children 5-10 are now free when accompanied by an adult; children 11-15 usually get half-price fares. To qualify for half-price fares, full-time students at London universities must obtain a **Student Photocard.** These can be a pain to get (you must send away for them), but the discounts are generally worth it. Ask your London university about the Student Discount Scheme.

DAY TRAVELCARDS. Day Travelcards are valid for bus, Tube, DLR, and commuter rail services for one day. You can also get one-third off Riverboat prices and free travel on some national rail lines (excluding Heathrow Express and Connect). There are two types of Day Travelcards: **Anytime** (all day; £7.20) and **Off-Peak** (M-F after 9:30am, Sa-Su all day; £5.60). Both Anytime and Off-Peak Travelcards are valid until 4:30am the morning after the printed expiration date. Fares are subject to change; see www.tfl.gov.uk.

THREE-DAY TRAVELCARDS. These have the same application as day Travel-cards. Anytime three-day cards cost £19 for zones 1-2, £43 for zones 1-6; Off-Peak zones 1-6 are £22. Fares are subject to change; see www.tfl.gov.uk.

SEASON TICKETS. Weekly, monthly, and annual Travelcards can be purchased at any time and are valid for seven days, one month, or one year, respectively, from the date of purchase. A matching Photocard is required, free from Tube stations with an ID photo. See www.tfl.gov.uk for fares.

OYSTER CARD. Most long-term Londoners hold an Oyster Card, a plastic card which allows you to touch and go on Tube station entrances and on buses. Oyster Cards can act either as a normal Travelcard (week or month) or as a "Pre-Pay," with discounted adult fares. "Day Capping" promises that you will never pay more in a single day than you would with a Travelcard. Be sure to register your card (£3 deposit)—if it's lost or stolen, you'll be able to recover pre-paid funds to your account that way.

 THE WORLD IS YOUR OYSTER CARD. Don't forget to return your Oyster Card at the end of your time in London to receive your £3 deposit back.

THE UNDERGROUND

Universally known as "the Tube," the Underground provides the fastest and most convenient way of getting around London. Within Zone 1, use the Tube only when traveling more than 2 stations (unless you're in a real hurry); adjacent stations are so close together that walking or taking a bus makes more sense.

 GETTING HOME. The Tube closes around midnight, so planning transportation home is important. Let's Go includes local Night Bus routes for most nightlife listings—excluding pubs, which mostly close around 11pm. Coordinate the best Night Bus route by matching route numbers in nightlife listings with route numbers in accommodation listings. If you don't find a perfect fit, head toward a major transportation hub (Trafalgar Sq., Oxford Circus, Liverpool St., or Victoria) for a transfer.

CARNET. A carnet is a book of 10 singles, available only for a Tube journey starting and finishing in Zone 1; they cannot be used as extensions, nor can you purchase extensions for them. Each ticket must be validated at the station before you use it; failure to do so counts as fare evasion. Purchasing a carnet is cheaper than buying individual singles, but unless you plan to do a lot of walking, a Travelcard is definitely better. See www.tfl.gov.uk.

NAVIGATING THE SYSTEM. Color-coding makes navigating the 12 lines a breeze. Platforms are labeled by line name and general direction, and most have a digital sign indicating the minutes until the next train arrives. If you are traveling on one of the lines that splits into two or more branches, check the platform indicators or the front of the train.

 NO EXIT. You need a valid ticket to enter and *exit* the tube. Hold onto your Oyster card, paper ticket, or Travelcard until you leave the station at your destination. Otherwise, you'll have to ride forever 'neath the streets of London.

HOURS OF OPERATION. The Tube runs daily from approximately 5:30am to midnight, giving clubbers that extra incentive to party till dawn. The exact time of the first and last train from each station should be posted in the ticket hall; check if you think you'll be taking the Tube any time after 11:30pm. Trains run less frequently early mornings, late nights, and Sundays.

TICKETS. You can buy tickets from ticket counters or machines in all stations. Tickets must be purchased at the start of a journey and are valid only for the day of purchase (including round-trip tickets, but excluding carnets). Keep your ticket for the entire journey; it will be checked on the way out and may be checked at any time. There's a £20 on-the-spot fine for traveling without a valid ticket.

 PAY ATTENTION. Many Tube stations post arrival times and destinations for upcoming trains. If a destination conflicts with what it says on the train, Tube officials recommend always following what is posted on the train. This is especially important when heading to Heathrow on the Piccadilly line.

BUSES

Only tourists use the Tube for short trips in central London—chances are you'll spend half as long walking underground as it would take to get to your destination. If it's only a couple of Tube stops, or if it involves more than one change, taking a bus (or even walking) will likely get you there faster. Bus riders can save money with Travelcards (p. 56).

NAVIGATING THE SYSTEM. Most bus stops display a map of local routes and nearby stops together with a key to help you find the bus and stop you need.

 I FOUGHT THE LAW AND THE LAW WON. While it may seem easy to hop on or off of a bus or subway without paying, ticket officials perform random checks on passengers that can result in a £20 fine.

HOURS OF OPERATION. Buses run approximately 5:30am to midnight; a reduced network of Night Buses (see below) fills in the gap. During the day, double-deckers generally run every 10-15min., while single-decker "Hoppers" leave every 5-10min.

NIGHT BUSES. Because the Tube closes around midnight, Night Buses are a necessary form of nighttime transportation (taxis can get quite pricey). Night Bus route numbers are prefixed with an N; they typically operate the same route as their daytime equivalents, but occasionally start and finish at different points. Buses that run 24hr. have no N in front. Most Night Buses operate every 30-60min. from midnight to 5:30am.

TICKETS. Bus and Night Bus fares are the same: £2, children 11-15 50p, children under 11 free; discounts on Oyster pre-pay. All tickets are good for traveling across the network and can be purchased at roadside machines or on the bus. Older buses still use conductors, who make the rounds between stops to collect fares. Keep your ticket until you get off the bus; otherwise you may face a £5 on-the-spot fine.

DOCKLANDS LIGHT RAILWAY

The toy-like driverless cabs of this elevated railway provide a vital link in the transport network of East London. Obvious physical differences aside, the network is basically an extension of the Tube, with the same tickets and pricing structure; with a valid ticket, you can transfer from Tube to DLR at no charge. Travelers visiting both Greenwich and Docklands in one day should inquire about **Rail and Sail** tickets. For costumer service, call ☎020 7363 9700 (M-F 8:30am-5:30pm); for the Docklands travel hotline, call ☎020 7918 4000 (24hr.).

7 PRACTICAL INFORMATION

TOURIST AND FINANCIAL SERVICES

There are 16 Tourist Information Centres spotted around Greater London. Check www.britainexpress.com/TIC/London.htm for a complete list or contact these central offices in the city center.

Tourist Information Centre: Britain Visitor Centres, 1 Regent St. (www.visitbritain.com), ⊖Piccadilly Circus. Open M 9:30am-6:30pm, Tu-F 9am-6:30pm, Sa-Su 10am-4pm. **London Information Centre,** 1 Leicester Pl. (☎020 7930 6769; www.londoninformationcentre.com), ⊖Leicester Sq. Open M-F 8am-midnight, Sa-Su 9am-6pm.

Tours: Big Bus Company, 35-37 Grosvenor Gardens (☎020 7233 7797; www.bigbus.co.uk), ⊖Victoria. Multiple routes and buses every 5-15min. 1hr. walking tours and Thames mini-cruise. Buses start at central office and at hubs throughout the city. £20. £2 discount for online purchase. AmEx/MC/V. **Original London Walks** (☎020 7624 3978, recorded info 7624 9255; www.walks.com) runs themed walks, from "Haunted London" to "Slice of India." Most 2hr. £6, concessions £5, under 16 free.

American Express: 84 Kensington High St. (☎020 7795 6703; www.americanexpress.com), ⊖High St. Kensington. Open M-Sa 9am-5:30pm. 30-31 Haymarket (☎020 7484 9610), ⊖Piccadilly Circus. Open M-F 9am-7pm, Sa 9am-6pm, Su 10am-5pm.

LOCAL SERVICES

Transport for London: Access and Mobility (☎020 7222 1234; www.tfl.gov.uk/tfl/ph_accessibility.shtml). Provides info on public transportation accessibility.

GLBT Resources: Gay London (www.gaylondon.co.uk) is an online community for gays and lesbians. A web portal for lesbian and bisexual women, **Gingerbeer** (www.gingerbeer.co.uk), lists clubs, bars, restaurants, and community resources.

EMERGENCY AND COMMUNICATIONS

Emergency: ☎999 from any landline or 122 from a mobile phone.

Police: City of London Police (☎020 7601 2222) for the City and the **Metropolitan Police** (☎020 7230 1212) for everywhere else. At least 1 station in each of the 32 boroughs is open 24hr. Call to find the nearest station.

Pharmacies: Open M-Sa 9:30am-5:30pm; a "duty" chemist in each neighborhood opens Su, but hours may be limited. Late-night chemists are rare. A 24hr. option is **Zafash Pharmacy,** 233 Old Brompton Rd. (☎020 7373 2798), ⊖Earl's Court. **Bliss,** 5-6 Marble Arch (☎020 7723 6116), ⊖Marble Arch. Open daily 9am-midnight.

Hospitals: Charing Cross, Fulham Palace Rd. (☎020 8846 1234), entrance on St. Dunstan's Rd., ⊖Hammersmith. **Royal Free,** Pond St. (☎020 7794 0500), ⊖Belsize Park. **St. Thomas's,** Lambeth Palace Rd. (☎020 7188 7188), ⊖Waterloo. **University College London Hospital,** Grafton Way (☎0845 1555 000), ⊖Warren St.

Internet Access: If you're paying more than £2 per hr., you're paying too much. Try the ubiquitous **easyEverything** (☎020 7241 9000; www.easyeverything.com). Locations include: 9-16 Tottenham Ct. Rd. (⊖Tottenham Court Rd.); 456-459 Strand (⊖Charing

LONDON

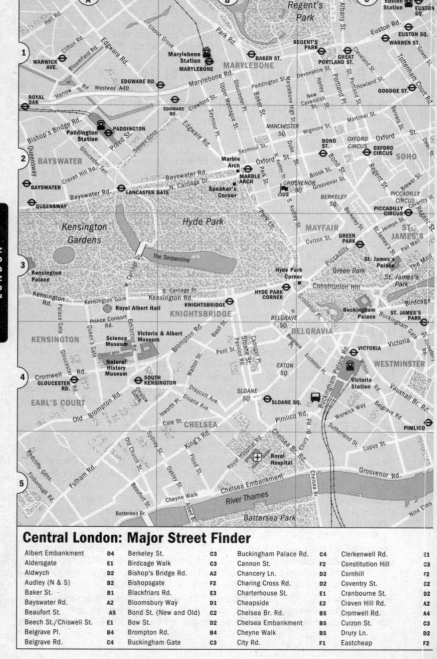

Central London: Major Street Finder

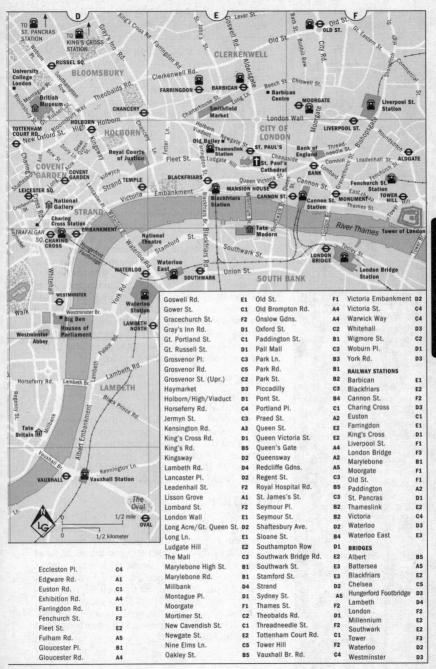

LONDON

Goswell Rd.	E1	Old St.	F1	Victoria Embankment	D2
Gower St.	C1	Old Brompton Rd.	A4	Victoria St.	C4
Gracechurch St.	F2	Onslow Gdns.	A4	Warwick Way	C4
Gray's Inn Rd.	D1	Oxford St.	C2	Whitehall	D3
Gt. Portland St.	C1	Paddington St.	B1	Wigmore St.	C2
Gt. Russell St.	D1	Pall Mall	C3	Woburn Pl.	D1
Grosvenor Pl.	C3	Park Ln.	B3	York Rd.	D3
Grosvenor Rd.	C5	Park Rd.	B1	**RAILWAY STATIONS**	
Grosvenor St. (Upr.)	C2	Park St.	B2	Barbican	E1
Haymarket	D3	Piccadilly	C3	Blackfriars	E2
Holborn/High/Viaduct	D1	Pont St.	B4	Cannon St.	F2
Horseferry Rd.	C4	Portland Pl.	C1	Charing Cross	D3
Jermyn St.	C3	Praed St.	A2	Euston	C1
Kensington Rd.	A3	Queen St.	E2	Farringdon	E1
King's Cross Rd.	D1	Queen Victoria St.	E2	King's Cross	D1
King's Rd.	B5	Queen's Gate	A4	Liverpool St.	F1
Kingsway	D2	Queensway	A2	London Bridge	F3
Lambeth Rd.	D4	Redcliffe Gdns.	A5	Marylebone	B1
Lancaster Pl.	D2	Regent St.	C3	Moorgate	F1
Leadenhall St.	F2	Royal Hospital Rd.	B5	Old St.	F1
Lisson Grove	A1	St. James's St.	C3	Paddington	A2
Lombard St.	F2	Seymour Pl.	B2	St. Pancras	D1
London Rd.	E1	Seymour St.	B2	Thameslink	E2
Long Acre/Gt. Queen St.	D2	Shaftesbury Ave.	D2	Victoria	C4
Long Ln.	E1	Sloane St.	B4	Waterloo	D3
Ludgate Hill	E2	Southampton Row	D1	Waterloo East	E3
The Mall	C3	Southwark Bridge Rd.	E3	**BRIDGES**	
Marylebone High St.	B1	Southwark St.	E3	Albert	B5
Marylebone Rd.	B1	Stamford St.	E3	Battersea	A5
Millbank	D4	Strand	D2	Blackfriars	E2
Montague Pl.	D1	Sydney St.	A5	Chelsea	C5
Moorgate	F1	Thames St.	F2	Hungerford Footbridge	D3
Mortimer St.	C2	Theobalds Rd.	D1	Lambeth	D4
New Cavendish St.	C1	Threadneedle St.	F2	London	F2
Newgate St.	E2	Tottenham Court Rd.	C1	Millennium	E2
Nine Elms Ln.	C5	Tower Hill	F2	Southwark	E2
Oakley St.	B5	Vauxhall Br. Rd.	C4	Tower	F3
				Waterloo	D2
				Westminster	D3

Eccleston Pl.	C4
Edgware Rd.	A1
Euston Rd.	C1
Exhibition Rd.	A4
Farringdon Rd.	E1
Fenchurch St.	F2
Fleet St.	E2
Fulham Rd.	A5
Gloucester Pl.	B1
Gloucester Rd.	A4

THE INSIDER'S CITY

5 PLACES TO WI-FIND YOUR WAY

Internet cafes are simply not the scene Londoners envision for a relaxed hour of checking email and Facebook-stalking one's ex. Here are a couple reliable and more enjoyable chains where the internets run free (or, for a small cost).

1. **Le Pain Quotidien:** This rustic French cafe chain has delicious baked goods at 12 locations in the city, 11 of which have free Wi-Fi. Some include: 201-203 Kings Rd., Chelsea (☎020 7486 6154) and 174 High Holborn, Holborn (☎020 7486 6154).

2. **McDonald's:** Legend goes that no two countries that both have McDonald's will ever go to war. That's not true, but this is a place where the cyber-world is always safe and free. Locations are all over the city.

3. **Pret A Manger:** These small sandwich shops are as ubiquitous as Starbucks, and most of the 130 locations have Wi-Fi. Walk a couple blocks and you should find one. Avoid ritzy residential areas if you want free access.

4. **Starbucks:** The coffee giant is slowly but surely dragging its feet into a free Wi-Fi world. Currently, it's just a BT Openzone hotspot, but they constantly promise that with a Starbucks card the wide, wide world of the internet will be soon accessible sans quid.

5. **Leon:** A healthy, Mediterranean restaurant with 9 locations and counting. Try the one in Soho: 35 Great Marlborough St., Soho (☎020 7437 5280).

Cross); 358 Oxford St. (⊖Bond St.); 160-166 Kensington High St. (⊖High St. Kensington). Prices vary with demand, from £1 per 15min. during busy times; usually around £1.60 per hr. Min. 50p-£1. Generally open until 11pm.

Post Office: Post offices are on almost every major road. When sending mail to London, include the full postcode, since London encompasses several. The largest office is the **Trafalgar Square Post Office,** 24-28 William IV St., WC2N 4DL. ⊖Charing Cross. Open M and W-F 8:30am-6:30pm, Tu 9:15am-6:30pm, Sa 9am-5:30pm.

▐ ACCOMMODATIONS

London's short-term living and real estate alike are notoriously expensive. However, with a little bit of searching and a lot of planning, it is possible to find rooms that are both comfortable and affordable—although you will usually be somewhat separated from the heart of the action. Bloomsbury is by far the budget traveler's best option. In a close second, Kensington and Earl's Court have a number of mid-range, high-quality digs, while Bayswater has less expensive options that are also a step down in quality. Below are some starting points for accommodations across a variety of price ranges and comfort levels. Specific listings appear later in the chapter organized by neighborhood.

CLERKENWELL

Clerkenwell does not have, well, anything in the way of affordable hotels and B&Bs (look to nearby Bloomsbury and King's Cross), but it does have a couple bargains in its inexpensive university dormitories (only open during the summer and Christmas holidays), such as those at **Rosebury Hall** (90 Rosebery Ave. (☎020 7955 7575; ⊖Angel. Night Bus #N19, N38, 341.)

HOLBORN

With a relatively central location near the City, Trafalgar, and the West End, Holborn's location is ideal, but the few rooms that are available are likely to fill up fast. **Guilford Bed and Breakfast Hotel** ❸ offers clean carpeted rooms with small showers and TVs. (4-6 Guilford St. ☎020 7430 2504; www.guilfordhotel.co.uk. ⊖Russell Sq. or Chancery Ln. Night Bus #N19, N35, N38, N43, N55, N243 all stop at the corner of Gray's Inn Rd. and Theobald's Rd. Singles £58; doubles £74; triples £99. AmEx/MC/V.)

THE SOUTH BANK

The South Bank is a mix of two worlds, the industrial inland and the cultural riverside. As a result, it mostly offers expensive chain hotels. It's best to just visit here for the day.

SOUTH LONDON

With multiple Tube stops and the expansive, picturesque Clapham Common nearby, South London is a nicer—and pricier—place to stay than one might guess. Come here to get away from the rush of the city.

The Gateway Hotel, 14 Balham Hill, Clapham Common (☎020 8673 7001; www.gatewayhotel.co.uk). ⊖Clapham South. Just down the street from the Common. 20 clean, comfortable, and coordinated rooms all come with radio, satellite TV, heating, coffee facility, and full baths. Some have CD/DVD players. Continental breakfast £5.50. Free Wi-Fi. Singles from £55; doubles from £70; triples from £75. AmEx/MC/V. ❺

The Windmill Hotel, Clapham Common South Side (☎020 8673 4578; www.windmillclapham.co.uk). ⊖Clapham South or Clapham Common. Walk along the right side of Clapham Common South Side and you'll come to Windmill Dr. on the right. Situated on the edge of Clapham Common, this quiet hotel has a luxurious country feel. Spacious and sophisticated rooms have high windows, large beds, immaculate modern baths, armchairs, and flatscreen TVs. Executive suites are sleek and modern, much larger, and have mini-fridges. Also has an attached restaurant and pub. Free parking. Free Wi-Fi. Breakfast included. Singles £100, doubles £110-130; extra person £15. Prices increase on weekends. AmEx/MC/V. ❺

THE WEST END

Unless you have tons of money, accommodations in the West End are scarce. Be sure to book months in advance, or you won't find a bed here. You may get lucky on short-term notice, but don't count on it. If you want to be close to the action of Soho, don't forget that many Bloomsbury accommodations are a short walk away and probably cheaper.

▨ **YHA Oxford Street (HI),** 14 Noel St. (☎020 7734 1618; www.yha.org.uk). ⊖Oxford Circus. Night Bus: more than 10 Night Buses run along Oxford St., including #N7, N8, and N207. Small, clean, bright rooms with limited facilities but an unbeatable location for nightlife. Some doubles have bunk beds, sink, mirror, and wardrobe; others have single beds and wardrobes. Clean communal toilets and showers. Spacious, comfy TV lounge. Huge, well-equipped kitchen. Laundry available. Towels £3.50. Wi-Fi £3 per hr. Travelcards sold at reception; discount tickets to popular attractions. Reserve at least 2 weeks in advance. 3- to 4-bed dorms £22-27, under 18 £17-21; 2-bed dorms £27-34. MC/V. ❷

BLOOMSBURY

Bloomsbury's quiet squares and Georgian terraces are home to an endless and varied assortment of accommodations. An abundance of quasi-affordable B&Bs line leafy **Cartwright Gardens, Bedford Place, Gower Street, and Montague Street.** During the summer, vacant university halls appear in the area around UCL. While in general King's Cross and its environs can no longer be considered "dodgy" due to a massive redevelopment project, it is best to avoid dark side streets at night.

▨ **The Generator,** 37 Tavistock Pl. (☎020 7388 7666; www.generatorhostels.com). ⊖Russell Sq. or King's Cross St. Pancras. Night Bus #N19, N35, N38, N41, N55, N91, N243. At the ultimate party hostel in London, you'll be greeted by the "Welcome Host" and shortly after offered a complimentary beer. Co-ed dorms (women-only available),

LONDON

Bloomsbury

🏠 ACCOMMODATIONS

Ashlee House, **1**	D1
Astor's Museum Hostel, **2**	C3
Carr-Saunders Hall, **3**	A3
Commonwealth Hall, **4**	C2
The Generator, **5**	C2
George Hotel, **6**	C2
Jenkins Hotel, **7**	C2
The Langland Hotel, **8**	B3
Pickwick Hall International Backpackers, **9**	C3
Thanet Hotel, **10**	C3
YHA St. Pancras International, **11**	C1

🍎 FOOD

Diwana Bhel Poori House, **12**	B2
ICCo, **13**	B4
Navarro's Tapas Bar, **14**	B4
Newman Arms, **15**	B4
North Sea Fish Restaurant, **16**	C2
Savoir Faire, **17**	C4
Wagamama, **18**	C4

⚫ SIGHTS

British Library, **19**	C1
Coram's Fields, **20**	D3
Senate House, **21**	C3
St. George's Bloomsbury, **22**	C4
St. Pancras Station, **23**	C1
University College London, **24**	B2

🏛 MUSEUMS

British Library Galleries, **25**	C1
British Museum, **26**	C4
Brunei Gallery, **27**	C3
Percival David Foundation of Chinese Art, **28**	C2
Pollock's Toy Museum, **29**	B3

🎭 ENTERTAINMENT

The Place, **30**	C2
RADA, **31**	B3
Renoir, **32**	C3
The Water Rats, **33**	D1

🛍 SHOPPING

Gay's the Word, **34**	C2
James Smith & Sons, **35**	C4
L. Cornelissen & Son, **36**	C4
Ulysses, **37**	C4
Oxfam Books, **38**	C4

⭐ NIGHTLIFE

Vats, **39**	D3

🍺 PUBS

Fitzroy Tavern, **40**	B4
The Jeremy Beutham, **41**	B3
The Queen's Larder, **42**	C3

a bar with nightly events (6pm-2am), cheap pints (6-9pm, £1.50), a full cafeteria-style dining area with dinner specials (from £4.50), and well-equipped lounge areas make this one of the best places to meet fellow travelers. All rooms have sinks; private doubles have tables and chairs. New clean showers. Continental breakfast included. Lockers (padlocks £4), free towels and linens, laundry (wash £2; dry £0.50 per 10min.), cash machine, charge station (for any phone or iPod) and an in-house travel shop that sells Tube, train, and theater tickets. Small safes £1 per day, £5 per week.; larger safes £3/10. Internet £1 per 30min. Wi-Fi £1.50 per hr.; £4 per 3hr. Reception 24hr. Reserve 1 week in advance for Sa-Su. Online booking. Credit card required with reservation. 4- to 12-bed dorms £15-25; singles £50-65; doubles with 2 twin beds £50-65; triples £60-75; quads £80-100; 6-bed private rooms £120-150. Discounts for long stays. 18+. MC/V. ❶

YHA St. Pancras International, 79-81 Euston Rd. (☎020 7388 9998; www.yha.org.uk). ⊖King's Cross St. Pancras. Night Bus #N10, N73, N91, 390. Opposite the British Library and St. Pancras Tube. After a £1.6 million refurbishment, this hostel has come out sparkling, with a sunken bar-cafe (beers from £2.20; pub style mains £5.50) and clean, spacious rooms with plush wall-to-wall carpets and wooden bunks. Family bunk rooms, single-sex dorms, basic doubles, and premium doubles (with bath and TV) are sparkling. Kitchen and elevators available. Breakfast £3.50-5. Linens included. Laundry (wash and dry £4.50). Wi-Fi £1.50 per 15min.; £3 per 30min. 1 week max. stay. Reserve dorms 1 week in advance for Sa-Su or summer, 2 weeks for doubles. 4- to 6-bed dorms £23-32, under 18 £18-25; doubles £63, with bath £68. £3 discount with HI, ISIC, or NUS card. MC/V. ❷

George Hotel, 58-60 Cartwright Gardens (☎020 7387 8777; www.georgehotel.com). ⊖Russell Sq. Night Bus #N10, N73, N91, 390. Spacious rooms with flatscreen satellite TV, radio, tea/coffee facilities, phone, and alarm clock, plus hair dryer and iron on request. The front rooms on the 1st fl. have high ceilings and tall windows; others have bay windows. Full English breakfast included. Free internet and Wi-Fi. Reserve 3 weeks in advance for summer; 48hr. cancellation policy. Singles £50, with shower £75; doubles £69/75, with bath £89; triples £79/89/99; basic quads £89. Discounts for stays over 4 days. MC/V. ❸

Astor's Museum Hostel, 27 Montague St. (☎7580 5360; www.astorhostels.co.uk). ⊖Tottenham Court Rd., Russell Sq., or Goodge St. Night Bus #N19, N35, N38, N41, N55, N91, N243. In a converted Victorian house, this rough-and-tumble hostel is not brand new, but it's still comfortable and has a fun, rambunctious feel. Spacious rooms, a fully-stocked communal kitchen and free DVDs, books, and board games to enjoy in the downstairs lounge. Hosts occasional dinners and events. English breakfast included. Luggage bins in room; padlock £3. Free luggage storage before check-in and after check-out. Safes £1.50 per day; £7 per week. Linens included; towel £5. Laundry £2.50 per wash, £0.50 per dry. Wi-Fi free for first 40min.; £1 per 40min. thereafter. Reception 24hr. Reservations recommended. 12-bed dorms £18-21; 10-bed £19-22; 8-bed £20-23; 6-bed £21-24; 4-bed (some female only) £25-26; private doubles £25-40. Rates fall £2 in winter. AmEx/MC/V. ❶

Thanet Hotel, 8 Bedford Pl., Russell Sq. (☎020 7636 2869; www.thanethotel.co.uk). ⊖Russell Sq. or Holborn. Night Bus #N19, N35, N38, N41, N55, N91, N243. A homey B&B. Bright, spacious rooms with fireplaces, large mirrors, and pleasant decor. All rooms have bath, TV, radio, hair dryer, tea/coffee facilities, and phone; some have balconies and garden views. Full English breakfast included. Free Wi-Fi in lobby. Reserve 1 month in advance. Singles £78; doubles £106; triples £125; quads £140. AmEx/MC/V. ❹

Ashlee House, 261-265 Gray's Inn Rd. (☎020 7833 9400; www.ashleehouse.co.uk). ⊖King's Cross St. Pancras. Night Bus #N10, N63, N73, N91, 390. A friendly budget accommodation with rather small but bright dorms and a number of perks, including deals at pubs and restaurants around town, occasional events, and free movie nights (from 8pm). Private rooms include table, sink, and kettle. Well-stocked kitchen available.

Free luggage storage and safe. Laundry £2 per wash, £2 per dry. Continental break-fast included. Linens included; towels £1. Internet £2 per hr.; Wi-Fi £1 per hr. 2-week max. stay. Reception 24hr. 16-bed dorms £14-20; 8- to 10-bed £16-24; 4- to 6-bed £18-26; singles £40; doubles £55; triples £70. MC/V. ❶

Wardornia Hotel, 46-54 Argyll St. (☎020 7837 3944; www.wardorniahotel.com). ⊖King's Cross St. Pancras. The rooms might be small, but they are bright, spotless, comfortable, and inexpensive. All come with digital TV, shelves, a nightstand, and a small bathroom. Singles £40; doubles £55-60; triples £70. AmEx/MC/V. ❷

The Langland Hotel, 29-31 Gower St. (☎020 7636 5801; www.langlandhotel.com). ⊖Goodge St. Night Bus #N5, N10, N20, 24, N29, N73, 134, N253, N279, 390. A comfortable B&B that distinguishes itself with lower rates. Rooms are clean and all have TV, kettle, and fan. Only 3 rooms with ensuite bathrooms. Lounge with satellite TV. Full English breakfast included. Luggage storage. Reserve a room away from street to avoid noise. 48hr. cancellation policy. Singles £45-75; doubles from £65, with bath £75; tri-ples from £70/85; quads from £85. Rates increase significantly in summer. Discounts for longer stays, students, and advance booking. AmEx/MC/V. ❸

Pickwick Hall International Backpackers, 7 Bedford Pl. (☎020 7323 4958; www.pickwickhall.co.uk). ⊖Russell Sq. or Holborn. Night Bus #N7, N91. Bright, small rooms may seem a bit worn but endearingly so. All have mini-fridge and microwave. Coin laundry, kitchen, TV lounge, and internet available. Continental breakfast included. Linens included. Reception 8am-10pm. Book 2-3 days in advance, 3 weeks in advance for July-Aug. Singles £37, with bath £55; doubles £50/66; triples £66/75; quads £100/88. MC/V. ❷

University of College London Garden Halls, 1-11 Cartwright Gardens (☎020 7121 7000; www.halls.london.ac.uk/visitor/garden/Default.aspx). ⊖Russell Sq. Night Bus #N10, N73, N91, 390. 3 post-WWII block residential halls: Commonwealth, Hughes Parry, and Canterbury. Nicely sized student singles with telephones. Public garden out front. Fridge and microwave on each floor, elevator and dining room in each hall. Access to study and library free, to tennis and squash courts for a fee. Dinner option included. Open from mid-Mar. to late Apr. and from mid-June to mid-Sept. Reserve at least 3 months in advance for July-Aug. Walk-ins only accommodated M-F 9am-5pm. Singles from £30, with dinner from £35. AmEx/MC/V. ❷

Carr-Saunders Hall, 18-24 Fitzroy St. (☎020 7955 7575; www.lse.ac.uk/vacations). ⊖Warren St. Night Bus #N7, N8, N10, 25, N55, N73, N98, 176, N207, 390. Old stu-dent residential hall with the inevitable industrial feel, but rooms are large and clean and include sink and phone. TV lounge, game room, and elevator to all floors, including the panoramic roof terrace. Laundry £1.60 per wash, £1 per dry. 1 computer with Inter-net; £1 per 20min. Reserve 6-8 weeks in advance for July-Aug., but check for openings any time. Open from late Mar. to late Apr., from late June to late Sept., and from mid-Dec. to early Jan. 30% deposit required. Singles from £31, with breakfast £33; doubles £40-50/45-55. Discounts for stays over 5 weeks. MC/V. ❷

NORTH LONDON

CAMDEN TOWN, KING'S CROSS, AND ISLINGTON

Home to a few cheap options, North London can be a good home for students, especially given the vibrant nightlife of Camden and Clerkenwell. Many afford-able accommodations, however, are in residential suburban areas, so increased transportation costs may offset some of the money saved.

🛏 **Kandara Guesthouse,** 68 Ockendon Rd. (☎020 7226 5721; www.kandara.co.uk). From ⊖Angel, take Bus #38, 56, 73, 341 to the Ockendon Rd. stop. Night Bus #N38, N73, 341. Far from the Tube but with ample access to downtown. Family-run B&B with 12 sparkling and comfortable rooms on a residential street. All rooms have flatscreen TV and tea/coffee facilities; guests share 6 communal baths. Bicycle storage. Internet cafe down the street. Full English or Continental breakfast included. Free overnight parking. Reserve well in advance. 1-night deposit required with reservation; 1-week cancellation policy. Singles £49-63; doubles £69-86; triples £79-93. Discounts with longer stays. MC/V. ❸

St. Christopher's Inn, 48-50 Camden High St. (☎020 7388 1012; www.st-christophers.co.uk). ⊖Mornington Crescent. Night Bus #N5, N20, N253. The reception in Belushi's Bar downstairs serves as a fitting entrance to this party-friendly backpacker hostel. Nicknamed the "hostel with attitude," this particular location is perfect for hitting the Camden Town bars and Clerkenwell clubs. Especially after a new paint job, rooms are surprisingly bright and spacious and all but 1 have private bath. Comfy common room with futons, flatscreen TV, and microwave. 10% off all food and drinks at the bar. Continental breakfast included. Luggage storage. Safety deposit boxes and lockers. Linens included. Laundry £2 per wash, £0.50 per dry. Free internet. Wi-Fi £1 per 20min. Reception 24hr. 10-bed dorms £19-25; 8-bed £20-26; 6-bed £21-27; women-only 6-bed £22-28; doubles £27-33. Rates depend on day of week and season; discount with online booking. MC/V. ❶

MARYLEBONE AND REGENT'S PARK

Marylebone's ritzy residential feel and proximity to the West End means that, while there are plenty of accommodations, they tend to be beyond the budget of the average traveler. There are a number of attractive B&Bs, but don't expect the deals you'll find in Bloomsbury or Bayswater. Here, you're paying to be within walking distance of **Oxford Street,** which makes up for the no-frills accommodations. The area's student rooms are a good deal, though they're often in the grittier parts of the neighborhood.

International Student House, 229 Great Portland St. (☎020 7631 8310; www.ish.org.uk). ⊖Great Portland St. Night Bus #N18. Large, institutional dorm. Decent selection of rooms during summer; limited options during school year. Most rooms have desk, sink, phone, and fridge; some have private bath. Modern bar with regular events. Nightclub, cafeteria, fitness center (£6 per day), and cinema that hosts free Su film viewings. Free safe in reception. Continental breakfast included except for dorms (£2.50); English breakfast £3.20. Luggage storage £1 per item; £5 per item over night. Laundry: wash £2, dry £0.20 per 15min. Internet £2 per hr. £20 key deposit. Some rooms wheelchair-accessible. 3-week max. stay. Reception open M-F 8am-7pm, Sa-Su 9am-5pm. Advance booking recommended. Dorms £13; singles £37-41; doubles £56-63; triples £68; quads £83. 10% discount on singles, doubles, and triples with ISIC. MC/V. ❶

University of Westminster Halls, 35 Marylebone Rd. (☎020 7911 5181; www.wmin.ac.uk/comserv). ⊖Baker St. Night Bus #N18. Clean, bright, and colorful rooms with Ikea-esque furnishings. Laundry, kitchen, lounges, and shared baths. Linens and towels included. Wi-Fi available. 1-week advance booking recommended; occasional last-minute availability. Singles from £27; doubles from £32. Students only. Rates lower over month-long stays. MC/V. ❷

Lincoln House Hotel, 33 Gloucester Pl. (☎020 7486 7630; www.lincoln-house-hotel.co.uk). ⊖Marble Arch or Bond St. Night Bus #6, N7, N15, 23, N36, N74, 94, N98. With a location near the Tube and Hyde Park, pleasant maritime-themed decor, and small conveniences like free Wi-Fi and A/C, Lincoln House is one of the better values in Marylebone. Clean and tidy, if a bit small, rooms, all with phone, TV, fridge, and ensuite bathrooms. Continental breakfast £2.90; full English or vegetarian breakfast £3.90. Some rooms wheelchair-accessible. Singles £55-95; doubles £89-130; triples £119-135; quads £129-145. Prices vary by season and length of stay; check website for details. Discounts for theater tickets and attractions. AmEx/MC/V. ❺

Hart House Hotel, 51 Gloucester Pl. (☎020 7935 2288; www.harthouse.co.uk). ⊖Marble Arch or Bond St. Night Bus #6, N7, N15, 23, N36, N74, 94, N98. Once a Revolution-era home for French nobility, this recently remodeled hotel is now a cheerful place to spend the night if money is no object. Comfortable rooms with sophisticated furnishings, TV, and private bath. Recipient of the "Sparkling Diamond" award, it is also squeaky clean. Full English breakfast included. Internet access. Online booking available. Singles £85; doubles £125; triples £145; quads £175. AmEx/MC/V. ❺

 DOUBLE FOR PLEASURE, TWIN FOR FUN. Unlike in the States, hotels in Britain distinguish between doubles (with 1 bed) and twins (with 2 single beds). Sometimes the latter is cheaper, so make sure you clarify if you prefer one bed, or if you're indifferent and want to take advantage of lower prices.

BAYSWATER

Flanked by expansive Hyde Park and posh Notting Hill, Bayswater offers a great location and an abundance of accommodations to fit the student's budget. Almost every side street is lined with bright white Victorian houses that have been converted into hotels or hostels. The greatest variety of rooms, and all the cheaper hostels, can be found around **Queensway;** try **Inverness Terrace** and **Leinster Square.** In **Kensington Gardens Square** and **Prince Square,** you pay for the location, but the amenities usually match or even outdo the price. On the other side of Bayswater, the area around **Paddington** is convenient for travelers arriving

LONDON

READY. SET.

LET'S GO

www.letsgo.com

THE STUDENT TRAVEL GUIDE

on the Heathrow Express: **Sussex Gardens** is lined with affordable B&Bs, while slightly cheaper hotels surround the Tube station.

> **DON'T JUDGE A BOOK...AND BOOK EARLY!** As most of the hotels and hostels in Bayswater are constructed out of similar Victorian houses, it may seem that they're all essentially the same in quality, but this couldn't be further from the truth. Decor, amenities, and general comfort and cleanliness all vary widely, and if you're not careful, you'll end up paying lots for a horrible experience. Its best to do your research and book ahead in this area, especially as rooms in the better-quality hotels get snatched up quickly.

The Pavilion, 34-36 Sussex Gardens (☎020 7262 0905; www.pavilionhoteluk.com). ⊖Paddington or Edgeware Rd. With over 30 themed rooms, including "Honky Tonk Afro" (dedicated to the 70s), "Casablanca Nights" (recalling a Moorish fantasy), and 2 James Bond inspired pads ("Gold Finger" and "Diamonds Are Forever"), this is the place to come for a hilariously sumptuous hotel experience. Decadent decor with funky additions like zebra print, Grecian busts, or Warhol-esque Marilyn photos accompany flatscreen TVs. Priding itself on its connection to all things art, fashion, and rock & roll, the Pavilion has hosted a number of celebrity visitors and fashion shoots: a naked Naomi Campbell and an impatient Kate Beckinsale both posed here. Continental breakfast included. Parking £10 per day. Reception 24hr. Singles £60-85; doubles £100; triples £130. AmEx/MC/V. **⑤**

Quest Hostel, 45 Queensborough Terr. (☎020 7229 7782; www.astorhostels.com). ⊖Queensway. Night Bus #N15, 94, 148. A chummy staff operates this simple backpacker hostel with a blackboard welcoming new check-ins by name. Mostly co-ed dorms (1 female-only room). Nearly all have bath; otherwise, facilities on every other fl. Recently refurbished kitchen. Continental breakfast included. Under-bed luggage storage; padlocks £2 (£5 deposit). Lockers £1.50 per day; £7 per week. Linens included. Laundry £2.50 per wash, £0.50 per dry. Wi-Fi £1 per 40min. Max stay 2 weeks in summer; longer in winter. Reception 24hr. 4- to 9-bed dorms £16-25; doubles £35-40. Rates increase July-Aug. and on weekends. Ages 18-35 only. MC/V. **①**

Admiral Hotel, 143 Sussex Gardens (☎020 7723 7309; www.admiral-hotel.com). ⊖Paddington. Night Bus #N15, 94, 148. Beautifully kept B&B. A sleek bar adds an unexpected modern touch. Recently redecorated rooms with bath, hair dryer, satellite TV, and kettle for tea or coffee. Owner's own artwork often appears on the walls. English breakfast included. Free Wi-Fi. Reception 24hr.; often at next door Kingsway Park Hotel. 4-day cancellation policy. Singles £40-50; doubles £58-75; triples £75-90; quads £88-110; quints £100-130. Ask about winter and long-stay discounts. MC/V. **③**

Garden Court Hotel, 30-31 Kensington Gardens Sq. (☎020 7229 2553; www.gardencourthotel.co.uk). ⊖Bayswater or Queensway. Night Bus #N15, 94, 148. Overlooking leafy Kensington Garden Sq. and with a patio garden of its own, this hotel offers 32 newly refurbished rooms with simple but pretty decor. Rooms vary in size but all have sink, flatscreen TV, and hair dryer. Many have beautifully restored crown molding and fireplaces. Wheelchair-accessible. Strict 2-week cancellation policy. Singles £48, with bath £73; doubles £76/118; triples £90/150; family quads £100/170. MC/V. **③**

Balmoral House Hotel, 156 Sussex Gardens (☎020 7723 7445; www.balmoralhousehotel.co.uk), another location across the street. ⊖Paddington. Night Bus #N15, 94, 148. Well-kept rooms with plush red carpets, floral wallpaper, and white beds welcome guests at this family-run hotel. All have satellite TV, complimentary tea and cookies, and hair dryer.

English breakfast included. Reserve months in advance. Singles £55; doubles £85; triples £105; quads £120; quints £135. 5% surcharge for MC/V. ❸

Hyde Park Hostel, 2-6 Inverness Terr. (☎020 3355 1441; www.hydeparkhostel.net). ⊖Bayswater or Queensway. Though it might show its age, this hostel has spacious dorms with sink and fridge. Large communal kitchen with 8 ovens and 2 microwaves; communal TV room with flatscreen. Well located just off Hyde Park. Breakfast, luggage storage, and linens included. Laundry: £3 per wash, £1.50 per dry. Internet £1 per 1¼hr.; Wi-Fi £5 per 5hr., £10 per 11hr. Reception 24hr. 8-bed dorms £14; 6-bed dorms £15; 4-bed dorms £17; doubles £25; singles £40. ❶

Vancouver Studios, 30 Prince's Sq. (☎020 7243 1270; www.vancouverstudios.co.uk). ⊖Bayswater and Queensway. This hotel might be on the pricey side, but it remains one of the best deals in the area. Located between beautiful Kensington Gardens Sq. and Prince's Sq., Vancouver's bright, spacious rooms come with modern bathrooms, a small kitchen area, flatscreen TV and DVD player, safe, and complimentary tea and shortbread. Delicate decorations befit a home more than a hotel. A sitting room with fireplace and walled English garden with fountain add to the luxury. Some rooms come with balconies. Services include bikes for hire, dry cleaning, self-service laundry, and DVD rental. Extra bed £20. Reception 24hr. Singles £89; doubles £130-145, with balcony £160; triples £170; 3-bedroom apartment £350. AmEx. ❺

Queensway, 147-149 Sussex Gardens (☎020 7723 7749; www.queenswayhotel.co.uk). ⊖Paddington. A professional feel and tidy rooms with high ceilings, flatscreen TVs, and color-coordinated decor make this hotel a pleasant, dependable choice. Continental breakfast included. Reception 24hr. Reserve 2 weeks in advance. Singles £69; doubles £89; triples £109. ❹

> **SCALING THE HEIGHTS.** Most accommodations in Bayswater are converted townhouses with long and narrow staircases. Those who have trouble with stairs may want to consider staying elsewhere.

NOTTING HILL

Although a lovely residential neighborhood, Notting Hill has no budget accommodations. Try nearby Bayswater for better deals, or bring lots of friends to defray costs.

■ **Portobello Gold Rooms,** 97 Portobello Rd. (☎020 7460 4910; www.portobellogold.com). ⊖Notting Hill Gate. Night Bus #N52. Encouraging visitors to "work, party, and sleep—all under one roof," the Gold hotel is very much in tune with the light-hearted vibe of the pub downstairs. 6 well-maintained, if small, rooms with TV, bath, phone, and a healthy dose of character. If you can find a group of 4-6, the family flat may be ideal: though a bit pricey, it spans 2 fl. and includes a kitchen, private rooftop terrace (with putting green), and mosaic-tiled bath. Continental breakfast included. Doubles £70 when booking online, £80 in person; apartment for 4 £170, each additional person £5. Discounts available for stays of a week or longer. AmEx/MC/V. ●

■ **The Gate Hotel,** 6 Portobello Rd. (☎020 7221 0707; www.gatehotel.co.uk). ⊖Notting Hill Gate. Night Bus #N52. 6 clean, relatively spacious rooms with brand new carpets make this a good deal for the area, even if the bathrooms are tiny. Rooms have TV/DVD, desk, mini-fridge, and phone. Continental breakfast included, served in-room. 48hr. cancellation policy. Singles M-F £60, Sa-Su £70; doubles £80/90. AmEx/MC/V. ●

KENSINGTON AND EARL'S COURT

For such an upscale neighborhood, Kensington is not entirely devoid of affordable accommodations—mid-priced B&Bs sit just a few blocks away from the mansions. The area is pretty large, however, and a Kensington address doesn't necessarily put you within walking distance of the main sights and shops. Decidedly less exclusive Earl's Court (to the west of **Collingham Road** and south of **Cromwell Road**) remains popular with backpackers and budget travelers, though its prices are on the rise, too.

■ **Astor Hyde Park,** 191 Queensgate (☎020 7581 0103; www.astorhostels.co.uk). ⊖South Kensington or Gloucester Rd. Set in a recently renovated Victorian walk-up, this social backpacker's hostel offers clean, spacious rooms outfitted with full ensuite baths and decorated with modern art. Sleek lounge with flatscreen TV and dining hall with pool table. Regular F night parties. Breakfast included; occasional hostel dinners £3-4. Lockers under beds; padlock £2. Safes £1.50 per day, £7 per week. Free luggage storage before check-in and after check-out. Wash £2.50; dry 50p per 20min. Internet 50p per 15min. Free Wi-Fi. Reception 24hr. Dorms in summer £15-25, in winter £13-20; doubles £35-40/25-30. Ages 18-35 only. AmEx/MC/V. ●

■ **Vicarage Hotel,** 10 Vicarage Gate (☎020 7229 4030; www.londonvicaragehotel.com). ⊖High St. Kensington. Night Bus #27, N28, N31, N52. Walking on Kensington Church St. from Kensington High St., you'll see 2 streets marked Vicarage Gate; take the 2nd on your right. Immaculately maintained Victorian house with ornate hallways, TV lounge, and elegant bedrooms; all have shiny wood furnishings, tea and coffee sundries, and hair dryers. Rooms with private baths have TV. Full English breakfast included. Free Wi-Fi. Best to reserve 2 months in advance with 1 night's deposit; personal checks accepted for deposit with at least 6 weeks notice. Singles £55, with private bathroom £93; doubles £93/122; triples £117/156; quads £128/172. AmEx/MC/V. ●

YHA Holland House, Holland Walk (☎020 7937 0748; www.hihostels.com). ⊖High St. Kensington or Holland Park. Night Bus #27, 94, 148. A picturesque location in the center of Holland Park makes this one of the better hostels in the city. Many of the surprisingly spacious rooms are in a beautiful 17th-century mansion overlooking a courtyard; others are in an attached building with an institutional feel. Standard (but very clean) 12- to 20-bed single-sex dorms (some bunks are 3-tiered). Caters mostly to groups of high school and college student. Bright TV room. Cafeteria-style restaurant. Full English breakfast included; 3-course dinners £6.70. In-room luggage storage; padlocks £3. Larger lockers £2 per use. Linens included; towels £3.50. Laundry: wash £1.50; dry 20p per 15min. Free Wi-Fi; internet £4 per hr. 7-day max stay. Reception 24hr. Book 2-3 weeks in advance for summer. Dorms £22-28; under 18 £18-22. Prices vary by season and day of week. £3 discount per night for members. AmEx/MC/V. ❷

Oxford Hotel, 16-18 and 24 Penywern Rd. (☎020 7370 1161; www.the-oxford-hotel.com). ⊖Earl's Court. Night Bus #N31, N74, N97. Sir William Ramsay, the physicist who discovered helium, once lived here. In 2 Victorian houses on the same block, the Oxford offers bright, comfortable, mid-sized rooms. Each room has flatscreen TV, tea and coffee, safe, and shower; some have full bath. Breakfast included. Reception 24hr. Singles with shower £45-75, with bath £60-90; doubles £65-95/75-105; triples with bath £83-113; quads £92-130. Prices fluctuate; reserve 2-3 weeks in advance to get the lowest prices. MC/V. ❹

YHA Earl's Court, 38 Bolton Gardens (☎020 7373 7083; www.hihostels.com). ⊖Earl's Court. Night Bus #N31, N74, N97. Sprawling Victorian townhouse considerably better-equipped than most YHAs. Bright, tidy, 4- to 10-bed single-sex dorms have wooden bunks, lockers (padlock £3), and sinks. Features a courtyard garden, spacious communal kitchen, 2 TV lounges, and small cafe (organic espresso £1). Breakfast included for private rooms only; otherwise £4. Luggage storage available. Linens included; towels £3.50. Coin laundry. Internet £1 per 15min. 2-week max. stay. Book private rooms at least 24hr. in advance. Dorms £18-29, under 18 £18-25; doubles £47-77; triples £69-111; quads £81-130. Rates vary by season and day of week. £3 discount per night for YHA members. MC/V. ❷

Mowbray Court Hotel, 28-32 Penywern Rd. (☎020 7373 8285; www.mowbraycourthotel.co.uk). ⊖Earl's Court. Night Bus #N31, N74, N97. Large B&B with elevator, lounge, and modern bar. Rooms range from small to enormous. Each has TV, radio, trouser press, hair dryer, safe, and phone. Continental breakfast included. Wi-Fi £6 per 3hr.; £15 per week. Reception 24hr. Reserve 1 week in advance. Singles £60, with bath £70; doubles £76/86; triples £89/96; quads £100/120; quints £120/130; 6-bed rooms with bath £144. AmEx/MC/V. ❹

KNIGHTSBRIDGE AND BELGRAVIA

Belgravia's B&Bs are concentrated on **Ebury Street,** a fairly busy road as close to Victoria and Sloane Square as it is to Belgravia proper. And that's not a disadvantage: with Westminster's sights and Chelsea's shops both within walking distance, you'd be hard-pressed to do better. We've listed three of Ebury's best, but if none of these is available, chances are you'll find a vacancy in a comparable establishment somewhere else on the street.

▨ **Morgan House,** 120 Ebury St. (☎020 7730 2384; www.morganhouse.co.uk). ⊖Victoria. A touch of pizzazz makes this B&B a neighborhood standout. A boisterous couple rents mid-sized rooms with floral decor and country-style furnishings. Many have fireplaces and all have TV, kettle, and phone for incoming calls (pay phone downstairs). English breakfast included. Wi-Fi available. Reserve 2-3 months in advance. 48hr. cancellation policy. Singles with sink £52; doubles with sink £72, with bath £92; triples £92/112; quads with bath £132. MC/V. ❸

Westminster House Hotel, 96 Ebury St. (☎020 7730 4302; www.westminsterhousehotel.co.uk). ⊖Victoria. A prime location and friendly staff paired with 12 mid-sized, endearingly

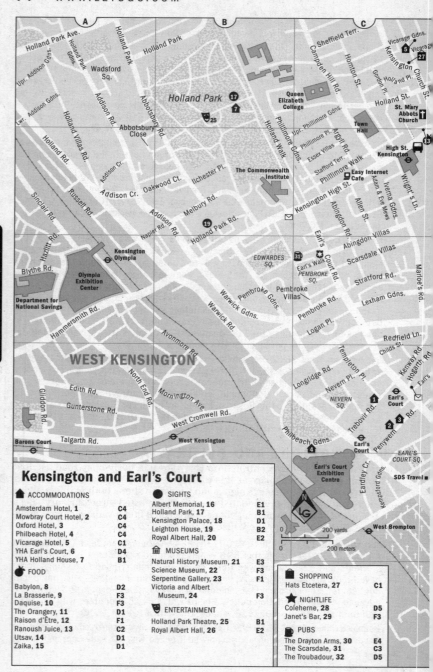

Kensington and Earl's Court

ACCOMMODATIONS

Amsterdam Hotel, 1	C4
Mowbray Court Hotel, 2	C4
Oxford Hotel, 3	C4
Philbeach Hotel, 4	C4
Vicarage Hotel, 5	C1
YHA Earl's Court, 6	D4
YHA Holland House, 7	B1

FOOD

Babylon, 8	D2
La Brasserie, 9	F3
Daquise, 10	F3
The Orangery, 11	D1
Raison d'Être, 12	F1
Ranoush Juice, 13	C2
Utsav, 14	D1
Zaika, 15	D1

SIGHTS

Albert Memorial, 16	E1
Holland Park, 17	B1
Kensington Palace, 18	D1
Leighton House, 19	B2
Royal Albert Hall, 20	E2

MUSEUMS

Natural History Museum, 21	E3
Science Museum, 22	F3
Serpentine Gallery, 23	F1
Victoria and Albert Museum, 24	F3

ENTERTAINMENT

Holland Park Theatre, 25	B1
Royal Albert Hall, 26	E2

SHOPPING

Hats Etcetera, 27	C1

NIGHTLIFE

Coleherne, 28	D5
Janet's Bar, 29	F3

PUBS

The Drayton Arms, 30	E4
The Scarsdale, 31	C3
The Troubadour, 32	D5

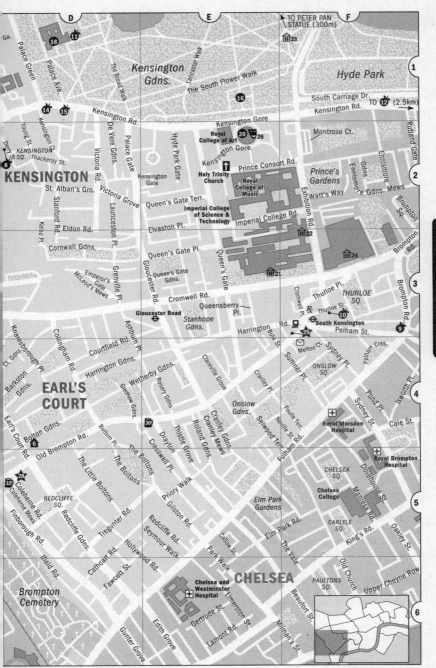

LONDON

quirky rooms. Delicious full English breakfast included. Reserve well in advance. 48hr. cancellation policy. Singles £50, with bath £60; doubles £70/80; triples £90/100; quads with bath £120. AmEx/MC/V. ❸

Belgravia Rooms, 104 Ebury St. (☎020 7730 1011; www.belgraviarooms.com). ⊖Victoria. Clean rooms with pleasant decor vary in size. All but the most basic have TVs, safes, ensuite baths, and Wi-Fi. 5- and 6-bed rooms are ideal for groups. Luggage storage £1 during stay; £2 after checkout. Free Internet at reception. Reception 24hr. 5-bed dorms from £90, 6-bed dorms from £100; singles from £20, with bath £45; doubles from £30/65; studios from £75; triples from £60/75; quads from £72/88. Discounts for stays longer than 1 week. MC/V. ❸

CHELSEA

Chelsea is practically devoid of accommodations and offers little for those on a student's budget. However, those who dream of calling Chelsea their temporary home have one great option:

IES Chelsea Pointe, (☎020 7808 9200; www.iesreshall.com), corner of Manresa Rd. and King's Rd., entrance on Manresa Rd. ⊖Sloane Sq., then Bus #11, 19, 22, 319; ⊖South Kensington, then Bus #49. Night Bus #N11, N19, N22. Brand new university residence offers clean, basic dorms. Amenities include phones, a modern kitchen, laundry service, and 5 TV/DVD lounges. Linens provided but guests must wash them. Free Wi-Fi. 1 week min. stay. Reservations recommended. 72hr. cancellation policy. Wheelchair-accessible. More availability during summer and winter school breaks. Singles £300-360 per week; doubles £394 per week. In the heart of trendy Chelsea, these prices are unheard of. AmEx/MC/V. ❸

WEST LONDON

Relative proximity to Notting Hill and Hyde Park, along with affordable prices and good transportation, make **Shepherd's Bush** and **Hammersmith** popular with student travelers. There are plenty of B&Bs, some small, independent hotels, and two vibrant hostels to choose from.

▨ **St. Christopher's Inn Hammersmith,** 28 Hammersmith Broadway (☎020 8600 7500, bookings 7407 1856; www.st-christophers.co.uk). ⊖Hammersmith. Steps away from the Tube, this brand new Aussie-inspired hostel has bright rooms with wood floors, yellow bedspreads, and the occasional pink wall. Bathrooms, too, are also recently redone. Set above the attached bar and restaurant, there is no shortage of entertainment. Breakfast and linens included. Luggage storage and laundry facilities available. Office safe for valuables. Wi-Fi in lobby. Airport pickup available; see website for details. 10% discount on Belushi's food and drinks. 8-bed dorms £16-23; 6-bed dorms £17-24; 4-bed dorms £19-28; doubles £50. Discounts available through hostelworld.com. 18+. MC/V. ❶

Euro Hotel, 31 Shepherd's Bush Rd. (☎020 7603 4721; www.euro-hotel.co.uk). ⊖Shepherd's Bush. Located 2 blocks from Shepherd's Bush Green, this hotel offers bright, spacious ensuite rooms with plush carpets, crisp coordinated decor, complimentary teas and soaps, free Wi-Fi, and satellite TV. Free parking 6:30pm-7:30am. Reception 24hr. Reserve weeks in advance for June-Aug stays. Singles £47; doubles £67; triples £89; quads £115; family studio £140. Discounts for stays of 4 nights or more. MC/V. ❸

St. Christopher's Inn Shepard's Bush, 13-15 Shepherd's Bush Green (☎020 8735 0270, bookings 7407 1856; www.st-christophers.co.uk). ⊖Shepherd's Bush. Night Bus #N72 or N97. Also above a Belushi's restaurant, but one that's recently been refurbished and offers nightly themed events, this crowded hangout is perfect for social backpackers. Relatively spacious but basic rooms with wood floors, red bunk beds, and sinks. A 24hr. downstairs lounge has ping pong, pool tables, a flatscreen TV, comfy couches, and internet access. Breakfast and linens included. Luggage storage; padlock £3. Office safe for valuables. Laundry £2 per wash, £1 per dry. Wi-Fi in lobby. Airport pickup available; see website for details. 10% discount on Belushi's food and drinks with key card. 8-bed dorms £16-23, 6-bed dorms £17-24, 4-bed dorms £18.50-28; doubles £50. 18+ unless accompanied by adult. MC/V. ➊

Star Hotel, 97-99 Shepherd's Bush Rd. (☎020 7603 2755; www.star-hotel.net). ⊖Hammersmith. Night Bus #9, 10, 11, 24. Family-run B&B. Rooms are clean, bright, and relatively spacious; all have TV, kettle, hair dryer, and large bath. Full English breakfast included, served in dining area with skylight. Book 1-2 months in advance for July-Aug. and Easter stays. Pay in advance. 72hr. cancellation policy. Singles £42-49; doubles £62-72; triples £80-93; quads £105. Stays over 2 nights receive a substantial discount. 3% surcharge for MC/V. ➌

Windsor Guest House, 43 Shepherd's Bush Rd. (☎020 7603 2116; www.windsorghs.co.uk). ⊖Shepherd's Bush or Hammersmith. This small, unpretentious, family-run B&B offers rooms with plush carpets and TV. Rooms on the bay window are especially spacious; some singles are small. Full English breakfast included; served in bright dining area. Reserve 1-2 months ahead for June-Aug stays. Singles £40; doubles £60; triples £75. Cash only. ➋

Hotel Orlando, 83 Shepherd's Bush Rd. (☎020 7603 4890; www.hotelorlando.co.uk). ⊖Shepherd's Bush or Hammersmith. Night Bus #N220. Clean, pleasant, decently-sized rooms are decent-sized with TV, phone, and bath; most have mini-fridge. Continental or full English breakfast included. Pay in advance. 5-day cancellation policy. Singles (some with double beds) £45-48; doubles £60-68; triples £80-88; quads £95-110. AmEx/MC/V. ➌

Dalmacia Hotel, 71 Shepherd's Bush Rd. (☎020 7603 2887; www.dalmacia-hotel.co.uk). ⊖Shepherd's Bush or Hammersmith. Nirvana's pre-stardom accommodation of choice, Dalmacia offers niceties like toiletries and tea kettles, decent-sized bathrooms, free Wi-Fi, and in-room safes. It does, however, have a no visitors policy, unconventional bed configurations ("doubles" are twins pushed together), and a non-complimentary breakfast (£3 for Continental; £5 for full English). All rooms have TVs and hair dryers. Singles £49-55; doubles £69-75; triples £81. Discounts depending on season. MC/V. ➌

☐ FOOD

While insiders have known London as a hot spot for inventive, internationally influenced cuisine for years, it has taken a little while to spread the word to tourists that Great Britain is more than just bangers and mash. London's thriving and enormously diverse food scene is fueled by its growing ethnic communities, many of which use their culinary traditions to maintain ties to their own culture while introducing others to their cuisine. Head to Whitechapel for the region's best Baltic food, to Chinatown for traditional dim sum, to South Kensington for French pastries, and to Edgware Rd. for a stunning assortment of Lebanese Shawarma. As London continues to become more diverse, the assortment and fusion of the dizzying number of food styles will most likely keep growing. That said, it would be a shame to come to the home of proper afternoon tea and fish 'n' chips and deny yourself these delicious and long-standing British traditions. The moral of the story: try everything.

CHECK, PLEASE. In most restaurants, it's considered rude for the waiter to give a patron their bill, since it implies they should hurry and give up the table. If you would like to pay, you will most likely have to ask for the check.

THE CITY OF LONDON

When in the City, do as the City-ers do: eat at one of the many chain restaurants. Eat, Pret a Manger, Costa Coffee, and Starbucks all hold court here, so don't get your hopes up for that perfect hole-in-the-wall. If you want a nice sit-down lunch, you'll most likely be surrounded by businessmen, while at dinner you might be all by your lonesome, as the workers clear out and most restaurants are only open through lunch hours. Your best bet is to take a gander at the options listed below or try a pub, most of which are open and serve decent food well into the evenings. If you still can't decide what to eat, the alleyways of Leadenhall Market pack in numerous mid-range chain restaurants, cafes, and pubs.

■ **CafeSpice Namaste,** 16 Prescot St. (☎020 7488 9242; www.cafespice.co.uk). ⊖Tower Hill or DLR: Tower Gateway. Somewhat out of the way, but well worth the trek. Bright, festive decorations bring a zany feel to this old Victorian warehouse with courtyard seating. Extensive menu of Goan and Parsi specialties. Meat mains are on the pricey side (from £14.30), but vegetarian dishes (from £5.50) are tasty and affordable. Varied wine list and excellent, if expensive, desserts. Open M-F noon-3pm and 6:15-10:30pm, Sa 6:30-10:30pm. Reservations recommended. AmEx/MC/V. ❸

The Place Below, St. Mary le Bow Church (☎020 7329 0789; www.theplacebelow.co.uk), on Cheapside, in the basement of the Church. ⊖St. Paul's or Mansion House. A definite step up from the chains, both in setting and quality. Climb down the winding steps from the foyer of St. Mary-le-Bow, and you'll find yourself in a fantastic vegetarian restaurant set in the vaulted crypt. Choose from constantly changing menu of veggie entrees like spinach, mushroom and stilton quiche (from £6.10), as well as creative salads (from £6.50), soups (£3.20), and sandwiches (£3-4). Or, try the daily health bowl, a concoction of various healthful foods (from £4.70). There are also pastries (from £1.40) and plenty of hot drinks. Be prepared to wait at lunchtime and count on taking your food with you. Seating in pleasant courtyard available. Open M-F 7:30am-3pm. ❶

Futures, 8 Botolph Alley (☎020 7623 4529; www.futures-vta.net), between Botolph Ln. and Lovat Ln. ⊖Monument. London's workforce besieges this tiny takeaway joint during lunch; come before noon to take advantage. Vegetarian soups (from £2.60), salads (£2.50-4), and hot dishes (from £5.70) change weekly. Wheat-free, gluten-free, and vegan options, and offers a wide variety of pastries (from £0.90) or porridges and cereals (from £1.40) for breakfast. Wheelchair-accessible. Open M-F 8-10am and 11:30am-2:15pm. AmEx/MC/V. ❶

Napket, 34 Leadenhall St. (☎020 7621 1831; www.napket.com), inside the Royal Exchange. ⊖Bond St. Decked out in slick black and proclaiming to serve "Snob Food," Napket is the Saks Fifth Avenue of sandwich and salad bars. But though it's made with busy executives in mind, it's neither exclusive nor expensive—and the gourmet food is delicious. Salads (from £3.90). Ciabatta and focaccia sandwiches (from £4.50) include chicken curry, New York club, or grilled veggies with goat cheese. Also serves pastas, pastries, smoothies, and coffee drinks. Wheelchair-accessible. Open M-F 6:30am-6pm. AmEx/MC/V. ❶

Spianata & Co., 73a Watling St. (☎020 7236 3666; www.spianata.com). ⊖Mansion House. With only a handful of places to sit, this sandwich shop is less about atmosphere and all about homemade flatbread piled with Italian ingredients. Classic mozzarella and tomato, ham with parmesan and artichoke, or smoked salmon with a gourmet cheese spread. £3-4 takeaway, £4-5 eat-in. Pizza £2 per slice. Wheelchair-accessible. Open M-F 7:30am-3pm. ❶

FOOD OR POCKET CHANGE. Pub grub is often the cheapest way to eat in London without having to cook for yourself. Head to one of the pubs recommended by *Let's Go,* listed in the Nightlife section (p. 186).

EAST LONDON

WHITECHAPEL AND THE EAST END

As with all things East End, diversity is the name of the game when it comes to food. Whether you're looking for a £2 market-gathered picnic, a cheap and filling curry lunch, vegan fare in a hip and crowded cafe, or a refined sit-down British meal, you'll find it here. **Brick Lane** has long been known as one of the most mouth-watering destinations in London; while it got on the map for its spectacular curries, it's also home to some of the best Jewish bakeries, hip coffee shops, and alternative cafe scene. Aspiring chefs can stock up on fresh, organic food at **Spitalfields Market** (p. 174), an Edwardian hall teeming with creatively decorated international food stalls. Finally, Hoxton and Shoreditch are the places to go for *haute cuisine* in the area's bars. A growing number of trendy restaurants on **Hoxton Square** and **Shoreditch High Street** also offer excellent pre-club fuel, and **Kingsland Road** boasts a treasure trove of affordable Vietnamese eateries. (⊖Old St., ⊖Shoreditch, or a 10min. walk from ⊖Aldgate East or ⊖Liverpool St.)

⊠ **Café 1001,** 91 Brick Lane, Dray Walk (☎7247 9679; www.cafe1001.co.uk), in an alley just off Brick Ln. ⊖Aldgate East. This massive warehouse-turned-artists' den feels more like a never-ending block party than a cafe. Students, artists and assorted hipster types lounge in couches in the spacious upstairs or at the numerous picnic tables that dominate the alleyway, while staff dole out fresh homemade food to eat in or take away. Choose from a variety of premade salads (3 for £3.50) and healthy main dishes (£5.95 including 3 side salads) at the buffet, or grab a massive sandwich (from £3.50) and pastry (from £.80) at the cafe side. Selections of wine and beer (£2-4). Outdoor barbecue weather permitting (burgers £4, with fries £4.50). Nightly DJs or live bands 8pm-close, W live jazz. Open M-Th and Su 6am-midnight, F-Sa 6am-12:30am. ❶

⊠ **Chaat,** 36 Redchurch St. (☎020 7739 9595; www.chaatlondon.com). ⊖Liverpool St. A sleek but cozy restaurant, tea room, and bar, Chaat serves delicious Bangladeshi food. Start with a "Chit Chaat" like samosas or tomato, ginger, and coriander soup; follow it with a veggie or meat dish; add a "Mopper" (rice or bread) and an accompaniment like dhal or pan-fried okra; and finish with a homemade dip. Doubles as an art gallery. 5-course meals £14. Reservations recommended. Open M-Sa 6:30-11pm. AmEx/MC/V. ❷

CLERKENWELL

There's no shortage of deliciously diverse dining experiences in Clerkenwell, from pitch-black fine dining to cafes focused first and foremost on local and organic fare. Sandwich bars and quick cafes cluster around Farringdon station and along St. John Street for the business lunch hour, while near West Smithfield you'll find inexpensive snack bars, pubs, and Chinese takeaways. For a proper sit-down meal, your best bet is either Charterhouse Street or Exmouth Market, a pedestrian street north of Clerkenwell Rd. with both eateries and adorable shops. Tucked between fine dining options, Clerkenwell's pubs (p. 190) are some of London's oldest, and they afford great options for those in the mood for something less formal than the area's posh restaurants.

⊠ **Dans Le Noir,** 30-31 Clerkenwell Green (☎020 7253 1100; www.danslenoir.com). Aimed at providing the ultimate sensory experience (and raising awareness about the visually impaired), the name says it all: dine in pitch black darkness while being served by blind waiters. All you know is that your 2- or 3-course menu is either meat, fish, veggie, or a "complete surprise," so you have only your taste buds to trust. For those who are afraid of the dark, the downstairs bar is lit, but your drink comes with a secret treat. Reserve 1 week in advance for a weekday, 2 weeks in advance for the weekend.

2-course meal £32, 3-course meal £38. Open M-Sa 6:30pm-midnight; 1st sitting 6:45-7:15pm, 2nd sitting 9-9:30pm. AmEx/MC/V. ❺

🏴 **The Clerkenwell Kitchen,** 31 Clerkenwell Close (☎020 7101 9959; www.theclerkenwellkitchen.co.uk). ⊖Farringdon. Hidden in a former warehouse among the twists and turns of the Close, this hip cafe specializes in sustainable food production. Every day the staff prepares 6 dishes, 2 puddings, and a selection of takeaway sanwiches, pastries, and tarts, almost all of which are made with organic and local ingredients. Dishes like spinach, onion, and feta tart and crab and fennel linguini £4.50-11. Open M-W and F 8am-5pm, Th 8am-11pm; breakfast 8-11am, lunch noon-3pm, snacks 3-5pm. MC/V. ❷

🏴 **Anexo,** 61 Turnmill St. (☎020 7250 3401; www.anexo.co.uk). ⊖Farringdon. With whimsically indulgent, Gaudí-esque decor and a spirited but laid-back attitude, this Spanish restaurant and bar serves tasty paella (£8.50-11.50), fajitas (£7.50-11.50), and tapas (from £3.25-6.50). The lunch special is hard to beat (£6.50 for 2 courses, £8.50 for 3 courses), and the mixed drinks menu is exhaustive (2 glasses £5-6.50, jug £16-20). Takeaway available. Wheelchair-accessible. Happy hour M-Sa 5-7pm: 2-for-1 on selected beers, wines, and mixed drinks. Open M-F 10am-11pm, Sa 6-11pm, Su 4:30-11pm. Bar open 11am-2am. AmEx/MC/V. ❷

Little Bay Restaurant, 171 Farringdon Rd. (☎020 278 1234; www.littlebay.co.uk). ⊖Farringdon. Part of the Little Bay mini-empire, this small restaurant serves delicious European food in a sumptuous interior filled with enormous gold masks, velvet drapes, and paintings of dancing Greek goddesses. During certain months, the restaurant famously invites you to "pay what you think it's worth." Mains like pan fried cod with chorizo stew, grilled lamb with balsamic vegetables, and paupiette of salmon with new potatoes and avocado salsa £5.25 noon-7pm, £7.45 after 7pm. Burgers £5.80. All-you-can-eat buffet with specialty salads (before 6pm) £6 eat in, £5 take-away. Open M-Sa noon-midnight, Su noon-11pm. AmEx/MC/V. ❷

St. John Restaurant and Bar, 26 St. John St. (☎020 7251 0848; www.stjohnrestaurant.com). ⊖Farringdon. Set in a towering former smokehouse, this bright, minimalist restaurant serves up unusual dishes that reward the adventurous eater. Menu changes daily, but standards include starters like roast bone marrow (£6.90) and entrees like pigeon with green beans (£15.90), blood cake and fried eggs (£16.20), or the less adventurous roast lamb and *courgettes* (£21.80). Bakery at the back of the bar churns out delicious loaves of bread (from £2). More familiar and less intimidating desserts £6.40-7.40. Enormous wine list. Open M-F noon-3pm

ON THE MENU

CHICKEN TIKKA MASALA

Yorkshire pudding, roast beef, fish and chips—all of these are quintessentially English dishes. But it is chicken tikka masala, a curry whose shadowy origins lie somewhere between India and the UK, that a recent survey identifies as Britain's most popular. With over 23 million portions sold per year, the stuff is everywhere: in sandwiches, on pizzas, and even flavoring potato chips.

Some say the creamy, red-and-orange mixture was invented by a chef in a fit of spontaneous creativity; when a dissatisfied customer demanded gravy on his chicken tandoori, the chef poured tomato soup and some spices over it. Several chefs have claimed to be the inspired originators, but one thing is certain: the innovation occurred somewhere in Britain, sometime in the mid-20th century. The recipe for the dish itself is uncertain. It is made of tikka (bite-size pieces of tandoori chicken) and masala ("spices," usually in a tomato-based sauce).

As a fusion of Asian and European elements, the meal has taken on even wider significance. The late Foreign Secretary Robin Cook called chicken tikka masala "a true British national dish, not only because it is the most popular, but because it is a perfect illustration of the way Britain absorbs and adapts external influences." Whatever its origins, chicken tikka masala is certainly a highlight of British cuisine.

and 6-11pm, Sa 6-11pm, Su 1-3pm. Bar open M-Sa 11am-11pm, Sa 6-11pm, Su noon-5pm. AmEx/MC/V. ❸

CAFES AND SPECIALTY SHOPS

▨ **Kipferl,** 70 Long Ln. (☎020 7796 2229; www.kipferl.co.uk). ⊖Barbican. London's only Austrian deli-cafe, the tiny Kipferl serves delicious sandwiches, soups, salads, and platters (£2.80-6.50) made with imported Austrian ingredients, many of which are organic. Choose from Austrian specialties like smoked salmon on quark bretzel roll (bagel-pretzel), Austrian sausage with sauerkraut and pickles, or Fritatten soup (savory pancake soup). Open M-F 8am-5pm, Sa 9am-5pm. AmEx/MC/V. ❶

▨ **Farm Collective,** 91 Cowcross St. (☎020 7253 2142; www.farmcollective.com). ⊖Barbican. This small cafe serves takeaway salads, sandwiches, soups, and hot mains made solely from UK-grown ingredients. Choose from among salads like the Herefordshire Ragstone goat's cheese with roasted tomatoes, walnuts and beets (£3.90-4.50), sandwiches like the Red Ruby beef and horseradish (£2.70-3.60), or a weekly selection of pies and mash (£6). Also serves a selection of breakfast foods and pastries. If you make it in time, you might get a spot at one of 10 tables. Open M-F 7:30am-4:30pm. ❶

The Curved Angel, 53 Clerkenwell Close (☎020 7502 3380; www.curvedangel.co.uk), by St. James Church. ⊖Farringdon. There's no sign on the door, but you won't want to miss this small cafe, which serves hearty homemade paninis, sandwiches, and ciabattas (£2-4.50), as well as entrees like Greek shepherd's pie, stuffed jacket potatoes, and spicy sausage penne (£4.20-5.20). A small lounge in the back and picnic tables outside offer great places to rest with a coffee and homemade scone or muffin. Also serves breakfast. Open M-F 8am-7pm, Sa-Su 9am-5pm. MC/V. ❶

HOLBORN

In the 18th century, there was one tavern in Holborn for every five homes; although the ratio has since diminished, pubs still occupy many a street corner, catering to the working Fleet Street crowd. You don't have to look hard to find cozy enclaves of smoke-blackened wood, traditional fare, and hand-pulled ales. For those not up for pub grub, affordable eateries line the alleys around **Red Lion Street** and **Theobald's Road,** and small cafes cater to the shoppers at **Leather Lane Market.** Whatever your cuisine, if it's in a box or a bag, take it over to **Lincoln's Inn Fields** or **Gray's Inn** for a fair-weather picnic.

▨ **Bleeding Heart Tavern** (☎020 7404 0333), on the corner of Greville St. and Bleeding Heart Yard. ⊖Farringdon. This jovial pub has guarded the entrance to Bleeding Heart Yard since 1746, and maintains the same motto: "drunk for a penny and dead drunk for two." Roast suckling pig with sage, apple, and onion stuffing (£14). Classic beer-battered haddock with marrow fat peas (£11). Open M-F 7-10:30am, noon-2:30pm, 6-10:30pm. Upstairs pub open M-F 11:30am-11pm. AmEx/MC/V. ❷

Bleeding Heart Bistro and Restaurant, Bleeding Heart Yard (bistro ☎020 7242 8238, restaurant 7242 2056). ⊖Farringdon. Around the corner from the Tavern; follow the signs. With over 450 options, their wine list has been named "one of the finest in the world" by *Wine Spectator* magazine. The more informal Bistro features French favorites like omelettes, char-grilled steak *haché*, and tuna *tartare* (£9-15). The dressy restaurant serves more ambitious entrees like pan-fried calf's liver with *ventreche* bacon, *pomme purée*, and *shallot jus* (£13-25). Vegetarian options available. Outdoor seating wheelchair-accessible. Dress business casual. Bistro and restaurant open M-F noon-2:30pm and 6-10:30pm. AmEx/MC/V. ❹

Aki, 182 Gray's Inn Rd. (☎020 7837 9281). ⊖Chancery Ln. A small, timbered room outfitted in Japanese lanterns, fans, and parasols. Best known for its delicious but affordable noodles (from £5.30), meat dishes (£8-13.50), and sushi (from £1.70-3).

Bento box lunch from £6. Takeaway available. Wheelchair-accessible. Open M-F noon-2:30pm and 6-11pm, Sa 6-10:30pm. AmEx/MC/V. ❷

Chutney Raj, 137 Gray's Inn Rd. (☎020 7831 1149). ⊖Chancery Ln. Traditional *tandoori* and Balti dishes (from £6), plenty of vegetarian dishes, and over 10 varieties of curry (£5-9). Lunch special includes *papadams,* a starter, and an entree (daily noon-2:30pm; £6). Similar "student offer" (daily noon-2pm and 5:30-11:30pm; £5). Takeaway and delivery available. Open M-Sa noon-2:30pm and 5:30-11:30pm, Su noon-2pm and 5:30-11pm. MC/V. ❷

THE SOUTH BANK

Although the views of the Thames often outdo the quality of the food, the South Bank is perfect for a small snack or a riverside picnic. Eateries on the wharf are generally either chains, or pricey, or both; consider buying food elsewhere and eating on one of the waterside benches. Should you venture inland, there are a couple restaurants that are both delicious and reasonably priced, though you'll want to have a place in mind—this area does not reward wanderers. If you insist on spontaneity, **Bermondsey Street, Tabard Street,** and **Borough High Street** have a handful of solid options. Meanwhile, those who prefer to assemble their own meals can turn to the **◪Borough Market,** where stalls lay out fresh and often organic gourmet cheeses, breads, fruits, and cured meats. (Off Borough High St. www.boroughmarket.org.uk. ⊖London Bridge. Open Th 11am-5pm, F noon-6pm, Sa 9am-4pm, some stalls open daily; best on 3rd Sa of every month.)

◪ **Bermondsey Kitchen,** 194 Bermondsey St. (☎020 7407 5719; www.bermondseykitchen.co.uk). ⊖London Bridge. On up-and-coming Bermondsey St., this lively restaurant offers a classy but casual dining experience, with heavy wooden tables and nice leather couches. A fresh, largely organic menu changes daily and features such delights as crab *pâté* with toast and gherkins or wild boar and apple sausages with thyme *au jus.* Also offers a small selection of tapas (£2-3.50). Appetizers £5.50-7. Entrees £9.50-14. Happy hour M-Sa 5-7pm; mixed drinks £5. Open M-F noon-3pm and 6:30-10:30pm, Sa 9:30am-3:30pm and 6:30am-10:30pm. AmEx/MC/V. ❷

Cubana, 48 Lower Marsh (☎020 7928 8778; www.cubana.co.uk). ⊖Waterloo. Parrots and dancing Cuban women, a Cuban flag, and lots of Che set the tone at this fun and lively restaurant-bar. Cuban tapas and mains like the *camarones criollos* (creole-style king prawns; £10) take 2nd place to the popular frozen mixed drinks (from £6, 2-pint jug £14). At lunch (M-F noon-3pm), get 2 tapas for £8, a 2-course meal for £7, and 3 courses for £9. Happy hour M-Sa 5-6:30pm; 2 mixed drinks for £6. W-Sa live salsa and Latin music. Cover F-Sa after 11pm £5. Open M-Tu noon-midnight, W-Th noon-1am, F noon-3am, Sa 5pm-3am. Reservations recommended. AmEx/MC/V. ❷

CAFES AND SPECIALTY SHOPS

The Island Cafe, 1 Flat Iron Sq. (☎020 7407 2224; www.cafetakeaway.co.uk). ⊖Southwark. At the junction of Union St. and Southwark Bridge Rd. This small diner-style hut and neighborhood hangout is famous for its delicious and cheap sandwiches, but offers much more, from ciabattas to pasta to jacket potatoes. Sandwiches (£2.10-£2.70) come with everything from cheddar and cream cheese to smoked salmon and minted lamb. Hot meals £3.80-4.80. Pastries £1.20. Breakfasts £2.40-3.60. Wheelchair-accessible. Open daily 6am-4:30pm. MC/V. ❶

Bermondsey Street Coffee, 167 Bermondsey Street (☎020 7408 7655). ⊖London Bridge. Organic fair trade coffee as cheap as can be, with the "flat broke" (espresso and steamed milk) starting at 80p. "Award-winning" sandwiches from £1.80. Dirty Sanchez (white and dark chocolate, espresso, milk, and whipped cream) £3. Smoothies £3. Open daily 7am-8pm. AmEx/MC/V. ❶

SOUTH LONDON

Despite sometimes gritty surroundings, Clapham and Brixton are packed with cute cafes and restaurants. Fish 'n' chips joints, rustic-gourmet cafes, hole-in-the-wall bakeries, classy Italian dinners, trendy brunch places... the list goes on, and you'll certainly find what you're looking for, especially if you didn't know you were looking for it. Visit **Brixton Market** for contained chaos and traditional delights like curry goat or saltfish with ackee.

 MAKE A NIGHT OF IT. Because it's a little out of the way, the best way to experience all that South London has to offer is to make dinner reservations at one of its great restaurants and continue on to the bars and clubs; if you come for daylight sightseeing, you might be disappointed.

BRIXTON

🏶 **Lounge,** 56-58 Atlantic Rd. (☎020 7733 5229; www.loungebrixton.com). ⊖Brixton. A self-described "urban retreat," this open restaurant features large windows, vibrant orange walls, and a laid-back vibe in which locals check email, chat over a drink, or feast on all-day breakfasts (full £6.95) and snacks. Free Wi-Fi. Open M-W 11am-11pm, Th-Sa 11am-midnight, Su 11am-5:30pm. MC/V. ❷

🏶 **Rosie's Deli Cafe,** 14e Market Row (☎020 7287 7490; www.rosiesdelicafe.com), off Coldharbour Ln. ⊖Brixton. Owned indeed by a surprisingly young Rosie, this tiny and somewhat hidden deli-cafe has become a local hit, serving up fresh ciabattas and breads loaded with the rarities like chicken liver, pate and olives; hummus and sun-dried tomatoes; and salt beef and gherkin (£3.50-4.50). Also serves serious salads and big plates (£6-6.50), as well as tons of specialty goods from around the world, which are packed into the overflowing shelves. Only a couple tables inside and in the market. Open Tu-Sa 9:30am-5:30pm. MC/V. ❶

THE WEST END

MAYFAIR AND SAINT JAMES'S

Mayfair and St. James are generally pricey neighborhoods: even cute holes-in-the-wall can run a bit steep. Yet, there are a couple areas where the atmosphere is great, the prices are lower, and the crowds are larger. These include the lively courtyard of **St. Christopher's Place,** the tiny **Kingly Street,** between Regent and Carnaby, and the tucked-away cobblestone streets of **Shepherd's Market** where pubs and cute cafes coexist.

🏶 **Busaba Eathai,** 8-13 Bird St. (☎020 7518 8080; www.busaba.com). ⊖Oxford St. Also at 106-110 Wardour St., Soho (☎7255 8686). Incense, floating candles, and slick wood paneling make you feel like you're dining in a Buddhist temple. Large, tightly-packed communal tables ensure a lively wait for the affordable, filling dishes. Students and locals line up for stir fry, curry, pad thai, and other wok creations (£6.20-11). Tons of vegetarian dishes. Open M-Th noon-11pm, F-Sa noon-11:30pm, Su noon-10pm. AmEx/MC/V. ❷

Mo Tearoom, 23 Heddon St. (☎020 7434 3999; www.momoresto.com). ⊖Piccadilly Circus or Oxford Circus. Based on a Moroccan *souq*, this restaurant-tea room-bar-bazaar is an authentic slice of Marrakesh. Carved chairs, floor cushions, low tables, and Moroccan crafts add to the ambience. Mix and match tapas-style appetizers (£7-11) including the popular *harira*, wood pidgeon pastilla, and mini chicken tagine. Hookah £9. Wheelchair-accessible outside seating. Come early in the evening to avoid a wait.

Entrees £15-23. Open daily noon-midnight. Restaurant open M-Sa noon-2:30pm and 6:30-11:30pm, Su 6:30-11pm. AmEx/MC/V. ❹

L'Autre, 5B Shepherd St. (☎020 7499 4680), in Shepherd's Market. ⊖Hyde Park Corner or Green Park. Charming and eccentric restaurant with Mexican and Polish dishes served in a cozy Victorian dining room. Specializes in fresh, seasonal game. Try the wild boar sausage or the special beef enchiladas (both £13). Open M-F noon-3pm and 6-11pm, Sa-Su 1-11pm. AmEx/MC/V. ❸

Sofra, 18 Shepherd St. (☎020 7493 3320; www.sofra.co.uk), in Shepherd's Market. ⊖Hyde Park Corner or Green Park. Also at 1 St. Christopher's Pl. One of the area's most popular restaurants, Sofra offers fine Turkish cuisine at reasonable prices. Nonstop hummus and bread is an added bonus. Their most popular dish: the mixed grill (minced lamb and chicken on a skewer; £15). Try the healthy menu or the crunch menu (both menus lunch £13, dinner £15). Lots of vegetarian dishes. Entrees £12-22. Open daily 8:30am-midnight. AmEx/MC/V. ❷

Tamarind, 20 Queen St. (☎020 7629 3561). ⊖Green Park. A sumptuous interior and classy, modern decor come at a price, but the inspired Indian dishes are worth their weight in gold. Vegetarian dishes from £7. Meat kebabs from £16. Curries from £17. Weekday *prix-fixe* lunch (2 courses £15, 3 £19, tasting menu £25). Open M-F noon-2:45pm and 6-11:30pm, Sa 5-11:30pm, Su noon-2:45pm and 6-10:30pm. Reserve ahead. AmEx/MC/V. ❸

SPECIALTY SHOPS AND CAFES

Paxton & Whitfield, 93 Jermyn St. (☎020 7930 0259; www.paxtonandwhitfield.co.uk). ⊖Piccadilly Circus. Winston Churchill once observed that "a gentleman only buys his cheese at Paxton & Whitfield." Founded in 1797, Paxton & Whitfield is still selling some of the best British and imported cheeses in the city. Have a visit—your nose will either thank or resent you. Most cheeses £5-10 per 250g. Also sells fresh sandwiches (£6-8) and cheese accessories like knives and graters. Open M-Sa 9:30am-6pm. AmEx/MC/V. ❷

Richoux, 41A South Audley St. (☎020 7629 5228; www.richoux.co.uk). ⊖Hyde Park Corner or Marble Arch. Also at 172 Piccadilly. ⊖Piccadilly Circus. Afternoon tea in a sumptuous environment. Attracts an international crowd from the nearby embassies. The Richoux Cream tea with scones and preserves is pricey at £8.30, as is the traditional afternoon tea (sandwiches, scones, and pastries; £16.50, £30 for 2). A normal pot of tea, however, costs only £2.90. Also serves lunch (sandwiches and salads £7.40-10). Open M-F 8am-11pm, Sa 8am-11:30pm, Su 9am-11pm. AmEx/MC/V. ❹

 FOOD FOR POCKET CHANGE. Takeaway is cheaper than staying in for many lunch places. Save yourself a few quid by getting your grub to go and settling in on a nearby bench instead.

SOHO

One of the best places in London to eat and drink, Soho has restaurants, cafes, and bars to suit every taste and budget. **Chinatown** is located on Gerrard St. and Lisle St., while Frith St. offers pizza, pasta, and garlic goodness in **Little Italy. Wardour Street** is a new hot spot for everything from vegetarian food to creperies and Asian cuisine. The southern side of **Shaftesbury Avenue** feeds hungry clubbers post-club. Around **Carnaby Street,** cute cafes and coffee shops welcome tired shoppers, while a little farther east lie holes-in-the-wall and edgier local spots.

The Breakfast Club, 33 D'Arblay St. (☎020 726 5454; www.thebreakfastclubsoho.com). A favorite spot for the irreverent brunch-goer, serving creative twists on classics like eggs benedict, pancakes, burritos and burgers. Large family-style tables with red-checkered table cloths. Specials like The Full Monty (bacon, sausage, beans, tomatoes, mushrooms; £6.20) or The Number wrap (goat cheese, roasted red peppers and eggplant, pesto, tomato chutney; £6). Full Metal Jacket Potatoes with a variety of toppings £4.50-5.50. Super smoothies £3.50. Open M-F 8am-6pm, Sa 9:30am-5pm, Su 10am-4pm. Cash only. ❶

Golden Dragon, 28-29 Gerrard St. (☎020 1705 2503). ⊖Leicester Sq. The ritziest and best-known dim sum joint in Chinatown. Golden Dragon's 2 large red-and-gold rooms (yes, there are dragons) are packed on the weekends with families and couples taking in the cheery atmosphere and shoveling in the dumplings—from veggie staples to minced prawn and sugar cane treats (each dish £2.40-3.20). Regular dinner items £6.20-22. Dim sum £15-25. Open M-Th noon-11:30pm, F-Sa noon-midnight, Su 11am-11pm. Dim sum served M-Sa noon-5pm, Su 11am-5pm. AmEx/MC/V. ❹

Cha Cha Moon, 15-21 Ganton St. (☎020 7297 9800; www.chachamoon.com). ⊖ Oxford St. Also at 151 Queensway (☎020 7792 0088). One of the area's more raucous spots with communal tables and a lively atmosphere. Low ceilings, brick columns, and bright red fixtures. The lo mein and wok creations are inexpensive (£4.80-7.50), and the atmosphere is perfect for a fun date or night out with friends. Open M-Th noon-11pm, F-Sa noon-11:30pm, Su noon-10:30pm. AmEx/MC/V. ❷

Vitaorganic, 74 Wardour St., (☎020 773 489 86; www.vitaorganic.co.uk), ⊖Tottenham Court Rd. or Leicester Sq. It doesn't get earthier than this: vegetarians and vegans unite in this jungle-esque cafe for organic, raw, and "gently cooked" dishes or healthier-than-thou juices. Served buffet style, dishes like veggie stroganoff, lentil daal, couscous, and moussaka are mouthwatering despite their health benefits. Try one of the specialty juices, with names like Red Purifier (beetroot, celery, carrot, apple, milk thistle) and Wisdom Eye (blackberry, blueberry, raspberry, grapes, gingkoba biloba). Or, make your own: choose a flavor (chai, earl grey, rooibus, masala), a style (hot or cold), a milk, a frappé, and a sweetening. Dairy, wheat, and gluten-free desserts available. Hot food £5-7. Juices £4-5. Open M-Sa noon-10pm, Su noon-9pm. Cash only. ❷

Jerk City, 189 Wardour St. (☎020 7287 2878). ⊖Tottenham Court Rd. The name refers to the food, not the service: a small and simple restaurant that lets its fine Caribbean fare do the talking. Feast on house specialties like jerk chicken (£7.50), Trinidadian mutton roti (£6), or one of several vegetarian options (£6-8). All entrees come with a hearty portion of rice and peas. Add fried plantains (£1) or delicious baked mac 'n cheese (£2.50). Halal meat used in all dishes. Takeaway available. Open M-Sa 10am-11pm, Su noon-8pm. AmEx/MC/V. ❷

Soba Noodle Bar, 11/13 Soho St. (☎020 7827 7300; www.soba.co.uk). ⊖Tottenham Court Rd. Narrow noodle bar with a long communal table, bench seating, and cork trimmings. Big bowls of wok-fried noodles and rice plates (both from £6.20). In nice weather, crowds gather at the outside tables overlooking Soho Square. Lots of vegetarian dishes. Happy hour (all mains £4.50) M-W 4-7:30pm, Sa and Su all day. Open M-F noon-3:30pm and 5:30-11pm, Sa noon-10pm, Su noon-9pm. AmEx/MC/V. ❷

Hummus Bros., 88 Wardour St. (☎020 7734 1311). ⊖Oxford Circus or Tottenham Court Rd. The 1st restaurant of its kind, Hummus Bros. offers variations on the versatile dip. Top it with everything from spiced chicken to veggie salad and pair it with warm pita bread. Sides like tabouleh, greek salad, and smoked BBQ aubergine. Environmentally friendly (completely carbon-neutral). Small, bright space with red-lacquered tables. Sides £2.50-3.20. Small dishes £3-6.50; regular dishes £4-8. Free Wi-Fi. Open M-W and Su noon-10pm, Th-Sa Sa noon-11pm. AmEx/MC/V. ❶

Masala Zone, 9 Marshall St. (☎020 7287 9966; www.realindianfood.com). ⊖Oxford Circus. Also in Islington at 80 Upper St. (☎7359 3399). Despite its status as a quasi-chain, Masala Zone manages to be hip and relaxed, with a softly lit interior and sunken dining room. The food is authentic, delicious, and cooked in an open kitchen. The focus is on *thalis*, platters that come with a variety of smaller dishes and a larger fish, chicken, meat, or veggie entree (£11-13). Also serves Indian street food (£4.20 each), including samosas. Vegetarian friendly. Open M-F noon-2:45pm and 5:30-11pm, Sa 12:30-11pm, Su 12:30-3:30pm and 6-10:30pm. MC/V. ❷

Boulevard Bar and Dining Room, 57-59 Old Compton St. (☎020 7287 0770). ⊖Leicester Sq. Fresh creative twists on standard English and American cuisine in American-sized portions. Try the jumbalaya (£10), Texas omelette with chorizo and potatoes (£9), or a steak (£13-20). Add in a hip atmosphere and you've got a nice pre-theater or pre-club spot for those who aren't up for Chinese. Starters like butternut squash soup with mascarpone £4.30-8. Desserts £5. AmEx/MC/V. ❸

CAFES AND SPECIALTY FOODS

▨ **Mrs. Marengo's,** 53 Lexington St. (☎020 7287 2544; www.mrsmarengos.co.uk). A refined pink diner serving healthy vegetarian takes on classics like burgers, quesadillas, falafel, and tajines (£4-7) as well as fresh, gourmet salads (£7). Beautiful but massive cakes and pastries (£3) in carrot, pecan, and triple chocolate varieties (£3). Eat-in or takeaway. Open M-F 8am-6pm, Sa noon-6pm. AmEx/MC/V. ❷

▨ **Snog,** 9 Brewer St. (www.ifancyasnog.com) ⊖Piccadilly Circus. Also at 32 Thurloe Pl., South Kensington. Opened in March 2009, Snog is another one of those guilt-free frozen yogurt havens. It has more of an attitude (colorful ceilings with myriad plays on the word snog) and toppings you can't get elsewhere, like an espresso shot, dates, and gogi berries. Choose from original, green tea, or chocolate. "Little" with 1 topping £3.60, 2 toppings £4.20, 3 toppings £4.80; "Classic" £4/4.60/5.20; "Massive" £8.60/9.30/9.10. Open daily 11am-midnight. AmEx/MC/V. ❶

Carlton Coffee House, 41 Broadwick St. (☎020 7437 3807). ⊖Oxford Circus or Tottenham Court Rd. Couples and groups hungry from a hectic day of shopping gather in this understated diner for sandwiches and panini (£2-5). Flavors vary from simple (like goat cheese or veggie) to indulgent (like bacon, brie, and cranberry or mozzarella and sundried tomato basil). Also serves homemade soups (£4-6) and salads (£4.90). Milkshakes £2.20. Delicious homemade desserts £2.30. Takeaway and delivery available. Bring your own wine. Open M-F 7am-5:30pm, Sa 8:30am-6:30pm. MC/V. ❶

ON THE MENU

BANGERS AND MASH

"What? Sunday morning in an English family and no sausages? God bless my soul, what's the world coming to, eh?" 20th century British writer Dorothy Sayers once said. Whether for breakfast or dinner, the English consume over a billion sausages annually.

The lesser known cousin of fish and chips and the most common sausage dish, bangers and mash is a London pub staple. Popular enough to have spawned a Radiohead song, the dish was voted as Britain's favorite comfort food, according to the *Telegraph*.

Sausages, commonly known by the British code word "bangers," were first introduced to Britain by the Romans. During WWII, sausages were filled with so much water that they would explode when cooked, spawning the name bangers. Others point to the appearance of bangers and mash on pub menus as early as WWI. Mash is, well, just mashed potatoes. Bangers and mash are typically smothered in onion gravy and frequently go hand-in-hand with the most popular pub item—the pint.

The English answer to hamburgers and French fries, bangers and mash is a cheap alternative to fish and chips at a local public house. With over 400 varieties of sausage available in the United Kingdom, travelers should be cautious about the kind they select—some have been maligned for containing less than 25% of meat.

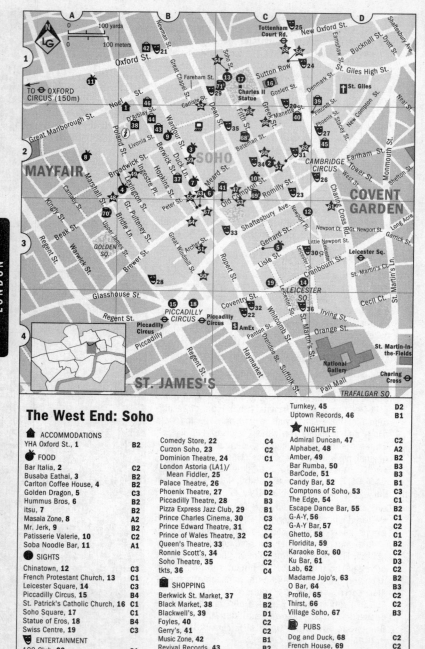

The West End: Soho

🏠 ACCOMMODATIONS

YHA Oxford St., **1**	B2

🍴 FOOD

Bar Italia, **2**	C2
Busaba Eathai, **3**	B2
Carlton Coffee House, **4**	B2
Golden Dragon, **5**	C3
Hummus Bros, **6**	B2
itsu, **7**	B2
Masala Zone, **8**	A2
Mr. Jerk, **9**	B2
Patisserie Valerie, **10**	C2
Soba Noodle Bar, **11**	A1

⭐ SIGHTS

Chinatown, **12**	C3
French Protestant Church, **13**	C1
Leicester Square, **14**	C3
Piccadilly Circus, **15**	B4
St. Patrick's Catholic Church, **16**	C1
Soho Square, **17**	C1
Statue of Eros, **18**	B4
Swiss Centre, **19**	C3

🎭 ENTERTAINMENT

100 Club, **20**	C1
Borderline, **21**	B1
Comedy Store, **22**	C4
Curzon Soho, **23**	C2
Dominion Theatre, **24**	C1
London Astoria (LA1)/ Mean Fiddler, **25**	C1
Palace Theatre, **26**	D2
Phoenix Theatre, **27**	D2
Piccadilly Theatre, **28**	B3
Pizza Express Jazz Club, **29**	B1
Prince Charles Cinema, **30**	C3
Prince Edward Theatre, **31**	B2
Prince of Wales Theatre, **32**	C4
Queen's Theatre, **33**	C3
Ronnie Scott's, **34**	C2
Soho Theatre, **35**	C2
tkts, **36**	C4

🛍 SHOPPING

Berkwick St. Market, **37**	B2
Black Market, **38**	B2
Blackwell's, **39**	D1
Foyles, **40**	C2
Gerry's, **41**	C2
Music Zone, **42**	B1
Revival Records, **43**	B2
Sister Ray, **44**	B2
Turnkey, **45**	D2
Uptown Records, **46**	B1

⭐ NIGHTLIFE

Admiral Duncan, **47**	C2
Alphabet, **48**	A2
Amber, **49**	B2
Bar Rumba, **50**	B3
BarCode, **51**	B3
Candy Bar, **52**	B1
Comptons of Soho, **53**	C3
The Edge, **54**	C1
Escape Dance Bar, **55**	B2
G-A-Y, **56**	C1
G-A-Y Bar, **57**	C2
Ghetto, **58**	C1
Floridita, **59**	B2
Karaoke Box, **60**	C2
Ku Bar, **61**	D3
Lab, **62**	C2
Madame Jojo's, **63**	B2
O Bar, **64**	B3
Profile, **65**	C2
Thirst, **66**	C2
Village Soho, **67**	B3

🍺 PUBS

Dog and Duck, **68**	C2
French House, **69**	C2
Old Coffee House, **70**	A3
The Toucan, **71**	C1

Bar Italia, 22 Frith St. (☎020 7437 4520). ⊖Piccadilly Circus or Leicester Sq. This 50s-style coffee bar—adorned with garlic, coffee beans, and soccer jerseys—is a Soho hallmark and go-to local spot for an espresso (£2-3.20), *panino* (£5.50-7), or pizza (£9.50-12). Outdoor seating perfect for people-watching in good weather. Accepts euro. Open M-Th 7:30am-4:30am, F-Sa 7:30am-6am, Su 7:30am-3am. Alcohol served 10am-11pm. MC/V over £10. ❷

Patisserie Valerie, 44 Old Compton St. (☎020 7437 3466; www.patisserie-valerie.co.uk). ⊖Piccadilly Circus or Leicester Sq. Other branches at 27 Kensington Church St., 215 Brompton Rd., 8 Russell St., and 105 Marylebone High St. A delicious taste (and even better whiff) of France in the center of London. Croissants, mousse cakes, eclaires (£2.30-4.50) and truffles (£4.25 per 100g) to die for. Excellent English breakfasts and lunches. Entrees £4-8. Cakes £18-30. Open M-Tu 7:30am-9pm, W-Sa 7:30am-11pm, Su 9am-8pm. AmEx/MC/V. ❶

COVENT GARDEN AND THE STRAND

In spite of its trendiness—or perhaps because of it—Covent Garden is not known for its cuisine. The **Piazza** within has unremarkable tourist-oriented cafes and overpriced restaurants catering to theater- and opera-goers, while sandwich bars and themed pubs prevail on side streets. Two exceptions are **Neal's Yard,** a small open courtyard that has evolved into a wholesome haven of vegetarian, vegan, and organic delights, and the side streets surrounding **Seven Dials.** Since the **Strand** is essentially one busy thoroughfare, it's not surprising that the majority of dining is mediocre at best. Head to **Craven Passage** and **Villiers Street,** between the Strand and Victoria Embankment, if you're looking to grab a bite.

▨ **Rock and Sole Place,** 47 Endell St. (☎020 7836 3785). ⊖Covent Garden. There's a reason Rock and Sole's been around since 1871: messy and delicious fried fish in an equally no-frills environment. A self-proclaimed "master fryer" (qualifications unclear) turns out tasty haddock, cod, halibut, and sole filets (all with chips; £9 takeaway, £11 sit down), while customers gather around the crowded diner tables inside, or the large wooden picnic tables under the giant tree outside. Extras like mushy peas, baked beans, coleslaw, or curry or gravy sauce £0.50-1.50. Open M-Sa 11:30am-11:45pm, Su noon-10:30pm. MC/V. ❷

▨ **Neal's Yard Salad Bar,** 1, 2, 8-10 Neal's Yard (☎020 7836 3233; www.nealsyardsaladbar.co.uk). ⊖Covent Garden. Not so much a salad bar as a hidden community feasting spot. A 3-building complex of vegetarian and vegan fare, the Salad Bar fills up an entire pastel-inspired courtyard with its picnic tables and colorful garbage bins planted with trees. The food is no less inspired: special salads (£3-5), hearty soups (£5.50), and slices of homemade quiche (£4.50) are all delicious. Specialty breads £1.50. Fresh juices like passion fruit, acai-banana, and carrot £3. Open daily 8am-9pm. Cash only. ❶

The Ivy, 1-5 West St. (☎020 7836 4751). ⊖Leicester Sq. Ivy's tables are highly sought-after, and for good reason: the modern British food is mouth-watering and the service (starting with the doorman) will make you feel like Queen Elizabeth. However, the steep prices (entrees £13-39) make the Ivy more appropriate as an occasional splurge. All the more reason to indulge—whether it be on the traditional shepherd's pie (£17), the Bannockburn rib steak (£28), or a delicious dessert (sticky toffee pudding; £7). Dress code classy, but no ties required. Wheelchair-accessible. Open daily noon-3pm and 5:30pm-midnight. Dinner reservations require booking up to 3 months in advance, but lunch tables are much easier to come by and have excellent views. AmEx/MC/V. ❺

Food for Thought, 31 Neal St. (☎020 0872 148 4061). A tiny vegetarian lunch haven that draws a crowd at noontime. Choose from stir-fried vegetables (£4.50), an Indian-inspired platter (£4.70), or one of the many specialty salads (£3.50-7). Don't forget vegan desserts like whole wheat brownies (£3.20-3.80). Open M-Sa noon-8:30pm, Su noon-5pm. Cash only. ❶

Cafe in the Crypt, Duncannon St. (☎020 7839 4342). ⊖Charing Cross. In the basement of St.-Martins-in-the-Fields Church. Eating in this spacious, exposed-brick cellar, with vaulted ceilings and subdued lighting, is an amped-up cafeteria experience. With a variety of fresh sandwiches (£5.20), dishes from the gourmet salad bar (£6.60), and hot meat and vegetarian dishes (£8.50 and £6.20, respectively), the Crypt is the perfect lunch stop during a day around Trafalgar. Linger with a glass of wine (from £4). Jazz some W nights. Open M-W 8am-8pm, Th-Sa 8am-9pm, Su 11am-6pm. AmEx/MC/V over £5. ❷

Cafe Pacifico, 5 Langley St. (☎020 7379 7728; www.cafepacifico-laperla.com). ⊖Covent Garden. A rare touch of Cabo in Covent Garden, this Mexican cantina is the most authentic in town. Pacifico's tequilas have been recognized as one of the top 3 most authentic by the Tequila Regulatory Council of Mexico. Take a shopping break with chips and salsa (free with meal) and a cold Corona (£3); heartier lunch special (£6; £10 with 2 beers or a margarita) M-F noon-4:30pm. Dinner entrees include fajitas (£14-17), tostadas (£11-12), and enchiladas (£8-13). Open Tu-Sa noon-11:30pm, Su noon-10:30pm. AmEx/MC/V. ❸

 RESTAURANT SECURITY. Many restaurants have security clips underneath the tables to thwart would-be thieves. Attach your purse or backpack straps to them to ease your mind.

CAFES AND SPECIALTY SHOPS

▨ **Yuforia,** Covent Garden Piazza (☎020 7240 5532; www.yu-foria.com). ⊖Covent Garden. This take on an American yogurt craze (a la PinkBerry) just opened in June 2009. Women especially (but men too) will know this gig from a mile away and swoon upon sight: 100% natural fat-free frozen yogurt, 3 flavors (original, chocolate, and a weekly special), tons of toppings (nuts, fruit, granola, chocolate chips, etc.), zero guilt. Too good to be true? Come taste for yourself. Small £2.80, medium £3, large £3.20. Toppings £0.40 each. AmEx/MC/V. ❶

▨ **Ben's Cookies,** Covent Garden Piazza (☎020 7240 6123; www.benscookies.com). ⊖Covent Garden. Other locations on High Kensington St. (☎020 7376 0559), South Kensington (☎020 7589 9155), and Leadenhall Market (☎020 7929 7631). You can smell these delicious, oozing treats from miles away. Attracts parents, children, lovers, and haters in flocks. 16 kinds including fruit and nut, lemon, oatmeal raisin, white chocolate and cranberry, double and triple chocolate chunk, peanut butter, and coconut. Also creamy ice creams to glob on top. Cookies priced by kg; approx. £1.20-1.30 each. Ben's Box of 7 £6.50. Cookie monster (cookie and ice cream) £2.80-3.50. AmEx/MC/V. ❶

▨ **Scoop,** 40 Shorts Gardens (☎020 7240 7086; www.scoopgelato.com). ⊖Covent Garden. From afar, Scoop seems like just another boutique, but it only takes a taste to realize that its creamy gelato and sorbet are not like the others. Only fresh ingredients are used, many of which are imported from the owner's home in Tuscany, and flavors range from *pompelmo* (grapefruit) to *cioccolato al latte* (milk chocolate). Pastries, coffee, and tea also available. Cups and cones from £2.50. Open M-Th 11:30am-9:30pm, F-Sa 11:30am-10:30pm, Su 11:30am-10pm. MC/V. ❶

Primrose Bakery, 42 Tavistock St. (☎020 7836 3638; www.primrosebakery.org.uk). ⊖Covent Garden. Also at 69 Gloucester Ave, Primrose Hill (☎020 7483 4222). Easy on the eyes and heavenly to the nose, this petite bakery on the corner of Tavistock and Catherine could give a sweet tooth to the scroogiest of scrooges. Specialty cupcakes (regular £1.80, mini £1.20) and cakes (slices from £1.50) of all sorts—plum, orange, chocolate and vanilla, coffee and walnut, to name a few. Open M-Sa 10:30am-7:30pm, Su noon-5pm. ❶

Monmouth Coffee Shop, 27 Monmouth Street (☎020 7379 3516; www.monmouthcoffee.co.uk). ⊖Covent Garden. One of the 1st businesses to lead to the turnaround of once rough-riding Neal's Yard, Monmouth Coffee is now a rustic-prep local favorite. Come for no-frills but oh-so-good coffee (espresso £1.30, latte £2.30) and accompany it with one of the many homemade pastries, brownies, and croissants (£0.80-3.10). ❶

BLOOMSBURY

At the heart of London's student community, Bloomsbury is overflowing with top-notch budget food. Running parallel to Tottenham Court Rd., **Charlotte Street** is one of London's best-known culinary stretches, with fashionable restaurants to suit every budget. A slew of extremely cheap vegetarian Indian eateries and sweet shops lines **Drummond Street,** while on the other side of Bloomsbury, **Sicilian Avenue** has great sandwich and snack shops. **Euston Road, Museum Street,** and **Cosmo Place** boast particularly flavorful ethnic food. Of course, on a sunny day, the ideal meal only requires a bit of takeaway and a patch of grass on one of the numerous squares and gardens that dot the neighborhood.

🎟 **Navarro's Tapas Bar,** 67 Charlotte St. (☎020 7637 7713; www.navarros.co.uk). ⊖Goodge St. Colorful, bustling tapas restaurant with blue tiled walls, brightly painted furniture, and flamenco music straight from Seville. The authenticity carries over to the excellent food—try the spicy fried potatoes (*patatas bravas;* £4.90), spinach with chickpeas (*espinacas con garbanzos;* £5) or one of the many brochettes of lamb, chicken, or prawns (£12-15). Tapas £4-15; 2-3 per person is plenty. £10 min. purchase. Reservations recommended for dinner. Open M-F noon-3pm and 6-10pm, Sa 6-10pm. AmEx/MC/V. ❸

🎟 **Newman Arms,** 23 Rathbone St., (☎020 7636 1127). ⊖Tottenham Court Rd. or Goodge St. A pub with a famous upstairs pie room and restaurant. Connoisseurs at 10 sought-after tables dig into homemade pies (with potatoes and vegetables; £10). Most are filled with seasonal game, but there's always a vegetarian option. Just-as-comforting desserts like spotted dick, puddings, and crumbles. Pints from £3. Book in advance. Pub open M-F noon-12:30am. Restaurant open M-Th noon-3pm and 6-9pm, F noon-3pm. MC/V. ❷

Savoir Faire, 42 New Oxford St. (☎020 7436 0707). ⊖Tottenham Court Rd. or Holborn. A fun French place with a sense of humor and sophistication: colorful murals of dance-hall women and theater-goers cover the walls and handwritten notes are scrawled across the ceiling. Continental favorites include steak frites and salad (£13) and pan-fried *foie gras* with caramelized apples (£7). 2-course vegetarian dinner £12. Also a popular brunch spot. Open daily noon-4pm and 5-11:30pm. AmEx/MC/V. ❷

North Sea Fish Restaurant, 7-8 Leigh St. (☎020 7387 5892; www.northseafishrestaurant.co.uk). ⊖Russell Sq. or King's Cross St. Pancras. Fish and chips done right in a classy and warm atmosphere. Offers a boatload of fresh, tasty fish, fried in crispy batter or matzot and egg (£11-20); grilled fish available too. For much lower prices and a more casual scene, order from the takeaway shop next door (cod fillets; £4.30-6). Restaurant open M-Sa noon-2:30pm and 5-11pm. Takeaway M-Sa noon-2:30pm and 5-11pm. AmEx/MC/V. ❸

Andreas, 40 Charlotte St. (☎020 7580 8971; www.andreas-restaurant.com). ⊖Tottenham Court Rd. or Goodge St. On popular Charlotte St., this bright, comfortable restaurant serves heaping portions of tasty Greek food for reasonable prices. Try the *mezze* for 2 (£22 per person), which includes 3 courses of salads, dips, meats, chicken, fish, and warm pita. Outdoor seating overlooks the street. Entrees £13-18. Open M-F noon-11:30pm, Su 5-11:30pm. AmEx/MC/V. ❸

Diwana Bhel-Poori House, 121-123 Drummond St. (☎020 7387 5556; www.diwanarestaurant.com). ⊖Euston or Euston Sq. Tasty, cheap South Indian vegetarian food in a quiet, bright, no-frills environment. Try the excellent all-you-can-eat lunch buffet (£6.50, served daily noon-2:30pm) or the set *thali* (£6-9). BYOB. Open daily noon-11:30pm. AmEx/MC/V. ❷

NORTH LONDON

CAMDEN TOWN, KING'S CROSS, AND ISLINGTON

If there were a word stronger than diverse, we would use it; this area of North London offers every type of cuisine, atmosphere, and price range, often all on the same street. In Camden Town, the delicious smells from the market stalls travel all the way down **Camden High Street,** and your hardest decision will be whether you feel like Thai, Brazilian, or Italian. If you want something more subdued, restaurants and cafes abound: **Parkway,** running from the Tube toward Regent's Park, is home to tapas, Indian, and noodle bars, and Camden High and **Kentish Town Road** also have some good cafes. In nearby Islington, **Upper Street** has over 100 restaurants, with close to 200 more in the surrounding area, ranging from Turkish to French, dirt cheap to exorbitant, and boisterous to romantic. For a taste of the ungentrified, pre-yuppie Islington, head to **Chapel Market,** just off Liverpool St. opposite the Angel Tube station. Here you can have an English meal with all the fixings for under £3 in any of the hole-in-the-wall restaurants that line the street. Just don't expect linen tablecloths.

☒ **Gallipoli Cafe Bistory,** 102 Upper St. (☎020 7359 0630), **Gallipoli Again,** 120 Upper St. (☎0207 359 1578), and **Gallipoli Bazaar,** 107 Upper St. (☎020 7226 5333). ⊖Angel. Three's usually a crowd, but not with this group of tasty Upper St. eateries. In fact, they only bring the crowds. Dark walls, patterned tiles, and hanging lamp and lanterns provide the background to spectacular Lebanese, Turkish, and Mediterranean delights like hummus, falafel, *kisir* (similiar to tabouleh), kebab, and *moussaka.* Try one of the set meals for 2, which come with a selection of hot and cold appetizers (£11-15 per person). Gallipoli Cafe was the original; Gallipoli Again opened in response to its immense popularity (with the added bonus of an outdoor patio); and Gallipoli Bazaar, which sits between the other two, serves up *sheesha* and food in tea-room surroundings. Again and Bazaar wheelchair-accessible. Open M-Th 10:30am-11pm, F-Sa 10:30am-midnight, Su 10:30am-11pm. Reservations recommended F-Sa. MC/V. ❷

☒ **Mango Room,** 10-12 Kentish Town Rd. (☎020 7482 5065; www.mangoroom.co.uk). ⊖Camden Town. A neighborhood favorite that's been around for almost a decade in an area where few restaurants last more than a year. Dark wood tables are accompanied by fine linen tablecloths and funky modern paintings. The brief but delicious menu features modern takes on Caribbean appetizers like plantain and sweet potato fritters (£7). Entrees include roast honey and ginger duck breast with potatoes and juniper berries *jus* (£12), or seabass, tiger prawns, and scallops with papaya *sambale* and fried *cassava* (£13). The tiny bar serves a wide array of potent tropical drinks at night. Wheelchair-accessible. Reservations recommended Sa-Su. Open daily noon-midnight. MC/V. ❷

Le Mercury, 140A Upper St. (☎020 7354 4088). ⊖Angel. This sunny, sophisticated little corner restaurant offers delicious and delightfully presented French food at extremely affordable prices. Dig into delicacies like *foie gras* and duck *ballontine* with roasted dates and slow roasted honeyed pork with granny smith apples. Perfect for a romantic date. Starters £3.50; entrees £6.50; desserts £3. Wheelchair-accessible. Open M-Sa noon-1am, Su noon-11:30pm. Dinner reservations recommended. MC/V. ❷

Camden Bar and Kitchen, 102 Camden High St. (☎020 7485 2744; www.camden-barandkitchen.com). ⊖Camden Town. By day, a sleek and funky eatery serving up Mediterranean dishes; by night a cool pre- or post-performace bar. A mixed Camden crowd of artists, students, and shoppers feast on entrees like *haloumi* and vegetable kebabs with pesto dressing (£8.50), free-range jerk chicken with mango salsa (£11), or spaghetti with blue swimmer crab, chili and garlic (£9.50). Also serves brunch Sa-Su until 4pm. Mixed drinks £5 per glass, £13 per pitcher. Open M-Th 10am-10:30pm, F-Sa 10am-11pm, Su 10am-10pm. MC/V. ❷

Cuba Libre, 72 Upper St. (☎020 7354 9998; cubalibrelondon.co.uk). ⊖Angel. A colorful and spirited restaurant packed with Cuban character: Che's friendly face, Havana posters, and other random kitsch abounds, accompanied by rambunctious salsa music. The menu features specialties like fried plantains and "old rags" (shredded braised beef with yuca and plantains), and also offers a selection of tapas (M-F 6 for £12). The bar in the back has some dance space and the paved terrace is perfect for outdoor revelry. Starters £6.50-7.50; entrees £12-14. Paella night M: order paella for 2 and get a bottle of wine free. Wheelchair-accessible. Happy hour M-F 5-8pm, Sa-Su noon-8pm (2 for £8.50 among the 241 different mixed drinks). Open M-Sa 10am-2am, Su 10:30am-10:30pm. MC/V. ❷

Ziloufs, 270 Upper St. (☎020 726 1118; www.ziloufs.com). ⊖Angel. A marriage of Thai and Western cuisine in an atmosphere of subdued sleek. Serious dishes like rare Thai beef salad with cashews, *penang* curry duck with lychee and bean sprouts, or the specialty pork belly with Thai spices, are accompanied by wrought-iron tables, gold trimmings, and chandeliers. After dinner, move to one of the leather couches and enjoy DJs or live music (Th and Su). Entrees from £7. Mixed drinks £4 before 9pm. Open Tu-Th 5-10pm, F-Sa 5-11pm, Su noon-8pm. Bar open until midnight. AmEx/MC/V.

Afghan Kitchen, 35 Islington Green (☎020 7359 8019). ⊖Angel. This tiny restaurant sits on a busy street, but the simple decor makes it feel serene. Share wooden benches with others downstairs, or have a table to yourself upstairs. "Traditional Afghan home cooking" means manageable portions of spicy meat and vegetarian dishes with sides like *daal*, spinach, or yogurt; most are £5-6.50. Sides £2-3.50, yummy baklava £1. Partially wheelchair-accessible. Open Tu-Sa noon-3:30pm and 5:30-11pm. Cash only. ❶

Trojka, 101 Regent's Park Rd. (☎020 7483 3765; www.trojka.co.uk). ⊖Camden Town. The name of this restaurant and Russian tea room means "three": an apt moniker, given the menu's Russian, Ukrainian, and Polish influences. If you're too broke for the *sevruga* caviar (£42 for 2 people), the lumpfish caviar (£10 for 2 people) does the trick. Other specialties include blintzes, borscht, smoked mackerel, beef stroganoff, schnitzel, and chicken Kiev. Coffees, teas, and homemade desserts are also served. 2-course lunch menu M-F £10, Sa-Su £8. Entrees £6-9. Live Russian music F-Sa nights. Open daily 9am-10:30pm. MC/V. ❷

Pizzeria Oregano, 18-19 St. Alban's Pl. (☎020 7288 1123). ⊖Angel. 2 steps away but almost hidden from Upper St. A step above cafeteria-style decor is simple enough, but the wood-grilled pizzas (from £6.50) and entrees, including their specialty seafood pastas (from £9) are top-notch. Nice *antipasti* selection (from £5.50). Open Tu-Th 5:30-11pm, F 5:30-11:30pm, Sa 12:30-11:30pm, Su 12:30-10:30pm. MC/V over £15. ❷

CAFES AND SPECIALTY SHOPS

Candid Cafe, 3 Torrens St. (☎020 7837 4237). ⊖Angel. Signs point to the door beneath the horse sculpture; go up 2 fl. to reach the cafe, part of the Candid Arts Trust. What you'd expect from an artists' cafe: antique sofas and Victorian candlesticks decorate a rustic wooden room. Watercolors and sexually provocative paintings provide the perfect backdrop for candid conversation. Leafy courtyard open in the summer. Baguette sandwiches from £2.80. Simple but healthy entrees like mixed vegetables with couscous and coconut sauce £5-10. Open M-Sa noon-10pm, Su noon-5pm. ❶

paul.a.young, 33 Camden Passage (☎020 7424 5750; www.paulayoung.co.uk). ⊖Angel. Former celebrity pastry chef Paul A. Young makes some of the best and most creative chocolates in the UK. His shop was voted one of the top ten chocolate shops in the world. Come in for the densest brownies you've tasted (£3 each), a box of melt-in-your-mouth truffles (£6 for 4 pieces) or a bag of delicious *pavé* bars in daring flavors like the award-winning Black Cardamom and Chinese Stem Ginger (£11). Open M-Th and Sa 10am-6pm, F 11am-7pm, Su noon-5pm. AmEx/MC/V. ❶

HAMPSTEAD, HIGHGATE, AND GOLDER'S GREEN

Hampstead High Street has no shortage of eating opportunities for the area's wealthy residents. There are a couple tourist traps, but most of the places, while high-end, are very good. Sugar abounds, with countless bakeries and patisseries selling inexpensive sweets. For a cluster of cheap restaurants, head to **South End Road** near the Hampstead Heath train station. Highgate is short on eats, as you'll mostly find pubs and convenience stores, but bakeries in the Jewish neighborhood **Golders Green** make some of the best challah, bagels, and pastries in the city.

🍽 **Le Crêperie de Hampstead,** 77 Hampstead High St. (www.hampsteadcreperie.com). ⊖Hampstead. Proof that good things come in small packages, this metal stand, topped with a traditional Parisian street sign, serves phenomenal crepes that are worth the wait. Most savory crepes are made with some combination of spinach, mushroom, ratatouille, asparagus, cream, egg, cheese and ham (£3.40-4.50). The most popular sweet crepe is the Banana Maple Cream Dream, with banana, walnuts, maple syrup, and cream (£4.30). Open M-Th 11:45am-11pm, F-Su 11:45am-11:30pm. Cash only. ❶

🍽 **Carmelli Bakery,** 128 Golders Green Rd. (☎020 8455 2074; www.carmelli.co.uk). ⊖Golders Green (Zone 3). Carmelli's golden egg-glazed challah (from £1.50) is some of London's best. With a pastry case filled to the brim with goodies large and small (from £1.50), it's hard to go wrong here. F afternoons are packed as people prepare for the Sabbath. Kosher. Wheelchair-accessible. Open M-W and F 6am-1am, Th 24hr. Cash only. ❶

Bloom's, 130 Golders Green Rd. (☎020 8455 1338). ⊖Golders Green. Sleek black booths and waiters in black bow ties. The takeaway shop in the front serves freshly made dishes like potato salad and sandwich fillers (from £4.50), while the restaurant in back has traditional deli dishes like chopped liver sandwiches (£8.50) and chicken schnitzel (£12.50). Favorites like gefilte fish (£4.50) and latkes (£2) served as side orders. Kosher. Wheelchair-accessible. Open M-Th and Su noon-11pm, F 11am-3pm. ❷

Gail's Bread, 64 Hampstead High St. (☎020 7794 5700; www.gailsbread.co.uk). ⊖Hampstead. Specializes in handmade bread. Also offers a delicious array of fresh salads like feta, mango and pecan (£3.30-5.30); baguettes stuffed with veggies, meats and cheeses (from £2.90); and hefty pastries, cookies, brownies and cakes (from £1.50). Open M-F 7am-7pm, Sa-Su 8am-7pm. AmEx/MC/V.

La Palmeraie, 42 Hampstead High St. (☎020 7435 7632). ⊖Hampstead. Amid Middle Eastern music and cushioned stools, the Moroccan chef serves an array of mixed *grillades* (from £2.10 each; min. 4), couscous (from £11.60), and *tajines* (from £13), all filled with fresh meat, lamb, chicken, fish, or vegetables. Occasional belly dancing. Open daily 9am-11pm. MC/V. ❸

MARYLEBONE AND REGENT'S PARK

Marylebone's culinary landscape is ever-changing. The many restaurants, delis, and bakeries clustered around **Edgware Road,** including the Maroush food empire, serve up some of the best Middle Eastern food in London, while a growing number of fashionable cafes and restaurants around **Marylebone High Street** cater to a crowd with a light appetite and a heavy wallet. Beyond the bourgeois facade, a few spectacular and inexpensive gems do exist.

🍽 **Le Relais de Venise "L'Entrecote,"** 120 Marylebone Ln. (☎020 7486 0878; www.relaisdevenise.com). ⊖Bond St. 2nd location at 5 Throgmorton St., The City

(☎020 7638 6325). This wildly popular French restaurant ventures across the channel; the queue is usually down the street. There's only one dish on the menu: steak, fries, and salad (£19). Pace yourself: as soon as you're done, they'll bring you more. Delicious desserts £5. Open M-Th noon-2:30pm and 6-10:45pm, F noon-2:45pm and 6-10:45pm, Sa 12:30-3:30pm and 6:30-10:45pm, Su 12:30-3:30pm and 6:30-10:30pm. AmEx/MC/V. ❹

🔲 **Patogh,** 8 Crawford Pl. (☎020 7262 4015). ⊖Edgware Rd. With just 10 tables and a cave-like interior, this charming Persian restaurant gives new meaning to "hole in the wall." Generous portions of sesame-seed flatbread (£2) and freshly prepared starters (£2-4) will whet your appetite; flame-grilled kebabs like kebab *koobideh* (minced lamb kebab) with bread, rice, or salad (£5-12) could feed you for days. Takeaway available. Open daily noon-midnight. Cash only. ❷

🔲 **The Golden Hind,** 73 Marylebone Ln. (☎020 7486 3644). ⊖Baker St. or Bond St. Open since 1914, the Hind has a strong claim to be the best "chippie" in London. This no-nonsense fish and chips joint serves up steamed or fried cod, haddock, salmon, and fishcakes (£4-£5.90) to a local clientele and travelers who are in on the secret. Chips (£1.30) and steamed or mushy peas (£0.90) round out the barebones menu. Takeaway available. Open M-F noon-3pm and 6-10pm, Sa 6-10pm. Reservations recommended after 7pm. AmEx/MC/V. ❷

Mandalay, 444 Edgware Rd. (☎020 7258 3696; www.mandalayway.com). ⊖Edgware Rd. 5min. walk north from the Tube. This Burmese restaurant is justly plastered with awards for its cheap and delicious food—think a mix between Chinese and Indian, with a sprinkle of Thai thrown in. Though it's clean and the atmosphere calm, the place is tiny and its decorations are sparse, save for a few pictures of Burma. Entrees £4.80-7.90. Open M-Sa noon-2:30pm and 6-10:30pm. Dinner reservations recommended. MC/V over £10. ❷

Royal China, 24-26 Baker St. (☎020 7487 4688; www.royalchinagroup.co.uk). ⊖Baker St. The less expensive sibling of the Royal China Club at no. 40-42, this sleek branch of the micro-chain renowned for London's best dim sum (served until 5pm) straddles the line between faux and real elegance. The food is reliable, but you pay for the experience. Keep your eyes open—this restaurant is crawling with MPs and minor celebs. If you're with a group and looking to splurge, try the 5-course seafood menu (£38). Most entrees and dim sum £5.50-23. Open M-Th noon-11pm, F-Sa noon-11:30pm, Su 11am-10pm. AmEx/MC/V. ❸

BAYSWATER

Cheap and central, Bayswater was an immigrant destination after WWII and played a large role in developing Britain's taste buds beyond meat pie and spotted dick. Hummus, kebabs, and other Middle Eastern delights came to Londoners through Bayswater's large Arab population. **Westbourne Grove, Queensway,** and the streets nearby, offer plenty of cheap Chinese, Indian, and Middle Eastern restaurants.

MIND THE CRAP. Many restaurants near Paddington Station serve mediocre, expensive food to tired Londoners just off the Tube. If you venture away from Paddington, you will be rewarded with more interesting choices.

Aphrodite Taverna, 15 Hereford Rd. (☎020 7229 2206). ⊖Bayswater or Notting Hill Gate. Zealously decorated walls feature an abundance of Aphrodite sculptures. Fabulous menu includes traditional favorites like *dolmedes* (stuffed grape leaves; £8.50), *keftedes* (Greek meatballs; £8.50), hummus, *tzaziki,* and *tambouli.* £1 cover is amply rewarded with baskets of freshly baked pita and other appetizers. Cafe Aphrodite next door offers some of Taverna's specialties at cheaper prices as well as a full sandwich menu (from £3). Takeaway available. Restaurant open M-Sa noon-midnight. Cafe open daily 8am-5pm. AmEx/MC/V. Restaurant ❷. Cafe ❶

Durbar Tandoori, 24 Hereford St. (☎020 7727 1947; www.durbartandoori.co.uk). ⊖Bayswater. Enjoy the refined dining room and revel in the inexpensive goodness of London's oldest family-owned Indian restaurant, which celebrated 50 years in 2006. Generous portions of dishes from regions throughout India. Vegetarian and meat entrees from £6. Bargain take-away lunch box £6. Chef's special dinner for 2 £25. Open M-Th and Sa-Su noon-2:30pm and 5:30-11:30pm, F 5:30-11:30 pm. AmEx/MC/V. ❷

Khan's Restaurant, 13-15 Westbourne Grove (☎020 7727 5420; www.khansrestaurant.com). ⊖Bayswater. This family-run restaurant celebrated its 30th birthday in 2009. Hearty portions of Indian favorites served among faux palm tree pillars. The extensive menu features tandoori specialties (chicken tikka; £5.80) as well as other meat, chicken, and seafood dishes (fish curry; £6.40). Thalis £9.50-£11. Takeaway available. Open M-Th noon-2:45pm and 6-11:45pm; F-Su 6pm-midnight. AmEx/MC/V. ❷

CAFES AND SPECIALTY SHOPS

🏴 **La Bottega del Gelato,** 127 Bayswater Rd. (☎020 7243 2443; www.labottegadelgelato.com). ⊖Queensway. Armed with over 50 flavors of creamy handmade gelato, La Bottega is not for the indecisive. Try the best-selling Ferrero Rocher, a chocolate hazelnut concoction. 1-3 scoops £2-4. Open daily Apr.-Aug. 10am-10pm; Sept.-Mar. closes early depending on weather. ❶

The Bathurst Deli, 3 Bathurst St. (☎020 7262 1888). ⊖Lancaster Gate. On a quiet cul-de-sac near Bayswater Rd., you'll know this small deli-cafe from its shocking orange-and-green exterior. Inside, however, its all about authentic and cozy: delicious meats, cheeses, pastries, *pâtés,* and homemade dishes sit front and center; rustic wooden tables and antique chairs round out the decor. Croissants, pastries, cookies, and cakes from £0.70. Lasagna, quiche, and cannoli £2.20-7. Meat and cheese platters £6-13. Open M-Sa 7am-11pm, Su 8am-10:30pm. ❷

NOTTING HILL

Dining in Notting Hill basically comes down to a choice between high-priced bistros and the inexpensive but excellent bites serving the market crowds around **Portobello Road.** For the widest variety of food, hunt around at the southern end of the general market and under the Westway.

🏴 **George's Portobello Fish Bar,** 329 Portobello Rd. (☎020 8969 7895). ⊖Ladbroke Grove. A London institution, George's garners praise from all who enter: Naked Chef Jamie Oliver, for one, raves about the place. George opened up here in 1961, and with his daughter now at the helm, the fish and chips are still as good as ever. Cod, rockfish, plaice, and skate come with a huge serving of chunky chips (from £7) and the popular barbecue ribs (£7) are made according to a secret recipe. With only a couple outdoor tables, seating is so scarce that on Sa, a seat costs £3 per person. Open M-F 11am-11:45pm, Sa 11am-9pm, Su noon-9:30pm. Cash only. ❷

🏴 **Charlie's Portobello Road Cafe,** 59a Portobello Rd. (☎020 7221 2422; charliesporto-belloroadcafe.co.uk). ⊖Notting Hill Gate. Tucked away behind a teal door and through a small alleyway courtyard, this is a perfect (if preppy) cafe retreat. Minimalist rustic-chic interior with wooden tables and chairs and white walls. Charlie's prides itself above all on its use of local and artisanal products, from the veggies and meats to the plates and the light fixtures. What results are delicious gourmet baguettes (£4.50) and salads (£7.50), mouthwatering breakfasts (entrees £9.50), and velvety pastries and cakes (£2.80). Open M-Sa 9am-5pm, Su 10am-2:30pm. AmEx/MC/V. ❷

Tom's Delicatessen, 226 Westbourne Grove (☎020 7221 8818). ⊖Ladbroke Grove or Notting Hill Gate. Looks like an old-fashioned candy shop but contains much more: an upstairs bakery and diner and a downstairs deli and salad bar with imported foods from around the world. Fills quickly during busy times, and the table-sharing policy means you might make a meal-time friend. Homemade cakes and pastries from £2; fresh takeaway sandwiches £2.80-4.30; takeaway from salad bar £2.50-6.50. Full English breakfast £12. Open M-F 8am-6:30pm, Sa 8am-6:30pm, Su 9am-6:30pm. MC/V. ❷

Manzara, 24 Pembridge Rd. (☎020 7727 3062). ⊖Notting Hill Gate. Street-side cafe serving Turkish delicacies. Besides standard kebabs (1 skewer £4.60, 2 skewers £6.60), the cafe specializes in *pide* (rolled pizza-like pastries filled with various delicacies, from eggplant and spinach to pepperoni; takeaway £5, eat-in £7). You'll also find organic Welsh beef burgers (from £4.60). Stop by for a quick bite on the way to the markets, or stay for a longer lunch in the small back dining room. Open M-Sa 8am-1am, Su 8am-11:30pm. MC/V. ❷

The Grain Shop, 269a Portobello Rd. (☎020 7229 5571). ⊖Ladbroke Grove. The aromatic smells of this vegetarian-vegan lunch counter are irresistible, and the queue snakes onto Portobello Rd. around noon. Organic breads and numerous filling dishes and cold side salads draw tourists and loyal locals. Mix as many dishes as you like in a takeaway box for £4-5.20. Homemade cakes and pastries from £0.80. Open M-Sa 9am-6pm, Su 10am-5pm. MC/V. ❶

CAFES AND SPECIALTY FOOD SHOPS

▨ **The Hummingbird Bakery,** 133 Portobello Rd. (☎020 7229 6446; www.hummingbirdbakery.com). ⊖Ladbroke Grove or Notting Hill Gate. 2nd location at 47 Old Brompton Rd. (☎020 7584 0055), in South Kensington. Many know this as the Gwyneth Paltrow and Elle Macpherson fave, but Hummingbird stands on its own as well. The cupcake-lined windows and the smell of buttercream and vanilla waft from out of this pink-and-chocolate colored shop, luring in anyone with even the slightest sweet tooth. With flavors such as lavender, caramel heart, black bottom, and red velvet with cream cheese frosting (their best-seller), the toughest decision will be which to try. Daily specials £2. Red velvet cupcakes £1.90, all others £1.60. Open M-Sa 10am-5:30pm, Su 11am-5pm. ❶

The Tea and Coffee Plant, 180 Portobello Rd. (☎020 7221 8137). ⊖Ladbroke Grove. A small eco-friendly shop that's permeated by the rich smell of its teas (from £1), freshly ground coffees (from £1.10), and takeaway concoctions of organic chocolate, caramel, and nuts (from £3.60). All are fair trade and organic. Chew on some beans before committing to a kilo (from £4.30), smell the tea varieties, or sip on a fresh espresso (£1). Mail order available. Open M-Sa 7:45am-5:30pm, Su 9am-4:30pm. MC/V. ❶

...melt..., 59 Ledbury Rd. (☎020 7727 5030; www.meltchocolates.com). ⊖Ladbroke Grove or Bayswater. If the name doesn't seduce you enough, the mouth-watering scent of award-winning chocolate should. This chocolate kitchen and boutique specializes in the "hot chocolate block" (£2 each), cubes of dark and milk chocolate swirled in warm milk, creating velvety liquid chocolate experience. Whimsical chocolate bars with flavors like blackberry and cinnamon, coconut, and chili £6.80. Holds intimate tastings that include chocolate, wine, and a gift to take home; £35. Open M-Sa 9am-6pm, Su 11-4pm. AmEx/MC/V. ❷

Lisboa Patisserie, 57 Golborne Rd. (☎020 8969 1052). ⊖Ladbroke Grove. A plain cafe mostly known as an afternoon hangout for local Portuguese and Moroccans, but it also has some of the best pastries in the area. If you're in the mood for puffy, gooey, or buttery, you'll find it here. Try the specialty: *pasteis de nasta,* small tarts filled with custard in flavors such as coconut and almond (£1.80). Open daily 8am-7:30pm. ❶

KENSINGTON AND EARL'S COURT

Kensington's prim and pretty character, along with attractions like Kensington Palace and the big three museums, make it ripe for pricey fine dining. Meanwhile, major thoroughfares like **Earls Court Road, Old Brompton Road,** and **Kensington High Street** host mostly chain restaurants and unappealing cafes. If you look hard enough, though, you'll find a couple reasonably priced and downright pleasant places to eat. **Kensington Court,** a short pedestrian street lined with budget and mid-range cafes, is always popular on warm summer evenings, while **Kensington Square's** environs provide decent sit-down options. In South Kensington, the area around the Tube station has some nicer chain cafes, and on francophone **Bute Street,** just opposite the Institut Français's *lycée* (high school), you'll find cheap patisseries and continental delis.

▧ **L Restaurant and Bar,** 2 Abingdon Rd. (☎020 7795 6969; www.l-restaurant.co.uk). ⊖High St. Kensington. L serves delicious modern European-Spanish fusion in a classy, comfortable atmosphere—and food critics rave. Indulge in entrees like oven-roasted stuffed squid with tomato and pepper salsa, chorizo, and saffron rice (£15), or go for a couple tapas like mussels with red pesto and *manchego* crust (£4.30-8). At lunch and early dinner 3 tapas £10, with drink £12. 2-course lunch menu £16; dinner £20. Entrees £13-20. Open M 6pm-midnight, Tu-W noon-3pm and 6pm-midnight, Th-Sa noon-3pm and 5pm-midnight, Su noon-midnight. Reservations recommended F-Sa for dinner. AmEx/MC/V. ❸

▧ **Zaika,** 1 Kensington High St. (☎020 7795 6533; www.zaika-restaurant.co.uk). ⊖High St. Kensington. If you're looking to splurge, indulge at one of London's best Indian restaurants. Soaring ceilings, vibrant colors, sleek decor, and creative food served on silver platters. Appetizers £7.50-13. Entrees like coconut poached prawns with lime and curry leaves and rice £16-21. Excellent wine list. Desserts £6-12. 2-course lunch menu with wine £20, 3 courses £25; 6-course dinner menu £39, with wine £68; 9-course dinner menu £58/95. Formal dress. Open M 6-10:45pm, Tu-Sa noon-2:45pm and 6-10:45pm, Su noon-2:45pm and 6-9:45pm. Dinner reservations recommended. AmEx/MC/V. ❺

La Brasserie, 272 Brompton Rd. (☎020 7581 3089). ⊖South Kensington. Bustling, cheerful French *brasserie*, with the obligatory large mirrors, red leather booths, shiny dark wood tables, and greenery. Famous for its oyster bar (6 for £12, 12 for £23) and steak *tartare* (£19), La Brasserie serves large portions and usually buzzes with blazer-clad locals. Extensive French wine list. French favorites like goat cheese *salade* and *entrecôte* with *béarnaise* sauce and fries (£14-26). Appetizers £5.60-7.90. Best value are the menus (2 courses £19; 3 courses £23). Open M-Sa 8am-11:30pm, Su 9am-11:30pm. AmEx/MC/V. ❹

Babylon, Kensington Roof Gardens (☎020 7368 3993; www.roofgardens.com). ⊖High St. Kensington. 99 Kensington High St. entrance is on Derry St. 7 stories above Kensington in the sumptuous Roof Gardens, Babylon offers a fresh, modern atmosphere to accompany its equally fresh cuisine. Appetizers like whipped Perroche goat cheese with asparagus, marmalade, and gingerbread £9-14. Entrees like roast lamb with aubergine chutney, spring onions and madeira *jus* £18-25. Best deals are the weekend lunch menus (Sa 2-course £18, 3-course £21; Su £22/25). Open M-Sa noon-2:30pm and 7-10:30pm, Su noon-2:30pm. Reservations recommended. AmEx/MC/V. ❹

CAFES AND SPECIALTY SHOPS

▧ **Oddono's Gelati,** 14 Bute St. (☎020 7052 0732; www.oddonos.com). ⊖South Kensington. Intriguing tastes include cinnamon, basil, chocolate and cognac, chili, and vodka lemon. At the back, you can watch the gelato chefs in action. Small £2, with waffle £3; medium £3/3.70; large £4; grandissimo £5. Open M-Sa 11:30am-8pm, Su 11:30am-6pm. MC/V. ❶

▩ **The Orangery,** Kensington Palace (☎020 7376 0239). ⊖High St. Kensington. Built for Queen Anne's dinner parties, this stately, white Neoclassical hall boasts soaring ceilings, 2-story windows, columns, statues, and greenery. Afternoon teas range from £14 for the Orangery Tea to £29 for a full selection of tea sandwiches, scones, pastries, cakes, tea, and champagne. Open daily 10am-noon for breakfast, noon-3pm for lunch, 3-6pm for tea. MC/V. ❸

KNIGHTSBRIDGE AND BELGRAVIA

In the home of Harrods and Harvey Nichols, touristy and overpriced are easy to come by, but there are also some affordable and delicious Knightsbridge institutions. Even within Harrods, the bakery and select stands in the awe-inspiring food halls approach affordable. **Beauchamp** (BEE-cham) **Place,** off Old Brompton Rd., and the surrounding streets are lined with cafes, noodle bars, and sandwich shops. **Belgravia** is a bit tougher; there's little chance of getting a sit-down meal at a restaurant for under £15, unless you go for a cafe or salt a £10 note and eat it straight. The mews behind **Grosvenor Place** cradle some popular pubs, and the gourmet delis and specialty food stores on **Elizabeth Street** will furnish a picnic basket fit for a prince. Some cheaper ethnic restaurants can be found on the side streets between **Sloane Square** and **Victoria Station.**

▩ **Jenny Lo's Teahouse,** 14 Eccleston St. (☎020 7259 0399). ⊖Victoria. The daughter of the late Ken Lo, at one point one of the most famous Cantonese chefs in the UK, Jenny Lo serves some of the best noodles in town. A healthy variety of Vietnamese, Thai, and Wok noodles (everything from *ho fun* to *wun tun*) brings a crowd every time the clock strikes noon. Of course, to top off the meal, Jenny offers a selection of Chinese, mint, and "therapeutic" teas (£1.90). Vegetarian options abound. Takeaway and delivery available over £5 per person. Noodles £7-8.50. Open M-F noon-3pm and 6-10pm. Cash only. ❷

▩ **Da Scalzo,** 2 Eccleston Pl. (☎020 7730 5498; www.dascalzo.com). ⊖Victoria. After selling their Patisserie Valerie, brothers Enzo and Roberto Scalzo strike again with a restaurant that marries their 2 passions: delicious homemade Mediterranean food and cutting edge contemporary art. The menu features a sweeping selection of fresh pizzas and pastas (£7.50-11), as well as ambitious main dishes like *fegato alla veneziana* (grilled liver, crispy bacon, and onions) and creamed potatoes (£13-16). If the artwork on the wall looks familiar to you, that's because many of the artists are also showing at the Saatchi, Tate, or National Portrait Gallery. Open M-Sa 8am-11pm, Su 8am-8pm. AmEx/MC/V. ❸

Haandi, 7 Cheval Pl. (☎020 7823 7373; www.haandi-restaurants.com). ⊖Hyde Park Corner or Knightsbridge. A restaurant with a regional specialty—North Indian cuisine—and a global presence, with locations in Nairobi, Juba, and Kampala. In a refined but casual atmosphere off of touristy Brompton Rd., feast on all the traditional favorites like samosas, chicken tikka, masalas, and curries. Entrees £6.50-11. Lunch special with entree, side, rice, and naan £9-13. Open M-Th and Su noon-3pm and 5:30-11pm, F-Sa 5:30-11pm. MC/V. ❷

CAFES AND SPECIALTY SHOPS

Poilâne, 46 Elizabeth St. (☎7808 4910; www.poilane.fr). ⊖Victoria or Sloane Sq. Paris's most famous *boulangerie* brings freshly baked delights to Belgravia. The shop is *très petit* and offers a selection of scrumptious breads and pastries for takeaway service only. Traditional sourdough country loaves £4 per kg. Buttery *pain au chocolat* £1.20. Specialty apple tart £11-22. Open M-F 7:30am-7pm, Sa 7:30am-6pm. MC/V. ❶

CHELSEA

Though it's becoming more and more trendy, Chelsea still has a number of quirky, delicious, and downright adorable restaurants and cafes that are easy on the wallet. While the eastern part of **King's Road** is dominated by chains, away from **Sloane Square** you'll find an appealing place every 30 ft.; between **Sydney Street** and the **World's End** area the chic thoroughfare includes quality, affordable restaurants to suit a wide range of tastes. The **Chelsea Farmer's Market** (open M-Su 8:30am-9pm) and **Duke of York Square,** both just off King's Road, are a good bet for stylish outdoor cafes.

Buona Sera, at the Jam, 289A King's Rd. (☎020 7352 8827). ⊖Sloane Sq., then Bus #19 or 319 (or a 10-15min. walk along King's). With patented "bunk" tables stacked high into the air and plants for effect, the treetop-esque dining experience alone justifies a visit; the mouth-watering Italian fare makes it practically mandatory. Waiters climb small wooden ladders to deliver generous plates of pasta (£8.20-11) along with fish and steak dishes (£12-15). Enjoy, but don't drop your fork. Open M 6pm-midnight, Tu-F noon-3pm and 6pm-midnight, Sa-Su noon-midnight. Reservations recommended F-Sa; for a higher bunk always reserve. AmEx/MC/V. ❸

Chelsea Bun, 9A Limerston St. (☎020 7352 3635). ⊖Sloane Sq., then Bus #11 or 22. Chelsea-ites spill into this spirited and casual Anglo-American diner, which serves heaping portions of everything from the "Ultimate Breakfast" (3 eggs, 3 pancakes, sausages, hash browns, bacon, burger, french toast, kitchen sink; £11) to Tijuana Benedict (eggs with chorizo sausage and tomato; £0). Also serves a plethora of sandwiches, salads, pasta, and burgers £2.80-9.20. Extensive vegetarian and vegan options. Early-bird specials available M-F 7am-noon (£2.20-3.20) and breakfast (from £4) served until 6pm. £3.50 min. per person lunch, £5.50 dinner. Open M-Sa 7am-midnight, Su 8am-7pm. MC/V. ❷

Gordon Ramsay, 68 Royal Hospital Rd. (☎020 7352 4441 or 7592 1373; www.gordonramsay.com). ⊖Sloane Sq., then Bus #137 or 360. Founded by Gordon Ramsay— artist, footballer, reality TV star—this sophisticated restaurant serves light and innovative French concoctions. The restaurant has been awarded 3 Michelin stars (only 2 other UK restaurants can match that), and Ramsay is widely considered to be England's best chef. Lunch menu £45. Multi-course dinner £85-120. Open M-F noon-2:30pm and 6:30-11pm. Smart jackets for men; nice slacks, skirts, or dresses for women; no jeans or T-shirts. Reserve 1 month in advance. AmEx/MC/V. ❺

Phật Phúc, The Courtyard at 250 King's Rd. (☎020 7832 199 738), entrance on Sydney St. ⊖Sloane Sq., then Bus #11, 19, 22, 319. Most giggly diners only eat here because of the witty name, but the courtyard seating and heaping portions of Vietnamese pho (noodle soup) are more than just a gimmick. Choose from starters like chicken satay and dim sum (£2.60), noodle salads (£5.50), and chicken, beef, or vegetable pho (£6.50). Open daily noon-5pm. Cash only. ❷

new culture revolution, 305 Kings Rd. (020 7352 9281; www.www.newculturerevolution.co.uk). ⊖Sloane Sq., then Bus #11. Other locations at 157-159 Nottinghill Gate (☎020 7313 9688) and 42 Duncan St. (☎020 7833 9083). The first noodle and dumpling bar in London, this sleek but casual cafe focuses on creating healthy, balanced Chinese dishes with natural ingredients (i.e. no MSG). Choose from pan-fried or boiled dumplings (£3-4.80); chow, tong, lao, or char mein (£6-7.80); and chicken, meat, or seafood dishes (£7.40-8.20). Vegetarian options available. Open daily 11am-11pm. AmEx/MC/V. ❷

My Old Dutch, 221 King's Rd. (☎020 7376 5650; www.myolddutch.com). ⊖Sloane Sq. One of 3 locations in London, My Old Dutch offers delicious Dutch food in a simple, quiet, and cheery environment. Choose from starters like *kaasballen* (deep fried cheese balls) and *bitterballen* (meat balls and mustard), savory pancakes (chicken curry, apple and smoked bacon; £8-10), and sweet pancakes with fruit and ice cream (£5.50-7.30). Open M-Sa 11am-11pm, Su 11am-10pm; sometimes closes early. MC/V. ❷

CAFES AND SPECIALTY SHOPS

◪ **The Chelsea Tea Pot,** 402 Kings Rd. (☎020 7751 5975). ⊖Sloane Sq. Newly opened in June 2009, this small, pastel cafe is all sugary sweetness and charm. The windows are piled high with colorful cakes, cookies, and pastries handcrafted by Italian chefs. The unique teas are only served here and at Harrods, and the organic Auntie Vals jams come from little known fruits like damson and greengage. Also serves gourmet sandwiches and salads. Full High Tea, with tea sandwiches, scones, and pastries £15; Cupcake Tea £6. Open M-Sa 8:30am-6pm. Cash only. ❷

WEST LONDON

The many chain restaurants around **Turnham Green** are fine places for a reliable bite, while **Goldhawk Road** provides a wealth of cheap ethnic eateries in the Shepherd's Bush neighborhood. **Hammersmith** is famous for the riverside pubs along the **Upper and Lower Malls,** west of the bridge.

◪ **The Gate,** 51 Queen Caroline St., 2nd fl. (☎020 8748 6932; www.gateveg.tv). ⊖Hammersmith. From the Tube, follow signs for Riverside Studios to Queen Caroline St., then head toward the Thames. The entrance is on the left, to the left of a church, 3 blocks before the river. The definition of hidden gem. One of London's top spots for gourmet vegetarian fare, served in an elegant minimalist dining room or a green garden courtyard in the summer. Appetizers such as fig and goat cheese galette £5-6. Entrees (e.g. shiitake wonton and pumpkin laksa) £11-14. Extensive wine list. Reservations recommended for dinner. Open M-F noon-2:45pm and 6-10:45pm, Sa 6-10:30pm. AmEx/MC/V. ❸

Patio, 5 Goldhawk Rd. (☎020 8743 5194). ⊖Shepard's Bush or Goldhawk Rd. You wouldn't notice this place if you walked by it, save for the windows crowded with starred reviews and awards. A quirky establishment that resembles grandma's living room, where servers dole out huge portions of Polish specialties like bortsch, pierogi, and beef stroganoff. No nonsense here in food or drink: heavy 3-course menu includes an after-dinner shot of vodka (£17). Wheelchair-accessible. Entrees £8.50-15. Open M-F noon-3pm and 6pm-midnight, Sa and Su 6pm-midnight. AmEx/MC/V. ❸

◎ SIGHTS

From the hints of the city's Roman past that poke through the ground at the London Wall to the reminders of the Blitz etched on the face of every church, London wears every period of its long history for the present to see; to walk from east to west is to watch the city unfold through time. Christopher Wren's work continues to marvel all around the City of London. Holborn's Fleet St. was long associated with the London press and the Royal Courts. Down in Westminster, you will hold court with the regents, royals, and ruffians who run this fair capital, and up in Bloomsbury you'll mingle with the students and youth who hold the future of London in their eager grasp.

Unlike London's museums, sights tend to be expensive. There is no reason to spend £30 on tourist trips to the Tower of London, St. Paul's Cathedral, and the London Eye, only to be left wondering what to do for the rest of your trip with just pocket change to spare. Be your own tour guide (with Let's Go in hand). From avant-garde architecture in Islington to the urban wilderness of Hampstead Heath, the best of London's sights are often those seen via excursions on foot. No matter what path you choose, whether you're strolling down small cobblestone streets or briskly marching down a modern thoroughfare, your exploration will be rewarded. There is no wrong turn.

LONDON

THE CITY OF LONDON

The City of London (usually shortened to "the City") is the oldest part of London; all other districts are simply outlying villages. Striking a delicate balance between traditional and modern, manmade and natural, in the City, 400-year-old churches and colorful gardens share sidewalks with modern office buildings. The most interesting sights, sounds, and smells are located within walking distance of each other in what is called the **Square Mile;** the stately dome of St. Paul's and the weathered battlements of the Tower of London rise above it all. The 39 churches and the labyrinthine alleyways that have survived fires and wars are almost the only reminders of the area's former role as the beating heart of London.

SAINT PAUL'S CATHEDRAL

St. Paul's Churchyard. ⊖St. Paul's. ☎020 7246 8350; www.stpauls.co.uk. Open M-Sa 8:30am-4pm; last entry 3:45pm. Dome and galleries open M-Sa 8:30am-4pm. Open for worship daily 7:15am-6pm. Partially wheelchair-accessible. Admission £11, students £8.50, children 7-16 £3.50, worshippers free. Group of 10 or more £0.50 discount per ticket. 1½-2hr. "Supertour" M-F 10:45, 11:30am, 1:30, 2pm; £3, students £2.50, children 7-16 £1; English only. Audio tours in English, Chinese, French, German, Italian, Japanese, Russian, and Spanish; 9am-3:30pm; £4, students £3.50.

Majestic St. Paul's remains a cornerstone of London's architectural and historical legacy, as well as an obvious tourist magnet. Architect Christopher Wren's masterpiece is the fifth cathedral to occupy the site; the original was built in AD 604. In 1668, after Old St. Paul's was swept away in the Great Fire, construction began on the current cathedral. The Church and architect were at odds from the start. When the bishops finally approved his third design, Wren started building. Sneakily, Wren had persuaded the King to let him make "necessary alterations" as work progressed, and the building that emerged in 1708 bore a close resemblance to Wren's second "Great Model" design, the architect's favorite.

> **TIP**
> **SAINT PAUL'S FOR POCKET CHANGE.** To gain access to the Cathedral's nave for free, attend an Evensong service (M-Sa 5pm, 45min.). Arrive at 4:50pm to be admitted to seats in the choir.

INTERIOR. The entrance leads to the **nave,** the largest space in the cathedral; an enormous memorial to the Duke of Wellington completely fills one of its arches. The nave leads to the second tallest freestanding dome in Europe (after St. Peter's in the Vatican). The north transept functions as the **baptistry.** Opposite the font hangs the third version of William Holman Hunt's ethereal *The Light of the World.* The south transept holds the larger-than-life **Nelson Memorial,** hailing Britain's most famous naval hero. During the Blitz, the stalls in the choir narrowly escaped a bomb, but the old altar was destroyed. It was replaced by the current high altar, above which looms the fiery ceiling mosaic of *Christ Seated in Majesty.* The north choir aisle holds Henry Moore's *Mother and Child,* one of the church's best sculptures. The south choir aisle contains one of the only statues to survive from Old St. Paul's: a swaddled tomb effigy of **John Donne,** once dean of the Cathedral. The monument to Donne almost didn't make it; burn marks can be seen at its base.

SCALING THE HEIGHTS. The cathedral's dome is built in three parts: an inner brick dome, visible from the inside of the cathedral; an outer timber structure; and, between the two, a brick cone that carries the weight of the lantern on top. The first stop on the way up is the narrow **Whispering**

LONDON

Gallery, reached by 259 shallow wood steps. If you whisper into the wall, you can be heard perfectly on the other side. From here, it's 119 steps more to the **Stone Gallery,** and 152 more to the **Golden Gallery.**

PLUMBING THE DEPTHS. The **crypt** is packed wall-to-wall with plaques and tombs of the great Britons. **Admiral Nelson's** enormous porcelain and marble tomb dominates the center; it was originally made for Cardinal Wolesy, who ended up falling out of Henry VIII's favor. Maritime-themed mosaics surround the tomb to commemorate his life at sea. The **Duke of Wellington's** tomb is notable for the ominous sleeping lions at its base. Above the black slab that forms **Sir Christopher Wren's** tomb is inscribed his famous epitaph: *Lector, si monumentum requiris circumspice* ("Reader, if you seek his monument, look around"). In the rear of the crypt are artists **Sir William Blake, J.M.W. Turner,** and **Henry Moore.**

◪THE TOWER OF LONDON

Tower Hill, next to Tower Bridge, within easy reach of the South Bank and the East End.
⊖Tower Hill or DLR: Tower Gateway. ☎0870 751 5175, ticket sales 0870 756 6060;
www.hrp.org.uk. Open Mar.-Oct. M and Su 10am-6pm, Tu-Sa 9am-6pm; buildings close
at 5:30pm, last entry 5pm. Nov.-Feb. M and Su 10am-5pm, Tu-Sa 9am-5pm; build-
ings close at 4:30pm, last entry 4pm. Tower Green open only by Yeoman tours, after
4:30pm, or for daily services. £17, concessions £15, children 5-15 £9.50, children
under 5 free, families of 5 £47. Tickets also sold at Tube stations; buy them in advance
to avoid long queues at the door. "Yeoman Warders' Tours" meet near entrance; 45min.-
1hr., every 30min. M and Su 10am-3:30pm, Tu-Sa 9:30am-3:30pm. Audio tours in 9
languages including English. £4, concessions £3.

The turrets and towers of this multi-functional block—it has served as palace, prison, royal mint, and living museum over the past 900 years—are impressive not only for their appearance and their integral role in England's history. Beginning with William the Conqueror's 1067 wooden structure and soon thereafter replaced with stone, the tower has remained essentially unchanged since medieval times. The whole castle used to be surrounded by a broad moat, but severe contamination led to its draining in 1843. "Beefeaters"—whose nickname may be a reference to their diet of meat in former times—still guard the fortress.

TRAITOR'S GATE. This gate was once known as Watergate, a fact the guards love to tell American tourists. Queen Anne Boleyn passed through here just before her death. Today, to enter after closing time, one still needs a top-secret password: known only to the Yeoman and other high-ranking officials, it has changed daily since 1327.

BLOODY TOWER. William Shakespeare's *Richard III* give this tower its name. The two young princes, Richard, age nine, and Edward V, the 12-year-old rightful heir, were "allegedly" murdered here—their bodies weren't found until 191 years after their deaths. The murder remains a mystery, though many suspect that Richard III, their uncle, killed the boys. Today, exhibits allow you to play detective and vote for who you think "dunnit." Sir Walter Raleigh was also imprisoned in the tower for 13 years.

MEDIEVAL PALACE. Begin at **Saint Thomas's Tower.** The rooms in this palace at first appear bare but are progressively filled with 13th-century decor and furniture.

WALL WALK. A series of eight towers that runs along the eastern wall, the walk originally housed guests before it became a prison. Inscriptions scratched by inmates, including religious messages from persecuted Catholics, are still legible.

THE WHITE TOWER. This was William's residence—the top floor holds the royal apartments. Inside, you'll find the royal armories and the **Chapel of Saint John**

the Evangelist, a stunning but simple 11th-century Norman chapel with Roman undertones. It's one of the oldest and most beautiful spaces in the Tower.

JEWEL HOUSE. What we've all been waiting for: the Crown Jewels. With the exception of the Coronation Spoon, everything dates from after 1660, when Oliver Cromwell melted down the original treasure. While you might be naturally drawn to the **Imperial State Crown,** don't miss the **Sceptre with the Cross,** topped with the First Star of Africa, the largest quality-cut diamond in the world. **Saint Martin's Tower** is home to a fascinating collection of retired crowns; documentation is much better here than in the Jewel House.

TOWER GREEN. Not so much a tower as it is a lovely grassy lawn, this was once the site of private beheadings (marked by the scaffold), an honor reserved for important guests. North of Tower Green is the **Chapel Royal of St. Peter and Vincula,** the last resting place of many Tower Green unfortunates. Three queens of England—Anne Boleyn, Catherine Howard, and Lady Jane Grey—are buried here, as well as saints Thomas More and John Fisher.

OUTSIDE THE TOWER. Directly outside the Tower walls across Tower Hill Rd., is **Tower Hill,** the traditional site for public beheadings (unlike private beheadings, they were not at all honorable). The most recent execution was that of 80-year-old Lord Lovat, leader of the 1745 Jacobite rebellion. Ceremonial salutes are fired from the river bank on royal birthdays and during state visits. One of the most popular ceremonies is the **Ceremony of the Keys,** a nightly locking-up ritual that has been performed every night for over 700 years. At precisely 9:53pm, the Chief Warder locks the outer gates of the Tower before presenting the keys to the Governor amid much marching and salutation. *(For tickets, write at least 2 months in advance with the full names of those attending, a choice of at least 3 dates, and a stamped addressed envelope or international response coupon to: Ceremony of the Keys, Waterloo Block, HM Tower of London, EC3N 4AB. Free.)*

OTHER CITY OF LONDON SIGHTS

GUILDHALL. Guildhall used to be the administrative center of the Corporation of London, but the lord mayor and his associates have since moved to more modern environs in the surrounding area in the City and on the South Bank. The outer courtyard, **Guildhall Yard,** is reason enough to stop, as it feels strangely removed from the City's bustle. Excavations in the 1990s revealed the remains of a Roman amphitheater below the Yard; its ruins are on display in the **Guildhall Art Gallery** on the Yard's eastern side. The towering Gothic building dates from 1440, and though little of the original remains, there are statues and gargoyles inside to preserve the Gothic image. Now a banquet hall for visiting heads of state and other dignitaries, Guildhall is more often than not closed to the public (the downstairs crypt is open by guided tour only). But if you arrive early, you might be able to pop in for a look. The **Guildhall Library,** in the 1970s annex and accessed via Aldermanbury or the Yard, specializes in the history of London and has an unparalleled collection of microfilm and books. The **Guildhall Clockmaker's Museum** is also housed here. *(Off Gresham St. Enter the Guildhall through the low, modern annex; entrance for library on Aldermanbury.* ⊖*St. Paul's, Moorgate, or Bank. Guildhall:* ☎*020 7606 3030, for tour info 7606 3030, ext. 1463. Open May-Sept. daily 10am-5pm; Oct.-Apr. M-Sa 10am-5pm. Last entry 4:30pm. Sept. Sa-Su are open-house. Free. Library* ☎*7332 1862. Open M-Sa 9:30am-5pm. Free.)*

ALL HALLOWS-BY-THE-TOWER. Nearly hidden by development projects and nearby office buildings, All Hallows bears its age with pride. Just inside the entrance to the left stands the oldest part of the church, a **Saxon arch** dating from AD 675, while in the main chapel, the right and left transepts date from the 13th and 14th centuries, respectively. The central ceiling is a 20th-century addition. The **Undercroft Museum** is home to a diverse collection of Roman and Saxon artifacts, medieval art, and church record books from the time of the plague, while the spectacular **Lady Chapel** holds a magnificent altarpiece dating from the 15th century. The church dealt with the beheading of Thomas More, while William Penn was baptized here and John Quincy Adams married Louisa Catherine Johnson here in 1797. (*Byward St. ⊖Tower Hill. ☎020 7481 2928; www.allhallowsbythetower.org.uk. Church open M-F 8:30am-5:45pm, Su 9:30am-5pm; crypt and museum open daily 10:30am-4pm. Free.*)

MONUMENT. The only non-ecclesiastical Wren building in the City, the Monument was built to commemorate the devastating Great Fire of 1666. It can only be scaled by climbing up 311 steps in the very narrow spiral staircase, but at the top (160 ft. tall), you'll be rewarded with an unparalleled panorama of the city. (*Monument St. ⊖Monument. ☎020 7626 2717. Open daily 9:30am-5:30pm; last admission 5pm. £3, students £2. The Monument and the Tower Bridge Exhibition (p. 105) offer joint admission £8, students £5.50.*)

TOWER BRIDGE. Not to be mistaken for its plainer sibling, London Bridge, Tower Bridge is the one you know from all the London-based movies. A relatively new construction—built in 1894—its impressive stature and bright blue suspension cables connect the banks of the Thames and tower above neighboring bridges. The steam-powered lifting mechanism remained in use until 1973, when electric motors took over; there's still enough large river traffic for the bridge to be lifted around 1000 times per year and five or six times per day in the summer. Call for the drawbridge schedule or check the signs posted at each entrance. The **Tower Bridge Exhibition,** which offers a view of London's skyline and a history of the bridge, is pricey and probably best enjoyed by historians and technophiles. (*Entrance to the Tower Bridge Exhibition is through the west side (upriver) of the North Tower. ⊖Tower Hill or London Bridge. ☎020 7403 3761, for lifting schedule 7940 3984; www.towerbridge.org.uk. Open daily Apr.-Sept. 10am-5:30pm; Oct.-Mar. 9:30am-5pm. Wheelchair-accessible. £7, students £5, children 5-16 £3.*)

SAINT MARY-LE-BOW. Another Wren construction, St. Mary's is most famous for its Great Bell, which rang the City curfew and wake-up call daily from 1334 to 1874. To be a true Cockney, one must have been born within earshot of the bells. The interior is strikingly modern, with bright blue walls and ceiling, gold-lined columns, geometric stained glass, an imposing hanging crucifix dominating the room, and a starkly simple altar and soundboard. Since the 12th century, the small 11th-century crypt, whose "bows" (arches) gave the church its epithet, has hosted the ecclesiastical Court of Arches, during which the Archbishop of Canterbury swears in bishops. (*Cheapside, by Bow Ln. Access the crypt via stairs in the west courtyard. ⊖St. Paul's or Mansion House. ☎020 7248 5139; www.stmarylebow.co.uk. Open M-W 8:15am-6:30pm, Th 7:30am-6:30pm, F 8:15am-1:30pm. Occasional Th concerts 1:05pm. Free.*)

SAINT STEPHEN WALBROOK. On the site of a seventh-century Saxon church, St. Stephen (built 1672-79) was Wren's personal favorite and boasts "the most perfectly proportioned interior in the world"—you can decide for yourself. The church's Classical simplicity complements Henry Moore's freeform altar, dedicated in 1987, which resembles wavy marshmallow. (*39 Walbrook. ⊖Bank or Cannon St. ☎020 7606 3998. Open M-F 10am-4pm. Wheelchair-accessible. Free.*)

ORGAN MUSIC FOR POCKET CHANGE. For pipe music fans, St. Stephen Walbrook church provides free 1hr. organ concerts on Friday at 12:30pm.

SAINT MARY WOOLNOTH. The dearth of lower windows is due to the lack of open space around the site at the time of this church's construction (1716-27). Even with few windows, the domed design and semicircular windows up top fill the small church with light. The remarkable altarpiece and oak soundboard are particularly noteworthy. *(Intersection of King William and Lombard St. ⊖Bank or Monument. ☎020 7626 9701. Open M-F 9:30am-4:30pm.)*

STAIR MASTER. There are lots of sights in the City whose main draw is an "unparalleled view" of London. At the end of the day, however, one priceless view is much like another. Skip out on the overpriced Monument and Tower Bridge views, and go with the view from St. Pauls' Stone Gallery. Spend the extra pounds you save on a drink to reward yourself for the 376-step climb.

EAST LONDON

WHITECHAPEL AND THE EAST END

Although the East End and the City are neighbors on the map, the two areas are virtual opposites. The border is as clear as it was when Aldgate and Bishopsgate were actual gates in the wall separating the City from the poorer quarters to the east. The buttoned-up feeling of the City contrasts with the artsy, diverse, and edgy flavor of its neighbor. The oldest part of the East End, **Whitechapel,** is home to London's largest Bangladeshi community, as well as strong Pakistani and Afghani communities. This strong Middle Eastern influence is even visible in the neighborhood's skyline, punctuated by the minaret of the East London Mosque. *(45 Fieldgate St., off Whitechapel. ⊖Aldgate East.)* Years ago, the East End was also home to London's sizable Jewish community; beside the mosque stands the neighborhood synagogue. The **Bevis Marks Synagogue** is the largest of the area synagogues; other tiny synagogues are nestled into alleys all over Whitechapel. *(Bevis Marks Rd. ⊖Aldgate.)* The best reasons to visit the East End are its markets, restaurants, nightlife, and vintage stores and boutiques. Shoppers descend on **Spitalfields** (p. 174) each weekend in search of organic produce and high-quality crafts and clothing.

Brick Lane boasts a number of delicious ethnic eateries, and East London's bars and clubs constitute one of the best evening scenes in the city. A winding mass of curry houses, a few remaining Jewish bakeries, independent clothing boutiques, and popular nightlife destinations give Brick Lane a unique atmosphere. The blending of cultures has not always gone smoothly, however: the East End was long the center of London's gang activity, and the Aldgate Tube station was one of the three targeted by suicide bombers in July 2005. *(⊖Aldgate, ⊖Aldgate East, ⊖Liverpool St. or ⊖Shoreditch, open only at rush hour.)*

While remnants of an industrial past remain, **Hoxton** and **Shoreditch** have recently become some of London's trendiest neighborhoods. In the 1990s, struggling artists, including Damien Hirst and Tracey Emin, saw potential in the neighborhood's cheap property and vacant warehouses, and Hoxton became the focus of an underground art scene. Eventually, word about the neighborhood spread, bringing an influx of artists from all over the world, followed by graphic and web designers. **Hoxton Square,** the compact center of the

LONDON

restaurant, gallery, and nightlife scene, emerged as the place to be. Many artists have since fled to cheaper living, taking some of the edge with them, but the area still maintains a hip, independent vibe. (⊖*Old St. The center of the Hoxton and Shoreditch scene spreads out on either side of Old St. between the junction with Great Eastern St. and Kingsland Rd./Shoreditch High St.)*

CHRIST CHURCH SPITALFIELDS. Christ Church, the largest design by Christopher Wren's student Nicholas Hawksmoor, stands proudly above its East End surroundings. A recently completed £7 million renovation has returned the church's stone facade to its former glory, and the inside is nicely outfitted with white crown moldings and marble pillars. (*Commercial St., opposite Spitalfields Market.* ⊖*Liverpool St.* ☎*020 7247 7202. Services held Su 10:30am; Communion the 1st and 3rd Su of each month at 8:30am. Open Tu 11am-4pm and Su 1-4pm; M, W, Th-F 11am-4pm when not in use for church functions.)*

CHRIST CHURCH CONCERTS FOR POCKET CHANGE. Christ Church Spitalfields opens its doors for a series of excellent and mostly free concerts during the Spitalfields Festivals in both June and December. See www.spitalfieldsfestival.org.uk for upcoming dates and concert schedules.

GREENWICH

With many well-known sights and a spacious park, Maritime Greenwich, as it's officially known, offers a welcome retreat from the chaos of the city's center. The borough was initially the site of a royal palace; both philandering Henry VIII and his virgin daughter, Elizabeth I, were born here. After the royal family vacated the premises, Greenwich became home to the Royal Navy, which it remained until 1998; now, the buildings are open to visitors and also house the **Trinity College of Music** and **Greenwich University**. The **Royal Observatory** lies on the **Prime Meridian line,** atop a hill in beautiful Greenwich Park. (*DLR: Cutty Sark unless stated otherwise.* ☎*0870 608 2000. The Greenwich Tourist Information Center, Pepys House, 2 Cutty Sark Gardens, offers a helpful map of the area. Guided walking tours leave the center daily at 12:15pm for the town and observatory and at 2:15pm for the Royal Naval College. Open M-Sa 10am-5pm. £5, concessions £4, children under 14 free.)*

Many people choose to make the hour-long boat trip from Westminster or Tower Hill to Greenwich; boats also run to the Thames Barrier. Travelcard holders get 33% off riverboat trips from a variety of companies. (*Visit www.tfl.gov.uk/ gettingaround/1131.aspx for details.)* City Cruises operates from Westminster Pier to Greenwich via the Tower of London. (☎*020 7740 0400; www.citycruises.com. Schedule changes constantly; call for times. One-way £6, all-day "roamer" ticket £7; children £3/3.50).*

TIP-TOP SHAPE. If you're willing to make the trek, there are spots in Greenwich Park that offer particularly noteworthy views: the first is the hill where the Royal Observatory sits; you can see all of the Docklands and Westminster on a clear day. The other is One Tree Hill, from which, looking in the other direction, you can see all of Greenwich.

ROYAL OBSERVATORY GREENWICH. Charles II founded the Observatory in 1675 to accelerate the task of "finding the longitude" after one too many shipwrecks led to public outcry. Despite its importance, he insisted it be built for under £500, so beams from ships and other construction sites were brought in to offset costs. Even though the puzzle of longitude was eventually solved, Greenwich still plays an important role as the marker of hemispheres: the **Prime Merid-**

ian, or longitude 0°0'0", is marked by a constantly photographed red LED strip in the courtyard and allows you to occupy space in both hemispheres. Next, you must choose one of two routes. The Meridian route takes you through all aspects of time, beginning with the **Flamsteed House,** a Christopher Wren creation originally designed as a living space for John Hamsteed, the first Astronomer Royal; it's topped by the Time Ball, which climbs to full mast at 12:58pm, only to drop again at 1pm. The Astronomy route takes you through to the back building, where you'll find a number of interactive exhibits about space exploration and the popular **planetarium.** *(At the top of Greenwich Park, a short but steep climb from the National Maritime Museum or an easier walk up the Avenue from St. Mary's Gate at the top of King William Walk. Tram leaves from the back of the Museum every 30min. ☎ 020 8858 4422; www.nmm.ac.uk. Open daily in summer 10am-8pm, in winter 10am-5pm. Last entry 30min. before closing. Summer open 10am-8pm; check website to confirm. Planetarium £6, students and children £4. Royal Observatory free.)*

THE ROYAL NAVAL COLLEGE. On the site of Henry VIII's Palace of Placentia—where he and his daughters Mary and Elizabeth I were born—the Royal Naval College was built in 1696 as the Royal Hospital for Seamen, a naval retirement in the vein of the army's Royal Hospital in Chelsea. However, the strict regime proved unpopular with former seamen, and in 1873 it was converted into the Royal Naval College. In 1998, the Navy packed its bags and the newly formed University of Greenwich stepped in, along with the famed Trinity College of Music. Most of the buildings are closed to the public, but two are open and worth a stop: the first, the extravagant **Painted Hall,** took Sir James Thornhill 19 years to complete; the second, the brightly colored **chapel.** The **Queen Mary Bar** and **King William Restaurant** below the chapel and Painted Hall, respectively. *(King William Walk. ☎ 020 8269 4747; www.greenwichfoundation. org.uk. Chapel and Painted Hall open daily 10am-5pm; chapel may close for weddings. Su 11am worship service open to public. Guided tours of the College leave from the Painted Hall Th-Sa 11:30am and 2pm, Su 2pm. Free. Tours £5.)*

GREENWICH PARK. A former royal hunting ground, Greenwich Park is home to fun and relaxation as young people and families come out in droves to sunbathe, picnic, and play pick-up soccer. But recreation is nothing new to the park: on the east side, the now-horizontal **Queen Elizabeth Oak** marks the spot where Henry VIII once frolicked with an allegedly 11-fingered Anne Boleyn. A chestnut tree (that many have mistaken for oak) was planted in the spot as a replacement in 1992. The garden in the southeast corner of the park blends English garden and fairy tale, complete with a deer park, while down the hill from the observatory lie the remains of an AD first-century Roman settlement and Saxon burial mounds (tumuli).*(Open daily 7am-dusk. Children's Boating Pool, behind the observatory, open June-Aug. daily 10:30am-5pm; Sept.-May Sa-Su 10:30am-5pm. 20min. paddle boat rental £2.50, children £1.50.)*

CUTTY SARK. Before it was a Scotch, the Cutty Sark was the fastest of the British tea-liners. Built in 1869, she made the round-trip voyage from China in only 120 days, carrying over a million pounds of tea. Retired from the sea in the 1930s, the deck and cabins have been partially restored to their 19th-century prime. The hold houses an exhibit on the ship's history and a collection of figureheads, while the upper deck features the officer's quarters—a far cry, comfort-wise, from those of the crew. Due to a large-scale conservation project that began in 2006, the ship is closed to visitors until 2010. *(King William Walk, by Greenwich Pier. ☎ 020 8858 3445; www.cuttysark.org.uk. Will be open daily 10am-5pm. Call for opening updates and details.)*

CLERKENWELL

The mercurial popularity of now-hip Clerkenwell coincides, appropriately enough, with the fluctuating role that alcohol has played in the local economy. Clerkenwell was founded as a monastic hamlet in the 12th century, but in his rage against the Church, Henry VIII destroyed or secularized many of its properties. In the 17th century, Clerkenwell became a veritable resort town, with spas, tea gardens, and theaters; Oliver Cromwell lived on the Close. Soon after, an influx of brewers and distilleries brought a slew of liquor-centric jobs to the area, but the accompanying population boom resulted in the area becoming the notorious slum detailed in Charles Dickens's *Oliver Twist*. WWII and fires in the 1980s and 90s brought even more damage. Today, Clerkenwell is less chic than before but definitely more fun, with a lively population of young bars and nightclubs.

TAKE A HIKE. Many of the neighborhood's historic buildings are beautiful from the outside but are inaccessible to tourists; instead, you can either get a guided tour (W 11am, Su 2am; departing from ⊖Farringdon; £5, concessions £4) or attempt to navigate the **Clerkenwell Historic Trail,** a 2 mi. marked route that starts near the Grand Priory Church on Clerkenwell Close.

▨SAINT BARTHOLOMEW THE GREAT. A small, Norman church tucked away among brick buildings, St. Bartholomew's is packed with interesting tidbits. It is the oldest church in London (**All Hallows,** which claims to be older, is in fact the oldest church *site*), having been a place of worship for 886 years. Inside, the current nave was the chancel of the original 12th-century church, which reached all the way to the street until Henry VIII destroyed it in his rampage against the Catholic Church. William Hogarth was baptized in the 15th-century font, and at one time Benjamin Franklin worked as a printer's apprentice in the Lady Chapel. The tomb near the central altar is the resting place of Rahere, who in 1123 founded both the church and the neighboring St. Bartholomew's Hospital. More recently, a number of blockbusters have been filmed here. This is where Hugh Grant was slapped by Ducky in *Four Weddings and a Funeral*, where Joseph Fiennes repented in *Shakespeare in Love*, where Mary Queen of Scots was executed in *Elizabeth: the Golden Age*, and where Jude Law and Robert Downey Jr. played detectives in Guy Ritchie's recent film about Sherlock Holmes. The peaceful elevated courtyard provides a close view of its unique and eccentric exterior as well as a lovely place to sit and relax. (*Little Britain, off West Smithfield. ⊖Barbican. ☎020 7606 5171. Open M-F 8:30am-5pm, Sa 10:30am-4pm, Su 8:30am-8pm. £4, concessions £3.*)

SAINT JOHN'S SQUARE. Now populated with hip cafes and lunchtime crowds, St. John's Sq. occupies the site of the 12th-century Priory of St. John, former seat of the Knights Hospitallers. The Hospitallers (in full, the Order of the Hospital of St. John of Jerusalem) were founded in 1113 during the First Crusade to simultaneously tend to the sick and fight the heathens. What remains of their London seat is now in the hands of the British Order of St. John, a Protestant organization; in 1997, it founded the Ambulance Brigade to provide first-aid service to the public.

Built in 1504 as the main entrance to the priory, **Saint John's Gate** now arches grandly over the entrance to the square. The small museum on the ground floor displays artifacts relating to the original priory and Knights Hospitallers, though it is currently closed until late 2010 for a £1.6 million renovation project. At that time, you will also be able to tour the church and crypt, which are usually closed to the public. *(St. John's Ln.* ⊖*Farringdon.* ☎*020 7324 4070; www.sja.org. uk/history. Prices and opening hours to be determined.)*

On the other side of Clerkenwell Rd., cobblestones in St. John's Sq. mark the position of the original 12th-century church. The current building dates to the 16th century and lies at the end of the cloister's garden. Two panels of the 1480 Weston Triptych stand on their original altar, but the real treasure of the church is the crypt, one of London's few surviving pieces of Norman architecture. *(Open only to tours of St. John's Gate, unless by special arrangement; see above.)*

THE CHARTERHOUSE. Originally a 14th-century Carthusian monastery, the Charterhouse and its walls were built around the communal grave of thousands of victims of the 1349 Black Death. In 1611, Thomas Sutton bought the property and established a foundation for the education of boys and the care of impoverished old men. Charterhouse School rapidly established itself as one of the most prestigious (and expensive) schools in England, but in 1872 the school moved to Surrey, leaving the complex to the (still penniless) pensioners. Weekly tours guide you through the grounds and into some of the buildings, including the Duke of Norfolk's Great Hall and the chapel with Sutton's ornate tomb. *(On the north side of Charterhouse Sq.* ⊖*Barbican.* ☎*020 7251 5002. Partially wheelchair-accessible. Open only for 1hr. tours May-Aug. W 2:15pm. Book months in advance. £10.)*

HOLBORN

Holborn native Samuel Johnson once advised, "You must not be content with seeing Holborn's great streets and squares but must survey the innumerable little lanes and courts" (not one of his crispier *bons mots*). From the tiny, winding lanes of the Temple to the enormous and ornate Royal Courts of Justice and from the unexpected, jewel-like gardens to the sprawling office buildings, Holborn is a neighborhood of contrasts, with the modern skyline of London's commercial present rising above the Gothic remains of its past. Only in the Courtauld Galleries in Somerset House could a Modigliani share a floor with a Botticelli.

Running through the center of Holborn is **Fleet Street.** Named for the (now underground) tributary that flows from Hampstead to the Thames, the thoroughfare became synonymous with the London press in the 19th century, when it housed all of the major dailies. After a standoff with the printers in 1986, Rupert Murdoch moved all of his papers (including *The Times*) to Wapping, Docklands and initiated a mass exodus; nevertheless, "Fleet Street" is still used to describe London-based newspapers. Today, Fleet St. is home to churches, coffee shops, and photocopying stores—the street's final nod to the printing industry.

◪THE TEMPLE. The Temple is a complex of buildings that derives its name from the crusading Order of the Knights Templar, which embraced this site as its English seat in 1185. Today, the stately construct houses legal and parliamentary offices, but its medieval church and charming network of gardens remain open to the enterprising visitor. Highlights include the **Inner Temple Gateway,** between 16 and 17 Fleet St., the 1681 fountain of **Fountain Court** (featured in Dickens's *Martin Chizzlewit*), and **Elm Court,** tucked behind the church, a tiny yet exquisite garden ringed by massive stone structures. *(Between Essex St. and Temple Ave.; church courtyard off Middle Temple Ln.* ⊖*Temple or Blackfriars. Free.)*

Temple Church is one of the finest surviving medieval round churches and London's first Gothic church, completed in 1185 on the model of Jerusalem's Church of the Holy Sepulchre—an original Norman doorway and 10 armored effigies. Adjoining the round church is a rectangular Gothic choir, built in 1240, with an 1682 altar screen by Christopher Wren. The church hosts frequent recitals and musical services, including weekly organ recitals. *(*☎*020 7353 3470.*

Hours vary depending on the week's services and are posted outside the door of the church for the coming week. Organ recitals W 1:15-1:45pm; no services Aug.-Sept.)

The **Middle Temple** largely escaped the destruction of WWII and retains fine examples of 16th- and 17th-century architecture. In Middle Temple Hall (closed to the public), Elizabeth I saw Shakespeare act in the premiere of *Twelfth Night*, and his *Henry VI* points to Middle Temple Garden as the origin of the red and white flowers that served as emblems throughout the War of the Roses. *(Open May-Sept. M-F noon-3pm.)*

ROYAL COURTS OF JUSTICE. This massive Neo-Gothic structure, designed in 1874 by G.E. Street, holds its own among the distinguished facades of Fleet St. Inside, things get serious, with courtrooms, chambers for judges and court staff, and cells for defendants. The **Great Hall** features Europe's largest mosaic floor, surrounded by over 3½ mi. of corridors and over 1000 rooms. The back bench of every courtroom is open to the public during trials unless the courtroom door says "In Chambers," and notice boards beside the Enquiry Desk in the Great Hall display a list of cases being tried. *(Where the Strand becomes Fleet St.; rear entrance on Carey St. ⊖Temple or Chancery Ln. ☎020 7947 6000, tours 7947 7684. Open to the public M-F 10am-4:30pm; cases are heard 10:30am-1pm and 2-4:15pm. Tours 1st and 3rd Tu of the month. Wheelchair-accessible. Be prepared to go through a security checkpoint with metal detector. Free. Tours £6.)*

SAINT BRIDE'S CHURCH. The unusual spire of Christopher Wren's 1675 church is the most imitated piece of architecture in the world: a local baker used it as the model for the first multi-tiered wedding cake. Dubbed "the printers' cathedral" or "journalist's church" in 1531 when Wyken de Worde set up his press here, it has long been closely associated with nearby newspapermen. Some pews are dedicated to reporters who have "lost their lives in search of the truth." The literary connection runs even deeper: Milton lived in the courtyard, while Dickens and Johnson lived in the parish. Although the interior is disappointing, its underbelly is not: the crypt includes the baker's wife's wedding dress and bonnet, as well as the remains of a Roman pavement and ditch from about AD 180, all meticulously maintained by a baker and a candlestick maker. *(St. Bride's Ave., just off Fleet St. ⊖Blackfriars. ☎020 7427 0133; www.stbrides.com. Open daily 8am-4:45pm. Lunchtime concerts and nighttime classical music; call for details. Free.)*

SAINT CLEMENT DANES. Legend places this church over the tomb of Harold Harefoot, a Danish warlord who settled here in the ninth century. Its fame with Londoners derives from its opening role in the famous nursery rhyme: "Oranges and Lemons Say the Bells of St. Clement's"—and they still do, daily at 9am, noon, 3, and 6pm. With a long history of destruction and reconstruction, it was rebuilt most notably by Christopher Wren in 1681 and again after German bombs destroyed the interior during the Blitz. The official church of the Royal Air Force since 1948, its interior has now been restored to its white-and-gold splendor; it houses the RAF regimental standards and a small tribute to the American airmen who died in WWII, to the left of the inner doors. *(At the eastern junction of Aldwych and Strand. ⊖Temple. ☎020 7242 8282. Open daily 9am-4pm. Free.)*

SAINT DUNSTAN-IN-THE-WEST. An early Victorian church crammed between Fleet St. facades, St. Dunstan is most notable for its 1641 clock, whose bells are struck every 15min. by a pair of hammer-wielding musclemen (figurines) representing the mythical giant guardians of London, Gog and Magog. The statue of Elizabeth I on the porch was saved from the 16th-century Lud Gate that stood nearby. Handel was once invited to play here but no one knows if it happened. Milton met his publisher for *Paradise Lost* in the courtyard, and Sweeney Todd, the infamous barber-murderer, at one point set up shop right next door. Today, the church is a model of ecumenical worship—seven separate and lavish chapels house seven different faiths, and there is also a plaque dedicated to "The Honest Solicitor," that rarest inhabitant of Fleet St. *(186A Fleet St. ⊖Temple or Chancery Ln. ☎020 7405 1929; www.stdunstaninthewest.org. Free lunchtime recitals W 1:15pm. Open M and W-F 11am-2pm, Tu 11am-3pm. Free.)*

THE SOUTH BANK

During the Middle Ages, the South Bank was outside the jurisdiction of the Puritan city authorities, and thus, "the Borough" became the center of all manner of illicit attractions—drunken revelry, prostitution, and acting—that the Puritans considered ungodly. Blood sports like bear-baiting and cockfighting thrived, as did the then-epitome of low-brow—theater, dominated by the big three: the Rose, the Swan, and yes, Shakespeare's Globe. After the English Civil War in the 1640s, the South Bank's fortunes turned to the sea, as wharves groaned under the weight of cargoes from across the Empire. By the time shipping moved elsewhere in the late 1950s, the seeds of regeneration had been sown. From the 1951 Festival of Britain sprang the Royal Festival Hall, the nucleus of the South Bank Centre and heart of the new South Bank. The National Theatre followed 20 years later, and development has continued at such a pace that the South Bank is now once more the heart of the London cultural scene, with a visitor-friendly conglomeration of art galleries, theaters, and music halls, each with their own history—not to mention personality.

◾**SHAKESPEARE'S GLOBE THEATRE.** The most popular and successful of the "big three" theaters in the 1500s, the original Globe burned down in 1613 during a rehearsal for *Henry VIII*. This incarnation of the Globe, the brain-child of American actor/director Sam Wanamaker, is faithful to the original, thatched roof and all. It had its first full season in 1997 and now stands as the cornerstone of the International Shakespeare Globe Centre. The informative exhibit inside covers the theater's history and includes displays on costumes and customs of the theater, as well as information on other prominent playwrights of Shakespeare's era. There's also an interactive display where you get to trade lines with recorded Globe actors. But the real highlight of a Globe visit is a 40min. tour of the theater itself, which (if a matinee is not scheduled) allows access either into the theater to watch actors rehearsing whatever play is running, or into the nearby **Swan,** where both Shakespeare and Christopher Marlowe performed. For info on performances, see **Entertainment,** p. 160. *(Bankside, close to Bankside pier. ⊖Southwark or London Bridge. ☎020 7902 1400; www.shakespeares-globe.org. Open Mar. daily 9am-5pm (exhibit and tours); Apr.-Sept. M-Sa 9am-12:30pm (exhibit and Globe tour) and 12:30-5pm (exhibit and Rose Tour), Su 9-11:30am (exhibit and Globe) and noon-5pm (exhibit and Rose); Oct.-Apr. daily 10am-5pm (exhibit). Wheelchair-accessible. £11, concessions £8.50, children 5-15 £6.50, families of 5 £28.)*

◾**SOUTHWARK CATHEDRAL.** A site of worship since AD 606, the cathedral has undergone numerous transformations in the last 1400 years. The majestic main chapel has fascinating historical connections. For one, Shakespeare's brother Edmund is buried here: a rare stained-glass window along the right side of the nave depicts characters from Shakespearean plays, while a memorial to the Bard's brother lies below. John Harvard, benefactor of Harvard University, was baptized here in 1607, and a chapel to him stands in the front left of the nave. In the retrochoir, there are four smaller chapels; the southernmost, St. Christopher's, is dedicated to travelers. Near the center, the archaeological gallery is actually a small excavation revealing a first-century Roman road along with Saxon, Norman, and 18th-century remains. In 2001, a new conference center and cafe were opened on the grounds by Nelson

Mandela as part of the millennium celebrations. *(Montague Close.* ⊖*London Bridge.* ☎*020 7367 6700; www.southwark.anglican.org/cathedral. Open M-F 8am-6pm, Sa-Su 9am-6pm. Wheelchair-accessible. Free, suggested donation £4. Groups are asked to book in advance; group rates available. Camera permit £2; video permit £5.)*

LONDON EYE. Also called the Millennium Wheel, the 135m British Airways London Eye is the biggest observational wheel in the world, taller than St. Paul's Cathedral and visible itself from miles around. The lines are about a millennium long, so don't come in the middle of the day or you'll be there forever. The elliptical glass "pods" give uninterrupted views from the top of each 30min. revolution. On clear days, you can see Windsor in the west, though eastward views are blocked by skyscrapers farther down the river. *(Jubilee Gardens, between County Hall and the Festival Hall.* ⊖*Waterloo.* ☎*087 990 8883; www.londoneye.com. Open daily May-June 10am-9pm; July-Aug. 10am-9:30pm; Sept. 10am-9pm; Oct.-Apr. 10am-8pm. Wheelchair-accessible. Buy tickets from the box office at the corner of County Hall before joining the queue at the Eye. Advance booking recommended, but check the weather. £17, concessions £14, children under 16 £8.50.)*

GET HIGH FOR FREE. If paying £20 for the London Eye seems a bit steep for a bird's-eye view of the city, climb the tower at the nearby Tate Modern (p. 141), which gives a similar view for free.

GABRIEL'S WHARF AND OXO TOWER. One of the more colorful additions to the South Bank, Gabriel's Wharf is an artsy market area where little shops and restaurants stretch from the water down into the surrounding streets. A few steps away is the Art Deco OXO Tower, built by a company that once supplied instant beef stock to the entire British Empire. Famous for its clever subversion of rules prohibiting advertising on buildings, the Tower's windows subtly spell out "OXO." The Tower is now enveloped in the brick mass of the OXO Tower Wharf, which holds tiny boutiques, workshops, and galleries run by some of London's most innovative young artists and designers. A free public viewing gallery on the eighth floor provides prime views over the South Bank area. *(Between Upper Ground and the Thames.* ⊖*Blackfriars, Southwark, or Waterloo. Wheelchair-accessible.)*

SOUTH LONDON

Initially just another South London railway suburb, **Brixton** was at first nothing more than home to Electric Ave. and Electric Ln., the first streets in South London with electric lighting. In the early 20th century, the area attracted thousands of middle and working class citizens, but WWII bombing plunged it into urban decay. Beginning in 1948, a steady stream of Caribbean immigrants arrived, transforming Brixton into the heart of London's West Indian community, and simmering racial tensions erupted with major riots in 1981, 1985, and 1995. The flames have quelled, however, and Brixton is (after the recession, more slowly) developing into a fashionable area for young artists and students, aided by the rise of an impressive club scene. A stroll through the area highlights the unique qualities of a town in flux: Afro-Caribbean markets, trendy new cafes, and increasing numbers of chain stores share street space. You can see the best of old Brixton early in the day, when Brixton Market is in full swing, and the best of new Brixton late at night, when young Brixtonians pile out of work and into the clubs and bars.

Clapham, just to the east, has more old-time charm than Brixton, though it too is on the up and up. Attractive High Street is packed with even more elite bars and clubs, as well as eateries that run the gamut from old to new and from cheap to pricey. At the end of the High Street lie the rolling fields of **Clapham Common,** a popular place for athletes and locals.

In the south, **Dulwich** could hardly offer a greater contrast; not much has changed in this old-money mecca in about four centuries. South London's snobbiest suburb, Dulwich bumbled along as an unremarkable country village until 1605, when Elizabethan actor Edward Alleyn bought a local manor; wealth and sprawling estates soon followed. His legacy lives on in the **College of God's Gift,** established according to his will for the education of 12 poor children. The original Old College buildings, including the chapel where Alleyn is buried, still stand close to **Dulwich Picture Gallery.** Dulwich College, now with 1600 very wealthy pupils, has since moved south to a palatial 19th-century site on College Road, where it reaps benefits by holding the last tollgate in London. *(Rail: North or West Dulwich.)*

DULWICH PARK. Created in 1890 as fields and farmland, this expansive park was once the stomping grounds of Queen Mary, who was especially fond of the American garden. Thanks to its 2006 renovation, the park's 79 acres hold a number of soccer fields, tennis courts, bowling greens, playgrounds, cafes, and gardens. It also hosts regular activities and organized walks; check the website for more details. *(Entrances on College Rd., Dulwich Common, and Court Ln. ✪ Brixton, then bus #P4 to College Rd. Rail: North or West Dulwich. ☎ 020 7525 2000; www.southwark.gov.uk.)*

BROCKWELL PARK. This massive stretch of rolling grass sprinkled with leafy trees is perfect for joggers, unleashed dogs, and those looking to get away from the crowded London streets. Just past the gated entrance is the popular **Brockwell Lido,** a 1930s outdoor swimming pool often described as "London's beach." Every year from 2001 to 2004, the park hosted the infamous, if controversial, **Cannabis Festival** (also known as Jay Day), when police allowed public smoking of cannabis, but the borough of Lambeth has since killed the buzz. The park also boasts tennis courts, a children's playground, miles of walking paths, a BMX track, and a small cafe at its summit, from which you can catch a glimpse of the London Eye. It is currently undergoing a large renovation project that will bring even more greenery. *(Between Tulse Hill and Dulwich Rd. From ✪ Brixton, turn left out of the station, bear left at the fork onto Effra Rd., walk about 10min., then turn left again onto Brixton Water Lane. The entrance is on the right. www.brockwellpark.com. Open daily 7:30am-dusk.)*

CLAPHAM COMMON. The Common comprises over 200 acres of grassland shaped in a triangle and situated between Clapham, Battersea, and Balham. Apart from usual park offerings, the Common boasts three ponds, in two of which you can fish. The Common's most notable feature is its 100-year-old bandstand, which has played host to numerous open-air concerts and festivals. *(Between Clapham Common North Side Rd. and Clapham Common South Side Rd.; from ✪ Clapham North, turn left out of the station and walk about 10min. down Clapham High St.)*

 STRENGTH IN NUMBERS. At night the Common is not very well lit and should not be traversed alone. Unless you're with a friend, take the streets around it instead.

WESTMINSTER

Big Ben, the Houses of Parliament, Westminster Abbey, Buckingham Palace, and more all fall within the confines of this age-old neighborhood, a necessary stop for any visitor to the city.

◪WESTMINSTER ABBEY

Parliament Sq. Access Old Monastery, Cloister, and Garden from Dean's Yard, behind the Abbey. ⊖Westminster. Abbey ☎ 7654 4900, Chapter House 7222 5152; www.westminster-abbey.org. No photography. Abbey open M-Tu and Th-F 9:30am-3:45pm, W 9:30am-7pm, Sa 9:30am-1:45pm, Su open for services only. Museum open daily 10:30am-4pm. Partially wheelchair-accessible. Abbey and Museum £15, students and children 11-17 £12, families of 4 £36. Services free. 1hr. tours £3 Apr.-Oct. M-F 10, 10:30, 11am, 2, 2:30pm, Sa 10, 10:30, 11am; Oct.-Mar. M-F 10:30, 11am, 2, 2:30pm, Sa 10:30, 11am. Audio tours available; free. M-F 9:30am-3:30pm, Sa 9:30am-1pm. AmEx/MC/V.

Originally founded as a Benedictine monastery, Westminster Abbey has evolved into a house of kings and queens both living and dead. On December 28, 1065, St. Edward the Confessor, last Saxon King of England, was buried in the still-unfinished Abbey Church of the West Monastery. Almost exactly a year later, on Christmas Day, the Abbey saw the coronation of William the Conqueror. Even before it was completed, the Abbey's twin traditions as the birthplace and final resting place of royalty had been established, as evidenced by King Edward's Chair, the throne on which every British sovereign has been crowned since 1308. Little remains of St. Edward's Abbey: Henry III's 13th-century Gothic reworking created most of the grand structure you see today. In 1540, Henry VIII dissolved the monasteries, expelling the monks and seizing control of the Abbey. Fortunately, Henry's respect for his royal forbearers outweighed his vindictiveness against Catholicism, so Westminster escaped destruction and desecration. Much of the monastic artwork has been lost over time, but the structure and the vaulted Gothic architecture remain beautifully preserved. The Abbey became a "Royal Peculiar" under the direct control of Henry VIII. Under this ambiguous status, the Abbey has since become a ceremonial center for the nation. Every ruler since William I has been coronated here, and many have been married here as well. The Abbey has also held funerals for royals and state figures like Winston Churchill. The varied uses and styles in the Abbey have combined to make an intriguing mix of statues, tombs, and plaques.

Of the many Brits buried and commemorated inside the Abbey, highlights include statesmen (and -women) Henry VII, Bloody Mary, and Elizabeth I; scholars and artists in the "Poet's Corner" include Geoffrey Chaucer and George Handel. Also, the Brontë sisters, Jane Austen, and Shakespeare are honored with plaques, but not buried there.

OLD MONASTERY, CLOISTERS, AND GARDENS. Formerly a major monastery, the Abbey complex still stretches far beyond the church itself, including gardens and other structures. A door off the east cloister leads to the octagonal **Chapter House,** the original meeting place of the House of Commons, whose 13th-century tiled floor is the best preserved in Europe. The faded but still exquisite frescoes of the Book of Revelations around the walls date from this period, as do the sculpture and floor tiles. A passage running off the southeast corner leads to the **Little Cloister** courtyard, from which another passage leads to the 900-year-old **College Gardens.** *(Chapter House open daily 10:30am-4pm. Cloisters open daily 8am-6pm. Garden open Apr.-Sept. Tu-Th 10am-6pm, Oct.-Mar. daily 10am-4pm. Band concerts at lunch in July and Aug. Free.)*

SAINT MARGARET'S. Adjacent to the entrance of the Abbey, this church has a strange status: as a part of the Royal Peculiar, it is not under the jurisdiction of the diocese of England or even the archbishop of Canterbury. Beautifully restored in the past few years, it was built for local residents by Abbey monks tired of having to share their own church with laymen. Since 1614, it has been the official worshiping place of the House of Commons—the first few pews

LONDON

are cordoned off for the Speaker, Black Rod, and other dignitaries. At times, parts of the church seem to be at odds with one another: the Gothic columns and arches support a decidedly un-Gothic ceiling. Also, the noticeably different styles of stained-glass windows can feel mismatched, but with good reason, since the geometric, gray-and-green-hued Piper Windows replaced those destroyed in WWII. The **Milton Window** (1888), in the back above the North Aisle, shows the poet (married here in 1608) dictating *Paradise Lost* to his daughters. Stained-glass images from the book fill the surrounding panels. Winston Churchill married his beloved "Clemmie" in the chapel. In the summer months, free lunchtime concerts are offered on a weekly basis; call for more information. (☎ 7654 4840. *Open M-F 9:30am-3:45pm, Sa 9:30am-1:45pm, Su 2-5pm. Hours subject to change; call first. Concerts every M during the summer months. Wheelchair-accessible. Free.*)

BUCKINGHAM PALACE

At the end of the Mall, between Westminster, Belgravia, and Mayfair. ⊖*St. James's Park, Victoria, Green Park, or Hyde Park Corner.* ☎ *7766 7324; www.the-royal-collection.com.*

Originally built for the Dukes of Buckingham, Buckingham House was acquired by George III for his new wife, Queen Charlotte, in 1761. Charlotte gave birth to 14 of her 15 children at Buckingham House. George IV, the next sovereign, decided it wasn't nearly big enough to be a royal residence and commissioned John Nash to expand the existing building into a palace. Neither George IV nor his successor, William IV, ever lived in the palace; when the 1834 fire left Parliament without a home, William offered Buckingham. Three years later, however, Queen Victoria moved in, and it has been the royal residence ever since. The structure was too small for Victoria's rapidly growing family, a problem that was solved by removing Nash's Marble Arch (which now stands just north at Marble Arch) and building a fourth wall to enclose the courtyard.

THE STATE ROOMS. The Palace opens to visitors every August and September while the royals are off sunning themselves. Don't expect to find any insights into the Queen's personal life—the State Rooms are the only rooms on display, and they are used only for formal occasions, like entertaining visiting heads of state. Fortunately, they are also the most sumptuous in the Palace. After ascending the grand staircase, you can tour the chromatically labeled drawing rooms, bedecked in white, blue, and green. Look for the secret door concealed in one of the **White Drawing Room's** mirrors—the royals enter the state apartments through this door. You'll also see the **Throne Room** and the domed and glittering **Music Room.** The **Galleries** display many of the finest pieces in the Royal Collection, including works by Rembrandt, Rubens, Poussin, and Canaletto. Queen Elizabeth has graciously allowed commoners into the **Gardens,** home to rare flowers and birds—keep off the grass! (*Enter on Buckingham Palace Rd. Ticket office* ☎ *7766 7324. Tickets also available at Buckingham Palace. Open from late July to late Sept. daily 9:45am-6:30pm, last entry 4:15pm. £16.50, students £15, children 6-17 £9.50, under 5 free, families of 5 £44. Advance booking is recommended; required for disabled visitors. AmEx/MC/V.*)

THE ROYAL MEWS. The Mews has many hats: it acts as a museum, stable, riding school, and working carriage house. The main attraction is the Queen's collection of coaches, including the "Glass Coach" used to carry royal brides (including Diana) to their weddings, and the State Coaches of Australia, Ireland, and Scotland. The biggest draw is the four-ton **Gold State Coach,** which can occasionally be seen tooling around the streets in the early morning on practice runs for major events. The attendants on guard throughout the self-guided tour are gold mines of royal information, full of tips on when and where to catch glimpses of Their Royal Highnesses. Visitors can meet the carriage horses themselves, each named by the Queen. Each horse has undergone years of training to withstand the distractions of crowds, street traffic, and gun salutes. Displays regarding more modern forms of transportation (the royal fleet of Rolls Royces) and the training and garments of the carriage men are an interesting contrast. Note that horses and carriages are liable to be absent without notice, and opening hours are subject to change. (☎7766 7302. Open from late July to late Sept. daily 10am-5pm, last entry 4:15pm; from Mar. to July and from late Sept. to late Oct. M-Th and Sa-Su 11am-4pm, last entry 3:15pm. Wheelchair-accessible. £7.50, seniors £6.75, children under 17 £4.80, families £20. AmEx/MC/V.)

QUEENS GALLERY. "God Save the Queen" is the rallying cry at this gallery dedicated to temporary exhibitions of jaw-droppingly valuable items from the Royal Collection. Most recently, a collection of royal porcelain that was purchased from France after it went out of fashion following the Revolution was on display until January 2009. Five exquisite rooms are full of various artifacts dedicated to extolling the glory of the sovereign in numerous art forms. The friendly older guards can show you the finest pieces of the Royal Collection, with the exception of the State Room pieces. The rooms in this opulent museum are monochromatic and designed to look like the interior of the palace; a grand staircase and green marble pillars welcome visitors into the first room. Free audio tours

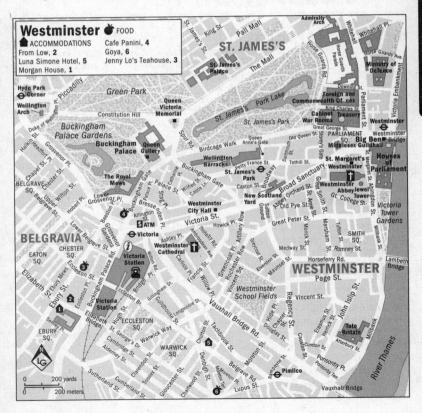

Westminster 🍎 FOOD

🏠 ACCOMMODATIONS
From Low, **2**
Luna Simone Hotel, **5**
Morgan House, **1**

Cafe Panini, **4**
Goya, **6**
Jenny Lo's Teahouse, **3**

typically accompany exhibits. Once purchased, passes may be registered online for 12 months of unlimited access. (☎7766 7301. Open daily 10am-5:30pm; last entry 4:30pm. Wheelchair-accessible. £8.50, concessions £7.50, families £21.50.)

CHANGING OF THE GUARD. The Palace is protected by a detachment of Foot Guards in full dress uniform, complete with highly impractical bearskin hats. "Changing of the Guard" refers not to replacing the sentries but to the exchange of guard duty between different regiments. When they meet at the central gates of the palace, the officers of the regiments touch hands, symbolically exchanging keys, and the guard is officially changed. Often, musical troops provide an accompanying soundtrack. To witness the 40min. spectacle, show up well before 11:30am and stand in front of the palace in view of the morning guards or use the steps of the Victoria Memorial as a vantage point. The middle of the week is the least crowded time to watch. (☎7766 7324. From Apr. to late July daily at 11:30am, From Aug. to Mar. every other day, excepting the Queen's absence, inclement weather, or pressing state functions. Free.)

CROWD CONTROL. If the crowds at Buckingham Palace are too much to bear, head to the Pall Mall side of St. James's Palace, where two guards keep watch and ceremoniously patrol the main entrance. Here, you'll encounter fewer crowds viewing the spectacle.

THE HOUSES OF PARLIAMENT

Parliament Sq., in Westminster. Queue for both Houses forms at St. Stephen's entrance, between Old and New Palace Yards. ⊖Westminster. ☎08709 063 773; www.parliament. uk/visiting/visiting.cfm. "Line of Route" Tour: includes both Houses. UK residents can contact their MPs for tours year-round, generally M-W mornings and F. Foreign visitors may tour Aug.-Sept. Book online, by phone, or in person at Abingdon Green ticket office (open mid-July) across from Palace of Westminster. Open Aug. M-Tu and F-Sa 9:15am-4:30pm, W-Th 1:15-4:30pm; Sept. M and F-Sa 9:15am-4:30pm, Tu-Th 1:15-4:30pm. 1¼hr. tours depart every few min. £12, students £8. MC/V.

The Palace of Westminster has been home to both the House of Lords and the House of Commons (together known as Parliament) since the 11th century, when Edward the Confessor established his court here. William the Conqueror added **Westminster Hall** in 1099—a wise move, since the rest of the Palace burned down in 1834. As a result, with the exception of Westminster Hall, everything you can see today was added in the 19th and 20th centuries. Two architects were commissioned for the rebuilding project—Classicist Charles Barry and Gothic champion Augustus Pugin—and a masterful combination of architectural styles resulted from their clash of temperaments. The exterior of the Palace is mostly Gothic, and the interior rooms and halls have a Classic dimension. Access has been restricted since a bomb killed an MP in 1979, but visitors can see some of the inside on the way to the galleries.

BIG BEN AND VICTORIA TOWER. The clock tower standing guard on the northern side of the building is famously nicknamed Big Ben, after the portly Benjamin Hall, a former Commissioner of Works. "Big Ben" actually refers only to the 14-ton bell that hangs inside the tower. The tower itself, Victoria Tower, was erected in 1834 to celebrate the emancipation of slaves in the British Empire. The tower contains copies of every Act of Parliament since 1497. A flag flown from the top indicates that Parliament is in session. When the Queen is in the building, a special royal banner is flown instead of the Union Jack.

WATERLOO VIEW. Sunset from the Waterloo Bridge is a must-see in London. With views of Parliament, Big Ben, the London Eye, and St. Paul's, there are few better places to soak in the city on a clear night.

DEBATING CHAMBERS. Visitors with enough patience or luck to make it inside the chambers can hear the occasional debate among members of both the House of Lords and the House of Commons—although the architecture of the palace is debatably more worthwhile than the debates themselves. The chambers are accessed via **St. Stephen's Hall,** which leads to the octagonal **Central Lobby**—the best example of the Gothic and Classical combination. The walls have ornate mosaics from 1870 depicting the kingdom's patron saints, while the Gothic archways hold stone sculptures of monarchs perched over the doors.

Access to the **House of Lords** is through the Peers' Lobby, which smug MPs have bedecked with scenes of Charles I's downfall. The ostentatious chamber itself is dominated by the sovereign's **Throne of State** under an elaborate gilt canopy—only when the golden throne is occupied can the Commons and the Lords congregate. The Lord Chancellor presides over the Peers from the **Woolsack,** a large red cushion that is quite the unusual post for a government official. Next to him rests the nearly 6 ft. gold **Mace,** which is brought in to open the House each morning. The lords face each other from their red leather benches arranged around the room. *(Lords Information Office ☎ 7219 3107. Chamber open Oct.-July M-Tu 2:30-10:30pm, W 3-10pm, Th 11am-7:30pm. Wait for Lords generally shorter than for Commons, although it still may not be possible to enter until after the 40min. "question time" M-W 2:30pm, Th-F 11am. Limited number of UK residents permitted for "question time." Foreign visitors must apply several weeks in advance for "question time" tickets through their embassy in London, or wait until questions are finished for entrance. Arrive in afternoon to minimize the wait, which regularly exceeds 2hr.)*

The contrast between the Lords and the **House of Commons**—with simple green-backed benches under an intricate (but comparatively plain) wooden roof—is not entirely due to differences in class; the Commons was destroyed by bombs in 1941, and rebuilding took place during a time of post-war austerity. The Speaker sits at the center-rear of the chamber, where he keeps order in the room. The government MPs sit to his right and the opposition to his left. However, with room for only 437 of the 635 MPs, things can get hectic when all are present. The front benches are reserved for government ministers and their opposition "shadows"; the Prime Minister and the Leader of the Opposition face off across their dispatch boxes. *(Commons Information Office ☎ 7219 4272. Chamber open Oct.-July M-Tu 2:30-10:30pm, W 11:30am-7:30pm, Th 10:30am-6:30pm, occasionally F 9:30am-3pm. Hours subject to change.)*

OTHER WESTMINSTER SIGHTS

⊠ SAINT JAMES'S PARK AND GREEN PARK. The streets leading up to Buckingham Palace are flanked by two sprawling, irregular quadrangles of greenery: St. James's Park and Green Park. In the middle of St. James's Park is the placid **St. James's Park Lake,** where you can catch glimpses of the pelicans that call it home—the lake and grassy area surrounding it are an official waterfowl preserve. Across the Mall, the lush Green Park is the creation of Charles II; it connects Westminster and St. James's. "Constitution Hill" refers not to the King's interest in political theory but to his daily exercises. If you sit on one of the lawn chairs scattered enticingly around both parks, an attendant will materialize out of thin air and demand money. Alternatively, act like a local and bring a blanket for a picnic, at no charge. *(The Mall. ⊖ St. James's Park or Green Park. Open* *daily 5am-midnight. Lawn chairs available, weather permitting, Mar.-Oct. 10am-6pm, June-Aug. 10am-10pm. £3 for 2hr., student deal £30 for the season. Last rental 2hr. before closing. Summer walks in the park some M 1-2pm, including tour of Guard's Palace and Victoria Tower Gardens. Book in advance by calling ☎ 7930 1793.)*

WESTMINSTER CATHEDRAL. Following Henry VIII's (and England's) break with the Catholic Church, London's Catholic community remained without a cathedral until 1884, when the Church purchased a derelict prison on the site of a former monastery. The Neo-Byzantine church looks somewhat like a fortress and is now one of London's great religious landmarks. Construction began in 1895, but the architect's plan quickly outran the funds available. When work stopped in 1903, the interior remained unfinished. The four blackened brick domes still await mosaic inlay and provide a striking contrast to the ornate trappings of the remainder. The front altar is covered with a marble canopy called a *baldachino;* above it hangs an imposing 10m cross. The brightness of the mosaics contrasts with the Colosseum-style marble arches and balconies. A lift carries visitors up the striped 273 ft. bell tower for an all-encompassing view of Westminster, the river, and Kensington. *(Cathedral Piazza, off Victoria St. ⊖Victoria. ☎7798 9055; www.westminstercathedral.org.uk. Open M-F 7am-7pm, Sa-Su 8am-7pm. Free, suggested donation £2. Bell tower open M-F 9:30am-5:15pm and Sa-Su 10am-4:45pm. Tower £5, students £2.50, families £11. Organ recitals in the winter Su 4:45pm.)*

WHITEHALL. Whitehall refers to the stretch of road connecting Trafalgar Sq. with Parliament Sq. and is synonymous with the British civil service. From 1532 until a devastating fire in 1698 it was the home of the monarchy and one of the grandest palaces in Europe, of which very little remains. Toward the north end of Whitehall, **Great Scotland Yard** marks the former headquarters of the Metropolitan Police. Nearer Parliament Sq., heavily guarded steel gates mark the entrance to **Downing Street.** In 1735, No. 10 was made the official residence of the First Lord of the Treasury, a position that soon became permanently identified with the Prime Minister. The Chancellor of the Exchequer traditionally resides at No. 11 and the Parliamentary Chief Whip at No. 12. The street is closed to visitors, but if you wait long enough you might see the PM going to or coming from work. South of Downing St., in the middle of Whitehall, stands Edward Lutyen's **Cenotaph** (1919), a proud commemoration to the soldiers who died in WWI. Many of the islands in the middle of the road hold statues honoring monarchs and military heroes, a testament to the avenue's identity as the center of civil service and the Ministry of Defence. *(Between Trafalgar Sq. and Parliament Sq. ⊖Westminster, Embankment, or Charing Cross.)*

LIFE GUARDS. The most photographed men in the area, the Queen's Life Guards, hold court in the center of Whitehall. Two mounted soldiers of the Household Cavalry, in shining breastplates and plumed helmets, guard a shortcut to The Mall and St. James's Park. While anyone can walk through, only those with a special ivory pass issued by the Queen herself may drive past the gates. The guards are posted from Monday to Saturday at 11am and Sunday at 10am, until they dismount for inspection daily at 4pm—a 200-year-old tradition broken only by WWII. Beyond the Neoclassical building is the pebbly expanse of **Horse Guards Parade,** where the Queen ceremonially sizes up her troops during the annual Trooping of the Colour ceremony on the second Saturday in June. *(Whitehall. ⊖Westminster, Embankment, or Charing Cross.)*

PARLIAMENT SQUARE. Conspiracy theorists will notice that this square, a center for anti-government protests over the last 250 years, is one of the few parks in the city without pedestrian access. Set in the middle of a busy traffic thoroughfare, would-be protesters must dodge traffic in all directions to reach this scruffy patch of grass where their voices can be heard. Until recently, anti-war activists displayed huge, eye-catching placards to passing motorists, but a law instated in August 2005 has prohibited all "unauthorized" protests. The law was designed to remove a single anti-war protester, Brian Haw, who spent an impressive four years in the square despite several attempts to evict him. The law notwithstanding, it's not unusual to find protesters camped out in support of their causes. If you make it to the square, you will see statues of Parliamentary greats, as well as a huge cast of ⬛"honest Abe" Lincoln across the road behind the square. *(Across the street from Parliament and Westminster Abbey. ↪Westminster.)*

VICTORIA TOWER GARDENS. South of the Palace of Westminster and overlooking the Thames, the open lawn and magnificent backdrop make the gardens a favorite spot for MPs, tourists, professionals, and TV crews running political features. For similar reasons, it is a first-rate picnic venue. Check out the superb cast of Rodin's *Burghers of Calais* and the memorial to suffragette Emmeline Pankhurst, which stands just inside the northwest gate. On the opposite side of the Palace, a tiny, slightly out-of-place Neo-Gothic gazebo commemorates the 1834 abolition of slavery on British territory. *(Millbank. ↪Westminster. Open daily until dusk. Wheelchair-accessible.)*

THE WEST END

MAYFAIR AND SAINT JAMES'S

The designer boutiques and prestigious gentlemen's clubs of Mayfair and St. James's are inaccessible to most budget-minded tourists, but the streets are perfect for afternoon strolls and window shopping. From the small alleys of Shepherd Market to the stately vista of Waterloo Place, Mayfair and St. James's are home to some of London's most impressive views and some of the its best people watching.

⬛**TRAFALGAR SQUARE.** London's largest traffic roundabout commemorates the victory over Napoleon's navy at Trafalgar, considered the British navy's finest hour. From the Chartist rallies of 1848 to the anti-apartheid vigils held outside South Africa House to London's largest protest over the war in Iraq in 2003, Trafalgar has traditionally been a site for public rallies and protest movements. The rest of the time, however, it functions as a favorite gathering place for Londoners. The masses congregate here on New Year's Eve to ring in midnight with the chimes of Big Ben and to honor the tradition of breaking the ice in the frozen fountains before the clock strikes twelve. Every December since the end of WWII, the square has hosted a giant Christmas tree, provided by Norway as thanks for British assistance against the Nazis.

In 1820, John Nash laid out the first plans for Trafalgar, but it took almost 50 years for the square to assume its current appearance. 51m **Nelson's Column,** a monument to naval hero Lord Nelson, arrived in 1843, while the larger-than-life lions were added in 1867. Four granite relief panels at the column's base were cast from captured French and Spanish cannons and to commemorate Nelson's victories at Cape St. Vincent, Copenhagen, the Nile, and Trafalgar. Meanwhile, to prove that the English can also be gracious losers, **George Washington** keeps watch in the east corner. Upon leaving England, Washington vowed never to set foot on English soil again, so the small plot of soil underneath his statue was brought over from the US. The statue of **George IV** in the northeastern corner was originally intended to top the Marble Arch but never made it. A sculpture of William IV was supposed to reign over the eastern corner, but was never built due to funding problems. Since 1999, modern pieces have occupied the corner, such as the Marc Quinn sculpture that has staked its claim since 2005. South of the square, a rare equestrian monument to **Charles I** stands on the site of the original Charing Cross. The statue escaped Cromwell's wrath when John Rivett bought it "for scrap" and did a roaring trade in souvenirs supposedly made from the figure. It was, in fact, hidden and later sold for a tidy profit to Charles II, who re-erected it in 1633. *(⊖Charing Cross or Leicester Sq.)*

CARLTON HOUSE TERRACE AND WATERLOO PLACE. Sweeping down from Piccadilly Circus, Regent St. comes to an abrupt halt at Waterloo Place, where steps lead to the Mall. Regent St. was built to be a triumphal route leading to the Prince Regent's residence at Carlton House, but by the time it was finished, the then-prince King George IV had moved on to Buckingham Palace. The aging royal architect John Nash was recommissioned to build something quickly on the site, and the result was Carlton House Terrace, a pair of imposing classical buildings that currently house the **Institute of Contemporary Arts**. Between the two Carlton House Terrace buildings, a statue of King Edward VII is dwarfed by a vast column topped with George IV's screw-up younger brother the "Grand Old" Duke of York, who docked his men's salaries in order to pay for the monument. The column's great height led many of the Duke's contemporaries to joke that he would climb it in order to flee his equally imposing debts.

Meanwhile, Waterloo remains steeped in tradition: on the west corner, the **Athenaeum Club,** England's most famous gentleman's club (think cigars and brandy, not strippers), has a 60-year waiting list. Around the corner is the **Carlton Club,** the conservative party's clubhouse; in 1979, the Club suffered a dilemma when two of its traditions—it males-only membership policy, and its admittance of all conservative leaders—collided with the nomination of Margaret Thatcher. The Club solved this problem by rather plausibly pretending that Margaret was a man. *(⊖Piccadilly Circus.)*

SAINT JAMES'S PALACE. Built in 1536 over the remains of a leper hospital, St. James's is London's only remaining intentionally-built palace; even Buckingham Palace was a rough-and-ready conversion of a Duke's house. Ever since Henry VIII chose it to be the site of the royal court, the palace has been London's most aristocratic address; foreign ambassadors to Britain are still officially called "Ambassadors to the Court of St. James." The official home of the Crown, St. James's current occupants include Prince Charles; the late Queen Mum lived in neighboring **Clarence House.** Royal proclamations are issued every Friday from St. James's balcony in the interior **Friary Court,** where the first announcement of the accession of a new monarch is made. The only part of the palace usually accessible to the public, however, is the **Chapel Royal,** open for Sunday services from October to Easter at 8:30 and 11:15am. From Easter to July, services are held in **Queen's Chapel,** across Marlborough Rd. from the palace, which was built in the 17th century for the marriage of Charles I. *(Best accessed from St. James's St. ⊖Green Park.)*

SAINT JAMES'S CHURCH, PICCADILLY. Poet William Blake was baptized in this church, the exterior of which is now darkened from the soot of London's mills. The current structure is largely a post-WWII reconstruction of what Sir Christopher Wren considered his greatest parish church; the original wooden flowers, garlands, and cherubs by master carver Grinling Gibbons managed to escape the Blitz. The churchyard is home to a cafe and a touristy craft market that sells antiques on Tuesdays. *(Enter at 197 Piccadilly or on Jermyn St. ⊖Piccadilly Circus or Green Park. ☎020 7734 4511; www.st-james-piccadilly.org. Church open M-Sa 9am-6:30pm, Su 1-4:30pm. Market open Tu 8am-6pm, W-Sa 10am-6pm. Cafe open M-F 7am-7:30pm, Sa 9am-7:30pm, Su 9am-6:30pm. Free.)*

SHEPHERD MARKET. This pedestrian area on the southern border of St. James's occupies the site of the May Fair that gave the neighborhood its name. In 1706, the infamously raucous fair was closed until native architect Edward Shepherd developed the area as a market later in the century. Today the tucked-away neighborhood is pleasantly abuzz at all hours, its 18th-century buildings housing pubs, restaurants, shops, and art galleries. *(⊖Hyde Park Corner or Green Park.)*

GROSVENOR SQUARE. One of the largest squares in central London, Grosvenor has gradually evolved into a North American diplomatic enclave, alongside its more popular role as a warm-weather picnic spot. John Adams lived at No. 9 while serving as the first US ambassador to England in 1785; a century and a half later, Dwight Eisenhower established his wartime headquarters at No. 20; today, the American Embassy towers at No. 1. At the eastern end of the square stands a garden memorial to the victims of September 11, while a monument to FDR is at the center of the park, across from a memorial pillar to the Eagel Squadron of WWII. *(⊖Bond St. or Marble Arch.)*

SPENCER HOUSE. At the end of a quiet, unassuming street near St. James's Palace lies the entrance to one of the finest 18th-century townhouses left in London. The home was built by the first Earl Spencer, Princess Diana's ancestor. The Spencer family kept the house as their London residence until 1926, after which it was used by the British intelligence service. Many of the finest rooms have been recently restored and are now rented out for private parties and receptions; they are open to the public only on Sundays. Though the required tour (1hr.) is overly detailed, the interiors are stunning and provide an excellent glimpse into the Spencer family's early history as well as 18th-century society at large. *(Enter at 27 St. James Place. ⊖Green Park. ☎020 7514 1958. Open Su 10:30am-5:30pm. £9, students £7.)*

SOHO

Soho is a place to be experienced, not toured. An extravaganza of trendy bars, cafes, restaurants, and shops, Soho is many things to many people. A concentration of gay-owned restaurants and bars has turned **Old Compton Street** into the heart of GLBT London, and a seemingly endless assortment of theaters and clubs around **Theatreland** keeps night owls of all persuasions entertained. **Berwick Street,** a remnant of Soho's seedy past, is now the nexus of the area's sex trade and plays host to a number of edgy music shops. **Carnaby** and **Kingly Court** form a shopping mecca, while the cafes around **Dean Street** are steeped in literary and music history. Media types and celebrities regularly visit the area, along with throngs of tourists looking for a wild night out.

CHINATOWN. It wasn't until the 1950s that immigrants from Hong Kong began moving en masse to the blocks just north of Leicester Square. Tiny and contained, this area is pleasant for a stroll or a dim sum brunch. Pedestrian-heavy **Gerrard Street**, with scroll-worked dragon gates and pagoda-capped phone booths, is the self-proclaimed center of this tiny slice of Canton. Grittier **Lisle Street,** one block to the south, is more authentic and less claustrophobic, with numerous specialty markets, bookshops, and craft stores to complement the food. The neighborhood is most exciting during the mid-Autumn Festival at the end of September and the raucous **Chinese New Year Festival** in February. *(Between Leicester Sq., Shaftesbury Ave., and Charing Cross Rd. ⊖Leicester Sq. or Piccadilly Circus.)*

SOHO SQUARE. First laid out in 1681, Soho Square is a rather unrefined hunk of grass popular for picnics and work breaks. Its removed location makes the square more hospitable and much less trafficked than its big brother, Leicester. Paul McCartney has his business headquarters at No. 1. Look for the quint-

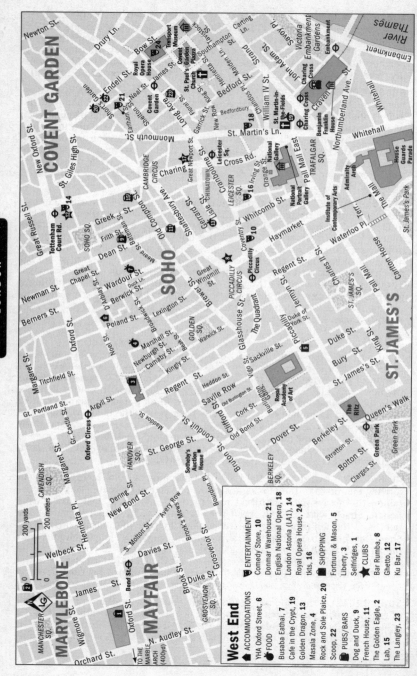

essential Twentieth Century Fox sign atop 31-32. Two monuments to Soho's cosmopolitan past border the square: London's only **French Protestant Church,** founded in 1550, and **St. Patrick's Catholic Church,** long the focal point of Soho's Irish and Italian communities. The petite, strange-looking mock-Tudor building in the center of the square is actually a Victorian garden shed that has never been removed. (⊖*Tottenham Court Rd. Park open daily 10am-dusk.*)

PICCADILLY CIRCUS. Piccadilly Circus is composed of four of the West End's major arteries: Piccadilly, Regent St., Shaftesbury Ave., and the Haymarket. It is the definition of touristy chaos, with all its excitement and hilarity. In the middle of all the glitz, kitsch, and neon stands the famous **Statue of Eros:** dedicated to the Victorian philanthropist Lord Shaftesbury, Eros was actually meant to be an "Angel of Christian Charity," but the aluminum figure has never been known as such. The archer originally pointed his bow and arrow down Shaftesbury Ave., but recent restoration work has put his aim significantly off. Behind Eros stands **Lillywhites,** the sports store giant, while **Ripley's Believe It Or Not! Museum** and **Trocadero,** the cheezy Paris-based arcade, stand on the northeast corner. (⊖*Piccadilly Circus.*)

LEICESTER SQUARE. A patch of greenery that is better for performance and protest than for pleasant relaxation, Leicester Square is lined with fast-food restaurants, tour buses, and London's most massive cinema. The Swiss Centre glockenspiel renders everything from pop songs to Beethoven's *Moonlight Sonata* in amusing, even if not quite in-tune, fashion. Get a henna tattoo, sit for a caricature, or enjoy one of the many preachers and performers. (*Glockenspiel rings M-F at noon, 6, 7, 8pm; Sa-Su noon, 2, 4, 5, 6, 7, 8pm.* ⊖*Piccadilly Circus or Leicester Sq.*)

SWEPT OFF YOUR FEET. If you'd rather not explore Soho on foot, flag down a pedicab driver to cart you around. Rickshaws congregate at various points around the West End, but the most popular pickup spot is the corner of Firth St. and Old Compton St. Short spins around Soho £3-4 per person; longer trips £5 per person per mi. 2 full-sized people per rickshaw. Agree on a price before you go. Available M-Th and Su 6pm-1am, F-Sa 6pm-4am.

COVENT GARDEN AND THE STRAND

Though it lacks the greenery suggested by its name, there are still plenty of reasons to come to Covent Garden, which retains its charm even as its shops become more mainstream. A central **piazza** hosts not only shops but markets and cafes—holdovers from the square's former role as London's main vegetable market (begun in medieval times, when it was just another "convent garden"). It was only in 1974 that the traders transferred to more spacious premises south of the river. On the very spot where Samuel Pepys saw the first "Punch and Judy" show in England 350 years ago, street performers entertain the hordes who flock here year-round, rain or shine.

Along Covent Garden's southern edge is the **Strand,** a busy road that is perhaps London's oldest, predating the Romans. Originally a riverside track, shifting watercourses and Victorian engineering dried it out. Now, several narrow passageways lead down to the Thames. As the main thoroughfare between Westminster and the City, it remains as busy as ever. Nearby street names are the only reminders of the many palaces that once made it London's most prestigious address: **Villiers Street** recalls George Villiers, while **Essex Street** honors Robert Devereux, Earl of Essex, Elizabeth I's favorite until she decided to cut his head off.

LONDON

THIS WAY, PLEASE. Since Covent Garden is an extremely popular destination in the city, its Tube station can be overcrowded during peak hours. An alternate route goes through Holborn or Leicester Sq., with signs posted to direct diverted travelers.

SAINT MARTIN-IN-THE-FIELDS. Though well-known for its history, the church has this past year become a must-see because of a striking new ▓window. Designed by Iranian Shirazeh Houshiary, the window shows the rippled image of a cross. The rest of the building is a 1726 James Gibbs creation: the rectangular portico supporting a soaring steeple served as a model for countless Georgian churches in Ireland and America. The front of the church sports Corinthian columns and George I's coat of arms, the church's first warden. St. Martin-in-the-Fields remains in the Queen's parish; look for the royal box above and to the left of the altar. Handel and Mozart both performed here, and the church hosts frequent concerts (see **Entertainment,** p. 160). In order to support the cost of keeping the church open, there is a **daily market** outside as well as a surprisingly extensive bookshop, a delicious cafe, and an art gallery in the crypt. The popular **London Brass Rubbing Centre** also is housed in undercroft, where you can create charcoal and pastel impressions of medieval brass plates as souvenirs. *(St. Martin's Ln., northeast corner of Trafalgar Sq.; crypt entrance on Duncannon St. ⊖ Leicester Sq. or Charing Cross. ☎ 020 7766 1100; www.smitf.org. Call or visit website for hours and further information.)*

ROYAL OPERA HOUSE. This house is home to the prestigious **Royal Opera, Royal Ballet,** and **ROH Orchestra.** The ROH's rehearsal studios and workshops are now behind the piazza's boutique-lined colonnade. It's worth a wander into the ornate lobby of the original 1858 theater and the impressive, glass-roofed Hamlyn Hall. From there, the escalator leads to a cafe, restaurant, and terrace overlooking the piazza. With occasional cheap concession tickets and free lunchtime concerts on some Monday afternoons, ROH is better attended for a performance than for a tour. *(Enter on Bow St. or through the northeast corner of the piazza. ⊖ Covent Garden. ☎ 020 7304 4000; www.roh.org.uk. Opera house, cafe, and restaurant open M-Sa 10am-3:30pm. Box office open M-Sa 10am-8pm. 75-90min. backstage tours M-F 10:30am, 12:30, 2:30pm; Sa 10:30, 11:30am, 12:30, 1:30pm except during daytime performances; reservations recommended. Wheelchair-accessible. Tours £8, students £7. Register online for student standbys. AmEx/MC/V.)*

SAINT PAUL'S. Not to be confused with St. Paul's Cathedral, this 1633 Inigo Jones church is now the sole remnant of the original square. A dearth of funds begot its simplicity: the Earl of Bedford instructed the architect to make it "not much better than a barn." Known as "the actors' church" for its long association with nearby theaters, the interior is festooned with plaques commemorating the achievements of such greats as Boris Karloff, Vivien Leigh, and Charlie Chaplin. Musical lovers take note: W.S. Gilbert (of Gilbert and Sullivan) was baptized here and George Bernard Shaw set the opening of *Pygmalion* (later remade as *My Fair Lady*) under St. Paul's front portico. To enter the church, first pass through the peaceful churchyard, where award-winning gardens provide a welcome shelter from the bustle of the surrounding streets. *(On Covent Garden Piazza; enter via the Piazza, King St., Henrietta St., or Bedford St. ⊖ Covent Garden. ☎ 020 7836 5221; www.actorschurch.org. Open M-F 8:30am-5:30pm. Morning prayer M-F 8:30am. Morning services Su 11am. Evensong 2nd Su of month 4pm. Free.)*

SAVOY. Considered the "fairest manor in all England," John of Gaunt's great Palace of Savoy was destroyed by a peasant revolt in 1381. Five hundred years later, the D'Oyly Carte Opera Company took its chances and moved into a newly constructed **Savoy Theatre,** the first in the world to be lit entirely by electricity. Managed by César Ritz, it is every bit as decadent as the Palace that once stood on the site, though today the building's elegance is partially obscured by ongoing construction. Despite it all, Savoy's grand foyer remains second only to the Ritz in popularity for afternoon tea (although not as good a value). Be careful as you cross the Savoy driveway: this short, narrow road is the only street in the UK where people drive on the right, a historical relic meant to ensure that chauffeured women riding behind their drivers (on the right) could exit cars easily onto the sidewalk. (⊖*Charing Cross. Walk 5min. east of the station on the south side of the Strand.)*

SEVEN DIALS. The radial configuration of six streets is a rare remnant of 16th-century town planning. Thomas Neale commissioned the central pillar in 1694, with one sundial facing each street; the seventh dial is the column itself. While the original was pulled down in 1773 to rid the area of the "undesirables" who congregated around it, a 1989 replica attracts all types, from lingering shoppers and busy businessmen to those simply trying to avoid the oncoming traffic. It tells the correct time to within 10 seconds—if you can figure out how to read it. *(Intersection of Monmouth, Earlham, and Mercer St. ⊖Covent Garden or Leicester Sq.)*

CHARING CROSS. Currently under construction, the tiered Gothic monument standing outside Charing Cross was the last of the 12 crosses erected by Edward I in 1290 to mark the passage of his wife's funeral procession (the cross itself is actually named "Eleanor's Cross"). The original was destroyed by Oliver Cromwell in 1647; the latest monument is a 19th-century replica. The first Cross stood on the spot now occupied by Charles I's statue in Trafalgar Square; its new location is the point from which all road distances to and from the city are measured. *(⊖Charing Cross.)*

CLEOPATRA'S NEEDLE. The oldest monument in London, this Egyptian obelisk, now oddly located on the side of the Thames, was first erected in Heliopolis in 1475 BC, making it some 1400 years older than Cleo herself. The Turkish Viceroy of Egypt presented it to Britain in 1819 in recognition of their help in booting Napoleon out of Africa. Shipped in 1877, the needle was almost lost when the ship sank en route, but a salvage operation recovered the obelisk and it was re-erected in 1879. Underneath the foundation is a Victorian time capsule containing a railway guide, several Bibles, and pictures of the 12 prettiest British women of the day. The scars at the needle's base and on the sphinx were left by the first bomb raid on London by German Zeppelins in 1917. *(North bank of the Thames between Hungerford and Waterloo Bridges. ⊖Charing Cross or Temple.)*

BLOOMSBURY

Home to both University College—London's first university—and the British Museum, Bloomsbury has long been the stomping ground of egg-heads and aspiring intellectuals. Farther down, **Bedford Square** is the only square in the city whose original Georgian buildings are all still standing. The student landscape around **Gower Street** is dotted with tourists, but the area's high concentration of academic and artistic institutions preserves its cerebral air. Scads of leafy green squares and gardens offer perfect spots for contemplation (or dozing). The somewhat gritty area around **King's Cross** and **Saint Pancras** is barely considered part of Bloomsbury (it's the border with North London), but it is home to the British Library.

BRITISH LIBRARY. Castigated during its long construction by traditionalists for being too modern and by modernists for being too traditional, the new

British Library building (opened in 1998) now impresses all nay-sayers with its stunning interior. The heart of the library is underground, with 12 million books on 200 miles of shelving; the above-ground brick building is home to cavernous reading rooms and an engrossing ▨**Museum**. Displayed in a glass cube toward the rear of the building, the 65,000 volumes of the King's Library were collected by George III and bequeathed to the nation in 1823 by his less bookish son, George IV. The sunken plaza out front features an enormous and somewhat strange statue of Newton, and also hosts a series of free concerts and events; its restaurant, cafes, and coffee bars are over-priced. *(96 Euston Rd. ⊖Euston Sq. or King's Cross St. Pancras. ☎020 7412 7332; www.bl.uk. Open M 9:30am-6pm, Tu 9:30am-8pm, W-F 9:30am-6pm, Sa 9:30am-5pm, Su 11am-5pm. Tours of public areas M, W, F 3pm; Sa 10:30am and 3pm. Tours including one of the reading rooms Su and bank holidays 11:30am and 3pm. Reservations recommended. Wheelchair-accessible. To use reading rooms, bring 2 forms of ID—1 with a signature and 1 with a home address. Free. Tours £8, concessions £6.50. Audio tours £3.50, concessions £2.50.)*

UNIVERSITY COLLEGE LONDON. Established in 1828 to provide an education to those rejected from Oxford and Cambridge, UCL was the first in Britain to ignore gender, race, creed, and politics in admissions. A co-founder and key advisor of the college, social philosopher **Jeremy Bentham**, still watches over his old haunts—per his will, his dressed skeleton has been on display in the South Cloister since 1850. Right now, Bentham has a wax head, but the original used to be propped between his feet until students staged regular attempts to steal it. At the southern end of Malet Street, the sight of UCL's massive central administrative building, **Senate House**, housed the BBC propaganda unit during WWII; George Orwell used his experiences there as inspiration for the "Ministry of Truth" in *1984*. *(Main entrance on Gower St. South Cloister entrance through the courtyard, in the back right corner. ⊖Euston. ☎020 7679 2000; www.ucl.ac.uk. Quadrangle gates close at midnight; access to Jeremy Bentham ends at 6pm. Wheelchair-accessible. Free.)*

SAINT PANCRAS STATION. Most visitors assume that the low concourse west of Midland Rd. is a railway station, and the soaring Gothic spires to the east are the British Library. In fact, the opposite is true: this Victorian extravaganza is the facade of St. Pancras Station, whose massive 1868 train shed was once the largest undivided indoor area in the world. *(Euston Rd. just west of the King's Cross St. Pancras Tube station. ⊖King's Cross St. Pancras.)*

SAINT GEORGE'S BLOOMSBURY. Time, the Blitz, and general disrepair took their toll on this 1730 Hawksmoor church—the last of its kind—but a £1 million restoration project brought it back to its former glory. The interior—the setting of Dickens's *Bloomsbury Christening*—offers an unusual flat ceiling undecorated except for a central plaster rose. The church's most unusual feature is its stepped spire, which is based on the ancient Mausoleum of Halikarnassos (one of the seven Wonders of the Ancient World, partially on display at the British Museum) and topped by a statue of George I. The restoration brought back the "beasts of Bloomsbury": the magnificent 10 ft. lions and unicorns that originally stood at George's feet. *(Bloomsbury Way, across from no. 2-12. ⊖Russell Sq. ☎020 7405 3044; www.stgeorgesbloomsbury.org.uk. Open daily 1-4pm when volunteers are present; guided tours by appointment.)*

NORTH LONDON

CAMDEN TOWN, KING'S CROSS, AND ISLINGTON

As North London becomes increasingly affluent, those in search of a slice of tawdriness come to Camden Town. The central Camden area, between Camden

Town and Chalk Farm, has thrown off attempts at gentrification thanks to the numerous street markets, now among London's most popular attractions.

SAINT PANCRAS OLD CHURCH. The first church on this site was reputedly founded by Roman legionaries in AD 314 for early Christian worship and became the first parish in London. The present building, though, dates from the 13th century—some of the Norman masonry is visible on the north wall of the nave. Don't miss the sixth-century altar stone, rumored to have belonged to St. Augustine of Canterbury. In the large and lovely churchyard is **Sir John Soanes's mausoleum** and the **Hardy Tree,** designed by a young Thomas Hardy long before he became a writer. It features hundreds of tightly clustered headstones that seem to spring from the roots. *(St. Pancras Rd. ⊖Mornington Crescent. ☎020 7424 0724. Wheelchair-accessible. Prayer services M-F 9am. Mass M 9:30am, Tu 7pm, Su 9:30am. Free.)*

SAINT JOHN'S WOOD AND MAIDA VALE

LORD'S CRICKET GROUND. The most famous cricket ground in England, Lord's is home to the local Marylebone Cricket Club (MCC) and hosts most of London's international matches. To see the Lord's Museum (home to the Ashes Urn as well as all the cricket-related memorabilia you could ever dream of) attend a match or take a 2hr. tour led by a senior club member. Included in the tours are the MCC members' Long Room, the ground, stands, and the striking space-age **NatWest Media Center.** On game days, tours after 10am skip the Long Room and media center, though visitors get a discount on game tickets as compensation (no tours during international test matches). Games take place on most summer days. *(10min. walk from ⊖St. John's Wood. Enter at Grace Gate, on St. John's Wood Rd. ☎020 7432 1000; www.lords.org.uk. Tours daily Oct.-Mar. noon and 2pm; Apr.-Sept. 10am, noon, 2pm. Wheelchair-accessible. Tours £10, concessions £7, children under 16 £6, families £27.)*

ABBEY ROAD. Don't worry, the traffic's used to slowing for the obligatory photo-op at the crosswalk where Abbey Rd. comes together with Grove End Rd. Stop to read the adulatory graffiti on the nearby street signs and walls—fans from all over the world have left marks here. Next to the crossing, the **Abbey Road Studios** (3 Abbey Rd.), where the Beatles made most of their recordings, are closed to the public but still in business. *(⊖St. John's Wood.)*

MARYLEBONE AND REGENT'S PARK

▧REGENT'S PARK

When Crown Architect John Nash designed Regent's Park, he envisioned a private residential development for the "wealthy and good." Fortunately for the rest of us, Parliament opened the space to the public in 1811, creating London's most popular and attractive recreational area. With 500 acres of jogging trails, football and cricket-scarred fields, lush gardens, and seven cafes, Regent's Park offers a range of not-to-be-missed sunny-day diversions.

▧GARDENS OF SAINT JOHN'S LODGE. While the two private villas in the park, Holme and St. John's Lodge, are owned by the unimaginably rich and closed to public viewing, these formal gardens, on the northern edge of the Inner Circle, provide a peek into the backyard of one such mansion, and look like something straight out of *The Secret Garden.*

THE INNER CIRCLE. You'll find that most attractions center on this road, which separates the regal, meticulously maintained ▧**Queen Mary's Gardens** from the rest of the grounds. Its **Rose Garden** and the chiseled subject of **Triton Fountain** are worth a visit, while the well-received **Open-Air Theatre** in the northwest quadrant provides fabulous summer entertainment.

BOATING LAKE AND THE CHILDREN'S BOATING LAKE. Around the Inner Circle, these lakes are home to rowboats and children's pedaloos. *(Open daily Apr.-Sept. 10:30am-5pm, July-Aug. closes later. Rowboats £4.50 for 30min., £6 for 1hr.; under 14 £3/4; £5 deposit. Pedaloos £3 for 20min. Discounts before 1pm. Under 16 with adult only. MC/V.)*

REGENT'S PARK TENNIS CENTRE. On the southeast side of the park, these courts can be booked year-round.*(☎020 7486 4216; www.tennisintheparks.co.uk. 1hr. non-member court use £7-9. 24hr. advance reservations required.)*

OTHER SIGHTS IN REGENT'S PARK. The **London Central Mosque** is also open to the public, while **Primrose Hill**, just north of Regent's Park proper, offers an impressive panoramic view of central London. The large red-brick complex of **Regent's College** lies south of Inner Circle, and neo-Georgian **Winfield House**, the private residence of the US ambassador, occupies 12½ acres in the northwest. *(❻Baker St., Regent's Park, Great Portland St., or Camden Town. ☎020 7486 7905; www.royalparks.org.uk/parks/regents_park. Open daily 5am-dusk. Free.)*

TO SIT OR NOT TO SIT. The oh-so-tempting desk chairs scattered through Regent's Park come with a price: £2 per 4hr. For a picturesque perch without a fee, head to the benches in the circular garden near the Inner Circle's eastern entrance.

OTHER SIGHTS

LONDON ZOO. First opened in 1826, the London Zoo has a range of modern exhibits as well as a few less current bars-and-cement enclosures. Either way, the diversity of its animal residents, which range from flamingos and pygmy hippos to African and Australian natives, is impressive for a city zoo. Perennial favorites include the itch-inducing corridors of BUGS!, the jungle-like primate house, and the komodo dragon exhibit. For up-close-and-personal interaction, head to Meet the Monkeys, an enclosed area where guests and playful squirrel monkeys can mingle. *(Main gate on Outer Circle, Regent's Park. ❻Camden Town plus a 10-15min. walk guided by signs or a short ride on Bus #274. ☎020 7722 3333; www.zsl.org. Open daily from Apr. to mid-July and from Sept. to mid-Oct. 10am-5:30pm; from mid-July to Aug. 10am-6pm; from mid-Oct. to late Oct. 10am-4:30pm; Nov.-Mar. 10am-4pm. Last entry 1hr. before closing. Wheelchair-accessible. £17, children 3-15 £13, students £15. AmEx/MC/V.)*

MADAME TUSSAUD'S. For those unwilling to pass up a £30 photo op with wax models of top celebs. *(Marylebone Rd. ❻Baker St. ☎0870 999 0293; www.madame-tussauds.com. Open Jan.-June and Sept.-Dec. M-F 9:30am-5:30pm, Sa-Su 9am-6pm; from mid-Feb. to late Feb., from early Apr. to mid-Apr., from mid-Oct. to late Oct., and from mid-Dec. to late Dec. daily 9am-6pm; from late Jul. to Aug. daily 9am-7pm. Wheelchair-accessible. Prices depend on day of the week, entrance time, package, and season. £23-40, under 16 £19-30. "Chamber Live" exhibit £2 extra. Advance booking by phone or online £2 extra; groups of more than 10 save approx. £1.50 per person. AmEx/MC/V.)*

PORTLAND PLACE. One of the most architecturally well-endowed streets in London, Portland Place was first laid out by Robert and James Adam in the 18th century. Today its draw lies in the great variety of building styles on display: design buffs will enjoy it, but others might not be overly dazzled. The street is the perfect home for the **Royal Institute of British Architects** (RIBA), whose 1932 headquarters is especially spectacular at night, when the Egyptian-inspired facade is lit with an eye-catching pink. Parts of the building are open to the public, including three exhibition galleries, an impressive architecture bookshop, and a cafe. *(66 Portland Pl. ❻Oxford Circus or Regent's Park. ☎020 7580 5533; www.architecture.com. Exhibits open M and W-Sa 9am-5pm, Tu 9am-9pm. Wheelchair-accessible.*

Free.) Guarding the entrance to Portland Place from Regent Street, the curved facade of the **British Broadcasting Center** is instantly recognizable to all Britons and remains the company's main center for radio production. On the facade is Eric Gill's sculpture of Shakespeare's Prospero and Ariel, together with the BBC motto, "Nation Shall Speak Peace Unto Nation." *(☎020 7580 3522; www.all-souls.org. Open M-F 9:30am-6pm, Su 9am-6:30pm.)*

HAMPSTEAD, HIGHGATE, AND GOLDERS GREEN

Home to the sprawling **Hampstead Heath**, Hampstead and Highgate is a great destination for a green getaway from central London. Above them, in a little corner of North London, **Golders Green** is the center of the city's Jewish community, with delicious specialty delis, excellent kosher restaurants, and Hebrew bookstores. **Golders Hill Park**—a western extension of Hampstead Heath—is the heart of the area.

HAMPSTEAD HEATH. Hampstead Heath is one of the last remaining traditional commons in England, open to all since at least 1312—thanks to the local residents, who successfully fought off attempts to develop it in the 19th century. Since Parliament declared in 1871 that the Heath should remain "forever open, un-enclosed, and un-built-upon," it has grown from 336 to 804 acres. Its imposing size can be daunting, but just spending a few hours enjoying the expansive, meadow-like green can be a lovely break from the city. Unlike so many other London parks, the Heath is not composed of manicured gardens and paths but rather of wild, spontaneous growth tumbling over rolling pastures and forested groves—perfect for picnicking. Dirt paths through the Heath are not well marked, but maps abound on the premise. On public holidays in spring and summer, fun fairs are held at South End Green and on the south side of Spaniards Rd. *(❸Hampstead. Rail: Hampstead Heath. Bus #210. Wheelchair-accessible. Open 24hr.)*

> **TIP** **SNAP THAT MAP.** If you have a digital camera, you might want to take a picture of one of the park maps and use it as a map along your hike.

HILL GARDEN. In this secret garden of sorts, a raised pergola bedecked in flowers of all sorts, passes over the former kitchen gardens of Lord Leverhulme's (founder of Lever Soap) mansion. The walkway was built to connect the mansion to his pleasure gardens. Sunsets here are spectacular. *(In Hampstead Heath; take North End Way to Inverforth Close. Open daily 8:30am-1hr. before sunset.)*

PARLIAMENT HILL. Legend claims that Guy Fawkes and his accomplices planned to watch their destruction of Parliament from atop Parliament Hill in 1605, but things didn't work out that way. The hike to the top takes you to sprawling fields and a vista that stretches to Westminster and beyond. At the foot of the hill, a series of ponds marks the final gasp of the River Westbourne before it vanishes into the Thames. The brave can swim for free in the waters of the single-sex bathing ponds, where some bathers choose to go nude. *(The southeastern part of the Heath; enter off of Downshire Rd. Rail: Gospel Oak or Hampstead Heath.)*

GOLDERS GREEN CREMATORIUM. Though visiting a crematorium may seem grim, don't let the Neo-Romanesque chapel buildings scare you. Behind them lie several acres of picturesque, beautifully maintained gardens; paths wander through leafy groves, water gardens, and open lawns. Each flower serves as a living grave for an individual; luminaries who came to rest here include T. S. Eliot, H. G. Wells, Peter Sellers, and five prime ministers. Sigmund Freud's ashes, in his favorite Greek vase, are locked in the Ernest George Columbarium; ask an attendant to let you in on weekdays. *(From ⊖Golders Green, turn right out of the exit, follow Finchley Rd. under the bridge, and continue for 5min. before turning right on Hoope Ln.; entrance is on the right. ☎020 8455 2374. Wheelchair-accessible. Grounds open daily in summer 9am-6pm; in winter 9am-4pm. Chapel and Hall of Memory open daily 9am-4pm. Free.)*

TWO WILLOW ROAD. Resembling an unimposing 1950s-style mini-block, Two Willow Road was actually built in 1939 as the avant-garde home of architect Ernö Goldfinger (Ian Fleming hated the design so much he named a James Bond villain after him). It stands apart quite visibly from the quaint Victorian facades that line the rest of the street. With clothes still in their plastic dry-cleaning sleeves, everything looks as if the family had just left. Family photos on the mantelpiece sit next to works of art by Max Ernst, Marchel Duchamp, Man Ray, and Goldfinger's wife, Ursula Blackwell. *(15min. walk from ⊖Hampstead; the best way is to take Hampstead High St. to Downshire Rd. and take a left. ☎020 7435 6166. Open Apr.-Oct. Th-F noon-5pm, Sa 11am-5pm. Timed ticket and 1hr. guided tours available Th-F at noon, 1, 2pm; Sa 11am, noon, 1, 2pm. £5.30, children £2.80, families £13.)*

KEATS HOUSE. The great Romantic poet John Keats produced some of his last and finest work, including "Ode to a Nightingale" in this house. Both the gardens and the house are lovely, although few original furnishings remain. A sparse recreation of its 1820 appearance (recently renovated in 2009), the current space is distinguished due to its literary history. Inside, copies of Keats's poems lie scattered about the well-kept rooms, together with Keats memorabilia and informative biographical displays. *(Keats Grove. ⊖Hampstead. ☎020 7435 2062; www.keatshouse.org.uk. Partially wheelchair-accessible. Closed as of summer 2009; call ahead.)*

KENSINGTON AND EARL'S COURT

Nobody took much notice of Kensington before 1689. But when newly crowned William III and Mary II decided to move into Kensington Palace following the Glorious Revolution of 1688, high society soon followed. Although today the area continues to be associated with the elite—from Queen Victoria's husband Albert (of "Albertopolis") to Princess Di—Kensington is also the center of national art, science, and culture. Not to be outdone by Paris's self-congratulatory exhibitions of French arts and industry in 1849, Prince Albert proposed to hold a bigger and better "Exhibition of All Nations" in London. Opened in Hyde Park in 1851, the Great Exhibition was housed in the Crystal Palace—a gigantic iron-and-glass structure 1848 ft. long, 408 ft. wide, and tall enough to enclose mature trees—and by the time it was dismantled a year later, six million people had passed through it and £200,000 had been raised. At Albert's suggestion, the money was used to buy 86 acres of land in South Kensington for institutions promoting British arts and sciences. Today, his vision has probably surpassed even his wildest dreams: on this land stands not only the quartet of the Royal Albert Hall (p. 135), Victoria and Albert Museum (p. 156), Science Museum (p. 158), and Natural History Museum (p. 158) but also the Royal College of Music, the Royal College of Art, and the Imperial College of Science and Technology, all world-renowned institutions in their respective fields. He might also be surprised to learn that "Albertopolis" is also known as "Coleville" after Sir Henry Cole, the man who actually implemented all of Albert's ideas after the Prince's untimely death in 1861. *(Kensington is roughly bound by Hyde Park to the north, Exhibition Rd. to the east, Cromwell Rd. to the south, and Queen's Gate to the west. ⊖South Kensington or High St. Kensington.)*

Blending into the neighborhood's southwestern corner, Earl's Court is a grimier, character-rich district still known by its nickname—"Kangaroo Valley"—an 80s-era testament to its popularity with Australian expats. The site of London's original gay village, the area also boasts a decent gay nightlife scene, though Soho is the clear favorite.

HYDE PARK AND KENSINGTON GARDENS

Framed by Kensington Rd., Knightsbridge, Park Ln., and Bayswater Rd. ⊖Queensway, Lancaster Gate, Marble Arch, Hyde Park Corner, or High St. Kensington. ☎020 7298 2100; www.royalparks.org.uk. Park open daily 6am-dusk. Free. "Liberty Drive" rides available Tu-F 10am-5pm for seniors and the disabled; ☎077 6749 8096. A full program of music, performance, and children's activities takes place during the summer; see park notice boards for details.

Surrounded by London's wealthiest neighborhoods, Hyde Park has served as the model for city parks around the world, including Central Park in New York and Paris's Bois de Boulogne. Henry VIII stole the land from Westminster Abbey in 1536, and James I opened it to the public in 1637—the first royal park to be the product of theft. During an outbreak of the plague in 1665, terrified inhabitants of the city camped out here for a year in an attempt to quarantine themselves. It's still the largest public space in central London, and the expansive grounds continue to be popular with tourists and locals. Kensington Gardens, originally part of Hyde Park and effectually still so, was created in the late 17th century when William and Mary set up house in Kensington Palace. In both parks, warm days attract swarms of sunbathers, along with people tossing frisbees, cycling, in-line skating, playing football, and horseback riding. A number of cafes and restaurants make a full day in the park easy— try **the Dell** or **the Lido**. *(Dell on the eastern side of the Serpentine. ⊖Hyde Park Corner. ☎020 7706 0464. Open daily in summer 9am-8pm; in winter 9am-4pm. Lido on the southern side of the Serpentine. ⊖Hyde Park Corner. ☎020 7706 7098. Open daily in summer 9am-8pm; in winter 9am-4pm.)*

THE SERPENTINE. Officially known as the "Long Water West of the Serpentine Bridge," that's... just what it is. The snaking, 41-acre body of water was created in 1730 as decoration, but today it's actually used quite a bit: dog-paddling tourists, rowers, and pedal boaters make it London's busiest swimming hole. Nowhere near the water, its namesake **Serpentine Gallery** (p. 159) is a leader in contemporary art. *(⊖Hyde Park Corner. Boating: ☎020 7262 1330. Open Apr.-Sept. daily 10am-5pm or later in fine weather. £5 per 30min., £7 per hr.; children £2/3. Deposit may be required for large groups. Swimming at the Lido, south shore: ☎020 7706 3422. Open from June to early Sept. daily 10am-5:30pm. Lockers and sun lounges available. £4, after 4pm £3; students £3/2; children 1p/80p; families £9. Gallery open daily 10am-5pm. Free.)*

TREE HUGGING

All across London, things are getting a little leafier. Through a new sidewalk-planting program, Conservative Mayor Boris Johnson hopes to add 10,000 trees to the city's streets; in the first year of his term alone, some 1500 new trees were planted. This greenery should certainly help liven up London's urban landscape, which distinctly lacks trees in certain areas; according to some estimates, nearly two million people in London live more than a kilometer away from any nature.

The program works on a voluntary basis: Londoners in "priority areas" register to have a tree planted outside their home. In May 2009, there were half a million residents eligible to sign up for a new tree. Meanwhile, the nonprofit organization Trees for Cities has begun a fundraising campaign to add another 37,000 trees to the 10,000 ones that Mayor Johnson has already promised.

Funding for Mayor Johnson's tree-planting project comes from another eco-friendly source—canceling the city-funded *Londoner* newspaper, started by Johnson's Labour predecessor. Johnson's environmental objectives dovetailed nicely with his political ones: he was a vocal opponent of *Londoner*, repeatedly calling it "communist propaganda." So instead of turning trees into paper, London will-for at least the next four years-be turning its paper into trees.

OTHER PARK SIGHTS. Running south of the Serpentine, the dirt horse track **Rotten Row** stretches west from Hyde Park Corner. The name is a corruption of Route du Roi, or King's Road, so named because this was the royal route from Kensington Palace to Whitehall. At the southern end of Hyde Park and into Kensington Gardens there's a cluster of statues: the goddess **Diana fountain;** the "family of man"; a likeness of **Lord Byron;** tiny **Peter Pan;** and a fig-leafed **Achilles** dedicated to the Duke of Wellington. The **Princess Diana Memorial Fountain** lies just south of the Serpentine while the **Diana, Princess of Wales Memorial Playground** is in the northwest corner of Kensington Gardens. Since 1872, **Speaker's Corner,** at the northeast corner of the park across from Marble Arch, has been the only place in London where demonstrators can assemble without a permit; on Sundays you can see free speech in action as proselytizers, politicos, and various crazies dispense the fruits of their knowledge to bemused tourists.

Looking rather out of place, **Marble Arch** was originally intended to be the front entrance to Buckingham Palace, but palace extensions and new roadways cut off John Nash's 1828 monument, leaving it stranded forlornly on a traffic roundabout. The arch now stands close to the former site of the Tyburn gallows, London's main execution site until 1783. *(Near the intersection of Park Ln., Oxford St., Edgware Rd., and Bayswater Rd. ⊖ Marble Arch.)*

OTHER SIGHTS IN KENSINGTON AND EARL'S COURT

KENSINGTON PALACE. In 1689, William and Mary commissioned Christopher Wren to remodel Nottingham House into a palace, and it remained the principal royal residence until George III decamped to Kew in 1760. Today, it's not technically for royals but is still in use—Princess Diana was its most famous recent inhabitant. Although the heart of the palace is closed to visitors, the Hanoverian **State Apartments,** with intricate decor and *trompe l'oeil* paintings by William Kent, are still open to the public. More impressive, however, is the **Royal Ceremonial Dress Collection,** a magnificent spread of beautifully tailored and embroidered garments. The hands-down favorite is the permanent display of Diana's decadent evening gowns, including the famous 1985 silk velvet number in which she shimmied alongside John Travolta. The visit's a bit pricey, though it includes a free audio guide. While those who love gowns, royalty, or both will be in heaven, others might want skip it and instead wander through the palace grounds, which encompass Sir John Vanbrugh's grand 1704 **Orangery,** initially built for Queen Anne's dinner parties and now a popular setting for afternoon tea. *(On the western edge of Kensington Gardens; enter through the park. ⊖ High St. Kensington, Notting Hill Gate, or Queensway. ☎ 020 7937 9561; www.hrp.org.uk/kensingtonpalace. Open daily 10am-6pm; last entry 1hr. before closing. Wheelchair-accessible. £13, students £11, children 5-15 £6.30, families of 5 £34. Combo passes with Tower of London or Hampton Court available; discounts for online purchases. MC/V.)*

HOLLAND PARK. Smaller and less crowded than Kensington Gardens, Holland Park probably makes for a better picnic spot or quiet stroll than does its famous cousin. Set off from Kensington High St. and full of shady paths, the grounds also offer open fields, football pitches, a golf bunker, cricket nets, tennis courts, Japanese gardens, cafes, an open-air opera venue (Holland Park Theatre, p. 164), and an adventure playground for the young or young at heart. Holland House, which sits at the center of the park, is home to the YHA hostel (p. 72). *(Bordered by Kensington High St., Holland Walk, and Abbotsbury Rd. Enter at Commonwealth Institute. ⊖ High St. Kensington. ☎ 020 7471 9813, police 7441 9811, sport league and recreation info 020 7602 2226; Open daily 7:30am-dusk. Free.)*

LEIGHTON HOUSE. Currently under renovation until April 2010, the house of painter Lord Fredric Leighton (1830-96) is a perfect example of all that is endearing and ridiculous in Victorian taste. Inspired by his trips to the Middle East, Leighton's home combines oriental pastiche, Neoclassicism, and English decor. The centerpiece is the **Arab Hall**, a Moorish extravaganza of tilework and mosaic complete with fountain and carpets—the walls bear one of Europe's best collections of medieval Arabian tile. Other rooms contain works by Leighton as well as other artists, including Millais, Tintoretto, and Edward Burne-Jones. *(12 Holland Park Rd. ⊖High St. Kensington. ☎020 7602 3316; www.rbkc.gov. uk/leightonhousemuseum/general. Open M and W-Su 11am-5:30pm. Call or check website for prices and tours after the reopening.)*

ROYAL ALBERT HALL. In contrast to the ornate Albert Memorial across the street, the classical Royal Albert Hall is one of the more restrained pieces of Victorian architecture, though perhaps not in size. Intended as an all-purpose venue, guests at the 1871 opening immediately noticed one shortcoming of the hall's elliptical design: a booming echo that made it next to useless for musical concerts. Acoustics experts finally solved the problem in 1968, installing dozens of sound-absorbing discs suspended in a haphazard fashion from the dome. The hall has hosted Britain's first full-length indoor marathon, the first public display of electric lighting, and the world premier of *Hiawatha*. It remains a versatile venue for everything from boxing matches to rock concerts, but it is best known as the seat of the Proms classical music festival (see p. 164). *(Kensington Gore, just south of Kensington Gardens and the Albert Memorial. ⊖High St. Kensington. ☎020 7589 8212; www.royalalberthall.com. Box office at Door 12 open daily 9am-9pm. 45min. tours M-Tu and F-Su 10:30am-3:30pm every 30min.; reserve space in advance by calling box office. £8, students £7.)*

ALBERT MEMORIAL. An ornate example of Victorian High Gothic style, this 1868 canopy by George Gilbert Scott was commissioned by Queen Victoria, who was so devastated by her dear husband's death that she decided to immortalize him in gigantic gold-plated detail. It recently underwent a 10-year, £11.2 million restoration project, making it shine even more (if that's possible). At Albert's blindingly gilded feet, friezes represent the Four Industries, the Four Sciences, and the Four Continents, themes seemingly chosen more for their symmetry than for their accuracy. Above, over-the-top ornamentation continues with a 180 ft. spire inlaid with semi-precious stones. Head across to the Royal Albert Hall for the best view of the monument in its full glory. *(Kensington Gore, on the edge of Kensington Gardens, just north of Royal Albert Hall. ⊖High St. Kensington. ☎020 7495 0916; www.royalparks.org.uk/parks/kensington_gardens. 45min. tours first Su of month Mar.-Dec. 2 and 3pm. Wheelchair-accessible. Free. Tours £5, concessions £4.50.)*

KNIGHTSBRIDGE AND BELGRAVIA

It's hard to imagine that in the 18th century, Knightsbridge, currently home to London's most expensive stores, was a district known for its taverns and for the salesmen taking advantage of the area's position just outside the City of London's jurisdiction. Gentrification has merely pushed highway robbery indoors: take a look at the price tags in **Harrods** and **Harvey Nichols.**

Squeezed between Knightsbridge, Chelsea, and Westminster, the wedge-shaped district of Belgravia was catapulted to respectability by the presence of royalty. When George IV decided to make **Buckingham Palace** his official residence in the 1820s, developers were quick to build suitably grand buildings for his aristocratic groupies nearby. **Belgrave Square,** the setting for *My Fair Lady,* is now so expensive that the aristocracy has had to sell out to foreign governments. The primary reason most travelers come here is to replace missing passports.

APSLEY HOUSE. Named for Baron Apsley, the house later known as "No. 1, London" was bought in 1817 by the Duke of Wellington, whose heirs still occupy a modest suite on the top floor. The opulent house itself warrants a visit: characterized by soaring ceilings, intricate chandeliers, and gilded mirrors, the mansion also boasts an oval spiral staircase. Most, though, come for Wellington's fine art collection, much of which was given to him by the crowned heads of Europe following the Battle of Waterloo. Most of the old masters hang in the **Waterloo Gallery** where the duke held his annual Waterloo banquet: Goya, LeFevre, Rubens, Van Dyck, and Velasquez are all here as is Correggio, who painted the Duke's favorite piece, *Christ's Agony in the Garden.* The dining room is dominated by a stupendous silver centerpiece, which was donated by the Portuguese government; spanning the entire table, it features dancing maidens, trumpeting cherubs, bird-like beasts, and winged Victory being saluted by four European countries. Downstairs you'll find less elaborate but still impressive centerpieces, such as the porcelain Egyptian Dessert Service Napoleon initially gave to Josephine as a divorce present. *(Hyde Park Corner. ⊖Hyde Park Corner. ☎020 7499 5676; www.english-heritage.org.uk/london. Open Apr.-Oct. W-Su 11am-5pm; Nov.-Mar. W-Su 11am-4pm. Wheelchair-accessible. £5.70, students £4.80, children 5-18 £2.90. Joint ticket with Wellington Arch £7/6/3.50. Audio tours free. MC/V.)*

WELLINGTON ARCH. Standing at the center of London's most infamous traffic intersection, the Wellington Arch was long ignored by tourists and Londoners until 2001, when the interior was revealed to the public for the first time. Built in 1825, the Green Park Arch was meant to constitute part of a processional route to London, a by-product of George IV's scheme to beautify the city. Beauty turned into self-aggrandizement, however, when the newly re-christened "Wellington Arch" was encumbered by an embarrassingly large statue of the duke. The government immediately ordered the statue's removal but desisted when Wellington threatened to resign from the army. The figure was replaced in 1912 by the even bigger (though less offensive) **Quadriga of Peace.** Inside the Arch, exhibitions on the building's history and the changing nature of war memorials play second fiddle to the two observation platforms with a bird's-eye (or rather, tree-level) view of Hyde Park Corner and Green Park. *(Hyde Park Corner. ⊖Hyde Park Corner. ☎020 7930 2726; www.english-heritage.org.uk/london. Open W-Su Apr.-Oct. 10am-5pm, Nov.-Mar. 10am-4pm. Wheelchair-accessible. £3.50, students £3, children 5-16 £1.80. Joint tickets with Apsley House available. MC/V.)*

BROMPTON ORATORY. Ornate Baroque flourishes like the soaring domed transept and marble, marble, marble overwhelm the visitor to this church, properly called the Oratory of St. Philip Neri. London's second largest Catholic church, the Oratory was built from 1874-1884 and was deliberately designed with a nave wider than St. Paul's. The KGB considered one of the church's altars to be the best dead drop in London: until 1985, agents left microfilm and other documents behind a statue for other agents to retrieve. The church lives up to its reputation for music during its Solemn Masses, sung in Latin. *(Thurloe Pl., Brompton Rd. ⊖South Kensington. ☎020 7808 0900; www.bromptonoratory.com. Open daily 7am-8pm, except during frequent short services. Mass Sa 6pm; Su 7, 8am, 12:30, 4:30, 7pm. Solemn Mass Su 11am. Call ahead for wheelchair access. Free.)*

CHELSEA

As wealthy as neighboring Belgravia and Kensington, Chelsea boasts a riverside location and a strong artistic heritage. Henry VIII's right-hand man (and later victim) Sir Thomas More was the first big-name resident in the 16th century, but it was in the 19th century that the neighborhood acquired its artistic reputation with the founding of the famous **Chelsea Arts Club. Cheyne** (CHAIN-ee)

Walk has been home to J.M.W. Turner, George Eliot, Dante Gabriel Rossetti, and more recently Mick Jagger (at No. 48). Oscar Wilde, John Singer Sargent, and James McNeill Whistler all lived on **Tite Street,** while Mark Twain, Henry James, and T.S. Eliot also called Chelsea home at various times. Chelsea's other distinguishing aspect is military: the **Chelsea Barracks,** the **Royal Hospital,** and the **National Army Museum** all happen to be stationed in this affluent artistic paradise.

CHELSEA PHYSIC GARDEN. Founded in 1673 to provide medicinal herbs to locals, the Physic Garden remains a carefully ordered living repository of useful, rare, and just plain interesting plants. It has also played an important historic role, serving as the staging post from which tea was introduced to India and cotton to America. Today, the garden is a quiet place for picnics, teas, and scenic walks. It also has a cafe. You can purchase flora on display, or buy some of the homemade honey from the bee hive. *(66 Royal Hospital Rd.; entrance on Swan Walk. ⊖Sloane Sq., then Bus #137. ☎020 7352 5646; www.chelseaphysicgarden.co.uk. Open from early Apr. to June and Sept.-Oct. W-F noon-5pm, Su noon-6pm; July-Aug. M-Tu and Th-F noon-5pm, W noon-10pm; Feb. Su 10am-4pm; during Chelsea Flower Show (late May) and Chelsea Festival (mid-June) M-F noon-5pm. Tea served M-Sa from 12:30pm, Su from noon. Call ahead for wheelchair access. £8, students and children under 16 £5.)*

CARLYLE'S HOUSE. In his time, Thomas Carlyle, the so-called "Sage of Chelsea," was England's most famous writer and historian. When he died in 1881, admirers purchased his house and obtained national monument status for it. The house and garden in which he entertained Dickens, Tennyson, and Ruskin are preserved more or less as they were during his lifetime. *(24 Cheyne Row. ⊖Sloane Sq., then Bus #19 or 319. ☎020 7352 7087. Open from mid-Mar. to Oct. W-F 2-5pm, Sa-Su 11am-5pm. Last entry 4:30pm. £4.90, children 5-16 £2.50.)*

CHELSEA OLD CHURCH. The quiet, unspectacular interior of this post-WWII-restored Saxon church won't do much for the lay observer. It's the history that's appealing: Sir Thomas More worshipped here in the 16th century, and Henry VIII is reported to have married Jane Seymour (number three of six) here before the official wedding took place. Just down the street is **Crosby Hall,** a 15th-century hall that was More's residence in Bishopsgate before its relocation in 1910. *(2 Old Church St. ⊖Sloane Sq., then Bus #19 or 319. ☎020 7795 1019; www.chelseaoldchurch.org.uk. Open Tu-Th 2-4pm. Services Su 8, 11am, 12:15pm. Evensong 6pm.)*

🏛 MUSEUMS

THE CITY OF LONDON

Although St. Paul's and the Tower get all the attention, the City's museums aren't too shabby. They're also less crowded and more affordable.

MUSEUM OF LONDON. Located in the southwest corner of the Barbican complex, the Museum of London resembles an industrial fortress from the outside. Inside, the engrossing collection traces the history of London from its Roman foundations to the present day. Most of the display consists of artifacts and models, but there are a couple worthwhile highlights: a reconstructed Roman dining room built over an original mosaic floor; a hefty model of St. Paul's; a life-size model of a London home in the 11th century; and the Cheapside Hoard, a 17th-century goldsmith's bounty uncovered in 1912. The current exhibit (London from 1666 to the Present) is undergoing a $20.5 million renovation set to end in 2010. It promises to be a real hit, with over 5000 objects, interactive displays, and the return of the favorite, gold-bedazzled Lord Mayer's Coach. *(London Wall. Enter through the Barbican or from Aldersgate; wheelchair-accessible via the elevator at*

Aldersgate entrance. ⊖St. Paul's or Barbican. ☎0870 4444 3851; www.museumoflondon.org.uk. Open daily 10am-6pm; last entry 5:30pm. Free. Audio tours £2. Free 1hr. Tours every day at noon and 4pm. Frequent demonstrations, talks, and guided walks; some are free, others up to £10.)

BANK OF ENGLAND MUSEUM. The Bank itself is only available to those on business; to get to the museum, you will be shuttled by security attendants. The museum traces the history of the Bank from its foundation (1694) to the present day. It's housed in a reconstruction of Sir John Soane's original domed Stock Office. *(Threadneedle St. ⊖Bank. ☎020 7601 5545; www.bankofengland.co.uk. Open M-F 10am-5pm. Wheelchair-accessible. Free.)*

THE CLOCKMAKERS' MUSEUM. A one-room museum measuring the 500-year history of clockmakers through clocks, watches, chronometers, and sundials—you won't lose track of time here. The display includes a watch that belonged to Mary Queen of Scots and the one worn by Sir Edmund Hillary when he climbed Everest. For a treat, be sure to visit on the hour. *(Enter through Guildhall Yard on Aldermanbury. ⊖St. Paul's or Moorgate. ☎020 7332 1868; www.clockmakers.org. Open M-Sa 9:30am-4:30pm. Wheelchair-accessible. Free.)*

THE CITY OF LONDON GALLERIES

BARBICAN ART GALLERY. Housing British and international art and photography, Barbican exhibits change every few months and generally include a variety of media. Call in advance for the season's exhibit; previous included "Folk Art," "Colour After Klein," and "Radical Nature." International pieces are showcased on the first floor behind the concert hall. *(Between London Wall, Beech St., Aldersgate, and Moorgate. ⊖Barbican or Moorgate. ☎020 7638 4141, box office 020 7638 8891; www.barbican.org.uk/gallery. Open M-Tu and Th-Sa 11am-8pm, W 11am-6pm. Wheelchair-accessible. Rates vary but are usually £8, students £6.)*

WHITECHAPEL AND THE EAST END

Home to a bustling contemporary art scene, Whitechapel and the East End house a number of museums, but the real gems are their art galleries, which range from remote and cutting-edge to established and edgy.

GEFFRYE MUSEUM. The Geffyre Museum is *the* place to unleash your inner Martha Stewart. This elaborately restored 17th-century almshouse holds a set of connecting rooms that have been painstakingly reconstructed to showcase specific periods in interior design. Move through Elizabethan parlors, Victorian studies, and stark post-WWI sitting rooms. If not informative, the obsessive attention to detail is certainly amusing: the radio in the "1990-2000" loft plays 1990s pop, and the table is strewn with glossy women's magazines. Downstairs you'll find temporary exhibits and a design center for local artists' displays. The manicured backyard garden is lovely and can be admired from the popular glassed-in lunch cafe. *(Kingsland Rd. ⊖Old St., then Bus #243 or 10min. walk along Old St. and left on Kingsland Rd., just past its intersection with Cremer Rd. or ⊖Liverpool St. and Bus #149 or 242. ☎020 7739 9893; www.geffrye-museum.org.uk. Open Tu-Sa 10am-5pm, Su noon-5pm. Cafe open 10am-4:45pm. Food £3-6. Admission free.)*

MUSEUM OF CHILDHOOD. Come here to visit the toys from your past, the toys you wish you had in your past, and some you didn't know existed. Housed in the original Victoria and Albert building, the museum holds puzzles, toys, dolls, and doll houses from the past few centuries. Play areas allow children to play dress up, perform puppet shows, build sandcastles, and generally exhaust themselves. Those over the age of five will appreciate fun facts about childhood favorites such as Barbie and GI Joe. *(Cambridge Heath Rd. ⊖Bethnal Green. ☎020 8983 5200; www.museumofchildhood.org.uk. Open daily 10am-5:45pm. Free.)*

GALLERIES

WHITE CUBE. A Hoxton Square (and art scene) institution, this stark white building has showcased some of the biggest names in international contemporary art. Housed in a former industrial building and opened in 2000, White Cube has an impressive list of alums, including Chuck Close and Damien Hirst. The Cube is small, but many consider it to be the preeminent contemporary art gallery in London. *(48 Hoxton Sq. ⊖Old St. ☎020 7930 5373; www.whitecube.com. Open Tu-Sa 10am-6pm. Sometimes closed for exhibit installation; call in advance. Wheelchair-accessible. Free.)*

WHITECHAPEL ART GALLERY. Reopened in Spring 2009 after doubling its size, this century-old gallery remains at the forefront of a buzzing East End art scene. Founded in 1901, Whitechapel was one of the first publicly funded galleries in London and served as an outlet for the area's political ferment, artistic innovation, and social change. It has since showcased art from Africa, India, the Middle East, and Latin America, and in the 1950s and 1960s it was at the heart of the Pop Art movement. Now, it displays everything from 19th-century Impressionist masterpieces to modern and contemporary art. The gallery also features a brand new dining area and cafe, and hosts regular talks, seminars, and poetry and music nights. *(Whitechapel High St. ⊖Aldgate East. ☎020 7522 7888; www.whitechapel.org. Open Tu-W and F-Su 11am-6pm, Th 11am-9pm. "Late nights" 7-11pm: poetry Th, music F. Dining room open Tu-F 11:30am-3pm and 5:30-11pm, Sa 11:30am-11pm, Su 11:30am-5:30pm; cafe and bar open Tu-W and Su 11am-5:30pm, Th 11am-10pm, F 11am-5:30pm and 7-11pm. Wheelchair-accessible. Call or check website for opening details. Free.)*

THANK GOD IT'S THURSDAY. Parasol Unit and the Whitechapel Art Gallery have recently teamed up to launch *First Thursdays:* they've convinced most East End galleries to stay open until 9pm on the first Thursday of every month to host exhibits, discussions, and other art-related events. Check specific gallery websites for more information.

VICTORIA MIRO. Though a bit out of the way, Victoria Miro is worth a visit. The gallery features works from young artists that make the most of its sprawling warehouse venue—think large installation pieces, not oil paintings. *(16 Wharf Rd. ⊖Old St. or ⊖Angel. From Old St., take Exit 8 and walk north up City Rd. toward Angel, pass the 230 address block, then turn right after the McDonald's; ring bell to enter. ☎020 7336 8109; www.victoria-miro.com. Open Tu-Sa 10am-6pm. Free.)*

PARISOL UNIT: FOUNDATION FOR CONTEMPORARY ART. Once a struggling art gallery, this privately funded charity has reestablished itself on the East End scene and now features four innovative exhibits per year, usually of work by international contemporary artists. *(14 Wharf Rd. ⊖Old St. or ⊖Angel. Just before Victoria Miro on Wharf. ☎020 7490 7373; www.parasol-unit.org. Open Tu-Sa 10am-6pm, Su noon-5pm. Wheelchair-accessible. Open until 9pm on First Thursdays. Other occasional late-night events Th at 7pm. Free. Events £3-5.)*

HALES GALLERY. First opened in South London in 1992, this small gallery has been a proving ground for many up-and-coming British artists. Since its move to the East End, it has taken on a number of established international talents as well. Showcases everything from oil on canvas to installation and sculpture. *(7 Bethnal Green Rd., in the Tea Building. ⊖Old St. ☎020 7033 1938; www.halesgallery.com. Open W-Sa 11am-6pm. Free.)*

ROCKET GALLERY. From furniture and photographs to screen prints and paintings, Rocket favors postmodern design and Minimalism, and in that genre doesn't disappoint. *(56 Shoreditch High St., in the Tea Building. ⊖Old St. ☎020 7729 7594; www.rocketgallery.com. Open Tu-F 10am-6pm, Su noon-6pm. Free.)*

GREENWICH

NATIONAL MARITIME MUSEUM. With around two million items in its possession, the National Maritime Museum covers almost every aspect of seafaring history, from the evolving conditions of maritime travel to the potential consequences of pollution and global warming. While most of the exhibits cater to those with a keen interest in the sea, there are highlights even for the seasick. The Maritime London room holds the uniform Admiral Nelson died in during the Battle of Trafalgar, the bullet hole still visible and the stockings stained with blood. Upstairs, you'll find over 400 objects from the museum's collection, a stained glass window designed by John Dudley Forsyth for the Baltic Exchange building, and an art gallery showcasing paintings inspired by the sea. The Bridge Gallery on the top floor features a virtual simulator that allows you to try your hand at steering a ship.*(Romney Rd. between the Royal Naval College and Greenwich Park. DLR: Cutty Sark. ☎020 8858 4422; www.nmm.ac.uk. Open daily Sept. 10am-5pm. Last entry 30min. before closing. Free.)*

HOLBORN

Holborn's museums may not be as famous as the Tate or the V&A, but they certainly deserve a visit. The post-Impressionist and modern art collections at the Somerset House museums are top-notch, and the Hunterian Museum offers odd but fascinating medical curiosities that are bound to intrigue even the most skeptical of visitors.

▨SOMERSET HOUSE

Strand, just east of Waterloo Bridge. ⊖Charing Cross or Temple. ☎020 7845 4600, events 020 7845 4670; www.somerset-house.org.uk. Courtyard open daily 7:30am-11pm. Tours 1st Sa of every month 1:30, 2:30, 3:45pm. Wheelchair-accessible. Ticket for 1 of the 3 collections £5, concessions £4, under 18 free; 2 collections £8/£7; 3 collections £12/11. MC/V.

Somerset House was London's first intentional office block. Originally home to the Royal Academy, the Royal Society, and the Navy Board, the elegant courtyard long induced a shiver of distaste in Londoners as the headquarters of the Inland Revenue. In December and January, the central **Fountain Courtyard** is iced over to make an open-air rink and in the summer months frolicking toddlers splash through the cool fountain jets. Thursday evenings from mid-June to mid-July feature classical music concerts, and in August there are open-air movie screenings. The annual Somerset House Concert Series features indie and pop bands in outdoor shows.

THE COURTAULD INSTITUTE GALLERIES. The Courtauld's outstanding collection ranges from 14th-century Italian religious works to 20th-century abstracts, but is most famous for its Impressionist and post-Impressionist pieces. The gang's all here: Manet's *A Bar at the Follies Bergères*, Van Gogh's *Self-Portrait with Bandaged Ear*, and an entire room devoted to Degas's bronzes, as well as pivotal works by Cézanne, Dufy, Gauguin, Kandinsky, Modigliani, Monet, and Renoir. The Renaissance galleries feature Rubens, Botticelli, and other renowned European artists. *(☎077 6427 3219; www.eastwing8.co.uk. Open last weekend of the month; Sa 10am-5pm, Su noon-5pm. Free.)*

THE EAST WING COLLECTION. Founded by a Courtauld art student, this student-curated show displays contemporary art by both students and established artists, with a particular focus on abstraction. (☎ *020 7848 2526; www.courtauld.ac.uk. Lunchtime talks free; check website for details. Wheelchair-accessible. Open 10am-6pm, last entry 30min. before closing. Free.)*

THE EMBANKMENT GALLERIES. Managed by the Courtauld Art Institute, these galleries showcase cutting edge exhibitions curated by the art students themselves. (☎ *020 7848 2526; www.courtauld.ac.uk. Wheelchair-accessible. Lunchtime talks free; check website for details. Open 10am-6pm, last entry 5:30pm. Free.)*

> **TIP** **COURTAULD FOR FREE.** The collection at the Courtauld Galleries is remarkable and worth every penny of the entrance fee. But why pay if you don't have to? Go by on Mondays between 10am and 2pm and get in for free.

OTHER MUSEUMS IN HOLBORN

HUNTERIAN MUSEUM. Buried within the grandiose **Royal College of Surgeons,** this museum is not for the squeamish. John Hunter, considered the founder of modern surgery, had a keen interest in the anatomy of all living things, expressed in his vast collection of both human and animal fetuses, stomachs, jaws, intestines, and teeth, all preserved in large glass jars. Only 3500 of his original 14,000 colorless pickled organs survived the Blitz. Galleries are devoted to subjects ranging from the ghastly history of surgical instruments to Hunter's personal art collection. Among the viscera are some genuine marvels, like the 7' 7" skeleton of Charles Byrne, the Irish Giant. *(35-43 Lincoln's Inn Fields. ⊖Holborn. Enter via the columned main entrance to the RCS building. ☎ 020 7869 6560; www.rcseng.ac.uk/services/museums. Open Tu-Sa 10am-5pm. Wheelchair-accessible. Free.)*

SIR JOHN SOANE'S MUSEUM. A somewhat incoherent but interesting maze of endlessly mirrored walls, opulent sky-lighted ceilings, beautiful artworks, and hundreds of marble and plaster fragments. Items of particular intrigue include the mummified corpse of Soane's wife's dog and an extraordinary sarcophagus of Seti I. *(13 Lincoln's Inn Fields. ⊖Holborn. ☎ 020 1405 2107. Open Tu-Sa 10am-5pm, 1st Tu of month 10am-5pm and 6-9pm. Tours Sa 10:30am. Free, £3 donation requested. Tours £5, students free.)*

THE SOUTH BANK

If the City and Westminster are London's historical centers, then the South Bank is the artistic center, with one of the highest concentrations of cutting-edge exhibits and museums in the world. Anchored by the gigantic Tate Modern, the area is home not only to top contemporary art, but to private galleries, each with its own specialty.

TATE MODERN

Main entrance on Bankside, on the South Bank; 2nd entrance on Queen's Walk. ⊖Southwark or Blackfriars. From the Southwark Tube, turn left up Union, then left on Great Suffolk, then left on Holland. ☎ 020 7887 8000; www.tate.org.uk. Open M-Th and Su 10am-6pm, F-Sa 10am-10pm. Free; special exhibits can be up to £10. Free tours meet on the gallery concourses: Level 3 at 11am and noon, Level 5 at 2 and 3pm. 5 types of audio tours include highlights, collection tour, architecture tour, children's tour, and tours for the visually impaired; £4, concessions £3.50. Free talks M-F 1pm; meet at the concourse on the appropriate level. Wheelchair-accessible on Holland St.

Considered the second half of the national collection (the first portion is held in the National Gallery), the Tate Modern is the most popular museum in

London and one of the most famous museums in the world. From the outside, it doesn't look like much: Sir Giles Gilbert Scott's boorish, mammoth building was formerly the Bankside power station. Inside, though, you'll find some of the world's most famous modern art, scattered among two floors and divided into six themes. By grouping works thematically, the Tate has turned itself into a work of conceptual art. The collection is enormous and gallery space limited, so works rotate frequently. If you're dying to see a particular piece, head to the museum's computer station on the fifth floor to browse through the entire collection. Meanwhile, the seventh floor bar boasts unblemished views of the Thames and the north and south of London, while **Turbine Hall** on the ground hall is now an immense atrium that inevitably dwarfs the (often interactive) installations it exhibits.

HIGHLIGHTS IN A HURRY: TATE MODERN. Collections on display at the Tate Modern are not enormous, and you should be able to get through all four sections within a few hours (although you could spend the whole day). Galleries not to be missed: Distinguished Voices and Expressionism in Material Gestures; Natural History in Poetry and Dream; Utopia and Abstraction in Idea and Object; and Roy Lichtenstein in States of Flux.

THIRD FLOOR. One of the four concept galleries, **Material Gestures** features post-war European and American painting and sculpture. The galleries within Material Gestures include artists such as Anish Kapoor, Claude Monet, and Douglas Gordon, as well as Mark Rothko's famous *Seagram Murals*. On the other side of Level 3 is the **Poetry and Dream** gallery, which is devoted to Surrealism and related works. Highlights include works by Francis Bacon, Joan Miró, Max Ernst, and Hans Arp. The small **Scale** room holds objects that play with perception; René Magritte, Auguste Rodin, and Claes Oldenburg all have works here.

FIFTH FLOOR. Energy and Process looks at artist's interaction with transformation and natural forces, and houses a series of works related to minimalism and conceptual art. Major artists include Kasimir Malevich, Richard Serra, and Anselm Keifer. **States of Flux** features Cubism, Vorticism, and Futurism alongside works that focus on change and modernity. Roy Lichtenstein, Jeff Koons, Andy Warhol, and Ed Ruscha are the chief artists on display.

OTHER MUSEUMS IN THE SOUTH BANK

IMPERIAL WAR MUSEUM. Massive naval guns guard the entrance to the building, formerly the infamous lunatic asylum known as Bedlam. In the basement, an exhaustive, labyrinthine exhibit takes you through every possible aspect of the World Wars, with accompanying uniforms, guns, video testimonials, and propaganda. The all-too-realistic **Trench Experience** recreates the conditions on the front lines in WWI, and the **Blitz Experience** details life on the home front in WWII. On the first floor, the remarkably high-tech **Secret War** is filled with gadgets and gizmos of espionage and a particularly gripping presentation of Operation NIMROD (the storming of a hostage-filled Iranian embassy in 1980 in London). The **Large Exhibits Hall** features an impressive array of military hardware, from "Little Boy" (an atomic bomb of the type dropped on Hiroshima) to Montgomery's tank to a German V-2 rocket, all clearly labeled and carefully explained. The best and most publicized exhibit, the **Holocaust Exhibition** on the third floor, provides a look at all the events surrounding the tragedy. If that sounds too upbeat, head to the fourth floor for **Crimes Against Humanity**, a sobering interactive display with a 30min. film at the back. The cinema shows historical documentaries. *(Lambeth Rd., Lambeth. ⊖Lambeth North or Elephant & Castle. ☎020 7416 5320; www.iwm.org.uk. Open daily 10am-6pm. Free.)*

⬛**DESIGN MUSEUM.** Housed in an arresting Art Deco riverfront building, this contemporary museum's installations fit right with its cutting-edge surroundings. Temporary exhibitions cover anything from avant-garde furniture and big-name graphic designers to as-yet-unseen fashions and industrial design and architecture. Everyone will enjoy the **Interaction Space** on the top floor, which includes a colorful variety of household items and a bay of vintage video games that inspired contemporary gaming. The Museum Café on the first floor serves sweet treats that are as aesthetically pleasing as anything you'll find in the galleries. *(28 Shad Thames, Butlers Wharf. ⊖Tower Hill or London Bridge. ☎020 7940 8783; www.designmuseum.org. Open daily 10am-5:45pm, last entry 5:15pm. Wheelchair-accessible. £8.50, concessions £5, under 12 free.)*

OLD OPERATING THEATRE AND HERB GARRET. Tucked into the loft of a 19th-century church, this is the oldest restored operating theater in the world. The surgeon's chair and restraining straps appear to await their next patient. A fearsome array of saws and knives are the core of the exhibit on surgical history, accompanied by plenty of hearts, brains, lungs, and intestines in glass jars. There's also a small display on Keats, who was a student here. The neighboring herb garret smells heavenly, filled with herbs, spices, and other creatures that were used by the hospital apothecary to prepare medicines. A 1718 cure for venereal disease (notepads out), for example, instructs the afflicted to ingest garden snails and earthworms, cloves, wormwood, and juniper berries. *(9A St. Thomas's St. ⊖London Bridge. ☎020 7955 4791; www.thegarret.org.uk. Open daily 10:30am-4:45pm. £5.50, concessions £4.45, children £3.25, families £13.80.)*

GALLERIES

⬛**HAYWARD GALLERY.** Hiding next to the Royal Festival Hall, this stark concrete building is a distinctive maze of blocks, which the brilliant curators fill with contemporary art and a few pieces from the early and mid-20th century. Two to three shows usually run concurrently. *(South Bank Centre. ⊖Waterloo, Embankment, or Temple. ☎0871 663 2501; www.hayward.org.uk. Call in advance, as the gallery closes between exhibits. Open M-Th and Sa-Su 10am-6pm, F 10am-10pm. £9, seniors £8, concessions £6, children 12-16 £4.50, children under 12 free.)*

JERWOOD SPACE. Primarily a rehearsal space for the performing arts, the Jerwood Space gives promising young artists a leg up, most famously by hosting the prestigious Jerwood Painting Prize exhibition (early May to mid-June). It also holds the Contemporary Makers (mid-June through mid-July) and Contemporary Painters (April) exhibitions. Works line the walls of the beautifully converted 2600 sq. ft. industrial space. *(171 Union St. ⊖Southwark or Borough. ☎020 7654 0171; www.jerwoodspace.co.uk. Open M-F 10am-5pm, Sa-Su 10am-3pm. Free.)*

POUSSIN GALLERY. Very much a hidden gem, this gallery specializes in contemporary abstract paintings and sculptures by British artists, many of whom also exhibit at the Hayward and Whitechapel. *(Block K, 13 Bell Yard Mews, 175 Bermondsey. In the back of parking lot. ⊖London Bridge. ☎020 7403 4444; www.poussin-gallery. com. Open during exhibitions W-Sa 1-7pm; call ahead to be sure.)*

SOUTH LONDON

DULWICH PICTURE GALLERY. England's first public gallery is the unlikely legacy of an ambitious actor and a Polish misfortune. In 1605, Edward Allyn,

Christopher Marlowe's leading actor, bought Dulwich manor in order to show-case his art collection, which was at that point minimal. Over 150 years later, King Stanisław August of Poland decided to invest in a national art collection and commissioned two London dealers to buy the best pictures available, but the partition of Poland in 1795 left them with a full-blown collection for which they had not paid. Rather than selling the art, they decided to put the 360 works on display in the manor. The main benefactor died before the project could be carried out, but his good friend Sir John Sloane finished the refurbishment for him. The high-ceilinged halls are famous for holding a fine collection by 17th- and 18th-century masters, including seven Poussins, three Rembrandts, and four Murillos, as well as works by Rubens, Van Dyke, and pieces from the Dutch, Spanish, Italian, French, and English schools of painting. The gallery also has a lesser known collection of 650 British works, collected over almost 400 years, which it uses for temporary exhibitions. *(Gallery Rd., Dulwich. ⊖Brixton, then Bus #P4 to Picture Gallery stop. Rail: North Dulwich or West Dulwich. From West Dulwich station, turn right onto Thurlow Park Rd. and left onto Gallery Rd. and follow the signs for 15min.; from North Dulwich, turn left out of the station and walk 10min. through Dulwich Village to the Gallery. ☎ 020 8693 5254; www.dulwichpicturegallery.org.uk. Open Tu-F 10am-5pm, Sa-Su 11am-5pm. Free tours Sa-Su 3pm. Wheelchair-accessible. Exhibitions and permanent collection £9, permanent collection only £5; seniors £8/4; students £4/free; children under 16 free.)*

HORNIMAN MUSEUM AND GARDENS. This museum is devoted to the small and fascinating collection of 19th-century tea merchant Frederick Horniman. The **African Worlds gallery** displays a rich selection of masks, costumes, and religious garb, including Egyptian sarcophagi and Haitian voodoo altars. Above, the **Textiles Display** showcases temporary exhibits formed from the collection of over 6500 textiles of different countries and fabrics. In the **Natural History collection,** you'll find giant stuffed sea and land animals, birds, and insects. The **Centenary Gallery,** filled with headdresses, masks, and figurines from around the UK, Australia and New Guinea, also traces the curatorial evolution of the museum. In the basement is a small aquarium, organized by habitat. The neighboring hillside garden holds a tiny domestic zoo where crowing roosters and goats make their homes; the 16 acres of colorful flower beds make for a charming stroll. *(100 London Rd. ⊖Brixton, then Bus #P4 to the Horniman stop. Rail: Forest Hill. Exit the station, cross Dartmouth Rd., and follow A205 for 5min. until it becomes London Rd. ☎ 020 8699 1872; www.horniman.ac.uk. Wheelchair-accessible. Open daily 10:30am-5:30pm. Gardens open M-Sa 7:30am-dusk, Su 8am-dusk. Free; temporary exhibitions around £5.)*

WESTMINSTER

Westminster's museums are really a *digestif* after the real meal, the sights.

◪CABINET WAR ROOMS
Clive Steps, far end of King Charles St. ⊖Westminster. ☎ 7930 6961; www.iwm.org.uk. Open daily 9:30am-6pm, last entry 5pm. £13, students £10.50, children under 16 free. MC/V.

From 1939 to 1945, what was previously a government coal storage basement was transformed into the bomb-proof nerve center of a nation at war. For six tense years, Winston Churchill, his cabinet and generals, and dozens of support staff lived and worked in this dark, underground labyrinth while bombs wreaked havoc above. The day after the war ended in August 1945, the Cabinet War Rooms were abandoned, shut up, and left undisturbed for decades until their reopening in 1984 by Margaret Thatcher. Thanks to journals, testimonies, and photos, the space has been preserved and displayed almost exactly as it was in wartime. An indispensable Churchillian-voiced audio tour talks you through the maze of rooms on show, supplemented by original recordings of

Churchill's speeches and recreations that bring them to life. Highlights include "Churchill's personal loo"—a small room containing the top-secret transatlantic hotline and massive encryption device—and the defense and map rooms that were in operation for six straight years, night and day. The clocks on display in Churchill's official meeting room read 4:58, the moment Churchill called the Cabinet's first official meeting, one day after a German air raid on London.

CHURCHILL MUSEUM. The connected museum, included in the admission to the War Rooms, holds many of Churchill's WWII possessions, along with remnants from his lesser-known days as a journalist, prisoner of war, amateur artist, and pro figure-skater. Alternately somber and amusing, it provides an in-depth look at the man whom many consider to be one of history's greatest leaders. Wander through five highly interactive sections, all profiling a distinct phase in the former Prime Minister's life. In the hot pink **1874-1900** area, peruse Winnie's famously lackluster report cards and stop to read about his daring escape from South Africa. The red-hued **1900-1929** section features his first love letter to his beloved "Clemmie" and profiles his early days as an extremely liberal social reformer. Be sure to check out the many political cartoons—funnier if you can read German—scattered throughout the exhibit alternatively depicting Churchill as a despondent infant and imperial slave-driver. The orange **Wilderness Years (1929-1940)** section profiles Churchill in his down-and-out days, with a hilarious interactive display of Churchill's witticisms and a computerized selection of his many amateur paintings. In the purple **1940-1945** section, visitors can immerse themselves in the 1940s wartime world. Hitler's anti-British propaganda, denouncing Churchill as "an utterly amoral repulsive creature," is also on view. Finally, the green **1945-1965** section, profiling Churchill's life as a statesmen and fashionista (he often donned one-piece zip-up velvet suits), explores his role in the Cold War and his honorary American citizenship, and ends with a somber video of his funeral. The best part of the museum, a giant interactive timeline table that runs diagonally across the room, connects all five of the displays and is filled with sound bites, newspaper clippings, and historical information that puts Churchill's life in a wider context. Generate all kinds of disruptive effects by selecting from the many dates along the timeline. Check out August 6th, 1945, but be prepared to draw stares from surrounding visitors.

 SCENIC MUSEUM HOPPING. Take the Tate Boat when traveling between Tate Modern and Tate Britain. The journey lasts 20min. and includes a stop at the London Eye. Book tickets at either the Tate museum, the Bankside Pier, or the London Eye, or online at www.tate.org.uk. Single adult trip £4, Transport for London Travelcard holders £2.75. Boats generally run 10am-5pm. Call ☎7887 8888 for more information.

OTHER WESTMINSTER MUSEUMS

TATE BRITAIN. The Tate Britain houses the foremost collection of British art, and also includes pieces from foreign artists working in Britain and Brits working abroad from 1500 to the present. Of the four Tate Galleries in England, this is the original Tate, opened in 1897 to house Sir Henry Tate's collection of "modern" British art and later expanded to include a gift from famed British painter J.M.W. Turner. Turner's donation of 282 oils and 19,000 watercolors can make the museum feel like one big tribute to the man. Skip the prolific collection of hazy British landscapes in the **Clore Galleries** if you don't like his style. Much of the **second floor** houses the permanent collection, loosely tracing the chronology of art in Britain from 1500 to 2004. Three subdivisions—Historic, Modern, and Contemporary—house themed rooms such as "Modern Landscapes" and "Art and Victorian Society," and allow visitors to grasp the breadth of the British artistic tradition in a single afternoon. These subdivisions also feature the fervent work of William Blake, as well as paintings by Pre-Raphaelites John Everett Millais, John Singer Sargent, and Frederic Lord Leighton on a rotating basis. Other artists on display include John Constable, William Hogarth, Richard Long, Ben Nicholson, and David Hockney. Beloved works include Henry Moore's incredible *Recumbent Figure* sculpture and John Singer Sargent's colorful Victorian portraits. The bulk of modern British art is absent, having been transferred to the Tate Modern at Bankside in 1999 (p. 141), but that doesn't mean that what remains here is static or stodgy; one of the most recent exhibitions was an exact recreation of an anti-war protester's demonstration that was removed from Parliament Sq. The annual and often controversial ■**Turner Prize** competition for contemporary visual art is still held here, the displays of which are worth a visit. Four contemporary British artists are nominated for the £40,000 prize; their short-listed works go on show from late October through late January. **Late at Tate Britain,** the first Friday night of every month, offers visitors an extended look at the museum's holdings in addition to live music and other performances. *(Millbank, near Vauxhall Bridge, in West-minster.* ⊖*Pimlico. Information* ☎ *7887 8008, M-F exhibition booking 7887 8888; www.tate.org. uk. Open daily 10am-5:50pm, last entry 5pm. Wheelchair-accessible via Clore Wing. Free; special exhibitions £7-11. Audio tours free. See website for free tours and lectures.)*

HIGHLIGHTS IN A HURRY: TATE BRITAIN. Get a taste of Turner and his contemporaries in the second-story **Clore Galleries,** then head over to John Singer Sargent's exquisite portraiture. Stop by the **second-story rooms** dedicated to John Constable and experience the joys of prudent restraint in the **Victorian Galleries.** From October through late January, the restraints are cast aside with modern, often controversial art in the **Turner Prize** exhibition.

THE WEST END

MAYFAIR AND SAINT JAMES'S

Auction houses and commercial galleries may outnumber museums in the West End, but Mayfair and St. James's is home to some of London's most recognizable art institutions: the National Gallery; its smaller (but just as worthwhile) counterpart, the National Portrait Gallery; and the Royal Academy of Art. Mayfair is the center of London's art market—and despite its genteel aura, it's not all Old Masters and watercolors. **Cork Street,** running parallel to Old Bond St. between Clifford St. and Burlington Gardens, is lined with dozens of small commercial galleries specializing in contemporary art of all types. The auction houses, like Christie's and Sotheby's, give insight into what is being bought and sold in the art world today.

■ NATIONAL GALLERY

Main entrance (Portico Entrance) on north side of Trafalgar Sq. ⊖*Charing Cross or Leicester Sq.* ☎ *020 7747 2885; www.nationalgallery.org.uk. Wheelchair-accessible at Sainsbury Wing on Pall Mall East, Orange St., and Getty Entrance. Open M-Th and Sa-Su 10am-6pm, F 10am-9pm. Special exhibitions in the Sainsbury Wing occasionally open until 10pm. Offers themed workshops (£30-40), lectures (£3-18), and courses (£30-45) to accompany exhibitions. Free, suggested donation £5; some temporary exhibitions £5-10, seniors £4-8, students and ages 12-18 £2-5. 1hr. tours start at Sainsbury Wing information desk. Tours daily 11:30am and 2:30pm. Audio guides £3.50, students £3. AmEx/MC/V for ticketed events.*

The National Gallery was founded by an Act of Parliament in 1824, with 38 pictures displayed in a townhouse. Over the years it has become one of the world's grandest museums. The Gallery has made numerous additions, the most recent and controversial being the massive, modern **Sainsbury Wing** (Prince Charles described an early version of the design as "a monstrous carbuncle on the face of a much-loved and elegant friend"). The Sainsbury Wing holds almost all of the museum's large exhibitions as well as its restaurants and lecture halls. If you're pressed for time, head to **Art Start** in the Sainsbury Wing, where you can design and print out a personalized tour of the paintings you want to see.

 HIGHLIGHTS IN A HURRY: NATIONAL GALLERY. Enter via the Sainsbury Wing. Pop up to **Room 56** on the 2nd fl. for a quick look at the *Arnolfini Portrait* by Jan van Eyck and then head to **Rooms 23** and **24** in the North Wing. See how well Rembrandt aged by comparing his self portraits, then move to **Rooms 2** and **8** in the west wing to take a look at a collection of Renaissance works that features pieces by Leornardo da Vinci and Michelangelo. Finally, wander through the Impressionist masterpieces in **Rooms 44** and **45,** which includes works by Degas, Gauguin, Manet, Monet, and Renoir, as well as Van Gogh's *Sunflowers.*

WEST WING: 16TH CENTURY. Dominated by works from the Italian High Renaissance, both Roman and Venetian, as well as from the first flowering of German and Flemish art. Religious motifs give way to domestic and rural themes. **Room 2** features one of the museum's most interesting works: the Leonardo Cartoon (*Virgin and Child with St. Anne*), a detailed preparatory drawing by Leonardo da Vinci for a never-executed painting. Other highlights include Leonardo's second *Virgin on the Rocks* and Parmigianino's nudes. **Room 8** includes works by Michelangelo and Raphael. **Rooms 9** and **10** focus on northern Italy, with works by Tintoretto, Veronese, Titian, and Piombo.

 THE AMBASSADORS. When perusing the paintings in Room 4 of the West Wing, you'll come across Hans Holbein's *The Ambassadors,* a work full of mystery and intrigue. At first glance the painting seems like a normal portrait of two men, until you notice the terribly skewed image of a human skull on the floor. The skull, signifying death, appears normal when viewed from the painting's left side. The various objects and decor surrounding Holbein's subjects have also been said to represent various religious theories and elements of discord. Just don't spend all day in front of the painting trying to decipher its mysteries—you'll miss out on the rest of the gallery!

EAST WING: 18TH TO EARLY 20TH CENTURIES. The National Gallery's most crowded wing houses the Impressionists. Stealing the show in **Room 45** is Van Gogh's *Sunflowers,* a painting which he originally hung in the guest room for his good friend Paul Gauguin, whose paintings are displayed nearby. Pissarro's landscapes and Cézanne's *Bathers* also are on display. **Room 44** contains Seurat's controversial *Bathers at Asnières* in addition to works by Manet, Monet, Pissarro, and Renoir. As a reminder that there was art on the English side of the Channel, **Rooms 34** and **35** feature portraits by Joshua Reynolds and Thomas Gainsborough as well as six luminescent Turners, including the stunning *The Fighting Temeraire.* **Room 41** will satisfy the classically-inclined, with works by Ingres and Delacroix.

NATIONAL PORTRAIT GALLERY

St. Martin's Pl., at the start of Charing Cross Rd., Trafalgar Sq. ☉Leicester Sq. or Charing Cross. ☎020 7312 2463; www.npg.org.uk. Open M-W and Sa-Su 10am-6pm, Th-F 10am-9pm. Wheelchair-accessible on Orange St. Free lectures Tu 3pm. Free gallery talks Sa-Su afternoons. Free live music F 6:30pm. General admission free; some special exhibitions free, others up to £6. Popular events require tickets, available from the information desk. Audio tours £2.

This artistic Who's Who in Britain began in 1856 and is now the place to see Britain's freshest new artwork as well as centuries-old portraiture. New facilities include the sleek **Ondaatje Wing,** completed in 2000: an IT Gallery with computers that allow you to search for pictures and print out a personalized tour. A restaurant on the third floor affords an excellent view of Westminster, although its high prices (meals around £15) will limit most visitors to coffee.

> **⯴TIP** **HIGHLIGHTS IN A HURRY: NATIONAL PORTRAIT GALLERY.** Visit Henry VIII and Queen Elizabeth I in the **Tudor Galleries** before heading downstairs for a glimpse of Charles Dickens and the Brontë Sisters in **Early Victorian Arts.** Stare real royalty in the face at the **Sovereign Gallery,** then pass by pseudo-royalty in the **Balcony Gallery,** which houses portraits of Sir Elton John and Sir Paul McCartney. Put your British pop culture knowledge to the test in the ground fl. **Contemporary Galleries.**

SECOND FLOOR. To see the paintings in historical order, take the escalator from the reception hall in the Ondaatje Wing to the top floor. Pay your respects to Henry VIII in **Room 1** and Shakespeare and Queen Elizabeth I in **Room 2** before making your way to the Stuarts and Hanoverians. *Pride and Prejudice* enthusiasts should stop off in **Room 18** and see the only known portrait of Jane Austen, not much bigger than a playing card, as well as portraits of the Romantics including Wordsworth, Coleridge, Byron, Keats, and others.

FIRST FLOOR. Explore the early Victorian arts in **Room 24,** including portraits of both Charles Dickens and all three Brontë sisters. The Brontës' portrait—crease lines and all—was discovered folded up on top of a dusty cupboard. The **Balcony Gallery** holds some of the gallery's most fun (and irreverent) works, including large, head-on portraits of Diana and Charles and Sam Walsh's painting of Paul McCartney, jokingly titled *Mike's Brother*—Walsh was friends with the slightly less-famous Mike McCartney.

GROUND FLOOR. Check out contemporary works in the ground floor gallery, which boasts work by the hottest artists and the most famous stars, from 1990 to the present.

OTHER MUSEUMS AND GALLERIES

▨ROYAL ACADEMY OF ARTS. Founded in 1768 under the patronage of King George III, the Academy was designed to cultivate sculpture, painting, and architecture. Today the Academy shares courtyard space with the Royal Societies of Geology, Chemistry, Antiquaries, and Astronomy. The academics in charge are all accomplished artists or architects. The incredibly popular **Summer Exhibition** (Jun.-Aug.), held every year since 1769, is open to any artist for submission. It showcases an unparalleled range of contemporary art in every medium, most of which is available for purchase. On Friday nights, the museum stays open until 10pm, with free jazz in the Friends Room after 6:30pm and candlelit suppers in the cafe. *(Burlington House, Piccadilly. ☉Piccadilly Circus or Green Park.*

☎ *020 7300 8000; www.royalacademy.org.uk. Open M-Th and Sa-Su 10am-6pm, F 10am-10pm. Wheelchair-accessible. Free. Exhibits in the Main Galleries £7, students £5.)*

INSTITUTE OF CONTEMPORARY ARTS (ICA). Housed in the grand Carlton House Terrace, the ICA is London's center for avant-garde artists. Never shying away from the controversial, the ICA usually displays artwork that challenges and explores contemporary issues. The building holds a large ground-level and small upstairs gallery with temporary exhibits, an art-house cinema, a theater, a trendy cafe, and a relaxed bar that hosts frequent club nights and gigs. The Institute also regularly features talks and lectures. *(The Mall. ⊖Charing Cross or Piccadilly Circus ☎020 7930 0493; www.ica.org.uk. Talks and lectures up to £10. Reduced prices M. Galleries open M-W and F-Su noon-7pm, Th noon-9pm. Cafe and bar open M noon-11pm, Tu-Sa noon-1am, Su noon-9pm. "Day membership," with access to galleries, cafe, and bar M-F £2, concessions £1.50, Sa-Su £3, concessions £2. Cinema £8, M-F before 5pm £7; concessions £7/6.)*

AUCTION HOUSES

CHRISTIE'S. Like a museum but more crowded and all for sale, Christie's is the best of the auction houses. The public can enter on days before an auction to peruse what's up for grabs. Lots range from busts of Greek gods to Monets to sports memorabilia. *(8 King St. ⊖Green Park. Smaller branch at 85 Old Brompton St. in Kensington. ☎020 7839 9060; www.christies.com. Open M-F 9am-5pm; call in advance for exact opening times. Public viewings can close early for evening auctions. Wheelchair-accessible. Admission free. Catalogues from £10.)*

SOTHEBY'S. Before each auction, the items to be sold are displayed for viewing in the many interlocking galleries. Aristocratic Sotheby's is a busy place; auctions occur within days of each other. *(34-35 New Bond St. ⊖Bond St. ☎020 7293 5000; www.sothebys.com. Open for viewing M-F 9am-4:30pm, Sa and the occasional Su noon-5pm; call in advance for exact hours. Public viewings can close early for evening auctions. Wheelchair-accessible. Admission free. Catalogues from £10.)*

GAGOSIAN GALLERY. A branch of the famed New York Gagosian, this gallery holds solo shows of famous artists like Willem de Kooning, Cy Twombly, Jeff Koons, Warhol, Lichtenstein, and Picasso. Sparse and spacious, the gallery space is completely visible from the street and contributes to an exciting stroll through Mayfair. It showcases contemporary and avant-garde art of every variety and material. Shows change monthly or every two months. *(17-19 Davies St. ⊖Hyde Park or Marble Arch. ☎020 7493 3020; www.gagosian.com. Open Tu-Sa 10am-6pm. Free.)*

TIMOTHY TAYLOR GALLERY. This gallery features exhibits based on individual artists or on common media or subjects. It recently brought in the largest collection of Andy Warhol's early drawings ever shown in Britain. *(21 Dering St. ⊖Oxford Circus or Bond Street. ☎020 7409 3344; www.timothytaylorgallery.com. Open M-F 10am-6pm, Sa 10am-1pm. Wheelchair-accessible. Free.)*

ADAM GALLERY. Specializing in 20th-century contemporary British and international artists, Adam showcases the likes of Arp, Dubuffet, Delaunay, and Calder alongside contemporary greats on two floors. *(24 Cork St. ⊖Bond St. or Green Park. ☎020 7439 6633; www.adamgallery.com. Open M-F 10am-6pm, Sa 11am-3pm. Free.)*

MARLBOROUGH FINE ARTS. This spacious gallery presents a variety of contemporary artists, including anything from sketches to mixed media and Lucian Freud to Frank Auerbach. The gallery also focuses on introducing new artists. *(6 Albemarle St. ⊖Green Park. ☎020 7629 5161; www.marlboroughfinearts.com. Open M-F 10am-5:30pm, Sa 10am-12:30pm. Wheelchair-accessible. Free.)*

FROM THE ROAD

THE ANATOMY OF AN AUCTION

As one of the centers of modern and contemporary art—not to mention artistic thought and creation in general—London is full of places and spaces in which one can observe art being made, discussed, or otherwise appreciated: museums, galleries, walls, the Tube, etc. There is one realm, however, in which it seems something of a mystery: that is the auction room, a realm that is for many beyond the reach of the human eye and for some, even imagination. After two nights at Sotheby's—one at an Impressionism and Modern Art auction, the other at an Contemporary Art auction—here's what I've discovered.

The auction is in a large, white room with subtle but bright lighting. At the front, the podium sits next to the "title" work for the show (the work that appeared on the cover, and which often is expected to go for the most money). On the left wall is the press, most of whom gather in a standing huddle and occasionally exchange bits of info.

The audience is in many ways hard to sum up: for one, there doesn't seem to be a dress code—many go business or cocktail attire, but skinny jeans are also common, especially among the New Yorkers. They mingle, chat, and otherwise distract themselves from the works of genius that abound in the room. The Sotheby's people, all in black, flit about among the crowd meeting with press to talk up the event,

ROBERT SANDELSON. This small gallery, spread out over two floors, contains exhibits of big-time modern and contemporary artists like Damien Hirst, Tamara de Lempicka, Sam Francis, and Howard Hodgkin. *(5A Cork St. ⊖Bond St. or Green Park. ☎020 7439 1001; www.robertsandelson.com. Open M-F 10am-6pm, Sa 11am-4pm. Free.)*

SOHO

THE PHOTOGRAPHERS' GALLERY. The largest public gallery in London devoted entirely to photography, the photographer's gallery never fails to please and inspire. Displays usually feature a single artist's work, ranging from classic landscape to socially conscious photography. A small cafe, print shop, and bookshop (named the "best photography bookshop in Europe" by the Times) are on the second floor. Frequent gallery talks, book readings, walking tours and film screenings are free; occasional photographers' talks may charge admission. *(16-18 Ramillies St. ⊖Oxford Circus. ☎020 0845 262 1618; www.photonet.org.uk. Open Tu-W, and Sa 11am-6pm; Th-F 11am-8pm; Su noon-6pm. Free.)*

 ART FOR POCKET CHANGE. The galleries and auction houses in Mayfair and Soho are often free and showcase museum-quality work from famous artists—, but without the lines you'll find at the big museums.

COVENT GARDEN AND THE STRAND

Covent Garden's museums are largely interactive, so get ready to get hands-on. They're also geared towards specialized interests: if you're not a transportation or history buff, you may want to stick to meandering, sight-seeing, and people-watching.

LONDON TRANSPORT MUSEUM. From tram to Tube, the museum takes visitors chronologically through the development of London's public transportation system over the last 200 years, tracing London's growth as a metropolis. Actual antique and modern carriages, trams, buses, trains, and Tube cars contain wax passengers and drivers, while a large screen plays live scenes from the Tube today. The last stop, "Fast Forward," explores the future of transport, from hovercars to teleportation. *(Southeast corner of Covent Garden Piazza. ⊖Covent Garden. ☎020 7565 7299; www.ltmuseum.co.uk. Open M-Th* *and Sa-Su 10am-6pm, F 11am-6pm; last entry 5:15pm. Wheel-chair-accessible. £8, students £6, children under 16 free with adult.)*

BLOOMSBURY

☒BRITISH MUSEUM

Great Russell St. ⊖Tottenham Court Rd., Russell Square, or Holborn. ☎020 7323 8000; www.british-museum.org. Great Court open M-W and Su 9am-6pm, Th-Sa 9am-11pm (9pm in winter); galleries open daily 10am-5:30pm, selected galleries open Th-F 10am-8:30pm; library open M-W and Sa 10am-5:30pm, Th 10am-8:30pm, F noon-8:30pm. Free 30-40min. tours daily starting at 11am from the Enlightenment Desk. "Highlights Tour" daily 10:30am, 1, 3pm; advanced booking recommended. Wheelchair-accessible. Free; £3 suggested donation. Temporary exhibitions around £5, concessions £3.50. "Highlights Tour" £8, concessions £5. Audio tours £3.50, family audio tours for 2 adults and up to 3 children £10. MC/V.

The funny thing about the British Museum is that there's almost nothing British in it. Founded in 1753 as the personal collection of Sir Hans Sloane, the museum juxtaposes Victorian Anglocentrism with a more modern, multicultural acceptance. The building itself, in all its Neoclassical splendor, is magnificent; a leisurely stroll through the less crowded galleries is well worth an afternoon visit. The many visitors who don't make it past the main floor miss out—the galleries above and below are some of the museum's best, if not the most famous.

 HIGHLIGHTS IN A HURRY: BRITISH MUSEUM. Gape at the grandness of the **Great Court,** then hit the closely packed stars of the **Egypt/Greece wings** (Rosetta Stone, Elgin Marbles). Take more time in the quieter **African** and **Islamic** galleries in the north wing. Head upstairs for actual British artifacts and for the **Clock Gallery.**

GREAT COURT. The largest covered square in Europe, the Great court is a must-see. Used as the British Library stacks for the past 150 years, the courtyard is still dominated by a gigantic **Reading Room.** The blue chairs and desks, set inside a towering dome of books, have shouldered the weight of research by Marx, Lenin, and Trotsky, as well as almost every major British writer and intellectual.

WEST GALLERIES. From the main entrance, the large double doors to the left of the Reading Room

making sure bidders are happy and primed to pay, and generally attempting to build the necessary mood, confidence, and energy.

The auctioneer, the man in the well-tailored suit, initially comes off as a bit of a stoic. As he begins to speak, though, a slight hum starts to gather and one feels the risk and excitement build: this event could explode or fizzle. There is a feeling that the millions that are being spent are as much based on the feel, energy, and rhythm of this room as they are on the months of deliberation and intellectual debate that precede the auction.

Some pieces garner no attention and fall flat—there is a feeling of general disappointment but also a shared sense that perhaps that was meant to happen: this is the market. And the one after it flails too, perhaps because of what preceded it. And then there are bidding wars—this man on the phone, that woman in the audience, back, forth, back, forth, ended by the gavel. The crowd, though largely still socializing, seems happier. The level of anticipation builds, then tapers again. This continues until the final gavel is heard, and we have reached the end. The room clears, the pieces come down, all is white again.

—Sara O'Rourke

lead to the Museum's most popular wing. The **Rosetta Stone** takes center stage in the **Egyptian Sculpture** rooms, while the less iconic but enduringly huge monumental friezes and reliefs of the Assyrian, Hittite, and other Ancient Near Eastern civilizations are worth more than a glance. Most famous (and controversial) of the massive array of Greek sculptures on display are the **Elgin Marbles** from the Parthenon, statues carved under the direction of Athens's greatest sculptor, Phidias (Room 18). The Greek government has been asking for the Marbles back for years, but the British government technically bought the Marbles (albeit for a measly price). Other Hellenic highlights include remnants of two of the seven Wonders of the Ancient World: the **Temple of Artemis** at Ephesus and the **Mausoleum of Halikarnassos** (Rooms 21-22). Upstairs, the **Portland Vase** presides over Roman ceramics and housewares (Room 70). When discovered in 1582, the vase had already been broken and reconstructed, and in 1845, it was shattered again by a drunk museum-goer. When it was put back together, 37 small chips were left over; two reconstructions have reincorporated more and more leftover chips, though some are still missing from the vase.

NORTH GALLERIES. Egyptian sarcophagi and mummies await in Rooms 61-66. The newer **African Galleries** display a fabulous collection accompanied by soft chanting, video displays, and abundant documentation (Room 25, lower floor). In Rooms 51-59, musical instruments and board games from the world's first city, Ur, show that leisure time is a historical constant, while nearby, **Mexico** dominates the **Americas** collection with extraordinary Aztec artifacts (Rooms 26-27). **Islamic** art resides in Room 34, and above it, the largest room in the museum holds **Chinese, South Asian,** and **Southeast Asian** artifacts alongside some particularly impressive Hindu sculpture (Room 33). The highlight of the **Korean** display, in Room 67, is a sarangbang house built on-site, while a tea house is the centerpiece of the **Japanese** galleries (Rooms 92-94).

SOUTH AND EAST GALLERIES. The **King's Library** gallery holds artifacts gathered from throughout the world by English explorers during the **Enlightenment.** While the labeling is poor (and in some places nonexistent), the collection itself is spectacular. The upper level of the museum's southeast corner is dedicated to ancient and medieval Europe, including most of the museum's British artifacts. A highlight of the collection is the treasure excavated from the **Sutton Hoo Burial Ship;** the magnificent inlaid helmet is the most famous example of Anglo-Saxon craftsmanship. Along with the ship is the **Mildenhall Treasure,** a trove of brilliantly preserved Roman artifacts (Room 41). Next door are the enigmatic and beautiful **Lewis Chessmen,** an 800-year-old Scandinavian chess set mysteriously abandoned on Scotland's Outer Hebrides (Room 42). Collectors and enthusiasts will also enjoy the comprehensive **Clock Gallery** (Room 44) and **Money Gallery** (Room 68).

TIP

DON'T BE MIS-GUIDED. The British Museum sells a number of items to assist the overwhelmed, including a map with color plans and illustrated visitor information (£2.50), a book of 15 Self-Guided Tours (£3.50), and a souvenir guide in 10 languages (£6). If you plan just to make a day of it, the most you would need (if anything) is the first—especially when paired with our own highlights. Also, keep in mind that a basic map is free.

OTHER MUSEUMS IN BLOOMSBURY

■BRITISH LIBRARY GALLERIES. Housed in a somber room the British Library (p. 127) is a sprawling collection of some of the most precious pieces of literature, music, religious texts, and notes in the world. In the **Literature Corner,** find Shakespeare's first folio, Lewis Carroll's handwritten manuscript of *Alice in Wonderland* (donated by the real life "Alice" herself), and Virginia Woolf's crazed handwritten notes for *Mrs. Dalloway* (then called *The Hours*). Music-lovers will enjoy Handel's handwritten *Messiah*, Mozart's marriage contract, Beethoven's tuning fork, and a whole display dedicated to the Beatles, including the original handwritten lyrics to *A Hard Days Night*—scrawled on the back of Lennon's son Julian's 1st birthday card. In **Illuminated Manuscripts and Sacred Texts,** you'll find the *Lindisfarne Gospels*, history's best-surviving Anglo-Saxon gospel, and Sultan Baybar's 1304 Qu'ran—some of the most beautiful texts in the world. The original copy of the Magna Carta has its own room with the accompanying Papal Bull that Pope Innocent III wrote in response. Leonardo da Vinci's notebooks are in the **Science** section, and one of 50 known original Gutenberg Bibles (1454) is in the **Printing** section. Sound archive jukeboxes allow visitors to hear snippets of the texts and music on display, and the **Turning the Page** computer enables anyone to (electronically) peruse the ancient tomes. Downstairs, the **Workshop of Sounds and Images** is aimed at a younger audience, with interactive displays charting the history of recording, from parchment to TV. *(96 Euston Rd.* ✪*King's Cross St. Pancras.* ☎*020 7412 7332; www.bl.uk. Grab a free map at the main info desk. Open M and W-F 9:30am-6pm, Tu 9:30am-8pm, Sa 9:30am-5pm, Su 11am-5pm. Wheelchair-accessible. Free.)*

THE CARTOON MUSEUM. This small, privately owned museum gives an insider's view of Britain's political pulse and its famous sense of humor. Two floors showcase over 200 British political cartoons, caricatures, and comics from 1700 to the present: think lots of dry humor and Margaret Thatcher sketches. *(35 Little Russel St.* ✪*Tottenham Court Rd., Russell Sq., or Holborn.* ☎*020 7580 8155; www.cartoonmuseum.org. Open Tu-Sa 10:30am-5:30pm, Su noon-5:30pm. Wheelchair-accessible. £5.50, concessions £4, students £3, under 18 free.)*

POLLOCK'S TOY MUSEUM. A maze of tiny rooms and passageways, this museum is full of antique playthings of high kitsch value. *(1 Scala St., entrance on Whitfield St.* ✪*Goodge St.* ☎*020 7636 3452; www.pollockstoytheatres.com. Open M-Sa 10am-5pm; last entry 4:30pm. £5, concessions £4, under 18 £2. AmEx/MC/V.)*

GALLERIES

BRUNEI GALLERY. Affiliated with the SOAS, this beautiful three-story space is devoted to carefully and elaborately crafted exhibitions of African and Asian art and culture. As its patron is the Sultan of Brunei, you'd expect nothing less. In 2010, exhibits will include "Self & Other: Portraits From Asia And Europe" (Jan. 21-Mar. 27); "In The Middle Of Asia: Music & Poetry of Tajikistan" and "Contemporary Ethiopian Art From Addis Ababa, Ethiopia" (Apr.-June); and "The Hibakusha Portraits – Hiroshima" (Aug. 6 - Oct. 10). *(10 Thornhaugh St., opposite the main SOAS entrance.* ✪*Russell Sq.* ☎*020 7898 4915; www.soas.ac.uk/gallery. Open Tu-Sa 10:30am-5pm when exhibits are running; visit website or call for schedule. Wheelchair-accessible. Group tours upon request. Free.)*

WOOLFF GALLERY. This gallery features new and established contemporary artists and designers, including Banksy, David Wheeler, Victoria Rose, Ben Young and Russell Wes, and work in a variety of mediums, including paint,

print, photography, ceramic, porcelain, and graffiti. *(89 Charlotte St. ⊖Goodge.*
☎020 7631 0551; www.woolffgallery.co.uk. Open M-F 10:30am-6pm, Sa 11am-5pm. Free.)

NORTH LONDON

North London's small collection of museums is diverse in their subject matter,
and even though many tourists stay away, the savvy traveler will enjoy exploring the many hidden treasures, from RAF fighters to Rembrandts.

CAMDEN TOWN, KING'S CROSS, AND ISLINGTON

ESTORICK COLLECTION. One of the "finest collections of 20th-century Italian art in the world" according to the Tate's director, the Estorick showcases works owned by American sociologist and London gallery owner Eric
Estorick. Housed in an 18th-century Georgian mansion, the collection focuses
above all on the Futurists, who sought to develop an aesthetic based on modern life and technology, but also features some figurative and metaphysical
works: Buccioni, Campigli, de Chirico, Morandi, Modigliani, and others are
all here. Extensive temporary exhibits, which are integrated with the permanent works, have included spotlights on Marcello Levi, fashion designer Mis-
soni, and Italian photography and sculpture. The museum also has a pleasant
courtyard cafe. *(39A Canonbury Sq. ⊖Highbury and Islington. ☎020 7704 9522; www.*
estorickcollection.com. Open W-Sa 11am-6pm, Su noon-5pm. Partially wheelchair-accessible.
£5, concessions £3.50, students and children under 16 free.)

> **TIP** **DON'T ZONE OUT.** When traveling to Islington, remember that ⊖Angel
> lies within Zone 1, while ⊖Highbury and Islington is in Zone 2. If your des-
> tination is anywhere near Upper St., save the extra fare price, do a bit of
> walking, and spend the money on a coffee instead.

THE JEWISH MUSEUM. The Jewish Museum is actually composed of two com-
plementary museums with different collections. The first, **Camden,** focuses on
the history of Jews in Britain. Its crowning achievement is a magnificent 16th-
century Venetian synagogue ark discovered by accident while being used as a
lord's wardrobe. Special programs and workshops are offered for children and
adults. *(129-131 Albert St. ⊖Camden Town. ☎020 7284 1997; www.jewishmuseum.org.uk.*
Open M-Th 10am-4pm, Su 10am-5pm; last entry 30min. before closing; closed Jewish holidays.
Wheelchair-accessible. £4, seniors £3, students and children £2, families £9.) The smaller
Jewish Museum, **Finchley,** focuses on Jewish social history and 19th- and early
20th-century life in London's East End. Its small Holocaust Education gallery is
particularly moving. *(80 East End Rd. 10min. walk from ⊖Finchley Central; take the "Regent's*
Park Rd." exit from the Tube, turn left on Station Rd., and then right on Manor View, which runs into
East End Rd. by the museum. ☎020 8349 1143. Open M-Th 10:30am-5pm, Su 10:30am-4:30pm;
closed Su in Aug. and Jewish holidays. Partially wheelchair-accessible. £3, children free.)

SAINT JOHN'S WOOD AND MAIDA VALE

FREUD MUSEUM. The comfortable home in which Sigmund Freud spent the
last year of his life after fleeing the Nazis packs a bit more of a punch than
most celebrity houses. In his later years, Freud delved into cultural analysis,
evidenced by his anthropological collection of masks and random artifacts
(thus setting the obligatory interior design scheme for every therapist's office
in perpetuity). He didn't drop his patients, however, and the infamous Persian
rug-covered couch in his dark study stands ready for the next session. Upstairs

hangs Dalí's cranially exaggerated portrait of Freud alongside the bedroom of Anna Freud, Sigmund's youngest daughter, who was an eminent psychoanalyst in her own right. An audio guide, along with selected plaques, brings the house to life by tying certain objects to Freud's dreams, family stories, and patients. *(20 Maresfield Gardens. ⊖ Swiss Cottage or Finchley Rd. ☎ 020 7435 2002; www.freud.org.uk. Open W-Su noon-5pm. Wheelchair-accessible. £5, children under 12 free. Audio guide £2.)*

HAMPSTEAD, HIGHGATE, AND GOLDERS GREEN

■**THE IVEAGH BEQUEST.** The impressive Iveagh collection in Kenwood House was bequeathed to the nation by the Earl of Iveagh, who purchased the estate in 1922. Everything on the estate is a work of art, from the ponds and paths to the rooms in the house, especially the library. A free booklet guides you through highlights including *The Guitar Player*—one of 35 known Vermeers in the world—Rembrandt's compelling self-portraits, and a beautiful Botticelli. Georgian society portraits by Reynolds, Gainsborough, Hogarth, and Romney fill the walls with faces of people who look as though they might have called Kenwood home. Meanwhile, even if you can't get into the house, the surrounding grounds are breathtaking. *(Kenwood House. Road access from Hampstead Ln. Walk or take Bus #210 from North End Way or Spaniards Rd. or from ⊖ Archway or Golders Green. ☎ 020 8348 1286. Wheelchair-accessible. Open daily 11:30am-4pm. Free.)*

GALLERIES

While Hampstead is a tiny town, a handful of worthwhile galleries lie along **Heath Street.**

The Catto Gallery, 100 Heath St. (☎ 020 7435 6660; www.catto.co.uk). One of London's leading contemporary fine art galleries, Catto features over 50 internationally recognized artists. Open M-Sa 10am-6pm, Su 2:30-6pm.

gallery k, 101-103 Heath St. (☎ 020 7794 4949; www. gallery-k.co.uk). ⊖ Hampstead. With a mind toward making art "help you to feel that the world, especially your own personal space, is a better place to be," k presents the most promising and most established contemporary Greek artists. Almost always uplifting. Open Tu-F 10am-6pm, Sa 11am-6pm, Su 2:30-6:30pm.

MARYLEBONE AND REGENT'S PARK

Marylebone's museums, like its sights, display the best and the worst of London attractions: the classic and classy Wallace Collection alongside the cheesy Sherlock Holmes Museum.

■**THE WALLACE COLLECTION.** Housed in palatial Hertford House, this stunning array of paintings, porcelain, and armor was bequeathed to the nation by the widow of Sir Richard Wallace in 1897. Restored to much of its 19th-century glory, the mansion's impressive collection is rendered even more dazzling by its grand gilded setting. On the ground floor, four **Armoury Galleries** boast scads of richly decorated weapons and burnished suits of armor. The **State Rooms** hold a collection of sumptuous Sèvres porcelain from Catherine II of Russia's meal service and the study has furniture once owned by Marie Antoinette, the queen of indulgence. The **East Galleries** contain Dutch and Flemish art. The centerpiece of this collection is indisputably the **Great Gallery,** once called "the greatest picture gallery in Europe": it boasts a varied collection of 17th-century work by masters like Van Dyck, Rembrandt, Rubens, Ruisdael, Velázquez, Titian, and Gainsborough as well as the collection's most celebrated piece, Frans Hals's *Laughing Cavalier.* An ongoing refurbishment project means some rooms are closed, but with over 25 galleries in total, you won't feel like you've missed anything. Hungry art appreciators can plop down in the newly opened and ever-so-swanky sculpture garden restaurant, **The Wallace,** which serves gourmet French cuisine. *(Hertford House, Manchester Sq.* ⊖*Bond St., Baker St., or Marble Arch.* ☎*020 7563 9500; call for details. Wheelchair-accessible. Free (£2 suggested donation). Tours £6. Audio tours £3. Restaurant:* ☎*020 7563 9505. Entrees £12.50-18. Open M-Th and Su 10am-5pm; F-Sa 10am-11pm.)*

SHERLOCK HOLMES MUSEUM. With four floors of scenes and decor from Sir Arthur Conan Doyle's novels, this museum claims to be the real 19th-century residence of fictional characters Sherlock Holmes and Dr. Watson. Probably only die-hard fans who delight in the unabashedly corny will find a photo-op in Mr. Holmes's cap worth the six quid. *(221B Baker St.* ⊖*Baker St.* ☎*020 7935 8866; www.sherlock-holmes.co.uk. Open daily 9:30am-6pm. £6, children 7-16 £4.)*

GALLERIES

THOMPSON'S GALLERY. Priding itself on displaying 20th- and 21st-century British and Scottish artists, Thompson's features cutting-edge painting, sculpture, and photography. *(76 Marylebone High St.* ⊖*Baker St. or Bond St.* ☎*020 7935 3595; www.thompsonsgallery.com. Open M-F 10am-6pm, Sa 11am-5pm, Su 11am-4pm.)*

NOTTING HILL

GALLERIES

Hanina Fine Arts Ltd, 180 Westbourne Grove (☎020 7243 8877; www.haninafinearts.com). ⊖Ladbroke Grove. A well-established gallery with another location in New York City. Showcases work by modern and contemporary international artists. Open M-Sa 10am-6pm.

Stern Pissarro Gallery, 46 Ledbury Rd. (☎020 7729 6187; www.stern-art.com). ⊖Ladbroke Grove. Showcasing work from the master himself as well as 3 generations of his followers, Stern Pissarro is filled with oil paintings and works on paper. Open M-Sa 10am-6pm.

KENSINGTON AND EARL'S COURT

South Kensington's "Albertopolis" is home to a triumvirate of London's biggest and best museums: the Victoria and Albert Museum, the Natural History Museum, and the Science Museum. While it's tempting to try and "do" them in a day, visiting more than two is a feat of superhuman stamina (not to mention a waste of at least one perfectly good museum). For those in a hurry, we've provided highlights so you don't miss the must-see treasures.

RISE ABOVE. While most people just take the sign-posted "Subway" feeder tunnels from the Tube to the museums, it's just as quick (and far more pleasant in good weather) to use the above-ground route.

◪VICTORIA AND ALBERT MUSEUM

Main entrance on Cromwell Rd., wheelchair-accessible entrance on Exhibition Rd. ⊖*South Kensington.* ☎*020 7942 2000; www.vam.ac.uk. Open M-Th and Sa-Su 10am-5:45pm, F 10am-10pm. Wheelchair-accessible. Free tours meet at rear of main entrance: introductory tours daily 10:30, 11:30am, 1:30, 3:30pm, plus W 4:30pm; British gallery tours daily 12:30 and 2:30pm. Talks and events meet at rear of main entrance. Free lunchtime talks W 1:15pm; free gallery talks Th 1pm (45-60min); F talks 7-8pm with big names in art, design and fashion industries, £8, concessions £6. Admission free.*

When the V&A was founded in 1852 as the Museum of Manufactures, the curators were deluged with objects from around the globe. Today, as the largest museum of decorative (and not so decorative) arts in the world, the

V&A rivals the British Museum for the sheer size and diversity of its holdings—befitting an institution dedicated to displaying "the fine and applied arts of all countries, all styles, all periods." With consistently excellent content, the V&A's five million sq. m of galleries house the "world's greatest collection" of miniature portraits, including Holbein's *Anne of Cleves*, newly refurbished glass and architecture galleries, and an exhaustive showcase of fashion from the 16th century onward. Interactive displays, high-tech touchpoints, and engaging activities add to the treasures. Staff shortages can lead to the temporary closure of less popular galleries without notice; it's best to call in advance on the day of your visit if you want to see a specific gallery. Themed itineraries available at the desk can help streamline your visit, and Family Trail cards suggest routes through the museum with kids.

 HIGHLIGHTS IN A HURRY: VICTORIA AND ALBERT MUSEUM. Make a tour of the **Fashion Gallery** before heading over to see **Tippoo's Tiger,** the **Cast Courts,** and the collection of **Oriental Rugs.** Finish up with a trip through the **20th-Century** galleries or go further back in time in the **British Galleries.**

BRITISH GALLERIES. The beneficiary of a recent £31 million renovation, the vast British Galleries sprawl over three floors of reconstructed rooms, documenting the progression of British taste and fashion from 1500 to 1900. From clothing to furniture to innumerable fascinating gadgets, exhibits all begin by asking, "Who led taste?" (The answer, of course, is always the British.)

FASHION GALLERY. Nothing but the finest resides in this gallery, which showcases the V&A's world-famous costume collection, covering everything from 18th-century court mantuas to modern minimalist garments. In the outer circle of displays, the exquisite clothes are arranged by themes: Dressing Up, Undress, The Suit for Men, The Suit for Women, The Dress, and Sportswear. Inner displays feature the "fashion cities"—London, Milan, New York, Paris, and Tokyo—as well as famous designers that are based there. Temporary exhibits change once or twice a year; themes have included Vivienne Westwood, New Sixties Fashion, Jean Charles de Casteljabac, and most recently, Future Fashion Now.

ASIAN GALLERIES. The selection of objects in the V&A's Asian collections may rest on national clichés (Indian temple carvings, Chinese porcelain), but the objects themselves are still spectacular. The highlight here is **Tippoo's Tiger,** a fascinatingly graphic 1799 model of a tiger eating a man—complete with organ sounds and crunching noises. The excellent **Japanese Gallery** displays an array of contemporary ceramic sculpture and kimonos.

UPPER FLOORS. Arranged by material, the upper floors are home to galleries devoted to everything from musical instruments to stained glass. In the textile collection, you can try on kimonos and tweed jackets, while long cabinets contain swatches of thousands of different fabrics. Two exceptions to the materially themed galleries are the **Leighton Gallery,** with a fresco by the essential Victorian painter, and the sprawling and somewhat trippy **20th-century collections,** where you'll find design classics like Salvador Dalí's 1936 sofa modeled on Mae West's lips, a spiral bookshelf, and a pair of 1990s latex hotpants.

HENRY COLE WING. The six-level Henry Cole wing is home to the V&A's collection of British paintings, including some 350 works by Constable as well as numerous Turners. Also here is a display of Rodin bronzes, donated by the artist in 1914. In the library-like print room, anyone can ask to see original works from the prodigious collection. *(Print room open Tu-Sa 10am-5pm.)*

OTHER MUSEUMS IN KENSINGTON AND EARL'S COURT

◪SCIENCE MUSEUM. Dedicated to the Victorian ideal of progress, the Science Museum focuses on the transformative power of technology in all its guises and aims to "bring science to life and life to science." With five floors, a whole host of special exhibits and activities, and a melange of cutting-edge interactive displays and priceless historical artifacts, there's certainly something for everyone. The towering **Making of the Modern World** entrance hall houses a collection of pioneering contraptions, including the Apollo 10 command module, while the basement focuses on smaller inventions with the **Secret Life of the Home,** showcasing 100 years of household gadgets, including Sir Thomas Crapper's famed "valveless waste preventer" and a 1970s VCR the size of a large microwave.

In the first floor's **"Who am I?",** you can research your family tree, meet a 200-year-old skeleton, and participate in a series of (potentially demoralizing) games that test your levels of intelligence, beauty, success, and happiness. The **Flight Gallery** tells the story of air travel from Victorian attempts at steam-powered flight to modern jumbo jets, and holds dozens of airplanes and an interactive Flight Lab. The popular **Launchpad** offers over 50 interactive exhibits, plus lively shows and demos, all of which explore the world of physics: build your own magnetic building, watch the bubble wall appear and disappear around you, or make water dance using sound effects. The **Science and Art of Medicine,** on the top floor, chronicles in impressive detail the history of medicine in its modern and cross-cultural incarnations, with over 5000 objects. Alternatively, scorn the real world entirely and enter virtual reality with a **SimEx** simulator ride through Dino Island, or get a ticket to the 3D motion theater, **Force Field,** where you can smell, hear, and feel what it's like to venture into space on an Apollo mission. *(Exhibition Rd. ⊖South Kensington. ☎08708 704 868, IMAX 08708 704 771; www.sciencemuseum.org.uk. Open daily 10am-6pm; last entry 5:30pm. Wheelchair-accessible. Free. Audio tours: "Soundbytes" cover Power, Space, and Making the Modern World; £3.50 each. IMAX shows usually daily every 30min., 10am-5pm; £8, concessions £6.25. See website for showtimes and bookings. SimEx £2.50, concessions £2; Force Field £5/4; special exhibitions £9/7. Daily demonstrations and workshops in the basement galleries and theater. MC/V.)*

◪NATURAL HISTORY MUSEUM. Architecturally the most impressive of the South Kensington trio, this cathedral-like Romanesque museum has been a favorite with Londoners since 1880. The entrance hall is dedicated to the **Wonders of the Natural History Museum,** a series of prehistorically important skeletons including a Diplodocus and a moa (a giant, flightless bird once native to New Zealand, extinct since the early 16th century). Divided into four zones—blue, green, orange, and red—the rest of the museum is reasonably easy to navigate despite regular massive crowds.

In the **Blue Zone,** you'll find the dark and surreal **Dinosaur Galleries,** which won't disappoint the Jurassic Park generation: the animatronic T-rex is so popular that he's secured an exhibit entirely for himself, and he has smaller animatronic friends, too. The enormous **Human Biology** exhibit boasts an endless succession of interactive and high-tech displays, not to mention an extremely detailed reproduction gallery. Nearby, you'll find an exhaustive collection of reptile and mammal exhibits, which hold many obscure species as well. The decided favorite is the massive blue whale suspended from the ceiling.

The **Green Zone** is home to **Creepy Crawlies,** featuring an enormous model scorpion, vomiting fly models, and a live ant colony. The collection of stuffed and mounted birds features everything from the ostentatious peacock to the awkward ostrich. You'll also get a sense of our place in the world's history, with the primates and evolution exhibits.

The **Red Zone** is less comprehensive but a bit more dynamic. The **Earth Galleries** are reached via a long escalator that journeys through the center of a model Earth on its way to **The Power Within,** an exposition of the volcanic and tectonic forces beneath our planet's surface. A walk-through model of a Japanese supermarket provides a recreation of the 1995 Kobe earthquake, and, on the same floor, **Restless Surface** explores the gentler action of wind and water in reshaping the world. The first floor's **From the Beginning** tells the history of the Earth itself, while **The Earth's Treasury** presents an enormous and spectacular array of gems and minerals, from sandstone to diamonds to many jewels you've probably never seen.

The **Orange Zone** is set to open in fall 2009, and will hold the cocoon-inside-a-box that is the Darwin Centre, an eight-story, £78 million project—the largest expansion since the museum moved to South Kensington in 1881. Most of it is research and storage space for the largest insect collection in the world, but it will also be open for tours, where the public can see what goes on behind the scenes and engage in interactive activities about the natural world and its conservation. *(Cromwell Rd. ⊖South Kensington. ☎020 7942 5000; www.nhm.ac.uk. Open daily 10am-5:50pm; last entry 5:30pm. Wheelchair-accessible. Free; special exhibits usually £7, concessions £4.50. MC/V.)*

HIGHLIGHTS IN A HURRY: NATURAL HISTORY MUSEUM. Shudder from **Creepy Crawlies** to the **Dinosaur Galleries,** making sure to swing by the blue whale. Then gape at the gems in the **Earth's Treasury** on your way to the Kobe earthquake upstairs.

SERPENTINE GALLERY. This tiny 1934 tea pavilion in the middle of Kensington Gardens is the unlikely venue for some of London's top contemporary art shows; Jeff Koons's recent *Popeye* series, displayed here, was his first major exhibition in a public gallery in England. Summer nights in the park also include architecture talks, live readings, and open-air film screenings. *(Off West Carriage Dr., Kensington Gardens ⊖South Kensington or Lancaster Gate. ☎020 7402 6075; www.serpentinegallery.org. Open daily 10am-6pm. Wheelchair-accessible. Free; suggested donation £1.)*

CHELSEA

Chelsea is not a destination for historical museums: home to the infamous Saatchi Gallery and a number of other lesser-known fine art galleries, this is above all a place for aesthetic appreciation. That being said, those interested in the military may want to check out the National Army Museum.

NATIONAL ARMY MUSEUM. Starting with the Battle of Agincourt in 1415 and ending with "The Modern Army," the chronological displays feature life-size recreations, videos, and memorabilia of combat through the ages. Naturally, there's also a permanent Waterloo display, complete with the skeleton of Napoleon's favorite horse, Marengo. *(Royal Hospital Rd. ⊖Sloane Sq., then Bus #137 or 360. ☎020 7730 0717; www.national-army-museum.ac.uk. Open daily 10am-5:30pm. Wheelchair-accessible. Free.)*

GALLERIES

◾SAATCHI GALLERY. London's leading gallery for contemporary art opened its new Duke of York location, which is more like a monument, museum, or park than a gallery, in October 2008. Its 70,000 sq. ft. of exhibition space features work from up-and-coming as well as not yet discovered talents. A show in the Saatchi is not just an honor—it can change an artist's career. Along with its renowned collection, the new building includes a bookshop and a sophisticated cafe. *(Duke of York Pl. ⊖ Sloane Sq. www.saatchi-gallery.co.uk. Open daily 10am-6pm. Free.)*

GAGLIARDI GALLERY. Associated with the Museum of Art of Chianciano Terme in Tuscany, Gagliardi showcases both lesser-known and established Realist, Impressionist, post-Impressionist, and Surrealist artists. Collection includes works by Edvard Munch, Rene Magritte, and Salvador Dalí. *(509 King's Rd. ⊖ Sloane Sq., then bus #11 or 22. ☎ 020 7352 3663; www.gagliardi.org. Open M-Sa 10:30am-7pm, Su 11am-5pm. Free.)*

FLYING COLOURS GALLERY. Founded in Scotland, this small gallery displays contemporary pieces by local artists. Work ranges from abstracts to landscapes to figurative art. *(The Courtyard, 6 Burnsall St., off of King's Rd. ⊖ Sloane Sq. ☎ 020 7351 5558; www.flying-coloursgallery.com. Open M-F 10:30am-5:30pm; evenings and weekends by arrangement. Free.)*

FAIRFAX GALLERY. With 3 locations in London, Fairfax has built a reputation for showing award-winning new contemporary artists alongside more established names in its two spacious floors and outdoor sculpture garden. *(5 Park Walk. ⊖ South Kensington. ☎ 020 7751 4477; www.fairfaxgallery.com. Open M-F 10:30am-6pm, Sa 11am-6pm. Free.)*

🎵 ENTERTAINMENT

With West End ticket prices through the roof and the quality of some shows highly questionable (not that we don't enjoy a good song-and-dance routine), it may seem that the city that brought the world Shakespeare, the Sex Pistols, and even Andrew Lloyd Webber and Tim Rice has lost its originality and theatrical edge. But, forgetting the new wave of mega-musicals—where Hollywood B-listers come to revive careers, or to at least go down with a yelp—London is at its heart a city of immense talent: it is a classroom for student up-and-comers, proteges of London-based Rolling Stones, David Bowie, and The Police, who were themselves small fish at one time; it is the city of undergrounders who prefer to hear their names shouted by fans rather than showcased in neon lights; and a city of writers who experiment and constantly push the limits. Fringe venues in North, South, and East London still produce the cutting-edge, where smart and challenging performances shine particularly bright in comparison to lackluster actors who may fall over from boredom if they sing "Fame" just one more time.

We do not want to give you the impression that the West End is dead: although long-running, Les Misérables is one of the best shows around, while, new to the 2004-05 season, Billy Elliot and a dark and edgy Mary Poppins have gotten rave reviews. The Globe continues to put on Elizabethan classics, and famed British wit makes audiences belly-laugh in the same comedy clubs where Whose Line Is It, Anyway? got its start; the Royal Ballet is as notable as when Dame Margot Fonteyn headlined, while fans of punk rock still dance to their own beat. And, oh yeah, there's that whole sports phenomenon. Whatever your fancy, London is sure to keep you entertained.

METRO IN THE TUBE. You don't have to buy the newspaper every morning to find the day's exciting entertainment and nightlife listings. Free in most Tube stations is The Metro, a small newspaper with headlines and event information, so read for free as you ride.

CINEMA

The heart of the celluloid monster is Leicester Square, where the dominant chains like Odeon take hold. Tickets to West End cinemas cost £5-10; weekday screenings before 5pm (and all day Monday) are usually cheaper and many offer regular student discounts (except on the weekends). Time Out publishes reviews and schedules for films, as do many other newspapers. Online, www.viewlondon.com also posts schedules. For listings of film festivals, see Life and Times (p. 50).

 CHOOSING A CINEMA. Unless you've booked early for a premiere, it's best to avoid the megaplex cinemas directly on Leicester Square—they all charge a few pounds more than those on the surrounding streets. There is another Odeon right down the road on Tottenham Court Rd. in Bloomsbury.

■ **Electric Cinema,** 191 Portobello Rd. (☎7908 9696; www.the-electric.co.uk), in Notting Hill. ⊖Notting Hill Gate or Ladbroke Grove. The improved version of London's oldest cinema (built in 1910). The Baroque splendor of a stage theater paired with a sleek big screen and an in-theater bar. Leather armchairs and loveseats make for a luxurious cinematic experience. Independent and international films, including docu-dramas, classics, and recent hits. Wheelchair-accessible. Tickets M £7.50, Tu-Su £12.50. Front 3 rows M £5, Tu-Su £10, 2-seat sofa M £20, Tu-Su £30. Twinbills Su 2pm £5/7.50/20. Book online at least 2 weeks in advance. MC/V.

■ **National Film Theatre,** Belvedere Rd. (☎7928 3232; www.bfi.org.uk/nft), in the South Bank. ⊖Waterloo, Embankment, or Temple. Underneath Waterloo Bridge. This is a 1-stop shop for alternatives to the summer blockbusters: European art-house retrospectives, old American flicks, and special directors' series fill the program. 6 different shows hit 3 screens every evening (9 shows on weekends), starting around 6pm (2pm on weekends). The sprawling, super-popular cafe and bar on the ground floor serve up goodies to the masses. Annual membership (£22, concessions £14) gives £1 off movies, priority booking, and a free ticket when you join. All films £7.50, concessions £5.70. Wheelchair-accessible.

■ **Riverside Studios,** Crisp Rd. (☎8237 1111; www.riversidestudios.co.uk), in West London. ⊖Hammersmith. From the Tube, take Queen Caroline St. under the motorway and follow it past the Apollo (10min.) toward the Thames. Crisp Rd. is on the left, 1 block before the river. One of the best entertainment venues in London, Riverside is not well-known outside of West London—probably due to its less-than-aggressive marketing scheme and slightly hidden location—but its productions are very popular with locals. 2 theaters feature well-reviewed dramas, as well as homegrown fringe productions and comedy. The ■ **cinema** plays international art-house films, with an excellent film festival program featuring new international work and many classics (some with live piano) entirely in double bills. It also has an espresso cafe and cafeteria-style restaurant, convenient for mealtime shows. Plays £10-20, student prices vary with performance. Films £6.50; students, elderly, disabled, and unemployed £5.50. Wheelchair-accessible. Box office open daily noon-9pm. Schedules online. MC/V.

BFI London IMAX Cinema, 1 Charlie Chaplin Walk (☎0870 787 2525; www.bfi.org.uk/imax), in the South Bank. ⊖Waterloo. At the south end of Waterloo bridge, accessible via underground walkways from the South Bank and the Tube station. This theater sticks out like a glass-enclosed sore thumb, rising in the center of a traffic roundabout. It houses the UK's biggest screen, at 20m high and 26m wide—taller than 5 double-decker buses stacked on top of each other. Blockbusters and educational movies shown. Shows start every 1hr.; last show 8:15 or 8:45pm daily. £8.50, concessions (M-F only) £6.25, children under 16 £5. MC/V.

Curzon Soho, 93-107 Shaftesbury Ave. (☎7734 2255; www.curzoncinemas.com), in Soho. ⊖Leicester Sq. Retains good taste in films—watch the latest hot independent and international films from plush, high-backed seats. Sleek cafe on the ground fl., and bar on the lower level. Frequent talks and Q&A sessions from big-name indie directors. 3 screens. Su classic and repertory double bills. M-F before 5pm £7, all other times £10; Su £6.50. Concessions £7. Wheelchair-accessible. AmEx/MC/V.

Everyman Cinema, 5 Holly Bush Vale (☎08700 664 777; www.everymancinema.com), in North London. ⊖Hampstead. One of London's oldest movie theaters, this 1930s picture house was recently revamped and is now hipper and more comfortable than ever. Lean back on the pillowed leather sofas on the "luxury" balcony or snuggle into one of the velvet stall seats. Mostly new independent films. Bars and lounges offer pre- or post-show drinks. Gallery with drink £15, standard £12, M-F concessions and Sa-Su matinees £7.50. Wheelchair-accessible. Box office open daily noon-11pm. Bar open daily 2-11pm. MC/V.

Gate Cinema, 87 Notting Hill Gate (☎08707 550 063; www.picturehouses.co.uk), in Notting Hill. ⊖Notting Hill Gate. Opened in 1911, Gate's drab exterior is a result of post-war reconstruction. Fortunately, the lovely Victorian interior remains intact, with comfortable leather chairs a welcome addition. Admire the ceiling details while waiting for the film to start. Arthouse, international, and select Hollywood flicks on daily rotation. Wheelchair-accessible. M £7, concessions £4.75; Tu-F before 5pm £8/5; Tu-Th and Su after 5pm £10/8; F-Sa after 6pm £11/9. MC/V.

Odeon (☎08712 241 999; www.odeon.co.uk). 11 locations in central London. See website for showtimes and contact information for a specific theater.

MTR Studio 23, 23 Charlotte St. (☎7729 2323; www.mouthnthatroars.com), in Westminster. ⊖Old St. Founded to promote and develop independent film-making, this small studio offers free viewings and a snack bar serving cookies, coffee, and juice boxes (£1.20-1.80). Theater seats arranged in pods of 3-4 and flat screen TVs make for a unique experience. Free film workshops year-round for those under 19. Check website for screenings.

Prince Charles Cinema, 7 Leicester Pl. (film info ☎09012 727 007, booking 0878 112 559; www.princecharlescinema.com), in Soho. ⊖Leicester Sq. Just off blockbuster-ridden Leicester Sq., the Prince Charles couldn't offer more of a contrast. It features 2nd-run Hollywood films and recent independents for unbelievably low prices. For a truly unique experience, perfect your do-re-mis at monthly sing-along screenings of The Sound of Music (generally last F of month; £14), complete with a costumed host and dress competitions. Tickets £3-4. MC/V.

Renoir, Brunswick Sq. (☎7837 8402), in Bloomsbury. ⊖Russell Sq. This independent movie house emphasizes current European (especially French) cinema. Only 2 screens, but the regular turnover makes this a standout. Doors and bar-cafe open 30min. before each screening. Wheelchair-accessible. £9, 1st performance of the day M-F £6, students £6. AmEx/MC/V.

Ritzy Picturehouse, Brixton Oval, Coldharbour Ln. (☎0871 704 2065; www.ritzycinema.co.uk), in South London. ⊖Brixton. Dating from the 1920s, the Picturehouse shows new Hollywood and independent films in well-preserved Art Deco screening rooms. For a pre-show snack, head to the cafe upstairs. Special events include several summer film series, like the African Film Festival. Tickets £8.50, matinees £6.50; concessions £7.25/5.25. MC/V.

Tricycle Cinema, 269 Kilburn High Rd. (box office ☎7328 1000; film info 7328 1900; www.tricycle.co.uk), entrance on Buckley Rd.; in North London. ⊖Kilburn. Showing independent and foreign films as well as Hollywood blockbusters. Films stay for 1-2 weeks; buy tickets in advance for popular movies. Recline on the plush pink seats and enjoy the show. Tricycle-print rugs and decor complete the picture. Tu pay-what-you-can tickets available to seniors, children, and students. Regular features £8, bargain M and Tu-F before 5pm £4.50; concessions M-F before 8pm and Sa-Su before 5pm £1 off. Wheelchair-accessible. MC/V.

TRICYCLE FOR POCKET CHANGE. The Tricycle Theatre and Cinema offers occasional "pay-what-you-can" entry to films and plays. Although not to be taken advantage of, this system makes top-quality entertainment much more affordable to the budget-conscious.

COMEDY

Capital of a nation famed for its sophisticated sense of humor, London takes its comedy seriously. Standup is the mainstay, but improvisation fares well. Most clubs only run once a week or once a month, so call, or check listings in Time Out or a newspaper to keep up to speed. Summertime comedy seekers should note that London empties of comedians in August, when most head to Edinburgh to take part in the annual festival (trying to win an award); but June and July are full of feverish comic activity as performers test out new material prior to heading north.

▓ **Canal Cafe Theatre,** Delamere Terr. (☎7289 6054; www.canalcafetheatre.com), above the Bridge House pub; in North London. ⊖Warwick Ave. One of the few comedy venues to specialize in sketch comedy (as opposed to standup). Cozy red velvet chairs and a raised rear balcony means that everyone gets a good view. Grab dinner below and enjoy your drinks around the small tables. Box office opens 30min. before performance. Weekly changing shows W-Sa 7:30 and 9:30pm (£5, concessions £4). "Newsrevue," Th-Sa 9:30pm and Su 9pm, is London's longest-running comedy sketch show, a hilarious satire of weekly current events (£9, concessions £7). Both shows £14. £1.50 membership included in ticket price.

▓ **Comedy Store,** 1a Oxendon St. (club inquiries ☎7839 6642; tickets 08700 602 340; www.thecomedystore.biz), in Soho. ⊖Piccadilly Circus. The UK's top comedy club (founded in a former strip club) sowed the seeds that gave rise to Absolutely Fabulous and Whose Line is it Anyway? All 400 seats have decent views of stage. Grab food at the bar before the show and during the intermission (burgers £6). Tu Cutting Edge (contemporary news-based satire); W and Su London's well-reviewed ▓**Comedy Store Players improv**; Th-Sa standup. Shows Tu-Th and Su 8pm; F-Sa 8pm, midnight. Book in advance. 18+. Tu-W and F midnight shows and all Su shows £16; concessions £8; Th-F early show and all Sa shows £15. Happy hour 6:30-7:30pm. Box office open M-Th and Su 6:30-9:30pm, F-Sa 6:30pm-1:15am. AmEx/MC/V.

DANCE

"Ah, to be young and in love, twirling around on a dance floor as if the night would never end, laughing and embracing and dancing, dancing, dancing." For listings of dance classes, see **Practical Information** (p. 59). The **Barbican Theatre** (see p. 169) hosts touring contemporary companies.

Peacock Theatre, Portugal St. (☎0894 412 4322; www.sadlerswells.com), in Holborn. ⊖Holborn. Managed by Sadler's Wells, the program leans toward contemporary dance, ballet, popular dance-troupe shows, and children- and family-geared productions. Some wheelchair-accessible seats (£9) can be booked 24hr. in advance. Box office open M-F 10am-6:30pm, 10am-8:30pm on performance days. £8-35, cheaper rates M-Th and Sa matinee; fees for telephone and online booking. Standbys (1hr. before show) £15 and other discounts for students, seniors, and patrons under 16. AmEx/MC/V.

The Place, 16 Flaxman Terrace or 17 Duke's Rd. (☎020 7121 1100; www.theplace.org. uk), in Bloomsbury. ⊖Euston or King's Cross St. Pancras. A top venue for contemporary dance training and performance that attracts companies from the UK and abroad. Wheelchair-accessible. Online booking. Performances £5-15, depending on seats and advance booking; students £7. Day-of standbys (£15) available from 6pm. Box office and phone bookings open M-Sa noon-6pm, on performance nights noon-8pm. MC/V.

The Royal Opera House, Bow St. (☎020 7304 4000; www.roh.org.uk), in Covent Garden. ⊖Covent Garden. Housing both the Royal Opera and the Royal Ballet, the recently rede-signed Royal Opera House is a glamorous venue. Prices for the best seats (orchestra stalls) top £75 for the ballet and £100 for the opera, but standing room and restricted-view seat-ing in the upper balconies run for as little as £5.70. Seats available from 10am on day of performance, limit 1 per person. For student standby tickets (£10), register online at www. roh.org.uk/studentstandby. Box office open M-Sa 10am-8pm. AmEx/MC/V.

MUSIC

CLASSICAL AND OPERA

London boasts four world-class orchestras, three major concert halls, and two opera houses. Most venues have scads of cheap seats, and when music is the attraction, bad views of the stage are less important. To hear some of the world's top choirs, head to churches throughout the city, including Westminster Abbey (see p. 115) or St. Paul's Cathedral (p. 102), where, as a bonus, you'll also get into the cathedral for free. For listings of festivals, particularly in the summer, see **Life and Times** (p. 50).

Barbican Centre, see p. 169.

English National Opera, London Coliseum, St. Martin's Ln. (☎7632 8300; www. eno.org), in Covent Garden. ⊖Charing Cross or Leicester Sq. 500 balcony seats (£16-21) for sale every performance. Innovative, updated productions of classics as well as contemporary work. Wheelchair-accessible. Purchase best-available, standby student tickets (£15), and balcony tickets (£10) at box office 3hr. before show. Call to verify availability. Half-price tickets for those under 17. Box office open M-Sa 10am-8pm. AmEx/MC/V.

Holland Park Theatre, Holland Park (box office ☎0845 223 097; www.rbkc.gov.uk/hollandpark), in Kensington and Earl's Court. ⊖High St. Kensington or Holland Park. Open-air performance space in the atmospheric grounds of a Jacobean mansion. Performances from June to early Aug. Tu-Sa 7:30pm, occasional matinees Sa 2:30pm. Box office in the Old Stable Block just to the west of the opera open M-F 1-6pm, performance days until 8pm. Tickets £10-54; occasional concessions £3 off mid-price tickets. Special allocation of tickets for wheelchair users. AmEx/MC/V.

Royal Albert Hall, Kensington Gore (☎7589 8212; www.royalalberthall.com), in Kens-ington and Earl's Court. ⊖High St. Kensington. Best known for the ▓**Proms.** Box office at Door 12 open daily 9am-9pm. MC/V.

Royal Opera, Bow St. (☎7304 4000; www.royaloperahouse.org), in Covent Garden. ⊖Covent Garden. Prices for the best seats (orchestra stalls) typically top £150, but standing room and restricted-view seating in the upper balconies (if you're not afraid of heights) runs for as little as £4. For some performances, 100 of the very best seats are available for £10; apply a minimum of 2 weeks in advance at www.travelex.royalopera-house.org.uk. 67 seats available from 10am on day of performance, limit 1 per person. Box office open M-Sa 10am-8pm. AmEx/MC/V.

The South Bank Centre, Belvadere Rd. (☎0871 663 2501; www.rfh.org.uk), in the South Bank. ⊖Waterloo or Embankment. This megaplex of concert halls features all kinds of music. The main venue is the Royal Festival Hall—home to the Philharmonia and the London Philharmonic. Tickets can be purchased in person at the Royal Festival Hall (daily 10am-11pm) and Queen Elizabeth Hall (1½hr. before every performance), by telephone (☎0871 663 2500; daily 9am-8pm), or online (booking fee £1.45). Some £5-10 standby tickets available 2hr. before performance.

St. John's, Smith Sq. (☎7222 1061; www.sjss.org.uk), in Westminster. ⊖Westminster or St. James's Park. This former church is now a full-time concert venue with a program heavy on chamber and classical music: rarely sold out but highly regarded by critics. Concerts from Sept. to mid-July daily, from mid-July to Aug. once or twice per week. Performances generally M-F 7:30pm, Su 3pm. £9-20, concessions £5-10. Box office open M-F 10am-5pm, performance nights 10am-6pm. Online booking also available (£1.50 fee); phone booking £2 fee. MC/V.

St. Martin-in-the-Fields, Trafalgar Sq. (☎7839 8362; www.smitf.org), in Covent Garden. ⊖Charing Cross. Frequent lunch (1pm) and evening (7:30pm) concerts and recitals are given in this ornate 18th-century church. Music includes solo and group baroque and chamber recitals. Jazz also hosted occasionally in the crypt at 8pm, £8. Tickets usually £6-24. Call box office or visit website for show details.

Wigmore Hall, 36 Wigmore St. (☎020 7935 2141; www.wigmore-hall.org.uk), in Marylebone. ⊖Oxford Circus. London's premier chamber music venue. Wheelchair-accessible. Season Sept.-July; concerts most nights 7:30pm. Prices vary greatly with event (£2-35). Phone booking (£1.50 extra) daily 10am-7pm, days without evening concert 10am-5pm. In-person booking daily 10am-8:30pm, days without evening concert 10am-5pm. Student and senior standby tickets available 1hr. before (£10). Sales stop 30min. prior to performance. AmEx/MC/V.

JAZZ

London's jazz scene is small but serious; this isn't Chicago, but hallowed clubs nevertheless pull in big-name performers from around the world.

▩ **Jazz Café,** 5 Parkway (☎020 7534 6955; www.jazzcafe.co.uk), in North London. ⊖Camden Town. Famous and popular. Crowded front bar and balcony restaurant overlook the dance floor and stage. Shows can be pricey at this nightspot, but the top roster of jazz, hip-hop, funk, and Latin performers (£10-30) explains Jazz Café's popularity. F-Sa jazzy DJs spin following the show. Box office open M-Sa 10:30am-5:30pm. Cover £5-10. Open M-Th and Su 7pm-2am, F-Sa 7pm-3:30am. 18+. MC/V.

▩ **Ronnie Scott's,** 47 Frith St. (☎020 7439 0747; www.ronniescotts.co.uk), in Soho. ⊖Tottenham Court Rd. or Leicester Sq. London's oldest and most famous jazz club, having hosted everyone from Dizzy Gillespie to Jimi Hendrix. Supporting and main acts alternate throughout the night. Table reservations essential for big-name acts. There's limited unreserved standing room at the bar; if it's sold out, try coming back at the end of the headliner's first set, around midnight. Traditional English dishes £12-24, mixed drinks £5-11. Box office open M-F 9:30am-5:30pm. Club open M-Sa 6pm-3am, Su 6pm-midnight. Tickets £26, restricted viewing £20. AmEx/MC/V.

ROCK, POP, AND FOLK

Dates for the biggest acts are usually booked months in advance and often sell out within days. In other words, you'll need to start planning well before

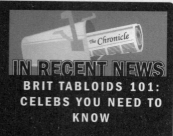

The Chronicle

IN RECENT NEWS

BRIT TABLOIDS 101: CELEBS YOU NEED TO KNOW

No visit to London is complete without insight into the celebrity scene. Here's a crash course in the Who's Who:

1. **The Royals:** Britain would not be Britain without its steamy Princes Harry and William, nor without the incessant speculation about their love lives. Harry (commonly known as the wild child recently tamed by his stint in the military) was for 4 years linked to beautiful blond Zimbabwean Chelsy Davy, who still appears in the papers from time to time. William (golden child and potential future king) is rumored to be hearing wedding bells whenever he looks at the classy brunette Kate Middleton, who he began dating in 2005.

2. **The WAGs:** A snarky if affectionate name for the Wives and Girlfriends of Sportsmen, the WAGs are in some ways the most exclusive sorority. With the untouchable Posh Spice as their Queen Bee (at least until her move to the States), the WAGs are all young, beautiful, and at the forefront of fashion. The press loves to document their every purchase, bridal shower, and most importantly, misstep. In 2007, there was a show "Wags Boutique," which pitted two teams of WAGs against each other, paralleling the 2002 soap opera entitled "Footballers' Wives," inspired by Posh. For the ladies, acronyms include: HABs (for husbands and

arriving in London to have a chance at bagging a seat. Folk (which in London usually means Irish) and world music usually keep a low profile; in general, outings are restricted to pubs and community centers.

The Monto Water Rats, 328 Grays Inn Rd. (☎020 7813 1079; www.themonto.com), in Bloomsbury. ⊖King's Cross St. Pancras. Where young indie rock bands come in search of a record deal. Bob Dylan had his UK debut here in 1962 and Oasis was signed here after their 1st London gig. Generous gastropub lunches (fish and chips £5-6) M-F noon-3pm. Tickets £6. Open for coffee M-F 8:30am-midnight. Music M-Sa 8pm-late (headliner 9:45pm). MC/V.

Borderline, Orange Yard (box office ☎020 7534 6970, 24hr. ticket line 08700 603 777), off Manette St. in Soho. ⊖Tottenham Court Rd. Warm basement space with 175 seats around a small stage. Well-known groups with strong folk-rock flavor. Past luminaries include Oasis, Pearl Jam, and Spinal Tap. W rock, Th emo or heavy metal, F indie, Sa "Christmas Club." Special acts other nights. Cover for theme nights from £5-10. Tickets £6-25. Online booking, fee £2.20. Box office open M-F 10am-6pm, Sa 10am-5pm. AmEx/MC/V.

02 Academy, Brixton, 211 Stockwell Rd. (☎020 7771 3000; www.brixton-academy.co.uk), in South London. ⊖Brixton. A fromer Art Deco cinema. The sloping floor ensures that even those at the back have a chance to see the band. Recent performers include Lenny Kravitz, Pink, the Offspring, and Franz Ferdinand. Box office open only on performance evenings; order online or by telephone. Tickets £20-40.

Apollo Hammersmith, Queen Caroline St. (☎020 8563 3800, 24hr. ticketmaster 0870 606 3400; www.hammersmith-apollo.com or www.ticketmaster.co.uk), in West London. ⊖Hammersmith. In the shadow of the Hammersmith Flyover, this utilitarian venue, seating up to 5000, hosts a huge array of major musical and theatrical diversions, from *Britain's Got Talent* to the Beach Boys to the Wu-Tang Clan. Box office open 4-8pm on performance days. Tickets from £19. AmEx/MC/V.

Forum, 9-17 Highgate Rd. (☎020 7284 1001, box office 0871 230 1093; www.kentishtownforum.com), in North London. ⊖Kentish Town. Turn right out of the Tube, go over the crest of the hill, and bear left—you'll see the marquee. The outside may not be beautiful, but inside is a lavish Art Deco theater. The great sound system and clear stage view has attracted some big names in the past: Van Morrison, Björk, Oasis, and Jamiroquai, among others. Tickets from £15. MC/V.

Hammersmith Irish Centre, Black's Rd. (☎020 8563 8232; www.irishculturalcentre.co.uk), in West London.

Hammersmith. From the District and Piccadilly Tube exit, head west on King St. Take your first left on Angel Walk and your first left again on Black's Rd.; Centre is on the right. Run by the local council, this claims to be London's foremost Irish center. Houses a small Irish lending library and frequently screens Irish films. Also hosts Irish bands, dance sessions, comedians, and literary readings. Wheelchair-accessible. Library open W 6pm-7pm, Sa 10am-2pm. Most performances Th and Su afternoons and Th-Sa nights; check online. Tickets up to £15; students usually £2 cheaper.

The Koko Club, 1A Camden High St. (☎0870 432 5527; www.koko.uk.com), in North London. Mornington Crescent. The newly reincarnated face of the old landmark Camden Palace, the Koko Club hosts a variety of acts. In a converted Victorian theater, now with space for 1600, it's an indie and rock venue that doubles as a dance club. Cover £3-15. Opening times vary.

SPECTATOR SPORTS

FOOTBALL

The vast majority of games take place on Saturdays, although there is the occasional Sunday or mid-week match. The big three London teams are Arsenal, Chelsea, and Tottenham Hotspur.

Arsenal, Emirates Stadium, 75 Drayton Park (box office ☎020 7704 4242; www.arsenal.com), in North London. Arsenal. The best way to ensure you'll get tickets is to become a "General Sale" members (free). £33-92. Online and phone booking fees £1-2. Box office open M-F 9:30am-5pm, Sa 9:30am-noon.

Chelsea, Stamford Bridge, Fulham Rd. (main switchboard ☎08703 001 212, box office 0870 300 2322; www.chelseafc.com), in West London. Fulham Broadway. £44-52, students £32-34. Box office open M-F 9am-5pm.

Tottenham Hotspur, White Hart Lane Stadium, 748 High Rd. (ticket office ☎08704 205 000; www.spurs.co.uk), in North London. Seven Sisters. Tickets £15-74; half-price tickets for senior citizens and children under 16 subject to availability. Box office open M-F 10am-6pm.

West Ham United, Boleyn Ground, Green St. (box office ☎08701 122 700; www.whufc.com), in East London. Upton Park. £21-63. Box office open M-F 9am-5pm, Sa 9am-1pm.

RUGBY

Three big London teams play from August to May on weekend afternoons.

boyfriends of Wimbledon women) and CHAPs (for celebrities' husbands and partners).

3. **The Sportsmen:** Here more than in America, sportsmen seem to be the subject of as much media attention as other entertainers. David Beckham is King to Posh's Queenship, but other Footballers like the freckled Wayne Rooney (Man U), the hot-tempered Christiano Ronaldo (who famously departed in June 2009 for Real Madrid, making him the most expensive player ever), and the short-shorts fan Rio Ferdinand, who consistently makes headlines. Otherwise, tennis prize child Andy Murray, with his extravagant purchases and consistent play, is always of interest.

4. **The Socialites:** Yep, this mostly-female pack is famous for being famous. The daughter of a business tycoon, Tamara Beckwith dropped out of school, gave birth to her daughter Anouska Poppy Pearl, and went on to guest-star in a number of reality TV shows. She's now nearly 40, but remains an original. Tara Palmer-Tomkinson (TPT), a friend of Tamara's, has been a model and TV personality, but made the most headlines for her struggles with drugs and her plastic surgery escapades. Now, 31-year-old Katie Price (a.k.a. Jordan) has taken center stage: the former model starred in a reality show with her husband Peter Andre, but now is mostly seen philandering on the beach while her son struggles with his parents' recent separation.

Boozing, posing, and otherwise intriguing, these celebs will only make your London stay that much more scandalous!

London Wasps, Sports Ground, Twyford Ave. (☎8993 8298, box office 0870 414 1515; www.wasps.co.uk), in West London. ⊖Ealing Common. £15-45, concessions £8-15.

NEC Harlequins, Stoop Memorial Ground, Langhorn Dr. (☎8410 6000, box office 08718 718 877; www.quins.co.uk), in West London. Rail: Twickenham. £20-40. Box office open M and F 9am-4:30pm, Tu-Th 10am-4:30pm.

Saracens, Vicarage Rd. Station (box office ☎01923 475 222; www.saracens.com), in North London. ⊖Watford. Tickets £20-60, advance £15-50; concessions £12-17/16-26.

CRICKET

Middlesex and **Surrey** are the main London teams; their grounds at Lord's and the Oval, respectively, are also used to host international test matches in which England traditionally loses abysmally.

Lord's Cricket Ground, St. John's Wood Rd. (☎7432 1000; www.lords.org), in North London. ⊖St. John's Wood.

Oval, Brit Oval, Surey County Cricket Club (☎08712 461 100, box office 7582 7764; www.surreycricket.com), in South London. ⊖Oval.

TENNIS

Demand for tickets at "The Championships" (Wimbledon) so exceeds supply that pre-sold tickets are lotteried in December; only 500 Centre, No. 1, and No. 2 Court tickets are saved for each day (except during the Final Four, when none are). To be assured one of these seats, overnight queuing is recommended. To see the big names in a more intimate environment, try the Stella Artois tournament, which precedes Wimbledon in June.

Stella Artois, Queen's Club, Palliser Rd. (☎020 7385 3421; www.queensclub.co.uk, for tickets to the tournament www.artoischampionship.com), in West London. ⊖Barons Crt.

Wimbledon, All England Lawn Tennis and Croquet Club (☎020 8971 2473; www.wimbledon.org), in West London. ⊖Southfields (Zone 3). 15min. walk along Wimbledon Park Rd. Wimbledon championship from late June to early July. Box office open M-F 9am-5pm.

WIMBLEDON. The Wimbledon finals are broadcast on a big screen in Covent Garden Piazza. Pack your own strawberries and cream and head there for an affordable afternoon of tennis.

THEATER

LONG-RUNNING SHOWS (THE WEST END)

London's West End is dominated by musicals and plays that run for years, if not decades. Below we list shows that have proved their staying power as well as recent arrivals that look ready for the long haul. Most long-running shows are in venues located in the West End.

tkts, south side of Leicester Sq. (www.tkts.co.uk). ⊖Leicester Sq. Also at Canary Wharf DLR Station, Platforms 4 and 5. Run by the Society of London Theatre, tkts is the only place where you can be sure your discounted tickets are genuine. The catch is that theaters only release the most expensive tickets to the booth, which means that it's a good deal for the best seats in the house, but they are rarely under £15 (most musicals around £27, plays £20-40). In addition, you can only buy day-of tickets in person, albeit with little seating choice. Notice boards display which shows are available. Booking fees vary but are typically £2.50 per ticket. Open M-Sa 10am-7pm, Su noon-3pm. MC/V.

PHONY DISCOUNTS. Many "discount" ticket booths will claim to offer you a reduced rate on tickets when in fact they are charging you more than the face value! Look for the logo of a white circle with a check mark on a ticket booth before purchasing—it denotes compliance with a set of rules and standards that ensures legitimate discounts.

REPERTORY

■ **Barbican Hall,** Silk St. (☎020 7638 4141; www.barbican.org.uk), in the City of London. ⊖Barbican or Moorgate. Recently refurbished, Barbican Hall is one of Europe's leading concert halls, with excellent acoustics and a nightly performance program. The resident London Symphony Orchestra plays here, and the hall also hosts concerts by international orchestras, jazz artists, and world musicians. Also has a cinema and the Barbican Centre for Arts.

■ **Royal Court Theatre,** Sloane Sq. (☎020 7565 5000; www.royalcourttheatre.com), in Chelsea. ⊖Sloane Sq. Dedicated to challenging new writing and innovative interpretations of classics. Their 1956 production of John Osborne's *Look Back in Anger* is universally acknowledged as the starting point of modern British drama. Main auditorium £10-25, concessions £10, standing room 10p 1hr. before curtain. 2nd venue upstairs £15, concessions £10. M all seats £10, with some advance tickets and some released 10am on day of performance. Wheelchair-accessible. Box office open M-Sa 10am-6pm, 10am-7:45pm performance weeks. AmEx/MC/V.

 TIX FOR POCKET CHANGE. Always ask at the box office for student discounts. Even if a theater does not advertise such discounts, they may give them (usually 1hr. before curtain). Most theaters will give the best seats available for standby. It's best to go in the middle of the week.

■ **Shakespeare's Globe Theatre,** 21 New Globe Walk (☎020 7087 7398; www.shakespeares-globe.org), in the South Bank. ⊖Southwark or London Bridge. Innovative, top-notch performances at this faithful reproduction of Shakespeare's original 16th-century playhouse. Choose among 3 covered tiers of hard, backless wooden benches (cushions £1 extra) or stand through a performance as a "groundling"; come 30min. before the show to get as close as you can. Should it rain, the show must go on, and umbrellas are prohibited. For tours of the Globe, see p. 112. Wheelchair-accessible. Performances from mid-May to late Sept. Tu-Sa 7:30pm, Su 6:30pm; June-Sept. Tu-Sa 2 and 7:30pm, Su 1 and 6:30pm. Box office open M-Sa 10am-6pm, 8pm on performance days; Su 10am-5pm, 7pm on performance days. New plays from £20, others from £15, yard (standing) £5.

National Theatre, South Bank (info ☎020 7452 3400, box office 7452 3000; www.nationaltheatre.org.uk), in the South Bank. ⊖Waterloo or Embankment. Founded by Laurence Olivier. Bigger shows are mostly staged on the Olivier, which seats 1160. The 890-seat Lyttleton is a proscenium theater, while the Cottesloe offers flexible staging for new works. Complicated pricing scheme; tickets typically start at £10, but contact box office for details. Wheelchair-accessible. Box office open M-Sa 9:30am-8pm, Su performance days noon-6pm. MC/V.

 NATIONAL THEATRE FOR POCKET CHANGE. Almost every day in the summer, the faux-grass courtyard at the National Theatre holds a free concert, film, or performance art exhibition. From magic shows to physical comedy to acrobatics, the Theatre will satisfy anyone looking for live entertainment.

LONDON

Open-Air Theatre, Inner Circle, Regent's Park (☎08700 601 811; www.openairtheatre.org), in Marylebone. ⊖Baker St. Charming open-air venue in the middle of Regent's Park. Bring blankets and rain gear; performances are canceled only in extreme weather conditions. Program runs June to early Sept. and includes 2 well-known plays, a musical, and a children's performance. Occasional Su night jazz and comedy shows. Bring your own picnic supplies or purchase barbecue or buffet dinner inside the venue. Wheelchair-accessible. Performances M-Sa 8pm, matinees Th and Sa 2:30pm; grounds open at 6:30pm and 1:30pm respectively. £10-38, discounts for groups and under 16 (with adult); student and senior standby £10 from 1hr. before curtain. Box office open Mar.-May M-Sa 10am-6pm; June-Sept. M-Sa 10am-8pm, Su (performance days only) 10am-8pm. AmEx/MC/V.

"OFF-WEST END"

New writers, smaller houses. *Time Out* has complete listings; these are a few of our favorites.

▨ **The Almeida,** Almeida St. (☎020 7359 4404; www.almeida.co.uk), in North London. ⊖Angel. The top fringe theater in London. Shows M-Sa 7:30pm, Sa matinees 3pm; occasional W matinees 3pm, other weekday matinees 2:30pm. Tickets usually £8-32, occasionally as high as £46. Wheelchair-accessible. MC/V.

▨ **The King's Head,** 115 Upper St. (☎020 7226 1916; www.kingsheadtheatre.org), in North London. ⊖Angel or Highbury and Islington. Above an attached pub, this theater focuses on new writing and rediscovered works. Alums include Hugh Grant, Gary Oldman, and Anthony Minghella. Shows Tu-Sa 8pm, Sa 3:30pm. £10-20, concessions £2.50 off; matinees £5 off. Occasional lunchtime shows and M night short-run shows; call for schedule. MC/V.

Battersea Arts Centre (BAC), Old Town Hall, 176 Lavender Hill (☎020 7223 2223; www.bac.org.uk), in South London. ⊖Clapham Common. One of London's top off-West End venues, best known for experimental theater. Box office open M 10:30am-6pm, Tu-F 10am-9pm, Sa-Su 4-9pm. Tickets from £10, concessions from £5. MC/V.

A NIGHT LESS ORDINARY. Until March 2011, 12 theaters around London are offering "A Night Less Ordinary" for groups of up to 6 under-26-year-old friends. Just visit freelondontheatre.com to get free tickets to shows at the Almeida Theatre, Battersea Arts Centre, Bush Theatre, Donmar Warehouse, Greenwich Theatre, Hampstead Theatre, Lyric Hammersmith, Royal Court, Soho Theatre, Theatre Royal Stratford East, Tricycle Theatre, or the Young Vic.

The Bush Theatre, Shepherd's Bush Green (☎020 7610 4224; www.bushtheatre.co.uk), in West London. ⊖Shepherd's Bush or Goldhawk Rd. Marked by a lime green and purple exterior, this theater's off-beat and cutting-edge shows derive from its policy of favoring new writers. Telephone booking M-Sa 10am-7pm. Box office open M-Sa 5-8pm. £13.50, students £9. AmEx/MC/V.

Donmar Warehouse, 41 Earlham St. (☎08700 606 624; www.donmarwarehouse.com), in Covent Garden. ⊖Covent Garden. In the mid-90s, artistic director Sam Mendes transformed this gritty space into one of the most excellent theaters in the country, featuring highly regarded contemporary shows with an edge. Tickets £13-29. Wheelchair-accessible. Box office open M-Sa 10am-7:30pm. AmEx/MC/V.

Old Vic, Waterloo Rd. (☎020 7369 1722; www.oldvictheatre.com), in the South Bank. ⊖Waterloo. Still in its original 1818 hall (the oldest theater in London), the Old Vic is one of London's most historic and beautiful theaters. Contact box office or check website for listings. Tickets £9.50-45. Box office M-Sa 10am-7pm. MC/V.

The Gate Theatre, 11 Pembridge Rd. (☎020 7229 0706; www.gatetheatre.co.uk), in Notting Hill. ⊖Notting Hill Gate. Often showcases new foreign works (in English) before they've been performed in their home countries. Jude Law and Rachel Weisz did some "emerging" here. Wheelchair-accessible. Performances typically M-F 7:30pm. £16, students £11. MC/V.

> **TIP**
>
> **THE GATE FOR POCKET CHANGE.** Happy Monday at The Gate means that the first 20 customers "pay what they can" at the door.

Hackney Empire, 291 Mare St. (☎020 8985 2424; www.hackneyempire.co.uk), in East London. ⊖Bethnal Green or DLR: Hackney Central, then Bus #D6, 106, 25. One of the best variety theaters around, featuring top comedy, musicals, opera, and drama. Charlie Chaplin performed here. Call or check website for shows and prices. Box office open M-Sa 10am-9pm on performance nights, Su noon-6pm. AmEx/MC/V.

SHOPPING

London has long been considered one of the fashion capitals of the world, up there with New York City, Paris, and Milan. Where else could seven-story department stores (Harrods and Harvey Nic's) draw tourists and locals for day-long extravaganzas? Unfortunately, in today's globalized economy, London features as many underwhelming chain stores as it does one-of-a-kind boutiques. Oxford St. is the place for a quick club-wear fix but is often overrun with teenagers and tourists who consider Topshop the new vogue simply because it's from London (don't get us wrong, it's still a good store). Meanwhile, price tags are ever-rising; the truly budget-conscious should forgo buying and stick to window shopping in Knightsbridge and Regent Street boutiques for ideas on how to mimic the fashion greats like Vivienne Westwood and Chanel.

That being said, designer brands also mean delightful vintage: secondhand and donation stores abound with great options, and they're only proliferating in recession times. For stunning vintage at surprisingly low prices, try the streets off Brick Lane in the East End, Camden Passage in Islington, or one of the Oxfam boutiques, Cancer Research UK shops, or Salvation Army stores in ritzier neighborhoods. And of course, there are always the markets: Portobello Rd. in Notting Hill and Spitalfields in the East End offer the best quality gear for fashionistas who need to return from a trip with something to show off.

Let's Go understands that shopping is a part of tourism, particularly in London, but we're generally broke. We therefore include a Notable Chains section for the best of high-end, then list our favorite vintage and other shops.

NOTABLE CHAINS

As in almost any major city, London's retail scene is dominated by chains. Fortunately, local shoppers are picky enough that buying from a chain doesn't mean abandoning the flair and quirky stylishness for which Londoners are famed. Plus, in such an expensive city, chain stores are often a great place for deals. Most chains have a flagship store on or near Oxford St., usually with a second branch in Covent Garden. The branches will have slightly different hours, but almost all the stores listed below are open daily 10am-7pm, starting later (noon) on Sunday and staying open an hour later one night of the week (usually Thursday).

BOOKS

Waterstone's (www.waterstones.co.uk). More than a dozen branches, including 203-206 Piccadilly (☎7851 2400; ⊖Piccadilly Circus) and 82 Gower St. (☎7636 1577; ⊖Goodge St.). Europe's largest bookstore, with specialty sections in just about everything. Comprehensive map and travel guide section for London and Britain, including 🔳 **Let's Go.** Many branches have cafe or restaurant. Frequent special events, including book signings by big-name authors (£2-4). Wheelchair-accessible. AmEx/MC/V.

CLOTHES AND ACCESSORIES

Jigsaw, flagship 126-127 New Bond St. (☎7491 4484; www.jigsaw-online.com). ⊖Bond St. 22 branches, including 449 Strand (☎7497 8663; ⊖Charing Cross) and 65 Kensington High St. (☎7937 3573; ⊖High St. Kensington). High-quality, mid-priced women's wear in feminine, classic cuts. Designs prize elegance over fad-based fashions, though there has been a move toward edgier designs. AmEx/MC/V.

Karen Millen (☎08701 601 830; www.karenmillen.co.uk). 17 branches including 247 Regent St. (⊖Oxford Circus), 22-23 James St. (⊖Covent Garden), 33 Kings Rd. (⊖Sloane Sq.), Jubilee Place (⊖Canary Wharf), and Barker's Arcade (⊖High St. Kensington). Best known for richly embroidered brocade suits and evening gowns, but recently edging toward a more casual line. Starting to expand their classic look to encompass a younger market. AmEx/MC/V.

Mango, flagship 106-112 Regent St. (☎7434 1384; www.mango.com). ⊖Piccadilly Circus. 2 other locations at 233 Oxford St. (☎7534 3505; ⊖Oxford Circus) and 8-12 Neal St. (☎7240 6099; ⊖Covent Garden). A UK foothold for a Spanish fashion empire that is quickly becoming a London mainstay, Mango carries a female line cut with classy, sensible designs appropriate for all occasions. Most casual tops and bottoms go for under £40, some as low as £10 during the summer sales. AmEx/MC/V.

Oasis, flagship Unit 12-14 Argyll St. (☎7434 1799; www.oasis-stores.com). ⊖Oxford Circus. 22 branches, including 13 James St. (☎7240 7445; ⊖Covent Garden) and 28a Kensington Church St. (☎7938 4019; ⊖High St. Kensington). Colorful, sexy clothes for work and play, plus shoes and accessories. A favorite with students and 20-somethings. AmEx/MC/V.

Topshop, flagship 36-38 Great Castle St. (☎7636 7700; www.topshop.co.uk). ⊖Oxford Circus. 2nd main location at 60-64 Strand (☎7839 4144; ⊖Charing Cross). Dozens of locations in central London. Cheap, popular fashions for young people; over-25s will feel middle-aged. Boasts a huge range of casual clothes, strappy shoes, and skimpy women's clubwear. Free Style Advisor personal shopping service. Many locations have adjoining Topman, for men. AmEx/MC/V.

Zara, flagship 118 Regent St. (☎7534 9500; www.zara.com). ⊖Piccadilly Circus. 9 branches including 215-219 Oxford St. (☎7534 2900; ⊖Oxford Circus). Yet another stylish Spanish brand that has taken Europe by storm with its sleek, relatively inexpensive clothing. Prices similar to its neighbor Mango, but with brighter and younger designs. AmEx/MC/V.

MUSIC

HMV, 150 Oxford St. (☎0845 602 7800; www.hmv.co.uk). ⊖Oxford Circus. Also at 40 King St. (⊖Covent Garden). 3 massive floors with a huge range of new vinyl, especially dance music. Music madness done right. Games department has playable consoles from every game maker. Wheelchair-accessible. Hours vary by store.

Virgin Megastore, flagship 1 Piccadilly (☎7439 2500). ⊖Piccadilly Circus. 13 branches including 213-219 Camden High St. (☎7482 5307; ⊖Camden Town) and 62-64 Kensington High St. (☎7938 3511; ⊖High St. Kensington). Covers the entire musical spectrum, including related books, magazines, and posters, DVDs, videos, and computer games. Internet cafe on ground fl. (£1 per 50min. before noon, £1 per min. after noon). Wheelchair-accessible. Hours vary by store.

WHITECHAPEL AND THE EAST END

In East London, street markets are lively and widespread, providing some of the most unique shopping in the area. **Spitalfields,** widely recognized as London's best market, offers a tasty weekend display of organic fruits and vegetables, along with trendy artwork, clothing, and jewelry. Just two blocks away, the new **Sunday (Up) Market** is a lesser-known alternative to the claustrophobia-inducing crowds of its neighbor. **Petticoat Lane** and **Brick Lane Market,** both popular tourist destinations, are unfortunately past their prime, but there's always the chance you'll find a diamond in the rough. In **Hoxton** and **Shoreditch,** as well as in the stretch of **Brick Lane** just north of the Truman Brewery, independent young designers have opened up gallery-esque boutiques frequented by local artists and artsy pretenders. The streets around Brick Lane feature some of the best secondhand, vintage, and thrift shops in town, and perhaps in general. More undiscovered gems than overpriced trends, the East End is a rare pocket of affordable style in London's otherwise hopped-up shopping scene.

CLOTHES

▨ **The Laden Showroom,** 103 Brick Ln. (☎020 7247 2431; www.laden.co.uk). ⊖Aldgate East or Liverpool St. A favorite of celeb trendsetters, Laden is the place to get your next flirty dress, sexy skirt, or flashy top. Selling for over 60 of the hippest independent fashion and accessory designers, each with a cube-like display space. Dedicated staff are highly knowledgeable. Dresses start at £45. New and recently used items under £70. Open M noon-6pm, Tu-F 11am-6:30pm, Sa 11am-7pm, Su 10:30am-6pm. AmEx/MC/V.

▨ **Absolute Vintage,** 15 Hanbury St. (☎020 7247 3883; www.absolutevintage.co.uk). ⊖Aldgate East or Liverpool St. Declared the best vintage shop in London, one of the top 100 stores to visit in the world, and the largest shoe collection in the UK, Absolute Vintage offers rows and rows of shoes organized by size, style, and color. From sleek silver heels to slouchy green leather boots and everything in between. Also endless racks of jeans, dresses, skirts, blazers, and army jackets—don't expect to leave empty-handed. Dresses and heels from £15; boots from £45. Open M-Sa noon-7pm, Su 10am-7pm. AmEx/MC/V.

Lily Bling, 11 Whitechapel Rd. (☎020 7247 4719; www.lillybling.com). ⊖ Liverpool St. Similar to Laden, Lily stocks pieces by some of best independent UK designers, except the selection is a little smaller and a little flirtier: think hip and tasteful (not gaudy) ruffles, stripes, prints, and florals. Dresses from £32. Open M-F 10am-7pm, Sa-Su noon-6pm. AmEx/MC/V.

GIFTS AND MISCELLANY

▨ **Sh! Women's Erotic Emporium,** 57 Hoxton Sq. (☎020 7613 5458; www.sh-womenstore. com). ⊖Old St. Founded as a "fresh alternative to Soho sleaze," this sex shop was the 1st in London to cater to women and was recently voted the "Best Sex Shop in London." Bubble-gum-pink walls, comfy lounge chairs, and a friendly staff offering hot tea put customers at ease while they browse the extensive selection of vibrators (Mistress

Twista, anyone?), condoms, gels, lingerie, and games. Men must be accompanied by a woman. Open daily noon-8pm. MC/V.

■ **Cinephilia,** 97 Sclater St., off Brick Lane (☎020 7729 9588; www.cinephilia.co.uk). ⊖Shoreditch, Liverpool St., or Aldgate East. Opened in October 2008, this small cinema bookshop has already become a go-to spot for anyone even remotely interested in the world of film. Featuring film criticism and film studies; works on selected actors, genres, and directors; books from leading publishers like WallFlower Press and Auteur Publishing. Also has a sizeable collection of independent films and other rare DVDs. A cozy feel and comfy couches invite in-store perusing. Books available to purchase or borrow. Open Tu-Su 12:30-7:30pm. AmEx/MC/V.

MARKETS

■ **Spitalfields Market,** Commercial St. ⊖Shoreditch (during rush hour), Liverpool St., or Aldgate East. Formerly one of London's main wholesale vegetable markets, Spitalfields has matured into the East End's best. It's now a dizzying array of clothes, crafts, books, albums, and food stalls selling everything from organic fruits to baked goods to freshly cooked ethnic dishes. Local independent designers showcase their work on Su. Crowds can be overwhelming: many head to the Sunday (Up) Market, but those in the know simply wait until late in the day for the scene to thin out. Antiques and vintage Th. Fashion and art F. Times vary but in general: shops open daily 11am-7pm; stalls open Th-F 10am-4pm, Su 9am-5pm.

Sunday (Up) Market, ⊖Shoreditch or Aldgate East. Housed in the old Truman Brewery just off Hanbury St., this Spitalfields neighbor offers more space than Spitalfield but slightly less inspiring goods. The market sells jewelry, handbags, art, housewares, clothing, and greeting cards by local designers. Excellent food. Held outdoors in good weather, indoors in winter. Open Su 10am-5pm.

Brick Lane Market, ⊖Shoreditch or Aldgate East. At the heart of Whitechapel's sizable Bangladeshi community, Brick Lane hosts a large Su market. Most of the stands sell bargain household goods and trinkets, along with annoying offers for cell-phone unlocking and pirated DVDs. It's a challenge to get out of the crowd once you're in the thick of it. Go for the experience but don't expect to find many treasures. Open Su 8am-2pm.

GREENWICH

While Greenwich's numerous weekend markets may not rival those of the East End, the longer trek tends to weed out the casual from the hard-core shoppers—you can expect Sundays to be less crowded here than at Spitalfields.

■ **Greenwich Market,** in the block surrounded by King William Walk, Greenwich Church St., College Approach, and Romney Rd. DLR: Cutty Sark. A worthwhile stop on the market crawl. Antiques and collectibles Th 7:30am-5:30pm; Arts and crafts and collectibles F 9am-5pm; Arts and crafts with an international food court Sa-Su 9:30am-5:30pm.

Antiques Market, Greenwich High Rd. Rail: Greenwich or DLR: Cutty Sark. Mostly 20th-century goods, many affordable. Open Sa-Su 10am-5pm.

Village Market, Stockwell St. (☎020 8858 0808). DLR: Cutty Sark. The international food court is the best part here, but there are also secondhand clothes and bric-a-brac in this indoor market. Everything from gramophones to used books. Open Sa-Su 8am-late afternoon.

HOLBORN

Holborn is not a top shopping destination, especially in comparison to nearby Covent Garden. **High Holborn** is a busy road with a few common chains, while **Fleet Street** hosts a number of indistinguishable clothing shops.

 BOOKWORMS REJOICE! The South Bank Book Market is the only established secondhand book market in Southern England. Situated just outside the BFI Theatre, the market is open daily.

THE SOUTH BANK

BOOKS

marcus campbell art books, 43 Holland St. (☎020 7261 0111; www.marcuscampbell. co.uk). ⊖Blackfriars or Southwark. Right behind the Tate and Bankside, this small shop specializes in out-of-print, secondhand, and rare books on 20th-century and contemporary art, design, and architecture. Most books £1-10. Open M-Sa 10:30am-6:30pm, Su noon-6pm. MC/V.

SOUTH LONDON

Brixton Market, along Electric Ave., Pope's Rd., and Brixton Station Rd., and inside markets in Granville Arcade and Market Row. ⊖Brixton. Packed with visitors most days, the vibrant stalls hawk everything from cheap household items to bootlegged films. The market carries London's best selection of Afro-Caribbean fruits, vegetables, spices, and fish. Negotiate with the vendors for some unbelievable deals on meat and produce. Open M-Tu and Th-Su 8am-6pm, W 8am-3pm.

 CASH MONEY. When visiting local markets, it's always wise to bring cash, especially in small denominations. While many vendors have begun accepting plastic, there is often a transaction fee incurred which can either be a fixed amount or a percentage of your total. Cash greases all wheels.

MAYFAIR AND SAINT JAMES'S

Shopping in London is concentrated around a number of posh high streets in Mayfair. The bonafide shopping nirvana, **Oxford Street**—appealing to chain-store aficionados and those who enjoy a crowd—betrays Mayfair's real character. **Regent** and **New Bond Street** are slightly more in line with the refined affairs of the neighborhood. **Avery Row** and **South Molton Street** host upscale shops and their outlets. **Carnaby Street** and **Kingly Court** have both adorable boutiques and hipster mainstays like Levi's and American Apparel.

Near Piccadilly, a number of Regency and Victorian **arcades** are lined with boutiques whose less interesting wares have changed little in the last hundred years. The oldest is the **Royal Opera Arcade,** between Pall Mall and Charles II St.; the most prestigious is the **Royal Arcade,** patronized by Queen Victoria and home of palace chocolatiers Charbonnel and Walker. The most famous, and longest, is the **Burlington Arcade,** next to the Royal Academy of the Arts, which houses several leather and jewelry shops. Shoppers take note: these and the other arcades have a bit of a stuffed-shirt feel; they're filled with high-brow clothing shops specializing in tweed and top hats. (Shops inside keep their own hours, but most are open M-Sa about 10am-7pm, Su noon-6pm.)

BOOKS

🔲 **Sotheran's of Sackville Street,** 2-5 Sackville St. (☎020 7439 6151; www.sotherans.co.uk). ⊖Piccadilly Circus. Founded in 1761 in York, Sotheran's moved to London in 1815; the selection of collectible and rare books hasn't changed much since. And while the atmosphere of hushed voices and locked shelves might be intimidating, its worth a peek inside. Also sells some newer books. Original of Jane Austen's *Guide to Manners* £15. Most books £10-35. Antique posters and prints available downstairs from £45. Open M-F 9:30am-6pm, Sa 10am-4pm. AmEx/MC/V.

Hatchard's, 187 Piccadilly (☎020 7439 9921; www.hatchards.co.uk). ⊖Green Park or Piccadilly Circus. Although London's oldest bookshop (est. 1797) has been bought by Waterstone's, it still maintains its sophistication and the respect of locals. Renowned for its selection of signed bestsellers. Prince Charles's official bookseller. Open M-Sa 9:30am-7pm, Su noon-6pm. AmEx/MC/V.

CLOTHES

Sam Greenberg, Unit 1.7 Kingly Court, Carnaby St. (☎020 7287 8474). ⊖Oxford Circus. Specializing in 80s T-shirts and old coats and jackets, this genuine vintage store sells post-rock throwbacks. Small collection of designer jeans from £50. T-shirts start at £10, and leather jackets are a real steal at £40. Most dresses and skirts £30-35. Open M-F 11am-7pm, Sa 10am-7pm, Su noon-6pm. MC/V.

Oscar Milo, 19 Avery Row (☎020 7495 5846; www.oscarmilo.com). ⊖Bond St. Also at 47 Brushfield St. (☎020 7655 4811). Particularly good menswear boutique with clothes that may not be cheap but are a good value. The 3 small floors are neatly organized and stacked with well-cut jeans, shirts, and seriously smooth footwear (separates and shoes £50-110). Open M-W and F-Sa 10:30am-6:30pm, Th 10:30am-7pm. AmEx/MC/V.

THE REAL DEAL. The areas around Oxford St. and Regent St. are dominated by enormous chain stores. If you are interested in buying anything from music to clothing, veer off this well-beaten path to find independently owned stores. They may have smaller collections, but the quality of goods and services are likely to be better and uniquely English.

CLOTHING OUTLETS

Paul Smith Sale Shop, 23 Avery Row (☎020 7493 1287; www.paulsmith.co.uk). ⊖Bond St. Small range of last-season and clearance items from the acknowledged master of modern British menswear. Decently sized stock of casual and formal wear at least 30% off original prices: grab a nice shirt or a pair of jeans for £50, or a tie or belt for £60. Open M-W 10am-6pm and F-Sa 10am-6pm, Th 10:30am-7pm, Su 1-5:30pm. AmEx/MC/V.

DEPARTMENT STORES

🔲 **Selfridges,** 400 Oxford St. (☎020 0870 837 7377; www.selfridges.com). ⊖Bond St. Tourists may flock to Harrods, but Londoners head to Selfridges. You'll find all the biggies here—Gucci, Chanel, Dior—but there are also more affordable brands. Styles run the gamut from traditional tweeds to space-age clubwear. Departments specialize in every product imaginable, from antiques and scented candles, not to mention key cutting and theater tickets. With 18 cafes and restaurants, a hair salon, an exchange bureau, and even a hotel, shopaholics need never leave. Massive Jan. and July sales. Wheelchair-accessible. Open M-Sa 9:30am-9pm, Su noon-6pm. AmEx/MC/V.

Liberty, 210-220 Regent St. (☎020 7734 1234; www.liberty.co.uk), main entrance on Marlborough St. ⊖Oxford Circus. Liberty's timbered, Tudor chalet (built in 1922) sets the regal tone. A focus on top-quality design and handcrafts makes it more like a giant boutique than a full-blown department store. Liberty is famous for custom fabric prints—10,000 now archived—sewn into everything from shirts to pillows. It also has a wide array of other high-end contemporary designer lines, home accessories, and hard-to-find beauty lines. Wheelchair-accessible. Open M-Sa 10am-9pm; Su noon-6pm, browsing only 11:30am-noon. AmEx/MC/V.

Fortnum & Mason, 181 Piccadilly (☎020 7734 8040; www.fortnumandmason.co.uk). ⊖Green Park or Piccadilly Circus. As the official grocer of the royal family, this gourmet department store provides quality foodstuffs fit for a queen. From *foie gras* to preserves and tea, the price tags are hefty, but the quality is top-notch. Don't come here to do your weekly shopping—prices aside, the focus is very much on gifts and luxury items. A complete renovation in 2007 added a basement wine bar to the existing 3 restaurants. The fancy **St. James Restaurant** serves a lovely Champagne Afternoon Tea (classic tea £38, without champagne £30; rare tea £42/30). Wheelchair-accessible. St. James Restaurant open for lunch daily noon-2:30pm, for tea M-Sa 2-7pm and Su noon-4:30pm. Store open M-Sa 10am-8pm, Su noon-6pm (browsing only 11:30-noon). AmEx/MC/V.

GIFTS AND MISCELLANY

Hamley's, 188-189 Regent St. (☎020 7734 3161; www.hamleys.co.uk). ⊖Oxford Circus. Quite simply one of the best toy shops in the world. Opened in 1760, Hamley's has 7 floors filled with every conceivable toy and game, plus dozens of strategically placed product demonstrations tempting the young (and not-so-young) with flying airplanes, chaotic robots, and rubber bugs that stick to the walls. Complete with a Build-a-Bear boutique and an overwhelmingly pink and glittery Barbie floor, even grown-ups may find themselves waxing nostalgic about childhood toys. Find the obligatory Sweet Shop, complete with huge candy sculptures, on the 2nd fl. Wheelchair-accessible. Open M-F 10am-8pm, Sa 9am-8pm, Su noon-6pm. AmEx/MC/V.

SOHO

Soho's eternal trendiness has made it one of the world's top shopping destinations. The record stores of **D'Arblay** and **Berwick Street** will please any music fan. **Denmark Street,** on the eastern fringe of Soho, has been dubbed London's "Tin Pan Alley" thanks to its many musical instrument and equipment shops, while **Charing Cross Road** remains London's bookshop center.

Gerry's, 74 Old Compton St. (☎020 7734 2053). ⊖Piccadilly Circus or Leicester Sq. Staggering selection of beer and hard liquor in all sizes, from miniatures to magnums. With 80 different tequilas, 170 vodkas, a revolving bottle display, and an incendiary Italian absinthe that's 89.9% alcohol by volume (½-liter £40), you can get drunk just looking. Open M-Th and Sa 9am-6:30pm, F 9am-7:30pm. MC/V.

MARKETS

Berwick Street Market, ⊖Leicester Sq. or Piccadilly Circus. Southernmost strip of Berwick St. One of central London's most well-known fruit and vegetable markets since the 1840s.

Disrupted a bit by nearby construction, its usually small selection is packed with fresh, quality merchandise. Especially lively at lunchtime. Open M-Sa 9am-5pm. Cash only.

BOOKS

Blackwell's, 100 Charing Cross Rd. (☎020 7292 5100; www.blackwell.co.uk). ⊖Tottenham Court Rd. or Leicester Sq. Get blissfully lost in the London flagship store of Oxford's top academic bookshop, with everything on one enormous floor. Wheelchair-accessible. Open M-Sa 9:30am-8pm, Su noon-6pm. AmEx/MC/V.

Foyles, 113-119 Charing Cross Rd. (☎020 7437 5660; www.foyles.co.uk). ⊖Tottenham Court Rd. or Leicester Sq. With over 30 mi. of recently renovated shelving, this labyrinthine bookshop spread over 5 fl. is exhaustive. A never-ending fiction department, a substantial GLBT section, and a small contemporary art gallery top off an already overwhelming selection. Free Wi-Fi. Wheelchair-accessible. Open M-Sa 9:30am-9pm, Su noon-6pm. AmEx/MC/V.

Grant and Cutler, 55-57 Great Marlborough St. ⊖Oxford Circus. This foreign language bookshop has extensive selections of French, German, Italian, Portuguese, Russian, and Spanish books. Also has tons of books in languages you may have never heard—or heard of. Open M-W and F-Sa 10am-6:30pm, Th 10am-7pm, Su noon-6pm. AmEx/MC/V.

MUSIC

Black Market, 25 D'Arblay St. (☎020 7437 0478; www.bm-soho.com). ⊖Oxford Circus. Metal-clad walls and massive speakers dominate the all-vinyl dance emporium, along with turntables ready for amateur or professional scratching. House and garage upstairs; phenomenal drum and bass section below with more underground garage. Also sells club tickets and merchandise from its own label (£12-30). Many albums are cheaper online. Open M-W and Sa 11am-7pm, Th-F 11am-8pm. AmEx/MC/V.

Sister Ray, 34-35 Berwick St. (☎020 7734 3297; www.sisterray.co.uk). ⊖Tottenham Court Rd. or Oxford Circus. The big daddy of the Berwick St. music shops emphasizes selection. Spacious compared to its competitors and packed with every genre. Often cheaper than other independent shops in the area (new releases £9-12). Strong vinyl and DVD offerings. Open M-Sa 10am-8pm, Su noon-6pm. MC/V.

Revival Records, 30 Berwick St. (☎020 7437 4271; www.revivalrecords.uk.com). ⊖Tottenham Court Rd. or Oxford Circus. Small secondhand shop boasts a varied collection of used CDs and vinyl. Recently revived under a new name and new ownership. CDs £4-10. Eclectic selection of used DVDs. Oasis box set £14. Open M-Sa 10am-7pm. AmEx/MC/V.

 SHOP TILL YOU DROP. Most shops in London stay open late 1 night per week. To continue your consumerism into the early evening, head to Chelsea and Knightsbridge on W and to Oxford St. and Covent Garden on Th.

COVENT GARDEN AND THE STRAND

Once the hottest proving ground for new designers, Covent Garden is gradually being overtaken by large clothing chains: almost every store with an eye on the youth market has more than one shop in the area, with a main branch on Oxford St. or Regent St. Mid-priced chains and tacky souvenir shops fill the piazza, though there are still enough quirky specialty shops left to make it worth a quick wander. However, in the mainstream mess there remains a haven of hope: the streets around **Neal's Yard** have some quasi-predictable chains, but also a handful of boutiques, specialty shops, and cafes. To the east, **Short's Gardens** has chic menswear and to the west, **Earlham** and **Monmouth Street** have a similarly stylish selection of women's clothing. (⊖*Covent Garden unless otherwise noted.*)

BOOKS

Stanfords, 12-14 Long Acre (☎020 7836 1321; www.stanfords.co.uk). Another location at 1 Regent St. A travel superstore, Stanfords covers every corner of the universe. With a sweeping range of hiking maps, city maps, road maps, flight maps, star maps, wall maps, and globes, you'll never be lost again. Travel books and travel writings cover the entire 1st fl. Huge selection of globes. Also has a Cafe Copia and a Craghoppers outdoor clothing store. Open M, W, F 9am-7:30pm, Tu 9:30am-7:30pm, Th 9am-8pm, Sa 10am-8pm, Su noon-6pm. MC/V.

CLOTHES

▨ **Apple Tree,** 62 Neal St. (☎020 7379 5944). Small boutique that specializes in upcoming and independent designers. Almost everything in the store is hand-sewn, and many items are one-of-a-kind. Selection ranges from beautiful eyelet dresses (£50-70) to printed tunics (£40) and ballet flats (£30). Quirky earrings £15. Many staff members are designers as well. Open M-Sa 10:30am-7:30pm, Su noon-6pm. AmEx/MC/V.

GIFTS AND MISCELLANY

▨ **Neal's Yard Dairy,** 17 Short's Gardens (☎020 7240 5700; www.nealsyarddairy.co.uk). Also at 6 Park St. (☎020 7367 0799). You'll smell it from a mile away—and that's a good thing. The enormous array of mostly British and Irish cheeses is entirely produced in small farms by traditional methods; massive wheels of Stilton and cheddar line the shelves and countertops. The staff is eager to slice off samples and compare types. Also sells preserves, organic milk, and yogurts. Call ☎7645 3555 for info on cheese tastings (from £40). Open M-Sa 10am-7pm. MC/V.

Spex in the City, 1 Shorts Gardens (☎020 7240 0243; www.spexinthecity.com). ⊖Covent Garden. This smooth and hip "independent optician" carries a selection of handmade glasses (no brands allowed!) and offers sight tests, style advice, frame settings, and individual lens fitting. The owner flies around the world to find the glasses she puts on the shelves, which begin at £40. AmEx/MC/V.

Penhaligon's, 41 Wellington St. (☎020 7836 2150; www.penhaligons.com). ⊖Charing Cross. Other locations on Bond St. and in Piccadilly Circus. Founded by former palace barber William Henry Penhaligon in 1870, Penhaligon's still provides elite men and women with perfumes and grooming products. Winston Churchill never left home without a dab of the English classic Blenheim Bouquet. Wheelchair-accessible. Open M-W and F-Sa 10am-6pm, Th 10am-7pm, Su noon-6pm. AmEx/MC/V.

Neal's Yard Remedies, 15 Neal's Yard (☎020 7379 7222; www.nealsyardremedies.com). An alternative to more mainstream bath and body stores, Neal's sells soaps, lotions, and fragrances incorporating everything from lavender to some of nature's lesser-known treasures (like bladder wrack and pilewort). Each Neal's has rooms for private therapeutic sessions; call ☎020 7379 7662 to reserve. Open M-Sa 10am-7pm, Su 11am-6pm. AmEx/MC/V.

The Tea House, 15 Neal St. (☎020 7240 7539). A small wooden store packed to the gills with tea, teapots, teacups, and tea cozies from around the world. Specializes in fine, classic, blended, scented, and flavored black teas, as well as caffeine free green and white teas. Teas £2.50-5.20 per lb. Open M-W 10am-7pm, Th-Sa 10am-8pm, Su 11am-7pm. MC/V.

MARKETS

Apple Market, inside the Covent Garden Piazza. Sells crafts, jewelry, and knick-knacks from artists and designers. Excellent finds, but expect to pay tourist prices. Wheelchair-accessible. Open daily 10:30am-6pm, some vendors until 7pm. Some vendors accept AmEx/MC/V.

Jubilee Market, Jubilee Hall on the corner of Covent Garden and Southampton. A rough-and-tumble market featuring clothing, albums, and accessories, along with quality arts and crafts (Tu-S) and antiques (M). Paintings, drawings, posters, and sketches also common finds. Wheelchair-accessible. Open daily 10:30am-6pm. Some vendors accept AmEx/MC/V.

> **TIP** **HIT IT AND QUID IT.** The slang for "pounds" is "quid," a more popular term in smaller shops or colloquial talk.

SHOES

The Natural Shoe Store, 13 Neal St. (☎020 7836 5254; www.thenaturalshoestore.com). ⊖Covent Garden. The 1st shoe store on Neal St. Smells like nature and looks like nature: a tree house, to be exact. If a brand makes you think "earthy" or "natural," you'll find it here: Teva, Think!, Patagonia, Toni Pons, Trippen, Arche, Frye. Enormous selection of Birkenstocks. Open M-W and Sa 10am-7pm, Th-F 10am-8pm, Su noon-6pm. AmEx/MC/V.

Office, 57 Neal St. (☎020 7379 1896; www.office.co.uk). One of London's foremost fashion footwear retailers, with a larger selection than most shoe stores on the street. Carries its own crazy-sexy-stylish brand as well as other brands like Camper and Lacoste. Women's shoes £20-145 (average £50-80), men's £60-130. The sale shop at 61 St. Martin's Ln. (☎020 7497 0390; ⊖Leicester Sq. or Covent Garden; open M-Sa 10am-7pm, Su noon-6pm) has good deals on all styles and includes midseason reductions. Wheelchair-accessible. Open M-W and F-Sa 10:30am-7:30pm, Th 10:30am-8pm, Su noon-6pm. 10% discount with student ID. AmEx/MC/V.

BLOOMSBURY

Not surprisingly, Bloomsbury's main commodity (other than A-level acumen) is books; it is commonly known as the heart of British bookselling. The streets around the British Museum are crammed with specialist and discount bookshops, while the **Waterstone's** on Gower St. (p. 172) is one of London's largest.

BOOKS

Gay's the Word, 66 Marchmont St. (☎020 7278 7654; www.gaystheword.co.uk). ⊖Russell Sq. The UK's largest gay and lesbian bookstore, GTW boasts a well-informed staff and an extensive collection including erotic fiction, detective stories, plays, poetry, and nonfiction, as well as movies and free magazines. Weekly events and discussion groups. Notice board with accommodations listings. Open M-Sa 10am-6:30pm, Su 2-6pm. AmEx/MC/V.

Gosh! 39 Great Russell St. (☎020 7636 1011; www.goshlondon.com). ⊖Tottenham Court Rd. With 2 fl. and 22 years of street cred, Gosh has any type of comic you'd ever want: tons of graphic novels, manga, vintage children's fiction, and cutting edge small press. Also features signed copies of new releases. Open M-W and Sa-Su 10am-6pm, F-Sa 10-7pm. AmEx/MC/V.

Persephone Books, 59 Lamb's Conduit St. (☎020 7242 9292; www.persephonebooks.co.uk). ⊖Russell Sq. A pretty lilac-gray bookshop that sells equally elegant reprints of "neglected" novels, diaries, short stories, and cookbooks, mostly by women and from the early to mid-20th century. All books £10; 3 for £27. Open M-F 10am-6pm, Sa noon-5pm.

Bookmarks, 1 Bloomsbury St. (☎020 7637 1848; www.bookmarksbookshop.co.uk). ⊖Tottenham Court Rd. A socialist bookstore. Open M noon-7pm, Tu-F 10am-7pm, Sa 10am-6pm; closed one week in early July for Marxism Festival. AmEx/MC/V.

GIFTS AND MISCELLANY

James Smith & Sons, 53 New Oxford St. (☎020 7836 4731; www.james-smith.co.uk). ⊖Tottenham Court Rd. Groucho Marx once quipped that he hated London when it wasn't raining. The Smith family, in the umbrella business since 1830, must surely agree. Their shop, unchanged with time, holds row after row of handmade brollies (from £85), walking sticks (from £20), and the newest rain-repelling models. Open M and W-F 9:30am-5:25pm, Tu and Sa 10am-5:25pm. AmEx/MC/V.

L. Cornelissen & Son, 105 Great Russell St. (☎020 7636 1045; www.cornelissen.com). ⊖Tottenham Court Rd. Straight out of the 19th-century, this tiny art shop will transport you back in time, and its selection will convince artists that they're dreaming. Jars of paints, pencils, raw pigments, gums, resins, crystals, inks, and lumps of foul-smelling "dragon's blood" reach to the ceilings. A feast for the imagination. Open M-Th 9:30am-5:30pm. MC/V.

CAMDEN TOWN, KING'S CROSS, AND ISLINGTON

North London offers a bevy of shopping options, from the upmarket boutiques in **Islington** to the outrageous alternative shops on **Camden High Street.** The **Camden Markets** are some of London's best; they sell everything from mouth-watering ethnic foods to handmade jewelry to fur and leather jackets. Serious music shoppers will revel in the vinyl shops on **Inverness Street,** while those looking for vintage should check out **Camden Passage,** near the Angel Tube. The stores on **Upper Street** range from popular chains to pricey specialty shops.

CLOTHES

▨ **Annie's,** 12 Camden Passage (☎020 7359 0796; www.anniesvintageclothing.co.uk), in Camden Passage Market. ⊖Angel. Vogue and Elle regularly use these lacy, beaded, or otherwise flirty vintage frocks in their photo shoots, while Alexander McQueen, John Galliano, Nicole Farhi, and Donna Karan come here to accessorize. 1920s dresses are too expensive to buy at £300-600; less flashy 1930s pieces are more affordable (£45-150). Bags, shoes, and hats from £30. Open M-Tu and Th-F 11am-6pm, W and Sa 8am-6pm, Su 11am-3pm. MC/V.

▨ **Equa,** 28 Camden Passage (☎020 7359 0955; www.equaclothing.com). ⊖Angel. The most responsible clothing shop in the city and perhaps the world, Equa sells only organic, fair trade, and otherwise morally superior pieces that are fashionable and sophisticated to boot. Each of the 30 designers has a different style and ethical specialty, from organic cotton skirts to worm-friendly silk dresses and vegan handbags. Dresses from £60; shoes and bags from £100. Open M-W and F-Sa 10am-6:30pm, Th 10am-7pm, Su noon-5pm. AmEx/MC/V.

LONDON

MARKETS

Camden Markets, ⊖Camden Town. Make a sharp right out of the Tube station to reach Camden High St., where most of the markets start. Though there's the obligatory onslaught of kitsch, these stalls house some great foods and handmade goods. Even if you don't find something you like, the atmosphere itself makes it worth a visit.

Camden Lock Market, from the railway bridge to Regent's Canal. This indoor-outdoor market is the largest and most diverse, selling everything from handmade jewelry and pocket mirrors to Banksy and Warhol prints to loose leaf teas. Also has an extensive selection of delicious food stalls. Open daily 10am-6pm.

Stables Market, farthest from the Tube station, right next to Camden Lock on the left. No matter which entrance you pick, you'll find yourself lost among the myriad stalls, shops, and food peddlers. Stables manages to avoid the tacky trap so many markets fall into. Toward the back, at the horse hospital, you'll find some remaining independent artists as well as a 2-story antique market. Wheelchair-accessible. Open daily 9:30am-5:30pm.

Camden Canal Market, opposite Camden Lock along the canal. Held in tiki-style huts, the Canal market offers tons of food—Thai, Mexican, Brazilian, Japanese, fish and chips, smoothies—and a long line of specialty shops, most selling clothes and bags, but others selling posters and some cute accessories. Wheelchair-accessible. Open daily 9am-6:30pm.

CAMDEN TOWN TUBE. Due to the hustle of the Sunday market crawl in Camden Town, ⊖Camden Town is only open to passengers disembarking, or changing from one train to another (1-5:30pm). No one can enter the station at that time from the street. You may have to take the bus back, or walk to ⊖Chalk Hill or Mornington Crescent.

Camden Passage Market, Islington High St. ⊖Angel. Turn right from the Tube; it's the alleyway that starts behind "The Mall" antiques gallery on Upper St. More for looking than for buying, London's premier antique shops line these quaint alleyways. Smaller items such as old prints, drawings, and small trinkets may dip into the realm of the affordable. Few stalls open daily, but all open W and Sa 8:30am-6pm.

MUSIC

Out on the Floor, 10 Inverness St. (☎020 7485 9958 or 7267 5989). ⊖Camden Town. 2 tiny fl. full of vinyl. Out on the Floor specializes in 60s-70s reggae, but also sell jazz, rock, soul, funk, and more (£5-100). Downstairs you'll find **Steam Power Poster Co.** (www.steampowerposters.com), one of the only places in the city where you can find handmade reprints of the greats of the 60s and 70s (£15). Also sells some originals (£10-150). Open daily 10am-6pm. AmEx/MC/V.

BAYSWATER

Catering more to chain stores, Bayswater offers little of London's unique shopping experience. There's a single exception: the weekly artists' market.

Bayswater Market, along Bayswater Rd. from Clarendon Pl. to Queensway. ⊖Queensway. Every Su for the past 50 years, this open-air art show—the largest weekly expo of its kind in the world—has been packed along the gates of Kensington Gardens. Over 250 painters, photographers, and various others ply their trade, sometimes with an overly firm eye on the tourist market. Despite this, surprises and delights abound, and the gardens add a touch of natural beauty. Shipping often available. Open Su 10am-6pm in any weather.

Adventure in Europe?
Do it by rail

With a Eurail Global or Select Pass you zoom fast from country to country, from city centre to city centre. So you can soak up hip street scenes. Shop till you drop. Explore the nightlife and meet cool people.

Why wait? Go to www.adventure-europe.com or contact your local travel agent now!

NOTTING HILL

Portobello Road is the undisputed center of Notting Hill shopping, with both its street market and its local boutiques, but the neighborhood has plenty of shopping to go around. **Golborne Road** has its own colorful street scene, with Moroccan, Lebanese and Portuguese shops and cafes, while book and antique lovers will enjoy the little shops lining **Blenheim Crescent**. A number of excellent (and affordable) vintage and secondhand stores are spread throughout the neighborhood, particularly at **Notting Hill Gate.**

ANTIQUES

Hirst Antiques, 59 Pembridge Rd. (☎020 7727 9364; www.hirstantiques.co.uk). ⊖Notting Hill Gate. Often featured in magazines and frequented by celebs (ahem, Sienna Miller, Keira Knightley, David Beckham), this shop is the place to go for antique jewelry. Among peacock blue walls, glass case after glass case is filled with quirky, chunky, understated, or just plain pretty rings, necklaces, brooches, and bracelets. Also sells sculptures and chandeliers. Earrings from £20, bracelets from £25. Open M-Sa 11am-6pm. MC/V.

BOOKS

Books for Cooks, 4 Blenheim Crescent (☎020 7221 1992; www.booksforcooks.com). ⊖Ladbroke Grove. An delightful shop devoted to all types of cookbooks, from breads and coffee to vegetarian dishes and desserts. Recipes from almost every world cuisine are available, and the knowledgeable staff is eager to help. MC/V.

The Travel Bookshop, 13-15 Blenheim Crescent (☎020 7229 5260; www.thetravel-bookshop.com). ⊖Ladbroke Grove. The inspiration for the bookshop in the 1999 film Notting Hill, The Travel Bookshop would be worth a visit even without Hollywood's seal of approval. Filled with travel books of all kinds, from love stories to phrase books to maps and guides. Open M-Sa 10am-6pm, Su 11am-5pm.

CLOTHES

Oxfam Boutique, 245 Westbourne Grove (☎020 7229 5000; www.oxfam.org.uk/fashion). One of three Oxfam boutiques opened in London in 2008, this shop takes only the best of what Notting Hill's well-heeled residents drop off, leaving the rest for non-boutique Oxfam stores. Wedged within a long line of designer boutiques on Westbourne, it's bound to carry many of the same names. Designer jeans from £15. Dresses from £10. Blazers from £30. Open M-Sa 10am-6pm, Su noon-4pm. AmEx/MC/V.

Dolly Diamond, 51 Pembridge Rd. (☎020 7792 2479; www.dollydiamond.com). ⊖Notting Hill Gate. This nostalgic shop specializes in men's and women's vintage clothing, from classic 50s to casual 70s wear and elegant evening gowns. Dresses start at around £65, but an upstairs sale room (open F-Sa) features pieces that start at £5. Open M-F 10:30am-6:30pm, Sa 9:30am-6:30pm, Su 11am-6:30pm. MC/V. 10% cash discount.

B Famous, 25 Pembridge Rd. (☎0790 0302 235; www.bfamouslondon.com). ⊖Notting Hill Gate. A striking yellow exterior with painted images of Blondie and Kiss belies what's inside—vintage T-shirts of all your favorite classic bands. Stones, Ramones, Hendrix, and Bowie are side-by-side with the Beatles, Run DMC, and AC/DC. Randomly, Che made the cut. T-shirts £20-35. Open M-F and Sa 10am-7pm, Su 9am-7pm. AmEx/MC/V.

THE HIDDEN DEAL

DOING GOOD, LOOKING GREAT

While London may not be the center of haute couture, it is the center of ethical fashion. Many of its charity shops rival the best vintage stores. In posh districts, these ethical stores regularly receive donations from the likes of Nicole Farhi and most carry designer labels.

Oxfam, for example, has begun a series of sustainable efforts—the organization now supports fair-trade labels like People Tree, Green Knickers, and Wright and Teague. Oxfam has also commissioned a series of designers like Junky Styling and students from the London College of Fashion to create new items from unsellable clothes—look for shoulder bags made out of old leather jackets.

The superstar of the ethical style is the new Equa (p. 181), a small boutique in Islington that features beautiful feminine fashions from 30 ethical designers. Each piece of clothing has a different story: sporty dresses are made with organic cotton; quirky heels are entirely vegan; gold necklaces are made by women in Nairobi through micro-finance efforts; a silk chiffon cocktail dress is made in India, Peru, Uganda, or Lesotho and distributed according to fair trade policies. Giving back and protecting the environment never looked so good.

Oxfam locations at 245 Westbourne Grove, Notting Hill (☎020 7229 5000); 123a Shawfield St., Chelsea (☎020 7351 7979); and 190 Chiswick High Rd. (☎020 8994 4888).

MARKETS

Portobello Road Markets. Home to a number of markets that occupy different parts of the street and operate on different days. In order to see it all, come F or Sa when everything is sure to be open. Stalls set their own times; hours below are approximate.

General Market. ⊖Westbourne Park or Ladbroke Grove. Farther north, from Elgin Crescent to Lancaster Rd. Sells fresh fruit, food, flowers, and household essentials. Gourmet stalls with breads and organic produce compete with local restaurants. Open M-W and F-Sa 8am-6:30pm, Th 8am-1pm.

Antiques Market. ⊖Notting Hill Gate. What most people associate with Portobello Rd. Stretches north from Chepstow Villas to Elgin Crescent. Most of what's on display is cheap bric-a-brac. Many stalls open at different points throughout the week; all Sa 7am-5pm.

Golborne Road Market. ⊖Ladbroke Grove. North of the Westway. Moroccan- and Lebanese-influenced stalls selling gourmet olives, sizzling kebabs, steaming couscous, and Berber handicrafts. Some stalls open at different points throughout the week; all are open F-Sa 9am-5pm.

Clothes Market. ⊖Ladbroke Grove. North of Lancaster Rd., with arms stretching along the Westway. A wide selection of secondhand clothes and jewelry, oddly interspersed with used electronics. Many stalls open at different points throughout the week; all F-Sa 8am-3pm.

MUSIC

Rough Trade, 130 Talbot Rd. (☎020 7229 8541). ⊖Ladbroke Grove. Don't be overwhelmed by the large selection—small reviews tacked to most CDs and records (from £5) will counsel you. Try the in-store turntables, test CDs at the listening station, or peruse the many leaflets advertising local bands and concerts. Downstairs, Rough Trade vintage sells secondhand vinyls, posters, and books from £10. Open M-Sa 10am-6:30pm, Su noon-5pm. AmEx/MC/V.

Honest Jon's, 276-278 Portobello Rd. (☎020 8969 9822). ⊖Ladbroke Grove. Laid-back and focused on the music, Jon's boasts an impressive collection of new and used jazz, Latin, reggae, hip hop, house, and garage vinyls and CDs. LPs and CDs start at £5. Open M-Sa 10am-6pm, Su 11am-5pm. AmEx/MC/V.

Intoxica, 231 Portobello Rd. (☎020 7229 8010; www.intoxica.co.uk). ⊖Ladbroke Grove. Outfitted like a tiki hut with leopard print and bamboo covered walls, Intoxica is unsurpassed in its international flair, with 2 fl. of new, collectible, and reissued vinyl LPs and 45s from around the world (from £6). Upstairs you'll find soul, funk, beat, Motown psych, reggae, ska, new wave, and more (all from the 50s onward); downstairs you'll see jazz, R&B, doo-wop, rock & roll, and an art gallery featuring up-and-coming artists. Open M-Sa 10:30am-6:30pm, Su noon-5pm. AmEx/MC/V.

MISCELLANY

Fussy Nation, 183 Portobello Rd. (☎020 7727 6426; www.fussynation.co.uk). ⊖Ladbroke Grove. A funky, somewhat saucy shop for boys and girls, with a selection of clothes (tops £65), shoes (£45), and risqué greeting cards and gift books. Other odds and ends include cutesy cupcake lipgloss, Wonder Woman toiletry cases (£15), political photo frames... the list goes on. Open M-Sa 10am-6:30pm, Su 10am-5:30pm. AmEx/MC/V.

KNIGHTSBRIDGE AND BELGRAVIA

Brompton Road dominates Knightsbridge's shopping arteries, with representatives of most upmarket chains featured between Harvey Nichols and Harrods. Explore the side streets for spectacular deals on designer clothing or blow a cool £1000 on ultra-exclusive **Sloane Street,** which rivals Bond St. for designer boutiques.

CLOTHES

▨ **Pandora,** 16-22 Cheval Pl. (☎020 7589 5289; www.pandoradressagency.com). ⊖Knightsbridge, take Harrods Exit. Secondhand designer clothes at affordable prices. Marc Jacobs skirts from £35; Prada, Jimmy Choo, and Ferragamo heels from £65. Sales Jan. and from late July to late Aug. Open M-Sa 10am-7pm, Su noon-6pm. MC/V.

DEPARTMENT STORES

▨ **Harrods,** 87-135 Brompton Rd. (☎020 7730 1234; www.harrods.com). ⊖Knightsbridge. In the Victorian era, this was *the* place for the wealthy to shop; over a century later, it is less of a provider of goods than a tourist extravaganza. Given the sky-high prices, it's no wonder that only souvenir-seekers and oil sheiks actually shop here. Open M-Sa 10am-8pm; Su 11:30am-6pm, browsing only 11:30am-noon. Wheelchair-accessible. AmEx/MC/V/gold/diamonds.

Harvey Nichols, 109-125 Knightsbridge (☎020 7235 5000; www.harveynichols.com). ⊖Knightsbridge. Imagine Bond St., Rue St. Honoré, and 5th Ave. all rolled up into one store: in contrast to the pomp and circumstance of the other H down the street, Harvey is about serious shopping. 5 of its 7 fl. are devoted to the sleekest, sharpest fashions from the biggest names to the hippest unknowns. Sales from late June to late July and from late Dec. to late Jan. Open M-Sa 10am-9pm, Su 11:30-6pm, browsing only 11:30am-noon. Wheelchair-accessible. AmEx/MC/V.

CHELSEA

Even if it has lost much of its punk-rock edge in recent years, Chelsea's abundance of quirky one-off boutiques and the relative dearth of upmarket chain stores lend the area a vitality and diversity absent from London's other shopping meccas. On the east side, **Sloane Square** is extremely "Sloaney" (the London equivalent of American "preppy"). To the west, **King's Road** gave us both the miniskirt and the Sex Pistols. Alternative styles have given way to more mainstream cuts, but the notorious Vivienne Westwood hasn't fled yet (see World's End, p. 186).

CLOTHES

Ad Hoc, 153 King's Rd. (☎020 7376 8829). ⊖Sloane Sq., then Bus #11, 19, 22, 211, 319. This store is a must for costume parties. Ad Hoc's scantily clad window mannequins display everything from candy bikinis to bling-heavy costume jewelry. Inside, a rainbow collection of wigs dominates the cluttered neon and sparkle-bedecked space. 10% student discount. Open M-Tu and Th-Sa 10am-6:30pm, W 10am-7pm, Su noon-6pm. AmEx/MC/V.

World's End, 430 King's Rd. (☎020 7352 6551). ⊖Sloane Sq., then Bus #11 or 22. This small store's legendary incarnations include SEX and Let it Rock. Today, little remains of the punk store that launched the career of the Sex Pistols, besides perhaps the zany clock above the doorway. Owned by the notorious Vivienne Westwood, the shop is now a pricey, funky showplace for her latest designs. Most items £100-300. Open M-Sa 10am-6pm. AmEx/MC/V.

SHOES

Sukie's, 285 King's Rd. (☎020 7352 3431). ⊖Sloane Sq., then Bus #19 or 319. Quirky British style and Italian quality. The heels, flats, loafers, and boots come in unusual colors, materials, and textures, and are specially designed for the store by Italian leather makers. Just a few pairs per size. Most start at £30. Wheelchair-accessible. Open M-Tu and Th-Sa 10am-7:30pm, W 10:30am-8pm, Su noon-6pm. MC/V.

WEST LONDON

Not much more than chain-store shopping exists in and around **Hammersmith** and **Shoreditch;** it may be the place to beat the crowds of **Oxford Street,** but not necessarily the place for bargains. The main roads of the suburbs of **Chiswick** and **Kew Gardens** feature an interesting enough mix of brand stores and unique shops to fill an afternoon—if you're willing to make the trek.

Fosters Bookshop, 183 Chiswick High Rd., Chiswick (☎020 8995 2768). ⊖Turnham Green. One of the most charming used bookshops in London. Shelves stacked to the brim with hardcovers. Originally specializing in children's literature, this tiny family-run shop is now a treasure trove for people all ages, offering many collector's editions of classics and out-of-print books. Everything from vintage fairy-tale compilations to old religious texts. Prices range from £2 to £2500 (for a signed John Lennon autobiography). Open Tu-Sa 10:30am-5pm. MC/V.

⊞ NIGHTLIFE

Whether you're ideal night out includes a chic ice bar or a secret speakeasy, a foosball-inspired latin bar or a sweatily chaotic club, the latest underground scene or a sprawling courtyard dance party, you're bound to find it in one of London's many nighttime hotspots. Pubs fill up even before the workday has ended, and the party more often than not continues on into the wee hours. But the rumor that Britain is primarily a place of pubbing falls away at the city limit: when the pubs close around 11pm, numerous bars and clubs take over, raging long into the night. Because there so many distinctive neighborhoods filled with diverse options, your best bet is just to pick one that matches your tastes and make a night of it: East London is for the edgy, artsy and hip, while North

London is the place to go for 70s-90s grundge and underground venues. Clerkenwell is well-known for clubbing, while Chelsea and Kensington offer more upscale and exclusive options. Soho takes the cake when it comes to GLBT nightlife, but also when it comes to a fun night of socializing: gay and straight clubs alike are filled with all sorts--so much so that most bars and clubs self-define as "polysexual." If you want something really quirky and up-and-coming, try the Southbank or South London--their distance makes them riskier, but that only means bigger reward. Remember to plan your Night Bus or (licensed) taxi trip home before you go out; Night Buses are listed with each establishment below.

 GETTING HOME. The Tube closes around midnight, so planning transportation home is important. Let's Go includes local Night Bus routes for most nightlife listings—excluding pubs, which mostly close around 11pm. Coordinate the best Night Bus route by matching route numbers in nightlife listings with route numbers in accommodation listings. If you don't find a perfect fit, head toward a major transportation hub (Trafalgar Sq., Oxford Circus, Liverpool St., or Victoria) for a transfer.

THE CITY OF LONDON

The City is a nice place to enjoy a pint, but it pretty much clears out after the work crowd has done its socializing. Even if establishments are open past 6pm, you may feel a little lonely in otherwise deserted streets on your walk home. The pubs are livelier in the mid-afternoon (noon to 4pm), making them fine spots for lunch or an afternoon beer.

PUBS

The Black Friar, 174 Queen Victoria St. (☎020 7236 5474). ⊖Blackfriars. The Black Friar's claim to fame is its Art Deco imitation of the 12th-century Dominican friary that once occupied this spot. Everything says friar, from the stained glass windows to the marble wall decorations. An open-front room and a back dining area outfitted in mirrors welcome visitors inside. Entrees from £7. Wheelchair-accessible. Open daily 11am-11pm. Kitchen open 10am-10pm. AmEx/MC/V.

The Walrus and the Carpenter, 45 Monument St. (☎020 7621 1647), at Lovat Ln. ⊖Monument.

IT'S THE MOST WONDERFUL TIME OF THE YEAR

I knew that it would take energy and determination to enter the heavy gilded doors of Harrods—but never could I have been prepared for what I encountered: it was Late June.

"Late June" is a vague label for many, but for Londoners, Late June means only one thing: sales. These sales happen at the centres (not centers) of the shopping world, the big tycoons, the two Hs: Harrods and Harvey Nichols. During the whirlwind weeks at the end of the month, sales creep upwards of 40% and 50% off, and the store culture responds accordingly. Dazed American tourists wander the Harrods Arcade, bags overflowing. Harvey's a bit more serious: wistful teenage girls and their well-heeled mothers "browse" aggressively in HN's Dior department, staking out the next cocktail dress. With a new crowd showing up, the atmosphere is hopeful, overwhelming, and chaotic. Even the mannequins, hanging over the balconies in the Harrods staircase and outfitted in the latest designer evening wear, seem to know what's up.

With all the excitement and confusion, it's worth at least a visit. Even as you get lost in the candy store, stumble through Luxury Room II, and end up next to the Miu Miu bags, you'll realize that the clutch you had your eye on is now selling for a mere £395!

This pub benefits above all from its proximity to the City center. Around lunch hour, patrons spill over into the cobblestone alleyway. A mix of young, old, and families. Traditional pub food from burgers (£8) to Oxford sausages (£7). Solid beer and wine selection. Ales and ciders £3.50. Wheelchair-accessible. Open M-F 11am-11pm. AmEx/MC/V.

PROACTIVE PUBBING. If you walk into a pub and set on down at the nearest table, you'll be waiting all night for a drink or a meal. Most pubs don't have wait staff, so you'll have to order at the bar. The menu is usually posted on a chalkboard nearby.

EAST LONDON

WHITECHAPEL AND THE EAST END

While Soho is considered London's nightlife capital, a younger, hipper, and edgier crowd flocks to Shoreditch every weekend. Years ago, Hoxton Square began building a reputation as the go-to spot for underground music and hipster gatherings, but this area is so up-and-coming that even Hoxton barely clings to its cooler than cool reputation. Meanwhile, the streets on and around **Brick Lane** bring the party every night; crowds gather in the streets from 9pm on. *Night Buses congregate at the Liverpool St. hub. #N8, N11, 23, N26, N35, N76, N133, 149, 214, 242, 271, unless otherwise indicated; additional Night Bus routes listed.)*

WHO'S A HIPSTER? While the East End is a haven for what Americans all affectionately call "hipsters," mention that word to Brits and they may look at you as if your furry American tail is poking out of your pants. Londoners don't have a comparable term ("fashionista" comes close). Hard to define, but you know it when you see it.

BARS

Vibe Bar, 91-95 Brick Ln. (☎020 7426 0491; www.vibe-bar.co.uk). ⊖Aldgate East or Liverpool St. Night Bus. Once the home of the Truman Brewery, this funky bar is heavy on style and light on pretension. Vibe prides itself on promoting new artists and combining music and visual displays. Dim lighting, brick interior, and mural-covered walls give the place an artsy, casual feel. In the summer, pour into the outdoor courtyard for drinking, BBQ, and general revelry. Free internet. DJs spin hip hop, garage, techno, and more M-Th and Su 11am-11:30pm. Cover F-Sa after 8pm £4. Open M-Th and Su 11am-11:30pm, F-Sa 11am-1am. AmEx/MC/V over £10.

Big Chill Bar, Dray Walk (☎020 7392 9180; www.bigchill.net), off Brick Ln. ⊖Liverpool St. or Aldgate East. Night Bus. No address? No problem: no one has trouble finding this watering hole off Brick Lane. DJs spin an eclectic mix nightly while famously friendly crowds chat or dance it up in the dark interior or on the outdoor patio. Stay all day during "Big Chill Sundae," with board games, brunch, and the market madness. Mixed drinks from £5.80. A menu of shareable foods such as pizza (£7-9) ensures no one goes hungry. Brunch Su noon-9pm. Open M-Th noon-midnight, F-Sa noon-1am, Su 11am-midnight. MC/V.

■ **Favela Chic,** 91-93 Great Eastern St. (☎020 7613 4228; www.favelachic.com/london). ⊖Old St. With a wildly popular location in Paris, this Franco-Brazilian restaurant-bar-dance club has exploded onto London's nightlife scene. Soaring ceilings and towering palm trees and pillars are hung with antique paintings, elaborate chandeliers, and an enormous disco ball. Everywhere else, an amped up crowd dances to everything from Motown to hip hop to Brit-pop to Baile Funk (if you have to ask, we can't explain). You will leave out of breath. Mixed drinks £7.50-8. Cover £10. Open M-Th 6pm-1am, F-Sa 6pm-2am. Kitchen open 7-11pm. AmEx/MC/V.

■ **Hoxton Square Bar & Kitchen,** 2-4 Hoxton Sq. (☎020 7613 0709). ⊖Old St. Night Bus. Consistently the most crowded place on Hoxton Square, this spacious bar manages to be a lounge, restaurant, and drinking destination at once. Three separate bars and DJs or live music on F-Sa nights bring masses of revelers. Low couches, a stark interior, and contemporary art make the bar feel like a warehouse; the restaurant is a bit cozier, with wooden tables, calmer artwork, and lighter walls. Head to the pleasant patio on summer evenings. Wheelchair-accessible. Open M 11am-midnight, Tu-Th 11am-1am, F-Sa 11am-2am, Su 11am-12:30am. No admission F-Su after midnight. MC/V.

Bar Music Hall, 134 Curtain Rd. (☎020 7729 7216; www.barmusichall.com). ⊖Old St. The enormous square bar may take center stage, but it only fuels the party happening all around. Live band or DJ plays as inhibitions are shaken off. Best of all, its always free. Occasional samba nights; live music or DJ almost every night. Beer and wine £3.20-4.70. Mixed drinks £6.50. Open M-Th and Su 11am-midnight, F-Sa 11am-1am. AmEx/MC/V.

Bar Kick, 127 Shoreditch High St. (☎020 7739 8700). ⊖Old St. Night Bus as well as #N55, N243. A dream come true for "table football" aficionados, this bar doesn't take itself too seriously. Foosball figurines, world flags, and football paraphernalia adorn the ceiling beams and walls while upbeat music favorites and 2 fl. of foosball keep crowds happy. Flatscreen TVs playing the latest (professional) sporting match entertain those not involved in competition. Tasty mixed drinks (mojitos and martinis; £7) and a heavy continental European influence. Nachos and burgers £4-5. Kitchen open M-F noon-3:30pm and 6-10pm, Sa-Su all day. Open M-W 10am-11pm, Th-F 10am-midnight, Sa noon-midnight, Su noon-10:30pm. Cash only.

Casa Blue, 120 Bethnal Green Rd. (☎020 7729 6444) ⊖Old St. or Liverpool St. Low scuffed-up couches, Christmas lights, candles propped in vodka bottles, hanging lanterns, disco balls: that's the furniture at this casa. Quirky mixed drinks (£5) go well with the house specialties. Chicken and lamb rolls £5. Platters of *haloumi,* samosas, falafel, and other Mediterranean staples £5 per person. Mixed drink fishbowls available; min. 4 people. Open M-Sa noon-midnight, Su noon-11pm.

Callooh Callay, 65 Rivington St. (☎020 7739 4781; www.calloohcallaybar.com). ⊖Old St. The favorite haunt of London's Jabberwockies. Why? Its list of over 38 mixed drinks, which arrives in newsletter format, includes creative concoctions like the Hibiscusaurus (El Jimidor Blanco, granny smith apple, lime, and hibiscus syrup) but makes sure to recall old favorites like the Mai-Thai and Manhattan. Mad Hatter's Tiki Punch for 3-5 people (£20) comes in a gramophone. Mixed drinks £7-8. Also serves snacks and tapas (£2.50-6). Dress is relaxed cocktail attire. Open M-Th 5-11pm, F noon-1am, Sa 6pm-1am, Su 6-11pm.

Comedy Cafe, 66 Rivington St. (☎020 7739 5706; www.comedycafe.co.uk). ⊖Old St. Night Bus. One of London's best venues for stand-up, featuring established stars and young talent alike. Enthusiastic 20- and 30-somethings grab a drink here (skip the food) before heading out for the rest of their night. Also has a bar and music space. Beers from £3.30. Wine from £4.30. New Act Night W; Best in Stand Up Th; Disco and dancing Sa. Cover W £4, Th £8, F £10, Sa £15. Group packages W-Sa £14-30. Doors open Tu-Th 7pm, F-Sa 6pm; show 9pm; dancing until 1am. Reserve F-Sa. Book online or over the phone. MC/V.

CLUBS

Aquarium, 256 Old St. (☎020 7253 3558; www.clubaquarium.co.uk. Tickets ☎08702 461 966; www.carwash.co.uk.). ⊖Old St.; Exit 3. Night Bus. The only club in London where bringing your bathing suit is par for the course: this club boasts a huge pool and hot tub. The 4 bars and many sofas keep non-swimmers occupied. Events here are campy affairs: "Carwash" Sa night (funky/retro-glam-funk fashion fest), "Redlight" Sa 4:30-11am (music electro/sexy; dress minimal), and "Wet Yourself" Su 10pm-4am provide one of the most awe-inspiring clubbing experiences in London. Join stilt walkers, performers, and dancers in your finest 70s, 80s, and 90s gear. Open F 10pm-4am, Sa 7pm-11am, Su 10pm-4am. Cover F men £15, women £10; Sa online £12, at door £15.

Cargo, Kingsland Viaduct, 83 Rivington St. (☎020 7739 3440; www.cargo-london.com). ⊖Old St. Night Bus as well as #N55, N243. Set in an enormous warehouse, Cargo remains a favorite among Londoners. Great acoustics, intimate candlelight, and a jungle-like outdoor garden with sunken benches. A mix of DJs and live music manages to drag almost every lounger onto the dance floor at some point. Wheelchair-accessible. Cover Sa £6 before 10pm, £12 after. No cover F, occasionally £3. Open M-Th noon-1am, F noon-3am, Sa 1pm-3am, Su 1pm-midnight.

93 Feet East, 150 Brick Ln. (☎020 7247 3293; www.93feeteast.com). ⊖Aldgate East or Liverpool St. Night Bus. Part of the old Truman Brewery complex, 93 rocks the post-tandoori Brick Lane night scene. With a bar and a DJ booth, the main dance floor is sparsely decorated but compensates with cool lighting; a separate room often hosts live music. Outside there's plenty of space to dance. Music style changes virtually every night; call or check website for details. Cover varies with act, usually around £10. Open M-Th 5-11pm, F 5pm-1am, Sa noon-1am, Su noon-10:30pm. MC/V over £10.

PUBS

The George and Dragon, 2 Hackney Rd. (☎020 7012 1100). ⊖Old St. Night Bus. The hidden secret of local artists and designers, this creatively remodeled pub proudly caters to an eclectic crowd. Gay-friendly, with a healthy dose of the 60s and 70s. On the wall, a horse that's constantly chewing, an angry Michelle Pfeiffer, and a bashful Smurf all watch over the crowd. Patrons often spill onto the surrounding sidewalks on warm evenings. Wheelchair-accessible. Beer £3.50. Wine £4. No mixed drinks. Open daily M-Sa 6pm-midnight. MC/V.

CLERKENWELL

The center for trendy nightclubs, Clerkenwell mostly caters to a young professional crowd. However, there are a few places to let loose and not break the bank—most notably, Fabric, arguably London's most outrageous club.

VERY OLD PUB

▧ The Jerusalem Tavern, 55 Britton St. (☎020 7490 4281; www.stpetersbrewery.co.uk). ⊖Farringdon. Tiny and wonderfully ancient, this showcase pub for the beers of the St. Peter's Brewery has many nooks and crannies, which fill with locals at lunchtime and at night. The availability of brews changes with the seasons and is advertised on a chalk-board outside. Specialty ales (£3.40) like grapefruit or cinnamon, several organic ales, Golden Ale, Honey Porter, Summer Ale, and Suffolk Gold are available in season. Pub grub £6.50-8.50. Sourdough sandwiches £6.80. Open M-F 11am-11pm. Lunch served daily noon-3pm, dinner served Tu-Th 5-9:30pm. MC/V.

IMPORTANT CLUB

▨ **Fabric,** 77a Charterhouse St. (☎020 7336 8898; www.fabriclondon.com). ⊖Farringdon. Night Bus #242. One of London's most hyped clubs, boasting Europe's first vibrat-ing "bodysonic" dance floor (actually one giant speaker). Add to that beds (you know, for all those naps); multiple bars, each with its own top DJ or artist; and 3 dance fl. crammed with close to 2000 hopping Londoners and curious tourists. Most in the young crowd dress to impress, but expect sweaty chaos. Cover varies, but usually £12-16, discounts after 3am; buy tickets in advance online. Open F 11pm-6am, Sa 11pm-8am, Su 10pm-5am. MC/V.

HOLBORN

Holborn is perhaps the best neighborhood for pubs, all of which are rich with history and decadent decor, but that's about the extent of its nightlife. Spend an early evening chatting with friends over a pint and then head elsewhere.

PUBS

▨ **Ye Olde Cheshire Cheese,** Wine Office Court. (☎020 7353 6170). Entrance in alley-way by 145 Fleet St. ⊖Blackfriars or St. Paul's. Dating from 1667, the Cheese was once a haunt of greats like Johnson, Dickens, Tennyson, Twain, Conan Doyle and Teddy Roosevelt. A dark labyrinth of oak-paneled, low-ceilinged rooms on 3 fl. Each room offers a different world cuisine. Front open M-Sa 11am-11pm, Su noon-6pm. Cellar Bar open M-Th noon-2:30pm and 5:30-11pm, F noon-2:30pm. Chop Room open M-F noon-9:30pm, Sa noon-2:30pm and 6-9:30pm, Su noon-5pm. AmEx/MC/V.

 HOW MUCH TO DRINK? Know your wine metrics! 175mL equals one small "pub" glass, 375mL is a half-bottle, and 750mL means one bottle.

▨ **The Old Bank of England,** 194 Fleet St. (☎020 7430 2255). ⊖Temple. Next to the Royal Courts of Justice and directly across from the entrance to the Temple. Opened on the premises of the 19th-century Bank of England (it still looks like a bank from the outside), this pub takes full advantage of its predecessor's towering ceilings, massive oil paintings, impressive chandeliers, and backyard garden. Meat pies (6 options in sum-mer, up to 11 in winter; £8.80-9.50). Afternoon tea M-F 2:30-5:30pm. Entrees £5-10, sandwiches £3-5. Reservations recommended for lunch. Open M-F 11am-11pm; kitchen open M-Th 11am-9pm, F 11am-8pm. AmEx/MC/V.

Ye Olde Mitre Tavern, 1 Ely Court (☎020 7405 4751), off #8 Hatton Garden. ⊖Chancery Ln. To find the alley down which this pub hides, look for the street lamp on Hatton Gar-den bearing a sign of a *mitre* (if you don't know what a *mitre* is, then good luck to you). This classic pub fully merits its "ye olde": the Bishop of Ely built the tavern in 1546, and Elizabeth I is reputed to have danced around the cherry tree in the corner. Superior

KEEP IT SECRET, KEEP IT SAFE

Who ever made up the ditty, "Secrets, secrets are no fun; secrets, secrets hurt someone" hadn't heard about the latest whisper on the London nightlife scene. The self-proclaimed "worst-kept secret in London" (after all, we know it...), **Bart's Speakeasy** opened this past February in South Ken.

Of course, much of the fun is in trying to figure out where it is and then seeing whether you make the cut for this funky Mickey-Mouse-themed bar.

Once inside, you'll find a sitting room with retro TVs, Prohibition-era music, and all the kitsch you'd expect from this kind of bar. Nevertheless, Bart's Speakeasy is classy and sleek. Most patrons grab one of the 20 mixed drinks (£6) and a highly-recommended cheese and charcuterie platter (£13) and toast to the excitement of being in on the secret.

So if you're looking for some late-night intrigue, this is the place to go—but if anyone asks, you didn't hear it from us!

Bart's Speakeasy, 87 Sloane Ave. (☎020 7581 3355; www. barts-london.com), in the Chelsea Cloisters. Open daily 5pm-late.

sandwiches, sausage rolls, and pork pie complete the limited menu (£2-4, served until 9:30pm). Open M-F 11am-11pm. AmEx/MC/V.

THE SOUTH BANK

Nightlife to most South Bankers means dinner and the theater or staying late at the Tate. Strangely enough, though, the South Bank is also home to one of the largest club venues in London, and has a couple bars worth checking out.

PUBS

The George Inn, 75-77 Borough High St. (☎020 7407 2056; www.traditionalpubslondon.co.uk). ⊖London Bridge. With a mention in Dickens's *Little Dorritt*, regular visits by Shakespeare, and the honor of remaining the only galleried inn in London, the George takes great pride in its history. A maze-like interior leads out into an enormous and popular patio, full of tourists as well as regulars from the City, just across the river. The ale (from £2.50) is excellent and the atmosphere is relaxed. Traditional pub food £5.50-8.30; sharing platters £8-9.40. In summer F BBQs from 6pm. Wheelchair-accessible patio. Open M-Sa 11am-11pm, Su noon-10:30pm. Kitchen open M-Sa noon-9pm, Su noon-5pm. AmEx/MC/V.

The Lord Nelson, 243 Union St. (☎020 7207 2701). ⊖Blackfriars. Tucked into the industrial buildings around it, this quirky pub has carved out space enough for an outdoor patio overflowing with flowers and personality. Work by well-known urban artists, as well as the owner himself, are plastered over the inside walls. Homemade vodka shots (from £4.10) come in flavors like rhubarb cream or cherry-chocolate-orange. M Poker. Su roasts. Summer BBQs. Wheelchair-accessible. Open M-F 11am-11pm, Sa 1-11pm, Su noon-3pm and 7-10:30pm. Kitchen open M-F noon-8pm, Sa-Su noon-5pm. MC/V.

BARS

The Old School Yard, 111 Long Ln. (☎020 7357 6281; www.theoldschoolyard.com). ⊖Borough. Just like Cat Stevens imagined it. Blue skies and fluffy clouds adorn the ceiling, sports trophies and Teenage Mutant Ninja Turtles paraphernalia cover the walls, and old-time tunes fill the air. The drink menu comes on notebook paper, organized by subject: don't know much about history? Go for geography and try a Manhattan. Beers from £3.30. Mixed drinks from £4.90. Happy Hour Tu-Sa 5:30-8pm, Su all day; mixed drinks £4.50, beers £2.50. Occasional events like Show-ke-oke (karaoke to Westerns) and Flair bartending competition. Open Tu-Th 5:30-11:30pm, F-Sa 5:30pm-12:30am, Su 5:30-10:30pm. AmEx/MC/V.

CLUBS

🔳 **Ministry of Sound,** 103 Gaunt St. (☎020 7378 6528; www.ministryofsound.com). ⊖Elephant and Castle; take the exit for South Bank University. Night Bus #N35, N133, N343. A mecca for serious clubbers worldwide—arrive before it opens or stand in line all night. Emphasis on dancing rather than decor, with a massive main room, smaller 2nd dance floor, and perpetually packed overhead balcony bar. Multiple artists often take over different venues on the same night. Dress to impress. Cover varies; usually £10-20. Hours depend on event; generally F 10pm-6am, Sa 11pm-7am, Su 10:30pm-3:30am. AmEx/MC/V.

SOUTH LONDON

Nightlife has featured prominently in Brixton and Clapham's renaissance, with an ever-increasing number of bars and clubs luring London's choosiest and largest concentration of under-35s. Since many clubs are small, lounging generally takes priority over dancing, though the recent proliferation of DJ bars in Brixton signals a shift back to sweaty chaos. While some Clapham nightspots are little different from their peers in Hoxton and Clerkenwell, there are destinations that have escaped yuppification.

BRIXTON

BARS

🔳 **Hootananny,** 95 Effra Rd. (☎020 773 772 73; www.hootanannybrixton.co.uk). ⊖Brixton, then 5-10min. walk along Effra Rd. Housed in an old brewery building with ample outdoor seating, Hootananny is halfway between a block party BBQ and a rowdy concert. A mixed crowd of old and young, hip and scruffy descend on all nights of the week to play pool and rock out. M-W live acoustic. Th reggae. F ska. Sa blues/soul/indie. Su Salsa. 1st W of month Karaoke. Usually free; occasional £5-12 cover. Open daily M-W and Su noon-2am, Th-Sa noon-3am. MC/V.

🔳 **Dogstar,** 389 Coldharbour Ln. (☎020 7733 7515; www.thedogstar.co.uk). ⊖Brixton. The crowd here runs the gamut from brooding artists to hardcore dancers, all of whom take clubbing Siriusly. 4 large rooms on 3 fl. host a dance floor with nightly DJs, pool and foosball, and live acts from comedy (Th) to spoken word to indie, hip hop, jazz, acoustic, and more. Wheelchair-accessible. Cover F-Sa after 10pm £5. Open M-F 4pm-2am, Sa-Su noon-4am. MC/V.

Fridge Bar, 1 Town Hall Parade, Brixton Hill (☎020 7326 5100; www.fridgebar. com). ⊖Brixton. Brixtonians from both sides of the fence mingle in this bright, narrow bar, which goes for good music and a scandalous vibe. Beer from £3. DJs spin nightly from 9pm: M and W roots and reggae; Tu salsa; Th soulful house and R&B; F-Sa hip hop, rap, and R&B (21+); Su 70s and 80s faves (22+). Dress code F-Sa: slinky dresses for girls and collared shirts for guys. Cover £5-10. Open M-Th and Su 9pm-3:30am, F-Sa 9pm-4:45am. MC/V.

Brixton Bar and Grill, 15 Atlantic Rd. (☎020 7737 6777; www.brixtonbarandgrill.co.uk). ⊖Brixton. Held in a candlelit, cave-like room with exposed brick and modern art, this is the perfect place for a quiet game of pool (£1) or relaxed drink—and after the DJs begin, for a wild dance party. Solid menu of upscale pub food and tapas, as well as some wild mixed drinks. W comedy nights bring some well-known names (doors 7:30pm, show 8:30pm; £7, £5 in advance). Th hip hop. 1st Sa of month funky house 9pm-4am. Happy Hour 5-7pm; 2-for-1 selected tapas and mixed drinks. Open M-W and Su 5pm-1am, Th-Sa 5pm-3am. MC/V.

CLUBS

▨ **Dex Club,** 467-469 Brixton Rd. (☎020 7326 4455; www.dexclub.co.uk). ⊖Brixton. With a huge, warehouse-esque dance floor, 2 roof terraces, outdoor jacuzzi, and DJs all through the weekend, the party never ends. 5 pimped-out hotel suites, 2 with jacuzzis, allow a lucky few never to leave. Attached Prince gastropub is the perfect pregame, serving food and drinks daily from noon-3am (DJs F-Sa). Weekly Su roof parties 2-10pm, with BBQ and live DJs. Occasional live music weekdays. Mixed drinks £7. Cover £5-10. Luxury suites from £100. Open F-Sa 10pm-6am, Su 2pm-3am. MC/V.

50/50 Bar, 50 Atlantic Rd. (☎020 7733 6189). ⊖Brixton. Humble but trendy club and bar where the revelry contines into the wee hours. Soak up the underground look and relax on huge black leather sofas lining one wall. Don't underestimate the mixed drinks (£7.50). Happy hour 5-10pm. Cover £5 after 10pm. Open Tu-Th and Su 9am-3am, F-Sa 9am-5am. MC/V.

CLAPHAM

BARS

The Landor, 70 Landor Rd. (☎020 7274 4328). ⊖Clapham North. Kayaks, sails, and hammocks hang from the ceiling and books populate the walls at this spacious, saloon-style bar, which caters to a cool 20-something crowd. The backyard beer garden, with greenery and country scenes, hosts BBQs on summer nights. The upstairs Landor Theatre puts on musical comedies and cabarets. Live music F-Sa. Free Wi-Fi. Beer from £3.20. Pub food M-F noon-2:30pm, Sa 1-8:30pm, Su 1-5pm; £3-6. MC/V.

CLUBS

The White House, 65 Clapham Park Rd. (☎7498 3388; www.thewhitehouselondon.co.uk). ⊖Clapham Common. Despite its name, it's the New York clubbing scene that the White House aims to bring to London, with sleek booths and candlelight. Constantly changing events make it one of the most popular dance haunts in the city, bringing a beautiful crowd from early on. The small roof terrace is perfect for long summer nights. Occasional cover £5-10. Open W-Th 5:30pm-2am, F-Sa 5:30pm-4am, Su 5pm-2am. MC/V.

Infernos, 146 Clapham High St. (☎7720 7633; www.infernos.co.uk). ⊖Clapham Common. Refers perhaps to disco fever that it hopes to inspire, with 9 fully-stocked bars and 3 DJs over 2 sweeping floors. Retro decor, fish tanks, hazy mist and colorful lights. Cover £10. Mixed drinks £7. Open F-Sa 9pm-3:30am. MC/V.

THE WEST END

MAYFAIR AND SAINT JAMES'S

While Mayfair and St. James's may not pack the nightlife punch of nearby Soho, Covent Garden, and the Strand, the area maintains a solid collection of both pubs and clubs. Try **Heddon Street** for a hipper bar scene and **Shepherd Market** area for a late afternoon drink.

PUBS

The Shepherds' Tavern, 50 Hertford St. (☎7499 3017). ⊖Green Park. With worn leather couches and antique chandeliers, this traditional tavern hasn't changed much since it opened in 1735. Local businessmen stop by for lunchtime pints, while 20-somethings gather for a pre-dinner drink. Linger by the downstairs bar with a pint or enjoy English fare (rump steak burger; £7.30) in the lounge upstairs. Wheelchair-accessible. Open M-Sa 11am-11pm, Su noon-10:30pm. AmEx/MC/V.

The Duke of York, 7 Dering St. (☎7629 0319). ⊖Bond St. This recently remodeled pub gives you plenty of choices for the perfect pint (£3). 3 floors are connected by a spiral wrought-iron staircase in the middle of the room: the ground fl. has old-fashioned arcade games and a big bar; the upstairs features small tables for socializing and dining; and the "comfort zone" basement is perfect for lounging and a game of darts. Open M-Sa 11am-11pm, Su noon-10:30pm. MC/V.

BARS

🎴 **Absolut Icebar,** 31-33 Heddon St. (☎7894 208 848; www.belowzerolondon.com). ⊖Oxford Circus. Because the only thing cooler than cool is ice cold. Absolut Icebar is kept just below freezing (-5°C) year-round, and guests are escorted in wearing special silver hooded capes (with fur trim) for their (usually) pre-booked 40min. time slot. The entire bar and its contents are constructed completely of Swedish-imported ice and undergo a complete renovation every 6 months. Entrance fee includes use of cape and hood, a personalized ice mug, and vodka cocktail: M-W and Su £13; Th-Sa £16 at door, £15 if reserved; special entrance Th-Sa at 8pm includes unlimited drinks, £23. Open M-W 3:30-11pm, Th 3:30-11:45pm, F 3:30pm-12:30am, Sa 12:30pm-1:15am, Su 3:30-11pm.

🎴 **22 Below,** 22 Great Marlborough St. (☎0871 223 5531; www.22below.co.uk). ⊖Oxford Circus, in a basement next to Cafe Libre and opposite Carnaby St. This hidden, amber-hued night spot is worth searching for. Entertaining comedy nights, oversized fresh fruit martinis (£7-9.50), and a friendly, casual crowd will make it hard to pull yourself off the comfy leather couches. DJs Th-Sa night. Tu comedy (£3.50). Open M-F 5pm-midnight, Sa 8pm-midnight. MC/V over £10.

SOHO

Considered the heart of London nightlife, Soho can be hit-or-miss for those who aren't in the know. Avoid the tourist crowds in Leicester Square and in places with tour buses out front. Head to the streets around **Old Compton Street** and **Soho Square** for gay and lesbian nightlife. Whatever your pleasure—feathered boas and sequins, karaoke, the latest Madonna hit, pleasant chit chat, or some good ol' rock and roll—Soho has it.

PUBS

🎴 **French House,** 49 Dean St. (☎020 7437 2799). ⊖Leicester Sq. or Piccadilly Circus. This small Soho landmark was once frequented by everyone from Maurice Chevalier and Charlie Chaplin to Salvador Dalí and Dylan Thomas. During WWII, it became the unofficial gathering place of the French Resistance. It's said that Charles de Gaulle wrote his "Appeal of 18 June" in this very pub. Enjoy beer or wine (all around £3-4) and hobnob with some of the most interesting characters in Soho. Wheelchair-accessible. Open M-W noon-11pm, Th-Sa noon-midnight, Su noon-11pm. Restaurant on 1st fl. open daily noon-3pm and 5:30-11pm. AmEx/MC/V.

🎴 **Dog and Duck,** 18 Bateman St. (☎020 7494 0697). ⊖Tottenham Court Rd. On the past site of the Duke of Monmouth's Soho house, and is the smallest and oldest pub in Soho. The name refers to Soho's original role as royal hunting grounds. The 1st fl. bar is named for George Orwell, who was once a regular. Look for the dog and duck tiles, installed in 1897. Wheelchair-accessible. Entrees £6.50-7.90. Beer and wine £3-4. Open M-Th 10am-11pm, F-Sa 11:30am-11pm, Su noon-11pm. Kitchen open daily noon-3pm and 5-9pm. MC/V.

The Toucan, 19 Carlisle St. (☎020 7437 4123). ⊖Tottenham Court Rd. A small pub right outside of Soho Sq., bursting with Irish pride. Named for the mascot of Guinness beer, the theme continues with posters, signs, and other testaments to the lager. In the basement bar, order from the extensive menu of classic or rare Irish whiskeys (£2.50-50). Many order their drinks to go and take them to Soho Park. Open M-F 11am-11pm, Sa noon-11pm. MC/V.

Old Coffee House, 49 Beak Street. (☎020 7437 2197). ⊖Oxford St. Don't let the name fool you: this down-to-earth pub is no coffee house but rather a jolly, rough-and-tumble drinking hole. A welcome relief from Soho's trendy atmosphere. Hosts a regular cast of Soho locals and some fabulous flair—old-fashioned posters, instruments, and pots and pans adorn the walls. Popular with the afterwork crowd. Open M-Sa 11am-11pm, Su noon-10:30pm. MC/V.

BARS

When bar-hopping through Soho's busy streets, keep in mind that some of the swankiest and most popular bars in the area, including The Player (8 Broadwich St.) become members-only after 11pm. Others, like Milk & Honey (61 Poland St.), have special members-only areas. You can enjoy their hip ambience—just make sure to call ahead or be prepared to leave when the clock strikes 11.

☒ **Lab,** 12 Old Compton St. (☎020 7437 7820; www.lab-townhouse.com). ⊖Leicester Sq. or Tottenham Court Rd. With restroom signs for "bitches" and "bastards," the only thing this bar takes seriously is its stellar drink selection. Drink sections like "high and mighty," "short and sexy," and "streets ahead" fill the book-length menu. Licensed mixologists serve up the award-winning concoctions (£6.80-7.50), while hip 20-somethings lounge in the colorful retro atmosphere. DJs spin house and funk nightly from 8pm. Open M-Sa 4pm-midnight, Su 4pm-10:30pm. Cash only.

☒ **Thirst,** 53 Greek St. (☎020 7437 1977; www.thirstbar.com), on the corner of Greek and Bateman. ⊖Oxford St. With all the drink specials at this trendy DJ bar, you'll come away anything but thirsty. This popular early evening watering hole turns into a late night dance scene downstairs, with DJs spinning house music every night from 9pm to 3am. The bar is small, so put your name on the online guest list, or show up early. Mixed drinks £7-9. "Stupid Hour" daily 5-7pm (½-price mixed drinks, beers, and house spirits £2.50, bottles of wine £10). Happy hour 7:30pm-close (mixed drinks £3). Cover M-Th after 10pm £3, F-Sa after 10pm £5. Open M-Sa 5pm-3am. AmEx/MC/V.

Alphabet, 61-63 Beak St. (☎020 7439 2190). ⊖Oxford St. or Piccadilly Circus. This lounge bar is *the* in-spot for the Soho in-crowd. Each weekend, the turquoise-tinged interior is filled with people sipping wine (£4.50-7 per glass) or tasty fruit and champagne cocktails (£6-7). Buy a piece of modern artwork off the upstairs walls, or head downstairs to plot your stumble home on the jumbo Soho street map underfoot. DJs spin eclectic tunes Th-Sa. Open M-F noon-11:30pm, Sa 5-11:30pm. AmEx/MC/V.

Club 49, 49 Greek St. (☎020 7439 4159; www.club49soho.com). ⊖ Tottenham Court Rd. With sleek leather booths, palm trees, crazy mixed drinks (like the Absinthe Mojito), and dark wood paneling, Club 49 brings a taste of the 70s to a hip club environment. 2 fl. (and 3 bars) of fun: lounge upstairs or hit the dance floor downstairs. Live DJs every night. Mixed drinks £8. Cover F £5 at 9pm, £10 at 10pm; Sa £5 at 10pm, £10 at 11pm. Happy hour M-Th 5-9:30pm, F-Sa 5-8:30pm; mixed drinks £7. Open M-Sa 5pm-3am. AmEx/MC/V.

Floridita, 100 Wardour St. (☎020 7314 4000), underneath Meza restaurant. ⊖Oxford St. or Piccadilly Circus. One of Soho's largest and swankiest bars, Cuban-themed Floridita's appeals to the classy set. A new house band every month provides live salsa music 6 nights a week for dancing, though many just come to lounge in one of the huge leather booths. Try their popular signature daiquiris (£8). Cover Th-Sa after 7pm £15. Open Tu-Th 5:30pm-2am, F-Sa 5:30pm-3am. AmEx/MC/V.

O Bar, 83-85 Wardour St. (☎020 7437 3490; www.the-obar.co.uk). ⊖Piccadilly Circus or Leicester Sq. Popular with tourists or those with a taste for the dramatic, O Bar features 3 fl. of candlelit elegance, comfy modern leather couches, and an antique bar. Enjoy a glass of wine on the ground fl. or get your groove on downstairs in the basement. Mixed drinks £6.50-7.50. Daily drink specials 4-8pm. DJs spin nightly. Swing dancing W. Karaoke Th 9pm. Open M-Th 5pm-3am, F 4pm-3am, Sa 3pm-3am, Su 4-10pm. AmEx/MC/V.

CLUBS

Madame Jojo's, 8-10 Brewer St. (☎020 7734 3040; www.madamejojos.com). ⊖Piccadilly Circus or Leicester Sq. Once a sleazy strip club, Jojo's maintains its endearingly gritty nature. Today, it does it all: comedy, disco, jazz, cabaret, and the famous deep funk. Tu "White Heat" (punk and New Wave 8pm-3am; bands play from 10:30pm); W "Tranny Shack" (10:30pm-3am) "releases the woman within"; 3rd Th of the month "Modern Love" (love songs throughout the decades; 10:30pm-3am); F "Deep Funk" (10pm-3am); Sa "Kitsch Cabaret" (blend of old-school music hall and Las Vegas floorshow); Su "Groove Sanctuary" (soulful house, disco, Latin 9:30pm-2am). Cover Tu £7; W £5; Th-F £8; Su £5 after 11am. Open Tu 8pm-3am, F-Sa 10pm-3am, Su 9:30pm-2am. AmEx/MC/V.

Bar Rumba, 36 Shaftesbury Ave. (☎020 7287 6933; www.barrumba.co.uk). ⊖Piccadilly Circus. A young crowd makes good use of the industrial-strength interior for dancing. Many of the best DJs spin here. Excellent sound system is often blasted at full volume—pick up earplugs from employees. Different theme every night, from Tu "Barrio Latino" to Su "Bubbling Over" (street soul and R&B). Student night Th. Cover varies but typically £6 before 11pm, £10 after. Opening hours vary; usually Tu-Su 9pm-2am. Check website for exact promotions, times, and prices. MC/V.

 DRESSING THE PART. Clubbing in London is an earnest endeavor, and some clubs take the dress code seriously. Although many will allow jeans, sneakers and baseball caps are usually not permitted. More upscale lounges may turn you away even in your best designer jeans. Girls, think about dresses and heels. Dress codes are far stricter on weekends.

GLBT

Check out Boy Magazine, available at many bars and clubs in Soho, for listings of GLBT events for the coming week—and for debaucherous photos of the past week's events.

The Edge, 11 Soho Sq. (☎020 7439 1313; www.edge.uk.com). ⊖Oxford Circus or Tottenham Court Rd. A friendly "polysexual" drinking spot just off Soho Sq. offers several types of venues, complete with Häagen Dazs ice cream and £14 bottles of wine. 4 floors of stylish brick, silver, or hot pink. Relaxed bar on the ground fl., sleek black lounge bar on the 1st fl., piano bar decked out in white on the 2nd, and a newly refurbished disco dance bar, with lit up dance floor, on the top fl. Piano bar Tu-Sa. Live jazz last W of the month. DJs and dancing F-Sa. Cover Th-Sa after 10pm £2. Open M-Sa noon-1am, Su noon-11pm. MC/V.

Profile, 56 Frith St. (☎020 7734 8300; www.profilesoho.com). ⊖Tottenham Court Rd. One of Soho's newest and most popular night spots, Profile is a joint venture with gay personals website www.gaydar.co.uk. Featuring 3 bars on 3 fl. as well as 2 of the most stylish internet cafes you're likely to encounter in London, this is definitely a place to see and be seen. DJs spin Th-Sa 8pm-1am. Happy hour M-Th 4-9pm. Open M-F 4pm-1am, Sa-Su noon-1am. AmEx/MC/V.

LOCAL LEGEND

HORROR MOVIE MATERIAL

Jack the Ripper has reigned as London's most infamous slasher for over a century. His identity was never confirmed, and he has gone down in history for slitting the throats of prostitutes after mutilating their bodies. With five confirmed victims and at least six others who were likely murdered by his hand, he was notorious for his brutality.

Although he was not the first serial killer, Jack was certainly the first to cause an international media frenzy, and some versions of his tale allege that his name was created to help sell more newspapers.

Visitors to London can track the legendary slasher by taking a night-time tour (www.jack-the-ripper-walk.co.uk), or following a newer local legend at the **Ten Bells,** 4 Commerical St. (☎20 73 66 17 21), in East London, the pub where he allegedly met two of his victims.

While most customers choose to consume pints of beer or cocktails, some opt for shots of absinthe. Some claim that Jack the Ripper's ghost will material-ize behind the bar after a few shots of the hallucinogenic drink. Beware: those who abstain from the liquorice-flavored drink may feel a tickle up their spine when wandering down to the dark, cellar bathrooms after a few drinks.

🏳️ **Candy Bar,** 4 Carlisle St. (☎020 7494 4041; www.thecandybar.co.uk). ⊖Tottenham Court Rd. or Oxford Circus. The self-proclaimed most prolific les-bian bar in the world, having allegedly "transformed the world of lesbian social opportunity," this estrogen-packed, pink-hued drinking spot is a one-stop shop for lesbian entertainment. Karaoke, striptease perfor-mances, DJs, and popular dance nights keep the young crowds happy 7 days a week. Guys allowed in only with a female escort. Mixed drinks £7. Theme nights every week. Cover F-Sa after 9pm £5. Open M-Th 5-11:30pm, F-Sa 5pm-2am, Su 5-11pm. MC/V.

🏳️ **G-A-Y Late,** 5 Goslett Yard (☎020 7434 9592; www.g-a-y.co.uk), off Charing Cross Rd. ⊖Tottenham Court Rd. Frequently besieged by teenage girls on weekends. Madonna previewed 6 songs from her new-est album here. G-A-Y (you spell it out when you say it) has become a Soho institution. Mixed drinks £5. Dancers on Tu, W "Slag Tags" (get a # at the door and when you see someone you like, text to the screen), Th "Porn Idol" ("Gay Girlz" in the pop room with a female stripper), F "Camp Attack" with 4 decades of music. Wheelchair-accessible. Cover varies from £1-15; check website for details. Open M, W-Th, and Su noon-2am; F-Sa noon-5am. Cash only.

Ku Bar, 30 Lilse St. (☎020 7600 4353; www.ku-bar.co.uk). ⊖Leicester Sq. Also at 25 Frith St., at the corner of Old Compton and Frith. A dark interior with neon lighting, dance space in the base-ment, a bar on the ground fl. and a lounge on the top fl. The crowd's age increases with the floor number. Mixed drinks £7. M "Major Mondays" (a live band followed by open mic); Tu "Ruby Tuesdays" (for girls and their guy friends); W "Shinky Shonky" (cabaret antics). Happy hour 5-8pm; ½-priced mixed drinks. Main bar open M-Sa noon-11pm, Su 1-10:30pm. Dance bar open M-Sa 8pm-3am. AmEx/MC/V.

Village Soho, 81 Wardour St. (☎020 7434 2124; www.village-soho.co.uk). ⊖Piccadilly Circus. Enter at the main door on Wardour St. or the slightly less-pol-ished back door around the corner on Berwick St. This Soho institution has been around for 15 years. Attracts a young crowd. Speedo-sporting superhero dancers along with cruising tourists make this bar consistently packed and always over the top. Mixed drinks £6-7. Tu Karaoke Night after 7pm. W Pink Poodle comedy club. F-Sa Discolicious. Cover F-Sa after 10pm £3. Happy hour 4-8pm; mixed drinks £4. Open M-Sa 3pm-1am, Su 3pm-11:30pm. AmEx/MC/V.

G-A-Y Bar, 30 Old Compton St. (☎020 7494 2756; www.g-a-y.co.uk), ⊖Leicester Sq. or Piccadilly Circus. A gay-and-lesbian feeder bar for the perennially popular G-A-Y Late, with the same fluorescent pop appeal and theme nights. Music videos of 80s classics and contemporary pop playing on video screens make way for as much dancing as drinking. Cheap drink specials attract a younger, broker set. Lesbian-dominated bar downstairs opens after 7pm. Plenty of straight folks tag along for the fluffy scene full of boas, hot pants, and the occasional bachelorette party. M-Th and Su "Illicit Eleven" mixed drinks and beers £1.60. Open M-Sa noon-midnight, Su noon-10:30pm. AmEx/MC/V.

Escape Dance Bar, 10A Brewer St. (☎020 7731 2626; www.kudosgroup.com). ⊖Leicester Sq. A small gay and lesbian dance bar with something for everyone. Running horses on the walls recall the club's spirit. Dance with young, friendly folks to the latest pop hits in an enjoyably cramped and sweaty space. A video DJ plays tunes with big, bright screens Th 8pm-3am. Open Tu-Sa 4pm-3am. AmEx/MC/V.

COVENT GARDEN AND THE STRAND

While serious partiers and wise locals head to Soho or over to Clerkenwell for a night out, the northern section of Covent Garden, close to Seven Dials, has several good bars and clubs.

PUBS

The Cross Keys, 31 Endell St. (☎020 7836 5185). ⊖Covent Garden. Covered in flowers and vines on the outside, and glowing a dark red within, this afterwork hangout is all about ambience. A collection of paintings, antiques, and Beatles memorabilia populate the walls, while copper kettles and pots hang from the ceiling. Bitters start around £3. Wheelchair-accessible. Open M-Sa 11am-11pm, Su noon-10:30pm. Kitchen open daily noon-2:30pm. AmEx/MC/V.

BARS

▨ **Gordon's Wine Bar,** 47 Villiers St. (☎020 7930 1408; www.gordonswinebar.co.uk). ⊖Embankment or Charing Cross. Once the home of Rudyard Kipling, this basement wine bar is the oldest in London. A honeycomb of low, candlelit vaults and aged brick walls will take you straight back to 1890. No beer or spirits—sherry and classy port from wood barrels around £3.50 per glass and a wide selection of international wine (from £3.80 per glass, £12 per bottle). Also serves traditional English fare (meat pies, stuffed potatoes) with an all-you-can-eat salad bar for £6-10. Roasted almonds £2.50. Cheese platter with 2 cheeses £7.60. Open M-Sa 11am-11pm, Su noon-10pm. AmEx/MC/V over £10.

▨ **The Langley,** 5 Langley St. (☎020 7836 5005). ⊖Covent Garden. This all-purpose basement party bar draws crowds in early and keeps them there. Friendly 20-somethings file in to the low-ceilinged lounge area for Happy Hour deals (daily 5-7pm; mixed drinks £3.30, margaritas and martinis £4.30) and then head to the Geneva Bar, a cavernous dance floor and bar in the back. Exposed brick and piping and chain-link chairs make for a sleek experience. The "vault," a small vaulted, cushioned room, offers a more intimate group experience. Bar food served until midnight. DJs Th-Sa from 9pm. Cover Th after 10pm £3, F-Sa after 10pm £7. Open M-Sa 4:30pm-1am, Su 4-10:30pm. AmEx/MC/V.

▨ **Freud,** 198 Shaftesbury Ave. (☎020 7240 9933). ⊖Covent Garden. Packed with hip 20-somethings. Sand-blasted walls exhibit works by contemporary artists. Drink a toast to Freud and invigorate your psyche with cheap but creative mixed drinks (£5-7). Not to be confused with the metalworks store on the ground fl. Most bottled beers less than £3.50. Salads, sandwiches, and soups (£3-6.30) noon-4:30pm. Occasional live jazz Su 5pm. Open M-W 11am-11pm, Th 11am-1am, F-Sa 11am-2am, Su noon-11:30pm. MC/V.

Detroit, 35 Earlham St. (☎020 7240 2662; www.detroit-bar.com). ⊖Covent Garden. Imposing double doors swing open to reveal a subterranean den full of cave-like enclaves. Low ceilings, orange lighting, and cushy, curtained-off booths add to the experience. Top-notch mixed drinks £7. Bar snacks £2-5. Happy hour 2-for-1 drinks until 7pm. Open M-Sa 5pm-midnight. AmEx/MC/V over £10.

CLUBS

The Den & Centro, 18 W. Central St. (www.thedenandcentro.com). ⊖Holborn or Tottenham Court Rd. From Holborn, walk along Holborn High St., take a right on Museum St., and look for a bright periwinkle building. With an upstairs bar and live stage that can hold 300, a downstairs dance area with one of the best sound systems in the world, and regular well-known DJs, Den & Centro is a 2-part venue you don't want to miss. Lipstick and Lashes W mixes fashion and music, with a different theme every week, and dancing, art, and fashion shows. Mixed drinks £4-5. Cover varies by act, usually £3-25. Open M-Th 10pm-4am, F-Sa 10pm-dawn. AmEx/MC/V.

> **TIP** **LIVIN' THE DREAM.** If you have your heart set on getting into an exclusive club, try asking your hotel concierge to call for a reservation or pick up the phone yourself; it's surprising what a bit of advanced planning can procure.

GLBT

 Box Bar, 32-34 Monmouth St. (☎020 7240 5828; www.boxbar.com). ⊖Covent Garden. Bright, friendly, and—despite the name—quite spacious, this gay-friendly bar and brasserie has an airy charm that turns hip and hot after hours, with blue and purple lighting and an attractive all-male crowd that spills onto and down the street (women still welcome of course). Also sells tickets to gay nightclubs. Open M-Sa 11am-11pm, Su noon-10:30pm. Kitchen open daily until 5pm; select menu afterward. MC/V.

■ **Heaven, The Arches,** Craven Terr. (☎020 7930 2020; www.heaven-london.com). ⊖Charing Cross or Embankment. The self-proclaimed "most famous gay nightclub in the world." Intricate interior rewards explorers—try unguarded doors to find the fantastically lit main fl., 5 additional bars and dance floors. Occasional big-name acts make this the place to be; don't be surprised to find security and metal detectors. M "Popcorn" (mixed crowd; chart-toppers, 70s-80s disco hits, and commercial house; £2-3 drinks); F "Camp Attack" (music from 70s till today; drinks from £3); Sa big-name acts like Lady Gaga. Cover M free before midnight, £8 after; on other nights, never over £10. Open M 10pm-5am, W 10:30pm-3:30am, F varies, Sa 10:30pm-5am.

BLOOMSBURY

Bloomsbury may be London's premier pub neighborhood: students in the classroom and library all day tend to hit the pubs hard every night of the week, which makes for an always exciting student evening scene. The pubs respond with cheaper prices and regular events. The places listed below offer a fair mix of drinking and eating.

PUBS

■ **The Court London,** 108A Tottenham Court Rd. (☎087 2148 1508). ⊖Goodge St. A lighthearted pub that's all about students, with pool tables, televised sporting events, regular DJ nights, and deals on drinks and food. Pleasant outdoor picnic-style seating area. Jukebox. Burger and beer £3.75. "Screaming" burger (with bacon, cheese, onion rings, and BBQ sauce) and beer £5.75. Wine from £1; beer from £2. Mixed drinks M £2.50. Open M-Th 11am-midnight, F-Sa 11am-1am, Su noon-6pm. AmEx/MC/V.

Fitzroy Tavern, 16 Charlotte St. (☎020 7580 3714). ⊖Goodge St., at the center of Bloomsbury's "Fitzrovia" neighborhood (guess where the name comes from). This pub was once popular with artists and writers (Dylan Thomas was a devoted patron). Its corner location affords it ample outdoor seating in summer. Traditional British lunches include bangers and mash, cottage pie, and baked pork chop (£5-6). Comedy night W 8:30pm (£6). Open M-Sa noon-11pm, Su noon-10:30pm. MC/V.

The Queen's Larder, 1 Queen's Sq. (☎020 7837 5627). ⊖Russell Sq. A pub has stood on this leafy square since 1710. The present incarnation dates to 1799, when Queen Charlotte rented out the cellar to store treats for her (temporarily) mad husband, King George III. Traditional English fare, including a popular roast with Yorkshire pudding, available in the tiny upstairs restaurant. Candlelit outdoor picnic tables perfect for warm nights. Entrees £7-9. Open M-Sa noon-11pm, Su noon-10:30pm. MC/V.

BARS

▨ **Vats,** 51 Lambs Conduit St. (☎020 7242 8963). ⊖Russell Sq. Move through the wooden foyer to the classic main bar, flanked by an antique reading desk piled high with wine-related volumes. Food is delicious and innovative, if a bit pricey. There are too many wines to fit them all on the list, so if you have something particular in mind, don't be afraid to ask. Occasional live music. "Good ordinary claret" £3.50 per glass, £14.50 per bottle. Burgundy from £15 per bottle. Appetizers £4-8. Meat entrees £10-16. Open M-F noon-11pm. MC/V.

NORTH LONDON

CAMDEN TOWN, KING'S CROSS, AND ISLINGTON

With swarms of young people in the area, it comes as a surprise that Camden Town's nightlife is centered on only a handful of clubs and bars. The local council is famously draconian: bars shut at 11pm, period. Though Camden's music scene is unbeatable, you may want to grab a few drinks here before heading to adjacent neighborhoods for your late-night fun. Though it's slowly begun to accumulate a couple popular spots, nightlife in Islington is usually good for loungers and drinkers who bar hop around Upper St. before heading to Clerkenwell's mega-clubs, just a short jaunt away.

PUBS

▨ **Duke of Cambridge,** 30 St. Peter's St. (☎020 7359 3066; www.dukeorganic.co.uk). ⊖Angel. Runner-up in the 2006 Observer Food Magazine "Best Pub in the UK" competition and London Dining's Pub of the Year in 2009, the Duke is dedicated to environmentally responsible dining. Sophisticated, exclusively organic menu and must-try organic beer and wine selection. Specializes in fresh dishes with surprise seasonal ingredients; the kitchen changes the menu twice per day. Game pie (venison, pigeon, and partridge) and more delicate entrees like haddock or pan fried polenta with mixed vegetables (£13.50). Open M-Sa noon-11pm, Su noon-10:30pm. Kitchen open M-F 12:30-3pm and 6:30-10:30pm, Sa-Su 12:30-3:30pm and 6:30-10:30pm. AmEx/MC/V.

▨ **The Castle,** 54 Pentonville Rd. (☎020 7713 1858; www.geronimo-inns.co.uk/thecastle). ⊖Angel. The mentality of a neighborhood bar and the style of a trendy gastro-pub. Chic decor and a roof terrace reminiscent of a tiki hut attract both subdued and boisterous crowds. Entrees like burger with tomato relish and pan-fried Coley fillet £9-13.50. Open M-Sa noon-midnight, Su noon-10:30pm. Kitchen open M-F 6-10pm, Sa-Su noon-9pm. MC/V.

- **Filthy MacNasty's Whiskey Cafe,** 68 Amwell St. (☎020 7837 6067; www.filthymacnastys.com). ⊖Angel or King's Cross. Night Bus #N10, N63, N73, N91, 390. Shane MacGowan, U2, and the Libertines have all played in this laid-back Irish pub, now a trendy neighborhood destination. Outside, red picnic benches support the rowdy overflow. Inside, there are 2 spaces: the bar area, with board games and classic rock, and a 2nd more intimate room, with live music and occasional literary readings that appeal to the hipster-intellectual. 14 varieties of whiskey from £2.30. Famous Pieminster pies from £5.50. Open M-Sa noon-11pm, Su noon-10:30pm.

- **Dublin Castle,** 94 Parkway (☎020 7485 1773). ⊖Camden Town. Night Bus #N5, N28, N31. Pretty-young-things, record execs, and talent scouts descend here regularly, looking for the next big act in rock and roll. After the bands finish, the pub turns into a dance club. 3 bands nightly 8:45-11pm; doors open 8:30pm. Wheelchair-accessible. Cover varies, usually around £6. Open M-Sa 11am-1am, Su 11am-midnight.

- **Compton Arms,** 4 Compton Ave. (☎020 7359 6883). ⊖Highbury or Islington. Once the favorite hangout of George Orwell, this 17th-century pub is now the go-to neighborhood spot on Arsenal home game night (oh, who are we kidding: it's the go-to spot most nights). Tucked away on a tiny side streets, its big draw is its beer garden, a picturesque outdoor patio where regulars enjoy one of the best Su roasts in the area, made by the owner's wife. Beer from £3. Open M-Sa noon-11pm, Su noon-10:30pm. Kitchen open M-F noon-2:30pm and 6-8:30pm, Sa-Su noon-4pm. MC/V.

BARS

- **Bar Vinyl,** 6 Inverness St. (☎020 7681 7898). ⊖Camden Town. Night Bus #N5, N28, N31. DJs spin loud music in a funky, narrow space. Tiny dancefloor always has a few takers; the rest of the crowd hangs out toward the quieter front of the room. During the day, it's a relaxed spot for coffee or lunch. Entrees £5-8. Drinks £5. DJs W-F night and Sa-Su from 3pm. Open daily M-W 2pm-midnight, Th-Sa noon-1am, Su noon-midnight. Kitchen open 11am-9pm.

- **The Purple Turtle,** 61-65 Crowndale Rd. (☎020 7383 4976; www.purpleturtlebar.com). ⊖Mornington Crescent. Night Bus #24, 27, N29. A young, eclectic crowd frequents this purple drinking haven, which turns into a packed dance or performance space for live acts F-Sa nights. An upstairs lounge area is more intimate, if you can hear people over the raging music. Close to 50 shooters to choose from at the bar. A more relaxed scene during the week. Cover varies; usually £3-10. Open M-Th 3pm-1am, F 3pm-3am, Sa 1pm-3am, Su 1pm-1am. MC/V.

CLUBS

- **Club Surya,** 156 Pentonville Rd. (☎020 8888 2333; www.club4climate.com/surya). ⊖King's Cross. The first ecological club in London, this nightclub seeks to enlighten (the name means Sun God). The bar area is made out of melted cell phones, the tables consist of old magazines, and downstairs, the music runs on the energy created by those on the electrifying dance floor. Also uses wind turbines and solar panels, hires local artists for the decor, and dedicates a portion of the profits to charity. Free entry for those who can prove they've traveled there by foot, bike, or public transport. Mixed drinks £7. Cover F-Sa £10-15. Open M-Th and Su 9am-11pm, F-Sa 9am-midnight. AmEx/MC/V.

- **The Black Cap,** 171 Camden High St. (☎020 7428 2721; www.theblackcap.com). ⊖Camden Town. North London's most popular gay bar and cabaret is always buzzing and draws an eclectic male and female crowd. The rooftop patio is the highlight of the place, with plenty of tables for outside revelry. Live shows and club scene downstairs F-Su nights and some weeknights (times vary; call for details). Cover for downstairs M-Th and Su before 11pm £2, 11pm-close £3; F-Sa before 11pm £3, 11pm-close £4. Open M-Th noon-2am, F-Sa noon-3am, Su noon-1am. Kitchen open noon-10pm.

Scala, 275 Pentonville Rd. (☎020 7833 2022; box office 0870 060 0100; www.scala-london.co.uk). Night Bus #N10, N63, N73, N91, 390. ⊖King's Cross. Once mainly a dance club, this has become a popular venue for live performances by acts like La Roux, special events like Miss Pole Dancing UK 2009, and well-known DJs. Tons of space means that it sometimes seems empty, but there's always room to dance. Check website for events schedule. No caps, sneakers, or sportswear. Cover varies; usually £10-15. Open only for events, usually 10pm-4am. 18+. MC/V.

Electric Ballroom, 184 Camden High St. (☎020 7485 9006; www.electric-ballroom.co.uk). ⊖Camden Town. Night Bus #N5, N28, N31. An octagonal bar and auditorium-sized dance floor downstairs; a more intimate lounge area with bar (and another dance area) upstairs. In the past, its hosted big names like The Clash and Run DMC, and most recently, it had The Killers and Paul McCartney. Club nights Sin City F with the latest hard rock, metal, ska, and underground; Shake Sa with DJs spinning beats from the 70s til today. Cover £7-10. Open F-Sa 10:30pm-3am. MC/V.

 MIND YOUR DRINK. A "pint" in England is 20 fl. oz. and generally contains 4-5% alcohol by volume. A "pint" in the US is 16 fl. oz. and tends to be less alcoholic. Fine. But who won the Revolution?

HAMPSTEAD, HIGHGATE, AND GOLDERS GREEN

ONE GASTRO-PUB IN HAMPSTEAD THAT DAVID BECKHAM LIKES

The Freemason's Arms, 32 Downshire Hill (☎020 7433 6811; www.freemasonsarms.co.uk), on the corner across from the Heath. ⊖Hampstead. With soaring ceilings, open kitchens, stone ovens, and wood fires, it's no wonder this gastro-pub is a favorite of Beckham and Posh when they're in town. The large stone patio regularly reels in the elite, and the beer garden in the back is one of the largest in London. Salads, pizzas, and pastas from £6; upscale pub mains from £10. Wheelchair-accessible. Open M-F noon-11pm, Sa 11am-11pm, Su 11am-10:30pm. MC/V. ❷

NEVER MIND THE BOLLOCKS, HERE'S.. SOME CONDOS?

Characterized by fire-ravaged buildings and a healthy dose of grunge, Camden has so far successfully maintained its endearing rough-and-tumble feel and kept its rep as a center for creativity and rebelliousness. A fire that took out much of the Camden market last year has instilled an endearing ugly-duckling sort of character and some raging parties. The question is, how long can Camden keep it up?

Just as Chelsea seems to have lost its rebellious underbelly, and Hoxton has become more and more preppy-artsy as opposed to actual-artsy, Camden, too, faces threats to its current state of play. For one, a number of architecture firms are proposing glass-and-steel environments that many fear would add sleek and chic at the expense of hot and hip. After all, Camden High St. has already—begrudgingly—allowed a number of retail chains to settle in.

And the reform spirit affects more than just the built environment: residents are starting to raise a fuss, arguing for the shut-down of many clubs and bars in order to eliminate the damaged property and occasional urine scent. A couple of residents are even threatening to sue for breach of human rights. Next year, Camden Council must meet to decide its next plan of action, and while liberal Matt Sanders insists that the "party is definitely not over," many wonder if for some places it soon will be. One can only hope that Camden hasn't yet given its last rager.

MARYLEBONE AND REGENT'S PARK

Like many of its West End neighbors, Marylebone doesn't boast a strong nightlife scene. Pubs are everywhere, but they all close by 11pm. Only a few places meet patrons halfway between pub and club, with a real bar, music, and dancing.

The Golden Eagle, 59 Marylebone Ln. (☎020 7935 3228). ⊖Bond St. The quintessence of "olde worlde"—both in terms of clientele and charm—this is one of the friendliest pubs around. Sidle up and join locals for the authentic pub sing-alongs (Tu and Th-F 8:30-11pm) around the piano in the corner. Beer and cider £2.40-3.50. Open M-Sa 11am-11pm, Su noon-7pm. MC/V.

The Coach Makers of Marylebone, 88 Marylebone Ln. (☎020 7224 4022). ⊖Bond St. Formerly O'Connor Don's, the most recent incarnation of this vibrant corner pub is a pleasant mix of upscale and relaxed. More of a gastro-pub than a pub, the Coach Makers offer an atmosphere fit for a drink or more. Its corner locale has translated into a nice outdoor socializing area. Tapas £4. Vegetable or meat platter £15. Entrees £9-19. Mixed drinks £7. Wine £4.75. Open M-Th noon-11:30pm, F-Sa noon-midnight, Su noon-10:30pm. AmEx/MC/V.

The Social, 5 Little Portland St. (☎020 7636 4992; www.thesocial.com). ⊖Oxford Circus. One of 3 UK Socials, this small, labyrinthine, and DJ-driven bar has a packed schedule of musical guests and special events like Hip Hop Karaoke and Comedy 2.0. A mixed crowd of 20- and 30-somethings fill the low-key, wood-paneled upstairs for grub and the more spacious and edgier downstairs for dancing. Mixed drinks £5.80-7.50. Shooters £3. Beers from £3.10. DJs spin nightly from 6 or 7pm. Cover usually free, sometimes £5-6. Open M-W noon-11pm, Th-F noon-1am, Sa 1pm-1am.

BAYSWATER

While Bayswater's nightlife scene offers a few pubs and bars, most people head elsewhere for a night out.

Arthur Baker's Harlem Soul Food, 78 Westbourne Grove (☎020 7985 0900; www.harlemsoulfood.com). ⊖Bayswater. The British just can't let 1776 go: now they want New York to come to London. Characterized by candles and leather booths cut into the walls, the intimate "Underground Bar" features live DJs spinning until 2:30am most nights; Diplo and the Loose Cannons are past performers. On the ground fl., the restaurant and bar serve an eclectic mix of drinks and comfort food, like balsamic and beer baby back ribs (£13) and Sugar Hill chicken pops (£7). M all-you-can-eat soul food buffet. Su American-style brunch with pancakes, omelettes and a "Bloody Mary Buffet." Open M-Tu 5pm-2am, W-F noon-2:30am, Sa 10am-2:30am, Su 10am-midnight. AmEx/MC/V.

Mitre, 24 Craven Terr. (☎020 7262 5240; www.mitrelancastergate.com). ⊖Lancaster Gate. Set in a sprawling Victorian mansion on a quiet corner, this comfortable pub is perfect for a lazy afternoon. Restored marble fireplaces, stained-glass skylights, a piano, and outdoor seating make it a cut above the rest. Made a cameo in Woody Allen's film *Match Point.* Upscale pub grub like rump steak with *beárnaise* or warm chicken and bacon salad £8-14. Beer from £3.20. Free Wi-Fi. Open M-Sa 11am-11:30pm, Su noon-11pm. Kitchen open noon-3pm and 6-10pm. AmEx/MC/V.

The Swan, 66 Bayswater Rd. (☎020 7262 5204). ⊖Lancaster Gate. Claims to have been the final drinking place for victims of the gallows that once stood nearby; now welcomes a slightly more upbeat crowd. A large patio and upstairs balcony are great places to relax with a pint (£3.10) and enjoy the view of Kensington Gardens directly across the street. Burgers and sandwiches £4.50-7; meat from the carvery with vegetables and potatoes £9. Public hangings M high noon. F-Su nights live acoustic music. Open M-Sa 10am-11:30pm, Su 10am-11pm. AmEx/MC/V.

NOTTING HILL

Dominated by young, artsy bohemians, Notting Hill stands in contrast to the clubs of the West End as the center of "alternative" nightlife culture. Even pubs in the area have their own distinct flavor.

PUBS

Prince Albert Pub, 11 Pembridge Rd. (☎020 7727 5244; www.the-prince-albert.co.uk). ⊖Notting Hill Gate. Always packed, the Prince has much to offer to his fellow pub-goers besides an endearingly chaotic atmosphere. In the pleasant backyard beer garden, crowds gather from afternoon on. On summer weekends there is BBQing (F 6-9pm, Sa-Su 3-9pm). Inside, wood floors and an assortment of comfy leather couches and booths set the tone for nighttime revelry or an afternoon meal or drink. Choose from over 40 beers, with 21 on tap (from £2.80). Open M-Sa noon-11pm, Su noon-10pm. MC/V.

Portobello Gold, 95-97 Portobello Rd. (☎020 7460 4900; www.portobellogold.com). ⊖Notting Hill Gate. Jolly pub with pineapple upholstery and a bright conservatory in the back, complete with palm trees and live birds, that's perfect for an afternoon tea. A healthy selection of draughts and ales (£3-4) and 20 varieties of whiskey rounds out the deal. Hosts rotating art exhibits. Regular live music on Su. Ploughman's Lunch £7. Oyster shooters from £3.50. Internet £1 per 30min. Wheelchair-accessible. Open daily 9:45am-midnight. MC/V.

Market Bar, 240a Portobello Rd. (☎020 7229 6472). ⊖Ladbroke Grove. Night Bus #N52. Look for the large, wrought-iron cornucopia above a bright red door. Consistently the loudest spot on Portobello, and that's saying a lot. Huge classic mirrors, dripped weeping-willow-esque candles, large toy horses stationed above the bar, and plenty of space. Try a Cool Cuban punch, caipirinha, or mojito (£5.50). Thai food upstairs M-F noon-3pm. DJs F-Sa. Open M noon-11pm, Tu-Th 11am-11pm, F 11am-12:30am, Sa 10am-12:30am, Su 11am-11pm.

Sun in Splendour, 7 Portobello Rd. (☎020 7792 0914; www.suninsplendourpub.co.uk). ⊖Notting Hill Gate. With its bright lilac facade, the oldest pub in Notting Hill looks brand-spanking new. A bit nicer than the Prince Albert and a little more low-key, this place is great for a chat over a beer or wine, or even a meal. The secret garden out back is prettier than Albert's, and the staff and loyal local following, mostly Aussie and American expats, are as friendly as they come. Pints £2.80-3.90. Mixed drinks £5.50. Burgers £6.50-8. Entrees £8. Open M-Th noon-11pm, F noon-midnight, Sa 11am-midnight, Su noon-10:30pm. AmEx/MC/V.

BARS

Mau Mau, 265 Portobello Rd. (☎020 7229 8528; www.maumaubar.com). ⊖Ladbroke Grove. Night Bus #N52. Known for its Bohemian vibe and live music, particularly the Th jazz nights, Mau Mau draws a crowd of local devotees. The bar in the front serves standard mixed drinks (£6.50) and a decent beer selection (from £3). A small stage and performance area occupies the back; get there early for a spot on the worn-in couches. Music starts at 8pm and ranges from funk to soul to R&B. Salsa nights M with lessons 7-8:30pm (£5) and dancing 8:30-11:30pm (£3). 18+. Open M-Th noon-11:30pm, F-Sa noon-2am, Su noon-10:30pm. Cash only.

CLUBS

Notting Hill Arts Club, 21 Notting Hill Gate (☎020 7598 5226; www.nottinghillartsclub.com). ⊖Notting Hill Gate. Night Bus #N94, 148, 207, 390. Where the newest of the underground bands are cultivated. Turntables, a dance floor, and distressed couches make this club the place to be. Arrive early to claim some space and avoid a wait. Beers and ciders from £3. Mixed drinks £6.90. Rotating art exhibits. Check out the free events (3 per week) online. Cover Th-Sa after 8pm £5-7. Happy hour M-F 6-9:30pm, Sa 4-9:30pm, Su 4-8pm; drinks half-priced. Open M-F 6pm-2am, Sa 4pm-2am, Su 4pm-1am. MC/V.

KENSINGTON AND EARL'S COURT

After a day of hard-core shopping or museum visiting, most people in the area prefer to go to sleep rather than to head out for the night. *Most* people.

PUBS

▨ **The Troubadour,** 265 Old Brompton Rd. (☎020 7370 1434; www.troubadour.co.uk). ⊖Earl's Court. Once upon a time this legendary pub, cafe, and deli hosted the likes of Bob Dylan (his first UK appearance) and (the almost as cool) Paul Simon, and it remains at the forefront with original music and spoken word events in the basement. The upstairs bar-cafe, decorated with hanging pitchforks, pots, and pans, is equally suited for morning espresso or evening vodka shots. An art gallery in the back displays other top talents, and the large courtyard garden is delightful in summer. Breakfast £5-10; lunch and dinner £8-15. Mixed drinks £8. Open daily 9am-midnight. Club open M-Th and Su 8:30am-12:30am, F-Sa 8:30am-2:30am. MC/V.

▨ **The Scarsdale,** 23A Edwardes Sq. (☎020 7937 1811). ⊖High St. Kensington. Hidden down an alleyway off Earl's Court Rd. Turn onto Earl's Walk (right next to the police stations), follow it to the end, and turn right; it's on the corner. Built during a bout of wishful thinking, this picture-perfect pub was initially intended to house Napoleon's officers after they "conquered" Britain. Now its elaborate decor and fantastic food make it a popular go-to place for locals of all ages. Delicious homemade meat and fish dishes (they don't do fish and chips; the favorite is the slow roasted lamb with rosemary and red currant *jus*) £10-15. Homemade sandwiches, burgers, and salads £8-12. Dinner reservations are essential. Open M-Sa noon-11pm, Su noon-10:30pm. Kitchen open noon-3pm and 6-9pm. MC/V.

The Pembroke, 261 Old Brompton Rd. (☎020 7373 8337; www.realpubs.co.uk). ⊖Earl's Court or West Brompton. Formerly the gay bar Colherne, the Pembroke is hipper, sleeker, and no longer exclusively gay. Now, you'll see men, women, lovers, and friends lounging among black leather couches, glowing chandeliers, and gilded trimmings. The outside seating area and upstairs roof terrace are especially popular in the summer. Delicate gourmet dishes like pan-fried pork *escalope* with apple and watercress £8.50-17. Board games available upon request. Free Wi-Fi. Open M-W and Su noon-11pm, Th noon-11:30pm, F-Sa noon-midnight. Kitchen open noon-2:30pm and 6-10pm. AmEx/MC/V.

The Drayton Arms, 153 Old Brompton Rd. (☎020 7835 2301; www.thedraytonarms-snorthkensington.co.uk). ⊖Gloucester Rd. or South Kensington. A spacious corner pub with relaxed but preppy (or "Sloaney") vibe. Well-dressed 20- and 30-somethings chat among velvet and leather couches, massive picture windows, and showy chandeliers, usually nursing a red or white (from £2.70) from the impressive wine list. Tasting platters £9-13. "Boutique" burgers and mains like beef bourguignon pie with homemade onion mash and steamed veggies £7-9. Sa DJs from 8pm. Su "Roast and Toast" with roast and wine pairing; noon-10pm. Open M-Sa noon-11pm, Su noon-10:30pm. Kitchen open M-F noon-4pm and 6-10pm, Sa noon-10pm, Su noon-9pm. MC/V.

BARS

Janet's Bar, 30 Old Brompton Rd. (☎020 7581 3160). ⊖South Kensington. Night Bus #14, N74, N97. Adorned with pink flamingos, sports memorabilia, balloons, streamers, random retro relics, and plenty of pictures of Janet herself, this local hole in the wall is a welcome alternative to the pubs and glamour bars in the area. Over 35 mixed drinks to choose from, including Janet's Love Lotion (malibu, vodka, mango, pineapple, and cranberry juice; £9.50). Wine £5.30. Beer £4. They don't do proper food, but nibblers like hot dogs, peanuts, and cheeses, are complimentary. Live music F-Sa 9:30pm. £3 cover if you don't order a drink. Open M-Th and Su 11:30am-1am, F-Sa 11:30-2:30am. MC/V.

KNIGHTSBRIDGE AND BELGRAVIA

Besides a couple of pubs that are more like institutions, Knightsbridge is not the place to go for a low-key night of inexpensive drinking. If you're going to go out on the town here, you might as well splurge and take your liquor with the celebrity and jet-setting crowds.

Talbot, Little Chester St. (☎020 7235 1639). ⊖Knightsbridge or Sloane Sq. This pub's outdoor patio beckons many a London professional for lunch and after-work drinks. Cheerful, bright setting topped off with a superior wine list. Sandwiches £4-5. Traditional British entrees £6.50-8.50. Pitcher of Pimm's and lemonade £10. Takeaway available. Open M-F 11am-11pm; outdoor seating open M-Th until 9pm, F until 10pm. AmEx/MC/V.

Wilton Arms, 71 Kinnerton St. (☎020 7235 4854). ⊖Knightsbridge or Hyde Park Corner. Claiming to be Britain's oldest Brewer, this refined pub actually encourages reading: bookshelves full of classic hardcover novels line the walls. Boozers and socializers won't feel out of place, though, thanks to a friendly crowd and a good selection of lagers and bitters (from £2.70). Outdoor seating under beautiful hanging flower baskets in nice weather. Plasma screen shows major sporting events. Entrees include shepherd's pie, fish and chips, and garlic battered chicken £6-7. Toasted sandwiches £3.30. Burgers £6. Open M-Sa 11am-11pm, Su noon-10:30pm. Kitchen open M-F noon-9:30pm, Sa noon-3pm. MC/V.

Nags Head, 53 Kinnerton St. (☎020 7235 1135). ⊖Hyde Park Corner or Knightsbridge. Head in through cascading flowers to this outstanding traditional pub. Model airplanes, Boston Red Sox gear (let it go, England: you lost the colonies), an eclectic collection of bronze beer mugs, and a couple antique fireplaces make this watering hole endearing. Sandwiches from £4.50. Entrees from £7. Open M-Sa 11am-11pm, Su noon-10:30pm. Cash only.

▓ DAYTRIPS FROM LONDON

BATH ☎(0)1225

The world's original tourist town, Bath has been a must-see since AD 43, when the Romans built an elaborate complex of baths to house the curative waters of the town they called *Aquae Sulis.* In the 18th and 19th centuries, Bath became a social capital second only to London, immortalized by Jane Austen and other literary greats. Today, hordes of tourists and backpackers admire the Georgian architecture by day and continue to create scandal by night.

▐ TRANSPORTATION

Trains: Bath Spa Station, Dorchester St., at the south end of Manvers St. Ticket office open M-F 5:30am-8:30pm, Sa 6am-8:30pm, Su 7:30am-8:30pm. Trains (☎08457 484 950) to: **Birmingham** (2hr., 2 per hr., £40); **Bristol** (15min., every 10-15min., £5.80-6); **Exeter** (1½-2hr., 2 per hr., £27); **London Paddington** (1¾hr., every hr., £17-74); **London Waterloo** (2½hr., every hr., £29); **Plymouth** (2½-3½hr., every hr., £45-53); **Salisbury** (1hr., 2 per hr., £7-14).

Buses: All buses depart from the **Bath Bus Station,** Churchill Bridge. Ticket office open M-Sa 8am-5:30pm. National Express (☎08717 818 181) to **London** (3hr., every hr., £18) and **Oxford** (2hr., 1 per day, £9.50). First (☎0871 200 2233) bus #X39 runs to **Bristol** (M-Sa every 12min. 6am-7pm, £4.30). Badgerline sells a **Day Explorer** ticket, good for 1 day of unlimited bus travel in the region (£6.30-7).

Taxis: Abbey Radio (☎01224 444 444). **V Cars** (☎01225 464 646).

◼★🛈 ORIENTATION AND PRACTICAL INFORMATION

The **Roman Baths,** the **Pump Room,** and **Bath Abbey** cluster in the city center, bounded by York St. and Cheap St. The River Avon flows just east of them and wraps around the south part of town near the train and bus stations. Uphill to the northwest, historic buildings lie on **Royal Crescent** and **The Circus.**

Tourist Information Centre: Abbey Chambers (☎09067 112 000; www.visitbath.co.uk). Town map and mini-guide £1. Books rooms for £3 plus a 10% deposit. Open June-Sept. M-Sa 9:30am-6pm, Su 10am-4pm; Oct.-May M-Sa 9:30am-5pm, Su 10am-4pm.

Tours: Several companies run tours of the city and surrounding sights.

Bizarre Bath (☎01225 335 124; www.bizarrebath.co.uk). The guides impart few historical facts on this comedic walk, but their tricks (including a bunny escape) prove entertaining. 1hr. tours begin at the Huntsman Inn at N. Parade Passage. Daily tours Apr.-Sept. 8pm. £8, concessions £5.

Ghost Walk (☎01225 350 512; www.ghostwalksofbath.co.uk). Tours leave the Nash Bar of Garrick's Head, near Theatre Royal. 2hr. tours. Apr.-Oct. M-Sa 8pm; Nov.-Mar. F 8pm. £7, concessions £5.

Mayor of Bath Tours (☎1225 477 411; www.visitbath.co.uk). Free walking tours leave from outside the Abbey Churchyard entrance to the Pump Room (on Stall St.). 2hr. M-F and Su 10:30am and 2pm, Sa 10:30 only. May-Sept. also Tu and F 7pm.

Jane Austen Tours (☎1225 443 000; www.janeausten.co.uk). Austen fans will need little persuasion to take this tour, which includes Austen's homes and favorite spots. Meet outside K.C. Change in the Abbey Churchyard. 1½hr. Daily 11am. Also July-Aug. F and Sa 6pm. Adults £4.50, concessions £3.50.

Bank: Barclays, Milsom St. (☎08457 555 555). Open M-F 9am-5pm, Sa 9am-3pm.

Library: Central Library, Podium Shopping Centre (☎01225 394 041). Free internet. Open M 9:30am-6pm, Tu-Th 9:30am-7pm, F-Sa 9:30am-5pm, Su 1-4pm.

Launderette: Spruce Goose, Margaret's Bldg. (☎01225 483 309), off Brock St. Open M-F and Su 8am-9pm, Sa 8am-8pm. Last wash 1hr. before close.

Police: Manvers St. (☎08454 567 000), near the train and bus stations.

Pharmacy: Boots, 33-35 Westgate St. (☎01225 482 069). Open M-Sa 8:30am-6pm, Su 10:30am-4:30pm.

Hospital: Royal United, Coombe Park (☎01225 428 331), in Weston. Take bus #14.

Internet Access: Free at the **Central Library** (p. 221). **@ Internet,** 13A Manvers St. (☎01225 443 181). £1 per 20min. Open daily 9am-10pm.

Post Office: 27 Northgate St. (☎08457 223 344), across from the Podium Shopping Centre. Open M and W-Sa 9am-5:30pm, Tu 9:30am-5:30pm. **Postcode:** BA1 1AJ.

◤ ACCOMMODATIONS

Well-to-do visitors drive up prices in Bath, but the city's location and sights bring in enough backpackers and passing travelers to sustain several budget accommodations. B&Bs cluster on **Pulteney Road** and **Pulteney Gardens. Marlborough Lane** and **Upper Bristol Road,** west of the city center, also have options.

YMCA, International House, Broad St. Pl. (☎01225 325 900; www.bathymca.co.uk). Up the stairs from High and Walcot St. Bright, clean, colorful dorms. Spacious rooms overlooking a courtyard garden. Continental breakfast included. Lockers £1.50-3 per day.

Internet 50p per 15min. Free Wi-Fi. Dorms £15-17; singles £27-31; triples £57-63; quads £68-76. MC/V. ❶

Bath Backpackers, 13 Pierrepont St. (☎01225 446 787; www.hostels.co.uk). Laid-back backpacker's lair with music-themed dorms. Hang out in the lounge with a big-screen TV or have a drink in the "Dungeon." Bathrooms may be less than shining and beds a bit creakier than at home, but still a solid budget option. Self-catering kitchen. Luggage storage £2 per bag. Internet £2 per hr. Reception open 8am-11pm. 10-bed dorms £13-15; 8-bed £14-16; 4-bed £16-18. MC/V. ❶

St. Christopher's Inn, 16 Green St. (☎01225 481 444; www.st-christophers.co.uk). Downstairs bar is an ideal hangout area for the young crowd. Simple and clean bunks, but not enough space to do much else but sleep. Free luggage storage. Internet £1 per 20min. Free Wi-Fi at the bar. Dorms £15-24. Online booking discounts. MC/V. ❶

YHA Bath, Bathwick Hill (☎01225 465 674). From N. Parade Rd., turn left on Pulteney Rd., swing right on Bathwick Hill, and climb the hill (40min.) or take bus #18 or 418 (every 20min.). Beautiful secluded Italianate mansion. Spacious facility frequented mostly by families and school groups. Kitchen available. Internet (terminal or Wi-Fi) £1 per 15min. Reception open 7am-11pm. Dorms £12-18, under 18 £9; private rooms £21-124. MC/V. ❶

Toad Hall Guest House, 6 Lime Grove (☎01225 423 254). Turn left off Pulteney Rd. after going under the overpass. Peaceful green carpet and pink rooms inspired by *The Wind in the Willows*. Hearty breakfast included. Singles £30; doubles £55. Cash only. ❸

🍴 FOOD

Although Bath restaurants tend to be expensive, reasonably priced eateries can be found throughout the city. For fruits and vegetables, visit the **Bath Guildhall Market.** (☎01225 477 945. Open M-Sa 9am-5:30pm.) Buy delicious vegetarian goodies at ⬛**Harvest,** 37 Walcot St., an inexpensive organic grocery with local produce and takeaway food. (☎01225 465 519; www.harvest-bath.coop. Sandwiches £2. Open M-Sa 9am-6pm, Tu 10am-6pm. MC/V.)

⬛ **The Eastern Eye,** 8A Quiet St. (☎01225 422 323; www.easterneye.com). Award-winning Indian cuisine in an elegant Georgian building with three domed skylights and murals covering the walls. The building has previously served as a casino, ballroom, and auction house. Vegetarian options available. Entrees £9-15. Open daily noon-2:30pm and 6-11:30pm. AmEx/MC/V. ❷

Cafe Retro, 18 York St. (☎07512 907 777; www.caferetro.co.uk). Mismatched chairs and wood floors give this cafe-bar a simultaneously hip and Old World feel. 2 floors and plenty of space to enjoy your sandwich (£4.60-6.20) or entree (£5.20-7). Breakfast served all day. Open M-Sa 9am-9pm, Su 10am-5pm. MC/V. ❷

Riverside Cafe (☎01225 480 532; www.riversidecafebar.co.uk), below Pulteney Bridge. Light dishes and coffee in a sheltered enclave overlooking the River Avon. If you can't get a table outside, take your food to the nearby park. Sandwiches and soups £5-6.20. Open M-Sa 9am-9pm, Su 9am-5pm. MC/V. ❶

Mai Thai, 6 Pierrepont St. (☎01225 445 557). Huge portions of Thai food at affordable prices. Ornate tables and authentic decorations make the atmosphere as rich as the food. Entrees £5-7.30. Lunch special £5.50. Open daily noon-2pm and 6-11pm. AmEx/MC/V. ❷

All Bar One, 11-13 High St. (☎01225 334 614; www.allbarone.co.uk). Spacious and swanky bar that serves handmade burgers (£7-9) and tapas from all over the world (£1.80-6). Vast wine selection and various European beers (pints £3-4). Open M-Th 10am-11pm, F-Sa 10am-midnight, Su 10am-10:30pm. Kitchen open M-Sa 10am-10pm, Su 10am-9pm. AmEx/MC/V. ❷

👁 SIGHTS

ROMAN BATHS. In 1880, sewer diggers uncovered an extravagant feat of Roman engineering. For 400 years, the Romans harnessed Bath's bubbling springs, which spew 264,000 gallons of 115°F (47°C) water every day. The city became a mecca for Britain's Roman elite. The ■museum has displays on excavated Roman artifacts and building design. It's also the only way to get up close and personal with the ancient baths (unfortunately, taking a dip is prohibited). Make sure to see the Roman curses (politely referred to as offerings to Minerva), wishing eternal damnation upon rival neighbors. Audio tours are a must, and the one narrated by Bill Bryson is excellent, if slightly random. (Stall St. ☎01225 477 785; www.romanbaths.co.uk. Open daily July-Aug. 9am-10pm; Sept.-Oct. and Mar.-June 9am-6pm; Nov.-Feb. 9am-5:30pm. Last entry 1hr. before close. £11, concessions £9.50, children £7.20, families £32. Joint ticket with Museum of Fashion £15/123/8.70/40.)

BATH ABBEY. Occupying the site where King Edgar was crowned the first king of England in AD 973, the 140 ft. abbey stands in the city center. Bishop Oliver King commissioned the abbey to replace a Norman cathedral, and the crowned olive tree on the ceiling symbolizes the message he heard from God: "let an Olive establish the Crown and a King restore the Church." A stunning stained-glass window contains 56 scenes from the life of Christ. Among the docents is an amateur campanologist who gives excellent tours of the ■bell tower. The underlying **Heritage Vaults** contain an exhibit on the abbey's uses through the ages. (Next to the Baths. ☎01225 422 462; www.bathabbey.org. Open M-Sa 9am-6pm, Su 1-2:30pm and 4:30-5:30pm. Suggested donation £2.50. Tower tours £5. Heritage Vaults open daily 10am-4pm. Sunday services at 8, 9:15, and 11am.)

MUSEUM OF FASHION AND ASSEMBLY ROOMS. The museum hosts a dazzling parade of 400 years of catwalk fashions, from 17th-century silver tissue garments to Jennifer Lopez's racy Versace jungle-print ensemble. Thematic displays show how fashion has changed through the years in everything from pockets to gloves, and interactive displays let visitors try on a corset and hoop skirt for a feel of how Victorian ladies felt. (Bennett St. ☎01225 477 785; www.fashionmuseum.co.uk. Open daily Mar.-Oct. 10:30am-6pm; Nov.-Feb. 10:30am-5pm. Last entry 1hr. before close. £7, concessions £6.30, children £5, families £20. Joint ticket with baths £14/12/8.30/38.) The museum is in the basement of the Assembly Rooms, which once held *fin de siècle* balls and concerts. Bombing during WWII ravaged the rooms, but a renovation has duplicated the originals. (☎01225 477 173. Open daily Mar.-Oct. 10:30am-6pm; Nov.-Feb. 10:30am-5pm. Sometimes closed for private functions. Free.)

OTHER MUSEUMS AND GALLERIES. Next to Pulteney Bridge, the **Victoria Art Gallery**, Bridge St., holds a collection of paintings from the mid-18th century to today. It houses Thomas Barker's *The Bride of Death*—Victorian melodrama at its sappiest. Rotating exhibits take place on the ground floor. (☎01225 477 244; www.victoriagal.org.uk. Open Tu-Sa 10am-5pm, Su 1:30-5pm. Free.) The **Jane Austen Centre** depicts Austen's time in Bath, where she visited her family and lived briefly. Ironically, she disliked living in Bath and wrote nothing while living here, but she frequently wrote about the city in her novels—most notably in *Persuasion* and *Northanger Abbey*. Tours of Bath sights mentioned in Austen's books and her family's homes are also available. (40 Gay St. ☎01225 443 000; www.janeausten.co.uk. Open July-Aug. M-W 9:45am-5:30pm, Th-Su 9:45am-7pm; Nov.-Mar. M-F and Su 11am4:30pm, Sa 9:45am-5:30pm. Last entry 1hr. before close. Tours Sa-Su 11am. Talks

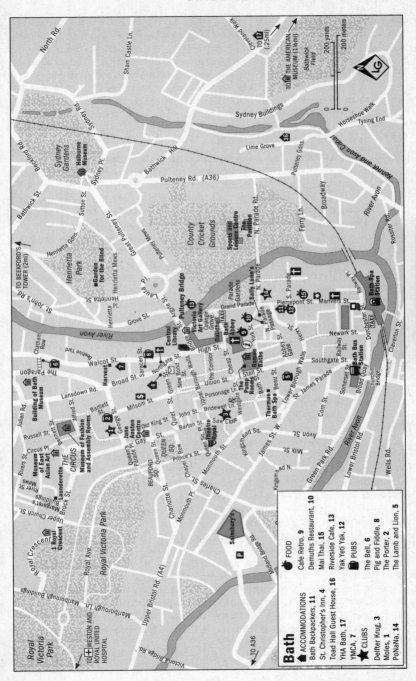

Bath

ACCOMMODATIONS
Bath Backpackers, 11
St. Christopher's Inn, 4
Toad Hall Guest House, 16
YHA Bath, 17
YMCA, 7

CLUBS
Delfter Krug, 3
Moles, 1
PoNaNa, 14

FOOD
Cafe Retro, 9
Demuths Restaurant, 10
Mai Thai, 15
Riverside Cafe, 13
Yak Yeti Yak, 12

PUBS
The Bell, 6
Pig and Fiddle, 8
The Porter, 2
The Lamb and Lion, 5

every 30min. £7, concessions £5.50. Walking tours £6, concessions £5.) Architecture buffs will enjoy the **Building of Bath Museum,** which explains the extensive planning of Bath as well as the history of the city's famous Georgian buildings. Check out the model of the city—it took 10,000 hours to perfect its 500:1 scale layout. (Countess of Huntingdon's Chapel, the Paragon. ☎01225 333 895; www.bath-preservation-trust. org.uk. Open from mid-Feb. to Nov. Sa-M 10am-5:30pm. £4, concessions £3.50.) The **American Museum,** Claverton Manor, has enough colonial relics to make any Yank feel at home. (☎01225 460 503; www.americanmuseum.org. Open from mid-Mar. to Oct. Tu-Su 2-5:30pm. Last entry 5pm. Gardens and tearoom open Tu-Su noon-5:30pm. £7.50, concessions £6.50. Grounds £5/4.)

HISTORIC BUILDINGS. The oldest house in Bath is **Sally Lunn's,** 4 North Parade Passage, built on the site of an old monastery. You can check out the ancient "faggot" oven used to bake her world-famous buns and buy a giant bun (£1.50) to take home. (Open M-Sa 10am-6pm, Su 11am-6pm. 30p, students and children free.) In the city's residential northwest corner are the **Georgian row houses,** built by famed architects John Wood the Elder and John Wood the Younger. One of the houses, **The Circus,** which has the same circumference as Stonehenge, has attracted illustrious inhabitants for two centuries; former residents include Thomas Gainsborough and William Pitt. Proceed up Brock St. to the **Royal Crescent,** a half-moon of 18th-century townhouses. The interior of **1 Royal Crescent** has been restored to the way it was in 1770, down to the last butter knife. (☎01225 428 126. Open from mid-Feb. to Oct. Tu-Su 10:30am-5pm; Nov. Tu-Su 10:30am-4pm. Last entry 30min. before close. £5, concessions £4, children £2.50, families £12.) For stupendous views, climb the 154 steps of **Beckford's Tower,** Lansdown Rd., 2 mi. north of town. (Take bus #2 or 702 to Ensleigh; otherwise, it's a 45min. walk. ☎01225 460 705. Open from Easter to Oct. Sa-Su 10:30am-5pm. £3, concessions £2, children £1.50, families £8.)

GARDENS AND PARKS. Consult a map or the TIC's *Borders, Beds, and Shrubberies* brochure to find the city's many stretches of cultivated green. High in the hills above above Bath, the ▨**Bathwick field** offered such stunning views of the city and surrounding area that it was made into National Trust land. Now, it's the perfect place to escape for a picnic, away from the touristy city center. (15min. walk up Bathwick Hill, across the river.) Next to the Royal Crescent, **Royal Victoria Park** contains rare trees and an aviary. (Open 24hr. Free.) **Henrietta Park,** laid in 1897 to celebrate Queen Victoria's Diamond Jubilee, was redesigned as a garden for the blind—only the most fragrant plants were chosen for its grounds. The **Parade Gardens,** at the base of N. Parade Bridge, won the Britain in Bloom competition so often that they were asked not to enter again. (☎01225 391 041. Open daily 10am-7pm. Apr.-Sept. £1, Oct.-Mar. free.)

🎵 🎆 ENTERTAINMENT AND FESTIVALS

In summer, **buskers** (street musicians) fill the streets with music, and a brass band often graces the Parade Gardens. The magnificent **Theatre Royal,** Saw Close, at the south end of Barton St., showcases opera and theater. (☎01225 448 844; www.theatreroyal.org.uk. Box office open M-Sa 10am-8pm, Su noon-8pm. Tickets £15-30.) The **Little Theatre Cinema,** St. Michael's Pl., Bath St., is Bath's local art-house cinema. (☎0871 704 2061. Tickets £6.20-7, concessions £5-5.70. Box office open daily 1-8pm.)

Bath hosts several festivals; for information or reservations, call the Bath Festivals Box Office, 2 Church St., Abbey Green. (☎01225 463 362; www.bath-festivals.org.uk. Open M-Sa 9:30am-5:30pm.) The **Bath International Music Festival** (typically May-June; check www.bathmusicfest.org.uk for updates) features world-class symphony orchestras, choruses, and jazz bands. The overlapping **Fringe Festival** (☎01225 480 079; www.bathfringearts.co.uk) celebrates the arts with over 200 live performances (May-June). The **Jane Austen Festival,** at the end of September, features Austen-themed walks, meals, and movies (contact the Jane Austen Centre; see **Sights,** p. 210). The **Literature Festival** is held in March, the **Balloon Fiesta** in mid-May, and the **Film Festival** in late October. Pick up the weekly *Venue* (£1.30), available at bookstores.

🍸🎵 PUBS AND CLUBS

Tourists and two universities keep this small town full of nightlife. Most pubs close around 11pm, and late-night clubs almost always charge a cover.

The Porter, 15 George St. (☎01225 424 104; www.theporter.co.uk). Offbeat vibe, a completely vegetarian menu, and live music M-Th nights in the basement. Pictures of artists who have performed at the Porter grace the walls, including such popular bands as The Killers. DJs F-Sa. Comedy Su 7pm (£7, students £5). Open M-Th 11am-midnight, F-Sa 11am-1am, Su 11am-11:30pm. Kitchen open daily 11am-9pm. AmEx/MC/V for food orders only.

Pig and Fiddle, 2 Saracen St. (☎01775 460 868), off Broad St. The 1st stop for many pub crawlers. The cozy interior and huge heated patio are always full of backpackers enjoying cider and local ales. £5 lunch special. Open-mic nights Tu. Movie nights Su 8pm. Happy hour M-F 3-7pm. Open M-Sa 11am-11:30pm, Su noon-10:30pm. Kitchen open M-F 11am-7pm, Sa-Su noon-6pm. MC/V.

The Lamb and Lion, 15 Lower Borough Walls (☎01225 334 617). Cheap pints (£1.70-2.80) and grub make this a popular pre-club pub with students and locals on weekends. Beer garden out back is fabulous in summer, as is the perfectly crafted fruit-filled Pimm's. £5 curry and a drink special Th. Open M-W 10am-11pm, Th-Sa 10am-12:30pm, Su noon-10:30pm. Kitchen open M-Sa 11am-8pm, Su noon-8pm. MC/V.

Moles, 14 George St. (☎01225 404 445; www.moles.co.uk). Pounds out soul, funk, and house in an underground setting. Up-and-coming live bands M and Th. Dance club night Tu and F-Sa. Cover £3-8. Open M-Th 9pm-2am, F-Sa 9pm-4am, Su 8pm-12:30am. Cash only.

The Bell, 103 Walcot St. (☎01225 460 426; www.walcotstreet.com). Challenges its clientele to talk over (or sing along with) the live folk, jazz, blues, funk, salsa, and reggae playing most nights. Pizza served in the garden on weekend evenings. Free Wi-Fi. Live music M and W evenings, Su lunch. Open daily noon-11pm. MC/V over £5.

PoNaNa, N. Parade and Pierrepont St. (☎01225 424 592; www.ponana.com/bath). Descend the staircase into a subterranean lair to find hot beats and sweaty dancers. "Squeeze the Cheese" F. Cover £3-5. Open Tu-Th 10pm-2am, F-Sa 10:30pm-2:30am.

Mandalyns, 13 Fountain Buildings, Lansdown Rd. (☎01225 425 403; www.mandalyns.com). Bath's most popular gay pub. Funky lighting and leopard-print sofas in the back. Drink specials every night of the week, such as karaoke and £1 shots on Th. Open M-Sa 4pm-2am, Su 6pm-1am. MC/V over £10.

BRIGHTON ☎(0)1273

Brighton (pop. 250,000) is one of Britain's largest seaside resorts. King George IV came to Brighton in 1783 and enjoyed the anything-goes atmosphere so much that he transformed a farmhouse into his headquarters for debauchery (the Royal Pavilion). A regal rumpus ensued. Since then, Brighton continues to turn a blind eye to some of the more scandalous activities that occur along its shores, as holidaymakers and locals alike peel it off—all off—at England's first bathing beach. Kemp Town (also known as Camp Town) has a thriving gay and lesbian population. The huge student crowd and flocks of foreign youth feed the notorious clubbing scene of this "London-by-the-Sea."

TRANSPORTATION

Trains: Brighton Station, uphill at the northern end of Queen's Rd. Ticket office open 24hr. Travel center open June-Sept. M-F 8am-5pm, Sa 9am-5pm, Su 9:30am-3pm; Oct.-May M-F 8am-5pm, Sa 9am-5pm. Trains (☎08451 272 920) to: **Arundel** (1¼hr., every hr., £8); **London Victoria** (1hr., 3 per hr., £13-20); **Portsmouth** (1½hr., 2 per hr., £16); **Rye** (1½hr., every hr., £5).

Buses: Tickets and info at **One Stop Travel,** 16 Old Steine (☎01273 700 406). Open June-Sept. M-Tu and Th-F 8:30am-5:45pm, W 9am-5:45pm, Sa 9am-5pm, Su 9:30am-3pm; Oct.-May M-Tu and Th-F 8:30am-5:45pm, W 9am-5:45pm, Sa 9am-5pm. National Express (☎08705 808 080) buses leave from Preston Park to **London Victoria** (2½hr., every hr., £12). Tickets available on board or online.

Public Transportation: Local **buses** operated by Brighton and Hove (☎01273 886 200; www.buses.co.uk) congregate around Old Steine. The Tourist Information Center (☎09067 112 255) at Royal Pavilion can give route and price information for most buses; all carriers charge £1.20 in the central area. Frequent local buses serve Brighton. Daysaver tickets before 9am £3.20, after 9am £3.

Taxis: Brighton Taxis (☎01273 202 020). Available 24hr.

ORIENTATION AND PRACTICAL INFORMATION

Brighton is easily explored on foot. **Queen's Road** connects the train station to the English Channel, and turns into **West Street** halfway down the slope at the intersection with Western Rd. Funky stores and restaurants cluster around **Trafalgar Street,** which runs east from the train station. From Queen's Rd., head east onto North St. to reach the narrow streets of the **Lanes,** a pedestrian shopping area by day and nightlife center after dark. **Old Steine,** a road and a square, runs in front of the **Royal Pavilion,** while **King's Road** runs parallel to the waterfront.

Tourist Information Centre: Royal Pavilion Shop, 4-5 Pavilion Bldg. (☎09067 112 255; www.visitbrighton.com). Staff sells guides and maps, books National Express tickets, and reserves rooms for £1.50 plus a 10% deposit. Open daily Apr.-Oct. 9:30am-5pm; Nov.-Mar. M-F 10am-5pm.

Tours: CitySightseeing (☎01708 886 200; www.city-sightseeing.com). 50min. bus tours leave from Brighton pier every 30min. with stops at Royal Pavilion, the railway station, and Brighton Marina. Apr.-Oct. £8, concessions £6, children £3, families £18.

Banks: All along North St., near Castle Sq. **ATMs** outside **Lloyds** (after hours ☎08453 000 000), at the corner of North St. and East St. Open M-Tu and Th-F 9am-5pm, W 10am-5pm, Sa 9:30am-1:30pm.

Library: Jubilee Library (☎01273 290 800, www.citylibraries.info), on Regent St. Open M-Tu 10am-7pm, W and F-Sa 10am-5pm, Th 10am-8pm, Su 10am-4pm.

Brighton

♦ ACCOMMODATIONS
Baggies Backpackers, **1**
Christina Guest House, **19**
Dorset Guest House, **17**
Hotel Pelirocco, **2**

◆ FOOD
Deli India Restaurant, **10**
Food for Friends, **7**
The Hop Poles, **6**
The Mock Turtle, **11**
Nia Restaurant and Cafe, **12**

▥ PUBS
The FishBowl, **9**
Fortune of War, **4**
The Mash Tun, **8**
Three and Ten, **15**
Ye Olde King and Queen, **13**

★ CLUBS
Audio, **18**
Candy Bar, **14**
Casablanca Jazz Club, **5**
Charles St., **16**
Coalition, **3**

English Channel

LONDON

GLBT Resources: Lesbian and Gay Switchboard (☎01273 204 050). Open daily 5pm-11pm. The TIC also (see above) stocks a list of gay-friendly accommodations, clubs, and shops.

Launderette: Preston St. Launderette, 75 Preston St. (☎01273 738 556). Wash and dry £4. Open M-Sa 8am-9pm, Su 9am-7pm. Last wash 1hr. before close.

Police: John St. (☎0845 607 0999).

Hospital: Royal Sussex County, Eastern Rd. (☎01273 696 955).

Pharmacy: Boots, 129 North St. (☎01273 207 461). Open M-Sa 8am-midnight, Su 11am-5pm.

Internet Access: Internet cafes cluster in the town center, especially along West St. and St. James's St. Try **Starnet,** 94 St. James's St. £1 per hr.

Post Office: 20 St. James's St. **Bureau de change.** Open M-F 8:30am-5:30pm, Sa 9am-2pm. **Postcode:** BN1 1BA.

ACCOMMODATIONS

On weekdays, accommodations in Brighton are discounted from their weekend markups. Brighton's best budget beds are in its hostels; the TIC has a complete list. The city's B&B's and hotels begin at £25-30 and skyrocket from there. Many midrange (£35-50) B&Bs line **Madeira Place;** cheaper establishments abound west of **West Pier** and east of **Palace Pier.** To the east, perpendicular to the shoreline, **Kemp Town** has a huge number of B&Bs.

Baggies Backpackers, 33 Oriental Pl. (☎01273 733 740). Join in the fun at this super-social hostel, where spontaneous parties on "Baggies Beach" are common. Racecar sheets and welcoming staff. Co-ed bathrooms. Kitchen with complimentary tea and coffee. Free Wi-Fi. Key deposit £5. Dorms £13; doubles £35. Cash only. ❶

Hotel Pelirocco, 10 Regency Sq. (☎01273 327 055; www.hotelpelirocco.co.uk). Wannabe rock stars will revel in the over-the-top, hip-to-be-different atmosphere. Each of 19 individually themed rooms (try the leopard-print "Betty's Boudoir" or Jamie Reid's "Magic Room," decorated by the Sex Pistols artist himself) has video games and a private bath. Singles £50-65; doubles £100-145. AmEx/MC/V. ❺

Christina Guest House, 20 St. George's Terr. (☎01273 690 862; www.christinaguesthousebrighton.co.uk). Family-run house a short walk from the seafront, with ensuite rooms. Full breakfast with vegetarian options included. Rooms £30-35 per person. MC/V. ❸

FOOD

Brighton has over 400 restaurants that will satisfy almost any craving. **Queen's Road** is lined with chain restaurants and fast food. Cheap ethnic eateries from Indian to Mediterranean to Moroccan can be found along **Preston Street.** Swanky patisseries and cafes fill the **Lanes,** which offer overpriced but memorable meals and people-watching. Get groceries at **Waitrose,** 130-134 Western Rd. (☎01273 326 549. Open M-Th and Sa 8am-8pm, F 8am-9pm, Su 11am-5pm.) Brighton's history as a health resort has not been forgotten—vegetarian options pervade the city. Satisfy sugar cravings with Brighton rock candy (foul and amazing) from any of the many shops that claim to have invented it.

Food for Friends, 17A-18A Prince Albert St. (☎01273 202 310; www.foodforfriends. com). Classy, bright corner restaurant serving tasty vegetarian tuck. Desserts are delectable, especially the baked chocolate pudding with homemade Bailey's ice cream (£5.80). Don't miss the Sunday "roast": all the fixings, none of the meat (£9.50).

Entrees £10-13. Live jazz Tu. Tea served 3-6pm. Open M-Th and Su noon-10pm, F-Sa noon-10:30pm. AmEx/MC/V. ❷

Mykonos Greek Tavern, 31 Preston St. (☎01273 329 918). Peaceful decor with the same color scheme as the Greek flag. Traditional Greek dishes (£7-12) and good wine might make you wish you were in the Greek Isles instead of Brighton. Open M-Th 5:30-11pm, F-Su noon-11pm. MC/V. ❷

Nia Restaurant and Cafe, 87 Trafalgar St. (☎01273 671 371), east of the train station. Elegant dishes (£8.30-15) like venison stew in a romantic cafe near the North Laines. International flavors, drawing from Japanese, French, and Mediterranean cuisine. Open M-Th and Su 9am-5pm, F-Sa 9am-10:30pm. MC/V. ❸

Banjo's Sandwich Shop, Norfolk Sq. (☎01273 772 836), near the corner of Upper North St. and Regent Hill. A tiny kiosk with inexpensive sandwiches made by perhaps the most polite man in Britain (that's saying something). Everything on the menu is less than £2.50. The adjacent Norfolk Sq. Park is a perfect place to enjoy a romantic lunch. Open M-F 7:30am-4pm, Sa 8am-3pm. Cash only. ❶

The Mock Turtle, 4 Pool Valley (☎01273 327 380). Half-hidden behind lace curtains, this tucked-away cafe is the perfect stop for a giant jelly doughnut or afternoon tea (£5.50). Open Tu-Su 9:30am-6pm, last orders 5:30pm. Cash only. ❶

The Hop Poles, 13 Middle St. (☎01273 710 444). Popular bar and hangout with a heated garden. Unique entrees like ham in plum ginger chili sauce and vegan dishes like Greek spanakopita (£7.50). Entrees £8-9. Kitchen open daily noon-9pm. MC/V. ❷

E-Kagen, 24 Sydney St. (☎01273 687 068). Japanese noodle bar on the hip and colorful Sydney St. Choose from numerous combinations of noodles, flavors, and ingredients, including the most expensive Ramen noodles you will ever eat (£6.50). Lunch specials £6.50-8. Sushi £3-4. Open Tu-W 11:30am-6pm, Th-F 11:30am-3:30pm and 6:30-10pm, Sa 11:30am-4pm and 6:30-10pm, Su noon-4pm. MC/V. ❷

🔄 🔖 SIGHTS AND BEACHES

▧ROYAL PAVILION. Brighton's Royal Pavilion is a touch of the Far East in the South of England. Much of Brighton's present extravagance can be traced to the construction of the unabashedly gaudy Royal Pavilion. In 1815, George IV enlisted architect John Nash to turn an ordinary farm villa into an ornate fantasy palace, with Taj Mahal-style architecture offset by Chinese interiors. The **Banquet Room** unfolds beneath a 30 ft. chandelier dangling in the claws of a black and gold dragon. Smaller dragons hold lotus lamps that, when lit, give the impression of breathing. In the music room, an exquisitely restored golden dragon-scale ceiling vaults over the prince regent's prize pipe organ. After your tour, find a seat on the balcony of the **Queen Adelaide Tea Room** for tea and scones or relax in the surrounding park. (☎01273 290 900. Open daily Apr.-Sept. 9:30am-5:45pm; Oct.-Mar. 10am-5:15pm. Last entry 45min. before close. Queen Adelaide Tea Room open daily Apr.-Sept. 9:30am-5pm; Oct.-Mar. 10am-4:30pm. Tours daily 11:30am, 2:30pm. £8.80, concessions £6.90. Free audio tour.)

▧DOWN BY THE SEA. Brighton's original attraction is, of course, the beach, but don't expect silky Southern California sand. Here, bikini-clad beachgoers must make do with fist-size rocks. But turquoise waters, beach bums, live bands, and umbrella-adorned drinks still make the seaside a must-visit. A debaucherous

Brighton weekend would not be complete without a visit to the **nude beach,** 20min. east of Brighton Pier, marked by green signs.

PIERS. The bright lights of the **Brighton Pier** give the oceanfront some kitsch and character. Past the slot machines, video games, and candy-colored condom dispensers is a mini amusement park complete with roller coaster, haunted house, and merry-go-round. Give weary legs a rest on **Volk's Railway,** the oldest electric railway in the world, which shuttles along the waterfront from the pier to the marina. *(☎01273 292 718. Open Apr.-Sept. M-F 11am-5pm, Sa-Su 11am-6pm. Round-trip £2.70.)* The **Grand Hotel** has been rebuilt since a 1984 IRA bombing that killed five but left target Margaret Thatcher unscathed. *(King's Rd.)* A walk along the coast past the ruins of **West Pier** leads to the residential community of **Hove.**

BRIGHTON MUSEUM AND ART GALLERY. This gallery holds English and international paintings, pottery, Art Deco, and an extensive Brighton historical exhibit that helpfully explicates the phrase "dirty weekend." The fine **Willett Collection of Pottery** has Neolithic relics and postmodern porcelains. *(Church St., around the corner from the Pavilion. ☎01273 292 882. Open Tu-Su 10am-5pm. Free.)*

LANES AND LAINES. Small fishermen's cottages once thronged the Lanes, an intricate maze of 17th-century streets (some no wider than 3 ft.) south of North St. in the heart of Old Brighton. Replace those cottages with touristy boutiques and chic restaurants and you have the Lanes today. For a less commercialized foray into shopping, head to **North Laines,** off Trafalgar St., where a variety of novelty shops crowd around colorful cafes and impromptu markets.

TOY AND MODEL MUSEUM. This collection of classic model trains, toy soldiers, and dolls is much bigger and older than the crate of Power Rangers in your basement. Reminisce about the days before the DVD player. And the CD player. And the 8-track. Don't miss the toy-soldier reenactments of famous battles on the ground floor. *(☎01273 749 494; www.brightontoymuseum.com. Open Tu-F 10am-5pm, Sa 11am-5pm. Last entry 4pm. £4, concessions £3, families £12.)*

🎵 🎆 ENTERTAINMENT AND FESTIVALS

Pick up the free *Events Guide* and *Theatre Royal Brighton* brochures at the TIC for the latest info on dates and locations. **Brighton Centre,** King's Rd. (☎0870 606 650; www.brightoncentre.co.uk; box office open M-Sa 10am-5:30pm), and **The Dome,** 29 New Rd. (☎01273 709 709; www.brighton-dome.org.uk; box office open 10am-6pm), host Brighton's biggest events, from Chippendales shows to big-name concerts. Local plays and London productions take the stage at the **Theatre Royal** on New Rd., a Victorian beauty with a plush interior. (☎01273 606 650; www.theatreroyalbrighton.co.uk. Tickets £10-25. Open M-Sa 10am6pm, performance days 10am-8pm.) **Komedia,** on Gardner St., houses a cafe with Wi-Fi, bar, comedy club, and cabaret. (☎01273 647 100; www.komedia.co.uk. Tickets £5-12; discounts available. Box office open Tu-Su noon-4pm, performance days noon-9pm.) The **Brighton Festival** (box office ☎01273 709 709), held each May, is one of the largest arts festivals in England, celebrating music, film, and other art forms. The **Brighton Pride Festival,** in late July, is the largest gay pride festival in the UK (☎01273 730 562; www.brightonpride.org).

🔲 NIGHTLIFE

For info on happening nightspots, check *Latest 7* or *The Source*, free at pubs, newsstands, and record stores, or *What's On*, a poster-size flyer also found at record stores and pubs. GLBT-friendly venues can be found in the free monthly issues of *G Scene* and *3Sixty*, available at newsstands; *What's On* also highlights gay-friendly events. Night buses N69, 85, and 98-99 run infrequently but reliably in the early morning, picking up at Old Steine, West St., Clock Tower, North St., the train station, and in front of many clubs, usually hitting each spot twice between 1 and 2:30am (£1-4).

PUBS

JB Priestley once noted that Brighton was "a fine place either to restore your health...or to ruin it again." The waterfront between West Pier and Brighton Pier is a good party spot, and there is a pub or bar on practically every corner of the city center. Many pubs host long happy hours during the week.

🔲 **The Fish Bowl,** 73 East St. (☎01273 777 505). Crowded by hip 20-somethings and students, this laid-back pub is a great spot to meet up with friends. They take their marine theme seriously, with turquoise paint and a beach ball-sized fish bowl on the bar. Pints £2.50-3.50. Pizza (£5) served until 2am. Free Wi-Fi. Open M-Sa 11am-2am, Su noon-late. Kitchen open noon-7pm. MC/V

🔲 **Fortune of War,** 157 King's Rd. Arches (☎01273 205 065), beneath King's Rd. Popular beachfront bar shaped like the hull of a 19th-century ship. Patrons sip their beverage of choice (pints £2.90-3.40) and watch the sun set over the Channel; night owls keep the place packed until it rises again. Free Wi-Fi. Open daily from noon until they feel like closing. AmEx/MC/V.

The Mash Tun, 1 Church St. (☎01273 684 951). Lounging in plush leather sofas and wooden church pews, a laid-back student crowd parties into the wee hours. Good food, graffiti-adorned walls, and music ranging from hip hop to rock to country. Happy hour M-Th and Su 3-9pm; £4 for a "double spirit and splash" (two shots with mixer). For £1, place your bet on which celebrity will die first for a chance to win big quid (no David Attenborough allowed). Open M-Th and Su noon-late, F-Sa noon-later. Kitchen open daily noon-6pm. AmEx/MC/V.

Three and Ten, 10 Steine St. (☎01273 609 777; www.threeandten.co.uk). Polished floor and cold pints. Fills early and stays busy with a mellow crowd of locals and tourists in the know. Cheap beer (£2-3) and mixed drinks (£3). Happy hour M-Sa 4-8pm, Su 4-10pm; all drinks £2.50. Open M-Th and Su 4pm-1am, F-Sa noon-3am. AmEx/MC/V.

Ye Olde King and Queen, Marlborough Pl. (☎01273 607 207). This 1779 farmhouse now has a beer garden and multiple bars. With the TV tuned to sports, the place is packed during football matches. Billiards and foosball tables upstairs. Pints £3. Open M-Th noon-11pm, F-Sa noon-late, Su noon-10:30pm. Kitchen open M-F noon-8pm, Sa-Su noon-6pm. AmEx/MC/V over £10.

CLUBS

The clubbing capital of the south, Brighton is also the hometown of Fatboy Slim and major dance label Skint Records—it's no surprise that Brightonians know their dance music. Most clubs are open Monday through Saturday 10pm-2am; after 2am, the party moves to bonfires and revels on the waterfront.

Revenge, 37 Old Stein St. (☎01273 606 064). Head upstairs for disco balls, dance platforms, and techno beats. GLBT-friendly. Open Tu and Th-Sa 10:30pm-late, W 11pm-late. AmEx/MC/V.

Audio, 10 Marine Parade (☎01273 606 906; www.audiobrighton.com). This nightlife fixture is the place to be in Brighton. Bar upstairs, dancing downstairs. Cover M-Th £3-4, F £5, Sa free. Open M-Th 11pm-2:30am, F-Su 10pm-4am. Bar open M-Th 1pm-2am, F-Sa 1pm-3am, Su 2pm-1am. AmEx/MC/V over £10 on weekdays, over £20 on weekends.

Coalition, 171-181 King's Rd. Arches (☎01273 772 842; www.thebrightoncoalition.co.uk). Restaurant by day and wild club scene by night. Big beats right on the shore. Salsa Tu 8-10pm. Cover £4-8. Open daily 9am-late. Kitchen open noon-10pm. MC/V over £5.

Charles Street, 8-9 Marine Parade (☎01273 624 091). Wild party with DJs and dance tracks. Cover Th £1, F-Sa £1-5. Open M-W noon-1am, Th-Su noon-3am. AmEx/MC/V.

Casablanca Jazz Club, 3 Middle St. (☎01273 321 817). One of the few clubs in Brighton that regularly offers live bands. Jazz, funk, disco, and Latin tunes for a mix of students and 20-somethings. Dance floor, DJ, and bar upstairs. Bands in the basement. Cover Th £2, F-Sa £5-7. MC/V.

Ghetto, 129 St. James's St. (☎01273 622 424; www.ghetto.co.uk). Caters mainly to lesbian clubbers with always entertaining, often risqué theme nights. Swirling disco and pink lights. "Pop Stars" party F. 80s Tropicana Night 3rd Su of the month. Cover £3-6 on weekends. Open M-Th 9pm-2am, F-Su 9pm-late. MC/V over £10.

STRATFORD-UPON-AVON   ☎(0)1789

Shakespeare was born here. This fluke of fate has made Stratford-upon-Avon a major stop on the tourist superhighway. Proprietors tout the dozen-odd properties linked, however remotely, to the Bard and his extended family; shops and restaurants devotedly stencil his prose and poetry on their windows and walls. Beyond the sound and fury of rumbling tour buses and chaotic swarms of daytrippers, there lies a town worth seeing for the beauty of the River Avon and riveting performances in the Royal Shakespeare Theatre.

HENCE, AWAY!

Trains: Station Rd., off Alcester Rd. Office open M-Sa 6am-8:15pm, Su 9am-8pm. Trains (☎08457 484 950) to **Birmingham** (50min., 2 per hr., £6), **London Marylebone** (2¼hr., 2 per hr., £17-45), and **Warwick** (25min., 9 per day, £4.50).

Buses: Depart from **Riverside Coach Park,** off Bridgeway Rd. near the Leisure Centre. National Express (☎08717 818 181; www.nationalexpress.com) to **London** (3-4hr., 4 per day, £16) and **Oxford** (1hr., 1 per day, £8). Stagecoach (☎08456 001 314) to **Birmingham** (1hr., 1 per hr., £3.60), **Chipping Norton** (45min., 3 per day, £4.50), and **Oxford** (1½hr., 3 per day, £6). Stagecoach #1618 services **Coventry** (2hr., every hr., £3.50) via **Warwick** (20-40min., every hr., £3). Buy bus tickets at the TIC.

Taxis: 007 Taxis (☎01789 414 007). **Shakespeare Taxis** (☎01789 266 100).

Bike Rental: Stratford Bike Hire, Guild St. (☎07711 776 340; www.stratfordbikehire. com). Mountain bikes £13 per day, £7 per ½-day. Delivers and picks up bikes within a 6 mi. radius of Stratford-upon-Avon; call in advance.

Boat Rental: Avon Boating, Swan's Nest Ln. (☎01789 267 073; www.avon-boating. co.uk), by Clopton Bridge. Rents rowboats (£4 per hr.) and motorboats (£25 per hr.). 30min. river trips £4, concessions £3. Open daily Apr.-Oct. 9am-dusk.

▐ WHO IS'T THAT CAN INFORM ME?

Tourist Information Centre: Bridgefoot (☎0870 160 7930; www.shakespeare-country. co.uk). Furnishes maps (£0.80-1.20), guidebooks, tickets, and accommodations lists. Books rooms for £4 and a 10% deposit. Open Apr.-Oct. M-Sa 9am-5:30pm, Su 10am4pm; Nov.-Mar. M-Sa 9am-5pm, Su 10am-3:30pm.

Tours: City Sightseeing Bus Tours, Civic Hall, 14 Rother St. (☎01789 412 680; www. citysightseeing-stratford.com), heads to Bard-related houses every 20-30min. from the front of the Pen and Parchment next to the TIC. £11, concessions £9, children £5.50. Office open daily 9am-5pm. **Stratford Town Walk** (☎01789 292 478; www.stratford-townwalk.com) arranges various walking tours throughout the city, including the popular Ghost Walks. All walks depart from Waterside St. opposite Sheep St., near the Royal Shakespeare Theatre. Regular town walk M-W 9am-5pm, Sa 9am-noon; Ghost Walk Th 7:30pm. Advanced booking required for Ghost Walk. £5, children £2, concessions £4.

Banks: Barclays (☎08457 555 555), at the intersection of Henley and Wood St. Open M-F 9am-5pm, Sa 9am-noon. **Thomas Cook,** 37 Wood St. (☎01789 293 582). Open M and W-Sa 9am-5:30pm, Tu 10am-5:30pm.

Library: Central Library, 12 Henley St. (☎01789 292 209). Internet £3 per hr. Open M and W-F 9am-5:30pm, Tu 10am-5:30pm, Sa 9:30am-5pm, Su noon-4pm.

Launderette: 34 Greenhill St. (☎07870 425 043). Open daily 8am-10pm.

Police: Rother St. (☎01789 414 111).

Pharmacy: Boots, 11 Bridge St. (☎01789 292 173). Open M-Sa 8:45am-5:30pm, Su 10:30am-4:30pm.

Hospital: Arden St. (☎01789 205 831), off Alcester Rd.

Internet Access: At **Central Library** (above). **Cyber Junction,** 28 Greenhill St. (☎01789 263 400). £4 per hr. Open M-F 10am-6pm, Sa 10:30am-5:30pm.

Post Office: 2-3 Henley St. (☎08457 223 344). **Bureau de change.** Open M and W-Sa 8:30am-6pm, Tu 9:30am-6pm. **Postcode:** CV37 6PU.

▐ TO SLEEP, PERCHANCE TO DREAM

B&Bs are common, but singles are rare. Accommodations in the £25-35 range line **Evesham Place, Evesham Road,** and **Grove Road.** Also try **Shipston Road** across the river, a 15-20min. walk from the station.

▧ **Carlton Guest House,** 22 Evesham Pl. (☎01789 293 548). Spacious rooms and spectacular service. Singles £24-30; doubles £52; triples £60-78. Cash only. ❸

YHA Stratford, Wellesbourne Rd., Alveston (☎01789 297 093; www.stratfordyha.org.uk), a little less than 2 mi. from Clopton Bridge. Follow the B4086 from town center (35min.) or take bus #X18 or 15 from Bridge St. (10min., every hr., £2). Isolated hostel catering mostly to school groups and families. A solid, inexpensive option for longer stays. Full English breakfast included. Laundry. Internet £1 per 15min. Dorms £23-28; doubles from £57; triples from £85. £3 YHA discount. MC/V. ❸

Melita Hotel, 37 Shipston Rd. (☎01789 292 432; www.melitaguesthouse.co.uk). Upscale B&B with gorgeous garden, retreat-like atmosphere, and great breakfast. Guests relax on the patio with less-than-intimidating guard dog Harvey and his accomplice, Daisy. Singles £49-54; doubles £75-89; triples £98; family rooms £120. AmEx/MC/V. ❺

Penshurst Guest House, 34 Evesham Pl. (☎01789 205 259; www.penshurst.net). 4 distinctly decorated rooms. Self-catering kitchen. Ensuite doubles and triples £39; ensuite family rooms £45-52. Prices vary; call ahead. Cash only. ❹

IN THE CAULDRON BOIL AND BAKE

Baguette stores and bakeries are scattered throughout the town center; there's a **Somerfield** supermarket in Town Sq. (☎01789 292 604. Open M-Sa 8am-7pm, Su 10am-4pm.) A traditional town **market** is held every Friday on Rother St. in Market Pl. On the first and third Saturdays of every month, the River Avon's banks welcome a bustling **farmers' market**.

The Oppo, 13 Sheep St. (☎01789 269 980; www.theoppo.co.uk). Low 16th-century-style ceilings and candles. Try the grilled goat cheese and artichoke salad (£9). Open M-Th noon-2pm and 5-9:30pm, F-Sa noon-2pm and 5-10:30pm, Su 5:30-9:30pm. MC/V. ❷

Hussain's, 6A Chapel St. (☎01789 267 506; www.hussainsindiancuisine.co.uk). Stratford's best Indian menu and a favorite of actor Ben Kingsley. Tandoori with homemade spices served in a red dining room. Entrees from £6. 10% discount for takeaway and pre-theater dining. Open daily 12:30-2:30pm and 5pm-midnight. AmEx/MC/V. ❷

Cafe Bar, inside the Courtyard Theatre (☎01789 403 415). Riverside pastries and homemade sandwiches. A perfect spot for a drink during matinee intermission, but be prepared to wait in line. Sandwiches £3.80. Open daily 10:30am-8:30pm. AmEx/MC/V. ❷

Must Go, 21 Windsor St. (☎01789 293 679). It's true; you must. After inspecting the 4 ft. long menu outside, enter the "Eat Out" doorway for takeaway or the "Eat In" door for a meal in surprisingly comfortable quarters. "Meal deals" £5-7. Open daily noon-2pm, Su-Th 5pm-midnight, F-Sa 5pm-12:30am. AmEx/MC/V. ❷

Hathaway Tea Rooms, 19 High St. (☎01789 292 404). Watch tourists scurry to and fro on High St. as you enjoy cream tea and a scone (£5.30) in this 17th-century Jacobean building. Sandwiches (£4.50-6) and decadent homemade pastries also available. Entrees (£6.10-8) are standard British fare with a few surprises (*lasagne verdi*) thrown in. Open daily 8:30am-5:45pm. Cash only. ❷

THE GILDED MONUMENTS

TO BARD...

Stratford's Will-centered sights are best seen before 11am, when the day-trippers arrive, or after 4pm, when the crowds disperse. The five official **Shakespeare properties** are Shakespeare's Birthplace, Mary Arden's House, Nash's House and New Place, Hall's Croft, and Anne Hathaway's Cottage. The only way to get into the **Three In-Town Houses** (the Birthplace, Hall's Croft, and Nash's House and New Place) is to buy a pass for all of them at once (£12, concessions £11, children £7, families £31). Diehards should get the **All Five Houses** ticket (£17/16/10/45).

SHAKESPEARE'S BIRTHPLACE. The only in-town sight directly associated with him includes an exhibit on his father's glove-making business, a peaceful garden, and the requisite walkthrough on the Bard's documented life, including a First Folio and records of his father's illegal refuse dumping. Videos tell his life story in several rooms featuring fragments of his possessions that have been excavated at the site over the years. You might catch some actors having a conversation in iambic pentameter in the courtyard. Join such distinguished pilgrims as Charles Dickens in signing the guestbook. (Henley St. ☎01789 201 806. Open in summer M-Sa 9am-5pm, Su 9:30am-5pm; in fall and spring daily 10am-5pm; in winter M-Sa 10am-4pm, Su 10:30am-4pm.)

SHAKESPEARE'S GRAVE. The least crowded and most authentic way to pay homage to the Bard is to visit his grave inside the quiet **Holy Trinity Church**— although here, too, groups pack the arched door at peak hours. Rumor has it that Shakespeare was buried 17 ft. underground by request, so that he would sleep undisturbed. To the left is a large bust of Shakespeare and his birth and death records. The church also harbors the graves of wife Anne and daughter Susanna. *(Trinity St. ☎01789 290 128; www.shakespearechurch.org.uk. Entrance to church free; grave £1.50, students and children 50p. Open daily 8:30am-6pm, except during Su services at 8, 10:30am, and 6pm.)*

NASH'S HOUSE AND NEW PLACE. Tourists flock to the home of Shakespeare's last descendent, his granddaughter Elizabeth's first husband. Nash's House has been restored to its Elizabethan grandeur and holds temporary exhibits on the Bard, but most want to see New Place, Shakespeare's retirement home and, at the time, Stratford's finest house. Today, only the foundations and a garden remain due to a disgruntled 19th-century owner named Gastrell who razed the building and cut down Shakespeare's mulberry tree in order to spite Bard tourists. Gastrell was run out of town, and to this day Gastrells are not allowed in Stratford. *(Chapel St. ☎01789 292 325. Open daily Apr-Oct 10am-5pm, Nov-Mar 11am-4pm.*

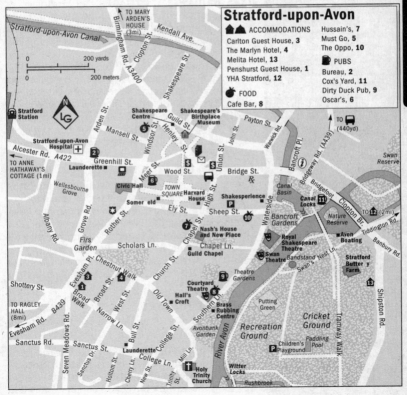

Stratford-upon-Avon

ACCOMMODATIONS
Carlton Guest House, **3**
The Marlyn Hotel, **4**
Melita Hotel, **13**
Penshurst Guest House, **1**
YHA Stratford, **12**

FOOD
Cafe Bar, **8**

Hussain's, **7**
Must Go, **5**
The Oppo, **10**

PUBS
Bureau, **2**
Cox's Yard, **11**
Dirty Duck Pub, **9**
Oscar's, **6**

SHAKESPEAREAN DISSES

In Stratford-upon-Avon, you can see where Shakespeare is buried, walk through the house where he grew up, and sit on a bench where he kissed his sweetheart. But what no tour guide will tell you is how Will slung out insults. Any of the following might come in handy, in Stratford and beyond:

1. Wipe thy ugly face, thou logger-headed toad-spotted barnacle! I'm sorry, you're just not that attractive.

2. Bathe thyself, thou rank reeling-ripe boar-pig! One way to tell that guy in your hostel that he could use a shower.

3. Thou puny milk-livered measel! You're a coward!

4. Thou dost intrude, thou infectious fat-kidneyed woldwarp! Sometimes, you just need some personal space.

5. Thou vain idle-headed strumpet! You spend too much time in front of that mirror.

6. Clean thine ears, thou lumpish boil-brained lout! What? You didn't hear me the first time?

7. Thy breath stinks with eating toasted cheese. Your breath is offensive. Brush your teeth.

8. Remove thine ass hence, thou beslubbering beetle-headed clotpole! For that drunkard in the club who just won't leave you alone.

9. Thou droning boil-brained harpy! To let your tour guide know that you're not that interested.

10. I'll see thee hang'd, thou villainous ill-breeding ratsbane! Only to be used when you're truly furious.

£3.80, concessions £3, children £1.80.) Down Chapel St. from Nash's House, the hedges and abundant flowers of the **Great Garden of New Place** offer a respite from the mobbed streets and hold a mulberry tree said to be grown from the one Gastrell chopped down. *(Open daily 10am-3:45pm. Free.)*

MARY ARDEN'S HOUSE. This farmhouse in Wilmcote, a village 3 mi. from Stratford, was only recently determined to be the childhood home of Mary Arden (Shakespeare's mother). Historians thought she grew up in the stately building next door. She didn't. Cattle roam the farm, and a display recounts how Mary fell in love with the elder Shakespeare. *(Connected by footpath to Anne Hathaway's Cottage, or take the train from Stratford 1 stop north. ☎ 01789 293 455. Open daily in summer 9:30am-5pm; in fall and spring 10am-5pm; in winter 10am4pm. £8, concessions £7, children £5, families £21.)*

ANNE HATHAWAY'S COTTAGE. The birthplace of Shakespeare's wife, about a mile away in Shottery, is a thatched-roof cottage out of a fairy tale. It boasts original Hathaway furniture (including William's "courting chair" near her bed) and a hedge maze. Entrance entitles you to sit on a bench Will may or may not also have sat on. *(Take the hop-on, hop-off Guide Friday tour bus or head west out of town on Alcester Rd. and look for the sign on the left to the cottage. ☎ 01789 292 100. Open in summer M-Sa 9am-5pm, Su 9am-5pm; in fall and spring M-Sa 9:30am-5pm, Su 10am-5pm; in winter daily 10am-4pm. £6.50, concessions £5.50, children £3.50, families £16.)*

SHAKESPEARIENCE. A Shakespearean extravaganza, if you will, and the most unique exhibit in town. A two-act show starting with a visual tour of Shakespeare's life and times and featuring a holographic summary of his most famous works. The blasting winds and surround sound may seem a bit over the top, but it's definitely a fun way to chill with Will. *(Waterside, across from the Bancroft gardens and carousel. ☎ 01789 290 111. Shows daily every hr. 10am-5pm. £8, children £7.)*

...OR NOT TO BARD

Believe it or not, non-Shakespearean sights do exist in Stratford.

STRATFORD BUTTERFLY FARM. Europe's largest collection of butterflies flutters through tropical surroundings. Less beautiful creepy-crawlies—like the salmon pink bird-eating spider—dwell in glass boxes nearby. *(Off Swan's Nest Ln. at Tramway Walk, across the river from the TIC.* ☎ *01789 299 288; www.butterflyfarm.co.uk. Open daily in summer 10am-6pm; in winter 10am-dusk. £5.80, concessions £5.30, children £4.80, families £17.)*

RAGLEY HALL. Eight miles from Stratford on Evesham Rd. (A435), Ragley Hall houses the earl and countess of Yarmouth. Set in a stunning 400-acre park, the estate has an art collection and a sculpture park. *(Bus #246 (M-Sa 5 per day) runs to Alcester Police Station. Walk 1 mi. to the gates, then ½ mi. up the drive.* ☎ *01789 762 090; www. ragleyhall.com. Park open Mar.-Nov. Sa-Su and holidays 10am-6pm. House and state rooms open from mid-July. to Nov. M-F and Su noon-4pm. £8.50, concessions £7, children £5, families £27.)*

🎵 ALL THE WORLD'S A STAGE

One of the world's most acclaimed repertories, the **Royal Shakespeare Company (RSC)** sells well over one million tickets each year. The **Royal Shakespeare Theatre** is currently undergoing a £100 million renovation and will re-open in 2010 with a 1000-seat thrust stage, bringing the whole audience within 50 ft. of the action. The construction has also closed the **Swan Theatre,** the RSC's more intimate neighbor, until 2010. The company continues to perform shows down the road at **The Courtyard Theatre.** Visitors can get backstage tours and a glimpse at the high-tech stage to be installed at the Royal Shakespeare Theatre. The box office in the Courtyard Theatre handles the ticketing for all theaters. (Ticket hotline ☎0844 800 1110; www.rsc.org.uk. Tickets £10-48, concessions £5. Standing room £5. Standby tickets in summer £15, in winter £12. Open M-Sa 9:30am-8pm. AmEx/MC/V.)

🌿 OUR RUSTIC REVELRY

Stratford's biggest festival begins on the weekend nearest April 23, **Shakespeare's birthday.** On Saturday there's a parade through town from his birthplace to his tomb, followed by a marathon race on Sunday. The modern, well-respected Shakespeare Birthplace Trust, Henley St., hosts a **Poetry Festival** every Sunday evening in July and August. It features poetry readings, book signings, and lectures on topics like "Shakespeare's Sonnets and Sex." Past participants include poet bigwigs Seamus Heaney, Ted Hughes, and Derek Walcott. (☎01789 292 176. Tickets £7-15.)

OXFORD

For nearly a millennium, the University of Oxford has been churning out talent, including 47 Nobel Prize winners, 25 British prime ministers, 86 Archbishops of Canterbury, 12 saints, six kings, and Hugh Grant. Its 38 colleges are home to impossibly intricate church ceilings, serene quads, and paintings that are older than many countries. But don't forget to come down from the ivory tower and explore the city of Oxford—a surprisingly modern metropolis of 150,000, where scaffolding creeps up ancient spires and even 11th-century buildings have been retrofitted with Wi-Fi. Those who avoid the crowds choking Cornmarket St. and explore the city's cobbled alleyways will be rewarded with historic bookshops, picturesque riverbanks, and, of course, legendary pubs inviting you to sample their brews.

LIFE AND TIMES

HISTORY

TIMES OF TUMULT: EARLY OXFORD. Known to its first Saxon occupants as Oxenaforda (which means "Ford of the Ox"), the town of Oxford was formally founded in the AD ninth century by the Saxon king **Alfred the Great.** A couple of invasions later, the oldest university in the English-speaking world opened its doors in 1167. From the beginning, tensions ran high between the students and the townspeople. Riots, student hangings, and the like were frequent and culminated in the 1355 **Saint Scholastica Day Riot,** during which as many as 93 individuals, students and townsfolk alike, were killed.

OXFORD: A SCHOOL FOR KIDS WHO WANT TO LEARN HOW TO READ GOOD. The introduction of the **printing press** in 1476 by William Caxton strengthened the university movement, which, thankfully, eased the strain of town and gown relations. In 1542, the crown granted Oxford an official charter. In 1547, the crown *really* outdid itself, giving Oxford its very own diocese. Oxford's economy slowly began to switch from industries like textile and leather manufacturing toward those that catered to students, such as clothing and beer manufacturing.

In 1646, Charles I sought refuge in Oxford after his deposition and exile from London during the **English Civil War.** The **Siege of Oxford** ended Oxford's stint as a prominent stronghold, but the onset of the **Great Plague** sent another King Charles—this time Charles II—running from London to the university town. The following centuries would be marked by expansion, as Oxford built connections with neighboring cities like Coventry and London.

The 19th and early 20th centuries witnessed several groundbreaking historical moments. The **University Act** of 1854 allowed those who weren't members of the Church of England to study at the University. In 1902, diamond baron and Anglo-Saxon supremacist Cecil Rhodes endowed the Rhodes Scholarship. Oxford went co-ed in 1884. Perhaps most importantly, the **Oxford Union Society,** current World Debating Champions, was founded in 1823.

OXFORD UNIVERSITY AND THE ORDER OF THE PHOENIX. Oxford experienced a burst of national prominence following William Morris's founding of the **Morris Motor**

Company. Morris's factory, in the Cowley neighborhood of southeast Oxford, divided the city into its western university neighborhood and its eastern car town.

The city managed to escape major damage during WWII. It went on to develop a substantial biotechnology industry. Recent attempts at the city's economic and social revival have resulted in the **"Transform Oxford"** plan, which kicked off with major construction projects near Westgate in 2004. Under Lord Mayor Susanna Pressel, the city of Oxford continues to build its economy, but the university remains its major attraction.

CULTURE AND THE ARTS

LITERATURE

OXONIAN POETIC PROLIFERATION. Eleven of Britain's poet laureates studied at Oxford. **John Donne** made a name for himself as a metaphysical poet; his works include "The Sunne Rising" and "The Flea." **Richard Lovelace,** who came to prominence shortly after Donne's death, began writing during his time at Oxford and continued Donne's tradition with politically informed metaphysical poetry, such as 1642's "To Althea, From Prison," which he wrote from inside a cell. **Percy Bysshe Shelley,** one of the major poets of the English Romantic tradition, carried the torch with poems like "Ozymandias" (1818).

T.S. Eliot, who spent his graduate years at Oxford, was the proverbial big man on campus in the early 20th century, garnering the 1948 Nobel Prize for *The Love Song of J. Alfred Prufrock, The Wasteland,* and existential plays like *Murder in the Cathedral.* Though an American by birth, Eliot would end his life as a British citizen. Eliot's contemporary and fellow Oxonian **W.H. Auden,** whose poetic style fluctuated wildly between the adapted Eliot-like style seen in 1928's *Poems* and more traditional British fare, did T.S. one better by ending his life as an American citizen.

OXFORD: FOUNDRY OF THE FANTASTICAL. In the mid-19th century, writer **Lewis Carroll** abandoned his track toward priesthood and instead captured the imagination of children, defining a whimsical genre known to some as "literary nonsense" with such classics as "The Jabberwocky" and *Alice's Adventures in Wonderland.* The Irish wit **Oscar Wilde,** Carroll's contemporary, defined a genre of a different sort of whimsy through dense, decadent writing in plays such as 1895's *The Importance of Being Earnest.* Wilde's trial on charges of "gross indecency" landed him in jail, where, separated from his lover Alfred Douglas, he wrote one of his most moving works, the long letter "De Profundis."

The modern political novel gained equal traction thanks to several Oxonians: **Harper Lee** wrote the classic commentary on the American south, *To Kill A Mockingbird;* **Aldous Huxley** wrote *Brave New World,* a critique of uniformity and mechanization; and **Joseph Heller** penned a 1961 depiction of the social question of bureaucracy with *Catch-22.* The modern children's book was equally influenced by Theodor Geisel, a noted Oxford alum more commonly known as **Dr. Seuss,** who, in 1954's *The Cat in the Hat,* followed orders from his publisher to produce a rhyming children's book using fewer than 250 words to help solve American literacy. Fantasy literature was equally revolutionized by Oxonians: **J.R.R. Tolkien, Richard Adams, Phillip Pullman,** and **C.S. Lewis** all studied at Oxford.

THEATER AND FILM

Oxford, while primarily an institution of learning, also has bred its fair share of comedic and dramatic screen actors. **Rowan Atkinson,** of *Blackadder* and *Mr. Bean* fame, was one of several famous British comics to come out of Oxford. Others include **Terry Jones** (a member of the famed comedy troupe *Monty Python*) and **Hugh Grant**.

As for the theater, notable drop-out **Andrew Lloyd Webber** has composed 13 musicals, including *Jesus Christ Superstar*, *Evita*, and *Cats* (based on fellow Oxonian T.S. Eliot's short *Old Possum's Book*.

▣ TRANSPORTATION

Trains: Station on Botley Rd., down Park End. Ticket office open M-F 5:45am-8pm, Sa 7:30am-8pm, Su 7:15am-8pm. Trains (☎08457 000 125) to: **Birmingham** (1hr., 2 per hr., £23); **Glasgow** (5-7hr., every hr., £93); **London Paddington** (1hr., 2-4 per hr., £19-24); **Manchester** (3hr., 2 per hr., £57).

Buses: Station on Gloucester Green. Stagecoach (☎01865 772 250; www.stagecoachbus.com; ticket office open M-F 9am-5pm, Sa 9:30am-1pm) runs to **Cambridge** (3hr., every hr., £9) and operates the Oxford Tube (☎01865 772 250) to **London** (1hr.; 3-4 per hr.; £13, students £9). National Express (☎08717 818 181; www.nationalexpress.com; ticket office open M-Th 8:30am-5:45pm, F-Sa 8:30am-6pm, Su 9am-4:30pm) runs to **Bath** (2hr., 5 per day, £11); **Birmingham** (2hr., 5 per day, £12.20); **Bristol** (3hr., 2 per hr., £14); **Stratford-upon-Avon** (2hr., 1 per day, £15). The Oxford Bus Company (☎01865 785 400; www.oxfordbus. co.uk; ticket office in Debenhams Department store, at the corner of George St. and Magdalen St., open M-W 9:30am-6pm, Th 9am-8pm, F-Sa 9am-7pm) runs to **London** (1hr.; 3-5 per hr.; £13, students £9), **Gatwick** (2hr.; every hr. 8am-9pm; £22, concessions £11), and **Heathrow** (1hr.; 3 per hr.; £18, concessions £9).

Public Transportation: The Oxford Bus Company Cityline (☎01865 785 400) and Stagecoach Oxford (☎01865 772 250) offer frequent service to: **Abingdon Road** (Stagecoach #32, 33, Oxford Bus X3); **Banbury Road** (Stagecoach #2, 2A, 2B, 2D); **Cowley Road** (Stagecoach #1, 5A, 5B, 10, Oxford Bus #5); **Iffley Road** (Stagecoach #3, Oxford Bus #4, 4A, 4B, 4C). Fares are low (£0.60-£1.40). Stagecoach offers a **DayRider ticket** (£3.50 day, £15-23 week) and the Oxford Bus Company a **Freedom ticket** (£3.30 day, £17 week), which give unlimited travel on the respective company's local routes. A **Plus Pass** grants unlimited travel on all Oxford Bus Company and Stagecoach buses and can be purchased on board (☎01865 785 410; £6 per day, £19 per week).

Taxis: Radio Taxis (☎01865 242 424). **ABC** (☎01865 770 077). Both 24hr.

Boat Rental: Magdalen Bridge Boat House, Magdalen Bridge (☎01865 202 643; www.oxfordpunting.co.uk). Rents punts and rowboats (£14 per hr.) or chauffered punts (£20 per 30min.). Open daily 9:30am-9pm or dusk (whichever comes first).

◪ ORIENTATION

Oxford's colleges stand around **Saint Mary's Church,** which is the spiritual heart of both the university and the greater city. The city's center is bounded by **George Street** and connecting **Broad Street** to the north and **Cornmarket** and **High Street** in the center. Directly south of the city center, the wide open spaces of **Christ Church Meadow** are surrounded by a horseshoe-shaped bend in the Thames. To the northwest, the district of **Jericho** is less touristed and is the unofficial hub of student life. Across Magdalen bridge, the corridor surrounding **Cowley Road** is a vibrant and diverse residential area that feels like its own city. **Banbury** to the north and **Abingdon** to the south are quieter, quainter towns surrounded by gorgeous countryside.

○ COLLEGES

All Souls College, T
Balliol College, H
Brasenose College, S
Christ Church, Z
Corpus Christi College, AA
Exeter College, O
Hertford College, P
Jesus College, N
Keble College, B
Lincoln College, R
Magdalen College, X
Harris Manchester College, K
Mansfield College, F
Merton College, BB

New College, Q
Nuffield College, L
Oriel College, V
Pembroke College, Y
Queen's College, U
Regent's Park College, C
Somerville College, A
St. Cross College, D
St. Hilda's College, CC
St. John's College, E
St. Peter's College, M
Trinity College, I
University College, W
Wadham College, J
Worcester College, G

OXFORD

Oxford

⚑ ACCOMMODATIONS
Oxford Backpackers Hostel, 3
YHA Oxford, 2

● FOOD
Pierre Victoire Bistrot, 1

Magdalene Bridge Boat Company
Magdalen Bridge
Pedestrian Bridges

Magdalen Grove Deer Park

Botanic Gardens

Rose Ln.

Longwall St.

Merton Field

Dead Man's Walk

Mansfield Rd.

Savile Rd.

University Museum of Natural History and Pitt-Rivers Museum

Rhodes House

South Parks Rd.

Parks Rd.

Museum Rd.

Holywell Music Rooms

Bath Pl.

Holywell St.

New College Ln.

Queens Ln.

St. Edmund Hall

High St. ("The High")

Merton St.

Christ Church Picture Gallery

Christ Church Chapel

Blackhall Rd.

Blackwell's

Sheldonian Theatre

Catte St.

St. Mary's Passage

St. Mary's

Radcliffe Camera

Bodleian Library

Brasenose Ln.

Oriel St.

Magpie Ln.

King Edward St.

Bear Ln.

Picklefast Quad

Tom Quad

Broad St.

Museum of the History of Science

Turl St.

Ship St.

Market St.

Alfred St.

Blue Boat St.

Painted Room

Town Hall

Museum of Oxford

Cornmarket St.

Carfax Tower

Queen St.

Marks and Spencer

Museum of Modern Art

Pembroke St.

Brewer St.

TO ABINGDON, READING, LONDON, M4

St. Giles

Martyr's Memorial

Magdalen St.

Ashmolean Museum

Beaumont St.

Oxford Playhouse

Friars' Entry

Victoria Ct.

Apollo Theatre

St. Michael's St.

Oxford Union

New Inn Hall

St. Ebbe's St.

Sainsbury's

Westgate Shopping Centre

Old Greyfriars

Castle St.

Norfolk St.

Paradise St.

Paradise Sq.

Banbury Rd.

Woodstock Rd.

Pusey St.

Alfred Ln.

St. John St.

Gloucester St.

Gloucester Green

STA Travel

George St.

New Rd.

Remains of Oxford Castle

Quaking Bridge

Worcester St.

Chain Alley

Oxford University Press

Walton St.

Wellington Pl.

Walton St.

Richmond Rd.

Worcester Pl.

Nelson St.

JobCentre

Hythe Bridge St.

Park End St.

St. Thomas St.

Osney Ln.

Oxpens Rd.

Hart St.

Albert St.

Canal St.

Cardigan St.

Victor St.

Great Clarendon St.

Wellington St.

St. Barn'.

Hollybush Row

Becket St.

Railway Station

Bletley Rd.

Oxford Canal

Castle Mill Stream

200 meters
200 yards

⚡ PRACTICAL INFORMATION

Tourist Information Centre: 15-16 Broad St. (☎01865 252 200; www.visitoxford.org). The busy staff books rooms for £4 plus a 10% deposit. Distributes free black-and-white maps (nicer colored maps £1.30), restaurant lists, accommodation lists, and monthly *In Oxford* guides. Job listings, long-term accommodations listings, and entertainment news posted daily at the TIC and at www.dailyinfo.co.uk. Open M-Sa 9:30am-5pm.

Tours: The 2hr. official Oxford University and city **walking tour** (☎01865 252 200) leaves from the TIC and provides access to some colleges otherwise closed to visitors. Tours only allow up to 19 people and are booked on a first-come, first-served basis, so get tickets early in the day. Daily in summer 10:30, 11am, 1, 2pm; in winter 11am, 2pm. £7, children £3.50. **Blackwell's** (☎01865 333 606) walking tours leave from Canterbury Gate at Christ Church. Literary tour of Oxford Tu 2pm, Th 11am; "Inklings" tours about CS Lewis, JRR Tolkien, and their circle of friends W 11:45am; Town and Gown Tour about the relationship between the university and the city F 2pm. All tours 1hr. £7, concessions £6.50. **Guided Tours** (☎07810 402 757), 1hr., depart from outside Trinity College on Broad St. and offer access to some colleges and other university buildings. Daily noon, 2, 4pm. £7, children £3. Evening 1hr. Ghost Tours in summer F-Sa 7:45pm. £5, children £3. **City Sightseeing** (☎01865 790 522; www.citysightseeingoxford.com) offers hop-on, hop-off bus tours of the city with 20 stops. Every 10-15min. from bay 14 of the bus station. Pick up tickets from bus drivers or stands around the city. £12, concessions £9.50, children £6, families £31.

Banks: Lining Cornmarket St. The **TIC** (p. 230) has a commission-free **bureau de change,** as does **Marks & Spencer,** 13-18 Queen St. (☎01865 248 075). Open M-W and F-Sa 8am-7pm, Th 8am-8pm, Su 10:30am-5pm.

Beyond Tourism: JobCentre Plus, 7 Worcester St. (☎01865 445 000). Open M-Tu and Th-F 9am-5pm, W 10am-5pm.

Library: Oxford Central Library, Queen St. (☎01865 815 549), near Westgate Shopping Centre. Free Internet. Open M-Th and Su 9am-7pm, F-Sa 9am-5:30pm.

Launderette: 127 Cowley Rd. (☎01865 778 847). Open daily 8am-10pm.

Police: St. Aldates and Speedwell St. (☎01865 505 505).

Pharmacy: Boots, Cornmarket St. (☎01865 247 461). Open M-W and F-Sa 8:30am-6pm, Th 8:30am-7pm, Su 11am-5pm.

Hospital: John Radcliffe Hospital, Headley Way (☎01865 741 166). Take bus #13.

Internet Access: Free at the **Oxford Central Library** (above). **Links Communications,** 33 High St. (☎01865 204 207). £1 per 45min. Open M-Sa 10am-8:30pm, Su 11am-8:30pm.

Post Office: 102-104 St. Aldates (☎08457 223 344). **Bureau de change.** Open M and W-Sa 9am-5:30pm, Tu 9:30am-5:30pm. **Postcode:** OX1 1ZZ.

🏠 🏕 ACCOMMODATIONS AND CAMPING

Book at least a week ahead from June to September, especially for singles. B&Bs (from £30) line the main roads out of town. Try www.stayoxford.com for affordable options. The 300s on **Banbury Road** are accessible by buses #2, 2A, 2B, and 2D. Cheaper B&Bs lie in the 200s and 300s on **Iffley Road** (bus #4, 4A, 4B, or 4C to Rose Hill) and on **Abingdon Road** in South Oxford (bus #X13). If it's late and you can't find a room, call the **Oxford Association of Hotels and Guest Houses** (East Oxford ☎01865 721 561, West Oxford 01865 862 138, North Oxford 01865 244 691, South Oxford 01865 244 268).

Central Backpackers, 13 Park End St. (☎01865 242 288; www.centralbackpackers.co.uk), a short walk from the train station. Spacious rooms and clean bathrooms. Have a few drinks on the rooftop terrace—where guests frequently barbecue in the summer time. Light sleepers beware: booming bass from nearby clubs may keep you awake on weekends (but shouldn't you be out partying anyway?). Kitchen available. Female-only dorms available. Continental breakfast included. Free luggage storage and lockers. Laundry £3.50. Free internet and Wi-Fi. 12-bed dorms £16; 8-bed £17; 6-bed £18; 4-bed £19. MC/V. ❶

Oxford Backpackers Hostel, 9A Hythe Bridge St. (☎01865 721 761; www.hostels.co.uk), halfway between the bus and train stations. A self-proclaimed "funky hostel" with murals and music playing in the hallway. The bathrooms may be a little dirty, and the chairs in the common area may be losing their stuffing, but after a few drinks from the inexpensive bar, who's going to notice? Self-catering kitchen. Female-only dorm available. Continental breakfast included. Luggage storage £2. Laundry £2.50. Internet £1 per 30min. 8-bed dorms £15-16; 4-bed £17-19. MC/V. ❶

Nanford Guest House, 137 Iffley Rd. (☎01865 244 743; www.nanfordguesthouse.com). Cross the Magdalen Bridge and bear right at the roundabout onto Iffley Rd., or take bus #4, 4A, 4B, or 4C to James St. This B&B is less quaint English countryside inn and more American roadside motel. The prices are below average, but the rooms are indistinguishable from the competition. Rooms have TVs and private baths. Free Wi-Fi and parking. Singles £30; doubles £40; quads £80. AmEx/MC/V. ❸

YHA Oxford, 2A Botley Rd. (☎01865 727 275). From the train station, turn right onto Botley Rd. Photos of famous Oxfordians line the walls. The quietest and most spacious of Oxford's 3 hostels. TV room, pool room, library, and ensuite bathrooms. Kitchen available. Full English breakfast included. Lockers £1. Towels £0.50. Laundry £3. 1hr. Wi-Fi free with purchase from the coffee shop. Wheelchair-accessible. Reception 24hr. Single-sex 6-bed dorms £19-30; doubles £43-63. £3 YHA discount. MC/V. ❷

Oxford Camping and Caravanning, 426 Abingdon Rd. (☎01865 244 088), about 1 mi. from the city center behind Go Outdoors camping store. Walk down St. Aldates to Abingdon Rd. or take bus 35, 35A, or 35B. Wi-Fi £4 per hr. or £7 per day. Reception 9-10:30am and 4-5:30pm. £8-17 per person and £6.50 per unit. Electricity £3.13. MC/V. ❶

The Isis, 45-53 Iffley Rd. (☎01865 248 894), just down the road from Nanford Guest House. Open July-Sept; used to house students in June as they prepare for exams. Clean, well-lit rooms with TV. Breakfast included. Singles £35, ensuite £42; doubles £70/76. MC/V. ❹

Westgate Hotel, 1 Botley Rd. (☎01865 726 721). From the train station, turn right on Botley Rd. An old-fashioned inn full of Oxford history. Cozy rooms with TVs and coffee makers. Features a restaurant (dinner from £6.50), bar, and pleasant outdoor patio. Breakfast included. Singles £44, ensuite £54; ensuite doubles £76. Cheaper rooms with shared bathrooms available in the "Annexe" across the street. AmEx/MC/V. ❹

Sportsview Guest House, 106-110 Abingdon Rd. (☎01865 244 268; www.sportsviewguesthouse.co.uk). Walk down St. Aldates to Abingdon Rd. or take bus #X13. Quaint B&B in row houses across the street from the Queen's College sporting grounds. Rooms are on the small side, but you can sit in the beautifully decorated lounge if you're feeling claustrophobic. Internet available. Free parking. Singles £42-50, ensuite £52-60; ensuite doubles £74-80. MC/V with 2% surcharge. ❺

Heather House, 192 Iffley Rd. (☎01865 249 757; www.heatherhouseoxford.com). A 10min. walk from Magdalen Bridge, or take the bus marked Rose Hill from the bus or train station or from Carfax Tower. Spotless ensuite rooms complete with small flatscreen TVs. Soft carpet, floral color scheme. Wi-Fi. Singles £37-47; doubles £67-80; triples £81-105; family rooms £96-120. MC/V. ❺

FOOD

Gloucester Green Market, behind the bus station, is full of tasty treats, fresh fruit, and assorted junk (Open W 9am-5pm). The **Covered Market** has produce and deli goods. Enter on High St. between Cornmarket St. and Turl St. (open M-Sa 8:30am-5:30pm, Su 10am-4pm). Across Magdalen Bridge, you'll find cheap restaurants on **Cowley Road** that serve international food in addition to fish and chips. For a meal on the go, try a sandwich from a **kebab van,** usually found on Broad St., High St., Queen St., or St. Aldates.

Chiang Mai Kitchen, Kemp Hall Passage (☎01865 202 233), hidden in an alley to the right of the Starbucks at 127 High St. Tasty Thai cuisine at unbeatable prices. Enjoy the fresh herbs and spices (flown in weekly from Bangkok) while soaking up the peaceful decor. Play it safe with pad thai (£9) or get exotic with jungle curry with wild venison (£9.50). Special vegetarian menu. Open M-Sa noon-2:30pm and 6-10:30pm, Su noon-2:30pm and 6-10pm. AmEx/MC/V. ❷

Edamame, 15 Holywell St. (☎08165 246 916; www.edamame.co.uk). This hip Japanese spot is popular with students and 20-somethings. Get there early on sushi night (Th 5:30-8pm) to avoid the line. Plenty of vegetarian options. Tongue-twisting entrees like *ikanoshogayaki* (stir-fried squid) for £6-7. Sushi £3-8. Wash it down with sake (£3). Open for lunch W-Sa 11:30am-2:30pm, sushi Th 5-8:30pm, dinner F-Sat 5-8:30pm. Cash only at lunch, MC/V over £10 in evenings. ❷

Frevd, 119 Walton St. (☎01865 311 171; www.freud.eu). Beneath the vaulted ceiling of a 19th-century church sits the club-bar-cafe-art gallery known to locals as Freud. Live music and dancing at night, but you can still get a gourmet pizza (£5-8.50) or a mixed drink (£5) during the day. Check website for live music schedule. Open M-Th 10:30am-midnight, F-Sa 10:30pm-2am, Su 10am-midnight. MC/V. ❷

The Alternative Tuck Shop, 24 Holywell St. (☎01865 792 054). Behind an unassuming veneer lies Oxford's most popular sandwich shop. Students and residents alike line up for a variety of delicious made-to-order sandwiches (under £3.50) and panini (£3), along with a sinful assortment of baked goods. Excellent ciabatta sandwiches with warm fillings. Open M-Sa 8:15am-6pm. Cash only. ❶

Kazbar, 25-27 Cowley Rd. (☎01865 202 920). Spanish-style decor, burning incense, and Moorish cushions, all accentuated by sexy lighting. Tasty tapas (£3.10-4.60) like *patatas con chorizo.* Free tapas with drink M-F 4-7pm, Sa-Su noon-4pm. Open M-Th 4pm-midnight, F 4pm-12:30am, Sa noon-12:30am, Su noon-midnight. AmEx/MC/V. ❷

G&D's Cafe, 55 Little Clarendon St. (☎01865 516 652). Superb homemade ice cream (£2), pizza bagels (£3.60-4.25), and a boisterous student atmosphere. Founded by an Oxford student in the early 90s, G&D's ice cream is affectionately known as "Oxford's Own." Tu "cow night": bring something with a cow on it (or a real one) and get 20% off (4-7pm). Open daily 8am-midnight. Branches at 94 St. Aldates (☎01865 245 952) and 104 Cowley Rd. (☎01865 727 111). Cash only. ❶

The Nosebag, 6-8 St. Michael's St. (☎01865 721 033). Cafeteria-style service on the 2nd fl. of a 15th-century stone building. Eclectic menu includes great vegan and vegetarian dishes for under £9. Don't miss homemade soups (£4.20). Indulge in a scrumptious dessert such as chocolate fudge cake (£3.20). Open Tu-Th 9:30am-9:30pm, F-Sa 9:30am-10pm, Su 9:30am-8:30pm. AmEx/MC/V. ❷

Vaults & Garden, Radcliffe Sq. (☎01865 279 112; www.university-church.ox.ac.uk/ info/vaults.htm), inside St. Mary's Church. Follow your nose to delectable homemade soups and organic entrees (£2-6). Cozy booths in the vaults and outdoor tables in the garden overlooking the iconic Radcliffe Camera. Open daily 9am-6pm. Cash only. ❷

Queen's Lane Coffee House, 40 High St. (☎01865 240 082). Opened in 1654, Oxford's oldest coffee house and quite possibly the oldest in the UK. You can still get a good cup of coffee here as well as a delicious sandwich (£2.30-5.30) and dessert (£1.50-3.80). Discounts for takeaway. Open M-Sa 7:30am-8pm, Su 9am-8pm. MC/V. ❶

Kebab Kid, Gloucester Green. (☎01865 200 121; www.kebabkid.com), adjacent to the bus station. A cultural crossroads of tasty meat dishes, including doner burgers, kebabs, curry, American-style fried chicken, and other greasy indulgences. Nourishes tired clubbers and stays open later than just about any place in Oxford. Value meals with fries and drink £3.40-7.50. 10% student discount. Open M-Th and Su 11am-3am, F-Sa 11am-5am. Another location at 146 Cowley Rd. Cash only. ❷

Rainbow, 19 Magdalen St. (☎01865 250 656). Escape the heat and hustle of the city center with a scoop of ice cream (£2-4). The eclectic menu also features panini sandwiches (£3), milkshakes (£2.20), and Cornish pasties with a variety of fillings, including spicy chicken or cheese and bacon (£2.80). Open M-Th 9am-11pm, F-Sa 9am-11:30pm, Su 9am-10pm. Cash only. ❶

Posh Fish, 109 Walton St. (☎01865 310 355). Greasy, delicious fish and chips in hearty portions (£5.30). If you're tired of that already, try jacket potatoes with a variety of fillings from *chili con carne* to chicken curry (£1.50-4.50). Doner kebabs (£4) add an international twist. Open M and Su 5-10:30pm, Tu-Th noon-2pm, F noon-2pm and 5pm-midnight, Sa noon-midnight. Cash only. ❶

The Standard Tandoori, 117 Walton (☎01865 553 557). A local favorite. Serves standard Indian dishes like tandoori, madras, and vindaloo alongside chef's specials (£7) like Lamb Passanda. Many dishes are deceptively cheap (£3.70-5.40) because rice costs £1.50 extra. Discounts for takeout. Open daily noon-2:30 and 6-11:30pm. MC/V. ❷

The Salad Bar, 131 Cowley Rd. (☎01865 240 026). A sandwich shop with a Mediterranean twist. Panini and ciabatta sandwiches (£1.70-2.60) with fresh ingredients made to order. Enjoy your food with some hookah (£9.50) on a couch in the open-air smoking lounge in the back. Jacket potatoes and salads £3. Open daily 7am-11pm. Cash only. ❶

Tick Tock Cafe, 3-5 Cowley Rd. (☎01865 200 777). A collection of pop-culture-themed clocks (Shrek, Chicago Bulls, etc.) adorns the walls of this breakfast nook—but bring a watch if you're on a schedule, because they all display different times. Full English

ON THE MENU

LIGHT BEER? GET REAL!

Weight-watching pub-goers may be dismayed to find that in Britain, light beer means beer with less alcohol, not calories. Just about every British brew has a sturdy, full flavor and the nutrition facts to go with it. But some connoisseurs demand a greater degree of authenticity in their beer. In the early seventies, a group of four drinkers decided they were tired of the homogenous, bland, and processed beer that was being churned out by huge distributors. They wanted to get back to the authentic ales produced by local brewers, without artificial carbonation or ingredients. In 1973, the Campaign for Real Ale was born. Today, the organization boasts more than 95,000 members in England and elsewhere.

Cask ale (referred to as "real ale" by enthusiasts) is thicker, darker, and less carbonated than traditional lagers. It has a shorter shelf life than keg beer and must be kept at correct temperatures. It is sometimes served at room temperature and has a variety of complex flavors, some of which come from the wooden casks that hold it.

Any Oxford pub worth its hops will offer several real ales, many from local breweries. Usually there will be a rotating selection. Try a pint of Old Hooky, brewed in North Oxfordshire, for a real Oxford pub experience.

breakfast (£4.50-6) served all day. Bacon and avocado sandwich on ciabatta bread £2.60. Open M-Sa 8am-9pm, Su 8am-6pm. MC/V. ❶

Al-Shami, 25 Walton Crescent (☎01865 310 066; www.al-shami.co.uk). Tucked away in a residential area of Jericho, this place serves up inexpensive and flavorful Lebanese food in an ornate Middle Eastern setting. Start off with a few *mezze* (small dishes similar to tapas; £2.40-3.60). Most meat dishes come on skewers (£6.20-7.40). Vegetarian dishes available. Open daily noon-midnight. Cash only. ❷

Pizza Express, 8A Golden Cross (☎01865 790 442; www.pizzaexpress.com). Across the street from McDonald's on Cornmarket St. This popular pizza chain occupies a recently restored 15th-century building. The original brick walls still stand inside. Innovative pizzas (£6-9.40) include the "devilishly hot" Diavolo. For calorie counters, the *leggera* (Italian for "light") is a spring-themed pizza with a hole in the middle filled with salad. Open M-W and Su 11:30am-11pm, Th-Sa 11:30am-11:30pm. 2nd location in Oxford Castle (☎01865 723 400). AmEx/MC/V. ❷

Jericho Cafe, 112 Walton St. (☎01865 310 840; www.thejerichocafe.co.uk). The calmer and more refined counterpart of the nearby Jericho Tavern. Enjoy homemade soups (£4) or a full breakfast (£7) in the peaceful basement dining room. Several light and vegetarian dishes, along with creative burgers like a lamb, feta, and mint burger served on pita (£8.30). Entrees £7-9. Open M-W 8am-9:30pm, Th-Sa 8am-10pm, Su 9am-8pm. MC/V. ❷

Harveys, 89 Gloucester Green (☎01865 793 963), next to the bus station. This local no-frills deli is the perfect stop after a long and dreary bus ride. Quick and tasty sandwiches at great prices (£2.30-4.20). English breakfast £2.90. Open M-Sa 7am-7pm, Su 8am-5:30pm. Branches at 19 and 58 High St. Cash only. ❶

MARKETS

Sainsbury's, 7 Magdalen St. (☎01865 204 969; www.sainsburys.co.uk). The smaller, more "local" of 2 Oxford branches in the national, all-purpose grocery chain. Open M-Sa 7am-11pm, Su 11am-5pm. AmEx/MC/V. Another branch in the Westgate Shopping Center, near the corner of Queen St. and Catte St., with a bigger selection and bigger crowds is open M-Sa 7am-8pm, Su 11am-5pm.

Co-Op Swift Shop, 42 Walton St. (☎01865 511 884; www.cooponline.coop). A small and socially responsible grocery store serving the Jericho neighborhood. Organic, free-range, cage-free, and other morally pleasing foods at financially pleasing prices. Democratically run by Co-Op members, but anyone can shop. Conveniently open until midnight every night, so no need to worry if you're still hungry when the pubs on Walton St. stop serving food. Open M-Sa 7am-midnight, Su 8am-midnight. MC/V.

Maroc Deli, 66 Cowley Rd. (☎01865 247 707). Colorful and aromatic Moroccan grocery shop featuring Middle Eastern standards like halal meat, dates, spices, and hookah. Sample a wide selection of olives for £0.75 per 100g. Open M-Sa 9:30am-7pm, Su 10am-6pm. AmEx/MC/V

🎓 COLLEGES

The 🏛Tourist Information Centre sells a map (£1.25) and gives out the *Welcome to Oxford* guide, which lists the visiting hours for all of the colleges. Hours can also be accessed online at www.ox.ac.uk/visitors/colls.html. Note that those hours change without explanation or notice, so confirm in advance. Some colleges charge admission, while others are only accessible through Blue Badge tours, booked at the TIC. Don't bother trying to sneak into Christ Church outside open hours—bouncers, affectionately known as "bulldogs," in bowler hats and stationed 50 ft. apart, will squint their eyes and kick you out.

CHRIST CHURCH

COLLEGE. "The House" has Oxford's grandest quad and its most distinguished students, counting 13 past prime ministers among its alumni. Charles I made Christ Church his headquarters for three and a half years during the Civil Wars and escaped dressed as a servant when the city was besieged. Lewis Carroll first met Alice, the dean's daughter, here. The dining hall and Tom Quad serve as shooting locations for Harry Potter films. If you visit in June, be respectful of undergrads prepping for exams as you navigate the narrow strip open to tourists. Through an archway, to your left as you face the cathedral, lie Peckwater Quad and the most elegant Palladian building in Oxford. Look for rowing standings chalked on the walls and for the beautiful exterior of Christ Church's **library.** Spreading east and south from the main entrance, **Christ Church Meadow** compensates for Oxford's lack of "backs" (the riverside gardens in Cambridge). The meadows are beautiful and afford great views of Christ Church College for those who don't want to pay to go inside. *(Down St. Aldates from Carfax. ☎ 01865 286 573; www.chch.ox.ac.uk. Open M-F 10:15am-11:45am and 2:15-4:30pm, Sa-Su 2:15-4:30pm. Last entry 4pm. Dining hall open 10:30am-noon and 2:30-4:30pm. Chapel services M-F 6pm; Su 8, 10, 11:15am, 6pm. £6, concessions £4.50.)*

CHRIST CHURCH CHAPEL. The only church in England to serve as both a cathedral and college chapel, Christ Church Chapel was founded in AD 730 by Oxford's patron saint, St. Frideswide, who built a nunnery here in honor of two miracles: the blinding of her persistent suitor and his subsequent recovery. A stained-glass window (c. 1320) contains a rare panel depicting St. Thomas Becket, archbishop of Canterbury, kneeling moments before his death. Many clergy are buried here, but the most aesthetically interesting tomb is the sculpture of a dead knight (John de Nowers, who died in 1386). He was 6'6" tall, a giant in his day. Look for the floating toilet in the bottom right of a window showing St. Frideswide's death and the White Rabbit fretting in the windows in the hall.

TOM QUAD. The site of undergraduate lily-pond dunking, Tom Quad adjoins the chapel grounds. The quad takes its name from Great Tom, the seven-ton bell, that has rung 101 (the original number of students) times at 9:05pm (the original undergraduate curfew) every evening since 1682. The bell rings at 9:05pm because, technically, Oxford should be 5min. past Greenwich Mean Time. Nearby, the college hall displays portraits of

THE LOCAL STORY

ELEMENTARY, MY DEAR MORSE

Readers worldwide are familiar with gentlemanly British crime-fighters like Sherlock Holmes and James Bond. While Oxford's own Inspector Morse isn't as well-known outside the UK, his legacy looms large over Oxford.

The protagonist of Colin Dexter's series of detective novels, Morse is much like any 60-year-old man you might find in the back of the White Horse pub. His high-brow interests include cask ale, classical music, and crosswords. When he's not cruising around in his Jaguar or lounging around at home with a pint and a book, he solves mysteries for the Thames Valley Police.

Occasionally, Morse bags the wrong suspect in a crime, but he's got a knack for finding clues in seemingly mundane details and has managed to keep Oxford safe for 13 novels.

The novels were adapted into a successful TV series that ran between 1987 and 2000. Much of it was filmed on location everywhere from the Ashmolean Museum to the Turf Tavern. Corpus Christi College served as the setting for the book's fictional Beaumont College. The Tourist Information Center offers weekly Inspector Morse-themed tours that visit the filming locations. To get a ticket, you have to solve a cryptic crossword after drinking a pint of ale (just kidding—you only have to fork over a few pounds).

some of Christ Church's famous alums—Sir Philip Sidney, William Penn, John Locke, and a bored-looking W.H. Auden—in a corner by the kitchen.

CHRIST CHURCH PICTURE GALLERY. Generous alumni gifts have established a small but noteworthy collection of works by Tintoretto, Vermeer, and Leonardo da Vinci, among others. *(In the Canterbury quad. Entrances on Oriel Sq. and at Canterbury Gate; visitors to the gallery should enter through Canterbury Gate. ☎ 01865 276 172; www.chch. ox.ac.uk/gallery. Open M-Sa 10:30am-5pm, Su 2-5pm. Tours M 2:30pm. £3, concessions £2.)*

OTHER COLLEGES

Oxford's extensive college system (totaling 39 official Colleges of the University) means that there are plenty of beautiful grounds to stroll year-round. The following is a selection of the most popular colleges. For information on others, check one of the many guides found at the TIC (p. 230).

ALL SOULS COLLEGE. The most prestigious of the colleges, All Souls does not even consider high school applicants. Only Oxford's best and brightest students receive an invitation-only admission offer. Candidates who survive the entrance exams are invited to a dinner, where the dons confirm that they are "well-born, well-bred, and only moderately learned." It was named for all the souls who perished in the English Civil War. All Souls is also reported to have the most heavenly wine cellar in the city. The Great Quad may be Oxford's most serene, as hardly a living soul passes over it. *(Corner of High St. and Catte St. ☎ 01865 279 379; www.all-souls.ox.ac.uk. Open Sept.-July M-F 2-4pm. Free.)*

BALLIOL COLLEGE. When Lord John de Balliol insulted the Bishop of Durham, he was assigned two penances: a public whipping at Durham Cathedral and an act of charity. For charity, he bought a small house outside the Oxford city walls and gave scholars a few pence a week to study there. This community officially became Balliol College in 1266. Students at Balliol preserve tradition by hurling abuse over the wall at their Trinity College rivals. Matthew Arnold, Gerard Manley Hopkins, Aldous Huxley, and Adam Smith were all sons of Balliol's mismatched spires. The interior gates of the college supposedly bear lingering scorch marks from the executions of 16th-century Protestants, and a mulberry tree planted by Elizabeth I still shades slumbering students. The beautiful Garden Quad is full of picnickers on pleasant days. *(Broad St. ☎ 01865 277 777; www.balliol.ox.ac.uk. Open daily 2-5pm. £1, students £0.50.)*

MAGDALEN COLLEGE. With extensive grounds and flower-laced quads, Magdalen (MAUD-lin) is considered Oxford's handsomest college. It has a deer park flanked by the River Cherwell and Addison's Walk, a circular path that touches the river's opposite bank. The college's most famous alumnus is wit and playwright Oscar Wilde. Its choir is one of three at the university that still uses young boys to sing the high notes, a relic from the era when women were not allowed; they attend the Magdalen College School across the bridge. *(On High St., near the Cherwell. ☎ 01865 276 000; www.magd.ox.ac.uk. Open daily July-Sept. noon-6pm; Oct.-Mar. 1pm-dusk; Apr.--June 1-6pm. £4, concessions £3.)*

MERTON COLLEGE. Merton's library houses the first printed Welsh Bible. Tolkien lectured here, inventing the Elven language in his spare time. The college's 14th-century **Mob Quad** is Oxford's oldest and least impressive, but nearby **Saint Alban's Quad** has grimacing gargoyles with drainpipes running out of their mouths. *(Merton St. ☎ 01865 276 310; www.merton.ox.ac.uk. Open M-F 2-4pm, Sa-Su 10am-4pm. Free. Library tours £2.)*

NEW COLLEGE. This is the self-proclaimed first real college of Oxford. It was here, in 1379, that William of Wykeham dreamed up an institution that would offer a comprehensive undergraduate education under one roof. The bell tower has gargoyles of the seven deadly sins on one side and the seven heavenly virtues on the other—all equally grotesque. *(New College Ln. gate in summer, Holywell St. Gate in winter. ☎01865 279 555. Open daily from Easter to mid-Oct. 11am-5pm; from Nov. to Easter 2-4pm. £2, concessions £1.)*

QUEEN'S COLLEGE. Although the college dates back to 1341, Queen's was rebuilt by Christopher Wren and Nicholas Hawksmoor in the 17th and 18th centuries in the distinctive Queen Anne style. A trumpet call summons students to dinner, where a boar's head graces the table at Christmas. That tradition supposedly commemorates a student who, attacked by a boar on the outskirts of Oxford, choked the beast to death with a volume of Aristotle—probably the nerdiest slaughter ever. *(High St. ☎01865 279 120; www.queens.ox.ac.uk. Open to Blue-Badge tours only.)*

TRINITY COLLEGE. Founded in 1555, Trinity has a Baroque chapel with a limewood altarpiece, cedar latticework, and cherub-spotted pediments. The college's series of eccentric presidents includes Ralph Kettell, who would come to dinner with a pair of scissors to chop anyone's hair that he deemed too long. The four statues on top of the chapel tower represent Geometry, Astronomy, Theology, and Medicine. The chapel's interior is notable for its intricate wood carvings by Grinling Gibbons. *(Broad St. ☎01865 279 900; www.trinity.ox.ac.uk. Open daily 10am-noon and 2-4pm. £1.50, concessions £0.80.)*

UNIVERSITY COLLEGE. Built in 1249, this soot-blackened college vies with Merton for the title of oldest, claiming Alfred the Great as its founder. Percy Bysshe Shelley was expelled for writing the pamphlet *The Necessity of Atheism* but was later immortalized in a monument, on the right as you enter. Bill Clinton spent his Rhodes days here. *(High St. ☎01865 276 602; www.univ.ox.ac.uk. Entries for individuals at the discretion of the lodge porter.)*

◉ SIGHTS

CARFAX TOWER. The tower marks the center of the premodern city. A climb up its 99 (very narrow) stairs affords a superb view of the dreaming spires and surrounding countryside. The only remnant of medieval St. Martin's Church, Carfax gets its name from the French Carrefour, referring to the intersection of the North, South, East, and West Gates. *(Corner of Queen St. and Cornmarket St. ☎01865 792 653. Open daily Apr.-Sept. 10am-5:30pm; Oct. and Mar. 10am-4:30pm; Nov.-Feb. 10am-3:30pm. £2.10, children £1.)*

BOTANIC GARDEN. Green things have flourished for three centuries in Oxford University's botanical gardens, the oldest in the British Isles. The path connecting the garden to Christ Church Meadow provides a view of the Thames and the cricket grounds on the opposite bank. On pleasant days, students and tourists alike come to picnic, read, and doze off on the lawn. Highlights include the oldest tree in the garden (an English Yew planted during the English Civil War in 1645) and J.R.R. Tolkien's favorite tree. *(Between Rose Lane and the Madgalen Bridge; from Carfax, head down High St. ☎01865 286 690; www.botanic-garden.ox.ac.uk. Open daily May-Aug. 9am-6pm, last entry 5:15pm; Sept.-Oct. and Mar.-Apr. 9am-5pm, last entry 4:15pm; Nov.-Feb. 9am-4:30pm, last entry 4:15pm. Glass houses open daily 10am-4pm. Throwing stones in glass houses is not advised. £3, concessions £2.50, children free.)*

OXFORD CASTLE Oxford's newest attraction, the castle has been an Anglo-Saxon church, a Norman castle commissioned by William the Conqueror, a courthouse, and (until 1996) a prison. Now the complex houses restaurants,

The Chronicle

IN RECENT NEWS

TRASHED AT OXFORD

It's summertime, the sun is shining, and you've just completed your final exam at prestigious Oxford University. The first thing you can look forward to in your new-found freedom? A face-full of raw fish and custard.

At least, that's the way things were up until a few years ago. The tradition of "trashing," which originated in the 1990s, refers to Oxford students' curious practice of throwing food at their friends who've just completed their last university exams. The messy projectiles ranged from champagne, beer, and eggs to flour, liver, and dog food—one unlucky undergrad even got an octopus thrown through his window.

But in the new millenium, the tradition started to get out of hand. Street cleanups after trashing cost the Oxford city council as much as £20,000, and several locals suffered broken limbs after slipping on the food mess trashers left behind. Fines for trashing had little effect at first, because university police had trouble catching the culprits in the act. But in 2008, the Oxford proctors found a new way to nab the trashers: they searched Facebook for pictures of food-throwing undergraduates.

Despite student outcry over what many saw as an invasion of privacy, the university collected over £10,000 in fines from graduating students—more than five times the total from any other year. It looks like the tradition may be on its way out; if you want to get trashed at Oxford, you better do it soon!

an open-air theater, and a luxury hotel (where you can stay in a converted prison cell). You can climb to the top of St. George's Tower for a view of the city formerly enjoyed only by prison guards. Back downstairs, the dark church crypt is one of the most haunted places in Oxford. *(Corner of Queen St. and Cornmarket St. ☎01865 792 653. Open daily Apr.-Sept. 10am-5:30pm; Oct. and Mar. 10am-4:30pm; Nov.-Feb. 10am-3:30pm. £2.10, children £1.)*

SHELDONIAN THEATRE. This Romanesque auditorium was designed by a teenage Christopher Wren. Graduation ceremonies, conducted in Latin, take place in the Sheldonian, as does everything from student recitals to world-class opera performances. The elaborate graduation ceremonies are so behind schedule that students often don't get their degree until 6 months after they complete their final exams. *The Red Violin* and *Quills*, as well as numerous other movies, were filmed here. Climb up to the cupola for views of Oxford's quads. The ivy-crowned stone heads on the fence behind the Sheldonian are a 20th-century "study in beards." *(Broad St. ☎01865 277 299. Open in summer M-Sa 10am-12:30pm and 2-4:30pm; in winter M-Sa 10am-12:30pm and 2-3:30pm. £2.50, concessions £1.50. Purchase tickets for shows from Oxford Playhouse at ☎01865 305 305. Box office open M-Sa 10am-6pm. Shows £15.)*

OXFORD CANAL. This 78 mi., nearly stagnant waterway was built in the 18th century to connect Coventry to the Thames. Today, people park long, eccentrically decorated houseboats along its banks as ducks paddle around to avoid their propellers. A gravel path along the west bank (great for jogging) is the most scenic route to Jehrico from the city center. *(Enter on Hythe Bridge St. or Park End St.)*

MAGDALEN BRIDGE BOATHOUSE. A summer weekend in Oxford isn't complete without an afternoon of punting on the Thames. Punts are gondola-style boats that are propelled by pushing a long pole against the riverbed. Be on the lookout for hard-charging crew races if you're punting during Eights Week. *(At Magdalen Bridge off High St. ☎01865 202 643. Open daily 10am-dusk. Chauffered punts for up to 4 £22 for 30min., £27 with a bottle of wine. Self-drive £16 per hour, 5-person max. Straw hats £3.)*

UNIVERSITY CHURCH OF SAINT MARY THE VIRGIN. This 11th-century church was once the academic center of Oxford University. Meetings and exams were held here, and it was later the site of executions during the Reformation. The magnificent spire, completed in 1320, holds one of the best views of the city for those who can make the climb. The colossal Swiss-made organ is one of only two of its kind in the United Kingdom (the other is in Cambridge). *(Radcliffe Sq., off High St. ☎01865 279 111; www.university-church.ox.ac.uk. Open M-Sa 9am-5pm, Su 11:30am-5pm. Last entry 30min. before closing. Free. Tower £3, concessions £2.50.)*

🏛 MUSEUMS

ASHMOLEAN MUSEUM. The grand Ashmolean—Britain's finest collection of arts and antiquities outside London and the country's oldest public museum—opened in 1683. The museum is undergoing extensive renovations until November 2009. *(Beaumont St. ☎01865 278 000. Open Tu-Sa 10am-5pm, Su noon-5pm. Free. Tours £2.)*

BODLEIAN LIBRARY. Oxford's principal reading and research library has over five million books and 50,000 manuscripts. It receives a copy of every book printed in Great Britain. Though he was not the original founder, Sir Thomas Bodley revived the library after 95% of the books were burned during the English Reformation. Downstairs in the Divinity School, aspiring clergy took lengthy oral exams called "disputations" where the discussed such weighty questions as "How many angels can fit on the head of a pin?" The institution has since grown to fill the immense **Old Library** complex, the **Radcliffe Camera** next door, and two newer buildings on Broad St. Admission to the reading rooms is by ticket only. Each case is assessed individually by the Admissions Officer: check the library's website for details. No one has ever been permitted to take out a book, not even Cromwell. Well, especially not Cromwell. *(Enter on Catte St. opposite Hertford College. ☎01865 277 000; www.bodley. ox.ac.uk. Library open in summer M-F 9am-4:45pm, Sa 9am4:30pm; during term-time M-F 9am-10pm, Sa 9am-1pm. Tours leave the Divinity School in the main quad in summer M-Sa 10:30, 11:30am, 2, 3pm. Tours £6. Audio tour £2.50.)*

MUSEUM OF OXFORD. With all the university's grandeur and history, it's easy to forget that the city of Oxford was there first. From hands-on exhibits to a murderer's skeleton, the museum provides an in-depth look at Oxford's rich history from Roman times to the present. Some highlights include an ancient Roman pottery kiln and a stone coat of arms for Merton College dating back to 1500. You can also see what dorm life was like for an upper-crust Oxford chap in the early 20th century. *(St. Aldates. Enter at corner of St. Aldates and Blue Boar. ☎01865 252 761; www.museumoxford.org.uk. Open Tu-F 10am-5pm, Sa-Su noon-5pm. Last entry 30min. before close. Free.)*

MODERN ART OXFORD. This trendy museum shows paintings, videos, sculptures, and other things you didn't even know were art. Rotating exhibits aim to bring the best in international art to Oxford. *(30 Pembroke St. ☎01865 722 733; www.modernartoxford.org.uk. Open Tu-Sa 10am-5pm, Su noon-5pm. Wheelchair-accessible. Free. Downstairs cafe open Tu-Sa 11:30am-2:30pm.)*

MUSEUM OF HISTORY OF SCIENCE. This collection of mostly pre-Victorian gadgets includes one of the earliest pendulum clocks in England. Appreciate the wonders of the Information Age as you imagine how difficult it was to make a (generally) accurate globe in the 17th century. You'll be glad that some of these relics—like the saws used for limb amputation—are obsolete and secure in their glass cases. *(Broad St., across from Blackwell's Books. ☎01865 277 280; www.mhs.ox.ac.uk. Open Tu-F noon-5pm, Sa 10am-5pm, Su 2-5pm. Free.)*

⚑ ENTERTAINMENT

Centuries of tradition give Oxford a solid music scene. Colleges offer concerts and evensong services; **New College** (p. 236) has an excellent boys' choir, and performances at the **Holywell Music Room,** on Holywell St., are worth checking out. Theater groups stage plays in gardens or cloisters. Pick up *This Month in Oxford,* free at the TIC, or *Daily Information,* posted all over town and online (www.dailyinfo.co.uk), for event listings.

■ **The Cellar,** Frewin Ct. (☎01865 766 766; www.cellarmusic.co.uk), in an alley off Cornmarket St. next to the Gap. Basement venue that hosts rock, indie, and electro-themed nights. Beers £2.90-3.80. Tickets £4-8. AmEx/MC/V.

Oxford Coffee Concerts (☎07976 740 024; www.coffeeconcerts.com) at the Holywell Music Room. Famous musicians and ensembles every Su at 11:15am. Tickets £9, concessions £8.

City of Oxford Orchestra (☎01865 744 457; www.cityofoxfordorchestra.co.uk). A professional symphony orchestra. Plays a subscription series at the Sheldonian and in college chapels during the summer. Tickets £10-27, concessions £2 less. Buy tickets at Oxford Playhouse (see below).

New Theatre, George St. (☎01865 320 760; www.newtheatreoxford.org.uk). Everything from jazz to musicals to the Welsh National Opera. Also occasionally hosts pop acts (Bryan Adams and Seal were recent headliners). Tickets £10-50. Box office open M-Sa 10am-6pm, performance days 10am-8pm.

Oxford Playhouse, 11-12 Beaumont St. (☎01865 305 305; www.oxfordplayhouse.com, www.ticketsoxford.com). Hosts amateur and professional musicians and dance performances. The playhouse also sells discounted tickets for venues citywide. Box office open M-Sa 10am-6pm, performance days 10am-8pm.

O2 Academy, 190 Cowley Rd. (☎01865 813 500; www.o2academyoxford.co.uk). Bus #5 to Cowley Rd. Larger venue that hosts the biggest-name acts that come to Oxford. AmEx/MC/V.

The Backroom at the Bullingdon, 162 Cowley (☎01865 244 516). Bus #5 to Cowley Rd. Behind the bar known locally as "The Bully," a fairly large music room is well-known for its Monday blues jams (£10). Tu free Jazz. F club nights with £4 cover.

The Wheatsheaf, 124 High St. (☎01865 721 156), down Wheatsheaf Yard Alley. Downstairs is a normal-looking pub, which dubiously claims to have one of the only pool tables in Oxford. Upstairs is a spacious music room with its own bar, where you can hear everything from metal to jazz. Tickets to shows are usually £4-5 and sold at the door. M comedy night. Open M-Th noon-11pm, F-Sa noon-midnight, Su noon-10:30pm. MC/V.

▯ SHOPPING

On a busy tourist day in Oxford, the biggest crowds won't be in line to tour Christ Church. They'll be milling around **Cornmarket Street,** the city's main shopping avenue. Buses and taxis are allowed in the city center, but only pedestrians cruise down Cornmarket. Shoppers from Oxfordshire and beyond come to the city for everything from major department stores to hidden vintage shops. For air-conditioned mall shopping, stop by **Westgate** or **Clarendon Centre.** Upscale boutiques can be found on **Queen Street, High Street,** and **Cornmarket Street.** Head down **Cowley Road** for inexpensive shops with some international flair.

MAJOR CHAINS

Debenham's (☎01865 255 060; www.debenhams.com), corner of Cornmarket St. and George St. An old stone building houses this sleek and modern department store. Stylish clothes for men, women, and children on 3 floors. Open M-W 9:30am-6pm, Th 9:30am-6pm, F 9:30am-7pm, Sa 9am-7pm, Su 11am-5pm. AmEx/MC/V.

Blackwell's, 48-51 Broad St. (☎01865-792-792; www.blackwell.com). The monster British entertainment chain got its start with this bookshop in Oxford. Also offers themed literary walking tours. Literature tour Tu and Th 11am; inklings tour W 11:45am; historic Oxford tour F 2pm. All tours £7.

British Home Stores (Bhs), Queen St. (☎01865 242 661; www.bhs.co.uk), next to Westgate. Basic department store with nice wares and decent prices. Cafe in the basement for exhausted bargain-hunters. Open M, W, and F-Sa 9am-6pm; Tu 9:30am-6pm; Th 9am-8pm; Su 11am-5pm. AmEx/MC/V.

HMV, 44-46 Cornmarket St. (☎01865 728 190; www.hmv.co.uk). Music, movies, and video games on multiple floors. M-W and F 8:30am-6:30pm, Th 8:30am-7pm, Su 11am-5pm. AmEx/MC/V.

Oxfam, 17 Broad St. (☎01865 241 333; www.oxfam.org.uk). Fair trade clothes, energy-saving gadgets, and recycled goods on the ground floor. Vintage clothes upstairs (dresses around £20), and used music in the basement, (CDs £1-5, vinyl also available). Sales benefit Oxfam's charitable activities all around the world. Open M-Sa 9:30am-5:30pm, Su 11am-4pm. MC/V.

CLOTHING AND GIFTS

Unicorn, 5 Ship St. (☎01865 240 568). There's not much room to walk around in this vintage shop, where mounds of clothing from the 50s-80s nearly touch the ceiling (only the owner herself ever reaches the back of the store). But for over 30 years, Oxford students have been braving the dust for great deals on funky dresses (£10-12), shirts (£6.50-8.50), and just about everything else. Open M-Sa 11am-5:30pm. Cash only.

Habibi, 21 Little Clarendon St. (☎01865 558 077). Habibi, which means "beloved one" in Arabic, is a great place to buy a unique gift for someone special back home. Art, jewelry, and clothing imported from all over the world, including Thailand, India, and Morocco. Handmade necklaces (£8-25) and silk dresses (£39). Open daily 10am-5:30pm. AmEx/MC/V.

Galeria Brasil, 33 Cowley Rd. (☎01865 240 568; www.galeriabrasiloxford.net). Across Magdalen Bridge, or take bus #5. Colorful Brazilian clothes and jewelry, ranging from well-known designers (in Brazil, at least) to community artisans. Traditional Brazilian prints hang in a gallery in the back. Open Tu-Sa 10:30am-6pm. AmEx/MC/V.

The Last Bookshop, 126 Walton St. How does a one-room bookshop compete with Blackwell's? By selling every single book for £2 (and they're all new). The store buys remainders from bigger bookshops and stocks a diverse, if limited, selection. Open M-F 9am-6pm, Sa 10am-6pm, Su 11am-5pm. Cash only.

Uncle Sam's, 29 Little Clarendon St. (☎01865 510 759). If the inventory of this shop is any indication, Brits must think everyone in America dresses like a Hell's Angel, cowboy, or both. Vintage American clothes, like leather jackets (£23-35), and fun Western accessories. Most shirts under £10. Open M-Sa 10:30am-6pm, Su 1-5pm. Cash only (no US dollars please).

OXFORD

THE INKLINGS

Oxford's intellectual history has been made as much in its pubs as in its colleges. The epicenter of this city's beer-soaked literary tradition is a short walk up St. Giles St, where two pubs have attracted writers for decades.

From 1939 to 1962, J.R.R. Tolkien, C.S. Lewis, and other members of Oxford's literati met at the Eagle and Child pub every Tuesday to discuss their writing and shoot the breeze. Branding themselves "The Inklings," they had several things in common: they were all male, British, Christian, and proponents of fantasy writing. These writers met in the Rabbit Room; once a private space in the back of the pub, this room is now open to the public and is lined with Inkling memorabilia. They referred to the pub as the Bird and Baby, but it has since accrued several more explicit alliterative nicknames like the Bustard and Bastard and the Fowl and Fetus.

In 1962, the Inklings migrated across the street to the Lamb and Flag, which has its own share of literary tradition. Thomas Hardy is said to have written the majority of his final novel *Jude the Obscure* there. In the book, he refers to the pub as an "obscure tavern in a rough place."

▼ PUBS

In Oxford, pubs far outnumber colleges—some even consider them the city's prime attraction. They often hold as much history as the colleges themselves. Most open by noon, begin to fill around 5pm, and close around midnight (earlier on Sunday). Recent legislation has allowed pubs to stay open later, but there may be conditions, including an earlier door-closing time or a small cover charge. Be ready to pub crawl—many pubs are so small that a single band of celebrating students will squeeze out other patrons.

The Turf Tavern, 4 Bath Pl. (☎01865 243 235; www.theturftavern.co.uk), hidden off Holywell St. Arguably the most popular student bar in Oxford, this 13th-century pub is tucked in an alley off an alley, but that doesn't stop just about everybody in Oxford from partaking of its 11 different ales. Bob Hawke, future prime minister of Australia, downed a yard of ale (over 2 pints) in a record 11 seconds here while at the university. The Turf is also allegedly the spot where Bill Clinton "didn't inhale" as a Rhodes Scholar. Quiz night Tu 8:30pm. Open M-Sa 11am-11pm, Su noon-10:30pm. Kitchen open noon-7pm.

The King's Arms, 40 Holywell St. (☎01865 242 369; www.kingsarmsoxford.co.uk). Oxford's unofficial student union. Until 1973, the bar was the last male-only pub in the UK. Now, the "KA" has plenty of large tables for all patrons even when it's busy. Features a rotating selection of tasty Young's cask ale. Open daily 10:30am-midnight. Kitchen open 11:30am-9pm. MC/V.

The Bear, 6 Alfred St. (☎01865 728 164). Patrons once exchanged their club neckties for a pint at this oldest (est. 1242) of Oxford's many pubs. Over 4500 adorn the walls and ceiling of the pub. Unfortunately, the deal no longer applies. Seating inside is scarce, but the heated garden has plenty of picnic tables. Open M-Th 11am-11pm, F-Sa 11am-midnight, Su 11am-10:30pm. MC/V.

Lamb and Flag, 12 St. Giles St. (☎01865 515 787). A sign outside gives this down-to-earth watering hole's succinct mission statement: "Honest Pub." Founded in 1617 as the Lamb Inn, this pub also has its share of literary history. Graham Greene was a regular, and Thomas Hardy set part of *Jude the Obscure* here. Open M-Sa noon-11pm, Su noon-10:30pm. Cash only.

Jericho Tavern, 56 Walton St. (☎01865 311 775). An upstairs venue where Radiohead had its debut gig in 1984. Downstairs, patrons enjoy the sleek decor, specialty draft beer, and heated beer garden. Live music

F-Sa and some weeknights with a £5-8 cover. Open M-F noon-midnight, Sa-Su 10am-midnight. AmEx/MC/V.

The White Horse, 52 Broad St. (☎01865 722 393; www.whitehorseoxford.co.uk), between the 2 entrances of Blackwell's. This tiny, historic pub favored by locals is haunted by a witch whose broomstick was found in the living room upstairs (where it remains untouched, for fear of provoking her ghost). Open daily 11am-11pm. Kitchen closes 9pm. MC/V.

The Jolly Farmers, 20 Paradise St. (☎07771 651 848). Oxford's 1st gay and lesbian pub. Popular with students and 20-somethings, especially on weekends. The landlord's standard poodle, Benson, is a regular attraction. Come early for a seat in the garden. Open M-Th 4pm-midnight, F-Su noon-midnight. Cash only.

Castle Tavern, 24 Paradise St. (☎07771 651 848). Recently converted into a gay-friendly pub after it was purchased by the current owner of the Jolly Farmers next door. On weekends, a DJ turns the basement into a club-style dance floor. Open M-Th noon-midnight, F-Sa noon-3am, Su noon-7pm. Cash only.

The Eagle and Child, 49 St. Giles (☎01865 302 925). The dark-paneled back (now middle) room of this historic pub hosted "The Inklings," a group of 20th-century writers including C.S. Lewis and J.R.R. Tolkien, who referred to it as the "Bird and Baby." *The Chronicles of Narnia* and *The Hobbit* were first read aloud here. Open M-Th 10am-11pm, F-Sa 10am-11:30pm, Su 10am-10:30pm. Breakfast served until noon. Kitchen closes 9pm. AmEx/MC/V.

The Red Lion, 14 Gloucester St. (☎01865 726 255). Popular for its spacious garden, above-average food, plasma TVs, and some of the cheapest pints in town. Sandwich and drink combo £4. Tu curry and drink special £5. Open daily 9am-12:30am. Kitchen open daily until 10pm. MC/V over £5.

The Head of the River, Folly Bridge, St. Aldates (☎01865 721 600). This aptly named pub has the best location in all of Oxford to view the Thames, known locally as the Isis. Much bigger than the pubs closer to the town center, so you can be sure you'll find a seat. The large beer garden fills up quickly in the early evening. Open M-Sa 11am-11pm, Su 11:30am-10:30pm. Kitchen open daily noon-2:30pm and 5-9pm. AmEx/MC/V.

St. Aldates Tavern, 108 St. Aldates (☎01865 250 201). Local charm and regional ales. Formerly called "the Hobgoblin," this pub has long been haunted. The ceiling is plastered with over 1200 labels from ales, all of which were consumed in the pub in 1 year. Student discount 10%. Open M-Th noon-11pm, F-Sa noon-midnight, Su noon-10:30pm.

THE LOCAL STORY

MORE THAN MUTTON

Spend any time in England and it will become apparent that pubs are more than just spots to watch football and drink a pint. Much like the French cafe, the English pub serves as a community center: a place for intellectual communion, political caballing, and literary gruntwork. Few pubs epitomize the institution as well as Oxford's **Lamb and Flag,** 12 St. Giles St., Oxford.

Originally a coach inn in the 15th century, the pub didn't begin to attract star clientele until the 19th century, when Thomas Hardy, the author of such grim classics as the *The Mayor of Casterbridge* and *Tess of the D'Ubervilles*, frequented its shadow-filled interior. Supposedly, it is there that he dreamt up his masterpiece, *Jude the Obscure*, a nightmarish novel about the hypocrisy of Oxford and the cruelty of the world. Another unhappy writer, Graham Greene, the chronicler of British international intrigue—see *The Quiet American, Our Man in Havana*, and *The Heart of the Matter*—also found solace under the pub's sign after releasing his first literary assay as an undergraduate at Oxford, which was universally panned.

But the pub hasn't only served as a place of consolation. In the 40s and 50s, it was the headquarters for the Coalbiters, the mythologically-minded coterie of C.S. Lewis and J.R.R. Tolkien, who switched their allegiances after their previous haunt, **The Eagle and Child** (across the street at 49 St. Giles St.) became too crowded.

Chequers Inn, 131 High St. (☎01865 727 463). Leather couches, brick fireplaces, and a heated beer garden make this a great place to kick off a pub crawl. Rustic decor and an energetic atmosphere. Built in 1260, the building was originally home to a money-lender; the name comes from the checkerboard, the ancient Roman symbol of that line of work. During the Reformation, Henry VIII's knights forced monks into underground tunnels across the street. Supposedly, when the pub is quiet, you can still hear their screams. More than 10 different English sausages available with your bangers and mash. Sausage tastings Tu 6-8pm. Open M-Th 10am-11pm, F-Sa 10am-midnight, Su 11am-10:30pm.

The Grapes, 7 George St. (☎01865 793 380). This Victorian pub hasn't changed much since the 19th century. A popular afterparty destination for actors and audience members from the New Theatre across the street. Open M-Th and Su 11am-11pm, F-Sa 11am-midnight.

The Gloucester Arms, Friars entry (☎01865 241 177). In an alley off Gloucester St., behind the Red Lion. Calls itself "Oxford's No. 1 Rock Pub," and has the long hair, piercings, and beards to prove it. Music-themed posters cover the ceiling. Show off your best grunts and growls at M night heavy metal karaoke. Open M-Th 11am-midnight, F-Sa 11am-1am, Su noon-11pm. AmEx/MC/V.

O'Neills, 37 George St. (☎01865 250 708; www.oneills.co.uk). A place so Irish that even their fish and chips is battered in Guinness. Popular pre-club spot for students. Occasionally hosts live music. Open M-W and Su 11am-midnight, Th 11am-1am, F-Sa 11am-2am. AmEx/MC/V.

🔊 CLUBS

Despite recent changes in licensing laws, most traditionalist pubs have elected to keep closing around midnight or 1am. After last call, crowds of well-dressed students swagger down to **Park End Street** for the trendiest clubs—but there are plenty of hot spots scattered around the city center where you can dance to whatever your ears desire. Saturdays are the biggest party night, but themed parties (like R&B, international, and indie) are popular during the week. Check flyers for theme parties and discounts.

Lava/Ignite, Park End St. (☎01865 250 181; www.parkend.co.uk), across the street from Thirst. The epicenter of Oxford's student nightlife; be prepared to wait in line to get in. DJs on 3 different dance floors spin the latest techno, pop, and R&B. Look for promoters down the street handing out discount stickers. No sneakers. Cover £3-7.

Thirst, 7-8 Park End St. (☎01865 242 044; www.thirstbar.com). Lounge bar with a DJ and backdoor garden, where you can smoke hookah (£10) with your drinks. Arguably the most popular student hangout in Oxford. Student discount on mixed drinks (from £2.80) M-Th and Su with student ID. Open M-W and Su 7:30pm-2am, Th-Sa 7:30-3am. MC/V over £10.

The Bridge, 6-9 Hythe Bridge St. (☎01865 242 526; www.bridgeoxford.co.uk). Dance to R&B, hip hop, dance, and pop on 2 floors. Erratically frequented by big student crowds. Drinks £3-4. Cover £3-7. Open M-W 9pm-2am, Th 9pm-3am, F-Sa 10pm-3am. MC/V.

Mood, 29 George St. (☎01865 249 605). Mirrors make this urbane club look much bigger than it actually is. Plays the latest rap and R&B. Beers £2.20-3.50, mixed drinks £2.50-3.50, Dom Pérignon champagne £189. No sneakers. £3-6 cover on weekends. AmEx/MC/V.

Anuba, 11-13 Park End St. (☎01865 242 526; www.bridgeoxford.co.uk/anuba). Sister club to The Bridge. Intimate pre-club atmosphere. Small dance floor is a nice alternative to the huge clubs throughout the city. Beer and mixed drinks £3. Salsa night W (cover £3). Live music F. Happy hour M-Sa 8:30-10:30pm. Open M-Th 8pm-1am, F-Sa 8pm-3am. MC/V.

The Purple Turtle, Frewin Ct. (☎01865 247 007; www.purpleturtlebar.com). Well hidden in a basement in an alley off Cornmarket St., this spot has a funky 60s vibe. The decor has two main ingredients: posters of rock gods and lots of purple paint. Beers £2.50. Th Karaoke. Open M-W 5:30pm-4am, Th-Sa 4pm-4am, Su 5:30pm-2am. Cash only.

Baby Love, 3 King Edward St. (☎01865 200 011; www.baby-bar.net). Candles, red lighting, and a long list of specialty cocktails. Basement dance floor features a platform with a stripper pole for the most confident dancers. Drinks £2.80-4. Tu gay night. Happy hour M-Th 9-10pm. £3-5 cover some nights. Open daily 9pm-3am. MC/V.

Freud, 119 Walton St. (☎01865 311 171; www.freudliving.com). Cafe by day, bar by night (see **Food,** p. 232). Open M-Th and Su 10:30am-midnight, F-Sa 10:30am-2am. MC/V.

❊ FESTIVALS

May Day, May 1. Daybrake cues one of Oxford's most inspiring moments: the Magdalen College Choir sings madrigals from the top of the tower beginning at 6am, and the town indulges in Morris dancing, beating the bounds, and other age-old rituals of merry men. Pubs open at 7am.

Oxford Final Exams, from late May to early June. If you thought your final exams were stressful, imagine being an Oxford student: they get no official credits for the classes in which they are enrolled, and their entire degree rides on the grueling final exams they take as seniors. You're bound to see some students strolling around the city center in subfusc (dark, goofy outfits). Oxford is one of few colleges that still requires students to wear academic regalia to exams, and students recently voted to uphold the tradition. Exam-takers pin carnations to their chests representing their progress: a white carnation for their first exam, pink during the middle, and red for the last one.

Eights Week, late May. Oxford's colleges enter crews in rowing races and beautiful people sip Pimm's on the banks. Because the Thames (known to locals as the Isis) is too narrow for side-by-side races, the colleges have devised a new form of competition: in "bumping races," eight-person crews start off NASCAR-style, back to back, and try to eliminate the boat in front of them by bumping it with their own.

Saint Giles Fair, in early Sept. An old-fashioned English fun fair invades invades one of Oxford's main streets.

CAMBRIDGE

Unlike museum-oriented, metropolitan Oxford, Cambridge is a town for students before tourists. It was here that Newton's theory of gravity, Watson and Crick's model of DNA, Byron's and Milton's poetry, and Winnie the Pooh were born. No longer the exclusive academy of upper-class sons, the university feeds the minds of female, international, and state-school pupils alike. At exams' end, Cambridge explodes in Pimm's-soaked glee, and May Week is a swirl of celebration on the River Cam.

LIFE AND TIMES

HISTORY

ROMANS, SAXONS, NORMANS, AND SO ON. The **Romans** were the first to set up shop in Cambridge, and remnants of their society can still be seen today at St. Peter's Church. But the Roman settlement on Castle Hill was not long for this world, and the **Saxons**—always with an eye on the prize—swept in during the early Middle Ages. Under the Saxons, Cambridge enjoyed a prolific period of trade. In about 875, the **Vikings** occupied Cambridge and moved the town center to the left bank, or Quayside, only to be outdone once again by those fearsome Saxons. In 1068, William the Conqueror occupied Castle Hill, this time claiming it for the **Normans.** (Still with us?) Cambridge was granted a Royal Charter in 1207.

TOWN AND GOWN. Tensions between students and townspeople are as old as the college itself. In fact, the University was founded in 1209 by a band of Oxford students who were on the run from some angry neighbors of their own. Turns out the Oxonians only brought the turmoil with them: in 1381 tensions between town and gown exploded, and University property came under attack.

CROWN AND GOWN. Religion played a major role in the early development of the university, and it is no surprise that theology was once the primary subject of study. In 1352, **Corpus Christi College** was founded as an answer to the shortage of priests that resulted from the black plague.

In the 15th century, Henry VI designed Cambridge's most famous structure, **King's College Chapel.** Henry VII finished the project in 1515. Henry VIII, famed philanderer and dissolver of monasteries, did his part for Cambridge development by transforming abbeys, cloisters, and convents into educational institutions.

GOT GAME? Cambridge's first college for **women** was founded in the late Victorian era, but they were not allowed to receive degrees until 1948. As if to emphasize the lack of estrogen on campus, scholars at Cambridge were expected to remain celibate, a rule which persisted into the 19th century. Instead, students were encouraged to excel on the athletic fields. It is said that the rules of **football** (soccer) were first established at Cambridge and in 1839 Cambridge and Oxford first took to the River Thames for **"The Boat Race,"** a rowing contest that has occurred annually ever since.

FROM CROMWELL TO BORAT. The list of notable Cambridge University alumni is virtually endless. Trinity College boasts such alums as **Oliver Cromwell, Sir Isaac Newton,** and **Prince Charles.** Other Cambridge big-shots include **John Harvard** and **Charles Darwin. James Watson** and **Francis Crick,** who discovered the double helix structure of DNA, are also alums. In fact, you can still visit the Cambridge pub (p. 256) where the brainy duo reputedly revealed this groundbreaking discovery. Many former Cambridge scholars have made it to Hollywood, including **Sir Ian McKellen,** **Hugh Laurie, Emma Thompson,** and **Sacha Baron Cohen.**

CULTURE AND THE ARTS

LITERATURE

DEEP IN THE HUNDRED ACRE WOOD. Oxford's own **A. A. Milne** (1882-1956) provided us with one of the most beloved children's book characters of all time: Winnie the Pooh. Milne studied mathematics at Trinity College, but found time to contribute to a university literary magazine. Trinity's Wren Library actually has handwritten copies of Milne's *Winnie the Pooh* books.

POETIC PUPILS. Cambridge has produced its share of canonical British poets. Author of *The Faerie Queen,* **Edmund Spenser** was educated at Pembroke College, while Shakespeare's contemporary **Christopher Marlowe** studied at Corpus Christi. **John Milton** wrote perhaps greatest English epic poem, *Paradise Lost.* Both **William Wordsworth** and **Samuel Taylor Coleridge,** head honchos of Romantic poetry, were Cambridge alumni. Twentieth-century American poet and novelist **Sylvia Plath** attended Newnham College as a graduate student on a Fulbright scholarship. It was at Cambridge that Plath met her husband-to-be, poet **Ted Hughes,** who was a student at Pembroke College.

THE CAMBRIDGE APOSTLES. The Cambridge Coversazione Society, or simply, the **Cambridge Apostles,** is an elite intellectual society founded in 1820. The members of this secret club—students of Trinity, St. John's, and King's—would convene and discuss the most pressing and serious issues of the day. Famous members of the group include poet **Alfred Lord Tennyson** and novelist **E.M. Forster.** In fact, the society makes a cameo in Forster's *The Longest Journey.* Several of the Cambridge Apostles eventually formed the core of London's famous **Bloomsbury Group,** including art historian **Roger Fry,** writer and critic **Lytton Strachey,** and the future husband of Virginia, **Leonard Woolf.** The society garnered serious publicity in 1951 with the exposure of the **Cambridge Spy Ring,** when it was revealed that Apostle **Guy Burgess** was spying for the Soviets.

TRANSPORTATION

Bicycles are the primary mode of transportation in Cambridge, a city that claims more bikes per person than any other place in Britain. If you are prepared to face the maze of one-way streets by driving to Cambridge, take advantage of its efficient park-and-ride system.

Trains: (☎08456 007 245). Station on Station Rd. (How original.) Ticket office open daily 5am-11pm. Trains to **London King's Cross** (45min., 3 per hr., £14) and **Ely** (20min., 3 per hr., round-trip £3.70).

Buses: Station on Drummer St. Ticket booth open M-Sa 9am-5pm; tickets often available onboard. **National Express** (☎08705 808 080) buses and airport shuttles pick up at stands on Parkside St. along Parker's Piece park. Buses to: **London Victoria** (2hr.,

CAMBRIDGE

every hr., £12); **Gatwick** (4hr., every hr., £31); **Heathrow** (2½hr., 2 per hr., £28); **Stansted** (1hr., every hr., £12). **Stagecoach Express** (☎01604 676 060) runs to **Oxford** (3hr., every 30min., from £11).

Public Transportation: Stagecoach (☎01223 423 578) runs **CitiBus** from the train station to the city center and around town (£5 for all-day ticket).

Taxis: Cabco (☎01223 312 444) and **Camtax** (☎01223 313 131). Both available 24hr.

Bike Rental: Station Cycles, Corn Exchange St. (☎01223 307 125). £9 per day; £50 deposit. Lock included. Open M-Sa 8am-7pm and Su 10am-6pm. AmEx/MC/V.

ORIENTATION

Cambridge has two central avenues; the main shopping street starts at **Magdalene Bridge** and becomes **Bridge Street, Sidney Street, Saint Andrew's Street, Regent Street,** and **Hills Road.** The other main thoroughfare starts as **Saint John's Street,** becoming **Trinity Street, King's Parade,** and **Trumpington Street.** From the Drummer St. bus station, **Emmanuel Street** leads to the shopping district near the TIC. To get to the TIC from the train station, turn right onto Hills Rd. and follow it ¾ mi.

PRACTICAL INFORMATION

Tourist Information Centre: Wheeler St. (☎09065 268 006; www.visitcambridge.org), 1 block south of Market Sq. Books rooms for £5 and a 10% deposit. Local Secrets Card gives city-wide discounts. Sells National Express tickets. Open Easter-Oct. M-F 10am-5:30pm, Sa 10am-5pm, Su 11am-3pm; Nov.-Easter M-F 10am-5:30pm, Sa 10am-5pm.

Tours: 2hr. walking tours leave from the TIC daily (July-Aug. 4 per day). Tours include King's College (£10, concessions £8.50, children £5) and St. John's College (£8.50/£8/£5). Call for times and tickets (☎01223 457 574). **City Sightseeing** (☎01353 663 659) runs 1hr. hop-on, hop-off bus tours Apr.-Oct. every 15-30min. £12, families £30, concessions £8, children £6.

Budget Travel: STA Travel, 38 Sidney St. (☎01223 366 966; www.statravel.co.uk). Open M-Th 10am-7pm, F 10am-6pm, Sa 9am-6pm, Su 11am-5pm.

Currency Exchange: Banks and **ATMs** on Market Sq., or at the **Post Office.**

Beyond Tourism: Blue Arrow, 40 St. Andrews St. (☎01223 323 272 or 324 433; www.bluearrow.co.uk). Year-round temp work. Open M-F 8:30am-5:30pm.

Luggage Storage: Cambridge Station Cycles (☎01223 307 125), outside the train station. Open M-Tu and Th-F 8am-6pm, W 8am-7pm, Sa 9am-5pm, Su 10am-5pm. £3-4

Police: Parkside (☎01223 358 966).

Pharmacy: Boots, 65-67 Sidney St. (☎01223 350 213). Open M 9am-6pm, Tu 8:30am-6pm, W 8:30am-7pm, Th-Sa 8:30am-6pm, Su 11am-5pm.

Hospital: Addenbrookes Hospital, Long Rd. (☎01223 245 151). Take Cambus C1 or C2 from Emmanuel St. (£1) and get off where Hills Rd. intersects Long Rd.

Internet Access: Available at:

Jaffa Net Cafe, 22 Mill Rd. (☎01223 308 380). From £1 per hr. 10% student discount. Open daily 10am-10pm.

Budget Internet Cafe, 30 Hills Rd. (☎01223 362 214). 75p per 30min. Open daily 9am-11pm. AmEx/MC/V.

Web and Eat, 32 Hills Rd. (☎01223 314 168). 70p per 30min. Open daily 8am-11pm.

Post Office: 9-11 St. Andrew's St. (☎08457 223 344). **Bureau de change.** Open M and W-Sa 9am-5:30pm, Tu 9:30am-5:30pm. **Postcode:** CB2 3AA.

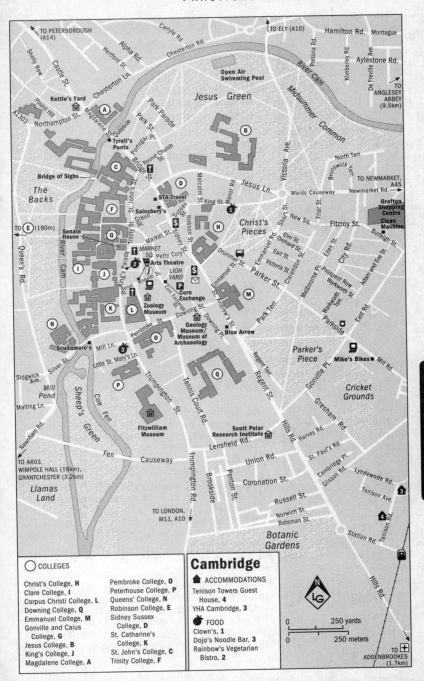

Cambridge

COLLEGES

Christ's College, **H**
Clare College, **I**
Corpus Christi College, **L**
Downing College, **Q**
Emmanuel College, **M**
Gonville and Caius College, **G**
Jesus College, **B**
King's College, **J**
Magdalene College, **A**

Pembroke College, **O**
Peterhouse College, **P**
Queens' College, **N**
Robinson College, **E**
Sidney Sussex College, **D**
St. Catharine's College, **K**
St. John's College, **C**
Trinity College, **F**

ACCOMMODATIONS
Tenison Towers Guest House, **4**
YHA Cambridge, **3**

FOOD
Clown's, **1**
Dojo's Noodle Bar, **3**
Rainbow's Vegetarian Bistro, **2**

0   250 yards
0   250 meters

CAMBRIDGE

IN RECENT NEWS

TUK-TUK...GOOSE?

Bicycles rule the road in Cambridge, but they may soon have a new motorized competitor. It's small, runs on three wheels, and is more a novelty than serious transportation.

No, it's not a tricycle–it's a *tuk-tuk*, a miniature cab popular in Southeast Asia. They can get up to about 30 mi. per hr., and they fit in narrow lanes that big-boy cars can't reach. In Asia, they are a serious mode of transportation, but in Europe they mostly serve as a joyride for tourists. Entrepreneur Malcolm Fulcher wants to expand the role of *tuk-tuks* by turning them into normal cabs.

Not everyone, however, is excited about sharing the road with these newcomers. The Cambridge Drivers Association, which represents taxi drivers, has challenged the project, citing safety concerns while avoiding mention of the competition regular cabs would face. Previous tourist *tuk-tuk* fleets have run into problems elsewhere in England—they were even kicked out of Bath after two riders were injured in an accident.

Proponents argue that accidents are relatively rare and that smaller vehicles are better for the environment. It's unknown yet whether the *tuk-tuks* will be approved, but if you're starving for slow and quirky transportation, there's always punting.

ACCOMMODATIONS AND CAMPING

Demand for accommodations in Cambridge is always high, and rooms are scarce. John Maynard Keynes, who studied and taught at Cambridge, tells us that low supply and high demand usually mean one thing: high prices. B&Bs cluster around **Portugal Street** and **Tenison Road** outside the city center.

Tenison Towers Guest House, 148 Tenison Rd. (☎01223 363 924; www.cambridgecitytenisontowers.com), 2 blocks from train station. Sunny rooms and freshly baked muffins in a Victorian house. Free Wi-Fi. Singles £40; doubles £60-66; triples £84. Cash only. ❹

Warkworth Guest House, Warkworth Terr. (☎01223 363 682). Spacious ensuite rooms near the bus station in a Victorian mansion. Breakfast included. Free Wi-Fi in lounge. Singles £55; twins and doubles £75; ensuite triples £90; families £95. MC/V. ❺

Travelodge, Clifton Way (☎0871 984 6101; www.travelodge.co.uk), down Hills Rd. past the train station. This big chain hotel is a bit of a hike to the city center but still a good option for students on a budget. Double rooms from £60. AmEx/MC/V. ❺

YHA Cambridge, 97 Tenison Rd. (☎01223 354 601), close to the train station. Relaxed, welcoming atmosphere draws a diverse clientele. 2 TV lounges and a kitchen. English breakfast included; other meals available. Lockers £1. Luggage storage £1-2. Laundry available. Internet £1 per 30 min. Reception 24hr. Dorms £20. MC/V. ❷

The Castle, 37 St. Andrews St. (☎01223 307 477; www.thecastlecambridge.com). When you first walk into this stylish restaurant and bar, you may not realize that there's a B&B upstairs. Closer to the city center than most accommodations. Shared bathrooms. Doubles £75. AmEx/MC/V. ❺

Highfield Farm Camping Park, Long Rd., Comberton (☎01223 262 308; www.highfieldfarmtouringpark. co.uk). Take Cambus #18 to Comberton (every 45min.) from Drummer St. Showers and laundry. Electricity £3. Sites May-Sept. £12-14; Apr. and Oct. £11. Cash only. ❶

FOOD

Market Square has bright pyramids of cheap fruit and vegetables. (Open M-Sa 9:30am-5pm.) Cheap Indian and Mediterranean fare on the edges of the city center satisfies hearty appetites. South of town, **Hills Road** and **Mill Road** are full of affordable restaurants popular

with the college crowd. Get groceries at **Sainsbury's**, 44 Sidney St.
(☎01223 366 891. Open M-Sa 8am-10pm, Su 11am-5pm.)

Clown's, 54 King St. (☎01223 355 711). The staff at this cozy Italian eatery will remember your name if you come more than once. Children's artwork plasters the orange walls. Huge portions of pasta and dessert (£2.50-7). Set menu includes a drink, salad, small pasta, and cake (£7.50). Open daily 8am-11pm. Cash only; accepts Euro. ❷

The Regal, 38-39 St. Andrews St. (☎01223 366 459). The largest pub in the UK. 3 floors, 2 bars, and lots of slot machines. Check out the value menu (£3-4) for classic fare. Cheap pints (£1.50-2.50) to accompany your meal. Free Wi-Fi. Open M-Th and Su 9am-midnight, F-Sa 9am-2am. AmEx/MC/V over £5. ❶

CB1, 32 Mill Rd. (☎01223 576 306). A student hangout coffee shop with hot drinks (£1-2) and walls crammed with books. Claims to be the oldest internet cafe in Cambridge (est. 1994). Enjoy free Wi-Fi while lounging on couches. Open M-Th 9am-8pm, F 9am-9pm, Sa-Su 10am-8pm. Cash only. ❶

CB2, 5-7 Norfolks St. (☎01223 508 503). Try the salmon niçoise or goat cheese parcels. Occasional art exhibits and a library in the back. Entrees are classy but a little pricey (£8-15). Open daily 10am-midnight; kitchen open until 10:30pm. MC/V. ❸

Dojo's Noodle Bar, 1-2 Mill Ln. (☎01223 363 471; www.dojonoodlebar.co.uk). Rave reviews bring long lines, but the enormous plates of wok-fried, soup-based, and sauce-based noodles are served quickly from the counter. Wide selection of vegetarian options and rice dishes. Everything under £8. Open M-Th noon-2:30pm and 5:30-11pm, F noon-4pm and 5:30-11pm, Sa-Su noon-11pm. MC/V. ❷

Eraina Tavern, 2 Free School Lane. (☎01223 368 786). Relaxed family-run eatery that serves up a little bit of everything (including Greek, Italian, and Indian). Entrees £7-14. Open M-F noon-2:30pm and 5:30-11:30pm, Sa noon-11:30pm, Su noon-11pm. AmEx/MC/V. ❸

Rainbow's Vegetarian Bistro, 9A King's Parade (☎01223 321 551; www.rainbowcafe.co.uk). Even carnivores enjoy this basement bistro. Serves Asian-inspired vegetarian fare, all for £8-9. Open Tu-Sa 10am-10pm and Su-M 10am-4pm. Kitchen open until 9:30pm. MC/V. ❷

Mai Thai Restaurant, Park Terr. (☎01223 367 480; www.mai-thai-restaurant.com). This stylish, colorful restaurant is home to great views across Parker's Piece and serves authentic Thai food with fresh ingredients. Entrees £7-16. Popular set lunch menu £10. Open daily noon-3pm and 6-11pm. AmEx/MC/V. ❸

La Raza, 4 Rose Crescent (☎01223 464 550; www.laraza.co.uk). Throbbing with live music every night. Affordable tapas menu (£3-14). Long glittering bar gilded with blue light. Open M-Th 11am-3:30pm and 7pm-1am, F-Sa 11am-4:30pm and 7pm-2am, Su noon-4pm. MC/V. ❷

The Curry King, 5 Jordan's Yard (☎01223 324 351). Head down the alley next to The Mitre on Bridge St. Watch yourself enjoy traditional Indian dishes through the mirror-covered walls of the upstairs dining room. Entrees £5.50-12. Open daily noon-2:30pm, 6pm-midnight. AmEx/MC/V. ❷

Sauce Bar, 1-3 Station Rd. (☎01223 360 268; www.club-salsa.co.uk). At night, this small restaurant turns into a spicy Latin club, with salsa classes (£5) M and W. Gourmet pizzas (£5) are a steal. Tapas £3-6. Entrees £7-12. Open M-Th noon-11pm and F-Sa noon-midnight. AmEx/MC/V. ❶

◎ SIGHTS

Cambridge is an architect's utopia, packing some of England's most impressive monuments into less than 1 sq. mi. The soaring King's College Chapel and St. John's Bridge of Sighs are sightseeing staples, while more obscure college quads open onto ornate courtyards and gardens. Most historic buildings are on the east bank of the Cam between Magdalene Bridge and Silver St. On the west bank, the meadowed Backs border the elegant Fellows' Gardens, giving the university a unique juxtaposition of cow and college.

The University of Cambridge has three eight-week terms: Michaelmas (Oct.-Dec.), Lent (Jan.-Mar.), and Easter (Apr.-June). Visitors can access most of the 31 colleges daily, although times vary; call the TIC (p. 248) for hours. Many are closed to sightseers during Easter term, virtually all are closed during exams (from mid-May to mid-June), and visiting hours are limited during May Week festivities. A visit to King's, Trinity, and St. John's Colleges should top your to-do list, as should a stroll or punt along the Cam. Porters (bowler-wearing ex-servicemen) maintain security. The fastest way to blow your tourist cover is to trample the grass of the courtyards, a privilege reserved for the elite. In July and August, most undergrads skip town, leaving it to PhD candidates, international students, and mobs of tourists.

COLLEGES

KING'S COLLEGE. King's College was founded by Henry VI in 1441 as a partner school to Eton: it was not until 1873 that students from other prep schools were admitted. Today, however, King's is the most socially liberal of the Cambridge colleges, drawing more of its students from state schools than any other. Its most stunning attraction is the Gothic **King's College Chapel.** From the southwest corner of the courtyard, you can see where Henry's master mason left off and the Tudors began work—the earlier stone is off-white. Inside, painted angels hover against the world's largest fan-vaulted ceiling. The nave is decorated with all the symbols of the triumphant Tudor family: wide-petaled roses, snarling dragons, and unicorns. Behind the altar hangs Peter Paul Rubens's *Adoration of the Magi* (1639). John Maynard Keynes, EM Forster, and Salman Rushdie all lived in King's College. In mid-June, university degree ceremonies are held in the Georgian Senate House. *(King's Parade.* ☎ *01223 331 100. Chapel and grounds open M-Sa 9:30am-5pm, Su 10am-5pm. Last entry 4:30pm. Contact TIC for tours. Listing of services and musical events available at porter's lodge. Choral services 10:30am, often 5:30pm. £5, students £3.50. Audio tour £2.50.)*

TRINITY COLLEGE. Henry VIII intended the College of the Holy and Undivided Trinity (founded in 1546) to be the largest and richest in Cambridge. Currently Britain's third-largest landowner (after the queen and the Church of England), the college has amply fulfilled his wish. The alma mater of Sir Isaac Newton, who lived in E staircase for 30 years, the college has many other equally illustrious alumni: literati Dryden, Byron, Tennyson, and Nabokov; atom-splitter Ernest Rutherford; philosopher Ludwig Wittgenstein; and Indian statesman Jawaharlal Nehru. The **Great Court,** the world's largest enclosed courtyard, is reached from Trinity St. through **Great Gate.** The castle-like gateway is fronted by a statue of Henry VIII grasping a wooden chair leg—the original scepter was stolen so frequently that the college administration was forced to remove it. The apple tree near the gate is supposedly a descendent of the tree that inspired Newton's theory of gravity; in the north cloister of **Nevile's Court,** Newton calculated the speed of sound by stamping his foot and timing the echo. On the west side of the court stand the dour **chapel** and the **King's Gate tower.** Lord Byron used to bathe nude in the **fountain,** the only one in Cambridge. The poet also kept a pet bear (college rules forbade only cats and dogs). The south side of the court is home to the **Master's Lodge** and the **Great Hall.** The **Wren Library** houses alumnus AA Milne's handwritten copies of *Winnie the Pooh* and Newton's personal copy of his *Principia.* Pass through the drab **New Court** (Prince

Charles's former residence) to get to the **Backs,** where you can enjoy the view from **Trinity Bridge.** *(Trinity St.* ☎ *01223 338 400. Chapel and courtyard open daily 10am-5pm. Easter-Oct. £2.50, concessions £1.30, children £1, families £4.40; Nov.-Easter free for all.)*

SAINT JOHN'S COLLEGE. Established in 1511 by Lady Margaret Beaufort, mother of Henry VIII, St. John's centers on a paved plaza rather than a grassy courtyard. The **Bridge of Sighs,** named after the Venetian original, connects the older part of the college with the towering Neo-Gothic extravagance of **New Court.** The **School of Pythagoras,** a 12th-century pile of wood and stone thought to be the oldest complete building in Cambridge, hides in St. John's Gardens. The college also boasts the longest room in the city—the **Fellows' Room** in Second Court spans 93 ft. and was the site of D-Day planning. *(St. John's St.* ☎ *01223 338 600. Open M-F 10am-5pm, Sa-Su 9:30am-5:30pm. Evensong Tu-Su 6:30pm. £3, concessions £2.)*

QUEENS' COLLEGE. Aptly named Queens' College was founded by two queens: Queen Margaret of Anjou in 1448 and Elizabeth Woodville (queen consort of Edward VI) in 1465. Queens' College has the only unaltered Tudor courtyard in Cambridge, but the main attraction is the **Mathematical Bridge.** *(Silver St.* ☎ *01223 335 511. Open Mar.-Oct. daily 10am-5pm. £2.)*

CLARE COLLEGE. Clare's coat of arms—golden teardrops ringing a black border—recalls the college's founding in 1326 by thrice-widowed, 29-year-old Lady Elizabeth de Clare. The college has some of the most cheerful **gardens** in Cambridge, and elegant **Clare Bridge,** dating from 1638, is the oldest surviving college bridge. Wander through Christopher Wren's **Old Court** for a view of the **University Library,** where 82 mi. of shelves hold books arranged by size rather than subject. *(Trinity Ln.* ☎ *01223 333 200. Open daily 10:45am-4:30pm. £2.50, under 12 free.)*

CHRIST'S COLLEGE. Founded as "God's house" in 1448 and renamed in 1505, Christ's has since won fame for its **gardens** and its association with John Milton and Charles Darwin. For $2.50, you can see the rooms where Darwin occasionally studied theology when he wasn't out drinking or hunting. *(Open W, Th, Sa 10am-noon and 2-4pm.)* **New Court,** on King St., is one of Cambridge's most modern structures, with symmetrical concrete walls and dark windows. Bowing to pressure from aesthetically offended Cantabrigians, the college built a wall to block the view of the building from all sides except the inner courtyard. *(St. Andrews St.* ☎ *01223 334 900. Gardens open daily term time 9am-4:30pm; summer 9:30am-noon. Fellows' Garden open M-F 9:30am-noon. Free.)*

JESUS COLLEGE. Beyond the walk called the "Chimney" lies a courtyard fringed with flowers. Through the arch on the right sit the remains of a gloomy medieval convent. *(Jesus Ln.* ☎ *01223 339 339. Courtyard open daily 10am-8pm. Free.)*

MAGDALENE COLLEGE. Located within a 15th-century Benedictine hostel, Magdalene (MAUD-lin) was the occasional home of Christian allegorist and Oxford man C.S. Lewis. **Pepys Library,** in the second court, displays the famous diarist's collections, including the five journals written in his secret shorthand code. *(Magdalene St.* ☎ *01223 332 100. Library open M-Sa Easter-Aug. 11:30am-12:30pm and 2:30-3:30pm; from Oct. to early Dec. 2:30-3:30pm. Courtyard open daily until 6pm. Free.)*

SMALLER COLLEGES. Thomas Gray wrote his "Elegy Written in a Country Churchyard" while staying in **Peterhouse College,** the smallest college, founded in 1294. *(Trumpington St.* ☎ *01223 338 200.)* The modern brick pastiche of **Robinson College** is the newest. In 1977, local self-made man David Robinson founded it for the bargain price of $17 million, the largest single gift ever received by the university. *(Across the river on Grange Rd.* ☎ *01223 339 100.)* **Corpus Christi College,** founded in 1352 by the townspeople, contains Cambridge's oldest courtyard, aptly named Old Court and unaltered since its enclosure. The library has a huge collection of Anglo-Saxon manuscripts. Alums include Sir Francis Drake and Christopher Marlowe. (*Trumpington St.* ☎ *01223 338 000.*) The 1347 **Pembroke College** holds the earliest work of Sir Christopher Wren and counts Edmund Spenser among its grads. (*Next to Corpus Christi.* ☎ *01223 338 100.*) A chapel designed by Wren dominates the front court of **Emmanuel College,** known as "Emma." John Harvard, benefactor of a different university in a different Cambridge, studied here and is commemorated in a stained-glass window in the chapel. (*St. Andrews St.* ☎ *01223 334 200.*) **Gonville and Caius College** (KEYS) was founded twice, once in 1348 by Edmund Gonville and again in 1557 by John Keys, who chose to use the Latin form of his name. (*Trinity St.* ☎ *01223 332 400.*)

MUSEUMS AND CHURCHES

⊠FITZWILLIAM MUSEUM. The museum fills an immense Neoclassical edifice, built in 1875 to house Viscount Fitzwilliam's collections. Egyptian, Chinese, Japanese, Middle Eastern, and Greek antiquities downstairs are joined by 16th-century German armor. Upstairs, galleries feature works by Rubens, Monet, Van Gogh, and Picasso. (*Trumpington St.* ☎ *01223 332 900. Open Tu-Sa 10am-5pm, Su noon-5pm. Call about lunchtime and evening concerts. Free; suggested donation £3.*)

UNIVERSITY MUSEUM OF ZOOLOGY. Explore the animal kingdoms of past and present with this impressive collection of preserved animals and fossils. Includes several of Darwin's famous finches. Don't miss the colossal finback whale skeleton hanging above the entrance, which originally washed ashore in Sussex. (*Downing St.* ☎ *01223 336 650; www.zoo.cam.ac.uk/museum. Open M-F 10am-4:45pm, Sa 11am-4pm. Free.*)

MUSEUM OF ARCHAEOLOGY AND ANTHROPOLOGY. The first floor of this museum holds archaeological treasures from all around the world, including a collection of intimidating primitive weapons. But the real highlight is upstairs, where an enormous totem pole from the Haida tribe of British Columbia will leave you wondering how the heck they got it in there. (*Downing St.* ☎ *01223 333 516; www.maa.cam.ac.uk. Open Tu-Sa 10:30am-4:30pm. Free.*)

SEDGWICK MUSEUM OF EARTH SCIENCES. As a young man, Charles Darwin accompanied Adam Sedgwick on geological expeditions to North Wales. Years later, the pious Sedgwick wrote Darwin to let him know that he read the Bible-defying *Origin of Species* "with more pain than pleasure." Today, Sedgwick's museum features an exhibit dedicated to his rebellious pupil's geological work. The museum also features a huge array of ancient rock samples and fossils, many of them from the Cambridge area. (*Downing St.* ☎ *01223 333 456. Open M-F 10am-1pm and 2-5pm, Sa 10am-4pm. Free.*)

WHIPPLE MUSEUM OF HISTORY OF SCIENCE. A smaller museum that show-cases gadgets of varying antiquity, the Whipple Museum features a collection of chunky calculators from the 1970s, including a TI-30. Upstairs, imagine yourself as Jane Austen in a recreated Victorian parlour. (*Free School Lane.* ☎ *01223 334 500. Open M-F 12:30-4:30pm. Free.*)

CAMBRIDGE AND COUNTY FOLK MUSEUM. Explore the social history of Cambridge in this 16th-century building located in the oldest part of the city. See how the living habits of Cantabridgians have change through history in several recreated living spaces. The museum is staffed by friendly volunteers. (*2/3 Castle St.* ☎ *01223 355 159; www.folkmuseum.org.uk. Open Tu-Sa 10:30am-5pm, Su 2-5pm. Last entry 4:30pm. £3.50, concessions £2, children £1.*)

OTHER SIGHTS

BOTANIC GARDEN. For those with a green thumb, this garden displays over 8000 plant species. It was opened in 1846 by John Henslow, Darwin's mentor. *(☎01223 336 265. Open daily Apr.-Sept. 10am-6pm; Oct. and Feb.-Mar. 10am-5pm; Nov.-Jan. 10am-4pm. £4, concessions £3.50.)*

KETTLE'S YARD. Kettle's Yard was founded by former Tate curator Jim Ede and displays an extensive collection of early 20th-century art. *(At the corner of Castle and Northampton St. ☎01223 352 124; www.kettlesyard.org.uk. House open Apr.-Sept. Tu-Su 1:30-4:30pm; Oct.-Mar. Tu-Su 2-4pm. Gallery open Tu-Su 11:30am-5pm. Free.)*

SCOTT POLAR RESEARCH INSTITUTE. The institute commemorates Arctic expeditions with photos and memorabilia. *(Lensfield Rd. ☎01223 336 540; www.spri.cam.ac.uk. Open Tu-F 11am-1pm and 2-4pm, Sa noon-4pm. Free.)*

ROUND CHURCH (HOLY SEPULCHRE). The Round Church is one of five surviving circular churches in England and the second-oldest building in Cambridge, predating even the university. Built in 1130, it is based on the pattern of the Holy Sepulchre in Jerusalem. *(On the corner of Bridge St. and St. John's St. ☎01223 311 602. Tours W 11am and Su 2:30pm. Open Tu-Sa 10am-5pm, Su 1-5pm. £2, students and children free. Tours £3.50.)*

SAINT BENET'S. The only building older than the Holy Sepulchre is this Saxon church on Benet St., built in 1025. *(☎01223 355 146. Open daily 8am-6pm. Free.)*

GREAT SAINT MARY'S CHURCH. The tower of Great Saint Mary's Church gives splendid views of the colleges. When you get there, pray that the 12 bells don't ring while you're ascending the 123 tightly packed spiral steps. *(Off King's Parade. Tower open M-Sa 9:30am-4:30pm, Su 12:30-4pm. £2.50, children £1.25. Church free.)*

▣ ENTERTAINMENT

CINEMA AND THEATER

The **Arts Box Office** (☎01223 503 333; open M-Sa noon-8pm), around the corner from the TIC on Pea's Hill, handles ticket sales for the **Arts Theatre,** which shows musicals, dramas, and pantomime. The **ADC Theatre** (Amateur Dramatic Club), Park St. (☎01223 300 085), puts up student-produced plays, term-time movies, and a folk festival during the summer months. The **Corn Exchange,** at the corner of Wheeler St. and Corn Exchange St. across from the TIC, is a popular venue for concerts. (☎01223 357 851. £10-30, concessions available. Box office open M-Sa 10am-6pm, until 9pm on performance days; Su 6-9pm on performance days only.) Independent and foreign-language films play at the **Arts Picture House,** 38-39 St. Andrews St. (☎01223 042 050; www.picturehouses. co.uk. M-F £6.40, Sa-Su £7.40, students £5.50.)

▣ PUNTING

Punting on the Cam is as traditional and obligatory as afternoon tea. Touristy and overrated? Maybe, but it's still a blast. Punters take two routes—from Magdalene Bridge to Silver St. or from Silver St. to Grantchester. The shorter, busier, and more interesting first route passes the colleges and the Backs. To propel your boat, thrust the pole behind the boat into the riverbed and rotate the pole in your hands as you push forward. Punt-bombing—jumping from bridges into the river alongside a punt to tip it—is an art form. Some more ambitious punters climb out midstream, scale a bridge while their boat passes underneath, and jump back down from the other side. Be wary of bridge-top pole-stealers. You can rent at **Scudamore's,** Silver St. Bridge. (☎01223 359 750; www.scudamores.com. M-F £16 per hr., Sa-Su £18 per hr. £80 deposit. MC/V.) Student-punted tours (£14, students £12) are another option.

SHOPPING

Cambridge's city center hosts most national chains as well as a few quirky local outfits. The main mall is **Lion Yard,** St. Andrews St. (www.thelionyard.co.uk). If you find yourself on the other side of town, **Grafton Centre** (East Rd.; www.graftoncentre.co.uk) has an impressive array of shops and restaurants. For a multicultural experience, try the international grocery shops that line Mill Rd.

MAJOR CHAINS

Zara, 66 St. Andrews St. (☎01223 558 570; www.zara.com). The same looks as the big designers, but cheaper. Open M-Tu and Th-Sa 9am-6pm, W 9am-8pm, Su 11am-5pm. AmEx/MC/V.

John Lewis, 10 Downing St. (☎01223 361 292; www.johnlewis.com). Not to be confused with 10 Downing St., London. 5-fl. department store with clothes, home furnishings, and much more. Open M-Tu and Th-Sa 9am-6pm, W 9am-8pm, Su 11am-5pm.

HMV, Lion Yard (☎01223 319 090; www.hmv.co.uk). Movies, music, and video games. Open M-Tu and Th-Sa 9am-6pm, W 9am-8pm, Su 11am-5pm. AmEx/MC/V.

Oxfam, 2 Mill Rd. (☎01223 321 921; www.oxfam.org). Ubiquitous British charity shop that sells vinyl records, clothes, postcards, and more. Open M-Sa 10am-6pm, Su 11am-4pm. MC/V.

CLOTHING AND GIFTS

Ark, 2 St. Mary's Passage (☎01223 363 372). Funky, friendly clothing shop with an eclectic collection. Climb the spiral staircase to reach the thrift racks on the top foor. Open M-Sa 9am-7pm, Su 10am-5pm. AmEx/MC/V.

The Magic Joke Shop, 29 Bridge St. (☎01223 353 003; www.jokeshop.co.uk). Magic tricks, prank supplies, scary masks, and more fun gifts. Pass through saloon-style doors to see the adult novelties in the back. Open M-Sa 9am-5:30pm, Su 10am-4pm. AmEx/MC/V.

Spice Gate, 14 Mill Rd. (☎01223 513 097). International grocery store with exotic meats, olives, sauces, and (of course) spices. Open daily 9am-1am. MC/V.

The Haunted Bookshop, 9 St. Edward's Passage (☎01223 312 913). Just off King's Parade, this 1-room used book shop specializes in old children's books. Watch out for the ghost that supposedly roams the shelves. Open M-Sa 10am-5pm. AmEx/MC/V.

🎭🎟 PUBS AND NIGHTLIFE

King Street has a diverse collection of pubs. Most stay open 11am-11pm (Su noon-10:30pm). The local brewery, **Greene King,** supplies many of them. Pubs are the core of Cambridge nightlife, but clubs are also on the curriculum. The city is small enough that a quick stroll will reveal the most popular venues.

The Eagle, 8 Benet St. (☎01223 505 020). Cambridge's oldest pub (in business since 1525) is in the heart of town and packed with boisterous tourists. When Watson and Crick rushed in to announce the discovery of DNA, the barmaid insisted they settle their 4-shilling tab. Check out the RAF room, where WWII pilots stood on each other's shoulders to burn their initials into the ceiling. Open M-Sa 11am-11pm, Su noon-10:30pm. AmEx/MC/V over £5.

The Anchor, Silver St. (☎01223 353 554). This jolly-looking pub, overflowing with beer and good cheer, is anchored right on the Cam. Scoff at amateur punters colliding under

Silver St. Bridge or savor a pint at the same spot from which Pink Floyd's Syd Barrett drew his inspiration. Open M-Th and Su 11am-11pm, F-Sa 11am-midnight. Kitchen open M-Sa noon-10pm, Su noon-9pm. AmEx/MC/V.

The Kings Street Run, 86-88 Kings St. (☎01223 328 900). Named for a famous pub crawl down Kings St. that usually ended in stumbling rather than running. Used to be a biker bar, and leather-clad riders still pop in occasionally. Open M-Th 11am-11pm, F-Sa 11am-midnight, Su noon-11pm. MC/V.

The Kingston Arms, 33 Kingston St. (☎01223 319 414; www.kingston-arms.co.uk). Friendly local watering hole with cheap ales and a sunny garden. Free internet and Wi-Fi. Open M-Th noon-2:30pm and 5-11pm, F-Sa noon-midnight, Su noon-11pm. AmEx/MC/V.

The Mill, 14 Mill Ln. (☎01223 357 026), off Silver St. Bridge. Low ceilings, wood interior, and great beer. Patrons relax outside for punt- and people-watching. Features a rotating selection of ales. Open daily noon-11pm. Kitchen open M-F noon-2:30pm and 6-8:30pm, Sa-Su noon-4pm. MC/V.

The Free Press, Prospect Row (☎01223 368 337). Named after an abolitionist rag and popular with locals. No pool table, no cell phones, no overwhelming music—just good beer and entertaining conversation. Open M-F noon-2:30pm and 6-11pm, Sa noon-3pm and 6-11pm, Su noon-3pm and 7-10:30pm. MC/V.

The Fez Club, 15 Market Passage (☎01223 519 224; www.cambridgefez.com). Moroccan setting complete with floor cushions. Dance to everything from Latin to trance. Cover M-Th and Su £2-5, F-Sa £5-8; students free W before 11pm. Open daily 10pm-3am. MC/V.

The Kambar Club, 1 Wheeler St. (☎01223 842 725), opposite the Corn Exchange box office. A mix of indie and electronica tunes. Drinks can be expensive, but the club's energy is great on weekends. Cover £5, students £3. Open M-Sa 10pm-2:30am. MC/V.

❈ FESTIVALS

May Week, actually in June—you would expect a better understanding of simple chronology from those bright Cambridge students. A celebration of the end of the term, the week is crammed with concerts, plays, and balls followed by recuperative riverside breakfasts and 5am punting. The boat clubs compete in races known as the **bumps.** Crews attempt to ram the boat in front before being bumped from behind. The celebration includes **Footlights Revue,** a series of skits by current undergrads. Past performers have included future *Monty Python* stars John Cleese and Eric Idle. £250 per person.

Strawberry Fair (www.strawberry-fair.org), on the 1st Sa in June. Attracts over 20,000 visitors with food, music, and body piercing. Free.

Midsummer Fair (☎01223 457 555; www.cambridge-summer.co.uk.), in the 3rd week of June. Dating from the 16th century, this festival fills the Midsummer Common with carnival rides and wholesome fun for 5 days.

Summer in the City (www.cambridge-summer.co.uk). Keeps Cambridge buzzing with a series of concerts and special exhibits culminating in a huge weekend celebration, the **Cambridge Folk Festival** (☎01223 357 851; www.cambridgefolkfestival.co.uk), on the last weekend of July. World-renowned musicians—past performers include James Taylor and Elvis Costello—gather for folk, jazz, and blues in Cherry Hinton Hall. Book tickets (about £43) well in advance; camping on the grounds is an additional £10-30.

Cambridge Shakespeare Festival (www.cambridgeshakespeare.com), throughout July and August. In association with the festival at Oxford, this festival features plays from the Bard. Tickets (£14, concessions £10) are available at the door and from the City Centre Box Office at the Corn Exchange.

DAYTRIPS FROM CAMBRIDGE

GRANTCHESTER

Take the marked path to Grantchester Meadows following the river. Grantchester village lies 1 mi. from the meadows; ask the way or follow the blue bike path signs (1½hr. by foot from Cambridge). If you have the energy to paddle your way, rent a punt or canoe. You can also hop on Stagecoach #18 or 18A (9-11 per day, round-trip £3.30).

"Grantchester! Ah Grantchester! There's peace and holy quiet there," wrote poet Rupert Brooke in 1912, and his words hold true today. This sweet, unsullied piece of bucolic England is still a mecca for Cambridge literary types. The golden meadows banking the Cam are a refuge from the University's intensity. The 14th-century **Parish Church of Saint Andrew and Saint Mary,** on Millway, is weathered and intimate. (☎01223 895 664. Free.) Have tea among the apple trees at lovely ⊠**Orchard Tea Gardens ❶,** 45 Millway, once a haunt of the "neopagans," a Grantchester offshoot of the famous Bloomsbury Group. Start your morning with scones (£2) and end your day with one of the occasional summer plays put on there. (☎01223 845 788; www.orchard-grantchester.com. Open daily 9:30am-7pm.) The main village pub, the **Rupert Brooke ❷,** 2 Broadway, is striving to improve the reputation of British cuisine. Its large beer garden overlooks Grantchester meadows. (☎01223 840 295; www.therupertbrooke.com. Open M-Sa noon-9:30pm, Su noon-8pm.)

ANGLESEY ABBEY

6 mi. northeast of Cambridge on the B1102 (signposted from A14). Bus #10 runs from Drummer St. (30min., 2 per hr.); ask to be let off at Lode Crossroads. ☎01223 810 080. House open Mar.-Nov. W-Su and bank holidays 1-5pm. Gardens open Apr.-Oct. W-Su and bank holidays 10:30am-5:30pm. £9.90, children £4.90. Garden and mill without house £5.80, children £2.90. Winter Garden Jan.-Mar. £4.40/£2.20; Nov.-Dec. £4.75/£2.40.

Northeast of Cambridge, 12th-century Anglesey Abbey has been remodeled to house the priceless exotica of the first Lord Fairhaven. The abbey has a collection of over 50 clocks, including the mesmerizing Congreve rolling ball clock in the library. If you have the time (get it?), make your own scavenger hunt and try to find all 50. After contemplating the 7000 volumes on the bookshelves, stroll through the 98 acres of gardens, where trees and statuary punctuate lines of clipped hedges and manicured lawns.

AUDLEY END AND SAFFRON WALDEN

Trains leave Cambridge for Audley End (15min., 3 per hr., round-trip £5.60). ☎01799 522 399. House open Apr.-Sept. W-F and Su 11am-5pm, Sa 11am-3pm. Grounds open Apr.-Sept. W-Su 10am-5pm, Oct. and Mar. 10am-4pm. Last entry 1hr. before closing. House can only be viewed as part of a 1hr. guided tour (10 per day). £10.70, concessions £9.10.

The magnificent Jacobean hall is only a quarter of Audley End's former size—it once extended down to the river, where part of the Cam was rerouted into an artificial lake. The grand halls display cases of stuffed critters, including some extinct species, amid paintings by Canaletto and Hans Holbein the Younger. One mile east of Audley End is the town of **Saffron Walden,** best known for the pargeting (plaster molding) of its Tudor buildings. The town is home to a Victorian hedge maze as well as England's largest turf maze, located on the town common. The **Tourist Information Centre** is on Market Sq. (☎01799 510 444. Open Easter-Oct. M-Sa 9:30am-5:30pm, Nov.-Mar. M-Sa 9:30am-5pm.) If you stay for the night, rest at the **YHA hostel ❶,** 1 Myddylton Pl. (☎0870 770 6014. Lockout 10am-5pm. Curfew 11pm. Open July-Aug. daily, Sept.-Oct. and Apr.-June Tu-Sa, Mar. F-Sa. Dorms from £12. MC/V.)

ELY
☎**(0)1353**

The prosperous town of Ely (EE-lee) was an island until steam power drained
the surrounding Fens in the early 1800s, creating a flat, reed-covered region
of rich farmland. Legend has it that the city got its name when St. Dunstan
transformed local monks into eels for their lack of piety. A more likely story
is that "Elig" (Isle of Eels) was named for the bountiful slitherers that infested
the surrounding waters—they were once so numerous that taxes were payable
in eels. Today, Ely remains proud of its eel-rich heritage. The local market sells
them fresh from the Great River Ouse, Eel Day celebrates the city's history, and
the Eel Heritage Walk snakes through all of the city's major sights.

⊏ TRANSPORTATION. Ely is the junction for **trains** (☎08457 484 950) between
London (1¼hr., 2 per hr., £22.40) and various points in East Anglia, including Cambridge (15min., 3 per hr., round-trip £4) and Norwich (1hr., 2 per hr.,
£13.50). Cambus **buses** (☎01223 423 554) #9, X9, and 12 leave from Market St.
to Cambridge (50min., 1 per hr., £3.70). The 17 mi. **walk** across the flat fens from
Cambridge to Ely is also an option. Ask at the TIC in Cambridge or Ely for a
copy of the helpful guide *The Fen Rivers Way* (£2).

⊟⊿ ORIENTATION AND PRACTICAL INFORMATION. Ely's two major
streets—**High Street** and **Market Street**—run parallel to the length of the cathedral. To reach the cathedral from the train station, walk up Station Rd., which
changes to Back Hill and then to The Gallery.

Oliver Cromwell's house is the current home of the **Tourist Information Centre,**
29 St. Mary's St., which books rooms for £2 plus a 10% deposit; call at least
two days ahead. (☎01353 662 062. Open Apr.-Oct. daily 10am-5pm; Nov.-Mar.
M-F and Su 11am-4pm, Sa 10am-5pm.) Other services include: **internet** access
at the **library,** 6 The Cloisters, just off Market Pl. (☎0345 045 5225; internet 50p
per 10min.; open Tu-W and F 10am-5pm, Th 9:30am-8pm, Sa 9:30am-4pm, Su
noon-4pm); **police,** Nutholt Ln. (☎0845 456 4564); **Prince of Wales Hospital,** Lynn
Rd. (☎01353 652 000); and the **post office,** 19-21 High St. (☎01353 669 946; open
M and Th-F 9am-5:30pm, W 9:30am-5:30pm, Sa 9am-1pm). **Postcode:** CB7 4LQ.

⌐⊡ ACCOMMODATIONS AND FOOD. Ely has few single rooms—your best
bet for finding one is the TIC accommodations booking service. **The Post House
❸,** 12A Egremont St., is a family home close to the city center. (☎01353 667
184. Singles £28; doubles £54, ensuite £60. Cash only.)

Many shops close on Tuesday afternoons, as they have for centuries. Stock
up on provisions at the **market** in Market Pl. (Open Th and Sa 8am-3pm.) **Tesco**
supermarket, Angel Drove, is next to the train station and has ATMs outside.
(☎08456 779 256. Open M-F 24hr., Sa 10pm-10am, Su 4pm-8am. AmEx/MC/V.)
Don't miss the Tea Guild's "Top Tearoom of 2007," **⊠Peacocks Tearoom ❶,** 65
Waterside, near the Babylon Gallery on the River Ouse. The teacup-size shop
has over 50 varieties of tea (£2.25) and sweet and savory snacks for £4-7.
(☎01353 661 100; www.peacockstearoom.co.uk. Open W-Su 10:30am-5pm.)
Although the river no longer oozes eels, the **Old Fire Engine House ❸,** 25 St. Mary's
St., often features the delicacy on its menu. The handwritten menu of the day
is posted in the window. (☎01353 662 582. Entrees £16. Lighter fare £5-9. Open
M-Sa 10:30-11:30am, 12:15-2pm, 3:45-5:30pm and 7:15-9pm; Su 12:15-5:15pm.
MC/V.) Affordable Indian restaurants line **Backhill Street.**

◙ SIGHTS. Let the tower of **⊠Ely Cathedral** guide you to the city center. When
lit, it can be seen for miles. The Saxon princess St. Etheldreda founded a monastery on the site in AD 673. Norman masons took a century to construct the

nave, and Victorian artists painted the ceiling and completed the stained glass. The **Octagon** replaced the original tower, which collapsed in 1322. Don't overlook the 215 ft. tiled **floor maze** or the movingly spare **Lady Chapel**, shorn of its original statuary. (☎01353 667 735. Open Apr.-Sept. daily 7am-7pm, Nov.-Mar. 7am-6:30pm. Octagon tours Apr.-Oct. 3 per day, Nov.-Mar. call ahead. West Tower tours Apr.-Oct. subject to guide availability. Evensong M-Sa 5:30pm, Su 3:45pm. Cathedral £5.50, concessions £4.70. Octagon tours £5. West Tower tours £5.) In the cathedral's brilliant ▊**Stained Glass Museum** are eight centuries of kaleidoscopic glass art. One hundred exquisite pieces detail the history of the art form, from yellow-toned medieval peasants to Victorian portraits. (☎01353 660 347; www.stainedglassmuseum.com. Open Easter-Oct. M-F 10:30am-5pm, Sa 10:30am-5:30pm, Su noon-6pm; Nov.-Easter M-Sa 10:30am-5pm, Su noon-4:30pm. Last entry 30min. before closing. £3.50, concessions £2.50, families £7. Museum and cathedral £8.30, concessions £6.70.) At the **brass rubbing center** in the cathedral, visitors can use chalk and paper to rub copies of engravings. (☎01353 660 345. Open M-Sa 10:30am-4pm, Su noon-3pm. Materials £2-7.)

For an architectural tour of Ely, follow the path outlined in the TIC's free *Eel Trail* pamphlet, which also highlights artwork related to the eel. **Oliver Cromwell's House,** 29 St. Mary's St., where the TIC is housed, still retains its 17th-century decor. The moving wax figures portraying Cromwellian domestic life and the distinctly un-creepy "haunted" bedrooms are not as much fun as the dress-up corner, where you can don plumed hats and military helmets. Fish and chips will look positively gourmet after a perusal of Lady Cromwell's recipe for eel pie with oysters. (☎01353 662 062. Open Apr.-Oct. daily 10am-5pm; Nov.-Mar. M-F and Su 11am-4pm, Sa 10am-5pm. £4.40, concessions £4, children £3, families £12.50. Free audio guide. MC/V over £10.) **Ely Museum,** at the Bishop's Gaol on the corner of Market St. and Lynn Rd., gives the history of the Fenland city. (☎01353 666 655; www.elymuseum. org.uk. Open in summer M-Sa 10:30am-5pm, Su 1-5pm; in winter M and W-Sa 10:30am-4pm, Su 1-4pm. £3.50, concessions £2.50.)

EDINBURGH

A city of elegant stone set between rolling hills and ancient volcanoes, Edinburgh (ED-in-bur-ra; pop. 500,000) is the pride of Scotland. Since King David I granted it "burgh" (town) status in 1130, Edinburgh has been a haven for forward-thinking intellectuals and innovative artists. Today, world-class universities craft the next generation of Edinburgh's thinkers. Businessmen, students, and lots of backpackers mix amid the city's medieval architecture and mingle in lively pubs and cutting-edge clubs. In August, Edinburgh becomes a mecca for the arts, drawing talent and crowds from around the globe to its International and Fringe Festivals.

LIFE AND TIMES

HISTORY

BEFORE EDINBURGH WAS EDINBURGH: THE PREHISTORY OF CASTLE ROCK. Little is known about Edinburgh's earliest inhabitants. The area's Roman relics date from the AD first century, but **Castle Rock** (known today as Edinburgh Castle) has been occupied continuously for 3000 years. By AD 600, the Scottish mainland was occupied by four warring tribes: the native **Picts,** the Celtic **Scots,** and the Germanic **Anglo-Saxons.**

Edinburgh was captured and fortified by **Edwin of Northumbria.** In AD 843, a Scottish victory over the Picts signaled the beginning of Scottish national consolidation.

THE ORIGINAL BRITISH INVASION. In 1286, **King Alexander III** died without a male heir. His two sons and his daughter all died in the last five years of his life. From 1286 to 1292, Alexander's granddaughter **Margaret** ruled during a period of interregnum, so called because she was never officially crowned Queen. The English seized this opportunity to snatch up Scotland. Margaret's brother, **Edward I of England,** appointed himself feudal overlord of Scotland in 1291. After a stint in England, Edward launched a full-on invasion of Scotland in 1296. This began Scotland's long history of oppression under the English. It also earned Edward the nickname "Hammer of the Scots."

The **Wars of Independence** that would ensue bred figures like **William Wallace** and **Robert the Bruce,** who emerged as Scotland's leader. Robert led the Scots to victory over Edward II in the 1314 **Battle of Bannockburn** and briefly won Scottish independence, though Edinburgh itself fell briefly again to England during the **Second War of Independence.**

BITTER ENEMIES, NEW ALLIES: ENGLISH UNIFICATION. The reigns of **James IV** and **James V** saw the arrival of the Renaissance and the Reformation. The royal court moved to Holyrood during this period and Edinburgh became Scotland's permanent capital. Shortly thereafter, when yet another Scottish leader (Elizabeth I) died without an heir in 1603, James VI of England became **James I** of Scotland. The **Parliament of Scotland,** seated in Edinburgh, was established after the Wars of Independence, but disputes over unifying **Scottish Presbyterianism** with the Anglican Church led to the Scots' initial backing of Oliver Cromwell during the English Civil War.

The victory of Protestant William of Orange in the Glorious Revolution prompted the Presbyterians to throw in their lot with the Anglicans, signing the 1707 **Act of Union.** Supporters of James II (the Jacobites) began a series of unsuccessful uprisings that ended in their expulsion from Edinburgh and the city's subsequent occupation by the British under Prince William. The Hanoverian British enacted new oppressive measures that included forbidding hereditary **tartans** and **bagpipes,** discouraging Gaelic, and even renaming the streets of Edinburgh after their royal British lineage. This would set the stage for the 18th-century Enlightenment, during which Scottish thinkers such as Edinburgh's own Adam Smith attempted to modernize the country by overhauling and improving agriculture, industry, and trade. The intellectual climate got an overhaul as well during what is commonly known as the **Scottish Enlightenment** (see **Scottish Letters,** p. 262).

MODERNIZED SCOTLAND. Economic problems in the 19th century were disastrous for rural Scotland. The **Industrial Revolution** transformed Edinburgh (particularly its port in Leith) into a cultural and economic powerhouse, while the rest of Scotland starved during the **Highland Potato Famine.**

Twentieth-century Scotland, like the rest of Europe, was defined by WWI and the Great Depression. A **Devolution** (home rule) movement called for a separate Scottish parliament to reside in Edinburgh. The **Scottish National Party** arose in 1934 on the strength of these sentiments, liberating the **Stone of Scone** (the traditional seat of coronation of the Scottish Monarch, removed under Edward I) in 1950 and calling for the separation of Scotland following the discovery of oil in the North Sea in the 1970s. Though a 1979 referendum failed, September 1997 marked a victory for devolution by a three-to-one margin. The **Scottish Parliament** was established in Holyrood, Edinburgh, and 1999 elections inaugurated the Labour-Liberal Democrat coalition. In spite of Scotland's renewed autonomy, it still holds several seats in the UK House of Commons.

CULTURE AND THE ARTS

SCOTTISH LETTERS

While the early Scottish literary tradition is a rich amalgamation of the Gaelic, French, Classical, and Chaucerian styles, Edinburgh's greatest works came from the Scottish Enlightenment.

David Hume, born in Edinburgh in 1711, produced subtle liberal tracts that pioneered the genre of the essay. His "An Enquiry Concerning Human Understanding" introduced us to sentimentalism as a moral philosophy. **Adam Smith,** also of Edinburgh stock, eulogized the free market in his 1776 *The Wealth of Nations.*

Edinburgh has contributed to Scotland's rich poetic and prose tradition as well. **James Boswell,** the biographer of Samuel Johnson, composed Scottish verse as well as a famous volume of journals about his travels with the Dr. Johnson. **Sir Walter Scott** was among the first Scottish authors to win international accolades for his work. His historical novels (such as *Waverley*) helped to spark the 19th-century revival of Highlands culture. **Robert Louis Stevenson** is most famous for his tales of high adventure, which include *Treasure Island.* His *Strange Case of Dr. Jekyll and Mr. Hyde* is nominally set in London, but you may recognize some of Edinburgh's streets in Stevenson's Gothic descriptions. Edinburgh's sons also include **Sir Arthur Conan Doyle,** whose Sherlock Holmes series is beloved by would-be gumshoes across the world.

Edinburgh's modern tradition is equally strong. Contemporary Scottish literature runs the gamut from **Irvine Welsh's** disjointed and gritty collection of short stories, *Trainspotting*, to **J.K. Rowling's** infamous canon. This strong and lasting tradition has led UNESCO to declare Edinburgh its first █ **City of Literature.**

THE HIGHLAND AESTHETES

In addition to hosting Scotland's five National Galleries (p. 279), the Royal Scottish Academy, and the Scottish National Gallery of Modern Art, Edinburgh has been responsible for some of Scotland's more famous visual artists. Eighteenth- and 19th-century painters like **Allan Ramsay** and **Sir Henry Raeburn** are known for their portraiture. The 20th century saw the development of the **Edinburgh School,** a group of artists who studied in Edinburgh College of Art around the time of WWI. The Edinburgh School has gained recognition for its application of non-natural techniques to still lifes and subjects from nature. **William Crozier,** for instance, employed a quasi-Cubist approach, while **Anne Redpath** drew inspiration from Matisse.

Edinburgh's Modern art is characterized by a vibrant grassroots tradition. The **Edinburgh Annuale** is an annual art festival that encourages the survival and growth of new, modern traditions. The event coincides with the International Festival and the Fringe Music Festival, which are both held in August.

FOOD AND DRINK

When it comes to local food, think **Scottish Breakfast** (beans, fried eggs, potato cakes, fried tomatoes, and bacon), **Scotch Eggs** (boiled eggs wrapped in a sausage meat mixture, breaded, and fried), and **haggis** (you don't even want to know). Edinburgh itself is the home of the **Edinburgh Rock,** first invented by Alexander Ferguson, who made the important discovery that sugar, water, cream of tartar, and colorings can be baked into create a soft, crumbly confection.

Interested in a bit more kick? Check out **White Horse** or **Glenkinchie,** two of Edinburgh's famous █ **whiskys** (spelled without the E). Remember: all Scotch is whiskey, but not all whiskey is whisky. Scotch whisky is either "single malt" (from a single distillery) or "blended" (a mixture of several brands). The malts are excellent and distinctive, with flavors and strengths varied enough to accommodate both novices and lifelong devotees.

TOP TEN LIST

TOP TEN USEFUL "SCOTTICISMS"

Though the philosophers of the Scottish Enlightenment attempted to eliminate words distinct to the Scottish dialect, an understanding of a few basic Scotticisms may help you blend in with the Edinburgh locals.

1. **Auld Reekie:** A slang term for Edinburgh that literally means "Old Smoky."

2. **Tassie:** A small cup or goblet. "Albert always orders a tassie of ale with his lunch."

3. **Swally:** An alcoholic beverage, short for "a swallow of," as in, "Ned bought swallys all around."

4. **Cludgie:** A toilet. "Harriet got a little flustered after she locked herself in the cludgie."

5. **Bampot:** A stupid or crazy person, often used affectionately. "Careful, our neighbor's a right bampot."

6. **Daud:** A sizeable portion of something, usually food. "Get Patrick to pass me a daud of bread!"

7. **Howff:** Literally a house or abode, colloquially refers to a pub or local haunt. "Let's hit up the howff for a few drinks, and I don't mean my house."

8. **Ginger:** A soda or other sweet beverage, such as lemonade. "Wallace is a teetotaler, but he still downs his share of gingers at the pub."

9. **High Do:** A commotion or state of excitement. "Hearts fans get up to high do after every win."

10. **Jiggered:** Exhausted. "Frances was completely jiggered after her night on the town."

TO 4 (3mi)

Edinburgh
ACCOMMODATIONS

Ardenlee Guest House,	1	D1
Argyle Backpackers,	2	C6
Caldeonian		
Backpackers,	3	B3
GlobeTrotter Inn,	4	A1
Greenside Hotel,	5	F2
Merlin Guest House,	6	A6
Robertson Guest House,	7	A6
SYHA Central,	8	F2

TO ROYAL BOTANIC GARDENS (¼mi) & EDINBURGH CARAVAN CLUB (2mi)

Henderson R

Raeburn Pl.

Dean St.
St. Bernard's Cr.

Leslie Pl.

Hamilton Pl.

Clarence St.

Henderson Pl.

Dean Terr.

Saunders St.

St. Stephen St.

Circus Lane

Dean St.

Dean Terr.

India Pl.

Doune Terr.

Glouster Pl.

Royal

N. W. Circus Pl.

Circus

Howe St.

DEAN VILLAGE

Orchard Brae

Dean Path

Water of Leith

Moray Pl.

Ainslie Pl.

Gloucester Ln.

India St.

Heriot Row

Queen Street Gardens

NEW TOWN

Dean Bridge

Randolph Cres.

Stuart St.

Queen St.

Young St.

Hill St.

Castle St.

George St.

Frederick St.

Thist

20

Australia

13

Belford Rd.

Douglas Cres.

Douglas Gdns.

Eglinton Cres.

Chester St.

Drumsheugh Gdns.

Queensferry St.

CHARLOTTE SQ.

S. Charlotte St.

10

Rose St.

R℞

TO 21 AND 25 (220yd)

Glencairn Cres.

Palmerston Pl.

St. Mary's Cathedral

Melville St.

WEST END

Alva St.

3

Princes St.

West Princes Street Gardens

TO EDINBURGH INTERNATIONAL AIRPORT (6½mi), EDINBURGH ZOO (2½mi)

Grosvenor St.

Manor Pl.

William St.

Coates Cres.

Shandwick Pl.

R℞

Rutland St.

S

Haymarket Terr.

HAYMARKET

West Maitland St.

Canning St.

King Stables Rd.

33

Esplanade Castlehi

Haymarket Station

Dalry Rd.

Morrison Link

W. Approach Rd.

Cambridge St.

Traverse Theatre

Canada

Royal Lyceum Theatre

Grindlay St.

Castle Terr.

King's Stables Rd.

Johnston Terr.

FOOD

The Basement,	9	E2
Candy Bar,	10	C2
Henderson's		
Salad Table,	11	D2
Mosque Kitchen,	12	D5
Mussel Inn,	13	C3
Sadivino,	14	E5

PUBS

Blue Moon Cafe,	15	E2
The Outhouse,	16	E2

CLUBS

Bongo Club,	17	E3
C. C. Bloom's,	18	E2
Ego,	19	E2
Po Na Na,	20	C2

Morrison St.

The Filmhouse

Lothian Rd.

Bread St.

Earl Grey St.

High Riggs

Lady Lawson St.

West Port

Grassmarke

FOUNTAIN-BRIDGE

Gardner's Cres.

Fountainbridge

Grove St.

Lauriston Pl.

TOLLCROSS

Chalmer's Hospital

TOLLCROSS

Gilmore Park

Union Canal

Leamington Terr.

West Tollcross

Biketrax

Lochrin Pl.

Home St.

Brougham St. Pl.

Lauriston Gdns.

Chalmers St.

Tarvit St.

Leven St.

King's Theatre

North Meadow Walk

The Meadows

Gilmor

Gillespie Cres.

Whitehouse Loan

Melville Dr.

Bruntsfield Links

Montpelier Park

6

Hartington Pl.

Viewforth

7

Hartington Gdns.

Warrender Park Terr.

Bruntsfield Pl.

Forbes Rd.

Bruntsfield Cres.

Warrender Park Rd.

BRUNTSFIELD

Spottiswoode St.

Arden St.

Marchmont Rd.

Marchmont Cres.

Sciennes Rd.

Argyle Pl.

2

N

0	200 yards
0	200 meters

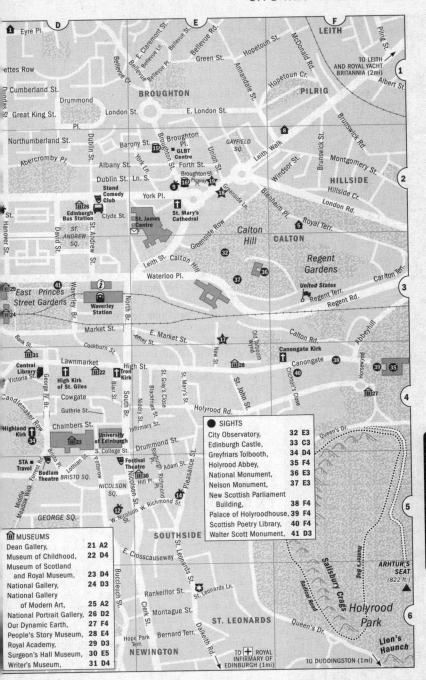

SIGHTS

City Observatory,	32 E3
Edinburgh Castle,	33 C3
Greyfriars Tolbooth,	34 D4
Holyrood Abbey,	35 F4
National Monument,	36 E3
Nelson Monument,	37 E3
New Scottish Parliament	
Building,	38 F4
Palace of Holyroodhouse,	39 F4
Scottish Poetry Library,	40 F4
Walter Scott Monument,	41 D3

MUSEUMS

Dean Gallery,	21 A2
Museum of Childhood,	22 D4
Museum of Scotland	
and Royal Museum,	23 D4
National Gallery,	24 D3
National Gallery	
of Modern Art,	25 A2
National Portrait Gallery,	26 D2
Our Dynamic Earth,	27 F4
People's Story Museum,	28 E4
Royal Academy,	29 D3
Surgeon's Hall Museum,	30 E5
Writer's Museum,	31 D4

EDINBURGH

TRAMS: THE WAVE OF HE (PAST AND) FUTURE

Princes Street, the main drag of Edinburgh's Old Town, currently looks like a war zone. Trenches in the pavement expose pipes and wires, and everything but the sidewalk is fenced off. In 2011, the street will reopen with a new addition—a tramway running from the airport to the Firth of Forth and passing through the city center. The £512 million main line will bring rail transport back to a city that, since 1956, has been served only by buses and cabs.

Like Los Angeles, Edinburgh once had a thriving and extensive railway system. But in the early 20th century, automobiles were the wave of the future. By 1956, all of the city's trams had shut down in favor of shiny diesel buses. Today, due to climate change and expensive gas, trains again are making a comeback.

Construction began shortly after the project received Royal Assent from the Queen in 2006. Building a new train in an old city isn't easy—underground utilities must be moved away from the tracks up the city's steep hills. Other obstacles include a global recession and an obstinate Scottish Parliament that wants to scrap the project to save money.

The lines may encourage adventurous tourists to explore remote parts of the city, but the day-trippers that stick to the Royal Mile won't even see it. In the meantime, the trendy clothing stores that line Princes Street will have to deal with construction workers' fashion faux pas across the street.

◼ INTERCITY TRANSPORTATION

Edinburgh lies 45 mi. east of Glasgow and 405 mi. northwest of London on Scotland's east coast, on the southern bank of the Firth of Forth.

Flights: Edinburgh International Airport (☎0870 040 0007), 7 mi. west of the city. Lothian Airlink (☎0131 555 6363) shuttles between the airport and Waverley Bridge (25min.; every 10-15min.; £3.50, children £2, round-trip £6/3). Flights to major international cities, including **New York City** (9hr.), as well as UK destinations such as **Birmingham, London Gatwick, London Heathrow,** and **Manchester.**

Trains: Waverley Station, between Princes St., Market St., and Waverley Bridge. Free bike storage beside platforms 1 and 11. Ticket office open M-Sa 4:45am-12:30am, Su 7am-12:30am. Trains (☎08457 484 950) to: **Aberdeen** (2½hr.; M-Sa every hr., Su 8 per day; £34); **Glasgow** (1hr., 4 per hr., £9.70); **Inverness** (3½hr., every 2hr., £32); **London King's Cross** (4¾hr., 2 per hr., £108); **Stirling** (50min., 2 per hr., £6.10).

Buses: The modern **Edinburgh Bus Station** is on the eastern side of St. Andrew Sq. Open daily 6am-midnight. Ticket office open daily 8am-8pm. National Express (☎08705 808 080) to **London** (10hr., 4 per day, £30). Scottish Citylink (☎08705 505 050; www.citylink.co.uk) to **Aberdeen** (2½hr., every hr., £23), **Glasgow** (1hr.; M-Sa 4 per hr., Su 2 per hr.; £6), and **Inverness** (4½hr., 8-10 per day, £25). A bus-ferry route via Stranraer goes to **Belfast** (2 per day, £28) and **Dublin, IRE** (2 per day, £32). Megabus also serves Edinburgh; for cheapest fares, book ahead online at www.megabus.com or call ☎0900 160 0900 (7am-10pm).

▣ LOCAL TRANSPORTATION

Public Transportation: Although walking is usually the fastest and easiest way around the city center, Edinburgh has a comprehensive bus system. Lothian (☎0131 555 6363; www.lothianbuses.com) operates most buses. Exact change required (£1.10, children 70p). Buy a 1-day **Daysaver** ticket (£3, children £2.40) from any driver or in the Lothian Travelshops (☎0131 555 6363) on Waverley Bridge, Hanover St., and Shandwick Pl. Open M-Sa 8:15am-6pm. **Night buses** cover selected routes after midnight (£3). First Edinburgh (☎0870 872 7271) also operates local buses. Traveline (☎0870 608 2608; www.traveline.co.uk) has more information.

Taxis: Stands located at all train and bus stations. **City Cabs** (☎0131 228 1211). **Central Radio Taxis** (☎0131 229 2468). **Central Taxis Edinburgh** (☎0131 229 2468; www.taxis-edinburgh.co.uk).

Car Rental: The TIC has a list of rental agencies, most from £25 per day. **Thrifty,** 42 Haymarket Terr. (☎0131 337 1319). **Avis,** 100 Dalry Rd. (☎0131 337 6363).

Bike Rental: Biketrax, 11-13 Lochrin Pl. (☎0131 228 6633; www.biketrax.co.uk). Mountain bikes £12 per ½-day, £16 per day. Open M-F 9:30am-6pm, Sa 9:30am-6pm, Su noon-5pm. **Edinburgh Cycle Hire,** 29 Blackfriars St. (☎01680 300 301), off High St., organizes cycle tours. Mountain bikes £10-15 per day, £50-70 per week. Open daily 10am-6pm.

⚜ ORIENTATION

Edinburgh's city center is divided into two halves, on either side of the train tracks, **Old Town** and **New Town.** The two are connected by three bridges: **North Bridge, Waverley Bridge,** and **The Mound.** The bridges cross over **Waverley Station,** which lies directly between Old Town and New Town. The **Royal Mile** and **Edinburgh Castle** are in Old Town and are the center of most tourist activities, while New Town plays host to upscale shopping. When reading maps, remember that Edinburgh is a multidimensional city—many streets that appear to intersect are actually on different levels. The terrain is hilly, and valleys are often spanned by bridges with streets running under them. Elevations are connected by many narrow stairway alleys known as "closes." Two miles northeast of New Town, **Leith** is the city's seaport on the Firth of Forth.

⓱ PRACTICAL INFORMATION

TOURIST AND FINANCIAL SERVICES

Tourist Information Centre: Waverley Market, 3 Princes St. (☎0845 22 55 121), north of Waverley Station. Helpful and often mobbed, the mother of all Scottish TICs books rooms for £4 plus a 10% deposit; sells bus, museum, tour, and theater tickets; and has free maps and pamphlets. **Bureau de change.** Open July-Aug. M-Sa 9am-7pm, Su 10am-7pm; Sept.-June M-Sa 9am-5pm, Su 10am-5pm.

Budget Travel: STA Travel, 27 Forrest Rd. and 72 Nicholson St. (both ☎0131 230 8569). Open M-Sa 10am-6pm, Su 11am-5pm.

Beyond Tourism: In the summer, young travelers are employed by festival organizers to help manage offices, set up, etc. Hostel notice boards often help employment agencies seeking temporary workers. **Temp Agency** (☎0131 478 5151). **Wesser and Partner** (☎01438 356 222, www.wesser.co.uk). **Kelly Services** (☎0131 220 2626).

LOCAL SERVICES

Luggage Storage: At the Waverley train station or the bus station. £5 per item per day.

Camping Gear: Millets the Outdoor Store, 12 Frederick St. (☎0131 220 1551). All the essentials, but no rentals. Open M-W and F-Sa 9am-6pm, Th 9am-8pm, Su 10:30am-5:30pm.

Library: Central Library (☎0131 242 8000), on George IV Bridge. Free Internet. Open M-Th 10am-8pm, F 10am-5pm, Sa 9am-1pm.

GLBT Resources: Edinburgh Lesbian, Gay, and Bisexual Centre, 58A-60 Broughton St. (☎0131 478 7069). **Gay Edinburgh** (www.visitscotland.com).

EDINBURGH

Disabled Services: Contact the TIC prior to traveling for a free *Accessible Scotland* guide or check www.edinburgh.org and www.capability-scotland.org.uk for info on access to restaurants and sights. **Shopmobility,** The Mound (☎0131 225 9559), by the National Gallery, lends motorized wheelchairs for free. Open Tu-Sa 10am-4pm.

Public Toilets and Showers: In the "Superloo" at the train station. Shower, toilet, and towel £3. Toilet 20p. Open daily 4am-12:45am.

EMERGENCY AND COMMUNICATIONS

Police: Headquarters at Fettes Ave. (☎0131 311 3131; www.lbp.police.uk). Other stations at 14 St. Leonard's St. (☎0131 662 5000) and 188 High St. (☎0131 226 6966). Blue **police information boxes** are scattered throughout the city center, with tourist information and an emergency assistance button.

Pharmacy: Boots, 48 Shandwick Pl. (☎0131 225 6757) and 101-103 Princes St. (☎0131 225 8331). Open M-W and F-Sa 8am-6:30pm, Th 8am-8pm, Su 10am-6pm.

Hospitals: Royal Infirmary of Edinburgh, 51 Little France Cres. (☎0131 536 1000, emergencies 536 6000). **Royal Hospital for Sick Children,** 9 Sciennes Rd. (☎0131 536 0000).

Internet Access: Signs to internet cafes are on every other corner along the Royal Mile. **E-Corner,** 54 Blackfriars St. (☎0131 558 7858). £1 per 30min. with terminals and Wi-Fi. Open M-F 10am-9pm, Sa 10am-8pm, Su noon-8pm. The **Bongo Club Cafe,** 6 New St. (☎0131 558 7604), has a few free terminals. Open M-F 11am-late, Sa 12:30pm-late. Free at the **Central Library** (p. 267). Many cafes throughout Old Town also offer internet access.

Post Office: St. James Centre (☎0131 556 9546). **Bureau de change.** Open M-Sa 9am-5:30pm. Branch at 46 St. Mary's St. (☎0131 556 6351). Open M-Tu and Th-F 9am-12:30pm and 1:30-5:30pm, Sa 9am-noon. **Postcode:** EH1 3SR.

⌂ ⚑ ACCOMMODATIONS AND CAMPING

Hostels and **hotels** are the only options in the city center; **B&Bs** and **guesthouses** appear on the edges of town. Be sure to ook ahead in summer. During the Festival (from late July to early Sept.) and New Year's, prices often rise significantly. Many locals let their apartments; the TIC's booking service works magic.

HOSTELS

Edinburgh is a backpacker's paradise, with a number of convenient hostels smack-dab in the middle of town. New hostels open all the time—check with the TIC for the latest listings. Hostels range from the small and cozy to the huge and party-oriented. Expect cliques of long-term residents. Several also offer more expensive private rooms with varying amenities.

▨ Scotland's Top Hostels (www.scotlands-top-hostels.com). This chain's 3 Edinburgh hostels all have a fun, relaxed environment and comfortable facilities. Also runs MacBackpacker tours in the city and around Scotland. All three run free Th pub crawls.

Royal Mile Backpackers, 105 High St. (☎0131 557 6120). The smallest of the chain's hostels. Well-kept and cozy, with a community feel (and free tea and coffee). Shared laundry facilities. Free Wi-Fi. 8-bed dorms £13-15. AmEx/MC/V. ❶

Castle Rock Hostel, 15 Johnston Terr. (☎0131 225 9666, www.castlerockedinburgh.com). Just steps from the castle, with a party atmosphere and a top-notch cinema room that shows nightly movies. Ask about their haircut offer: £10 with a complimentary shot of vodka. Breakfast £2. Free Wi-Fi. Dorms £13-15; doubles £30-34; triples £45-51. AmEx/MC/V. ❶

High St. Hostel, 8 Blackfriars St. (☎0131 557 3984). Ideally located just off the Royal Mile. Laid-back party environment and 16th-century architecture. Pub crawls, movie nights, and pool competitions. Free Wi-Fi. 4- to 18-bed dorms £13-15. AmEx/MC/V. ❶

Budget Backpackers, 37-39 Cowgate (☎0131 226 2351; www.budgetbackpackers.co.uk). The most modern of the Old Town hostels. Spacious 2- to 12-bed rooms; female-only dorms available. Free city tour daily; pub crawl M-Sa starting at 9pm. Breakfast £2. Lockers free (bring your own padlock). Laundry £1 each for washer and dryer. Internet £1 per 30min. Reception 24hr. Key-card access. Rooms £9-24. 18+. MC/V. ❷

Globetrotter Inn, 46 Marine Dr. (☎0131 336 1030; www.globetrotterinns.com), a 15min. bus ride from Waverley train station and Edinburgh International Airport. Large grounds next to the Firth of Forth. An hourly shuttle service runs to and from the city, although a shop, TV room, gym, hot tub, and 24hr. bar make it tempting to stay put. Curtained bunks offer privacy. Light breakfast included. Free Wi-Fi and internet terminals. Lockers free. Key-card access. Dorms £15-19; ensuite doubles and twins £46. MC/V. ❶

Edinburgh Backpackers, 65 Cockburn (CO-burn, you pervert) St. (☎0131 220 2200; www.hoppo.com). Lively clientele. Common areas, pool table, jukebox, and TV. 15% discount at the downstairs cafe. Co-ed dorms. Laundry and internet available. Check-out 10am. 8- to 16-bed dorms £10-19; private doubles £45-52. MC/V. ❶

Central (SYHA), 9 Haddington Pl. (☎0131 524 2090; www.syha.org.uk), off Leith Walk. Brand new, with modern ensuite rooms, bar, and bistro. Singles, doubles, and family rooms in addition to 4- to 8-bed dorms. Child-friendly. Laundry and internet £1 each. Dorms £10-25, under 18 £10-23. AmEx/MC/V. ❷

Argyle Backpackers, 14 Argyle Pl. (☎0131 667 9991; www.argyle-backpackers.co.uk). Take bus #41 from Market St. to Warrender Park Rd. 3 renovated townhouses with a backyard and free coffee. A B&B-like alternative to louder city hostels. Private rooms, many with TVs, along with 4- to 10-bed dorms. Lockable dorms. Laundry facilities available. Internet £1.50 per hr. Reception 9am-10pm. Check-in 2-11pm. Dorms £13-23; doubles and twins £43-60; triples £58-65. MC/V. ❷

Princes Street East Backpackers, 5 West Register St. (☎0131 556 6894; www.edinburghbackpackers.com). Climb the "77 steps to debauchery" to reach this lively top-floor lair. Bizarre murals cover the walls. Recently renovated bathrooms are spotless, and the dorms have plenty of elbow room. Lockers available; bring your

THE BIG SPLURGE

THE SCOTSMAN

Edinburgh's backpacker contingent loves the city's cheap hostel accommodations. But when high rollers like Sir Sean Connery come to town, they don't shack up at Budget Backpackers. Rather, they freqent the luxury hotels as historic as the city that surrounds them.

If you fancy a night of indulgence, book a night at The Scotsman. Be prepared to break you piggybank: rooms range from £300 for a basic single to £1300 for the penthouse suite. The hotel's century-old building was once the headquarters of Scotland's national newspaper of the same name. It has since been converted into a five-star hotel that remains proud of its journalistic heritage. Plates in the trendy North Bridge Brasserie downstairs are painted with old newsprint, while rooms include the Publisher's Suite, the Director's Suite, and the Baron's suite. The basement, where printing presses once thundered, now emits the humming sound of treadmills from a state-of-the-art gym and spa. You are invited to "detox" at the spa and to "retox" with a dram of 28-year-old Highland whisky, delivered to you room for £14.50.

The restaurant's marble staircase is perhaps the hotel's greatest luxury. In the past, only the editor-in-chief was allowed to scale the steps; other staff were allowed this privilege only once per year. Such light traffic has left the staircase in immaculate condition; you can now walk up and down it as you please.

THE LOCAL STORY

GARDY-LOO!

Edinburgh's nickname, **Auld Reekie** (Scottish for "Old Smokey") comes from its dark and dirty days as an industrial powerhouse. Much like Dickensian London, the city struggled to accommodate its booming population and filth. It was certainly reekie, but it reeked as well.

The deep ditch that now holds the train tracks and Princes Street Gardens was once the Nor'Loch, a lake that doubled as the community dumpster. After years of tossing nasty things into the loch (including witches, to see if they could float), the water got progressively more foul and, in 1759, was completely drained.

Falling into the Nor'Loch wasn't a germaphobe's only worry in Victorian Auld Reekie. Even walking the Royal Mile was hazardous. At the end of each day, residents emptied their chamber-pots out their windows and into the streets, where waste would stew until crews cleaned it up in the morning. To warn passers-by of falling crap, they would shout "Gardy-loo!" The expression derives from the French *gardez l'eau* (look out for the water). In fact, it is believed that the modern British slang for toilet—loo—derives from this warning. Rest assured that today the only remnants of Edinburgh's reeking past are the soot-stains on the Scott Monument.

own padlock. Wi-Fi £3 per day. Reception 24hr. Dorms £11-18. AmEx/MC/V. ❶

Belford Hostel, 6-8 Douglas Gardens (☎0131 225 6209). off Belford Rd. Cubicle-style walls divide the sanctuary of a huge church into dorms. Where else can you look up at a vaulted ceiling as you drift off to sleep these days? Bar and pool tables in the common room. Reception M-Th and Su 24hr., F-Sa until 3am. Breakfast £2.50. Luggage storage £1. Laundry £3. Dorms during the week £6-11, on weekends £15-20. MC/V. ❶

Cowgate Tourist Hostel, 96-112 Cowgate (☎0131 226 2153; www.cowgatehostel.com), just a block from the Royal Mile. Apartment-style living in 2- to -6 bed dorms. Mountains of flyers in the lobby let you know what's going down in town. Free internet. Dorms during the week £10-11, on weekends £13-14. MC/V. ❶

Caledonian Backpackers, 3 Queensferry St. (☎0131 476 7224; www.caledonianbackpackers. com), at the west end of Princes St. Join the chorus of snores in the 38-bed dorm. Backpackers' bar stays open late with open mic Tu and live music F-Sa. 284 beds. 2 kitchens. Lockers, laundry, and free Wi-Fi. Dorms £10-20; doubles £50-72. MC/V. ❶

HOTELS

Most of the independent hotels in the city center have stratospheric prices. At the affordable end are budget **chain hotels**—they may lack character, but they're comfortable.

Greenside Hotel, 9 Royal Terr. (☎0131 557 0121). A refurbished Georgian building with views of the Firth from its top floors. Free Wi-Fi. Singles £25-60. AmEx/MC/V. ❺

Grassmarket Hotel, 94 Grassmarket (☎0131 220 2299). Formerly Premier Lodge. In the heart of Old Town. Doubles £80-120. MC/V. ❺

B&BS AND GUESTHOUSES

B&Bs cluster in three colonies, all of which you can walk to or reach by bus from the city center. Try Gilmore Pl., Viewforth Terr., or Huntington Gardens in the **Bruntsfield** district, south from the west end of Princes St. (bus #11, 16, or 17 west/southbound); Dalkeith Rd. and Minto St. in **Newington**, south from the east end of Princes St. (bus #7, 31, or 37, among others); or **Pilrig**, northeast from the east end of Princes St. (bus #11 east/northbound). See www.visitscotland. com/listings/edinburgh-guest-houses.html for a complete list or call the TIC.

▓ **Ardenlee Guest House,** 9 Eyre Pl. (☎0131 556 2838; www.ardenlee.co.uk), near the beautiful Royal Botanic

Gardens. Take bus #23 or 27 from Hanover St. northbound to the corner of Dundas St. and Eyre Pl. In a Victorian building with a welcoming red carpet running up the stairs. Comfortable beds complete with teddy bears. £25-45 per person; prices rise during July and August. Free Wi-Fi. MC/V. ❹

Relax Guest House, 11 Eyre Place (☎0131 556 1433; www.relaxguesthouse.co.uk), in New Town. Ensuite rooms and a calm vibe. An impressive whisky selection in the fully licensed bar helps guests relax. Low-season £25-60 per person, high-season £45-60. AmEx/MC/V. ❹

Robertson Guest House, 5 Hartington Gardens (☎0131 229 2652; www.robertson-guesthouse.com). Bus #11, 16, or 17 from George St. Quiet and welcoming, with ensuite rooms and a relaxing garden patio. An original tile mosaic in front of the door has survived for 135 years. £29-75 per person. MC/V. ❹

Elder York Guest House, 38 Elder St. (☎0131 556 1926; www.elderyork.co.uk). One of Edinburgh's most centrally located B&Bs, across from St. James Shopping Centre in New Town. Ensuite rooms. Aug. £60 per person, Sept.-June £40, July £45. MC/V. ❺

Afton Guest House, 1 Hartington Gardens (☎0131 229 1019; www.aftonguesthouse.co.uk). Comfortable ensuite rooms in a Victorian building. Singles £30-70; doubles £50-130. MC/V. ❹

CAMPING

Edinburgh Caravan Club Site, Marine Dr. (☎0131 312 6874), by the Firth. Take bus #27 from The Mound, get off at Silvernose, and walk 15min. down Marine Dr. Clean and family-friendly. Electricity, shop, hot water, showers, and laundry. £4.60-6 per person; £4.80-7.60 per pitch for members. £7 per pitch for non-members. MC/V. ❶

Mortonhall Caravan and Camping Park, 38 Mortonhall Gate, Frogston Rd. (☎0131 664 1533; www.meadowhead.co.uk). Take bus #11 from George St. to Hyvots Bank. South of the city, near picturesque barley fields. Electricity, hot water, laundry. Wigwams £14-22. ❷

◨ FOOD

Edinburgh's restaurants offer a range of cuisines. If it's traditional fare you're after, find everything from pub haggis to creative "modern Scottish" at the city's top restaurants. For food on the cheap, many **pubs** offer student and hosteler discounts in the early evening, while fast-food joints are scattered across New Town. Takeaway shops on **South Clerk, Leith Street** and **Lothian Road** have affordable Chinese and Indian fare. For groceries, try **Sainsbury's,** 9-10 St. Andrew Sq. (☎0131 225 8400; open M-Sa 7am-10pm, Su 9am-8pm) or the **Tesco** on Earl Grey St. (☎0131 221 0650; open daily 6am-11pm).

OLD TOWN

▨ **The Mosque Kitchen,** 19A West Nicholson Street, tucked away in the courtyard of Edinburgh's modern central mosque. A jumble of long tables make up an outdoor cafeteria. Popular with students. Heaping plates of curry (£4) are hard to beat. Open M-Th and Sa-Su 11:30am-7pm, F noon-1pm and 1:45-7pm (closes briefly for F prayers). Cash only. ❶

▨ **The City Cafe,** 19 Blair St. (☎0131 220 0125), right off the Royal Mile behind Tron Kirk. This perennially popular Edinburgh institution is a cafe by day and a flashy pre-club spot by night. Sip a milkshake and people-watch from the cafe's heated street-side seating. Happy hour daily 5-8pm. Open daily during the festival 11am-3am; otherwise 11am-1am. Kitchen open M-Th until 10pm, F-Su until 10pm. MC/V. ❷

Maxies Bistro and Wine Bar, 5B Johnston Terrace (☎0131 226 7770, www.maxies.co.uk). For 35 years, this local institution has poured some of the world's tastiest wines on their romantic second-story patio overlooking Old Town. Eclectic menu with everything from pasta to Mexican (entrees £7-13). Vegetarian dishes £7. Open daily 11am-midnight. AmEx/MC/V. ❷

The Elephant House, 21 George IV Bridge (☎0131 220 5355). Harry Potter and Albus Dumbledore were born here on scribbled napkins. A perfect place to chill, chat, and read a newspaper. Exotic teas and coffees and the best shortbread in the universe. Great views of the castle. Coffee and 1hr. of internet £2.50. Open daily 8am-11pm. MC/V. ❶

David Bann, 56-58 St. Mary's St. (☎0131 556 5888; www.davidbann.com). Popular vegetarian restaurant that serves creative gourmet dishes (£8.50-13) and delectable desserts. Red mood lighting and modern decor. Vegan options available. Brunch Sa-Su £6. Open M-Th and Su 11am-10pm, F-Sa 11am-10:30pm. Reservations recommended. AmEx/MC/V. ❸

The Outsider, George IV Bridge (☎0131 226 3131). A stylish restaurant without the usual high price tag or attitude. Chunky kebabs (£9) and an excellent seafood section (£9-15). Open daily noon-11pm. Reservations recommended; request a window table for a view of the castle lit up at night. MC/V. ❷

Tang's, 44 Candlemaker Row (☎0131 220 5000). Small and polite Japanese restaurant with sushi, bento boxes, and noodle dishes. Chef's specials £9.50-12. Sushi platters (£7-8) are great for sharing. Vegetarian options available. Discounts for takeout (£4.50-6.50). Open M-Th and Su noon-2:30pm and 6-10pm, F-Sa noon-9:30pm. MC/V. ❷

Il Castello, 36 Castle Terrace (☎0131 229 2730). Authentic Italian cuisine in the shadow of Castle Rock. Innovative pizzas like *Gnocci al Pomodoro* are a nice break from the boring pies you get at kebab shops. Brush up on your Italian if you want to read the menu. Pizza and pasta dishes £7-9. Open daily noon-2:30pm and 5-11pm. AmEx/MC/V. ❷

NEW TOWN

☒ Valvonna & Crolla, 19 Elm Row (☎0131 556 6066; www.valvonacrolla.co.uk), off Leith Walk. Beloved of foodies across the UK, this deli has been selling Italian wine, gourmet meats, and other delicious groceries since 1934. In back, the cafe serves Scottish takes on Italian specialties, complete with wine pairings. Open M-Th 8:30am-5:30pm, F-Sa 8am-6pm, Su 10:30am-3:30pm. Reservations recommended on weekends. MC/V. ❷

The Basement, 10A-12A Broughton St. (☎0131 557 0097; www.thebasement.org.uk). Menu changes daily, with plenty of vegetarian options. Energetic vibe draws students, artists, performers, and other creative types. Entrees £6-9.50, set 2-course lunch £8. Mexican night Sa-Su. Kitchen open M-Sa noon-10:30pm, Su 12:30-10:30pm. Bar open until 1am. Reservations recommended on weekends. AmEx/MC/V. ❷

Henderson's Salad Table, 94 Hanover St. (☎0131 225 2131). The flagship of Edinburgh's vegetarian scene. The bar gets going at night, offering a range of organic wines, beers, and spirits. Free Wi-Fi. Seriously good salads £2.10-7.30. Open M-Sa 8am-11pm. Kitchen open 11:30am-10pm. AmEx/MC/V. ❶

Mussel Inn, 61-65 Rose St. (☎0131 225 5979; www.mussel-inn.com). Succulent local shellfish in a friendly, relaxed environment. Gourmet entrees £11-18. Open M-Th noon-3pm and 5:30-10pm, F-Sa noon-10pm, Su noon-10pm. MC/V. ❸

Tippoo Sahib, 129A Rose St. (☎0131 226 2862). Named for an Indian sultan who died defending his capital from the British East India Company in 1799; a mural of the martyred sultan meeting some friendlier Scotsmen covers the wall. Traditional Indian plates of tandoori, curry, and more £7.50-14. Open M-F noon-2:30pm and 5-11pm, Su 4-11pm. AmEx/MC/V. ❷

Great Grog, 43 Rose St. (☎0131 225 1616). Wine bar that also serves surprisingly cheap pub fare (£2-7). Comfy chairs in the back are perfect for socializing. Enjoy the

Scottish summer with a jug of sangria (£13) on the outdoor patio. Jazz W at 7pm. Open M-Th and Su 9am-10pm, F-Sa 9am-11pm. AmEx/MC/V. ❷

Candy Bar, 113-115 George St. (☎0131 225 9179). A world away from the Royal Mile, this modern bar serves burgers, noodles, and salads (most around £6.50-8). Excellent sharing platters £7.50-9.50. Steer clear of the tempting 14-page drink menu outside of happy hour (5-8pm) if you want to leave with your wallet intact. "Under £5" food menu during happy hour is a steal. Open daily noon-7pm. Bar open until 1am. MC/V. ❷

El Barrio, 47 Hanover St. (☎0131 220 6818; www.elbarrio.co.uk). "Loud Food, Spicy Music" in the middle of New Town. Standard Mexican dishes £8.50-14. Salsa classes M-Th and Su 7-9pm, £5. Open daily noon-3am. MC/V. ❷

◎ SIGHTS

TOURS

Edinburgh is best explored by foot, but Lothian buses run several hop-on, hop-off open-top bus tours around the major sights, beginning at Waverley Bridge. **City Sightseeing Edinburgh** is popular; others include the **Majestic Tour** to New Haven and the Royal Yacht Britannia, vintage **MacTours,** and **Edinburgh Tours.** (General tour bus information ☎0131 220 0770; www.edinburghtour.com. All tours run Apr.-Oct. every 20-30min. £10, concessions £9. Tickets can be used for reduced admission at many attractions.) A 24hr. Edinburgh **Grand Tour** ticket (£13, concessions £11) combines all four.

While a great array of tour companies in Edinburgh tout themselves as "the original" or "the scariest," the most worthwhile of the bunch is **◪McEwan's Edinburgh Literary Pub Tour.** Led by professional actors, this 2hr., booze-filled crash course in Scottish literature meets outside the Beehive Inn on Grassmarket. (☎0800 169 7410; www.edinburghliterarypubtour.co.uk. May-Sept. daily 7:30pm, Oct. and Mar.-Apr. Th-Su 7:30pm, Nov.-Feb. F 7:30pm. £8, concessions £7. £1 discount for online booking.) The popular **City of the Dead Tour,** which convenes nightly outside St. Giles's Cathedral, promises a one-on-one encounter with the MacKenzie poltergeist. (☎0131 225 9044; www.blackhart.uk.com. Daily Easter-Halloween 8:30, 9:15, 10pm; Halloween-Easter 7:30, 8:30pm. £8.50, concessions £6.50.) **Mercat Tours,** leaving from Mercat Cross, enters Edinburgh's spooky underground vaults, relying upon long ghost stories rather than staged frights. (☎0131 225 5445; www.mercattours.com. £7.50-8.50, families £20-23.)

OLD TOWN

Edinburgh's medieval center, the **Royal Mile,** is the heart of Old Town and home to many attractions—it's an energetic traveler's playground. The Mile gets its name from the royal edifices on either end: **Edinburgh Castle** on top of the hill and the **Palace of Holyrood** anchoring the bottom of the hill. The top of the Mile is known as **Castle Hill.** Continuing east downhill from the castle, the street becomes **Lawnmarket,** then **High Street,** then **Canongate,** and finally ends at **Holyrood.** Each segment is packed with attractions and souvenir shops.

CASTLE HILL AND LAWNMARKET

◪EDINBURGH CASTLE. Looming over the city center atop a dormant volcano, Edinburgh Castle dominates the skyline. Its oldest surviving building is tiny 12th-century **Saint Margaret's Chapel,** built by King David I of Scotland in memory of his mother. The castle compound developed over the course of centuries; the most recent additions date to the 1920s. The central **Palace,** begun in the 1430s, was home to Stuart kings and queens and contains the room where

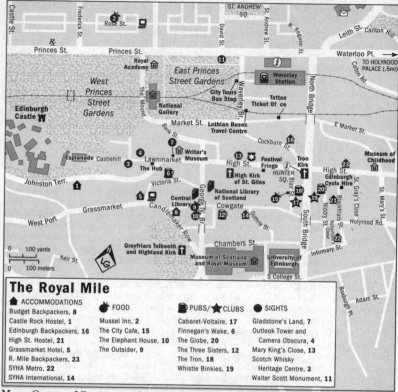

The Royal Mile

ACCOMMODATIONS
Budget Backpackers, 8
Castle Rock Hostel, 1
Edinburgh Backpackers, 16
High St. Hostel, 21
Grassmarket Hotel, 5
R. Mile Backpackers, 23
SYHA Metro, 22
SYHA International, 14

FOOD
Mussel Inn, 2
The City Cafe, 15
The Elephant House, 10
The Outsider, 9

PUBS/★CLUBS
Cabaret-Voltaire, 17
Finnegan's Wake, 6
The Globe, 20
The Three Sisters, 12
The Tron, 18
Whistle Binkies, 19

SIGHTS
Gladstone's Land, 7
Outlook Tower and
Camera Obscura, 4
Mary King's Close, 13
Scotch Whisky
Heritage Centre, 3
Walter Scott Monument, 11

Mary, Queen of Scots, gave birth to James VI. It also houses the **Scottish Crown Jewels,** which are older than those in London. The storied (although visually unspectacular) **Stone of Scone,** more commonly known as the Stone of Destiny, is also on permanent display. Other sections of the sprawling compound, like the Scottish National War Memorial, the National War Museum of Scotland, and the 15th-century monster cannon Mons Meg, definitely merit a visit, despite the uphill climb. The **One O'Clock Gun** fires from Monday to Saturday. Guess what time. Buy tickets online to skip the queues. (☎0131 225 9846; www.edinburghcastle. gov.uk. Open daily Apr.-Oct. 9:30am-6pm, Nov.-Mar. 9:30am-5pm. Last entry 45min. before closing. Free guided tours of the castle depart regularly from the entrance. £13, concessions £10.50, children £6.50. Excellent audio tour £3.50, concessions £2.50, children £1.50.)

■**CAMERA OBSCURA AND WORLD OF ILLUSIONS.** Climb **Outlook Tower** to see the 150-year-old camera obscura, which captures moving color images of the street below. On the top floor, a guide uses the lever-operated camera to show you around the city from the comfort of a darkroom. The museum's dazzling exhibits use lights, mirrors, lenses, and other 19th-century technology to create illusions that still manage to amaze and confound visitors; displays with more modern technology are equally astonishing and amusing, including a photographic face-morphing booth and a hall of holograms. (☎0131 226 3709. Open daily July 9:30am-7pm, Aug 9:30am-7:30pm, Sept.-Oct. and Apr.-June 9:30am-6pm, Nov.-Mar.

10am-5pm. Presentations every 20min., last presentation 1hr. before closing. £8.50, concessions £6.75, children £5.75.)

THE SCOTCH WHISKY EXPERIENCE. Learn about the "history and mystery" of Scotland's most famous export at the Scotch Whisky Heritage Centre, located right next to the castle. The first portion is a Disney-style barrel ride with animatronic displays that explain the careful process of distillation. Next, you're taught about the character of different regional whiskeys and left to choose the one that suits your fancy. *(350 Castle Hill. ☎0131 220 0441; www.scotchwhiskyexperience.co.uk. Open daily June-Sept. 10am-5:30pm, Oct.-May 10am-5pm. Tours every 15min. £11, concessions £8.50.)*

MARY KING'S CLOSE. Under the souvenir shops and cafes of the Royal Mile lies a long-abandoned underground neighborhood. Accessed just off the Mile via Warriston's Close, the narrow alley of Mary King's Close was sealed off when the Royal Exchange was built in 1753. Today, tours of the street and its dark dwellings allow a fascinating glimpse into the lives of its 19th-century residents. *(☎0870 243 0160. Open Apr.-June and Oct. daily 10am-9pm; Aug. 9am-9pm.; Nov.-Mar. M-F and Su 10am-5pm, Sa 10am-9pm. 1hr. tours every 20min. Book ahead. £10, concessions £9.)*

WRITER'S MUSEUM. Inspirational quotations are etched into the pavement of this tribute to literary greats, just off the Royal Mile down Lady Stair's Close. The museum contains memorabilia and manuscripts from three of Scotland's greatest wordsmiths: Robert Burns, Sir Walter Scott, and Robert Louis Stevenson. *(Lawnmarket. ☎0131 529 4901. Open M-Sa 10am-5pm; during the Festival M-Sa 10am-5pm, Su 2-5pm. Free.)*

PRINCES STREET GARDENS. The gardens are in the city center, with fantastic views of Old Town and the castle. The lush park stands on the site of now-drained Nor'Loch, where Edinburghers used to toss their refuse (and drown accused witches). The loch has been replaced with an impeccably manicured lawn, stone fountains, winding avenues with benches, and enough trees to provide shade from the Scottish "sun." *(Open daily. Hours vary; usually closes at dusk.)*

GLADSTONE'S LAND. Staffed with knowledgeable guides, the oldest surviving house on the Royal Mile (completed in 1620) has been carefully preserved, with hand-painted ceilings and period furniture. *(477B Lawnmarket. ☎0844 493 2120. Open daily July-Aug.*

FROM THE ROAD

TAKING A SEAT

Walking around Edinburgh is an easy way to get in shape. No matter where you go, your journey will probably involve climbing a hill. But the best natural exercise in the city comes from climbing Arthur's Seat, a dormant volcano southeast of Old Town.

Determined to get some pretty pictures of the ocean and church spires, I decided to climb the rocky peak. There is a gradually sloping path that leads in a wide circle around the mountain, but I was stupid and tried to take an extremely steep shortcut. The path was well-trodden, and there were muddy steps the whole way up. I basically felt like using the Stairmaster on the hardest level possible. Every time I looked back I had a more spectacular view of the city and the Firth of Forth, and the injuries I would endure if I slipped.

It was so incredibly windy when I got to the top that I was afraid my jacket would act as a parachute and sweep me off the cliff. I lay down on some cushiony moss and soaked in the breathtaking scenery.

The only thing more difficult that climbing up the steep side of the mountain is getting back down. I decided that constantly looking down at the hundreds of feet below me would be too unnerving, so I instead took a leisurely stroll down the gentle incline on the other side of the mountain. If you decide you want to summit the Seat, save yourself some pain and take the easy path both ways.

—Jack Holkeboer

10am-6:30pm, Sept.-Oct. and Apr.-June 10am-5pm. Last entry 30min. before closing. £5.50, concessions £4.50, families £14. Braille guidebook available.)

HIGH STREET

High St. marks the middle of the Royal Mile with *kirks* (churches) and monuments. Watch for sandwich board signs advertising ghost and underground tours—many convene throughout the day and night along High St.

■**HIGH KIRK OF SAINT GILES.** This *kirk* is Scotland's principal church, sometimes known as **Saint Giles's Cathedral.** From its pulpit, Protestant reformer John Knox delivered the sermons that drove the Catholic Mary, Queen of Scots, into exile. Stained-glass windows illuminate the structure, whose crown spire is one of Edinburgh's hallmarks. The 20th-century ■**Thistle Chapel** honors the Most Ancient and Most Noble Order of the Thistle, Scotland's prestigious chivalric order. The church is flanked on the east by the stone **Mercat Cross,** marking the site of the medieval market ("mercat"), and on the west by the **Heart of Midlothian,** inlaid in the pavement. According to legend, spitting on the Heart protects you from being hanged in the square. It appears as though many visitors are under the impression that they get extra protection if they spit their gum on the Heart. The cathedral hosts free concerts throughout the year. *(Where Lawnmarket becomes High St. ☎ 0131 225 9442. Open M-F 9am-7pm, Sa 9am-5pm, Su 1-5pm. Suggested donation £1.)*

CANONGATE

Canongate, the steep hill that constitutes the final segment of the Royal Mile, was once a separate burgh and part of an Augustinian abbey. Now it is home to cafes and shops that are quieter than their High St. counterparts.

CANONGATE KIRK. Royals used to worship in this 17th-century chapel. Adam Smith, founder of modern economics, is buried in the slope to the left of the entrance. Down the hill from his grave, find the joint effort of three literary Roberts: Robert Louis Stevenson commemorated a monument erected here by Robert Burns in memory of Robert Fergusson. *(Open from Apr. to mid-Sept. M-F 9am-7pm, Sa 9am-5pm, Su 1-5pm; from mid-Sept. to Mar. M-Sa 9am-5pm, Su 1-5pm. Free.)*

SCOTTISH POETRY LIBRARY. An award-winning piece of modern architecture, the library has a fine collection of Scottish and international poetry. *(5 Crichton's Close. ☎ 0131 557 2876; www.spl.org.uk. Open M-F 11am-6pm, Sa 1-5pm. Free.)*

HOLYROOD

Holyrood, at the lower end of the Royal Mile, is mostly occupied by the huge palace, park, and parliament.

PALACE OF HOLYROODHOUSE. This Stuart palace at the base of the Royal Mile remains Queen Elizabeth II's official Scottish residence. As a result, only parts of the ornate interior are open to the public. Once home to Mary, Queen of Scots, whose bedchamber is on display, the palace is every inch a kingly residence. Dozens of portraits inside the **Great Gallery** chronicle its proud history. On the palace grounds lie the ruins of **Holyrood Abbey,** built by King David I in 1128 and ransacked during the Reformation. Most of the ruins date from the 13th century, but only a single doorway remains from the original construction. Located in a recently renovated 17th-century schoolhouse near the palace entrance is the **Queen's Gallery,** which displays exhibits from the royal art collection. *(At the bottom of the Royal Mile. ☎ 0131 556 5100. Open daily Apr.-Sept. 9:30am-6pm; Nov.-Mar. 9:30am-4:30pm. Last entry 1hr. before closing. No entry while royals are in residence (often June-July). Palace £10, concessions £9, children £6, under 5 free, families £26.50. With admission to Queen's Gallery £14/12.50/8/free/38.50. Audio tour free.)*

HOLYROOD PARK. A true city oasis, Holyrood Park is filled with hills, moorland, and lochs. At 823 ft., ◼**Arthur's Seat,** the park's highest point, affords the best views of the city and Highlands. Considered a holy place by the Picts, the name "Arthur's Seat" is derived from "*Ard-na-Saigheid,*" Gaelic for "the height of the flight of arrows." Traces of forts and Bronze Age terraces dot the surrounding hillside. From the Palace of Holyroodhouse, the walk to the summit takes about 45min. **Queen's Drive** circles the park and intersects with Holyrood Rd. by the palace.

HOLYROOD SCOTTISH PARLIAMENT BUILDING. After years of controversy and massive budget overdraws, the new Scottish Parliament Building is functional and open to visitors. A winner of numerous architectural awards, the building is highly geometric, with steel, glass, oak, and stone fanning out every which way. Architect Enric Miralles was influenced by the surrounding landscapes, the paintings of Charles Rennie Mackintosh, and boats on the seashore. (☎0131 348 5200; www.scottish.parliament.uk. Open Apr.-Oct. M and F 10am-6pm, Tu-Th 9am-7pm, Sa-Su 10am-4pm; Nov.-Mar. M and F-Su 10am-4pm, Tu-Th 9am-7pm. Hours may vary; call ahead. Guided tours on non-business days £6, concessions and children £3.60, under 5 free. Free tickets to the parliamentary sessions; book in advance.)

ELSEWHERE IN THE OLD TOWN

Believe it or not, there is more to Old Town than the Royal Mile.

GREYFRIARS TOLBOOTH AND HIGHLAND KIRK. Off George IV Bridge, the 17th-century *kirk* rests in a churchyard that, while lovely, is estimated to contain 250,000 bodies and has long been considered haunted. A few centuries ago, the infamous body snatchers Burke and Hare dug up corpses here before resorting to murder in order to keep the Edinburgh Medical School's anatomy laboratories well supplied. A more endearing claim to fame is the loyal pooch Greyfriars Bobby, whose much-photographed statue sits at the southwestern corner of George IV Bridge in front of the churchyard's gates. (Beyond the gates, atop Candlemakers Row. ☎0131 225 1900. Open for touring Easter-Oct. M-F 10:30am-4:30pm and Sa 10:30am-2:30pm. Free.)

NATIONAL LIBRARY OF SCOTLAND. The library rotates exhibitions from its archives, which include a Gutenberg Bible, the last letter of Mary, Queen of Scots, and the original copy of *The Wallace,* an epic poem. (George IV Bridge. ☎0131 623 3700. Open M-Tu and Th-F 9:30am-8:30pm, W 10am-8:30pm, Sa 9:30am-1pm. Free.)

MUSEUM OF EDINBURGH. Walk around on creaky floors and trace the city's development and various inhabitants, including Celts, Romans, and Scots. A series of maps and drawings shows how Edinburgh's hilly cityscape has been changed by buildings over the years. On display is an original copy of the 1638 National Covenant, which boldly states Scotland's opposition to Charles I's Episcopaliansim. Edinburgh's "goldsmiths" actually worked mainly with silver, and the museum houses an impressive collection of their work. (142 Canongate. ☎0131 529 4143. Open M-Sa 10am-5pm, Su noon-5pm.)

SURGEON'S HALL MUSEUMS. Edinburgh's Royal College of Surgeons recently celebrated its 500th anniversary, and it has racked up a lot of medical artifacts on the way. One exhibit displays rusty amputation knives and other implements of military surgery. Squeamish types should avoid the real human remains and giant tumors. Due to the shortage of medical school cadavers in Scotland, every 500th visitor to the museum must donate his or her body to science. Just kidding. (18 Nicolson St. ☎0131 527 1600. £5, concessions £3, families £15. Open M-F noon-4pm.)

THE NEW TOWN

Don't be fooled by the name—Edinburgh's New Town, a masterpiece of Georgian design, has very few buildings with 20th-century birthdays. James Craig, an unknown 23-year-old architect, won the city-planning contest in 1767. His rectangular grid of three parallel streets (**Queen, George,** and **Princes**) linking two large squares (**Charlotte** and **Saint Andrew**) reflects the Scottish Enlightenment belief in order. Queen St. and Princes St., the outer streets, were built up on only one side to allow views of the Firth of Forth and Old Town. Princes St., Edinburgh's main shopping drag, is also home to the venerable **Jenners,** the Harrods of Scotland. (☎0131 225 2442. *Open M-W and F 9:30am-6pm, Th 9:30am-7pm, Sa 9am-6pm, Su 11:30am-5:30pm. AmEx/MC/V.*)

WALTER SCOTT MONUMENT. Statues of Sir Walter and his dog preside inside the spire of this Gothic "steeple without a church." Climb 287 narrow, winding steps past carved figures of Scott's most famous characters to reach the top. An eagle's-eye view of Princes St., the castle, and the surrounding city awaits. The journey to the top is not recommended for those who suffer from claustrophobia or vertigo. (*Princes St. between The Mound and Waverley Bridge.* ☎0131 529 4098. *Open daily Apr.-Sept. 10am-7pm, Oct.-Mar. 10am-4pm. £3.*)

CALTON HILL. This hill at the eastern end of New Town commands views of the city and the Firth of Forth. Climb 143 steps inside the **Nelson Monument,** built in 1807 in memory of the admiral and the Battle of Trafalgar. The hilltop is also home to two 19th-century landmarks: the old **City Observatory** and the **National Monument,** affectionately known as "Edinburgh's Disgrace." The structure, a poor man's Parthenon designed to commemorate those killed in the Napoleonic Wars, was scrapped when civic coffers ran dry after a mere 12 columns were built. For all its faults, the monument does offer beautiful views of the sunrise between its columns from Waverley Bridge. (*Nelson Monument:* ☎0131 556 2716. *Open Apr.-Sept. M 1-6pm, Tu-Sa 10am-6pm; Oct.-Mar. M-Sa 10am-3pm. £3.*)

BEYOND THE CITY CENTER

LEITH. Two miles northeast of the city center, the neighborhood of **Leith** has undergone a dramatic revival. Its abandoned warehouses have been replaced (or at least supplemented) by upscale flats, restaurants, and bars. The **Royal Yacht Britannia,** used by the royal family from 1953 to 1997 (when the government decided it was too expensive and decommissioned it), sailed around the world on state visits and royal holidays. Visitors can listen to a free audio tour of the entire flagship, which remains exactly as it was when decommissioned, and visit the royal apartments. Even the queen's bedroom, off-limits at every other royal residence, is open to visitors. Other highlights include the officers' mess and the engine room. *(Entrance on the 3rd fl. of the Ocean Terminal. Take bus #22 from George St. to Ocean Terminal. £1.10. ☎0131 555 5566; www.roya-lyachtbritannia.co.uk. Open daily Apr.-June and Oct. 10am-4pm, July 9:30am-4pm, Aug. 9:30am-4:30pm, Nov.-Mar. 10am-3:30pm. £10, concessions £8.75.)*

CRAIGMILLAR CASTLE. This 15th-century castle stands 3½ mi. southeast of central Edinburgh. Mary, Queen of Scots, fled here after the murder of her secretary at Holyroodhouse. While she was here, plans emerged for the murder of her second husband, Lord Darnley. Today, the castle is relatively safe: only two visits in the past 50 years have led to fatal entanglement in the ancient Scots-Darnley feud. *(Take bus #2, 14, or 30 from George St. to the corner of Old Dalkeith Rd. and Craigmillar Castle Rd., then walk 10min. up the castle road. ☎0131 661 4445. Open daily Apr.-Sept. 9:30am-5:30pm, Oct.-Mar. 9:30am-4:30pm. Last entry 30min. before closing. £4.20, concessions £3.70, children £2.10.)*

EDINBURGH ZOO. At long last, your search for the world's largest penguin pool has come to an end. You'll find it 2 mi. west of the city center, along with exhibits featuring some 1000 other animals. *(Take bus #12, 26, or 31 westbound from Princes St. ☎0131 334 9171. Open daily Apr.-Sept. 9am-6pm, Oct. and Mar. 9am-5pm, Nov.-Feb. 9am-4:30pm. £14, concessions £12, children £9.50; various family packages available.)*

ROYAL BOTANIC GARDENS. Edinburgh's herbaceous oasis has plants from around the world. Guided tours wander across lush grounds and greenhouses crammed with orchids, tree ferns, and towering palms. *(Inverleith Row. Take bus #23 or 27 from Hanover St. ☎0131 552 7171. Open daily Apr.-Sept. 10am-7pm, Oct. and Mar. 10am-6pm, Nov.-Feb. 10am-4pm. Free. Greenhouses £4, concessions £3, children £1.)*

🏛 MUSEUMS

NATIONAL GALLERIES OF SCOTLAND

Edinburgh's four major galleries are an elite group, housing work by Scots and non-Scots alike. *(☎0131 624 6200; www.nationalgalleries.org. All open daily 10am-5pm; during the festivals 10am-6pm. All free.)*

▨NATIONAL GALLERY OF SCOTLAND. Housed in a grand 19th-century building designed by William Playfair, this gallery has a superb collection of works by Renaissance, Romantic, and Impressionist masters, including Raphael, Titian, El Greco, Turner, and Gauguin. Sprawling, wall-sized works illustrate important moments in Scottish history. Don't miss the octagonal room, which displays Poussin's entire *Seven Sacraments*. The basement houses a selection of Scottish art. The impressionist room upstairs shows several works by Monet. *(On The Mound between the halves of the Princes St. Gardens.)*

Next door is the ▨Royal Academy, connected by an underground tunnel, which hosts exhibits from the National Gallery and runs a high-profile show each summer. *(At the corner of The Mound and Princes St. Special late night Th until 7pm. Exhibit prices vary, many are free; visit www.royalscottishacademy.org for information.)*

SCOTTISH NATIONAL PORTRAIT GALLERY. The gallery displays the stern faces of the famous men and women who have shaped Scotland's history. Military, political, and intellectual figures are all represented, including renegade Bonnie Prince Charlie, royal troublemaker Mary, Queen of Scots, and wordsmith Robert Louis Stevenson. (*1 Queen St., north of St. Andrew Sq. Exhibition prices vary, usually about £4-8; visit www.nationalgalleries.org.*)

SCOTTISH NATIONAL GALLERY OF MODERN ART. In the west end of town, this collection includes works by Braque, Matisse, Picasso, Warhol, and Hirst. The landscaping in front of the museum, a bizarre spiral of grass set into a pond, represents the concept of chaos theory with dirt and greenery. (*75 Belford Rd. Ride bus #13 from Hanover St. or walk along the Water of Leith Walkway. Special exhibits £5-10.*)

DEAN GALLERY. The newest addition to the National Galleries is dedicated to Surrealist and Dada art. The gallery owes much of its fine collection to the sculptor Eduardo Paolozzi, whose towering three-story statue, *Vulcan*, stands at the main entrance. Other sculptures dot the spacious and well-manicured front lawn. (*73 Belford Rd. Special exhibits £3.50.*)

OTHER MUSEUMS AND GALLERIES

MUSEUM OF SCOTLAND AND ROYAL MUSEUM. The superbly designed Museum of Scotland traces the whole of Scottish history through an impressive collection of treasured objects and decorative art. Highlights include the working **Corliss Steam Engine** and the **Maiden,** Edinburgh's guillotine, used on High St. around 1565. The rooftop terrace provides a 360° view. Gallery and audio tours in various languages are free. The Royal Museum has rotating exhibits on natural history, European art, and ancient Egypt, to name a few. The **Millennium Clock,** a towering, ghoulish display of figures representing human suffering in the 20th century, chimes three times per day. Free tours, from useful intros to 1hr. circuits of the highlights, leave from the Main Hall's totem pole in the Royal Museum and the Museum of Scotland's Hawthornden Court. (*Chambers St. ☎0131 247 4422; www.nms.ac.uk. Both open daily 10am-5pm. Free.*)

OUR DYNAMIC EARTH. This glitzy, high-tech lesson in geology is part amusement park, part science experiment, and appealing mainly to children. Look for the white tent-like structure next to Holyroodhouse. (*Holyrood Rd. ☎0131 550 7800; www.dynamicearth.co.uk. Open daily July-Aug. 10am-6pm, Sept.-June 10am-5pm. Last entry 70min. before closing. £9.50, concessions £7.50, children £6.*)

OTHER MUSEUMS. The **Museum of Childhood** displays an array of antique and contemporary childhood toys, from 19th-century dollhouses to 1990s Teletubbies. (*42 High St. ☎0131 529 4142. Open M-Sa 10am-5pm, Su noon-5pm. Last entry 15min. before closing. Free.*)

Canongate Tolbooth (c. 1591), with a beautiful clock face above the Royal Mile, once served as a prison and gallows for "elite" criminals. Now it houses the **People's Story Museum,** an eye-opening look at the life of Edinburgh's working classes. (*163 Canongate. ☎0131 529 4057. Open M-Sa 10am-5pm; daily 10am-5pm during the Festival Free.*)

⚏ ENTERTAINMENT

For all the latest listings and local events in Edinburgh, check out *The List* (£2.25; www.list.co.uk), available at newsstands, or *The Skinny*, a monthy music magazine with concert listings (free, available in most hostels; www.theskinny.co.uk). Watch for ads in pubs and clubs. The Fringe festival publishes its own program of activities, available in hard copy from the Fringe office and online at www.edfringe.com.

COMEDY, FILM, AND THEATER

For mainstream cinema, try **Odeon,** 7 Clerk St. (☎0131 667 0971) or **UGC Fountainpark,** Dundee St., Fountainbridge (bus #1, 28, 34, or 35; ☎0870 902 0417).

🎦 **The Stand Comedy Club,** 5 York Pl. (☎0131 558 7272; www.thestand.co.uk). Hilariously unhinged acts perform every night in front of a mural of a guy aiming a pistol at his own sombrero (that is, a mural of a guy watching bad standup comedy, likely at a lesser venue than The Stand). Free lunchtime improv Su 1:30pm. Special program with 17 shows per day for the Fringe Festival. Call ahead. Tickets £1-13. MC/V for tickets only.

Festival Theatre, 13-29 Nicholson St. (☎0131 529 6000; www.eft.co.uk). Stages predominantly ballet and opera, turning entirely to the Fringe in August. Box office open M-Sa 11am-8pm and before performances. Tickets £5-55. MC/V.

King's Theatre, 2 Leven St. (☎0131 529 6000; www.eft.co.uk). Promotes musicals, opera, and the occasional pantomime. Box office open 1hr. before show and between matinee and evening performances. Tickets also available through the Festival Theatre. MC/V.

Traverse Theatre, 10 Cambridge St. (☎0131 228 1404; www.traverse.co.uk). Presents almost exclusively new drama and experimental theater with lots of local Scottish work. Box office open daily 10am-6pm. Ticket prices vary, usually around £7-12, up to £18 during Festival. MC/V.

Royal Lyceum Theatre, 30 Grindlay St. (☎0131 248 4848; www.lyceum.org.uk). The finest in Scottish and English theater, with many international productions. Box office open M-Sa 10am-6pm, performance nights 10am-8pm. Tickets £4-26, students half-price. AmEx/MC/V.

Bedlam Theatre, 11B Bristo Pl. (☎0131 225 9893). A university theater with student productions, ranging from comedy and drama to F night improv, all in a converted church. A Fringe Festival hot spot. Box office open M-Sa 10am-6pm. Tickets £4-5.

Edinburgh Playhouse, 18-22 Greenside Place (☎0131 524 3333; www.edinburghplayhouse.org.uk), off Leith St. Shows big-budget commercial theatre, with productions like *The Lion King* and *The Sound of Music.* Occasionally hosts comedians. Box office open M-F 10am-6pm, or you can book online with Ticketmaster. Tickets £15-45. AmEx/MC/V.

The Filmhouse, 88 Lothian Rd. (☎0131 228 2688). European and arthouse films, though Hollywood fare appears as well. Also the main venue for the Edinburgh Film Festival. Tickets £4.40-6.50, concessions £3.30-4.90. MC/V.

Cameo, 38 Home St. (☎0131 228 2800). Screens mostly indie and foreign films, with the occasional Hollywood title. Cafe inside. Open daily 10am-midnight. AmEx/MC/V.

Jongleurs, Greenside Place (☎0844 499 4066; www.jongleurs.com), in the Omni Centre. Hosts 3-4 hilarious comics on weekend nights. Also has bar and occasional dance floor. Doors open F-Sa 7pm. Tickets £11-14. MC/V.

VUE Cinemas, Greenside Place. (☎08712 240 240; www.myvue.com). Located in the glass-and-steel Omni Centre. Screens standard Hollywood fare. Wheelchair-accessible. Tickets £7.30, students £6.20. MC/V.

Church Hill Theatre, 33A Morningside Rd. (☎0131 447 7597). Go south on Lothian Rd. Small theater that shows lots of local work. During the summer, American high school students move in and put on a variety of productions. Buy tickets at the Fringe office. Most shows £8-14. AmEx/MC/V.

LIVE MUSIC

Thanks to an abundance of university students who never let books get in the way of a good night out, Edinburgh's live music scene is vibrant and diverse. Excellent impromptu and professional folk sessions take place at pubs, and many university houses sponsor live shows—look for flyers near Bristol Sq. *The Skinny* has comprehensive listings. **Ripping Records,** 91 South Bridge (☎0131 226 7010), sells tickets to rock and pop performances.

The Jazz Bar, 1A Chambers St. (☎0131 220 4298). Not just a jazz venue: you can also see blues, hip-hop, funk, and more. Classy and relaxing vibe, with stone walls and red lighting. 3 shows most days: "Tea Time" (acoustic, T-Su 5-8:30pm, free entry, free Wi-Fi), "Early Gig" (mostly jazz, daily 8:30-11pm, cover £1-5), and "Late N' Live" (daily 11:30pm-3am, or 5am during Festival, cover £1-5). Always packed on weekends. Cash only for cover. MC/V at bar over £5.

Whistle Binkie's, 4-6 South Bridge (☎0131 557 5114). A subterranean pub with 2 live shows every night, open to bands of any genre. Mostly local rock cover bands, with some folk music thrown in. Gets busy later at night. Open daily until 3am. AmEx/MC/V over £5.

The Mitre, 131-133 High St. (☎0131 652 3902). Live music starts every night at 9:30pm in this traditional pub on the Royal Mile. Haunted by the ghost of 17th-century Bishop John Spottiswool, whose throne is buried under the bar in concrete that mysteriously repels the drills of workmen seeking to excavate. Beautiful Jacobean ceiling. Mostly acoustic folk and covers, with lots of Scottish ballad sing-alongs. Open M-Th and Su noon-midnight, F-Sa noon-1am. AmEx/MC/V.

The Ark, 5-7 Waterloo Pl. (www.myspace.com/thearkvenue). Showcases local rock, indie, and folk bands. Cover £2-5. Shows start around 8pm. Open daily 11am-1am. Cash only.

The Royal Oak, 1 Infirmary St. (☎0131 557 2976). Classic pub setting with live traditional and folk music every night. Live music from 9:30pm. Tickets £1-3. Open M-F 10am-2am, Sa 11:30am-2am, Su 12:30pm-2am. Cash only.

▐ SHOPPING

From ritzy department stores to funky vintage shops, Edinburgh has something for every shopper and every wallet. If you want to get in touch with your Scottish heritage, tourist shops along the **Royal Mile** sell Highland outfits, cashmere sweaters, tartan towels, and will even trace your family history for around £10. New Town generally caters to big spenders—major chains line **Princes Street,** and **Multrees Walk** off St. Andrew's Square houses upscale designer shops like Louis Vuitton. The pedestrian **Rose Street** has smaller boutiques and plenty of pubs to whet your whistle (while you can still afford a whistle). Big malls include **St. James Shopping Centre** (off Leith St.; open M-W and F 9am-6pm, Th 9am-8pm, Sa 9am-6:30pm, Su 10am-6pm) and **Princes Mall** (Princes St.; open M-W and F-Sa 9am-6pm, Th 9am-7pm, Su 11am-5pm). For (slightly) more affordable shopping, stick to **Old Town.** The **Grassmarket, Cockburn Street,** and **Lothian Road** are all full of diverse and interesting shops.

MAJOR CHAINS

Topshop, 30 Princes St. (☎0131 556 0151; www.topshop.com). Ladies and gentlemen of fashion swear by Topshop, which now offers a line designed by Kate Moss. A personal "style advisor" can educate you on what goes with what (no jeans under those kilts, boys). Open M-W and F 9am-6:30pm, Th 9am-8pm, Sa 9am-6pm, Su 11am-6pm. AmEx/MC/V.

John Lewis, Leith St. (☎0131 556 9121; www.johnlewis.com). In St. James Shopping Centre. Gigantic department store that has everything from clothes to laptops to Persian rugs. Open M-W and F 9am-6pm, Th 9am-8pm, Sa 9am-6:30pm, Su 10am-6pm. AmEx/MC/V.

USC, 97-98 Princes St. (☎0131 220 2210). Casual club wear for him and her, from big brands like Diesel. Open M-W and F-Sa 9am-6pm, Th 9am-8pm, Su 11am-5pm. MC/V.

H&M, (☎0208 382 3256; www.hm.com). All the latest trends at surprisingly affordable prices. Open M-W and Sa-Su 9am-6pm, Th 9am-8pm, F 9am-7pm. AmEx/MC/V.

STREET MARKETS

Edinburgh Farmers Market, Castle Terrace. Under the shadow of Castle Rock, local farmers sell a variety of fresh, tasty produce. Open Sa 9am-2pm.

The Eating Place, Castle St. A big market with produce from all around Scotland. Last Th of the month noon-6pm.

CLOTHING AND GIFTS

☒ **Armstrong's,** 83 Grassmarket (☎0131 220 5557). Colorful vintage store with combat boots, Christopher Columbus hats, silk ties, designer jeans, and more. Kilts (£20) are more affordable here than in tourist shops. Open M-Th 10am-5:30pm, F-Sa 10am-6pm, Su noon-6pm. MC/V.

Backbeat Records, 31 East Crosscauseway (☎0131 668 2666), off Nicolson St. Hitch your pony before entering—you'll need to be as nimble as possible to navigate the narrow aisles between boxes of records stacked above your head. Over 65,000 rare and not-so-rare vinyls, cassettes, and CDs. Open M-Sa 10am-5:30pm. AmEx/MC/V.

Fabhatrix, 13 Cowgatehead (☎0131 225 9222; fabhatrix.com). Long-necked mannequins model a variety of hats, from gentlemanly top hats to frilly numbers fit for the Queen herself. Most are hand-crafted in the shop's basement. Open M-Sa 10:30am-6pm, Su noon-5pm. AmEx/MC/V.

The Creepy Wee Shop, George IV Bridge (☎0131 225 9044). On the grounds of Highland Kirk. This small gift shop has much more than postcards. Lots of scary trinkets shaped like skulls, rats, black cats, and other macabre creatures. Open daily 11am-4pm.

▓ NIGHTLIFE

Edinburgh is known internationally for its festivals, but its nightly festivities are a big draw as well. Some Festival-goers even skip the theaters altogether and spend their time doing two things—sleeping and partying. During the Fringe, the city turns into a sort of month-long Mardi Gras, with packed streets, loud revelry, and nonstop performances. The sun rises around 4am in the summer, so partying until dawn is easy.

PUBS

Pubs on the **Royal Mile** tend to attract a mixed crowd of old and young, tourists and locals. Students and backpackers gather in force each night in the Old Town. Casual pub-goers groove to live music on **Grassmarket, Candlemaker Row,** and **Victoria Street.** The New Town also has its share of worthy watering holes, some historical and most strung along **Rose Street,** parallel to Princes St. Wherever you are, you'll usually hear last call sometime between 11pm and 1am, or 3am during the Festival.

The **Broughton Street** area of the New Town (better known as the Broughton Triangle) is also the center of Edinburgh's gay community. Lesbian club nights are held monthly—check *The List* (£2.25) for venues and times.

TOURIST TO PURIST. Don't order your Scotch on the rocks if you want to avoid looking like a tourist. Scotch whisky should be drunk neat—with no ice. Locals may mix with a splash of water—real pros ask for mineral water from the region in which the whisky was distilled.

The Tron, 9 Hunter Sq. (☎0131 226 0931), behind Tron Kirk. Friendly student bar. Downstairs is a mix of alcoves and pool tables. Frequent live music. Burger and a pint £3.50 after 3pm, or get 2 meals for just £6.50. "Pound-a-pint" W. Open M-Sa noon-1am, Su 12:30pm-1am; during the Festival daily 10am-3am. Kitchen open until 9pm. AmEx/MC/V over £5.

Royal Mile Tavern, 127 High St. (☎0131 557 9681). This easygoing pub has managed to avoid the high prices and tourist gimmicks of its Royal Mile neighbors. Live music every night (don't miss the popular "Acoustic Dave" Sa). Flash your hostel card for a £2.50 pint or to see the cheap "Backpacker food" menu. Open daily 8am-1:30pm. MC/V.

The Outhouse, 12A Broughton St. (☎0131 557 6668). Hidden up an alleyway off Broughton St. and well worth the hunt. More stylish than your average pub but just as cheap, with one of the best beer gardens in the city. Free Wi-Fi. Happy hour daily 5-8pm. Open daily noon-1am. Kitchen open M, W, Su 1-7pm; Tu, Th, F-Sa 1pm-late. MC/V over £5.

The Three Sisters, 139 Cowgate (☎0131 622 6801). Loads of space for dancing, drinking, and lounging. Attracts a young crowd to its 3 bars (Irish, Gothic, and American). Beer garden sees close to 1000 people pass through on Sa nights. Open daily 9am-1am. Kitchen open M-Th 9am-9pm, F-Su 9am-8pm. MC/V.

Blue Moon Cafe, 36 Broughton St. (☎0131 557 0911), entrance around the corner on Barony St. A popular GLBT pub serving food to a mixed gay and straight crowd in a chic setting. Open daily 10am-11pm. Kitchen open until 10pm. MC/V.

The Globe, 13 Niddry St. (☎0131 557 4670). Cheap pints (from £2.25) and a rowdy atmosphere make this a popular destination for students and backpackers. A selection of Aussie and South African beers. Quiz night M, karaoke Th (free shot if you sing). Occasional live entertainment. Open M-F 4pm-1am, Sa noon-1am, Su 12:30pm-1am; during the Festival M-F 4pm-3am, Sa noon-3am, Su 12:30pm-3am. MC/V.

Jolly Judge, 7 James Ct. (☎0131 225 2669). Hidden just off the Royal Mile, with a cozy atmosphere. One of the few pubs in Edinburgh that serves real cider, the apple equivalent of real ale. 17th-century painted ceiling. Free Wi-Fi with any purchase. Quiz night M 9pm. Live music Th 9pm. Open M and Th-Sa noon-midnight, Tu-W noon-11pm, Su 12:30-11pm. Kitchen open noon-3pm. MC/V over £5.

Maggie Dickson's, 92 Grassmarket (☎0131 225 6601). When 18th-century Edinburgh resident Maggie Dickson gave birth to an illegitimate stillborn baby and tried to dispose of it discreetly, she was found guilty under the Concealment of Pregnancy Act and hanged in the Grassmarket. But when family members heard a pounding from inside the coffin, they reopened it to find Maggie alive and well. She went on to live another 40 years. Today, backpackers can get a pint for £2 and relax in this wood-paneled watering hole, where a skeleton in stocks grimaces in a corner. Maggie's remains are on display in a glass case behind the bar. Just kidding. Open M-Sa 10am-1am, Su 9am-1am. Kitchen open M-Th and Su 10am-10pm, F-Sa 10am-9pm. MC/V.

CLUBS

Edinburgh may be best known for its pubs, but the club scene is none too shabby. It is, however, in constant flux. Consult *The List* (£2.25), a comprehensive events guide available from any local newsstand, for the night's hot spot. Clubs cluster around the city's once-disreputable **Cowgate,** just downhill from and parallel to the Royal Mile; most close at 3am (5am during the Festival).

Cabaret-Voltaire, 36-38 Blair St. (☎0131 220 6176; www.thecabaretvoltaire.com). Most clubbers agree that "Cab-Volt" is the place to be in Edinburgh. Playing everything from jazz to break beat, this innovative club knows how to throw a party. Cavernous interior packs a loyal crowd. Cover free-£2 on weeknights, £5-10 on weekends. Open daily 7pm-3am.

Bongo Club, 37 Holyrood Rd. (☎0131 558 7604), off Canongate. Particularly noted for its hip hop and immensely popular "Messenger" (reggae; 1 Sa per month) and "Headspin" (funk and dance; 1 Sa per month) nights. Occasionally hosts live music. Cafe with free internet during the day. Cover £3-7. Open M-W and Su 10am-midnight, Th-F 10am-3am. MC/V.

CC Bloom's, 23-24 Greenside Pl. (☎0131 556 9331), on Leith St. No cover and a new up-and-coming DJ each night at this gay club. Karaoke Th and Su nights. Open daily 4pm-3am. MC/V.

Po Na Na, 43B Frederick St. (☎0131 226 2224), beneath Cafe Rouge. Go down the steps to a yellow cartoon image of a man in a fez. Moroccan-themed, with parachute ceilings, red velvet couches, and an eclectic blend of R&B, hip hop, disco, and funk. Cover £3-6.50. Open M, Th, Su 11pm-3am, F-Sa 10:30pm-3am. Open during the Festival M, Th, and Su 11pm-5am; F-Sa 10:30pm-5am.

Ego, 14 Picardy Pl. (☎0131 478 7434; www.clubego.co.uk). Not strictly a gay club, but hosts gay nights, including Vibe (Tu) and Blaze (4th Sa of the month). Cover £3-10. Open M-W and Su 10pm-1am, Th-Sa 11pm-3am.

APPENDIX

CLIMATE

Winds from the Atlantic mix with seas surrounding the island country to produce the dense fog and low clouds characteristic of Britain's land- and cityscapes. Though notorious for a wet and climate, weather in London, Oxford, Cambridge, and Edinburgh is highly variable. Days are cool to mild with frequent clouds and rain and occasional calm spells. Visitors are often surprised by the long summer days, a happy consequence of Britain's northern latitude. Summers are cooler than in continental Europe, and winters are milder.

AVG. TEMP. (LOW/ HIGH), PRECIP.	JANUARY			APRIL			JULY			OCTOBER		
	°C	°F	mm	°C	°F	mm	°C	°F	mm	°C	°F	mm
London, Oxford, and Cambridge	2/6	36/43	54	6/13	43/55	37	14/22	57/72	57	8/14	46/57	57
Edinburgh	1/6	34/43	57	4/11	39/52	39	11/18	52/65	86	6/13	43/55	66

To convert from degrees Fahrenheit to degrees Celsius, subtract 32 and multiply by 5/9. To convert from Celsius to Fahrenheit, multiply by 9/5 and add 32.

°CELSIUS	-5	0	5	10	15	20	25	30	35	40
°FAHRENHEIT	23	32	41	50	59	68	77	86	95	104

MEASUREMENTS

Like the rest of the rational world, Britain uses the metric system. The basic unit of length is the meter (m), which is divided into 100 centimeters (cm) or 1000 millimeters (mm). One thousand meters make up one kilometer (km). Fluids are measured in liters (L), each divided into 1000 milliliters (mL). A liter of pure water weighs one kilogram (kg), or 1000 grams (g). One metric ton is 1000kg. Gallons in the US and those in Britain are not identical: one US gallon equals 0.83 Imperial gallons. You'll notice that Britain's longtime conversion to the metric system is still in progress—road signs still indicate distances in miles.

MEASUREMENT CONVERSIONS	
1 inch (in.) = 25.4mm	1 millimeter (mm) = 0.039 in.
1 foot (ft.) = 0.305m	1 meter (m) = 3.28 ft.
1 yard (yd.) = 0.914m	1 meter (m) = 1.094 yd.
1 mile (mi.) = 1.609km	1 kilometer (km) = 0.621 mi.
1 ounce (oz.) = 28.35g	1 gram (g) = 0.035 oz.
1 pound (lb.) = 0.454kg	1 kilogram (kg) = 2.205 lb.
1 fluid ounce (fl. oz.) = 29.57mL	1 milliliter (mL) = 0.034 fl. oz.
1 gallon (gal.) = 3.785L	1 liter (L) = 0.264 gal.

LANGUAGE

BRITISH PRONUNCIATION

Berkeley	BARK-lee	Magdalen	MAUD-lin
Berkshire	BARK-sher	Norwich	NOR-itch
Birmingham	BIRM-ing-um	Salisbury	SAULS-bree
Derby	DAR-bee	Shrewsbury	SHREWS-bree
Dulwich	DULL-idge	Southwark	SUTH-uk
Edinburgh	ED-in-bur-ra	Thames	Tems
Gloucester	GLOS-ter	Woolwich	WOOL-itch
Greenwich	GREN-itch	Worcester	WOO-ster
Hertfordshire	HART-ford-sher	gaol	jail
Grosvenor	GROV-nor	quay	key
Leicester	LES-ter	scones	skons

SCOTS WORDS AND PHRASES

Scots is a distinct dialect of English. Listed below are a few of the many Scots words and phrases used in standard Scottish English.

WORD/PHRASE	MEANING	WORD/PHRASE	MEANING
aye	yes	kirk	church
ben	mountain	lad	man, boy
blether, guide blether	talk idly, chat (good BLA-ther)	lass	woman, girl
breeks	pants	nae	no (nay)
bonnie	beautiful	nicht	night
brae	hill near water (bray)	sassenach	Lowlander (SAS-uh-natch)
braw	bright, strong, great	strath	broad valley
burn	stream	tatty	potato
cannae	cannot (CAN-eye)	thane	minor noble
eejit	idiot	tipple	a drink
gye	very	weegie	Glaswegian (WEE-gee)

INDEX

MAP INDEX

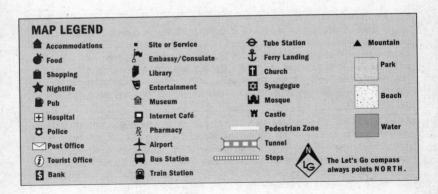

MAP LEGEND

Accommodations	Site or Service	Tube Station	Mountain
Food	Embassy/Consulate	Ferry Landing	Park
Shopping	Library	Church	
Nightlife	Entertainment	Synagogue	Beach
Pub	Museum	Mosque	
Hospital	Internet Café	Castle	Water
Police	Pharmacy	Pedestrian Zone	
Post Office	Airport	Tunnel	
Tourist Office	Bus Station	Steps	
Bank	Train Station		The Let's Go compass always points NORTH.

Maps by Let's Go copyright © 2010 by Let's Go, Inc.

Distributed by Publishers Group West.
Printed in Canada by Friesens Corp.

ISBN-13: 978-1-59880-303-7
ISBN-10: 1-59880-303-4
First edition
10 9 8 7 6 5 4 3 2 1

Let's Go London, Oxford, Cambridge & Edinburgh is written by Let's Go Publications, 67 Mount Auburn St., Cambridge, MA 02138, USA.